# Harvard™ Graphics:
# The Complete Reference

# Harvard™ Graphics: The Complete Reference

Cary Jensen
and
Loy Anderson

**Osborne McGraw-Hill**

Berkeley  New York  St. Louis  San Francisco
Auckland  Bogotá  Hamburg  London  Madrid
Mexico City  Milan  Montreal  New Delhi  Panama City
Paris  São Paulo  Singapore  Sydney
Tokyo  Toronto

Osborne **McGraw-Hill**
2600 Tenth Street
Berkeley, California 94710
U.S.A.

Osborne **McGraw-Hill** offers software for sale. For information on software, translations, or book distributors outside of the U.S.A., please write to Osborne **McGraw-Hill** at the above address.

**Harvard™ Graphics: The Complete Reference**

Copyright © 1990 by McGraw-Hill, Inc. All rights reserved. Printed in the United States of America. Except as permitted under the Copyright Act of 1976, no part of this publication may be reproduced or distributed in any form or by any means, or stored in a database or retrieval system, without the prior written permission of the publisher, with the exception that the program listings may be entered, stored, and executed in a computer system, but they may not be reproduced for publication.

 234567890 DOC 99876543210

ISBN 0-07-881621-1

Information has been obtained by Osborne **McGraw-Hill** from sources believed to be reliable. However, because of the possibility of human or mechanical error by our sources, Osborne **McGraw-Hill**, or others, Osborne **McGraw-Hill** does not guarantee the accuracy, adequacy, or completeness of any information and is not responsible for any errors or omissions or the results obtained from use of such information.

To our parents,
Gene and Carol Jensen
Lloyd and Dorothy Anderson

|          |                                              |     |
|----------|----------------------------------------------|-----|
|          | Why This Book Is for You                     | 1   |
| PART ONE | Harvard Graphics                             | 3   |
| One      | Overview                                     | 5   |
| Two      | Harvard Graphics Basics                      | 15  |
| Three    | Setup and Default Settings                   | 47  |
| Four     | Text Charts                                  | 73  |
| Five     | Organization Charts                          | 97  |
| Six      | XY Charts: Bar/Line, Area, and High/Low/Close | 125 |
| Seven    | Pie Charts                                   | 213 |
| Eight    | Producing Output                             | 247 |
| Nine     | Drawing and Annotating                       | 271 |
| Ten      | Multiple Charts                              | 331 |
| Eleven   | Templates and Chartbooks                     | 349 |
| Twelve   | Importing and Exporting                      | 369 |
| Thirteen | Slide Shows                                  | 403 |
| Fourteen | Macros                                       | 447 |
| PART TWO | Harvard Graphics 2.3                         | 469 |

| | | |
|---|---|---|
| **Fifteen** | Introduction to Harvard Graphics 2.3 .................. | 471 |
| **Sixteen** | Harvard Graphics 2.3 Features ..... | 489 |
| **PART THREE** | Draw Partner .................. | 523 |
| **Seventeen** | Introduction to Draw Partner ...... | 525 |
| **Eighteen** | Drawing and Editing with Draw Partner ......................... | 555 |
| **PART FOUR** | Effective Presentation Graphics .... | 623 |
| **Nineteen** | Effective Data Charts .............. | 625 |
| **Twenty** | Advanced Data Topics .............. | 683 |
| **Twenty-One** | Effective Text and Organization Charts ......................... | 699 |
| **Twenty-Two** | Common Charting Mistakes ........ | 715 |
| **Twenty-Three** | Using Charts in Presentations and Documents ....................... | 737 |
| **PART FIVE** | Reference ....................... | 749 |
| **Twenty-Four** | Harvard Graphics Forms and Function Keys .................... | 751 |

| | | |
|---|---|---|
| Twenty-Five | Draw Partner Forms and Function Keys | 971 |
| PART SIX | Appendixes | 995 |
| A | Additional Support for Harvard Graphics | 997 |
| B | Installation | 999 |
| C | Harvard Graphics Accessories | 1011 |
| D | Harvard Graphics Tables | 1035 |
| E | Harvard Graphics Menus | 1051 |
| | Index | 1061 |

|  |  |  |
|---|---|---|
|  | Introduction ............................. | xxxvii |
|  | Why This Book Is for You ............... | 1 |
| PART ONE | **Harvard Graphics** ................... | 3 |
| ONE | **Overview** ............................ | 5 |
|  | An Introduction to Harvard Graphics ........ | 5 |
|  | Harvard Graphics Features ............... | 7 |
|  |     Ease of Use ........................ | 8 |
|  |     Selecting from a Variety of Chart Styles ... | 8 |
|  |     Customizing Charts ................. | 9 |
|  |     Enhancing Charts with Drawings and Symbols ........................ | 11 |
|  |     Sharing Charts and Data Using Import/Export ..................... | 11 |
|  |     Improving Productivity with Templates ... | 12 |
|  |     Creating Computerized Presentations ..... | 12 |
|  |     Automating Tasks with Macros ........ | 13 |
|  |     Expanding Your Drawing Options with Draw Partner ........................ | 13 |
| TWO | **Harvard Graphics Basics** ........... | 15 |
|  | Harvard Graphics Menus, Forms, and Function Keys ..................... | 15 |
|  |     Menus ............................ | 16 |
|  |     Forms ............................ | 19 |
|  |     Types of Options on Forms ............ | 20 |
|  |     Function Key Banner ................ | 22 |
|  | Getting On-Line Help .................... | 23 |
|  | Cursor Control: Moving Around in Harvard Graphics ......................... | 24 |
|  |     The Keyboard ..................... | 24 |
|  |     Using a Mouse ..................... | 24 |
|  |     Using a Digital Tablet ................ | 25 |
|  | Control Keys .......................... | 26 |
|  | Starting Harvard Graphics ............... | 26 |
|  |     Quick Start ....................... | 28 |
|  |     Exiting Harvard Graphics ............ | 28 |
|  | The Main Menu ....................... | 29 |
|  |     Create New Chart .................. | 29 |

|  |  |
|---|---|
| Enter/Edit Chart | 29 |
| Draw/Annotate | 29 |
| Get/Save/Remove | 29 |
| Import/Export | 30 |
| Produce Output | 30 |
| Slide Show Menu | 30 |
| Chartbook Menu | 30 |
| Setup | 31 |
| Exit | 31 |
| Working with Charts | 31 |
| The Current Chart | 31 |
| Displaying the Current Chart | 33 |
| Creating a New Chart | 33 |
| Saving the Current Chart | 34 |
| Getting an Existing Chart | 36 |
| Deleting Files | 39 |
| Spell Checking the Current Chart | 41 |

### THREE  Setup and Default Settings ......... 47

|  |  |
|---|---|
| Setting Data and Display Defaults | 47 |
| Default Data Directory | 49 |
| Default Chartbook | 50 |
| Default Import Directory | 50 |
| Default Import File | 51 |
| Default Chart Orientation | 51 |
| Default Border | 52 |
| Default Font | 53 |
| Default Color Scheme | 53 |
| Setting Hardware Defaults | 54 |
| Default Printers | 55 |
| Default Plotter | 58 |
| Film Recorder Defaults | 59 |
| Default Screen (Graphics Adapter) | 61 |
| The Color Palette | 63 |
| Specifying a Palette Filename | 65 |
| Defining the Screen and Output Label Options | 65 |
| Modifying the CGA Color Settings | 65 |
| Modifying Color Palette Color Intensities | 67 |

|  |  |  |
|---|---|---|
|  | Overriding Default Chart Characteristics | 70 |
| **FOUR** | **Text Charts** | **73** |
|  | Creating Text Charts | 73 |
|  | Overview of Chart Forms | 76 |
|  |     Title Chart Form | 76 |
|  |     Simple Lists | 79 |
|  |     Bullet Lists | 79 |
|  |     Two- and Three-Column Charts | 79 |
|  |     Free-Form Charts | 82 |
|  | Modifying Text Attributes | 84 |
|  |     Highlighting Text to Change Attributes | 85 |
|  |     Setting Attributes for Highlighted Text | 86 |
|  | Modifying Text Size and Placement | 88 |
|  |     Setting Text Size | 89 |
|  |     Modifying Text Placement | 89 |
|  |     Setting Indentation | 90 |
|  |     Modifying Column Spacing | 90 |
|  | Using Bullets | 90 |
|  |     Changing the Bullet Type in a Bullet List | 91 |
|  |     Adding a Bullet to a Non-Bullet Chart | 93 |
|  |     Changing the Bullet Type on a Non-Bullet Chart | 93 |
|  | Clearing Text from Your Chart | 93 |
|  | Changing Text Chart Styles | 95 |
| **FIVE** | **Organization Charts** | **97** |
|  | Introduction to Organization Charts | 97 |
|  | Creating Organization Charts | 100 |
|  | The Organization Chart Form | 102 |
|  |     Entering a Title, Subtitle, and Footnote | 102 |
|  |     Entering a Name, Title, and Comment for the Current Manager | 107 |
|  |     Entering Abbreviations | 109 |
|  |     Entering Subordinates | 109 |
|  |     Adding Additional Organization Levels | 111 |
|  |     Adding a Title and Comment for Last Level Subordinates | 111 |
|  | Moving Around the Organization | 112 |

| | | |
|---|---|---|
| | Changing Levels in an Organization Chart | 112 |
| | Moving Between Individuals at the Same Level | 112 |
| | Editing an Organization Chart | 115 |
| |     Changing the Order of Subordinates | 115 |
| |     Inserting Additional Subordinates | 115 |
| |     Deleting a Subordinate | 116 |
| | The Org Chart Options Form | 116 |
| |     Displaying Less than the Entire Organization | 116 |
| |     Customizing the Information Displayed | 118 |
| | Clearing Values | 121 |
| **SIX** | **XY Charts: Bar/Line, Area, and High/Low/Close** | **125** |
| | Creating XY Charts | 126 |
| | XY Chart Styles Overview | 127 |
| |     Bar/Line Chart | 127 |
| |     Area Chart | 130 |
| |     High/Low/Close Chart | 130 |
| | Specifying the X Data Type | 130 |
| | Automatic X Data Entry | 136 |
| |     Changing the X Data Type | 137 |
| | Entering XY Chart Data | 138 |
| |     Entering X Axis Data | 140 |
| |     Entering Series Data | 144 |
| |     Changing the Order of X Axis Data | 145 |
| |     Deleting an X Data Value | 147 |
| |     Adding an X Data Value | 147 |
| | Using Calculations | 148 |
| |     Defining Series Legends Using Calculate | 149 |
| |     Formula Calculations | 151 |
| |     Keyword Calculations | 152 |
| |     Using Arguments in Calculations | 155 |
| |     Using Calculations that Refer to Calculated Series | 156 |
| | Specifying XY Chart Text | 157 |
| |     Entering a Chart Title, Subtitle, and Footnote | 158 |

|  |  |
|---|---|
| Specifying X and Y Axis Titles ........... | 158 |
| Specifying a Legend Title ............... | 159 |
| Changing the Series Legend ............. | 159 |
| Modifying XY Chart Text Attributes ...... | 160 |
| Modifying Size and Placement of Chart Text ....................... | 162 |
| Specifying XY Chart Characteristics ......... | 164 |
| Selecting Series Symbol Types .......... | 165 |
| Displaying Series Symbols ............. | 168 |
| Selecting the Series Axis .............. | 168 |
| Customizing the Series Symbol Style ..... | 168 |
| Changing the XY Chart Orientation ...... | 186 |
| Displaying Data Values on an XY Chart ... | 186 |
| Customizing the Chart Frame ........... | 188 |
| Customizing the Chart Legend .......... | 189 |
| Using a Data Table ................... | 192 |
| Applying Value Labels ................ | 194 |
| Using Grid Lines ..................... | 196 |
| Specifying Tick Mark Styles ........... | 196 |
| Customizing XY Chart Axes ............ | 196 |
| Page 4 Title, Subtitle, Footnote, Labels, and Legends ......................... | 205 |
| Creating a Cumulative Chart ........... | 206 |
| Setting Y Labels ..................... | 206 |
| Defining Chart Symbol Colors .......... | 207 |
| Defining Marker and Pattern Styles ...... | 209 |
| Clearing Data from XY Charts .............. | 210 |
| Changing Data Chart Styles ................ | 211 |
| Changing XY Chart Styles .............. | 211 |

## SEVEN  Pie Charts ....................... 213

|  |  |
|---|---|
| Pie Chart Overview ....................... | 213 |
| Creating Pie Charts ....................... | 215 |
| Pie Chart Data Form ..................... | 216 |
| Entering Pie Labels ................... | 219 |
| Entering Pie Values ................... | 219 |
| Adding Additional Series ............... | 221 |
| Modifying Pie Series .................. | 222 |
| Defining a Two-Pie Chart .............. | 223 |

| | |
|---|---|
| Exploding Slices of a Pie ................ | 223 |
| Selecting the Colors of Pie Slices ........ | 224 |
| Selecting Patterns for Pie Slices ......... | 225 |
| Pie Chart Titles & Options Form ............ | 225 |
| Entering a Title, Subtitle, and Footnote ... | 226 |
| Entering Titles for Pie 1 and Pie 2 ...... | 227 |
| Modifying Text Attributes .............. | 228 |
| Modifying the Size and Placement of Text .. | 230 |
| Adding a Three-Dimensional Effect to Pies .. | 232 |
| Creating Linked Pies ................. | 232 |
| Making Pies Proportional ............. | 234 |
| Selecting a Pie Fill Style ............... | 234 |
| Page 2 of the Pie Chart Titles & Options Form .. | 235 |
| Defining Pie Chart Styles .............. | 236 |
| Sorting Pie Slices .................... | 236 |
| Specifying the Starting Angle ........... | 238 |
| Defining the Pie Size ................. | 238 |
| Displaying Pie Labels ................ | 238 |
| Defining the Pie Label Size ............. | 239 |
| Displaying Pie Values ................ | 240 |
| Defining the Value Placement .......... | 240 |
| Formatting Pie Values ................ | 240 |
| Defining Pie Values as Currency ......... | 242 |
| Displaying Pie Value Percentages ....... | 242 |
| Defining the Placement of Percentage Values ................................. | 242 |
| Formatting Percentage Values .......... | 243 |
| Clearing Data from Your Pie Chart .......... | 244 |
| Changing Chart Styles .................... | 244 |
| Changing a Pie Chart to an XY Chart .... | 244 |
| Changing an XY Chart to a Pie Chart .... | 246 |

## EIGHT  Producing Output ................... 247

| | |
|---|---|
| The Produce Output Menu ................ | 247 |
| Preparations for Producing Chart Output ..... | 249 |
| Previewing Your Chart Before Outputting .. | 249 |
| Printing ............................... | 250 |
| Selecting Printing Quality ............. | 251 |
| Selecting Chart Size ................. | 252 |

| | |
|---|---|
| Selecting Paper Size | 253 |
| Selecting the Printer | 254 |
| Using Color | 254 |
| Printing Multiple Copies | 255 |
| Plotting | 255 |
| Selecting Plotter Quality | 256 |
| Plotting Transparencies | 256 |
| Pausing for Plotter Pens | 256 |
| Plotting Multiple Copies | 257 |
| Film Recording | 257 |
| Using a Slide Service | 258 |
| The Effects of Color Settings | 258 |
| Color Printing | 258 |
| Color Plotting | 259 |
| Color Film Recording | 259 |
| Color Settings and Grey Scale Using PostScript | 260 |
| Outputting the Charts in a Slide Show | 262 |
| Defining the Range of Slides | 264 |
| Collating Charts | 264 |
| Selecting a Slide Show Chart Size | 265 |
| Printing Non-Chart Text | 266 |
| Printing Chart Data | 267 |
| Printing Practice Cards | 267 |
| Printing a Slide Show List | 269 |

## NINE  Drawing and Annotating — 271

| | |
|---|---|
| Drawing Overview | 271 |
| Draw/Annotate and the Current Chart | 273 |
| The Drawing Area and Chart Image | 274 |
| Saving Drawings | 275 |
| Draw Menu Overview | 277 |
| Adding Objects to Your Chart | 277 |
| Moving the Cursor in the Drawing Area | 279 |
| Adding Text | 282 |
| Setting Text Options | 283 |
| Changing Text Attributes | 285 |
| Adding a Box | 287 |
| Setting Box Options | 288 |

|     |     |
| --- | --- |
| Adding a Polyline | 291 |
| Setting Polyline Options | 292 |
| Adding a Line or Arrow | 294 |
| Setting Line Options | 294 |
| Adding a Circle | 296 |
| Setting Circle Options | 297 |
| Adding a Polygon | 298 |
| Setting Polygon Options | 299 |
| Selecting Objects | 300 |
| Modifying Objects | 304 |
|    Moving an Object | 304 |
|    Changing the Size of an Object | 305 |
|    Modifying Options | 306 |
|    Changing Object Order | 308 |
| Copying Objects | 308 |
| Deleting Objects | 309 |
|    Deleting One or More Objects | 310 |
|    Recovering a Deleted Object | 310 |
|    Deleting All Objects | 311 |
| Using a Grid | 311 |
|    Changing Grid Size | 311 |
|    Displaying a Grid | 312 |
|    Using the Snap-to-Grid Feature | 312 |
| Using Symbols | 313 |
|    Retrieving a Symbol | 314 |
|    Saving a Symbol | 317 |
|    Grouping Objects | 318 |
|    Ungrouping Objects | 319 |
|    Removing Symbols from Symbol Files | 320 |
| Setting Default Options | 320 |
|    Setting Global Options | 321 |
| Advanced Draw/Annotate Topics | 323 |
|    Editing Symbols | 324 |
|    Creating Symbols | 324 |
|    Saving a Chart as a Symbol | 324 |
|    Using a Chart Saved as a Symbol | 327 |
|    Using Draw Partner with Symbols | 327 |
| Changing the Size and Placement of a Chart | 329 |

| | | |
|---|---|---|
| **TEN** | **Multiple Charts** .................... | **331** |
| | Multiple Chart Overview ................. | 331 |
| | Creating Multiple Charts ................ | 332 |
| |     Edit Multiple Chart Form ........... | 334 |
| | Sizing and Placing a Custom Multiple Chart ... | 341 |
| |     Using Quick Mode to Speed Up Custom Chart Layout ................... | 345 |
| | Changing Multiple Chart Styles ............ | 346 |
| **ELEVEN** | **Templates and Chartbooks** ......... | **349** |
| | Template Overview ..................... | 349 |
| | Saving a Template ..................... | 351 |
| |     Setting Options on the Save Template Overlay ......................... | 352 |
| | Retrieving a Template .................. | 354 |
| |     Creating a Chart from a Template ...... | 356 |
| |     Changing Default Chart Settings with a Template ...................... | 357 |
| |     Saving a Data Link in a Template ...... | 358 |
| |     Using Templates in a Slide Show ....... | 360 |
| | Chartbook Overview .................... | 360 |
| |     Creating a Chartbook ................ | 361 |
| |     Adding Templates to the Chartbook List .. | 364 |
| |     Selecting a Chartbook ............... | 364 |
| |     Editing a Chartbook ................ | 365 |
| | Creating a Chart from a Template in a Chartbook ......................... | 368 |
| **TWELVE** | **Importing and Exporting** ........... | **369** |
| | Importing and Exporting Overview ......... | 369 |
| | Importing Data ....................... | 370 |
| | Preparing a Harvard Graphics Chart for Importation ......................... | 371 |
| | Saving the Data Link ................... | 372 |
| | Importing Lotus Data .................. | 373 |
| |     Using the Import Lotus Data Form ...... | 375 |

| | | |
|---|---|---|
| Importing ASCII Text Files | ............... | 378 |
|    Using the Import ASCII Data Form | ..... | 379 |
|    Importing Tabular ASCII Data | .......... | 381 |
| Importing Delimited ASCII Files | ........... | 385 |
|    Defining ASCII Delimiters | ............. | 387 |
|    Importing Series Legends from Delimited ASCII Files | ..................... | 388 |
| Importing Graphs into Harvard Graphics | ..... | 389 |
|    Importing Lotus Graphs | ............... | 389 |
|    Importing Graphs from PFS:GRAPH | ..... | 392 |
|    Importing CGM Metafiles | ............. | 392 |
|    Importing CGM Metafiles Using VDI Device Drivers | ......................... | 394 |
| Exporting Charts | ....................... | 395 |
|    Using the Export Picture Overlay | ........ | 397 |
|    Exporting a Chart to a CGM Metafile | ..... | 401 |

## THIRTEEN    Slide Shows    403

| | | |
|---|---|---|
| Slide Show Overview | ..................... | 403 |
| Creating a Slide Show | .................... | 405 |
| The Create Slide Show Overlay | ............ | 407 |
| The Create/Edit Slide Show Form | ........... | 408 |
|    Entering Files in the Slide Show List | ..... | 409 |
| Selecting a Slide Show | .................... | 410 |
| Editing a Slide Show | ..................... | 411 |
|    Adding Files to a Slide Show | ........... | 412 |
|    Deleting Files from a Slide Show | ........ | 412 |
|    Changing the Order of Files in a Slide Show | ....................... | 412 |
| Including Bit-Mapped Files in a Slide Show | ... | 413 |
| Including a Template in a Slide Show | ........ | 414 |
|    Including a Title Chart Template in a Slide Show | ..................... | 416 |
|    Including a Data-Linked Template in a Slide Show | ..................... | 417 |
|    Including a Multiple Chart Template in a Slide Show | ..................... | 418 |
| Including Slide Show Files in a Slide Show | .... | 419 |
| Using Harvard Graphics Screenshows | ....... | 420 |

| | |
|---|---|
| Hardware Considerations for Screenshows | 420 |
| Displaying a Screenshow | 421 |
| Adding Screenshow Effects | 422 |
|     Previewing a Slide Show from the Screenshow Effects Form | 423 |
|     Changing the File Order from the Screenshow Effects Form | 424 |
|     Using Transitions to Enhance a Screenshow | 424 |
|     Using Go To Keys to Create Flexible Screenshows | 434 |
| Special Considerations for Very Large Slide Shows | 439 |
| Using Custom Palettes in a Screenshow | 439 |
|     Creating a Bit-Mapped File for an Alternate Palette | 440 |
| Creating Practice Cards for a Slide Show | 440 |
| Other Slide Show Topics | 444 |
|     Spell Checking Charts in a Slide Show | 444 |
|     Creating a Slide Show for Output | 445 |
|     Using a Screenshow to Review Charts | 445 |

## FOURTEEN

| | |
|---|---|
| **Macros** | **447** |
| Macro Overview | 447 |
|     Loading MACRO | 449 |
|     Unloading MACRO | 450 |
| Recording a Macro | 451 |
| Playing a Macro | 454 |
|     Changing the Macro Directory | 455 |
|     Pausing During Playback | 456 |
| Customizing a Macro | 458 |
|     Adding Delays to a Macro | 458 |
|     Displaying On-Screen Messages During Macro Playback | 460 |
|     Permitting User Input During Macro Playback | 460 |
|     Adding Comments to a Macro During Recording | 461 |
|     Including a Macro Within a Macro | 462 |

| | Editing and Writing Macros | 462 |
|---|---|---|
| |    Inserting a Macro Command While Recording a Macro | 464 |
| | Creating Macros that Run Continuously | 467 |

# PART TWO    Harvard Graphics 2.3    469

## FIFTEEN    Introduction to Harvard Graphics 2.3    471

| | |
|---|---|
| New Features Overview | 472 |
| Starting the On-Line Tutorial | 477 |
| Using Speed Keys | 477 |
| Default Settings | 478 |
| Defining International Formats | 483 |
| Setting Current Chart Options | 487 |

## SIXTEEN    Harvard Graphics 2.3 Features    489

| | |
|---|---|
| Chart Gallery Overview | 489 |
|    Using the Chart Gallery | 490 |
| Accessing Other Applications | 494 |
|    Specifying Applications | 495 |
| Changing the Applications Option | 497 |
|    Running Applications from Harvard Graphics | 499 |
| Including Multiple Fonts in One Chart | 500 |
|    Adding Text Using Different Fonts | 500 |
|    Modifying the Font of Existing Text | 502 |
|    Specifying a Default Font | 502 |
| ScreenShow Enhancements | 503 |
|    Using the ScreenShow Pointer | 503 |
|    Creating a HyperShow | 503 |
|    Using ShowCopy | 509 |
| Improved Palettes | 511 |
|    Selecting an Alternate Color Palette | 514 |
|    Creating a New Color Palette | 515 |
|    Changing an Existing Palette | 516 |
|    Printing Using Grey Scale | 517 |
| Improved Importing | 518 |

|  |  |  |
|---|---|---|
|  | Importing Excel Data | 518 |
|  | Importing Excel Charts | 519 |
|  | Selecting Lotus and Excel Named Ranges | 520 |
|  | Importing CGM Metafiles | 521 |

## PART THREE  Draw Partner ..... 523

### SEVENTEEN  Introduction to Draw Partner ..... 525

Draw Partner Overview ..... 526
    Starting Draw Partner ..... 527
    Exiting Draw Partner ..... 528
The Draw Partner Screen ..... 529
Draw Partner Menus ..... 530
    Selecting Menu Options from the Keyboard ..... 530
    Selecting Menu Options Using a Mouse ..... 531
Draw Partner Forms ..... 532
    Setting Form Options from the Keyboard ..... 532
    Setting Form Options Using a Mouse ..... 532
Using Function Keys ..... 532
    Using On-Line Help ..... 533
    Previewing a Drawing ..... 535
    Updating a Drawing Using Redraw ..... 535
    Adjusting the Mouse Speed ..... 535
    Saving a Drawing ..... 535
    Displaying the View Menu ..... 535
Changing the View with the View Menu ..... 536
    Using Zoom ..... 537
    Panning the Zoomed View ..... 538
    Using a Grid ..... 540
    Using the Snap-to-Grid Feature ..... 541
    Setting the Automatic Redraw ..... 542
Retrieving and Saving Files ..... 542
    Retrieving a File ..... 543
    Retrieving a File from a Different Directory ..... 545
    Saving a File ..... 547
Removing a Symbol from a Symbol File ..... 553

Using Harvard Graphics Drawings in Draw
    Partner Version 1.0 .................... 553
Using Draw Partner Drawings in Harvard
    Graphics ............................. 554

**EIGHTEEN** **Drawing and Editing with Draw Partner** ..................... **555**
    Drawing and Editing Overview ............ 555
    Moving the Cursor in the Drawing Area ...... 558
    Overview of Adding Objects ............... 559
        Adding Text ....................... 565
        Adding a Box ...................... 568
        Adding a Polyline .................. 572
        Adding a Line ..................... 574
        Adding a Circle ................... 575
        Adding a Polygon .................. 577
        Adding Circular Text ............... 578
        Adding an Arc .................... 581
        Adding a Wedge ................... 583
        Adding a Freehand Drawing ............ 584
        Adding Regular Polygons .............. 585
        Adding a Button ................... 587
    Selecting Objects ..................... 587
    Modifying Objects .................... 589
        Grouping Objects .................. 590
        Ungrouping Objects ................ 592
        Moving an Object ................. 592
        Changing the Size of an Object .......... 593
        Copying an Object ................. 594
        Deleting Objects .................. 595
        Rotating an Object ................. 596
        Flipping an Object ................. 598
        Modifying Object Options ............. 599
        Changing Object Order .............. 600
        Editing Text ...................... 602
        Sweeping Objects .................. 602
        Adding Shadows to Objects ............ 604
        Skewing Objects .................. 606
        Adding Perspective to Objects .......... 607

|     |     |
| --- | --- |
| Aligning Objects | 607 |
| Editing Polylines and Shapes | 610 |
|     Adding Points to a Polyline or Shape | 611 |
|     Moving Points in a Polyline or Shape | 614 |
|     Deleting Points from a Polyline or Shape | 614 |
|     Breaking a Polyline or Shape | 615 |
|     Combining Two Polylines | 616 |
|     Converting a Polyline to a Shape | 618 |
|     Aligning Points in a Polyline or Shape | 619 |
|     Converting Text, Lines, or Boxes to Polygons | 620 |

## PART FOUR   Effective Presentation Graphics    623

## NINETEEN   Effective Data Charts    625

|     |     |
| --- | --- |
| What Is a Chart? | 625 |
|     When to Use a Data Chart | 626 |
|     When to Avoid Using a Data Chart | 627 |
| Charts and Data | 628 |
|     Understanding Data | 628 |
|     Data with Multiple Series | 631 |
| Data Chart Elements | 634 |
|     Titles and Subtitles | 634 |
|     Descriptions | 636 |
|     Axes and Axis Titles | 637 |
|     Axis Labels | 638 |
|     Data Tables and Data Labels | 639 |
|     Tick Marks | 640 |
|     Grid Lines | 640 |
|     Line Styles and Point Markers | 641 |
|     Patterns and Shading | 642 |
|     Colors | 643 |
|     Legends | 644 |
|     Fonts and Text Attributes | 645 |
|     Text Sizes | 646 |
| Types of Data Charts | 648 |
|     Bar Charts | 648 |
|     Line Charts | 659 |
|     Point Charts | 663 |

|  |  |  |
|---|---|---|
|  | Area Charts | 667 |
|  | Pie Charts | 672 |
|  | Specialty Charts | 674 |
|  | Guidelines for Creating Data Charts | 678 |
|  | Before You Create Your Chart | 680 |
|  | After You Have Created Your Chart | 681 |
| **TWENTY** | **Advanced Data Topics** | **683** |
|  | Data Reduction | 684 |
|  | Averages and Totals | 684 |
|  | Minimums, Maximums, and Ranges | 685 |
|  | Frequency Counts | 687 |
|  | Regression and Regression Lines | 688 |
|  | Transformations and Adjustments | 691 |
|  | Weighting or Equalizing Data | 691 |
|  | Percentage Adjustments | 691 |
|  | Transformations | 693 |
|  | Logarithmic, Power, and Root Transformations | 694 |
|  | Other Data Topics | 695 |
|  | Cumulative Data | 695 |
|  | Moving Averages | 696 |
|  | Scientific Notation | 697 |
| **TWENTY-ONE** | **Effective Text and Organization Charts** | **699** |
|  | Types of Text Charts | 699 |
|  | Title Charts | 700 |
|  | List Charts | 700 |
|  | Column Charts | 702 |
|  | Free-Form Charts | 703 |
|  | Considerations for Designing Text Charts | 704 |
|  | Simplicity | 705 |
|  | Phrasing | 706 |
|  | Fonts and Text Attributes | 706 |
|  | Text Sizes | 708 |
|  | Color | 709 |

| | | |
|---|---|---|
| | Graphic Enhancements ................ | 710 |
| | Organization Charts .................... | 711 |
| | Considerations for Designing Organization Charts ............................. | 712 |

## TWENTY-TWO  Common Charting Mistakes ........ 715

| | |
|---|---|
| Introduction ........................... | 715 |
| Distortions ............................ | 716 |
|    Scaling Distortion ................... | 716 |
|    Text Omission Distortion ............ | 719 |
|    Misrepresentative Text Distortion ........ | 721 |
| Illusions .............................. | 723 |
|    Depth Illusion ..................... | 723 |
|    Size Illusion ....................... | 725 |
|    Color Illusion ..................... | 727 |
|    Shading Illusion ................... | 730 |
|    Pattern Illusion: The Moiré Effect ...... | 730 |
| Traps ................................. | 732 |
|    Artistic Trap ...................... | 733 |
|    Chart-Fixation Trap ................ | 733 |
|    Equipment/Software Trap ............ | 734 |

## TWENTY-THREE  Using Charts in Presentations and Documents ....................... 737

| | |
|---|---|
| Designing Effective Presentations .......... | 737 |
|    Putting It Together: Clarity, Consistency, and Context ..................... | 742 |
|    Incorporating Text Charts ............ | 743 |
|    Incorporating Data Charts ............ | 744 |
|    Incorporating Illustrations ............ | 745 |
|    Special Considerations for Computerized Presentations ................... | 745 |
| Using Charts in Documents ................ | 747 |
| Using Humor ........................... | 748 |

## PART FIVE  Reference ........................ 749

| TWENTY-FOUR | Harvard Graphics Forms and Function Keys | 751 |

| | |
|---|---|
| Harvard Graphics Forms | 751 |
| Application Options Overlay (Version 2.3) | 751 |
| Applications Form (Version 2.3) | 753 |
| Area Chart Data Form | 755 |
| Area Chart: Size/Place Overlay | 756 |
| Area Chart Titles & Options Form | 757 |
| ASCII Delimiters Overlay | 769 |
| Bar/Line Chart Data Form | 770 |
| Bar/Line Chart: Size/Place Overlay | 772 |
| Bar/Line Chart Titles & Options Form | 773 |
| Box Options Form | 786 |
| Box Styles Overlay | 789 |
| Bullet List Form | 789 |
| Bullet List: Size/Place Overlay | 791 |
| Bullet Shape Overlay | 792 |
| Button Options Form (Version 2.3) | 793 |
| Calculate Overlay | 794 |
| CGA Color Palette Overlay | 795 |
| Change Chart Type Overlay | 796 |
| Chart Data Option Overlay | 797 |
| Circle Options Form | 797 |
| Color Palette Setup Form | 799 |
| Color Selection Overlay | 802 |
| Create Chartbook Overlay | 802 |
| Create Palette Overlay (Version 2.3) | 803 |
| Create Slide Show Overlay | 805 |
| Create/Edit Chartbook Form | 806 |
| Create/Edit Slide Show Form | 807 |
| Current Chart Options Overlay | 809 |
| Current International Settings Overlay (Version 2.3) | 810 |
| Default International Settings Overlay (Version 2.3) | 813 |
| Default Settings Form | 816 |
| Delays Overlay | 819 |
| Directions Overlay | 821 |
| Export for Professional Write Overlay | 822 |
| Export Metafile Overlay | 823 |

| | |
|---|---|
| Export Picture Overlay | 824 |
| Film Recorder Setup Form | 826 |
| Fonts Overlay (Version 2.3) | 828 |
| Free Form Text Form | 828 |
| Free Form Text: Size/Place Overlay | 829 |
| Global Options Form | 831 |
| Go To Overlay (Version 2.13) | 832 |
| Group Options Form | 834 |
| High/Low/Close Chart Data Form | 835 |
| High/Low/Close Chart: Size/Place Overlay | 836 |
| High/Low/Close Chart Titles & Options Form | 838 |
| HyperShow Menu Overlay (Version 2.3) | 849 |
| Import ASCII Data Form | 851 |
| Import Excel Chart Overlay (Version 2.3) | 853 |
| Import Excel Data Form (Version 2.3) | 854 |
| Import Lotus Data Form | 856 |
| Import Lotus Graph Form | 859 |
| Import Titles and Legends Overlay | 860 |
| Line Options Form | 862 |
| New Symbol File Overlay | 864 |
| Organization Chart Form | 865 |
| Organization Chart: Size/Place Overlay | 866 |
| Org Chart Options Form | 867 |
| Parallel/Serial Overlay | 870 |
| Patterns Overlay | 872 |
| Pause Overlay | 873 |
| Pie Chart Data Form | 874 |
| Pie Chart: Size/Place Overlay | 877 |
| Pie Chart Titles & Options Form | 878 |
| Plot Chart Options Overlay | 884 |
| Plot Slide Show Options Overlay | 886 |
| Plotter Setup Form | 889 |
| Polygon Options Form | 890 |
| Polyline Options Form | 892 |
| Practice Cards Form | 894 |
| Practice Cards Options Overlay | 895 |
| Print Chart Options Overlay | 897 |
| Print Slide Show Options Overlay | 899 |
| Printer 1 Setup Form | 902 |
| Printer 2 Setup Form | 903 |

| | |
|---|---|
| Range Names Overlay (Version 2.3) | 904 |
| Record Chart Option Overlay | 905 |
| Record Slide Show Options Overlay | 905 |
| Save Chart As Symbol Overlay | 907 |
| Save Chart Overlay | 908 |
| Save Template Overlay | 910 |
| Screen Setup Form | 912 |
| ScreenShow Effects Form | 913 |
| Select CGM Metafile Form (Version 2.3) | 917 |
| Select Chart Form | 918 |
| Select Chartbook Form | 919 |
| Select Directory Form | 920 |
| Select Excel Chart Form (Version 2.3) | 922 |
| Select Excel Worksheet Form (Version 2.3) | 923 |
| Select File Form | 924 |
| Select Lotus Worksheet Form (Version 2.3) | 926 |
| Select Palette Form (Version 2.3) | 927 |
| Select Slide Show Form | 928 |
| Select Symbol File Form | 929 |
| Select Template Form (<Get template>) | 931 |
| Select Template Form (<From chartbook>) | 932 |
| Select Worksheet Form (Versions 2.13 and earlier) | 933 |
| Shaded Background Overlay | 933 |
| Simple List Form | 935 |
| Simple List: Size/Place Overlay | 936 |
| Size/Place Overlays | 937 |
| Slide Show List Option Overlay | 937 |
| Text Attributes Overlay | 938 |
| Text Options Form | 940 |
| Three Columns Form | 943 |
| Three-Column Chart: Size/Place Overlay | 944 |
| Title Chart Form | 945 |
| Title Chart: Size/Place Overlay | 946 |
| Titles & Options Forms | 947 |
| Transitions Overlay | 947 |
| Two Columns Form | 948 |
| Two-Column Chart: Size/Place Overlay | 949 |
| X Data Type Menu Overlay | 950 |

| | |
|---|---|
| Function Keys | 952 |
| F1-Help | 952 |
| F2-Draw chart (individual charts) | 952 |
| F2-Draw chart (multiple charts) | 953 |
| F2-Preview | 953 |
| F2-Preview show | 954 |
| F2-Show palette | 954 |
| F3-Applications (version 2.3) | 954 |
| F3-CGA palette | 955 |
| F3-Change dir | 955 |
| F3-Gallery (version 2.3) | 955 |
| F3-Intl formats (version 2.3) | 955 |
| F3-Save (version 2.3) | 956 |
| F3-Select files | 956 |
| F3-Set X type (versions 2.13 and earlier) | 957 |
| F3-XY position | 957 |
| F4-Calculate (versions 2.13 and earlier) | 957 |
| F4-Clear ranges | 958 |
| F4-Draw/Annot (version 2.3) | 958 |
| F4-Redraw | 958 |
| F4-Reselect | 959 |
| F4-Spell check | 959 |
| F5-Attributes | 960 |
| F5-Prev palette (version 2.3) | 961 |
| F5-Set X type (version 2.3) | 961 |
| F6-Calculate (version 2.3) | 961 |
| F6-Choices (Draw/Annotate) | 962 |
| F6-Choices (slide show) | 962 |
| F6-Colors | 963 |
| F6-Next palette (version 2.3) | 963 |
| F6-Range names (version 2.3) | 963 |
| F6-Shaded bkgd | 964 |
| F7-Data | 964 |
| F7-Size/Place (individual charts) | 965 |
| F7-Size/Place (Main Menu) | 965 |
| F7-Size/Place (multiple charts) | 965 |
| F8-Data | 966 |
| F8-Draw | 966 |
| F8-Final mode | 966 |
| F8-HyperShow menu (version 2.3) | 967 |

| | |
|---|---|
| F8-Options (Import ASCII Data form) | 967 |
| F8-Options (Main Menu) | 967 |
| F8-Options (Organization and Data Chart forms) | 968 |
| F8-Quick mode | 968 |
| F8-User menu (versions 2.13 and earlier) | 969 |
| F9-Edit (version 2.3) | 969 |
| F9-More series | 969 |
| F10-Continue | 970 |
| F10-Edit + Clear (version 2.3) | 970 |

## TWENTY-FIVE  Draw Partner Forms and Function Keys . . . . . . . . . . . . . . . . . . . . . . **971**

| | |
|---|---|
| Arc Options Form (Version 2.3) | 971 |
| Box Options Form | 972 |
| Button Options Form (Version 2.3) | 975 |
| Circle Options Form | 975 |
| Circular Text Options Form | 977 |
| Freehand Options Form (Version 2.3) | 979 |
| Line Options Form (Version 2.3) | 980 |
| Options Form (Version 2.3) | 982 |
| Polygon Options Form | 982 |
| Polyline Options Form | 984 |
| Regular Polygon Options Form (Version 2.3) | 985 |
| Text Options Form | 987 |
| Wedge Options Form (Version 2.3) | 989 |
| Function Keys | 990 |
|     F1-Help | 991 |
|     F2-Preview | 991 |
|     F3-Change dir | 991 |
|     F4-Redraw | 992 |
|     F5-Mouse speed | 992 |
|     F6-Choices | 992 |
|     F7-Save | 993 |
|     F8-Options | 993 |
|     F8-Draw | 994 |
|     F9-View | 994 |
|     F10-Continue | 994 |

| PART SIX | Appendixes | 995 |

## A — Additional Support for Harvard Graphics ... 997
Software Publishing Corporation ... 997
Slide Services ... 997

## B — Installation ... 999
What Comes with Harvard Graphics? ... 1000
Equipment Needed ... 1000
Equipment Options ... 1001
    Mouse ... 1001
    Digital Tablet ... 1001
    Hard Disk Options ... 1001
    LIM 4.0 Expanded Memory (Version 2.3) ... 1002
    Monitors ... 1002
    Output Devices ... 1002
Making Backup and Working Copies ... 1002
Installing Version 2.3 ... 1003
Installing Version 2.13 or Earlier on a Hard Disk ... 1004
    Preliminary Steps ... 1005
    Installation Instructions ... 1006
Preparing to Run Version 2.13 or Earlier from Two 3 1/2-Inch Disk Drives ... 1008
Installing Draw Partner Version 1.0 ... 1008
Installing the Virtual Device Interface (VDI) ... 1009
Harvard Graphics and Memory-Resident Programs ... 1010

## C — Harvard Graphics Accessories ... 1011
Using Business Symbols ... 1012
Designer Galleries ... 1013
    Installing Designer Galleries ... 1014
    Using Designer Galleries ... 1014
Military Symbols ... 1016
Quick-Charts ... 1016

|  |  |
|---|---|
| Installing Quick-Charts | 1017 |
| Using Quick-Charts | 1018 |
| ScreenShow Utilities | 1019 |
| Using the ScreenShow Projector | 1019 |
| The CAPTURE Utility | 1020 |
| U.S. MapMaker Overview | 1023 |
| Installing U.S. MapMaker | 1023 |
| Using U.S. MapMaker | 1024 |

## D  Harvard Graphics Tables ............ 1035

| | |
|---|---|
| Fonts and Text Attributes | 1035 |
| Text Sizes | 1042 |
| International Characters | 1043 |
| Line Styles | 1043 |
| Markers | 1044 |
| Screen Patterns | 1044 |
| Printer Patterns (HP LaserJet) | 1045 |
| Printer Patterns (PostScript) | 1045 |
| Grey Scale (Version 2.13 and Earlier) | 1046 |
| Symbols | 1046 |
| Animated Sequences (Version 2.3) | 1049 |

## E  Menus ............ 1051

| | |
|---|---|
| Harvard Graphics Version 2.1 - 2.13 Menus | 1051 |
| Harvard Graphics Version 2.3 Menus | 1054 |
| Draw Partner Version 1.0 Menus | 1057 |
| Draw Partner Version 1.1 Menus | 1059 |

## Index ............ 1061

# ACKNOWLEDGMENTS

We want to thank Dan Meub, Pat Hardee, Terri O'Neel, and Shirley Bunger, of Software Publishing Corporation for their valuable encouragement and assistance. In addition, Don Brenner and Peter Lawson of Software Publishing Corporation provided much-appreciated technical assistance along with all the rest of the helpful technical support people at SPC. Our appreciation also goes out to Lisa Biow, whose insightful criticisms of our writing greatly improved this book; Leslie Tilley, for her outstanding copy edit; and John Levy for his thorough technical review. We also want to thank Steve Hom for assisting us in the initial stages of this project.

Last, and most importantly, we want to thank the fine people at Osborne/McGraw-Hill for their hard work and dedication. Notably, Cindy Hudson, whose faith in this project made it a reality; Liz Fisher, our acquisitions editor, for her support and professionalism; Ilene Shapera and Judith Brown for their hard work; and to the many others at Osborne/McGraw-Hill who were involved in this project.

## About This Book

This book is a complete and up-to-date reference guide to Harvard Graphics. If you are currently using Harvard Graphics versions 2.0 through 2.13, you will find all of the necessary information to use Harvard Graphics effectively and efficiently. If you are using the newest release of Harvard Graphics, version 2.3, you will find all of the new features presented in detail in addition to the existing features which contributed to Harvard Graphics' success.

It is not necessary for you to have any previous experience with Harvard Graphics in order to use this book. If you are a beginner, you will want to pay attention to the first three chapters where the setup and general principles of Harvard Graphics usage are discussed. If you are an experienced user of Harvard Graphics, you too will benefit from the discussions of the many advanced features that Harvard Graphics has to offer.

Using this book does require that you know fundamental MS-DOS principles, however. At the very least, you should be familiar with file-naming conventions and how to reference your drive/directory paths. If you lack these skills, you should consult your DOS manual or an introductory DOS book before you continue.

By reading this book, you will be introduced to all elements of Harvard Graphics usage as well as principles of good chart production. You will want to keep this book handy whenever you are using Harvard Graphics. In particular, you will find that the reference section provides you with instant descriptions of all of the Harvard Graphics options. In addition, you may want to review some of the many tips and suggestions provided throughout this book, especially as you become more experienced with Harvard Graphics.

In writing this book, we have drawn on our years of experience with Harvard Graphics. Our experience as Harvard Graphics trainers in the corporate training environment has also influenced the style, layout, and content that you find here. Through our experiences, and those of the participants in our courses, we have tried to make your learning and use of Harvard Graphics as efficient and enjoyable as possible.

## How This Book Is Organized

To assist you in your use of Harvard Graphics, this book has been organized into six parts. The following is a description of each of these parts.

The first part describes the use of Harvard Graphics. The first three chapters introduce the basics of Harvard Graphics. These include creating and saving charts, defining your default settings, and configuring Harvard Graphics for your particular output devices. Chapters 4 through 7 provide you with detailed descriptions of the Harvard Graphics chart styles. Taken together, these chapters contain hundreds of charts that depict the influence of Harvard Graphics' many options and settings. In Chapters 8 through 14, each of Harvard Graphics' advanced features is described in detail. These discussions include working with templates, using macros, importing data, drawing and annotating on your charts, and creating slide shows.

The second part of this book focuses on the features and capabilities added to Harvard Graphics in the newest release, version 2.3. These features include the expanded color palette support, speed keys, the applications menu, and HyperShow, just to name a few. If you have been using an earlier version of Harvard Graphics, you can use this part of the book to quickly familiarize yourself with the new release.

Part Three contains a detailed guide to using the newest and most powerful addition to Harvard Graphics, Draw Partner. Draw Partner provides you with stunning drawing capabilities and a wide variety of special effects. Among these are the ability to add freehand drawings, zoom in for detailed drawing and editing, add a shadow to any object, create curved text, edit individual points in objects, create special effects called sweeps, or automatically align distant objects in the drawing area.

Principles of effective chart production are the focus of the fourth part of this book. Among the many topics discussed are recommendations for producing that perfect chart or presentation. Also covered are common charting mistakes that result in chart distortions and illusions. By learning how these mistakes reduce the effectiveness of your charts, you can become a better chart producer.

A complete reference book would not be complete without a handy reference to the many Harvard Graphics and Draw Partner forms and function keys. Part Five contains over three hundred pages devoted to describing the effects of every option found in Harvard Graphics. This part is organized alphabetically to help you quickly locate just the information you need.

Last, but not least, are the appendixes. Included are descriptions of installing Harvard Graphics and using the many Harvard Graphics accessories. Here is also where you will find examples of the Harvard Graphics fonts, markers, and patterns.

## Conventions Used in This Book

In order to be consistent in the discussion of the many Harvard Graphics features, the following conventions have been observed throughout this book.

- Any commands that you must enter on your keyboard are represented in boldface.

- Keys on your keyboard, such as ENTER and ESC, are represented in small caps.

- All menus, forms, and overlays are referred to by name. For example, the Main Menu, the Default Settings form, and the Save chart overlay are labeled as such in Harvard Graphics. The names of these objects, however, do not necessarily include the words "menu," "form," or "overlay" on your screen.

- Menu selections are enclosed in angle brackets. For instance, selecting <Create new chart> from the Main Menu causes Harvard Graphics to display the Create New Chart menu.

- Options on forms and overlays are referred to by enclosing the option name in quotation marks. For example, "Orientation" is an option on the Default Settings form.

- Function keys are represented using small caps for the function key followed by the description that appears in the function key banner on your screen. F1-Help, for example, is how the help function key is referenced.

## Additional Help from Osborne/McGraw-Hill

Osborne/McGraw-Hill provides top-quality books for computer users at every level of computing experience. To help you build your skills, we suggest that you look for the books in the following Osborne/McGraw-Hill series that best address your needs.

The "Teach Yourself" series is perfect for beginners who have never used a computer before or who want to gain confidence in using program basics. These books provide a simple, slow-paced introduction to the fundamental usage of popular software packages and programming languages. The "Mastery Learning" format ensures that concepts are learned thoroughly before progressing to new material. Plenty of exercises and examples (with answers at the back of the book) are used throughout the text.

The "Made Easy" series is also for beginners or users who may need a refresher on the new features of an upgraded product. These in-depth introductions guide users step-by-step from the program basics to intermediate-level usage. Plenty of "hands on" exercises and examples are used in every chapter.

The "Using" series presents fast-paced guides that quickly cover beginning concepts and move on to intermediate-level techniques, and even some advanced topics. These books are written for users already familiar with computers and software, and who want to get up to speed fast with a certain product.

The "Advanced" series assumes that the reader is already an experienced user who has reached at least an intermediate skill level, and is ready to learn more sophisticated techniques and refinements.

The "Complete Reference" books are a series of handy desktop references for popular software and programming languages that list every command, feature, and function of the product, along with brief, detailed descriptions of how they are used. Books are fully indexed and often include tear-out command cards. The "Complete Reference" series is ideal for all users, beginners and pros.

The "Pocket Reference" is a pocket-sized, shorter version of the "Complete Reference" series, and provides only the essential commands, features, and functions of software and programming languages for users who need a quick reminder of the most important commands. This series is also written for all users and every level of computing ability.

The "Secrets, Solutions, Shortcuts" series is written for beginning users who are already somewhat familiar with the software, and for experienced users at intermediate and advanced levels. This series provides clever tips and points out shortcuts for using the software to greater advantage. Traps to avoid are also mentioned.

Osborne/McGraw-Hill also publishes many fine books that are not included in the series described above. If you have questions about which Osborne book is right for you, ask the salesperson at your local book or computer store.

## Other Osborne/McGraw-Hill Books of Interest to You

We hope that *Harvard Graphics: The Complete Reference* will assist you in mastering this fine product and will also pique your interest in learning more about other ways to better use your computer.

If you're interested in expanding your skills so you can be even more "computer efficient," be sure to take advantage of Osborne/McGraw-Hill's large selection of top-quality computer books that cover all varieties of popular hardware, software, programming languages, and operating systems. While we cannot list every title here that may relate to Harvard Graphics and to your special computing needs, here are just a few of the books that complement *Harvard Graphics: The Complete Reference*.

If you're looking for intermediate-level books on Lotus 1-2-3, see *Using 1-2-3 Release 2.2*, by The LeBlond Group, or *Using 1-2-3 Release 3*, by Martin S. Matthews and Carole Boggs Matthews. Both are fast-paced, hands-on guides that quickly cover basics before discussing intermediate techniques and even some advanced topics. *Using 1-2-3 Release 2.2*, by The LeBlond Group, is a book/disk package that also features an add-in word processor to use with Lotus 1-2-3. The word processor is written by Geoff LeBlond, author of the outstanding book on using 1-2-3 that has sold over one million copies.

*1-2-3 Release 2.2: The Complete Reference*, by Mary Campbell, is an indispensable reference that covers Lotus Releases 2.0, 2.1, and 2.2. You'll find every feature, command, and function thoroughly described for beginners and advanced users alike. Campbell has organized the book so you can quickly find information on entering data, macros, graphics, printing, and more.

For all PC-DOS and MS-DOS users with any DOS version up to 3.3, see *DOS: The Complete Reference, Second Edition,* by Kris Jamsa. This book provides comprehensive coverage of every DOS command and feature. Whether you need an overview of the disk operating system or a reference for advanced programming and disk management techniques, you'll find it here.

## Companion Disk and Videos

The authors are making the following products available in conjunction with this book. These products can be purchased from Data Works of Houston by filling out the enclosed coupon or a facsimile.

**The Chart Advisor**   (5 1/4-inch disks, 3 1/2-inch on request) The Chart Advisor is a Harvard Graphics HyperShow that provides you with detailed descriptions of more than 35 different chart styles that you can create with Harvard Graphics. Chart Advisor provides descriptions of, and solutions for, eight common charting mistakes. System requirements: Harvard Graphics 2.3, EGA or VGA, and a hard disk.

**Making Charts with Harvard Graphics 2.3**   (VHS video tape) Ideal for the beginner, this video shows you the fundamentals of Harvard Graphics usage. Watch or work along as the tape shows you, step-by-step, how to create each category of chart using Harvard Graphics 2.3.

**Harvard Graphics 2.3 ScreenShows**   (VHS video tape) This video shows how to get the most out of Harvard Graphics' powerful Screen-Show and HyperShow capabilities. Learn how to produce interactive ScreenShows, create attention-catching animation, use templates in slide shows, as well as automate such tasks as printing and spell checking.

The Data Works of Houston video training tapes are designed to be both pleasing to watch and informative. Your TV displays an actual Harvard Graphics session as Harvard Graphics expert and author Cary Jensen demonstrates tips and techniques you can use to make more informative charts and presentations using Harvard Graphics.

## Order Form

| Product | Quantity | Amount |
|---|---|---|
| The Chart Advisor ($19.95 ea.) | _____ | _____ |
| Making Charts with Harvard Graphics 2.3 ($49.95 ea.) | _____ | _____ |
| Harvard Graphics 2.3 ScreenShows ($49.95 ea.) | _____ | _____ |
| Shipping and handling: add $5 per tape and $3 per disk. International orders add $10 per tape and $6 per disk. | | _____ |
| Texas residents please add 8.25% state sales tax | | _____ |
| | Total | _____ |

Please make your check or money order out to Data Works of Houston. All funds must be drawn on U.S. banks. Please allow two to four weeks for delivery. This offer expires June 30, 1991.

Send to: Data Works of Houston
P.O. Box 273283
Houston, Texas 77277-3283

Osborne/McGraw-Hill assumes NO responsibility for this offer. This is solely an offer of Data Works of Houston and not of Osborne/McGraw-Hill.

# WHY THIS BOOK IS FOR YOU

Whether you are an everyday Harvard Graphics user, an occasional user, or are merely thinking of purchasing Harvard Graphics, you will find this book to be an invaluable resource. This book is the most complete and up-to-date book available on Harvard Graphics. The use of every Harvard Graphics and Draw Partner feature is covered in detail. Have this book handy whenever you are using Harvard Graphics.

This book is actually three books in one. The first 18 chapters provide you with the most accurate and detailed description of using Harvard Graphics and Draw Partner you can buy. Each of these features is described using a combination of step-by-step instructions with detailed descriptions of special features, tricks, and solutions.

This book is also a guide to creating quality charts and presentations. If you have had formal training in graphic design and chart production, you will find Chapters 19 through 23 to be a handy refresher. If you are new to chart production, these chapters will provide you with an invaluable introduction to the art of graphic communication.

Finally, in Chapters 24 and 25 you will find a comprehensive, quick reference to the many forms and function keys in Harvard Graphics and Draw Partner. These forms and function keys are presented in alphabetical order for easy look-up. Each feature described in the reference section is presented in a compact yet informative fashion, permitting you to answer your Harvard Graphics and Draw Partner questions without resorting to time-consuming trial and error.

## Learn More About Harvard Graphics

Here is an excellent selection of other Osborne/McGraw-Hill books on Harvard Graphics and other compatible software that will help you build your skills and maximize the power of the graphics package you have selected.

*Harvard Graphics Made Easy,* by Mary Campbell, helps you learn Harvard Graphics step-by-step from the basics of creating charts and using the drawing feature to more advanced procedures such as developing presentation-quality slide shows and mastering macro techniques. You'll learn how to get great results with overhead transparencies and 35mm slides. With the handy supplementary disk that's included, all the sample programs used in the book will be instantly at your fingertips — what a time-saver!

If you are a beginning WordPerfect 5.1 user looking for an in-depth guide that leads you from basics to intermediate-level techniques, see *WordPerfect 5.1 Made Easy,* by Mella Mincberg. If you are using WordPerfect 5.0, look for *WordPerfect Made Easy, Series 5 Edition* or *WordPerfect Made Easy* if you have release 4.2. Both are by Mella Mincberg.

*WordPerfect 5.1: The Complete Reference,* by Karen Acerson, is ideal for all users, both beginners and pros. This desktop resource lists *every* WordPerfect 5.1 command, feature, and function along with in-depth discussions of how they are used. Acerson's *WordPerfect: The Complete Reference, Series 5 Edition* covers release 5.0 and *WordPerfect: The Complete Reference* covers release 4.2.

*1-2-3 Release 2.2 Made Easy,* by Mary Campbell, takes you through all the basics of working with Lotus 1-2-3 Releases 2.0, 2.01, and 2.2, the popular spreadsheets for the IBM PC and compatible computers. From beginning concepts to intermediate techniques, you'll learn 1-2-3 as you follow hands-on lessons filled with examples and exercises. Also see *1-2-3 Release 3 Made Easy* if you have Lotus 1-2-3 Release 3.0.

# Harvard Graphics

Overview
Harvard Graphics Basics
Setup and Default Settings
Text Charts
Organization Charts
XY Charts: Bar/Line, Area, and High/Low/Close
Pie Charts
Producing Output
Drawing and Annotating
Multiple Charts
Templates and Chartbooks
Importing and Exporting
Slide Shows
Macros

**PART ONE**

# Overview

An Introduction to Harvard Graphics
Harvard Graphics Features

This chapter provides an overview of Harvard Graphics, its origins, and its features. If you have little or no experience with Harvard Graphics, you will want to read this chapter to familiarize yourself with this software. If you are already an experienced Harvard Graphics user, you may want merely to scan this chapter before proceeding to the sections of this book that interest you most.

## An Introduction to Harvard Graphics

Harvard Graphics is a high-end chart production application, marketed by Software Publishing Corporation. With Harvard Graphics you can create presentation-quality charts, and then print, plot, or produce slides of them. You can even combine your charts into a computerized slide show that can be displayed on your monitor, often called a desktop presentation.

Harvard Graphics is the most popular presentation graphics application for DOS-based personal computers ever sold. It is popular because it is an intelligent and easy-to-use application that is packed with features. The first time you use Harvard Graphics you will be able to produce quality charts with a minimum of effort. As you gain more experience with the program, you will want to use its wide variety of features to create custom tailored charts and images. These features include capabilities for adding drawings and annotations to charts, importing and exporting charts and data, building computerized presentations, and creating customized symbols such as a company logo to include in charts. An example of a chart created with Harvard Graphics is shown in Figure 1-1.

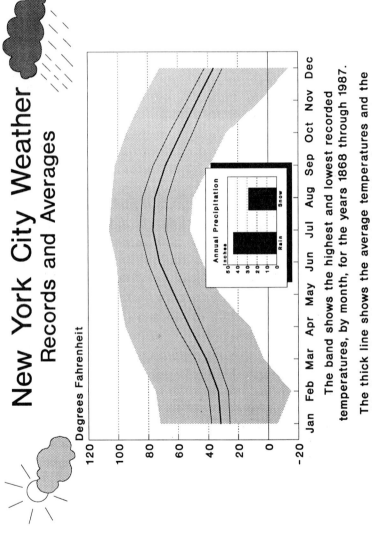

**Figure 1-1.** A chart made with Harvard Graphics

Before PC-graphing software like Harvard Graphics became available, you had three options when you needed a chart. One was to use paper, pens or pencils, stencils, and rulers to draw the chart yourself. This tedious process usually resulted in a chart that was usable, but probably not "presentation" quality. Your second option was to turn over the chore to graphic artists, who had the technical expertise, material and equipment, and talent necessary to produce presentation-quality charts, transparencies, and slides. The last alternative was to use a mainframe computer graphics package. Unfortunately, creating charts with mainframe systems was both costly and difficult.

Two developments in the computer industry are responsible for providing the capability to create high-quality charts on PCs. One of these was the availability of affordable output devices such as dot matrix and laser printers, pen plotters, and, increasingly, film recorders. The other was the development of graphing software for PCs.

The introduction of presentation graphics software for PCs has led to an increase in the volume and quality of the charts being used in business today. Not only has graphing software simplified the chart production process, but it has led to the development of new presentation technologies, such as desktop presentations.

Of all the presentation graphics packages available, none has had the impact of Harvard Graphics. Harvard Graphics has defined and extended the state of the art in business and presentation graphics and has consistently won praise and recognition as the presentation graphics software package of choice. Awards it has received include Editor's Choice (*PC Magazine,* 1987 and 1988), Top Rated (*Personal Computing,* 1989), Graphic Product of the Year (*InfoWorld,* 1988), and World Class Award *(PC World,* 1987, 1988, 1989), to mention a few.

That Harvard Graphics has earned this recognition is not an accident. It is the result of Software Publishing Corporation's commitment to providing ease of use and powerful features in one package. These ingredients have proven to be a winning combination for beginning chart producers and experienced graphics professionals alike.

## Harvard Graphics Features

The remainder of this chapter contains a brief overview of each of the major features of Harvard Graphics. Use these descriptions to familiarize yourself with the overall capabilities of the package. For specific information concerning any of the described features, refer to the appropriate chapter or chapters in this book.

## Ease of Use

In an age when the words *powerful software* often mean *complicated software,* Harvard Graphics stands out as a refreshing exception. The ease of use that has become synonymous with Harvard Graphics results from a combination of easy to follow menus and forms and a straightforward interface with other software applications and output devices.

Much of the chart creation process in Harvard Graphics involves making menu selections and changing settings on various forms. When you must make a choice, the alternatives are typically displayed before you, making your decisions easier. In addition, Harvard Graphics' online help can provide you with a wealth of information while you are creating your chart.

Using the program with output devices, such as printers, plotters, and film recorders, is often as easy as setting an option on one of Harvard Graphics' forms. And if you have a mouse connected to your computer, you can use it to perform most of the tasks in Harvard Graphics. About the only activity you cannot use a mouse for in Harvard Graphics is entering alphanumeric text or data.

The interface between Harvard Graphics and other software is another strong feature. Data used by other programs, such as a Lotus 1-2-3, can be easily incorporated into a Harvard Graphics chart. Likewise, the charts you create in Harvard Graphics can be exported for use with other software. This is a particularly useful feature if you want to use your chart with desktop publishing software, or include it in a report using word processing software.

## Selecting from a Variety of Chart Styles

Harvard Graphics can create many different types of charts. These include most of the popular chart styles, as well as many less common styles. The charts available in Harvard Graphics can be roughly divided into three categories: text charts, organization charts, and data charts. An example of each of these chart styles is shown in Figure 1-2.

As the name implies, *text charts* display words and numbers. Text charts are used when you want to present this type of information in an attractive and compact form. Most text charts are fairly brief and are used to summarize main ideas, present a title of a report or a presentation, or list text or numerical information. Text charts are ideal for creating handouts, creating slides, or for use in computerized presentations. Text chart styles available in Harvard Graphics include title charts, list charts, bullet charts, free-form text charts, and column charts with either two or three columns. These charts are covered in Chapter 4, "Text Charts."

*Organization charts* visually depict the structure and members of an organization. For example, they are often used to show the relative position of people in an organization. For each individual represented in an organization chart, his or her name, title, and a comment may be displayed. With Harvard Graphics you can create an organization chart containing as many as eight levels. This chart style is covered in Chapter 5, "Organization Charts."

*Data charts* graphically display numerical relationships. Numbers are represented by symbols such as lines, markers, pie slices, bars, and areas. Harvard Graphics can produce many types of data charts. Examples include pie charts, line charts, point charts, area charts, bar charts, band charts, needle charts, and high/low/close charts. Furthermore, with Harvard Graphics you can easily switch among most of these styles until you find the chart that best suits your needs. Pie charts are described in Chapter 7, "Pie Charts." The other data charts are covered in Chapter 6, "XY Charts."

## Customizing Charts

No matter which type of chart you decide to produce, Harvard Graphics provides you with many options for tailoring the chart to your specific needs. When you first create a chart, the program automatically selects default settings for each of the options for the selected chart type. In most cases, the Harvard Graphics default settings are tasteful and appropriate for that chart style. However, you will probably want to modify some options in order to customize your chart's appearance.

## Text Chart
### Text Chart Styles

*Title*
*Simple List*
*Bullet List*
*Two Column*
*Three Column*
*Free Form*

## Organization Chart

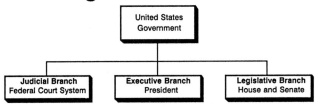

## Data Chart

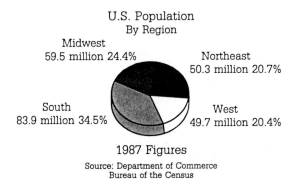

**Figure 1-2.** The three major categories of Harvard Graphics charts

The most common modification you will want to make is to provide a title for your chart. In addition, you can change colors and patterns, select three-dimensional effects for chart elements, label the axes, add a border, and so on. The combination of charting styles and the many options available give you nearly unlimited variety.

## Enhancing Charts with Drawings and Symbols

Harvard Graphics does the chart drawing for you. That is, on the basis of the data and/or text you enter and the options you select, it produces a professionally drawn chart. Sometimes you will want to add your own special touch to your chart. This enhancement may include an *annotation* (a description that clarifies or adds information), your company's logo, a detailed illustration, a pre-drawn image from Harvard Graphics' library of 300 symbols, or even a scanned photograph or drawing.

To assist you with these enhancements, Harvard Graphics provides drawing and symbol manipulation capabilities. These allow you to create sophisticated drawings to add to your chart. You can also use the drawing feature by itself to create a completely original chart or symbol. These topics are covered in Chapter 9, "Drawing and Annotating."

## Sharing Charts and Data Using Import/Export

Another valuable Harvard Graphics feature is its compatiblity with a variety of other software. This makes it easy to import both data and images, including charts, from other software, as well as to export Harvard Graphics charts for use by other software.

You can import data directly from a Lotus 1-2-3 spreadsheet or a file created by a database application. This saves you the time it would take to enter the data in a Harvard Graphics form and reduces data entry errors. You can also import charts or images created with other software. These importing techniques can just as easily be used to chart data that originated on a mainframe computer.

Sometimes you may want to use a Harvard Graphics chart or drawing in conjunction with other PC software, such as Ventura Publisher, PageMaker, OfficeWriter, Professional Write, WordPerfect, Microsoft Word, or AutoCAD, among others. Harvard Graphics can export your charts or symbols in a variety of file types that make using these images with other software easy. These topics are covered in Chapter 12, "Importing and Exporting."

## Improving Productivity with Templates

Harvard Graphics allows you to save a template for a chart. This feature is a real time-saver if you need to produce charts with certain characteristics on a regular basis. A template can keep track of where you want your title and legend placed on the chart, what font to use, the chart type and options, and even what drawings or annotations you want added to the chart.

If you regularly import data into Harvard Graphics, you will be pleased to learn that templates can be used to "remember" that you imported data for your chart. These templates are *linked* to the data set that contained the data. Each time you use a linked template, Harvard Graphics automatically imports the data all over again. If you update the data in your linked spreadsheet or other data file, you can instantly create a chart of the updated data by using the template.

If you make extensive use of templates, you can use *chartbooks* to keep your templates organized. Put simply, a chartbook contains a list of templates. You can organize your templates into chartbooks, each one relating to a different project or charting need, to make it easier to locate and choose the appropriate template. These topics are covered in Chapter 11, "Templates and Chartbooks."

## Creating Computerized Presentations

Computerized presentations are being used increasingly to aid people giving presentations, much like 35-mm slides or transparencies. Harvard Graphics can even be used to create automated presentations. A computerized slide show, called a Harvard Graphics Screenshow, consists of

Harvard Graphics charts stored on disk. You select the charts to be displayed, and in what order, for your slide show.

Harvard Graphics Screenshow supports a variety of special effects that you can use to control the transition from chart to chart. For example, the first chart in your slide show can *scroll* (slide) from the left onto your screen. This chart can then fade out as the second chart fades in. A well-planned series of transition effects can add a dramatic impact to your presentation.

If you want your slide show to be automated, Harvard Graphics permits you to specify how long each chart is displayed. Alternatively, you can set up the slide show to be interactive, going on to the next slide, or any other slide in the show, at the press of a key.

## Automating Tasks with Macros

Harvard Graphics permits you to create, save, and play a *macro*. A macro is a record of your keystrokes. Once you have created a macro, you can "play it," automatically performing an entire series of keystrokes as if you were pressing the keys one at a time. These macros are useful for automating a repetitive sequence of commands.

Most macros are created by recording keypresses while you are working with Harvard Graphics. It is also possible to write a macro much as you would a computer program, that is, by creating a file that consists of commands and keys to be pressed. This is especially useful when you want to create a fairly long or sophisticated macro. However, even when your macro is just a recorded macro, you can add features such as displaying customized messages to the screen, permitting user input, and pausing for specified time periods.

## Expanding Your Drawing Options with Draw Partner

In November 1989 Software Publishing Corporation began packaging a new drawing accessory called Draw Partner with Harvard Graphics. Draw Partner is a powerful drawing program that extends and complements Harvard Graphics' drawing capabilities. It permits you to create and edit Harvard Graphics symbols. Draw Partner provides you with a variety of state-of-the-art drawing features such as object rotation and flipping, object sweeping, curved text, and point editing, to name a few. However, because it is a separate program, it is necessary to exit Harvard Graphics in versions 2.13 and earlier, in order to use Draw Partner version 1.0.

If you purchased Harvard Graphics before Draw Partner was available, you can still purchase a copy from a software outlet, or contact Software Publishing Corporation for information. (See Appendix A for Software Publishing Corporation's address.) If you do a lot of drawing and annotating of Harvard Graphics charts, or simply want to work with the state of the art, you should seriously consider getting the Draw Partner accessory.

---

If you are new to Harvard Graphics, you will benefit by reading the next chapter, "Harvard Graphics Basics." If you are already comfortable with how the program works, you may want to skip to the chapters that interest you most.

# Harvard Graphics Basics

Harvard Graphics Menus, Forms, and Function Keys
Getting On-Line Help
Cursor Control: Moving Around in Harvard Graphics
Control Keys
Starting Harvard Graphics
The Main Menu
Working with Charts
Spell Checking the Current Chart

This chapter will show you how to use Harvard Graphics' menus and forms, tell you where to find the features that you need, and accustom you to the program's look and feel. The topics of getting, saving, and removing charts, and of using the spelling checker, are covered in detail in this chapter. The many other topics discussed, for example, creating charts, adding drawings, and outputting data, are intended only to familiarize you with Harvard Graphics' capabilities. These topics are discussed in detail in later chapters of this book. You will be referred to the appropriate chapters as these topics are covered.

This chapter assumes that you have installed Harvard Graphics on your hard disk or have prepared Harvard Graphics for a two-disk system. If you have not yet installed Harvard Graphics, refer to your Harvard Graphics manual or Appendix B, "Installation," for information on installing the program.

## Harvard Graphics Menus, Forms, and Function Keys

Almost everything you do in Harvard Graphics is through the use of menus, forms, and function keys. *Menus* allow you to choose other menus or forms. *Forms* are used to define chart characteristics, program parameters, and hardware settings. *Function keys* give you instant access to selected Harvard Graphics features. Menus, forms, and function keys are described in greater detail in the following sections.

## Menus

Harvard Graphics is a *menu-driven* program. This means that you tell it what charting facilities and utilities you want to use by making selections from menus. In Harvard Graphics, a menu is a vertical list of choices. When you first start Harvard Graphics, you will see the menu shown in Figure 2-1. This is the Main Menu.

In most situations, when you make a selection from the Main Menu, Harvard Graphics will display another menu, which permits you to further define your request. For instance, if you choose the first selection on the Main Menu, <Create new chart>, Harvard Graphics displays the Create New Chart menu, which allows you to select the type of chart. Likewise, a selection from a second-level menu may in turn

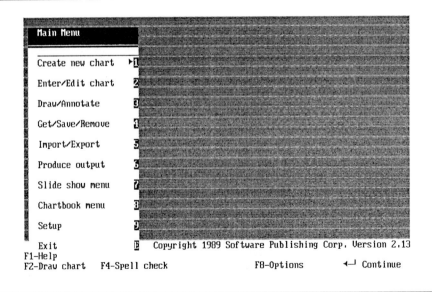

**Figure 2-1.** The Main Menu

produce yet another menu. Figure 2-2 shows the Text Chart Styles menu, which is displayed when you select <Text> from the Create New Chart menu. If you keep making menu selections, Harvard Graphics will eventually display a form rather than another menu (forms are described shortly).

It is best to think of the organization of the menus in Harvard Graphics as a tree, with the Main Menu acting as the trunk, and the various submenus representing the branches of the tree. When you make a selection from the Main Menu, you go to one of the branches. In order to return to the trunk, press the ESC key. ESC returns you to the immediately preceding menu. If your cursor is on a menu that is two levels below the Main Menu, you will need to press ESC twice to return to the Main Menu. To move from one branch of the menu system to another, you must first return to the trunk, that is, the Main Menu.

There are two ways to select one of the menu items from a menu: typing and highlighting.

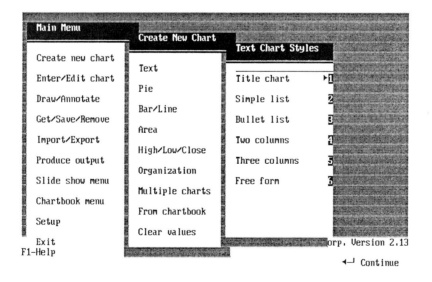

**Figure 2-2.** Text Chart Styles menu

### Selecting Menu Items by Typing

Each menu item has a number or letter printed to its right. If you type this number or letter, that menu item will immediately be selected. For example, if you press **1** at the Main Menu, Harvard Graphics will immediately display the Create New Chart menu. Typing is the quickest way to select a menu item using the keyboard.

### Selecting Menu Items by Highlighting

Selecting an item by highlighting requires two steps:

1. Highlight the menu items. Usually a menu item is highlighted when it is marked with an arrow and appears brighter than the other menu items. On monochrome monitors, a line is displayed above the menu item.

2. Press ENTER to select the highlighted item.

There are a number of ways to highlight a menu item. One is to press the SPACEBAR. Each time you press the SPACEBAR the cursor moves to the next item in the list and highlights it. If the last item in the menu is highlighted and you press the SPACEBAR, Harvard Graphics will highlight the first item in the menu.

Instead of using the SPACEBAR, you can also use the UP and DOWN cursor keys to move to the desired item. Or, if you use a mouse, you can highlight a menu item by using the mouse to move the cursor to the desired item.

The final way to highlight an item is to press the first letter of its name. If two or more menu items begin with the same first letter, pressing this letter repeatedly causes the highlighting to rotate through the alternatives. For example, pressing **S** repeatedly while at the Main Menu will cause the highlighting to alternate between <Setup> and <Slide show menu>.

*Caution:* This initial letter method generally works well, with one exception on the Main Menu. Because the E is used to select <Exit> using the typing method, you cannot highlight <Enter/Edit chart> by pressing **E**. When you press **E** while at the Main Menu, you will always exit Harvard Graphics.

## Forms

In Harvard Graphics all menus eventually lead to a form. There are forms for entering chart data, printing, saving, and for specifying default settings, to name a few. The form itself appears as a rectangular area on your screen. Each form displays one or more *options* within this area. An option is an area on the form where you choose what you want Harvard Graphics to do. The form shown in Figure 2-3, for example, was displayed after selecting <Get/Save/Remove> from the Main Menu, and then <Save chart> from the Get/Save/Remove menu. This form contains three options related to saving your chart, "Directory," "Chart will be saved as," and "Description," in which you enter the directory path, a filename, and a description of your chart. When you press F10-Continue, Harvard Graphics uses the values you entered to save your chart correctly.

Forms are referred to as *overlays* when they appear on top of, or over, other forms or menus. When you see a form referred to as an overlay, treat it exactly as you would any other form.

When a form is first displayed, the cursor appears on the form at the first option. You can easily move between options by using the TAB

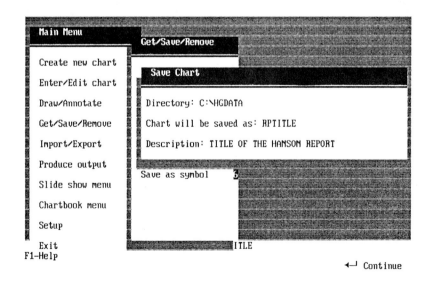

**Figure 2-3.**   Save Chart overlay

key to move to the next option and SHIFT-TAB to move to the previous option. TAB and SHIFT-TAB are usually the best keys for moving to options on forms because they will move the cursor directly to the next selection. You can also use the cursor keys (UP, DOWN, LEFT, and RIGHT arrows) and ENTER. ENTER moves the cursor to the next option, unless it is at the last one on the form, in which case ENTER acts like F10-Continue. If you have a mouse, you can use it to move the cursor. Additional detail on moving around on forms is provided later in this chapter in the section "Cursor Control: Moving Around in Harvard Graphics."

Once you have set the options on your form, press F10-Continue to go on to the next screen. Depending on the form, this next screen will contain either another form or a menu. To learn more about setting the options on a particular form, refer to the reference section or the chapter of this book where that form is discussed.

*Note:* Throughout this book you will see the instruction "press TAB" when you need to move the cursor to the next option on the form. This was done because TAB and SHIFT-TAB are preferred for moving to options. Keep in mind that you can also use the arrow keys (UP, DOWN, LEFT, and RIGHT arrows), or ENTER to move to the different options. However, when your cursor is on the last option on a form, pressing ENTER will have the same effect as F10-Continue.

## Types of Options on Forms

Options used on Harvard Graphics forms come in three types: entry options, list options, and toggle options. These types are described in the following sections.

### Entry Options

*Entry options* are those for which there exists an unlimited number of possible settings. Since the possible settings cannot be listed on screen, the option name is followed by a blank field, where you enter the desired setting. In some cases an entry option is provided with a default setting. To change a default value, press BACKSPACE, DEL, or CTRL-DEL to erase the option setting, and then enter the new setting. Examples of an entry option are shown in Figure 2-3. For instance, "Chart will be saved as" is an entry option since you must type in the chart name.

## List Options

In contrast to entry options, *list options* are accompanied by a list of all of the possible settings for that option. This list appears on the form next to the option name. When you display a form containing a list option, one of the alternatives for the option will already be selected (marked with an arrow). To select a different setting, first move your cursor to the option; the current settings will then be highlighted. Press the SPACEBAR repeatedly to move to the different settings. Each time you press the SPACEBAR, the next alternative becomes highlighted and selected. Examples of list options are shown in Figure 2-4. "Orientation," "Border," and "Font" are list options since you can see all the possible settings listed on the form next to the option names.

Instead of using the SPACEBAR, you can also move to a list option and press the first letter of a setting's name. This will automatically highlight and select that setting. If there is more than one setting with the same first letter, pressing that letter repeatedly will cycle through the settings, selecting and highlighting each one in turn.

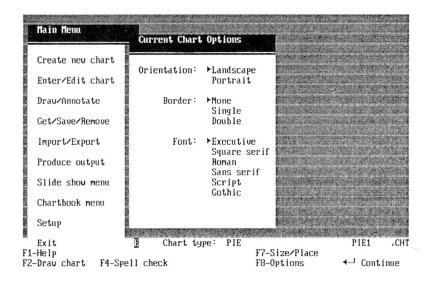

**Figure 2-4.** Current Chart Options overlay

There is yet another way to select list option settings. With the cursor at the option, use the arrow keys or the mouse to highlight the desired setting. Unlike using the SPACEBAR, highlighting a setting this way will not automatically select it. Select the highlighted setting by pressing ENTER or the SPACEBAR.

### Toggle Options

Like list options, *toggle options* also have a fixed number of settings to choose from. Unlike list options, however, all the possible settings are not displayed on the form at one time. Instead, only the current setting is displayed next to the option name. You can change the setting by first moving to the option, and then pressing the SPACEBAR to change the setting. Each time you press the SPACEBAR, a new setting is displayed.

All toggle options have a relatively small set of possible values. In many cases, there are only two settings: on and off. Pressing the SPACEBAR toggles (alternates) between these two settings, hence the name. In this case, an arrow precedes the option name when it is set to on, and is absent when it is off. Other toggle options have as many as 16 values. For these the current setting is displayed next to the option name.

Examples of toggle options can be seen on the Text Attributes overlay shown in Figure 2-5. "Fill," "Bold," "Italic," "Underline," and "Color" are all toggle options. The first four have only two settings, on or off. The "Color" option has 16 possible settings, 1 to 16. The current setting is indicated by the number to the right of the "Color" option.

## Function Key Banner

Every Harvard Graphics screen has a banner at the bottom of the screen. This banner lists the currently active function keys (F keys) along with a brief description of their functions. While several function keys are almost always present in the banner, such as F1-Help, and F10-Continue, others will only appear when you are performing certain functions. For example, the function key F8-Quick mode is only available when you are creating a custom multiple chart. The function keys used in Harvard Graphics are listed in Part Five, the reference section.

Harvard Graphics Basics 23

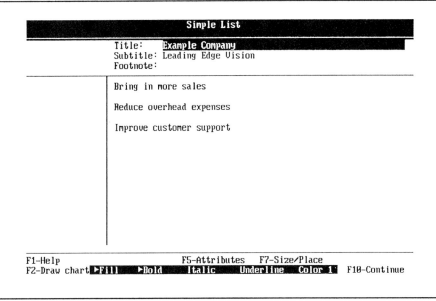

**Figure 2-5.** Text Attributes overlay

## Getting On-Line Help

Anytime during your Harvard Graphics session you can invoke the help system by pressing F1-Help. This will display a *context-sensitive* help screen. This means Harvard Graphics knows where you are in the program, and sometimes even what you are trying to do, and will provide specific information to help you perform your task.

There is no way to overemphasize the value of this on-line help. It is rich in content and well organized. In those instances where there is more information available than can fit on a single screen, Harvard Graphics instructs you to press PGUP and PGDN to display additional help screens. When you are through reading the screen(s), press ESC to return to your task.

## Cursor Control: Moving Around in Harvard Graphics

Harvard Graphics will accept cursor movement instructions from a number of sources. The primary source for most users is the standard computer keyboard. However, if you are one of the ever increasing number of mouse users, you will find that some capabilities can be accessed more quickly with the mouse. Many users alternate between keyboard and mouse.

Another device you can use for cursor control is a digital tablet. Since tablets are not nearly as popular as mice, Harvard Graphics directly supports only one digital tablet, the Kurta IS/ONE Tablet.

### The Keyboard

Harvard Graphics provides you with a number of quick and easy ways to move around menus and forms using a standard computer keyboard. These cursor movement keys are shown in Table 2-1. In some sections of Harvard Graphics there are additional key presses available. These special cases are discussed in the appropriate chapters of this book.

### Using a Mouse

When menus or forms are active, moving a mouse changes the cursor position. The movement of the cursor corresponds to the movement of your mouse. When you move your mouse to the left, the cursor moves to the left. When you move your mouse to the right, your cursor makes the corresponding movement. Up and down movements yield similar results.

If you are using a mouse on a multi-page form, moving your mouse above or below the boundary of the current page will cause the cursor to move to the next or previous page, respectively. In long lists, such as a list of files too long to display on one screen, moving your mouse beyond the bottom item will cause the list to scroll upward and display additional files. A similar effect occurs when additional items are listed above the first item displayed and you move your mouse up.

Besides using a mouse to move the cursor and to highlight items, the buttons of your mouse permit you to make selections from menus,

| Key | Function |
|---|---|
| CTRL-LEFT | Moves cursor to the previous word in the line. |
| CTRL-RIGHT | Moves cursor to next word in the line. |
| DOWN (arrow) | Moves cursor down one line, option, or menu item. |
| END | Moves cursor to the last option or line on a form. (*Note:* END does not work on the Select Chart, Select File, and Select Directory forms.) |
| ESC | Returns to the previous screen (press ESC multiple times to back up through previous menus and forms to the Main Menu), or cancels changes and returns to the previous screen. |
| HOME | Moves cursor to the first option or line on a form. |
| LEFT (arrow) | Moves cursor one character or option setting to the left. |
| PGDN | Displays the next page of a multi-page form or next screen of information on forms with a scrollable region. |
| PGUP | Displays previous page of a multi-page form or previous screen of information on forms with a scrollable region. |
| RIGHT (arrow) | Moves cursor one character or option setting to the right. |
| SHIFT-TAB | Moves cursor to the previous column or option on a form. |
| TAB | Moves cursor to the next column or option on a form. |
| UP (arrow) | Moves cursor down one line, option, or menu item. |

**Table 2-1.** Cursor Movement Key Functions

set list and toggle options on forms, and specify points while using Harvard Graphics' drawing utility. The effects of mouse button presses are listed in Table 2-2.

## Using a Digital Tablet

Harvard Graphics directly supports the Kurta IS/ONE graphics tablet. If you have a different digital tablet, you may find that some of the images you draw using Harvard Graphics' drawing utility are distorted.

| Button | Function |
|---|---|
| Left | Same as ENTER key. |
| Right | Same as ESC key. |
| Left and right combination | Activates cursor in the function key banner. To select an F key, move the mouse to highlight the desired key and press the left button to select it or the right button to escape. |

**Table 2-2.** Mouse Button Functions

The way you use a digital tablet pen is similar to the way you use a mouse. You may also be able to emulate ENTER and ESC keypresses using your digital tablet pen or cursor (see your digital tablet manual for instructions). However, you cannot trace or draw freehand using the digital tablet.

## Control Keys

Some of the editing capabilities in Harvard Graphics can only be accessed by using your keyboard. These control keys are listed in Table 2-3. Like the cursor keys, some of these keys are available only in certain sections of Harvard Graphics. These special uses will be discussed in the appropriate chapters of this book.

## Starting Harvard Graphics

If you have loaded Harvard Graphics onto your hard disk, the method you use to start will depend on whether the Harvard Graphics directory is included in your DOS path. You can see the path list by typing **PATH** at the DOS prompt. If your Harvard Graphics directory does not appear in the list, or DOS responds "No Path," then you must move to the Harvard Graphics directory before you can go further. Once you are in the Harvard Graphics directory, type **HG** to start the program. If the directory is on your DOS path, you can start Harvard Graphics from any directory by typing **HG**. Appendix B, "Installation," contains instructions on adding the Harvard Graphics directory to your DOS path.

If you are running the program from two 3 1/2-inch disks, after your computer has been turned on and you have loaded DOS, insert the Harvard Graphics Program disk in drive A. The chart disk that you prepared for storing chart files, which also contains the font and palette files, goes in drive B. If you have not yet prepared Harvard Graphics for use on a two-disk drive system, see Appendix B for this information.

If you do not use an AUTOEXEC.BAT file on your two-disk drive system, you will need to type the DOS command

PATH = A:\;B:\;

before you start Harvard Graphics. This command tells your computer to look for your Harvard Graphics files on both drive A and drive B. You can avoid having to enter this command every time you turn on your computer by adding this path statement to the AUTOEXEC.BAT file on your DOS disk, or creating this file if you do not already have one.

| Key | Function |
| --- | --- |
| BACKSPACE | Moves cursor back one space, deleting any character in that space. |
| CTRL-DEL | Deletes entire contents of line at the cursor. |
| CTRL-INS | Inserts a blank line above the line the cursor is on. |
| DEL | Deletes character at the cursor. |
| ENTER | Selects highlighted menu items on menus. Selects highlighted settings for form options and moves cursor to the next option on the form. |
| INS | Inserts character(s) at cursor. INS toggles on and off. The cursor appears as a block when INS is on, and as a small line when INS is off. |

**Table 2-3.**   Editing Control Key Functions

After you have completed any preparation to run Harvard Graphics on a two-disk drive system, type **HG** to start Harvard Graphics. Once you have done so, the Harvard Graphics logo displays on your screen while the program is loading. The Harvard Graphics' Main Menu is then displayed.

## Quick Start

Since Harvard Graphics version 2.1, it has been possible to start the program and have it immediately display a chart or a slide show without displaying the logo or Main Menu. This capability is called Quick Start.

Quick Start is very useful if you are presenting a slide show to an audience. In these situations you do not want to distract your audience, nor do you want to have to find and load the correct slide show. Instead, you want everyone, including yourself, to concentrate on the contents of your presentation. These same considerations apply even when you only need to display a single chart.

To start Harvard Graphics using Quick Start, add the name of the chart or slide show you want to display to the HG command. This name must include the chart or slide show extension, and needs to be separated from the HG command by at least one space. For example, your HG Quick Start command might look like this:

**HG MYSHOW.SHW**

When your slide show has finished and the last chart in the show is on the screen, or you no longer want to display a single chart, press any key to terminate the display. You will find yourself at the Main Menu.

You can also add the parameter /Q to the end of your Quick Start command to tell Harvard Graphics to return to DOS once the chart or slide show display is through. Then when you press any key at the end of your presentation, you will return directly to DOS. This statement might look like this:

**HG MYSHOW.SHW /Q**

## Exiting Harvard Graphics

To exit Harvard Graphics and return to DOS, select <Exit> from the Main Menu. Move your cursor to <Exit> and press ENTER or simply type **E**.

## The Main Menu

When you type **HG** at the DOS prompt, you start out at the Main Menu shown in Figure 2-1. The Harvard Graphics Main Menu is your starting place for any work you will do in the program. Each of the ten Main Menu selections is introduced in the following pages.

### Create New Chart

Select <Create new chart> in order to make a chart. When you choose this menu selection, Harvard Graphics will display a list of chart types to choose from. <Create new chart> can also be used to change the type of the chart you are currently working with.

### Enter/Edit Chart

<Enter/Edit chart> will return you to the form for the chart you are working on. For instance, if you create a bar/line chart, and then return to the Main Menu to perform a spell check, you will need to select <Enter/Edit chart> if you want to return to the chart form to modify the chart data or options.

### Draw/Annotate

<Draw/Annotate> takes you to Harvard Graphics' drawing screen, where you can add text (annotations) or drawings to your chart. In addition <Draw/Annotate> gives you access to the symbol files that came with your Harvard Graphics package. These symbols can be used as is, or they can be modified and incorporated into your own drawings. See Chapter 9, "Drawing and Annotating."

### Get/Save/Remove

<Get/Save/Remove> allows you to save and retrieve Harvard Graphics charts and chart templates, make symbols from your charts, and delete charts or other files from your disk. Chapter 11, "Templates and Chartbooks," and Chapter 9, "Drawing and Annotating," offer more details on these subjects.

## Import/Export

<Import/Export> allows you to import Lotus 1-2-3 data and charts, ASCII files, and PFS:GRAPH charts. It also enables you to export a Harvard Graphics chart in a number of graphics formats including encapsulated PostScript, HPGL (Hewlett-Packard Graphics Language), and CGM Metafile, as well as a special format for Software Publishing Corporation's Professional Write. See Chapter 12, "Importing and Exporting."

## Produce Output

Using the features found under <Produce output>, you can print, plot, or record the current chart, if you have the corresponding output device. You can also print, plot, or record a slide show. Other information you can print out includes chart data, a list of slides in a presentation, and practice cards, which you create for a slide show. See Chapter 8, "Producing Output."

## Slide Show Menu

Select <Slide show menu> to create, edit, or select a slide show. <Slide show menu> also permits you to display a slide show on your monitor or add special effects to a slide show. See Chapter 13, "Slide Shows."

## Chartbook Menu

<Chartbook menu> allows you to create, edit, or select a Harvard Graphics chartbook. A chartbook contains a list of templates. By organizing templates into different chartbooks, you can make it easier to locate and select the desired template. See Chapter 11, "Templates and Chartbooks."

## Setup

From <Setup>, you can modify your Harvard Graphics environment. This includes defining printers, plotter, and film recorders, choosing a default data directory, and selecting default chart options, as well as modifying the colors of the Harvard Graphics menus and forms. See Chapter 3, "Setup and Default Settings."

## Exit

Select <Exit> to leave Harvard Graphics and return to DOS. If you have not saved the most recent changes to your chart, Harvard Graphics will prompt you to either confirm that you want to exit, or allow you to continue so that you can save your work.

## Working with Charts

The following sections provide a general overview of Harvard Graphics charts. The first discusses the concept of the current chart. The remaining sections detail the basic procedures that you perform on charts. These include creating and saving charts, retrieving an existing chart, deleting charts, and spell checking a chart. Printing the current chart is discussed in Chapter 8, "Producing Output."

### The Current Chart

In Harvard Graphics you work with one chart at a time. This is called the *current chart*. When you first enter Harvard Graphics, there is no current chart. You can make a chart current either by creating a new chart or by retrieving an existing one.

Almost everything you do in Harvard Graphics happens to the current chart. When you print, you print the current chart; if you attempt to print a chart when there is no current chart, your printer will produce a blank page. Similarly, when you add drawings with <Draw/Annotate> those drawings are added to your current chart.

When you are viewing the Main Menu, the chart type of the current chart, if one exists, is shown centered at the top of the function key banner, and the name of the current chart is displayed to its right. Figure 2-6, for example, shows that a pie chart with the filename PIE1.CHT is the current chart. If you do not have a current chart, Harvard Graphics displays a copyright notice and the version number in place of the chart type and name (see Figure 2-1).

It is possible to have a current chart that has no name. This occurs when you have created a chart but not yet saved it. In these situations, the chart type is displayed in the usual place, while the location used for displaying the chart name will be blank until you save the chart the first time.

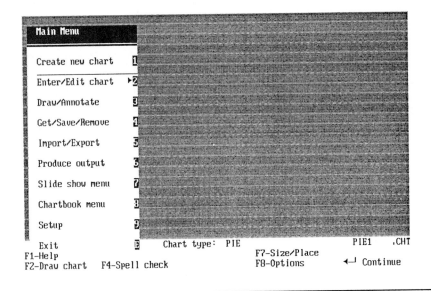

**Figure 2-6.** Current chart type and filename in the function key banner

## Displaying the Current Chart

While you are at the Main Menu or editing a chart, you can display the current chart image by pressing F2-Draw chart. If you press this key when there is no current chart, a blank screen will be displayed. After you press F2-Draw chart, the chart image or blank screen will remain on screen until you press any key.

Previewing a chart is particularly useful when you are setting options, since you can immediately see the effects of your settings.

## Creating a New Chart

Creating charts in Harvard Graphics involves five basic tasks. They are

1. Telling Harvard Graphics that you want to create a chart

2. Selecting a chart type

3. Entering text and/or numbers on a chart form

4. Changing chart options on forms to tailor the chart to your needs

5. Saving the chart to disk and/or printing, plotting, or recording the chart

The specific details of the third and fourth tasks vary depending on the type of chart you are creating. Refer to the appropriate chapter for information on these chart types. To create a new chart in Harvard Graphics, follow these steps:

1. At the Main Menu, select <Create new chart>. The Create New Chart menu shown in Figure 2-7 is displayed. This lists the general types of charts you can create in Harvard Graphics.

2. Select a chart type from this menu. To do so, move the cursor to the desired menu item using the SPACEBAR or cursor keys, and press ENTER. Or you can select a chart type directly by pressing the number associated with it.

3. Enter the data for the chart on the chart form. You can adjust the chart settings to suit your needs. For information about entering data and adjusting chart settings, see the chapters on individual chart types.

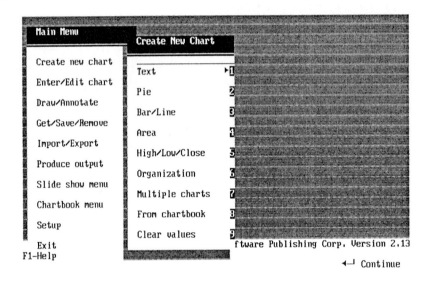

**Figure 2-7.** Create New Chart menu

## Saving the Current Chart

After you have created a new chart, you must save it if you want to use it later. Similarly, if you edit an existing chart, you must save those changes in order to make them permanent. The following steps assume you have just created or edited a chart:

1. If you are not at the Main Menu, press ESC until you return there.

2. Select <Get/Save/Remove>. The Get/Save/Remove menu, shown in Figure 2-8, is displayed.

3. Select <Save chart>. The Save Chart overlay, shown in Figure 2-9, is displayed. The current directory is listed at the "Directory" option.

4. If you want to save your chart to a different directory, press SHIFT-TAB to move to "Directory," and enter the full directory path. Then press TAB to move to the next option.

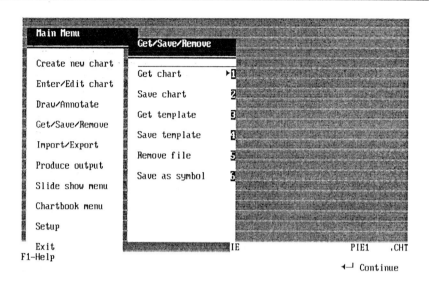

**Figure 2-8.**   Get/Save/Remove menu

5. At "Chart will be saved as" enter a name for your chart. This name is limited to eight characters and must conform to DOS filename conventions. Do not, however, include an extension with this name since Harvard Graphics automatically adds the extension .CHT to this chart name.

If this chart had previously been saved, the chart name that you had previously given the chart will appear in this field. If you want to replace the existing copy of your chart with the revised copy, keep the same chart name. If you would like to keep both old and revised charts, press CTRL-DEL to erase the contents of this field, and enter a new name for the chart.

6. Press TAB to move to "Description," and enter a description for the chart. If you provided a title for your chart on the chart form, the text from this title will already appear at the "Description"

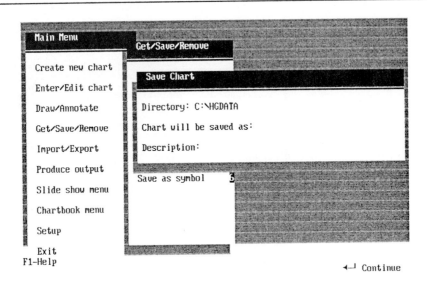

**Figure 2-9.**    Save Chart overlay

option. You may want to change this text (this will not change your chart title) or add a description, if there is not one. Descriptions can be helpful when you later need to retrieve your chart since they are displayed on the Select Chart form. The next section contains information on that form.

7. Press F10-Continue to save your chart and return to the Get/Save/Remove menu.

## Getting an Existing Chart

Use <Get chart> to retrieve a copy of an existing chart stored on disk. You would do this to view, print, or edit a chart created and saved earlier in the same work session or in a previous session. To get a chart that you have saved earlier, follow these steps:

1. At the Main Menu, select <Get/Save/Remove>. The Get/Save/Remove menu shown in Figure 2-8 is displayed.

Harvard Graphics Basics 37

2. Select <Get chart>. Harvard Graphics will display a Select Chart form similar to the one shown in Figure 2-10. The current directory is listed at the top of the form at the "Directory" option. Any chart files (files with the extension .CHT) in the current directory are displayed on the bottom part of the form. As you can see on your screen, the first chart file in the list is displayed at the "Filename" option (at the top of the form) and appears highlighted on the screen. The cursor is also positioned at "Filename."

3. Select the desired chart file in one of two ways. The most direct way is to position your cursor at "Filename," type in the name of the chart, with or without the extension, and then press ENTER. Alternatively, you can use the UP and DOWN arrow keys to highlight a chart file in the file list. Use PGUP and PGDN to display additional chart files in the directory if they do not all fit on one screen. As you move your cursor up and down the list, the chart file shown at "Filename" changes. When the chart file you want is displayed at "Filename," press ENTER.

```
                        Select Chart
Directory: C:\HGDATA
Filename:  PIE1     .CHT

Filename Ext  | Date     | Type  | Description
PIE1     .CHT | 12-03-89 | PIE   | Pie chart number 1.
HG       .CHT | 12-01-87 | CHART |
ANNOUNCE .CHT | 07-01-87 | CHART |
INTRO    .CHT | 07-01-87 | CHART |
OPENING  .CHT | 07-01-87 | CHART |
PRODS    .CHT | 07-01-87 | CHART |
REGIONS  .CHT | 07-01-87 | CHART |
SALES    .CHT | 07-01-87 | CHART |
TRISALES .CHT | 07-01-87 | CHART |

F1-Help      F3-Change dir
                                         F10-Continue
```

**Figure 2-10.**    Select Chart form

Once Harvard Graphics retrieves a chart, it displays it on the screen. Press any key to remove the chart and display the chart form appropriate to that chart type. You can then edit your chart or return to the Main Menu to produce output.

### Getting Files from Other Directories

You can retrieve a file from a directory other than the one shown at the "Directory" option in two different ways. The first is to press SHIFT-TAB to move your cursor to "Directory." Then use CTRL-DEL to erase the name of the directory shown. Type in the new drive and directory, and press ENTER.

*Note:* This is the only way to move to a directory that is on a drive different from that of the current directory.

The other way is to press F3-Change dir to display the Select Directory form shown in Figure 2-11. Again the current directory is

```
                       Select Directory
Directory: C:\HGDATA
Filename:  ..

  Filename Ext  |  Date    | Type |     Description
  ..            | 12-03-89 | DIR  | Parent Directory
  WEEKLY        | 12-03-89 | DIR  | Sub Directory
  3QRTRPT       | 12-03-89 | DIR  | Sub Directory
  STATS         | 12-03-89 | DIR  | Sub Directory




  F1-Help        F3-Select files
                                                      F10-Continue
```

**Figure 2-11.**   Select Directory form

displayed at "Directory." Any subdirectories of the current directory are shown on the bottom part of this form. The directory listed as ".." refers to the *parent directory*, the directory that is immediately above the current directory. (The current directory is a subdirectory of the parent directory.) If the current directory is the root directory of the current drive, there will be no parent directory (..) in the list.

Use the UP and DOWN cursor keys to highlight a directory in the list. Use PGUP and PGDN to display additional subdirectories if they do not all appear on the screen at one time. As you move your cursor to different directories, the directory shown at "Filename" changes. When the desired directory name appears at "Filename" press ENTER.

If the desired directory is not a subdirectory of the current directory, select the parent directory and press ENTER. The directory you selected will now be the current directory and will be displayed at the "Directory" option. The lower part of this form will then contain a list of the directories available under the new current directory. Repeat this process until you have selected the desired directory.

With the directory you want displayed at "Directory," press F3-Select chart. Harvard Graphics will return to the Select Chart form, and a list of all of the chart files in the selected directory will be displayed.

## Deleting Files

Use <Remove file> to delete a chart, symbol, slide show, or any other file from a disk. (You can also remove files directly from DOS using the DEL or ERASE commands, or by using another disk management utility.)

*Caution:* <Remove file> allows you to delete any kind of file that is stored on your disk. Use it with care.

To delete files from your disk using Harvard Graphics, follow these steps:

1. At the Main Menu, select <Get/Save/Remove>. The Get/Save /Remove menu shown in Figure 2-8 is displayed.

2. Select <Remove file>. A Select File form similar to the one shown in Figure 2-12 appears. The current directory is shown at the top of the form at the "Directory" option. If there are any files in the current directory, these files are listed in the bottom part of the form. The first file in the list is highlighted on your screen and is shown at the "Filename" option at the top of the form. The cursor is also positioned at "Filename."

3. Select a file to remove in one of two ways. The most direct way to remove a file is to position the cursor at "Filename," type in a filename (including the extension), and press ENTER.

Alternatively, you can use the UP and DOWN arrow keys to highlight a file in the file list. Use PGUP and PGDN to display additional files in the

```
                          Select File
Directory: C:\HG
Filename:  PLANSAMP.ASC

Filename Ext   | Date     | Type   | Description

ANNOUNCE.CHT   | 07-01-87 | CHART
INTRO   .CHT   | 07-01-87 | CHART
OPENING .CHT   | 07-01-87 | CHART
PRODS   .CHT   | 07-01-87 | CHART
REGIONS .CHT   | 07-01-87 | CHART
SALES   .CHT   | 07-01-87 | CHART
TRISALES.CHT   | 07-01-87 | CHART
SAMPLE  .SHW   | 04-20-87 | SHOW
PLANSAMP.ASC   | 03-18-87 | OTHER
UNITS   .ASC   | 04-12-87 | OTHER
UNITS   .WKS   | 05-07-87 | OTHER
HG      .PIF   | 07-02-87 | OTHER
AGX     .PAL   | 10-12-88 | OTHER
ASTTURBO.PAL   | 09-14-88 | OTHER
BH      .PAL   | 10-20-87 | OTHER

F1-Help      F3-Change dir                        F10-Continue
```

Figure 2-12.    Select File form

directory if they do not all fit on one screen. When the file you want to remove is displayed at "Filename" press ENTER.

In either case, Harvard Graphics will display this message:

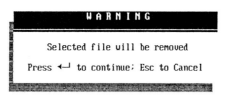

4. Press ENTER to verify that you want to delete the selected file or ESC to cancel. Harvard Graphics returns you to the Main Menu.

### Deleting Files from Other Directories

You can also delete files from directories other than the one shown at the "Directory" option on the Select File form. To change the directory, either enter a new directory path at the "Directory" option, or select a different directory from the Select Directory form. (This form is displayed when you press F3-Change dir from the Select File form.) These two methods of changing your directory are described in detail in the earlier section, "Getting Files from Other Directories."

Once you change directories, all of the files contained in the directory are displayed on the Select File form. You can now delete any of the files shown on the form. Refer to the preceding section, "Deleting Files."

## Spell Checking the Current Chart

Harvard Graphics' Spell Check feature (in versions 2.1 and later) allows you to check the spelling of all text that appears in the current chart. This includes checking the spelling of axis labels and legends, and even annotations and other text in drawings and symbols that you have placed on your chart. For information on using Spell Check to check all the charts in a slide show, see Chapter 13, "Slide Shows."

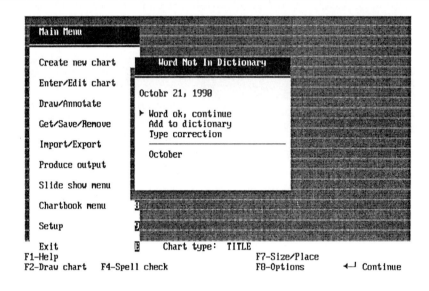

**Figure 2-13.** Word Not In Dictionary overlay

Checking the spelling of your chart is very simple and should be done before you produce your final output. This can save you the embarrassment of presenting a chart that contains simple spelling errors. It involves the following steps:

1. Start with the chart you want to spell check as your current chart.

2. If you are not at the Main Menu, return there by pressing ESC until it is displayed.

3. Press F4-Spell check.

Harvard Graphics loads the spelling dictionary and then checks spelling in the chart. If you want to cancel the spell checking, press ESC at any time. During the check, if Harvard Graphics finds a word it does not recognize, it displays the Word Not In Dictionary overlay. This overlay, shown in Figure 2-13, displays the word that is not recognized (in this case, "Octobr"), and waits for you to indicate a course of action. At a minimum, you may select one of the three alternatives: "Word ok, continue," "Add to dictionary," and "Type correction." Additionally, Harvard Graphics may suggest one or more words that are in the dictionary as possible correct spellings for the unrecognized word. Continue with the spelling check by positioning your cursor at one of the three alternatives or one of the suggested words and pressing ENTER.

If the highlighted word is spelled correctly, select "Word ok, continue." Alternatively, select "Add to dictionary" if the highlighted word is one you use frequently and want to add to Harvard Graphics' dictionary. However, use this feature with care. Make absolutely sure the word you are adding is spelled correctly. Once a word is added to the dictionary it cannot be removed.

If the highlighted word is not spelled correctly, and Harvard Graphics does not suggest the correct spelling, select "Type correction." Harvard Graphics will display a Type Spelling Correction overlay, shown in Figure 2-14, that permits you to edit or erase the word and retype it correctly. If you want to cancel typing a correction, press ESC to return to the Word Not In Dictionary overlay. When you have entered the correct spelling for the word in the Type Correction overlay, press ENTER to continue. Harvard Graphics will then check the spelling of the correction you have entered.

If Harvard Graphics detects a repeated word in your chart, such as "And and," the Repeated Word overlay, shown in Figure 2-15, will be displayed. When a word is repeated, Harvard Graphics displays the single word (in this case "And"), as the suggested spelling. To correct the mistake in this example, you would select the suggested word.

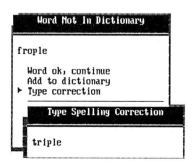

**Figure 2-14.**   Type Spelling Correction overlay

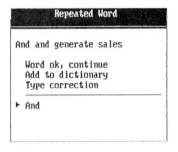

**Figure 2-15.**  Repeated Word overlay

Incorrect capitalization is another problem Spell Check will detect. For instance, "mR." will cause Harvard Graphics to display the Irregular Capitalization overlay shown in Figure 2-16. Incorrect punctuation in words or numbers will display the Irregular Punctuation overlay or the Irregular Number overlay. An example of the Irregular Number overlay is shown in Figure 2-17. Use each of these overlays the way you use the Word Not In Dictionary overlay. Select either "Word ok, continue," "Add to dictionary," "Type correction," or a suggested spelling or punctuation.

**Figure 2-16.**  Irregular Capitalization overlay

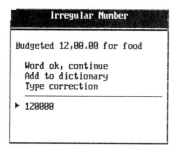

**Figure 2-17.**    Irregular Number overlay

Once the spelling check of your chart is completed, the message "Spell check complete" is displayed. Press ENTER to see the current chart form, or make another selection from the Main Menu.

Chapters 4 through 7 cover the chart styles available in Harvard Graphics. To see how to create these charts, refer to the appropriate chapter. If you have not yet set up Harvard Graphics for your computer and output device(s), refer to Chapter 3, "Setup and Default Settings." Chapter 3 also describes how to change the default settings Harvard Graphics uses to tailor the screen and charts to your own preferences.

# Setting and Default Settings

**Setting Data and Display Defaults**
**Setting Hardware Defaults**
**The Color Palette**
**Overriding Default Chart Characteristics**

When you start Harvard Graphics, you may notice that screens and charts have certain characteristics. For example, Harvard Graphics will use the Executive font when you first enter text on a chart, and it will display charts using landscape, or horizontal, orientation rather than portrait, or vertical. The characteristics that Harvard Graphics assumes when you begin a session are called *defaults*.

   This chapter describes how to change these default settings, both to customize Harvard Graphics to your particular computer and output devices and to tailor the screen and charts to your own preferences. At the very least you will need to specify devices, such as printers, plotters, and film recorders, that you will use to output your charts. Also, if your screen does not look normal when you run the program, you will need to adjust the Harvard Graphics screen defaults. Both of these topics are discussed in the "Setting Hardware Defaults" section. You may want to leave the rest of the defaults as they are until you have worked with the program for a while and determined which settings you want or need to adjust. At that time, read the sections in this chapter pertaining to the default settings you want to change.

## Setting Data and Display Defaults

To change Harvard Graphics default options, select <Setup> from the Main Menu. The Setup menu lists the major categories of the default options you can change. You can find a summary of these options in Table 3-1 and more detailed information in later sections of this chapter.

At the Setup menu, select <Defaults> to display the Default Settings form shown in Figure 3-1. The first four options allow you to simplify file management. The next three, "Orientation," "Border," and "Font," relate to chart format. The last option allows you to select a color scheme for the screen. Once you have set the desired options, press F10-Continue to return to the Setup menu.

| Setup Menu Item | Use | Options |
| --- | --- | --- |
| Defaults | File management | Data directory |
| | | Chartbook |
| | | Import directory |
| | | Import file |
| | Chart options | Orientation |
| | | Border |
| | | Font |
| | Screen colors | Menu colors |
| Printer 1 | Type of printer used most often | Printer |
| Printer 2 | Type of printer used occasionally | Printer |
| Plotter | Type of plotter used | Plotter |
| Film recorder | Type of film recorder used | Film recorder |
| | | Slide file directory |
| | | Film type |
| | | Use hardware fonts |
| Screen | Different graphics adapter from default | Screen |
| Color Palette | Create or change color palette file | Palette file |
| | | Screen |
| | | Recorder |
| | | 16 colors |

**Table 3-1.**   Setup Menu Options

## Setup and Default Settings

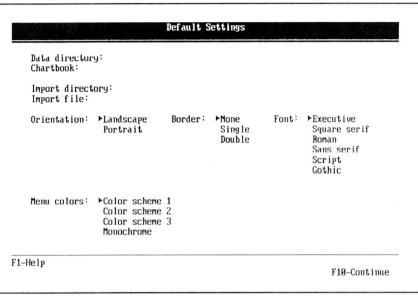

**Figure 3-1.** Default Settings form

As the name suggests, the options you set on the Default Settings form are default options for your Harvard Graphics sessions. Each of these options, except the last one, can be overridden for a specific chart. For instance, if you have specified a default data directory, you can still get charts from, or save charts to, any directory on your computer. Likewise, if you have set your default font to Executive, you can easily select Roman for a particular chart.

*Note:* None of the Default Settings form options that affect chart display characteristics (such as orientation and font) will have any influence on charts you have already created. These options will only determine the characteristics of new charts, as you create them.

## Default Data Directory

Most of the time you will want to save the charts you create in a separate directory. If you have not assigned a default data directory,

Harvard Graphics will assume you want to store your charts in the current directory—which may not be what you want. If you have created a directory specifically for storing Harvard Graphics charts, you will want to define this as your default data directory.

Enter a drive and directory path at "Data directory" to have Harvard Graphics automatically use this directory to store your charts. For example, type **C:\HGDATA** to store your charts in the directory named HGDATA on drive C.

You do not have to store all your charts in this directory; you can always enter a different directory path by typing an alternate drive and directory on the Select Chart and Save Chart forms. However, when you get a chart from, or save a chart to, a directory other than the default directory, Harvard Graphics will use that directory as the default for the remainder of the session or until you change it again. The next time you start Harvard Graphics, the default directory will again be the directory you specified as the default. See Chapter 2, "Harvard Graphics Basics," for more information on getting and saving charts.

## Default Chartbook

If you use chartbooks to organize templates, you can specify the name of the chartbook you use most often as the default. (Chartbooks are used to store related templates for easier retrieval.) At "Chartbook" on the Default Settings form, type in the name of this chartbook. Do not enter a drive, directory, or extension for the chartbook name. If you have defined a default directory, the chartbook must be stored in that directory. Otherwise, your default chartbook must be stored in the current directory. If you do not use a chartbook, leave this option blank.

The next time you create a new chart by selecting <From chartbook> from the Create New Chart menu, Harvard Graphics automatically gets the chartbook you specified as the default and lists all the templates it contains. You can always get a different chartbook by choosing <Select chartbook> from the Chartbook menu. See Chapter 11, "Templates and Chartbooks," for more information.

## Default Import Directory

If you usually import data or chart files from a directory other than your default directory, you can specify it at the "Import directory" option. If you do not use Harvard Graphics' importing utilities, leave this field blank. To enter a default import data directory, press TAB to move to "Import directory," and enter the directory path. For example, type **C:\LOTUS123** to specify the LOTUS123 directory on drive C as the directory from which you most often import data. You can import data from directories other than the default by specifying the appropriate directory path when setting up your data importation. For more information, see Chapter 12, "Importing and Exporting."

## Default Import File

If you tend to import data or charts from one particular file, for instance a specific spreadsheet, you can specify this filename at the "Import file" option. If you do not use Harvard Graphics' data importing utilities, leave this field blank.

To enter a default import file, press TAB to move to "Import file" and enter the filename, including the extension. For example, say you store weekly sales totals in a Lotus 1-2-3 spreadsheet file called WEEKLY.WKS. Periodically you want to create a chart showing these weekly sales figures. If WEEKLY.WKS is the only file you generally import from, you would enter **WEEKLY.WKS** at "Import file." Thereafter Harvard Graphics would automatically assume you want to import this file when you select <Import Lotus data> from the Import/Export menu.

If you specify a default import file, you will probably also want to specify a default import directory (see the preceding section, "Default Import Directory"). Otherwise, Harvard Graphics will assume your import file is in the current directory. You can find additional information about importing data and chart files in Chapter 12, "Importing and Exporting."

*Note:* You cannot define a delimited ASCII file as the default for the "Import file" option.

## Default Chart Orientation

Harvard Graphics uses your default *orientation* to determine which of two ways charts are displayed on the page: landscape or portrait.

Landscape orientation produces a chart wider than it is tall. Portrait orientation produces a chart that is taller than it is wide. Examples of these formats are shown in Figure 3-2.

Harvard Graphics defaults to landscape orientation. As you can see in Figure 3-1, an arrow points to "Landscape," indicating that it is the current setting. To change this setting, press TAB to move to "Orientation," and press the SPACEBAR to change the setting to "Portrait."

To use an orientation other than the default for a specific chart, select the orientation at the Current Chart Options form. See the "Overriding Default Chart Characteristics" section later in this chapter.

## Default Border

The "Border" option allows you to select a border to be drawn around charts when they are displayed on screen or sent to an output device. Harvard Graphics defaults to "None," which leaves your charts without borders. To draw single- or double-line borders around your charts, press TAB to move to the "Border" option on the Default Settings form, and press the SPACEBAR until the setting you want is highlighted and marked with the arrow. Figure 3-3 shows examples of chart borders.

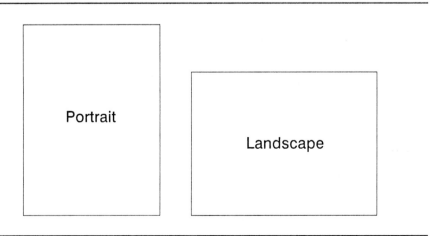

**Figure 3-2.**  Portrait and landscape orientations

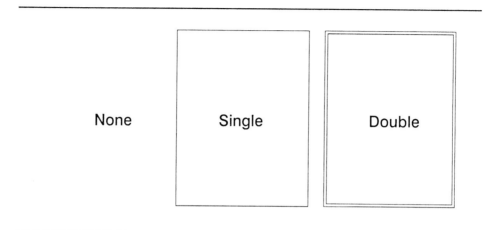

**Figure 3-3.**  Chart borders

To use a border other than the default for a specific chart, select a different border at the Current Chart Options form. See the "Overriding Default Chart Characteristics" section later in this chapter.

## Default Font

You can select one of the six fonts shown in Figure 3-4 as the default to be used for text on a chart. Harvard Graphics initially defaults to the Executive font. To change this, on the Default Settings form, press TAB to move to "Font" and press the SPACEBAR until the setting you want is highlighted and marked with the arrow.

*Note:*  Harvard Graphics allows you only one font per chart.

To use a font other than the default for a specific chart, select a different font at the Current Chart Options form. See the "Overriding Default Chart Characteristics" section later in this chapter.

## Default Color Scheme

You can change the colors used to display menus and forms by selecting one of four different color schemes. If you have a color monitor,

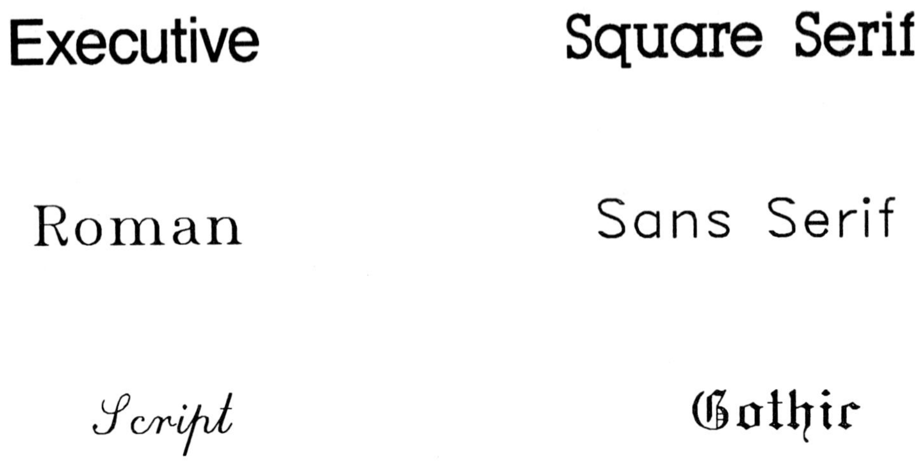

| Executive | Square Serif |

| Roman | Sans Serif |

| Script | Gothic |

**Figure 3-4.**   Fonts available in Harvard Graphics

Harvard Graphics defaults to Color scheme 1, the color scheme that is used when you first start up Harvard Graphics. To change this setting, at the Default Settings form, press TAB to move to "Menu colors," and press the SPACEBAR until the setting you want is highlighted and marked with the arrow.

*Hint:* Select "Monochrome" if you are using a monochrome monitor and a color graphics card. Doing so will improve the appearance of Harvard Graphics' screens by making the text darker and easier to read.

## Setting Hardware Defaults

Before you can produce output of your charts or slide shows, you will need to tailor Harvard Graphics to run with your particular computer and output devices. There are five menu selections on the Setup menu that allow you to do this.

| Menu Item | Specifies |
|---|---|
| Printer 1 | Type of printer most often used |
| Printer 2 | Type of printer used occasionally or as a backup |
| Plotter | Type of plotter |
| Film recorder | Type of film recorder |
| Screen | Type of graphics adapter card in computer |

These menu items are described in the following sections.

## Default Printers

You can set up Harvard Graphics to use two different printers: <Printer 1>, the printer you use most often, and <Printer 2>, your secondary or backup printer. Once you choose one of the two printer selections at the Setup menu, Harvard Graphics displays a Printer Setup form like the one in Figure 3-5. (If you select <Printer 2>, you will see "2" rather than "1" in the title banner at the top of the form.) The printer currently selected is highlighted on the screen and listed at the lower-left corner of the form at "Printer." To change this setting, use the arrow keys or press the SPACEBAR until the desired printer name is highlighted. Alternatively, you can press the first letter of the desired printer until that printer is highlighted.

You cannot type in a printer name directly; you must select one of the printers from the list. If your printer is not listed on the Printer 1 Setup form, shown in Figure 3-5, refer to your printer and Harvard Graphics manuals to see if your printer can emulate one of the printers that is listed. Once the appropriate printer name is shown at "Printer," press F10-Continue to set this as the default printer. Harvard Graphics will then display the Parallel/Serial overlay. See the next section, "Selecting an Output Device Port."

*Note:* If you select a printer (AST TurboLaser, CalComp ColorMaster, or Matrix TT200) that requires the VDI (Virtual Device Interface),

```
┌─────────────────────────── Printer 1 Setup ───────────────────────────┐
IBM Graphics Printer      EPSON   FX,LX,RX        TOSHIBA  P1340,P1350,P1351
    Proprinter,XL,II              EX,JX                    P321,P341,P351
    ProprinterX24,XL24            MX                       P351C
    QuietwriterII,III             LQ 800,1000              PageLaser12
    Color Printer                 LQ 1500
    Color Jetprinter              LQ 2500         QUME     LaserTEN,+
    Personal PagePrinter          GQ 3500
                                                  AST      TurboLaser
 HP LaserJet,+,500+,II    OKIDATA ML 84,92,93
    ThinkJet                      ML 182,183      APPLE    LaserWriter
    QuietJet,+                    ML 192,193
    PaintJet,XL                   ML 292,293      CALCOMP  ColorMaster
    PaintJet,XL (Trans.)          ML 294
    DeskJet,+                     LaserLine 6     MATRIX   TT200
NEC P5,P6,P7
    P5XL,P9XL,CP6,CP7     XEROX   4020            TEKTRONIX 4696
    LC-860 (LaserJet)             4045                     Phaser CP
    LC-890 (PostScript)
                          CANON   LBP8 II,III     VDI      Printer
 Printer: Graphics Printer

 F1-Help                                                       F10-Continue
```

**Figure 3-5.**    Printer 1 Setup form

you must install the specific VDI for your printer before you can print. See your Harvard Graphics manual for instructions on installing VDI device drivers.

### Selecting an Output Device Port

Most computers have two different types of ports that can be used to connect the computer with other pieces of hardware such as printers, plotters, and film recorders. These two port types are *serial ports* and *parallel ports*. Although most printers are connected to the computer using a parallel port, it is possible to connect many printer models to either serial or parallel computer ports. Plotters, on the other hand, usually are connected to a serial port.

You define the port your output device is attached to on the Parallel/Serial overlay, shown in Figure 3-6. Harvard Graphics displays this overlay automatically, after you set the defaults for your printer, plotter,

## Setup and Default Settings

```
                          Printer 1 Setup
 IBM Graphics Printer      EPSON   FX,LX,RX        TOSHIBA   P1340,P1350,P1351
     Proprinter,XL,II              EX,JX                     P321,P341,P351
     ProprinterX24,XL24            MX                        P351C
     QuietwriterII,III             LQ 800,1000              PageLaser12
     Color Printer                 LQ 1500
     Color Jetprinter              LQ 2500         QUME      LaserTEN,+
     Personal PagePrinter          GQ 3500
                                                   AST       TurboLaser
 HP  LaserJet,+,500+,II    OKIDATA ML 84,92,93
     Thi ┌─Parallel──────────────────Serial─────────────────────────────┐ ter
     Qu  │                                                              │
     Pa  │  ►LPT1              COM1      COM2                           │ ter
     Pa  │   LPT2        Baud rate: ►9600  4800  2400  1200  300       │
     De  │   LPT3        Parity:    ►None  Even  Odd                   │
 NEC P5  │               Data bits: ►8     7                           │
     P5  │               Stop bits: ►1     2                           │
     LC  │                                                              │ P
     LC  └──────────────────────────────────────────────────────────────┘
                          CANON    LBP8 II,III     UDI       Printer
 Printer: Graphics Printer

 F1-Help
                                                                F10-Continue
```

**Figure 3-6.** Parallel/Serial overlay

or film recorder. To set the port on this overlay, press the SPACEBAR until the port your output device is connected to is highlighted. (If you are not sure which port this is, check your printer, plotter, or film recorder manual and your computer manual for installation instructions or diagrams that indicate which port to use.)

If your output device uses a parallel port, choose the appropriate LPT setting (LPT1, LPT2, or LPT3). Alternatively, if a serial port is being used, select the appropriate COM port (COM1 or COM2). If you select one of the parallel ports, press F10-Continue to return to the Setup menu. If you select one of the serial ports, however, you will need to specify additional details. With a serial port, you must also set the speed of communication (*baud rate*), the type of error checking (*parity*), the length of information being sent (*data bits*), and transmission control characters (*stop bits*). Again, check your printer, plotter, or film recorder manual for this information.

## Default Plotter

To set up Harvard Graphics to use a plotter, select <Plotter> at the Setup menu. The Plotter Setup form, shown in Figure 3-7, is then displayed, listing the plotters Harvard Graphics supports. The plotter currently selected is highlighted on the screen and is listed at the lower-left corner of the form, at the "Plotter" option. To change this setting, use the arrow keys, the SPACEBAR, or press the first character of the displayed name of your plotter. When the plotter name is highlighted, it will appear at "Plotter." If your plotter is not listed on the Plotter Setup form, refer to your plotter and Harvard Graphics manuals to see if your plotter can emulate a listed one. When you have selected a plotter, press F10-Continue. Next, the Parallel/Serial overlay will appear. Specify the computer port your plotter is connected to on this overlay. See the previous section, "Selecting an Output Device Port," for a detailed description of this overlay.

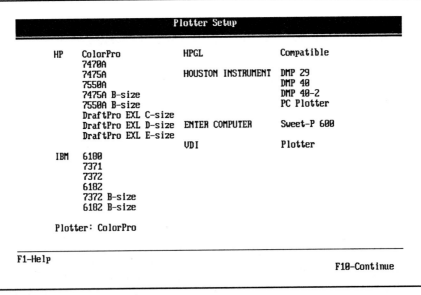

**Figure 3-7.** Plotter Setup form

*Note:* If your plotter is not listed on the Plotter Setup form and cannot emulate one of the plotters listed, you may be able to use the VDI. Refer to your plotter manual to see if your plotter is supported by the VDI. Also refer to your plotter and Harvard Graphics manuals for information on obtaining, installing, and setting up the VDI for your plotter. Then, in Harvard Graphics, select VDI Plotter as the default.

## Film Recorder Defaults

To set up Harvard Graphics to use a film recorder, select <Film recorder> at the Setup menu. The Film Recorder Setup form, shown in Figure 3-8, is then displayed, listing the film recorders Harvard Graphics supports. Use this form to specify the type of film recorder, the

```
                    Film Recorder Setup

        POLAROID       Palette (CGA)       MATRIX        PCR,QCR
                       PalettePlus (EGA)
                                           AUTOGRAPHIX   Slide Service
        LASERGRAPHICS  RASCOL II/PFR
                       Compatible          VDI           Camera

        BELL & HOWELL  CDI IV,1000         GENERAL       VideoShow
                                           PARAMETRICS   ColorMetric
        PTI            ImageMaker                        GPC file
                       Montage

        Film recorder: Palette (CGA)

        Slide file directory:

        Film type:         ▶Ektachrome     Polachrome  669   339
        Use hardware fonts: ▶Yes           No


  F1-Help
                                                          F10-Continue
```

**Figure 3-8.**   Film Recorder Setup form

directory in which slide files should be stored (if desired), the type of film, and whether the film recorder's own fonts (if available) should be used.

### Selecting a Default Film Recorder

As you can see in Figure 3-8, the film recorder currently selected is listed near the middle of the form, at "Film recorder." The selected recorder is also shown highlighted on screen. To set a different film recorder, use the arrow keys or press the SPACEBAR to see the name listed at "Film recorder" change as you cycle through the choices on the form. You cannot type in a film recorder name directly; you must select one from the list. If your film recorder is not listed on the Film Recorder Setup form, refer to your film recorder and Harvard Graphics manuals to see if your film recorder can emulate one of those listed. Once the appropriate film recorder is listed at the "Film recorder" option, press F10-Continue to set this as your default.

If the Parallel/Serial overlay appears (indicating that Harvard Graphics requires this information for your particular type of film recorder), set the port that your film recorder is connected to. Refer to "Selecting an Output Device Port," earlier in this chapter, for more information.

*Note:* If you select a film recorder that requires a VDI device driver (Bell & Howell CDI IV or 1080, Lasergraphics RASCOL II/PFR or compatible, PTI Montage, or Matrix PCR or QCR film recorders), you must install the appropriate VDI device driver before you can produce output with the film recorder. See the Harvard Graphics manual for instructions on installing the VDI device drivers. If you select one of General Parametrics' settings (VideoShow, ColorMetric, or GPC file), or select the Autographix Slide Service, you will need to refer to your Harvard Graphics manual for additional information about setting up and using these products with the package.

### Setting a Default Slide File Directory

In Harvard Graphics you can save slide files to disk and later use them with the Autographix Slide Service or with selected film recorders. (See the Harvard Graphics manual for information about saving files to disk for specific film recorders and the Autographix Slide Service.) When you create files of your slides, it is good practice to store these files in a directory different from the current one. To set a default directory for your slide files, press TAB to move to "Slide file directory," and enter the directory path. For example, type **C:\SLIDES** to specify a directory called SLIDES located on drive C as the default. Harvard Graphics will automatically use this directory when you save slide files. If you do not specify a directory, Harvard Graphics will save slide files to the current directory.

### Selecting a Default Film Type

For some film recorders, you must specify the type of film you are using. Harvard Graphics defaults to Ektachrome. To change this setting to either Polachrome, 669, or 339, move to "Film type" and press the SPACEBAR until the setting you want is highlighted and marked with the arrow. Refer to your film recorder and Harvard Graphics manuals for information on specifying film types for specific recorders.

### Setting the Use Hardware Fonts Default

Some film recorders can use either Harvard Graphics fonts or the film recorder's internal fonts. Harvard Graphics fonts typically provide more font size options, whereas hardware fonts that come with film recorders are typically faster to record and smoother in appearance. Harvard Graphics already defaults to using the hardware fonts. If you would rather use Harvard Graphics' fonts, set "Use hardware fonts" to No. Refer to your film recorder and Harvard Graphics manuals for more information on using your film recorder's hardware fonts.

## Default Screen (Graphics Adapter)

When you first run Harvard Graphics, the program automatically checks the graphics adapter attached to your computer and sets this graphics adapter type as its default screen. This means you do not need to set this default. If you select <Screen> from the Setup menu to display the Screen Setup form, shown in Figure 3-9, you will see "Default screen" listed at the "Screen" option. This is the graphics adapter Harvard Graphics automatically selected.

Usually you will not need to modify your screen default. However, if the Harvard Graphics menus look distorted or fuzzy, your screen setting may be incompatible with your computer's graphics adapter. To change this setting, press the SPACEBAR until the appropriate graphics adapter is listed at "Screen." Then press F10-Continue to return to the Setup menu.

You may also want to change this setting if you have a second adapter attached to your computer or if Screenshow special effects do not work on your computer. For VGA adapters, try setting "Screen" to EGA color. For other adapters, try setting "Screen" to CGA color or CGA monochrome.

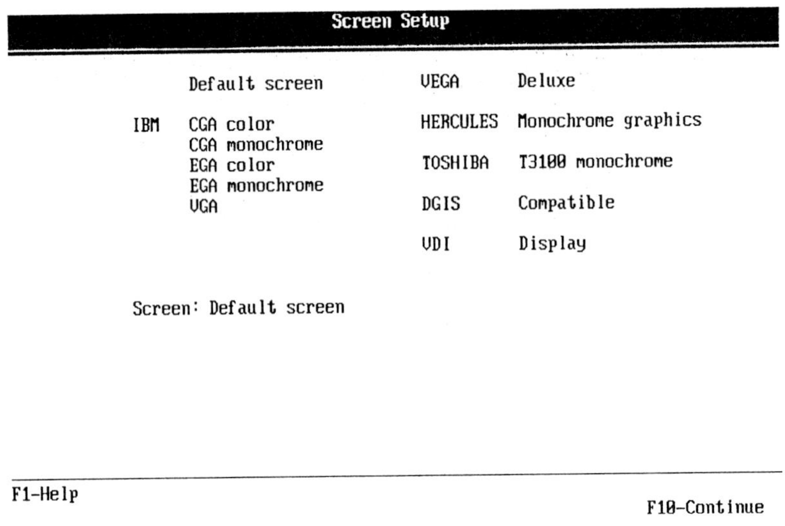

```
                          Screen Setup

              Default screen        VEGA      Deluxe

         IBM  CGA color             HERCULES  Monochrome graphics
              CGA monochrome
              EGA color             TOSHIBA   T3100 monochrome
              EGA monochrome
              VGA                   DGIS      Compatible

                                    VDI       Display


         Screen: Default screen




 F1-Help                                            F10-Continue
```

**Figure 3-9.**   Screen Setup form

## The Color Palette

Harvard Graphics allows you to create and customize 16-color palettes for your charts, and save them for later use. You can create as many different palettes as you like. Each palette definition is stored as a separate file, with the extension .PAL.

*Note:* The 16-color palette is not available if your graphics adapter is a CGA. If you have a CGA, you can only choose from three different CGA color definitions. Refer to the section, "Modifying the CGA Color Settings," later in this chapter.

The color palette defines the 16 colors used in charts when you display the chart on your monitor (using a color graphics adapter other than a CGA), or output the chart to a film recorder. The color palette has no effect on plotters and printers (except for the AST TurboLaser and the CalComp ColorMaster printers, which are able to use the color palette settings described in this section). Plotters use the color number to select plotter pens, and most color printers use a predefined color map (see Chapter 8, "Producing Output," for more information). Refer to the Harvard Graphics and output device manuals for information on how palette colors are set for your specific output device.

If you have selected a film recorder from the Film Recorder Setup form or the AST TurboLaser or the CalComp ColorMaster from the Printer 1 or Printer 2 Setup form, your palette will default to the palette designed for this device. If you have not selected one of these devices, your palette will be the HG.PAL palette.

Colors are defined in the color palette as mixtures of red, green, and blue. For each of the 16 colors listed on the palette, the particular blend of red, green, and blue intensities produces the actual color that appears on the screen or film. There are two sets of color blends on each palette, one for the screen and one for the output device. Each palette provided with Harvard Graphics uses the same set of color blends for the screen colors. The color blends for each output device are different, however, having been designed specifically for the particular device.

To create a new color palette, or modify an existing color palette, select <Color palette> from the Setup menu. The Color Palette Setup form, shown in Figure 3-10, is then displayed. On this form you can name a new or existing color palette, modify the color mix for each of the 16 colors in the palette, change the name of any of the colors, modify your chart background color, define a shaded background for film recorder output, and label the screen and film recorder for which you are designing the palette. When you are finished modifying your color palette, press F10-Continue to save the modified palette and return to the Setup menu.

As you modify the colors in your palette, you can check the results of your screen color blends by pressing F2-Show palette to preview the current color definitions. After displaying the screen colors, press any key to return to the Color Palette Setup form. It is not possible to preview your output color blends. You must use the particular output device to see these changes.

*Note:* Do not press F2-Show palette if you have a current chart and you have not saved it. Pressing F2-Show palette retrieves a chart called

---

**Color Palette Setup**

Palette file: HG

| | | Screen: EGA | | | Output: Polaroid | | |
|---|---|---|---|---|---|---|---|
| | | Red | Green | Blue | Red | Green | Blue |
| 1 | White | 1000 | 1000 | 1000 | 115 | 35 | 60 |
| 2 | Cyan | 0 | 1000 | 1000 | 0 | 20 | 47 |
| 3 | Magenta | 1000 | 0 | 1000 | 48 | 0 | 47 |
| 4 | Green | 0 | 1000 | 0 | 22 | 20 | 0 |
| 5 | Blue | 0 | 0 | 660 | 0 | 0 | 60 |
| 6 | Red | 1000 | 0 | 330 | 90 | 3 | 6 |
| 7 | Yellow | 1000 | 1000 | 330 | 115 | 35 | 0 |
| 8 | Orange | 1000 | 330 | 0 | 90 | 0 | 0 |
| 9 | Royal Blue | 0 | 0 | 1000 | 0 | 9 | 47 |
| 10 | Gold | 1000 | 660 | 0 | 115 | 24 | 0 |
| 11 | Violet | 660 | 0 | 660 | 20 | 0 | 14 |
| 12 | Pink | 1000 | 0 | 660 | 90 | 0 | 33 |
| 13 | Grey | 660 | 660 | 660 | 25 | 0 | 3 |
| 14 | Crimson | 660 | 0 | 0 | 30 | 1 | 0 |
| 15 | Dark Green | 0 | 330 | 0 | 9 | 0 | 0 |
| 16 | Black | 0 | 0 | 0 | 0 | 0 | 0 |

Background color number: 16

F1-Help
F2-Show palette          F6-Shaded bkgd          F10-Continue

**Figure 3-10.** Color Palette Setup form

HG.CHT, which displays the 16 palette colors. HG.CHT will replace your current chart.

### Specifying a Palette Filename

At "Palette file" enter the name of an existing color palette file or enter a new name to create a new color palette. This filename is limited to eight characters and must conform to MS-DOS file naming conventions. Do not, however, add an extension to this name; Harvard Graphics automatically adds the extension .PAL.

If you enter the name of an existing color palette, Harvard Graphics will load that palette from disk and display its color settings on the Color Palette Setup form. If you enter a name that does not correspond to an existing file, Harvard Graphics will create a palette with the given name using the settings of the current palette. In either case the palette will be loaded or created as soon as you move the cursor from the "Palette file" option on the Color Palette Setup form.

*Hint:* If you need to modify the color palette settings, it is a good idea to create a new palette and modify its settings rather than change the existing palette. This way you can define new color settings and still retain the original ones.

### Defining the Screen and Output Label Options

The "Screen" and "Output" options that appear at the top of the Color Palette Setup form, shown in Figure 3-10, are used to note the type of screen and output devices the palette is intended for. These labels have no impact on the colors that will be used for either the screen or the output device; they are intended as reminders only. If you define a new palette for a specific monitor or output device, you can supply a label of up to 12 characters at either "Screen" or "Output."

### Modifying the CGA Color Settings

If you have set your screen default to CGA, you can use the F3-CGA palette function key to select one of three color schemes and one of 16

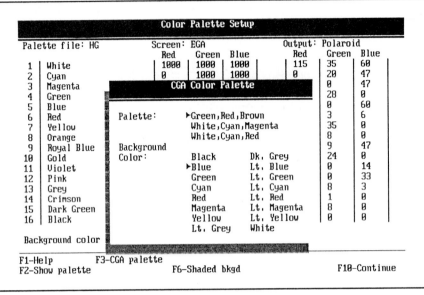

**Figure 3-11.**  CGA Color Palette overlay

possible background colors. Pressing F3-CGA palette displays the CGA Color Palette overlay shown in Figure 3-11. At "Palette" select one of the three color palettes. Next, set "Background color" to one of the 16 background colors. Press F10-Continue to return to the Color Palette Setup form.

### Effects of CGA Colors on Chart Elements

When your monitor and graphics adapter are set to use CGA colors, you can still define the various elements of your charts (text, bars, lines, and so on) to any of the 16 colors in the color palette. Since the CGA palette only supports three foreground and one background color, Harvard Graphics displays the different colors on your monitor using a process called *dithering*. Dithering is a process in which the colors of the dots (called *pixels*) that make up the on-screen image alternate to create the impression of additional colors.

When Harvard Graphics displays large objects that are dithered, the objects may seem to be a color other than one of the three foreground colors. However, when objects are small, the effects of the dithering may not be apparent. For example, although you can use any of the 16 colors for your text, when the text size option is set to 5 or lower, many different text colors will appear to be the same color on your monitor, since the effects of the dithering are not visible.

## Modifying Color Palette Color Intensities

The colors used for screen display and recording onto film can be changed by modifying the blend of red, green, and blue used to produce these colors. Color mixing for the screen involves defining the intensities of red, green, and blue using the color intensity columns on the Color Palette Setup form (see Figure 3-10). For the screen color definitions, the value 1000 defines full intensity, whereas 0 defines no intensity, or an absence of that color.

Although color mixing for an output device follows the same principles, the numbers you define will depend on the characteristics of the particular output device. (It is for this reason that palettes tend to be identified by the output device rather than the screen.) To define new colors for your film recorder or the CalComp ColorMaster printer, refer to your device manual and the Harvard Graphics manual for color intensity information.

*Note:* If you are using a CGA graphics adapter, use the CGA Color Palette overlay to define your screen colors and background color. You may, however, use the Color Palette Setup form to define the colors for your film recorder. This section, and the later section called "Changing the Background Color," do not apply to the screen display of CGA graphics adapters.

To change the setting for a particular color in the palette, use the UP and DOWN arrows to move to one of the 16 colors in the list, and press TAB to move to the red, green, and blue intensity-value columns. Change these values to create the new color. You may preview screen color settings by pressing F2-Show palette to view a pie chart that displays and labels each of the palette colors. Press any key to return to the Color Palette Setup form.

*Note:* If you press F2-Show palette, and no colored pies appear, it may be because you have removed the HG.CHT chart from your Harvard Graphics program directory. If this is the case, and you want to be able to preview your screen palette settings, you must copy the chart named HG.CHT back into the program directory from the original installation disks.

Although you can enter any number from 0 to 1000 for intensity values, Harvard Graphics only recognizes four levels of intensity for the screen color definitions. The screen intensities are defined as follows:

| Color Setting | Result |
|---|---|
| 0-249 | Off, no intensity |
| 250-499 | Low intensity |
| 500-749 | Moderate intensity |
| 750-1000 | High intensity |

### Changing Color Names

You can change the names of the 16 colors listed in the color palette. If you provide alternative color names, these new names will be displayed wherever the names are used.

To change the name of a color, use the cursor keys to move to the current name. Use CTRL-DEL to erase the existing name, and then enter a new color name.

### Changing the Background Color

The background color is the color displayed in the background of every chart. The default setting is black. To choose a different background color, use the cursor keys to move to "Background color number." Enter a number from 1 to 16 to specify a new color for chart backgrounds.

Although a colorful background can be quite appealing, especially when you are displaying a slide show, choosing a background color other than black can have unpredictable effects on the colors Harvard Graphics uses in its menus. The background color may also adversely affect your chart if you select a background color that either clashes with or is identical to colors used for your chart elements, such as frames and symbol colors. If the background color is identical to the color used for any chart elements, these elements will not be visible against the background of your chart.

### Creating a Shaded Background

Some film recorders permit you to give your chart a shaded background. This special effect will appear as a gradual blending from one color to another on your recorded chart, and can be quite impressive looking. If you have selected a film recorder that supports a shaded background, "F6-Shaded bkgd" will appear in the function key banner. If the film recorder you selected on the Film Recorder Setup form does not support a shaded background, this option will not be displayed.

To define a shaded background for your recorded charts, press F6-Shaded bkgd while the Color Palette Setup form is displayed. The Shaded Background overlay shown in Figure 3-12 will appear. Set "Use

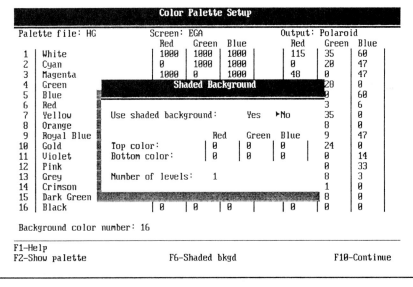

**Figure 3-12.** Shaded Background overlay

shaded background" to Yes. Next, identify the top and bottom background colors. Use the same color definition techniques you would use to define a new film recorder palette color. If you like, you can enter two of the color definitions from the Color Palette Setup form for use as the top color and bottom color. Finally, indicate how many levels you want to display between the top and bottom colors. The number of levels may be from 1 to 100. If you choose 50 or more, the background shading will appear as a continuous blend of color from top to bottom.

## Overriding Default Chart Characteristics

Harvard Graphics allows you to override default chart settings for your current chart. The default settings you can modify for your current chart are "Orientation," "Border," and "Font." See the first section in

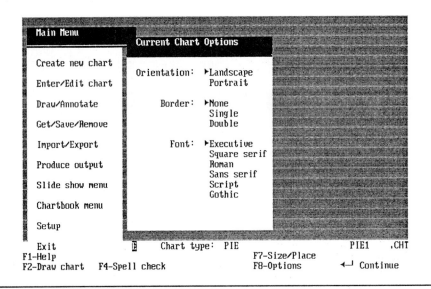

**Figure 3-13.** Current Chart Options overlay

this chapter, "Setting Data and Display Defaults," for a more detailed description of each of these options.

*Note:* If you want to change one or more of these settings for a chart other than the current one, you must first retrieve that chart, making it the current chart, before you continue.

The current chart options must be changed from the Main Menu rather than the Setup menu. If you are not already there, press ESC until you return to the Main Menu, and then press F8-Options. The Current Chart Options overlay, shown in Figure 3-13, is displayed. The current settings for each option are marked with an arrow.

If you want to change any of these options, press TAB to move to the option you want to set. Press the SPACEBAR until the desired setting is highlighted. When you are finished setting chart options, press F10-Continue to return to the Main Menu. To return to the Main Menu without changing the default options, press ESC.

# Text Charts

Creating Text Charts
Overview of Chart Forms
Modifying Text Attributes
Modifying Text Size and Placement
Using Bullets
Clearing Text from Your Chart
Changing Text Chart Styles

This chapter discusses the most frequently created of all Harvard Graphics charts—the text chart. As the name implies, text charts are used to display words and numbers. Most text charts are fairly brief and are used to summarize ideas, present a title of a report or a presentation, or list text or numerical information. They are ideal for creating handouts, for making slides for oral presentations, or for use in computerized presentations. It would be hard to imagine a presentation that did not include at least one text chart. At the very least, nearly every presentation will use a text chart as a title slide or other introductory screen.

This chapter starts with a brief overview on creating text charts. The rest of the chapter details the individual steps involved.

## Creating Text Charts

There are six different styles of text charts available in Harvard Graphics. These are listed in Table 4-1. Each of these styles is particularly useful for a certain task. Taken together, these chart styles provide a

| Chart Style | Description |
|---|---|
| Title chart | Title, affiliation, and author information |
| Simple list | List of items |
| Bullet list | Like the simple list, except bullets are automatically added before each list item |
| Two column | Chart with two columns |
| Three column | Chart with three columns |
| Free form | Charts with more than three columns, long descriptions, or quotations |

**Table 4-1.**   Text Chart Styles Available in Harvard Graphics

broad range of text charting capabilities. The steps involved in creating each of the text charts are fairly similar. They are summarized as follows:

1. At the Main Menu, select <Create new chart>.

2. At the Create New Chart menu, select <Text>.

3. At the Text Chart Styles menu, shown in Figure 4-1, select one of the six text chart styles. Harvard Graphics will display the chart form for the selected chart style.

4. Enter your text in the form as described in the next section, "Overview of Chart Forms."

5. Modify the size and placement of the text (using the Size/Place overlay) and the text attributes (using the Text Attributes overlay) as described later in this chapter.

At this point your text chart is complete. If you want to save your chart the way it is, skip to step 10. You may, however, want to consider some of the following optional steps to improve or enhance your chart. If you change or add to your chart, remember to save it to retain these changes.

6. To check the spelling of text in your chart, return to the Main Menu and press F4-Spell check. Additional information about spell checking your charts is provided in Chapter 2, "Harvard Graphics Basics."

7. To change the font used on your text chart or to select a different chart border or orientation, return to the Main Menu and press F8-Options. Set the "Orientation," "Border," and "Font" options on the displayed Current Chart Options overlay. See Chapter 3, "Setup and Default Settings," for additional details.

8. You may also want to embellish your text chart by using Harvard Graphics' drawing and annotating features to add lines, boxes, circles, squares, or incorporate Harvard Graphics symbols in your chart. You can also reduce the overall size of your chart. See Chapter 9, "Drawing and Annotating," for more information.

9. If you want to print, plot, or record your chart on film, return to the Main Menu and select <Produce output>. See Chapter 8, "Producing Output," for more information.

10. Save your chart to disk if you want to use it at a later time. See Chapter 2, "Harvard Graphics Basics," for information on saving charts.

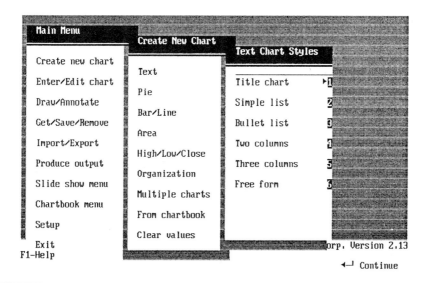

**Figure 4-1.**   Text Chart Styles menu

## Overview of Chart Forms

Chart forms are used to enter the text and numbers you want to display on your text chart. (Refer to Appendix D, "Harvard Graphics Tables," if you want to also use international text characters in your chart.) The keys listed in Table 4-2 control cursor movement and simplify text entry. While you are entering text on a chart form, use F2-Draw chart frequently to see the layout of the text chart you are creating. Then press any key to return to your chart form.

The forms for five of the six chart styles are very similar in structure. The chart forms for simple lists, bullet lists, two- and three-column charts, and free-form text charts contain three lines: one each for the title, subtitle, and footnote. They also contain an area where the bulk of the text is entered. The title is centered at the top of the chart, with the subtitle appearing just below it. The footnote is left-justified at the bottom of the chart. The text entered in the text area on the chart forms appears in the middle of the chart. (The sixth type of chart form, the Title Chart form, is described in the next section.)

The text area on these five chart forms is 16 lines long. That is, you can enter up to 16 lines of text in the text area before you reach the bottom of the text chart screen. You can, however, create simple, bullet, two-column, and free-form text charts with more than the 16 lines that initially appear in the text area. After you have entered 16 lines of text, pressing the DOWN arrow or PGDN will reveal additional lines for entering text. For simple lists, bullet lists, and free-form text charts, the maximum number of lines is 48. Two-column charts can display 24 lines, including the column header. Three-column charts are limited to the 16 lines that are initially displayed, while title charts are limited to only nine.

*Note:* The number of lines of text that can be displayed on a single page (either on the screen or output) depends on both the size selected for the text and the font. Use F2-Draw chart to see the effects of size and font settings. See Appendix D for examples of font styles and sizes.

### Title Chart Form

A title chart is used to display a title page for a report or presentation. A title chart often contains the title of a document or presentation, the name and affiliation of the author or presenter, and the date. The Title

| Key | Function |
|---|---|
| BACKSPACE | Moves cursor back one space, deleting any character in the space. |
| CTRL-B | Creates a bullet at the cursor position on chart forms. |
| CTRL-DEL | Deletes entire contents of line at the cursor. |
| CTRL-DOWN | At the text area of a chart form that contains more text lines, scrolls text up one line. |
| CTRL-INS | Inserts a blank line above the line the cursor is on in the text areas of chart forms. |
| CTRL-LEFT | Moves cursor to the previous word in the line. |
| CTRL-RIGHT | Moves cursor to the next word in the line. |
| CTRL-UP | At the text area of a chart form that contains more text lines, scrolls text down one line. |
| DEL | Deletes character at the cursor. |
| DOWN (arrow) | Moves cursor down one line, option, or menu item. |
| END | Moves cursor to the last option or line on a form. |
| ENTER | Selects highlighted menu items on menus. Selects highlighted settings for form options and moves cursor to the next option on the form. |
| ESC | Returns to the previous screen (press ESC multiple times to back up through previous forms and menus to the Main Menu) *or* cancels changes and returns to the previous screen. |
| HOME | Moves cursor to the first option or line on a form. |
| INS | Toggles insert mode on and off—the cursor appears as a block when INS is on, and as a small line when it is off. |
| LEFT (arrow) | Moves cursor to the left one character or option setting. |
| PGDN | Displays the next screenful of text in the text area of chart forms. |
| PGUP | Displays the previous screenful of text in the text area of chart forms. |
| RIGHT (arrow) | Moves cursor to the right one character or option setting. |
| SHIFT-TAB | Moves cursor to the previous column or option on a form. |
| TAB | Moves cursor to the next column or option on a form. |
| UP (arrow) | Moves cursor up one line, option, or menu item. |

**Table 4-2.** Cursor Control Keys and Functions for Text Charts

Chart form has three areas for entering text—top, middle, and bottom—corresponding to the relative placement of this text on the chart. Each of these areas can contain up to three lines of text, for a total of nine lines. By default, these lines are centered when displayed on the chart. An example of a Title Chart form and the resulting title chart are shown in Figures 4-2 and 4-3, respectively.

```
                    ┌─────────────── Title Chart ───────────────┐
                    
                     Size    Place    Top
                      8      L ►C R
                      8      L ►C R   Using A Title Chart:
                      5      L ►C R   The First Impression
                    
                                      Middle
                      4      L ►C R   Cary Jensen
                      4      L ►C R   &
                      4      L ►C R   Loy Anderson
                    
                                      Bottom
                      4      L ►C R   Harvard Graphics: The Complete Reference
                      4      L ►C R   Osborne/McGraw-Hill
                      4      L ►C R
                    
                     F1-Help                F5-Attributes  F7-Size/Place
                     F2-Draw chart                                        F10-Continue
```

**Figure 4-2.**   Title Chart form


# Using A Title Chart:
## The First Impression


Cary Jensen
&
Loy Anderson


**Harvard Graphics:   The Complete Reference**
Osborne/McGraw-Hill

**Figure 4-3.**   A title chart

## Simple Lists

A simple list is a series of lines of text, usually preceded by a title and subtitle, and followed by a footnote. By default, Harvard Graphics centers all text on a simple list chart, with the exception of the footnote, which is left-justified. Each line of text is entered on a separate line on the Simple List form. Figures 4-4 and 4-5 show an example of a Simple List form and the resulting simple list chart.

## Bullet Lists

A bullet list permits you to create a list of numbers, words, phrases, or sentences that are punctuated with a *bullet* (a mark or symbol) at the beginning of each new line. These charts are particularly well suited for listing a number of points that you want to make. There are five different types of bullets you can use: dots, dashes, check marks, boxes, and numbers. You select one of the bullet types on the Size/Place overlay for bullet lists, as described later in this chapter in the section "Changing the Bullet Type in a Bullet List." Use one of the first four types of bullet when you want to give your points equal emphasis. Use the # sign to create a numbered list, a variation of a bullet list in which each item is automatically numbered in sequence.

The Bullet List form is shown in Figure 4-6. Harvard Graphics automatically places a bullet before the first line you enter in the text area and on subsequent lines that follow a blank line. If text is placed on a line immediately below an existing line of text, no bullet will appear. You can use this characteristic to create a list of secondary points for each bullet item. See Figure 4-7 for an example of this effect.

You can also change the color of the bullet for emphasis, so the bullets appear in a different color than the text. See the section "Coloring Bullets in a Bullet List" later in this chapter.

## Two- and Three-Column Charts

Two- and three-column charts display text and/or numbers in columns. The chart forms for these two chart styles are shown in Figures 4-8 and

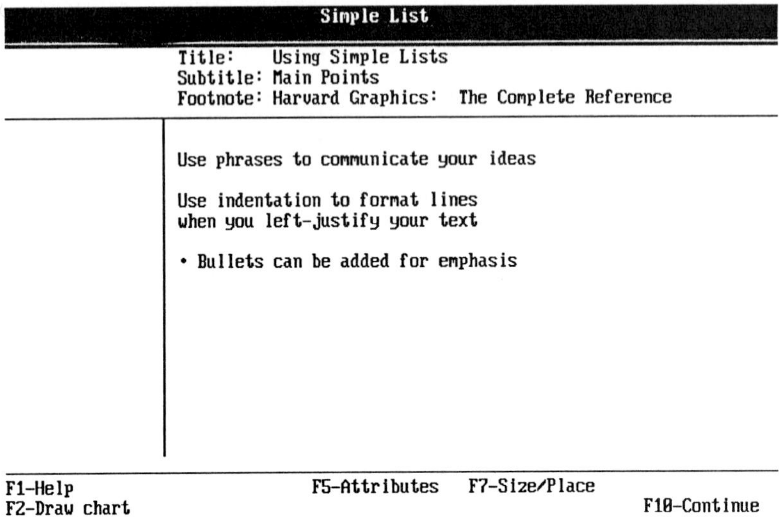

```
┌─────────────────────────────────────────────────────┐
│                    Simple List                       │
├─────────────────────────────────────────────────────┤
│     Title:    Using Simple Lists                     │
│     Subtitle: Main Points                            │
│     Footnote: Harvard Graphics:  The Complete Reference │
├─────────────────────────────────────────────────────┤
│   Use phrases to communicate your ideas              │
│                                                      │
│   Use indentation to format lines                    │
│   when you left-justify your text                    │
│                                                      │
│   • Bullets can be added for emphasis                │
│                                                      │
│                                                      │
│                                                      │
├─────────────────────────────────────────────────────┤
│ F1-Help              F5-Attributes   F7-Size/Place   │
│ F2-Draw chart                              F10-Continue │
└─────────────────────────────────────────────────────┘
```

**Figure 4-4.** Simple List form

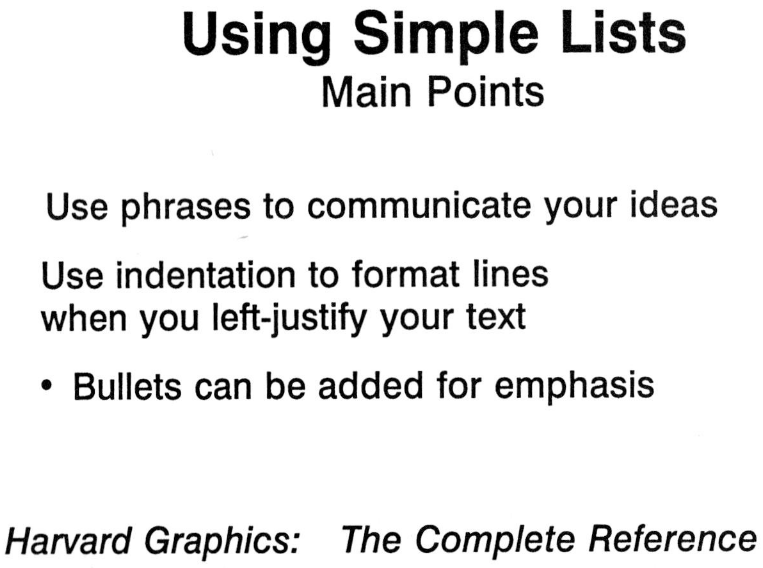

# Using Simple Lists
## Main Points

Use phrases to communicate your ideas

Use indentation to format lines
when you left-justify your text

• Bullets can be added for emphasis

*Harvard Graphics:   The Complete Reference*

**Figure 4-5.** A simple list chart

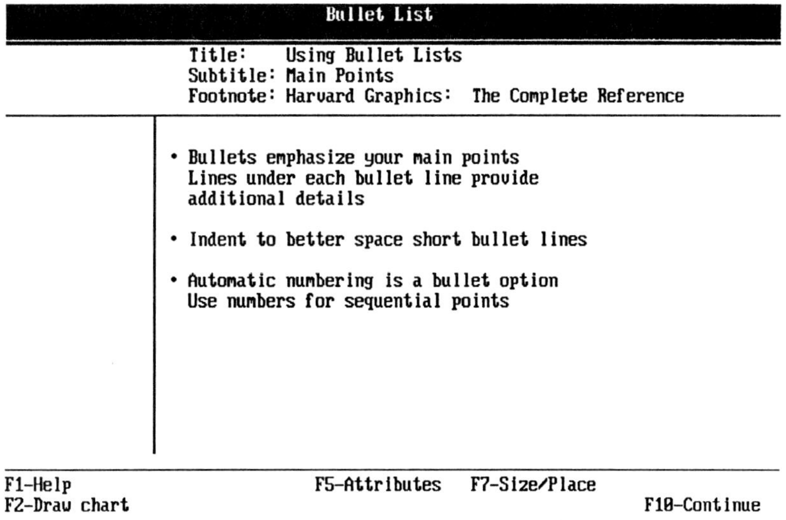

```
                    Bullet List
         Title:    Using Bullet Lists
         Subtitle: Main Points
         Footnote: Harvard Graphics:   The Complete Reference

         • Bullets emphasize your main points
           Lines under each bullet line provide
           additional details

         • Indent to better space short bullet lines

         • Automatic numbering is a bullet option
           Use numbers for sequential points




 F1-Help                   F5-Attributes   F7-Size/Place
 F2-Draw chart                                              F10-Continue
```

**Figure 4-6.**   Bullet List form

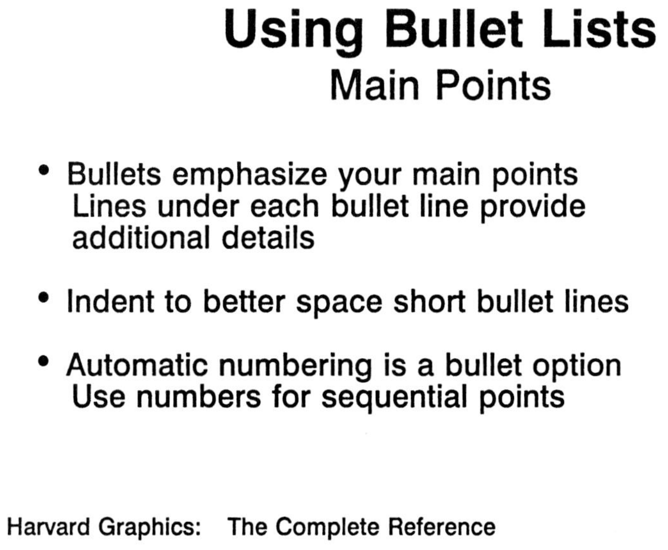

# Using Bullet Lists
## Main Points

- Bullets emphasize your main points
  Lines under each bullet line provide
  additional details

- Indent to better space short bullet lines

- Automatic numbering is a bullet option
  Use numbers for sequential points


Harvard Graphics:   The Complete Reference

**Figure 4-7.**   A bullet list chart

```
                    ┌─────────────────────────────────────────────────┐
                    │                  Two Columns                    │
                    │  Title:    Two and Three Column Charts          │
                    │  Subtitle: Number Tables or Text Tables         │
                    │  Footnote: Harvard Graphics: The Complete Reference │
                    ├──────────────────────┬──────────────────────────┤
                    │ Tables of Numbers    │ Tables of Text           │
                    │                      │                          │
                    │  $  1,546.34         │ Text is left justified   │
                    │  $ 10,500.43         │ Numbers are right justified │
                    │  $ 47,123.00         │ Column headings are underlined │
                    │  $ 87,409.53         │ Column spacing is adjustable │
                    │                      │                          │
                    └──────────────────────┴──────────────────────────┘
   F1-Help                      F5-Attributes    F7-Size/Place
   F2-Draw chart                                                F10-Continue
```

**Figure 4-8.**    Two Columns form

4-9. Text entered within each column is automatically left-justified when displayed on the chart. If an entire column consists of numbers, Harvard Graphics right-justifies the column on the chart. As you can see in the two-column chart in Figure 4-10, column titles can be entered and will appear above the corresponding column on the chart.

*Note:*   If you need to create a text chart with more than three columns, use a free-form chart.

## Free-Form Charts

Create a free-form chart when none of the other text chart formats suits your needs. As you can see in Figure 4-11, the Free Form Text form allows you to place text anywhere in the text area of the chart. Since this placement is user defined, you must space the text exactly as you want it to appear on the chart. If you include a title, subtitle, and footnote, the title and subtitle will be centered and the footnote will be

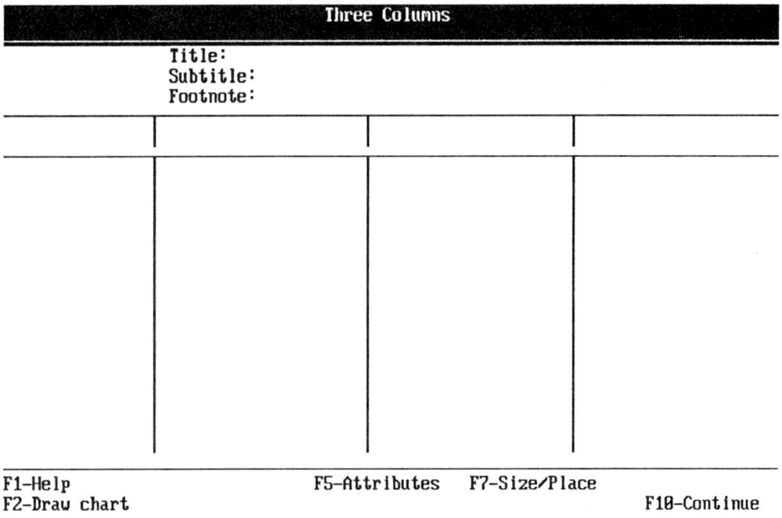

Text Charts 83

```
                      Three Columns
            Title:
            Subtitle:
            Footnote:


F1-Help                   F5-Attributes   F7-Size/Place
F2-Draw chart                                            F10-Continue
```

**Figure 4-9.**     Three Columns form

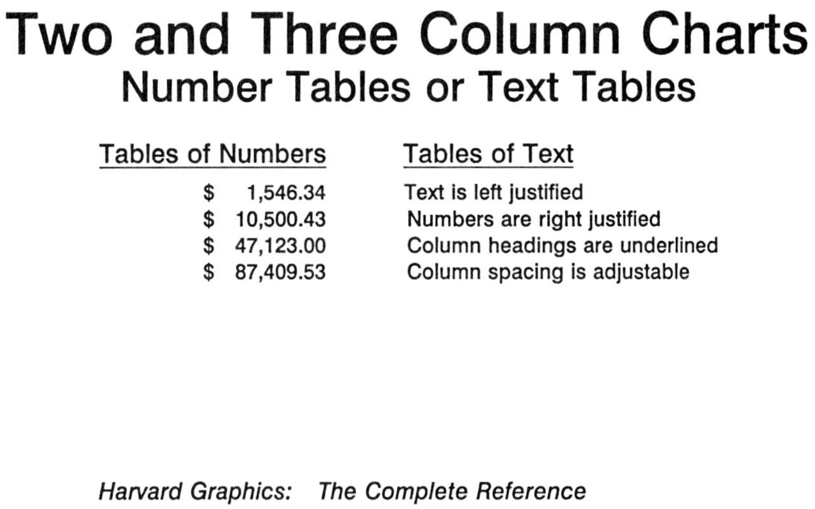

# Two and Three Column Charts
## Number Tables or Text Tables

| Tables of Numbers | Tables of Text |
|---|---|
| $   1,546.34 | Text is left justified |
| $  10,500.43 | Numbers are right justified |
| $  47,123.00 | Column headings are underlined |
| $  87,409.53 | Column spacing is adjustable |

*Harvard Graphics:   The Complete Reference*

**Figure 4-10.**     A two-column chart

```
              ┌─────────────Free Form Text─────────────┐
              Title:    Free Form Text Chart
              Subtitle: Uses For This Chart Style
              Footnote: Harvard Graphics:  The Complete Reference

              The free form text chart can be used to display
              entire paragraphs of information.  These
              paragraphs can define terms that you are using
              in your presentation, display quotations, or
              provide lengthy descriptions.

              The free form chart is often used when long
              text files are imported into Harvard Graphics
              for use in your presentation.

              You can also use free form charts when you want
              to create a column chart that contains more than
              three columns.

                  Column 1      Column 2     Column 3    Column 4
                   Item 1        100.0        100.12        15

     F1-Help                     F5-Attributes   F7-Size/Place
     F2-Draw chart                                          F10-Continue
```

**Figure 4-11.**     Free Form Text form

left-justified on the chart. The text entered into the form shown in Figure 4-11 results in the chart shown in Figure 4-12.

## Modifying Text Attributes

Text attributes include font weight (regular or bold), style (italics and fill), underlining, and color. Modifying one or more of these attributes requires two steps. The first involves selecting the text whose attributes you want to modify. The second step is to set the desired attributes on the Text Attributes overlay. See Appendix D, "Harvard Graphics Tables," for examples of attribute combinations for each of the six fonts available.

## Free Form Text Chart
### Uses For This Chart Style

The free form text chart can be used to display entire paragraphs of information. These paragraphs can define terms that you are using in your presentation, display quotations, or provide lengthy descriptions.

The free form chart is often used when long text files are imported into Harvard Graphics for use in your presentation.

You can also use free form charts when you want to create a column chart that contains more than three columns.

| Column 1 | Column 2 | Column 3 | Column 4 |
|----------|----------|----------|----------|
| Item 1   | 100.0    | 100.12   | 15       |
| Item 2   | 101.5    | 101.01   | 27       |
| Item 3   | 103.0    | 3,102.00 | 53       |
| Item 4   | 104.5    | 4,000.01 | 64       |

Harvard Graphics:   The Complete Reference

**Figure 4-12.**  A free-form text chart

## Highlighting Text to Change Attributes

Before you can modify text attributes, you must place your cursor at the correct location on the screen. If you want to modify only a portion of the text that appears on a line, first move the cursor to the left-most character of the text you want to modify. Then press F5-Attributes to highlight the character at your cursor and display the Text Attributes overlay (shown in Figure 4-13) at the bottom of the screen.

Alternatively, if you want to change the attributes of one or more entire lines of text, move your cursor to the top line that you want to

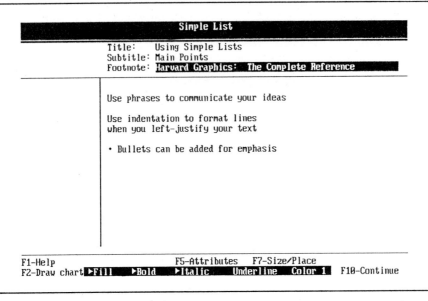

**Figure 4-13.**  Text Attributes overlay—footnote has been highlighted for an attribute change

highlight. Then press SHIFT-F5 to automatically highlight the entire current line and display the Text Attributes overlay at the bottom of the screen.

Use the RIGHT and DOWN arrow keys to highlight the desired text. Press RIGHT to highlight text to the right of the cursor. (Pressing F5-Attributes at this point is the same as pressing the RIGHT key.) Press DOWN (or SHIFT-F5) to highlight additional lines of text. If you try to highlight text to the left of where you began highlighting, no highlighting will appear and the Text Attributes overlay will be removed from the screen.

## Setting Attributes for Highlighted Text

Once you have highlighted the desired text, use the TAB key to move among the various attribute options on the Text Attributes overlay. The settings for these options are changed by pressing the SPACEBAR. For "Fill," "Bold," "Italic," and "Underline," when the attribute is turned on, an arrow appears to the left of its name.

There are two ways to change the setting for "Color." The first is to press the SPACEBAR until the desired color number appears to the right of "Color." The second way is to select a color from a list. With your cursor positioned on the "Color" option of the Text Attributes overlay, press F6-Colors. Harvard Graphics will display the Color Selection overlay, shown in Figure 4-14. This overlay lists the names of all 16 colors on your color palette. Select the desired color and then press ENTER or F10-Continue. The Color Selection overlay disappears from the screen and the cursor returns to the Text Attributes overlay.

When you are through setting text attribute options for the highlighted text, press F10-Continue to return to your chart form.

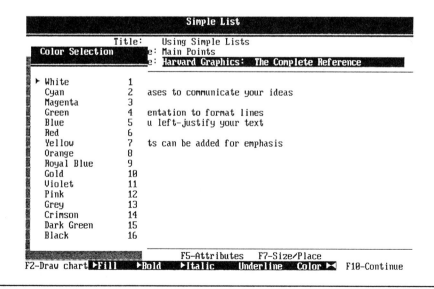

**Figure 4-14.** Color Selection overlay

## Modifying Text Size and Placement

You may want to change the text size or placement on your chart for emphasis, to create a well-balanced layout, or to add variety. While you are entering data into your chart, you can press F7-Size/Place to modify the size and placement of text on your chart. When you do so, the Size/Place overlay is displayed over the upper-left corner of the chart form. For example, Figure 4-15 displays the Size/Place overlay for a title chart.

Each chart uses a slightly different Size/Place overlay. Some of these overlays permit you to specify the indentation of the text (for simple and bullet lists), the shape of bullets (bullet lists), or the spacing of columns (two- and three-column charts). Each of these topics is covered in the following sections.

Once you set your desired options on the Size/Place overlay, press F7-Size/Place or F10-Continue to return to the chart form.

```
                         Title Chart

     Size    Place    Top
      8      L ►C R
      8      L ►C R
      8      L ►C R
                      Middle
      6      L ►C R
      6      L ►C R
      6      L ►C R
                      Bottom
      4      L ►C R
      4      L ►C R
      4      L ►C R

     F1-Help                    F5-Attributes  F7-Size/Place
     F2-Draw chart                                             F10-Continue
```

**Figure 4-15.**   Size/Place overlay for a title chart

## Setting Text Size

To adjust the text size of a particular line on your chart, you enter a number in the column on the Size/Place overlay. Each number in that "Size" column corresponds to the text that appears to the right of it. (In the simple list, bullet list, two- and three-column, and free-form chart, the last size setting on the Size/Place overlay defines the size of the text in the text area of the chart.) The number that you enter can be from .1 to 99. See Appendix D, "Harvard Graphics Tables," for examples of different sizes.

*Note:* The actual text size on your chart will depend both on the size you specify on the Size/Place overlay and on the font you specify on the Current Chart Options overlay. (For information about the Current Chart Options overlay, see "Overriding Default Chart Characteristics" in Chapter 3, "Setup and Default Settings.") In addition, if your text size is small, attributes of chart text may not be displayed on your monitor, although they will appear when output.

Once you have changed your text size, you can modify text placement options or press F7-Size/Place or F10-Continue to return to the chart form. After changing your text size, it is always a good idea to press F2-Draw chart to see how the new text size appears on your chart. Harvard Graphics will permit you to enter a text size that creates text so large it will not fit on your chart. If the size of your text is not satisfactory, press F7-Size/Place and adjust it again.

## Modifying Text Placement

The "Place" column on the Size/Place overlay permits you to select the placement of the text for the top, middle, and bottom sections of text on title charts, and for the title, subtitle, and footnote on all other charts. (You may also define the placement of the text in the text area of simple and bullet list text charts.) Corresponding to each of these text areas are the settings "L," "C," and "R" on the Size/Place overlay. These settings signify left-justified text, centered text, and right-justified text, respectively. To change the placement of text, move to the appropriate line in the "Place" column and press the SPACEBAR until the desired setting is marked with an arrow. Preview your text placement by pressing F2-Draw chart.

## Setting Indentation

Simple lists and bullet lists give you the option of indenting the text area of the chart by a specified percentage. This option will only have an effect if the placement of the text within this text area is left-justified. Otherwise, the indentation value is ignored.

To indent the text in the left-justified text area, move to the "Indent" option on the Size/Place overlay and enter a number from 0 to 100. This number specifies the percentage of the chart width that the text will be indented. For example, if you indent the text using the value 50, the text will begin at the middle of the chart (the 50% mark). If you indent 20, the text will begin one-fifth of the way across the chart.

## Modifying Column Spacing

The Size/Place overlays for two- and three-column charts permit you to specify the spacing between columns. To set the desired spacing, move to the "Column Spacing" option. Possible settings for column spacing are "S" (small), "M" (medium), "L" (large), or "X" (extra large). Press the SPACEBAR to set the desired spacing. Preview the chart by pressing F2-Draw chart to see the effects of your column spacing settings.

## Using Bullets

Bullets are symbols or markers placed at the beginning of lines of text to add emphasis, identify separate concepts or issues, or enumerate points. There are five different types of bullets you can use in Harvard Graphics: dots, dashes, check marks, boxes, and numbers.

There are two ways to make bullets appear in your Harvard Graphics charts. The first is to use a bullet list, a chart style specifically designed to include bullets. When you create a bullet list, Harvard Graphics automatically places bullets on your chart as described in the earlier section, "Bullet Lists." The second way is to manually add a bullet to your chart by pressing CTRL-B at the desired location of the bullet, as described in the upcoming section, "Adding a Bullet to a Non-Bullet Chart." By using this method, you can add a bullet to any style of text or data chart.

The bullets placed automatically on bullet lists and the bullets placed manually by pressing CTRL-B have different characteristics. The first difference is the overlay on which you select the bullet type. For bullet lists, it is selected at the "Bullet shape" option on the Size/Place overlay (see the next section, "Changing the Bullet Type in a Bullet List"). In addition, the bullet numbering feature (using the # sign) is only available with bullet lists, so you must choose this chart style and select the # to have Harvard Graphics automatically number your points. For bullets placed manually, you select the bullet type from the Bullet Shape overlay, which is displayed immediately after you press CTRL-B.

The second difference is the manner in which you modify a bullet's color or delete a bullet. The bullets you enter manually behave like any other text on the chart. Specifically, you can delete a bullet using DEL or change its color using F5-Attributes, just as you would for any text on the chart. Bullets in bullet lists, however, require additional steps. Because these bullets are placed automatically by Harvard Graphics you cannot move your cursor to the region on the Bullet List form where Harvard Graphics places these bullets. In order to delete these bullets, you must delete the entire line of text by pressing CTRL-DEL. Changing the color of bullets on bulleted lists is more involved and is described in the section, "Coloring Bullets in a Bullet List."

## Changing the Bullet Type in a Bullet List

The Size/Place overlay for the bullet list (shown in Figure 4-16) allows you to select the shape used for bullets: dot, dash, check mark, square, or numbered. The first four shapes can be used for bullets added to any type of chart. The numbering bullet can only be used in bullet lists.

```
   Size      Place  |             Bullet List               |
    8       L ▶C R  | Title:    Using Bullet Lists          |
    6       L ▶C R  | Subtitle: Main Points                 |
    3.5     ▶L C R  | Footnote: Harvard Graphics: The Complete Reference |

    5       ▶L C R
                    | • Bullets emphasize your main points
   Bullet Shape     |   Lines under each bullet line provide
                    |   additional details
   ▶•  -  ♪  ■  #   |
                    | • Indent to better space short bullet lines
   Indent: 15
                    | • Automatic numbering is a bullet option
                    |   Use numbers for sequential points



   F1-Help                    F5-Attributes    F7-Size/Place
   F2-Draw chart                                             F10-Continue
```

**Figure 4-16.**   Size/Place overlay for a bullet list

*Note:* The # sign will mark the location of numbered bullets on the Bullet List form, but will display as "1," "2," "3," and so on, on the chart.

To set or change a bullet type, press F7-Size/Place to display the Size/Place overlay for the bullet list. Move to the "Bullet shape" option and press the SPACEBAR to select a bullet shape. Press F7-Size/Place or F10-Continue to return to the Bullet List form.

### Coloring Bullets in a Bullet List

You may want to color the bullets on your bullet list for emphasis, making them a different color from the subsequent text. However, because you cannot move your cursor to the region that contains the bullets, you cannot highlight the bullet in order to change its color. Fortunately, there is a way to set the color of the bullet without necessarily setting the color of the text next to the bullet.

First, there must be at least one extra space between a bullet and the start of the text. Place the cursor as close as you can to the right of the bullet. If your cursor is at a text character, you will need to add an extra space before the start of the text, and then position the cursor on this space. Next, press F5-Attributes to highlight the space and to display the Text Attributes overlay. Only the single space at your cursor should be highlighted. Set a color for this space and press F10-Continue. Your bullet will now adopt the color you set for the space. Furthermore, the presence of the additional space will not affect the formatting of the text on the same line.

*Note:* It is necessary to color each bullet on the bullet list separately using this technique.

## Adding a Bullet to a Non-Bullet Chart

A bullet can be added to any style of text or data chart. To place a bullet, move your cursor to the desired location on the chart form and press CTRL-B to display the Bullet Shape overlay, shown in Figure 4-17. Press the SPACEBAR to select the bullet you want to place, and then press ENTER or F10-Continue. Harvard Graphics will place the selected bullet at the location of your cursor. To cancel adding a bullet once you have displayed the Bullet Shape overlay, press ESC.

## Changing the Bullet Type on a Non-Bullet Chart

Manually placed bullets have the same characteristics as any other text you place on your chart. Therefore, to delete a bullet, you delete the existing bullet using DEL and reenter the desired bullet when you want to change the bullet type.

## Clearing Text from Your Chart

It is possible to clear all the text entered on a chart while retaining the option settings. This feature is useful, for instance, when you need to

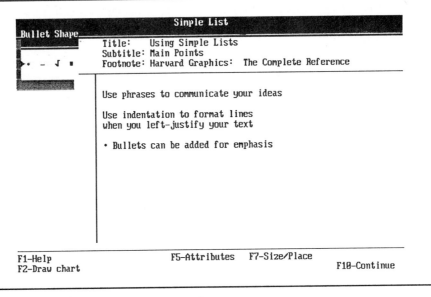

**Figure 4-17.**   Bullet Shape overlay

create several of the same type of text chart with the same Text Attribute and Size/Place settings. To clear text, press ESC until you return to the Main Menu. (If you have not saved your current chart and want to, use <Get/Save/Remove> to save your chart before continuing. See Chapter 2, "Harvard Graphics Basics.")

Select <Create new chart> from the Main Menu, and then select <Clear values>. If you have not saved your chart since creating or modifying it, Harvard Graphics will display the message "Chart values are about to be cleared. Press Enter to continue; Esc to Cancel."

When you use <Clear values> Harvard Graphics will remove all the text entered on your chart and display a blank chart form of the same style as your previous current chart. Enter your new text on this chart form. The text attributes set on the Text Attributes overlay and the text size and placement specified on the Size/Place overlay will be the same settings defined for your previous chart.

## Changing Text Chart Styles

Occasionally you will want to change a text chart from one style to another while retaining all the text you have entered on the chart form. Most of these changes work smoothly, especially changing from a simple list to a bullet list, for example. Other changes, such as changing from a three-column chart to a title chart, produce undesirable results.

To change text chart styles, start with the text chart in its original style as the current chart. If you have not saved this chart since you created or last modified it, save it before you continue. (See Chapter 2, "Harvard Graphics Basics," for information on saving charts.) Next, select <Create new chart> from the Main Menu, followed by <Text> from the Create New Chart menu.

If you select a text chart style that is different from the current one, Harvard Graphics will display the Change Chart Type overlay, shown in Figure 4-18, which asks you to indicate whether you want to keep the

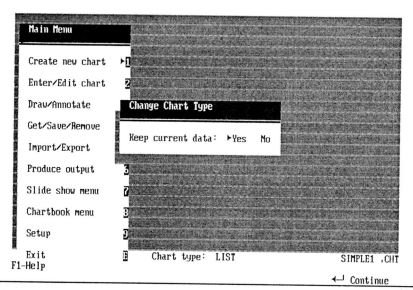

**Figure 4-18.**   Change Chart Type overlay

text entered for the current chart. If you select Yes, Harvard Graphics will use the text already entered for your current chart and copy it to the chart form for the new chart style. If you select No, the chart form for your new chart will be blank.

# Organization Charts

Introduction to Organization Charts
Creating Organization Charts
The Organization Chart Form
Moving Around the Organization
Editing an Organization Chart
The Org Chart Options Form
Clearing Values

Organization charts graphically depict the structure of an organization—the members and their relationships. This chapter describes organization charts, how to create them, and how to tailor them to suit your needs. The first section starts with an introduction to organization charts and an overview of the steps needed to create them. The rest of this chapter details the individual steps involved in creating organization charts.

## Introduction to Organization Charts

Organization charts allow you to define the relationships among members of an organization and display these relationships graphically. Figure 5-1 shows an example of an organization chart. Although the primary purpose of organization charts is to represent business structures, these charts are also useful for displaying other hierarchical relationships. These can include family trees, software program menu structures, or the organization of your computer's directories and subdirectories, just to name a few.

Designing an organization chart with Harvard Graphics involves two distinct steps. The first is to define the members of the organization

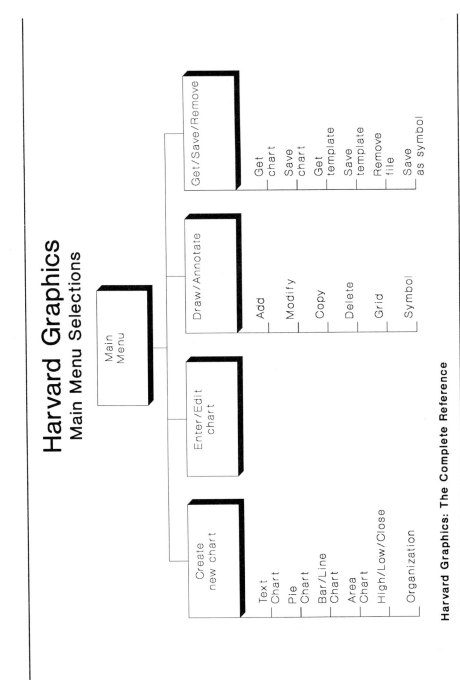

**Figure 5-1.** An organization chart

and their relationships to each other. This step is carried out using the Organization Chart form. The second step is to define how the organization chart will appear. This includes choosing the amount of data to display for each individual, the text attributes to use for the text, whether to use a drop shadow effect on the boxes, and whether to display the last level of the organization vertically or horizontally.

Before you begin entering data for your organization chart, you should be aware of the limitations of this chart type. Harvard Graphics organization charts are limited to a maximum of eight levels. There is also a limit to the size of the organization that can be displayed on a chart. For example, if you enter five levels, and each individual at each level has four subordinates, your chart would need to contain 341 names, with 256 people at the lowest level. This chart would be too large to display or print in its entirety. If your chart is too large to display on the screen (using F2-Draw chart), Harvard Graphics will display this message:

The maximum size of an organization chart depends on a number of factors. These include the type of graphics adapter you are using, the type of device you output your chart to, the size of the longest text field displayed in your chart, and the orientation of the lowest level. These combinations can lead to a situation where a chart will be too wide to display on your monitor, but can still be printed or plotted. If you think your chart is only slightly larger than can be displayed on your monitor, you may still want to try to print or plot it. Most of the time, however, you will not be abler to output your chart when it is too wide.

*Note:* You can display or print selected subsets of an organization even when the entire organization is too large to display in its entirety. See the section, "Displaying Less than the Entire Organization," later in this chapter.

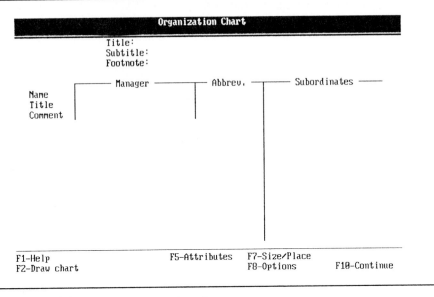

**Figure 5-2.**   Organization Chart form

## Creating Organization Charts

The following is a general overview of the steps involved in creating an organization chart. Refer to the remaining sections of this chapter for more details.

1. At the Main Menu, select <Create new chart>.

2. At the Create New Chart menu, select <Organization>, and Harvard Graphics will display the Organization Chart form, shown in Figure 5-2.

3. Enter a title, subtitle, and footnote to be used for the chart.

4. Modify the size and placement of the title, subtitle, and footnote (using the Size/Place overlay), and attributes for this text (using the Text Attributes overlay).

5. Define the members of the organization and their relationship to each other in the organization. This involves the following steps:

a. Define the top manager (to be displayed in the top level of the organization chart) in the "Manager" column on the Organization Chart form. Add a name, title, and comment for this person and, if desired, an abbreviated name, title, and comment for the top manager in the "Abbrev." column.

b. List the names of the individuals who are subordinate to the top manager in the "Subordinate" column.

c. Move your cursor to the name of one of the subordinates. Press CTRL-PGDN to move to this subordinate's level in the organization. This subordinate's name will now appear in the "Manager" column on the Organization Chart form. Add a title, comment, abbreviations, and list the subordinates for this individual.

d. Repeat this process for each individual in the organization, using CTRL-PGUP to move up one level and CTRL-PGDN to move down one level in the organization.

*Note:* You will not add names of subordinates to the individuals who are in the lowest level of the organization.

6. Define options for the organization chart as a whole on the Org Chart Options form.

At this point, your organization chart is finished. If you want to save your chart the way it is, skip to the last step. You may, however, want to consider some of the following optional steps to improve or enhance your chart. If you change or add to your chart, remember to save it to retain these changes.

7. If you want to check the spelling of text in your chart, return to the Main Menu and press F4-Spell check. Additional information about spell checking your charts is provided in Chapter 2, "Harvard Graphics Basics."

8. If you want to change the font used for text in your chart, or select a different chart border or orientation, return to the Main Menu and press F8-Options. Set "Orientation," "Border," and "Font"

on the displayed Current Chart Options overlay. See "Overriding Default Display Characteristics" in Chapter 3, "Setup and Default Settings," for additional detail.

9. If desired, you can enhance your chart by using Harvard Graphics' drawing and annotating features. You can also reduce the overall size of your chart. See Chapter 9, "Drawing and Annotating," for more information.

10. If you want to print, plot, or record your chart on film, return to the Main Menu and select <Produce output>. See Chapter 8, "Producing Output," for more information.

11. Save your chart to disk if you want to use it at a later time. See Chapter 2, "Harvard Graphics Basics," for information on saving charts.

## The Organization Chart Form

The Organization Chart form, shown in Figure 5-2, is used to define a title, subtitle, and footnote for the chart as a whole, as well as a name, title, and a comment for each individual in the organization. The title, subtitle, and footnote are entered on the top three lines of the form. The lower section of the form is used for adding individuals to the organization. This area has three columns labeled "Manager," "Abbrev.," and "Subordinates."

Use the keys listed in Table 5-1 to control cursor movement and simplify text entry on the Organization Chart form. While you are entering text on the form, use F2-Draw chart frequently to see the layout of the chart you are creating. Then press any key to return to the form.

*Note:* For information on using international text characters in your chart, refer to Appendix D, "Harvard Graphics Tables."

### Entering a Title, Subtitle, and Footnote

The title and subtitle are used to identify the name of the organization you are charting. The footnote is typically used to identify the source of the chart information or the date when the chart was last modified.

| Key | Function |
| --- | --- |
| BACKSPACE | Moves cursor back one space, deleting any character in the space. |
| CTRL-DEL | Deletes entire contents of line at the cursor. Deletes a subordinate in the "Subordinates" column on the Organization Chart form. |
| CTRL-DOWN | Moves subordinate down one position in the "Subordinates" column on the Organization Chart form. |
| CTRL-INS | Inserts a blank line above the line the cursor is on. Use it to insert a subordinate in the "Subordinates" column on the Organization Chart form. |
| CTRL-LEFT | Moves cursor to the previous word in the line. |
| CTRL-PGDN | Moves to a lower organizational level on the Organization Chart form. |
| CTRL-PGUP | Moves to a higher organizational level on the Organization Chart form. |
| CTRL-RIGHT | Moves cursor to next word in the line. |
| CTRL-UP | Moves subordinate up one position in the "Subordinates" column on the Organization Chart form. |
| DEL | Deletes character at the cursor. |
| DOWN (arrow) | Moves cursor down one line, option, or menu item. |
| END | Moves cursor to the last option or line on a form. |
| ENTER | Selects highlighted menu items on menus. Selects highlighted settings for form options and moves cursor to the next option on the form. |
| ESC | 1. Returns to the previous screen. Press ESC multiple times to back up through previous forms and menus to the Main Menu. 2. Cancels changes and returns to the previous screen. |
| HOME | Moves cursor to the first option or line on a form. |
| INS | Toggles insert mode on and off. Cursor appears as a block when it is on, and as a small line when it is off. |
| LEFT (arrow) | Moves cursor to the left one character or option setting. |
| PGDN | Moves to the next subordinate at the same organizational level on the Organization Chart form. |
| PGUP | Moves to the previous subordinate at the same organizational level on the Organization Chart form. |
| RIGHT (arrow) | Moves cursor to the right one character or option setting. |
| SHIFT-TAB | Moves cursor to the previous column or option on a form. |
| TAB | Moves cursor to the next column or option on a form. |
| UP (arrow) | Moves cursor up one line, option, or menu item. |

**Table 5-1.** Organization Chart Cursor Control Keys and Functions

The title, subtitle, and footnote are optional, and each is limited to a maximum of 40 characters. By default, the title and subtitle are centered at the top of the chart and the footnote is left-justified at the bottom.

## Modifying Text Attributes

After you have entered a title, subtitle, and footnote, you can modify the attributes of the text in these fields with the Text Attributes overlay. See Appendix D for examples of different attribute combinations.

In order to modify text attributes, you must first highlight the text to change. To highlight the entire title, subtitle, or footnote, move your cursor to the appropriate line and press SHIFT-F5. To highlight less than an entire line of text, move your cursor to the left-most character of the text you want to highlight and press F5-Attributes. Then use the RIGHT and DOWN arrow keys until all of the desired text is highlighted. (At this point, pressing F5-Attributes is the same as pressing the RIGHT key and pressing SHIFT-F5 is the same as pressing the DOWN key.)

Once you press F5-Attributes or SHIFT-F5, the Text Attributes overlay shown in Figure 5-3 is displayed at the bottom of the screen. To change the attributes of the highlighted text, move to the desired option on the Text Attributes overlay and press the SPACEBAR to set the attribute option to the desired setting. For "Fill," "Bold," "Italic," and "Underline," the option is set to on when an arrow appears to the left of the option name, and set to off if no arrow is visible. To change the text color, you can press the SPACEBAR until the desired color number is displayed at "Color." Alternatively, with the cursor positioned at "Color," you can press F6-Colors to select from the Color Selection overlay, shown in Figure 5-4. Highlight the desired color in the list and then press ENTER or F10-Continue to return to the Text Attributes overlay.

When you are done setting text attributes for the highlighted text, press F10-Continue to return to the Organization Chart form. If you press ESC while the Text Attributes overlay is displayed, your text attribute settings will be canceled.

*Note:* Attributes for other text in organization charts is set on the Org Chart Options form. See the section, "The Org Chart Options Form," later in this chapter.

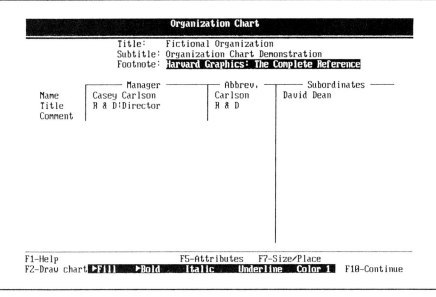

**Figure 5-3.**   Text Attributes overlay

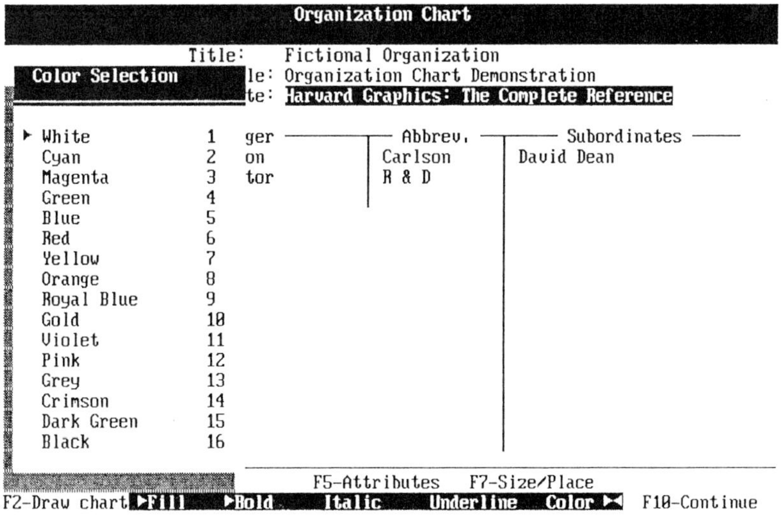

**Figure 5-4.**   Color Selection overlay

## Modifying Text Size and Placement

At the Organization Chart form, press F7-Size/Place to display the Size/Place overlay. This overlay, shown in Figure 5-5, contains two columns, "Size" and "Place," that allow you to define the size and placement for the title, subtitle, and footnote text. Set the size of text by moving to the "Size" column that corresponds to the text you want to modify, and entering a new size value. This value can be from .1 to 99. The larger the number, the larger the text. See Appendix D for examples of sizes.

*Note:*  If the text size is too small, text attributes applied to chart text may not be displayed on your monitor, although they will appear when output.

To change the placement of the text, move to the "Place" column corresponding to the text you want to move. Press the SPACEBAR to set the desired text placement to either "L" (left-justified), "C" (centered), or "R" (right-justified). Use F2-Draw chart to view your chart and ensure that your size and placement settings are satisfactory.

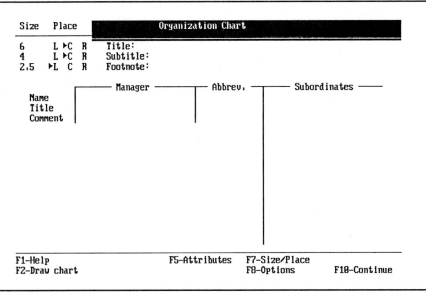

**Figure 5-5.**   Size/Place overlay

When you are done setting the size and placement of the title, subtitle, and footnote text, press F10-Continue to return to the Organization Chart form.

*Note:* Harvard Graphics automatically selects the text sizes used for the text entered in the "Manager," "Abbrev.," and "Subordinates" columns.

## Entering a Name, Title, and Comment for the Current Manager

When you first create an organization chart, the "Manager" column is blank. Enter the name of the top person in the organization in this column. Although it is not necessary to display the top manager on your chart, it is the highest position that *can* be displayed. You cannot add another level of organization above this first level.

At any given time, the name that appears in the "Manager" column is referred to as the *current manager*. When you first create an organization chart, the top manager is the current manager. Any individual in the organization can be made the current manager by moving down, up, or sideways within the organization. See the section "Moving Around the Organization" later in this chapter, for details.

The "Manager" column is used to enter the name, title, and a comment for the current manager. Each of these lines can contain up to 22 characters. Use the next column, "Abbrev.," to enter an abbreviated name, title, and comment for the current manager, as described in the section "Entering Abbreviations." The contents of the "Abbrev." column are used only if you later choose to display abbreviated names, titles, and comments on your chart. The final column, "Subordinates," is used to list the names of all of the individuals who are at the level directly under the current manager in the organization, as described in the later section "Entering Subordinates."

### Splitting a Name, Title, or Comment onto Two Lines

You can display the name, title, or comment for the current manager on two lines instead of one. There are two steps to this process. If you want to control where the line will be split, you must place the line-splitting character (¦) where you want Harvard Graphics to split the line. Move to the place in the row where you want the split to occur, and insert the ¦. Do not follow the ¦ with a space, or this space will be printed on the following line and cause the second line of the split field to appear off center. Figure 5-6 shows an appropriate placement of ¦ between the first and last names of the current manager, Allen Allbright.

The second step is to specify that the text be split on the Org Chart Options form. To do this, move to the "Split" option on the appropriate row of the Org Chart Options form. Then press the SPACEBAR to set "Split" to Yes. See the section "Setting Organization Text Attributes," later in this chapter, for more details on defining a split text field on the Org Chart Options form.

*Note:* If you use the ¦ character in a field, but then fail to set the corresponding "Split" option to Yes, the text will not be split, and the ¦ will appear on your chart. If you do not use the line-splitting character, but have set the "Split" option to Yes, Harvard Graphics will determine if and where the text will split.

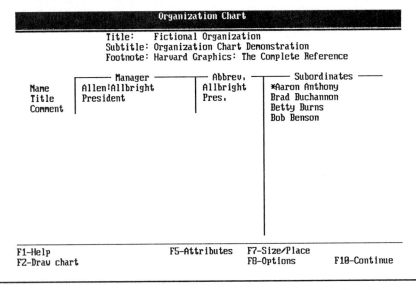

**Figure 5-6.** The ¦ and * symbols indicate text split and staff position, respectively

## Entering Abbreviations

When charts become large you may want to use abbreviated names, titles, and comments in order to save space on your chart. Each line in the "Abbrev." column is limited to 11 characters. The "Abbrev." column is used in conjunction with the "Abbreviations" option on the Org Chart Options form. When "Abbreviations" is set to Yes, the name, title, and comment values entered in the "Manager" column of the Organization Chart form will not be used in the chart. Instead, the corresponding values in the "Abbrev." column will appear in the chart.

## Entering Subordinates

Use the "Subordinates" column to enter the names of the individuals that will appear below the current manager in the organization chart. The names you enter will appear in a horizontal (left to right) orientation on the organization chart. If these subordinates are at the lowest level of your organization, you have the option of displaying their names vertically, as described in the section "Setting the Last Level Display Characteristics," later in this chapter.

### Defining a Staff Position

While you are entering the subordinates for the top manager, you may define *one* of the subordinates as a staff person—an assistant or secretary to the top manager. The staff person has no subordinates. To add a staff person, enter the name of the staff person in the "Subordinates" column, preceded by an asterisk. In Figure 5-6, the name of the first subordinate in the list is preceded by an asterisk. This staff position will appear to the right of the manager position on the chart, as is shown in Figure 5-7.

Only one staff position may be defined in your entire organization chart, and it must be associated with the top manager. If you define more than one staff position, all but the first one will be displayed as regular subordinates on the chart. Also, if you define a staff position for a manager who is not the highest manager displayed on the chart, the

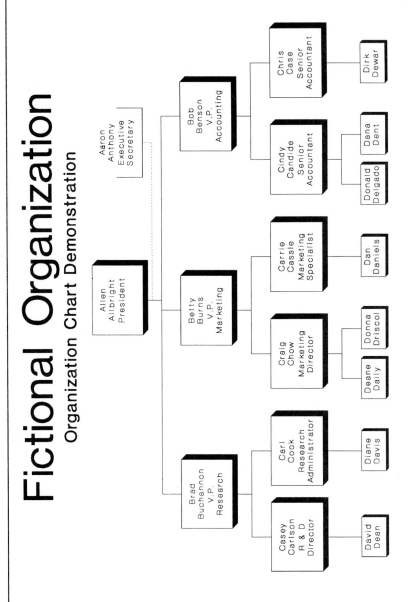

**Figure 5-7.** The staff position is displayed to the right of the President position

staff person will simply be displayed as a regular subordinate. Lastly, if you add subordinates to a staff position, the staff position will be displayed as a regular subordinate.

## Adding Additional Organization Levels

Additional levels are added to an organization by making one of the subordinates the current manager, then adding subordinates to this manager. This procedure involves the following steps:

1. Move to the name in the "Subordinates" column for which you want to add an additional level.

2. Press CTRL-PGDN. This moves you down one level in the organization, which makes the selected subordinate the current manager. The subordinate's name will now appear in the "Manager" column.

3. Enter a title and comment for the current manager.

4. If you will use abbreviations in your chart, move to the "Abbrev." column and enter an abbreviated name, title, and comment.

5. If there are individuals who report to the current manager, move to the "Subordinates" column and add their names.

This process can be repeated as many times as necessary, up to the limit of eight organizational levels.

## Adding a Title and Comment for Last Level Subordinates

The last level of the organization is the level where the individuals have no subordinates of their own. When you first display your organization chart, these individuals have names but no titles or comments. If you like, you can add titles and comments for the lowest level subordinates by making each of them in turn the current manager and adding a title and comment in the "Manager" column. You can also define an abbreviated name, title, and comment for each subordinate. Do not, however, enter any names in the "Subordinates" column, unless you want to add an additional organization level.

## Moving Around the Organization

The trick to effectively adding to and changing an organization chart lies in the ability to move among the different levels of the organization. The following sections describe the basics of movement in the Organization Chart form. You may also want to refer to Table 5-1 for a summary of the keys that can be used when working with organization charts.

### Changing Levels in an Organization Chart

There are two key combinations that permit you to quickly move between the various levels of your organization chart: CTRL-PGDN and CTRL-PGUP. If you are not in the "Subordinates" column of the Organization Chart form, pressing CTRL-PGDN will move you down one level, making the first entry in the "Subordinates" column the current manager. If the cursor is in the "Subordinates" column, you can move it to a specific subordinate and press CTRL-PGDN to make that individual the current manager. For example, if, in Figure 5-8, Allen Allbright is the current manager, you can make Betty Burns the current manager by moving to her name in the "Subordinates" column and pressing CTRL-PGDN. Figure 5-9 shows the result of this. If you are at the last level in the organization, CTRL-PGDN will have no effect.

Pressing CTRL-PGUP will move you up one level in the organization. However, if you are already at the top level in the organization, that is, the current manager is the top manager, pressing CTRL-PGUP will have no effect.

### Moving Between Individuals at the Same Level

Using PGUP and PGDN you can quickly move between two individuals at the same level in the organization when they are subordinate to the same manager. Moving to an individual who reports to a different manager requires you to first move up at least one organizational level before moving down to the desired individual.

Consider Figure 5-8 as an example. If your current manager on the

Organization Charts 113

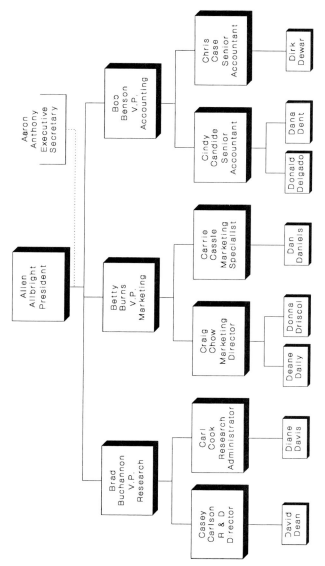

**Figure 5-8.** Betty Burns as a subordinate of Allen Allbright

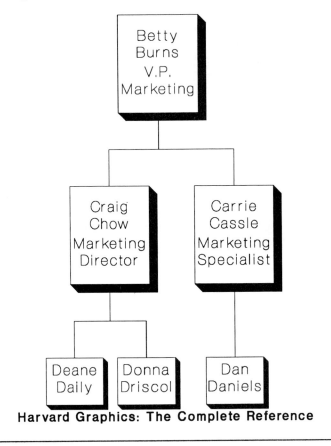

**Figure 5-9.**   Betty Burns as the current manager

Organization Chart form is Carrie Cassle, you can move to Craig Chow by pressing PGUP. You can tell that you need to press PGUP from the line connecting Cassle and Chow, which indicates that Craig is listed immediately before Carrie in the "Subordinates" column for their manager, Betty Burns. You cannot use PGDN to move to Cindy Candide, however, because she is not subordinate to Betty Burns. In this case, you must press CTRL-PGUP to move to Betty Burns, then press PGDN to move sideways to Bob Benson, and then press CTRL-PGDN to move to Cindy Candide.

## Editing an Organization Chart

Organizations tend to change on a regular basis. New people are hired and others leave. When your organization changes, your chart will need to be modified to reflect these changes. The simplest change to make is to a name, title, or description. To make these changes, simply display and then edit the appropriate text. However, many of the types of changes you will need to make involve more than just modifying the text descriptions. They will involve changing the relative positions of individuals in the organization chart, inserting new individuals, and removing old ones.

### Changing the Order of Subordinates

Changing the order of the subordinates in the "Subordinates" column modifies the order in which those subordinates appear on the organization chart. The first subordinate in the column will be the left-most subordinate on the chart at a given level, the second will be the second from the left, and so on. To change the order of subordinates move your cursor to the subordinate you want to move and press CTRL-UP or CTRL-DOWN to move this subordinate up or down in the "Subordinates" column.

### Inserting Additional Subordinates

To insert new subordinates, move to the location in the "Subordinates" column where you want to add a new subordinate and press CTRL-INS. This will open a new line above the line where you pressed CTRL-INS. Then enter the name of the subordinate. If desired, you can press CTRL-PGDN to make the newly added subordinate the current manager. With the new subordinate as the current manager, you can add a title, comment, and abbreviations, as well as subordinates for this individual.

## Deleting a Subordinate

To delete a subordinate from the list of subordinates in the "Subordinates" column, move the cursor to the name of the subordinate you want to delete and press CTRL-DEL. You cannot delete an individual who has subordinates. If you try to, Harvard Graphics will display this message:

> Cannot delete manager with subordinates

If you need to delete an individual who has been assigned subordinates, you must delete those subordinates first.

## The Org Chart Options Form

After you have entered data into the Organization Chart form, you will most likely want to set options for the chart. Options permit you to display or print only a part of the organization chart, select the fields you want to display, modify the attributes of text, and define how to display the lowest level of the organization.

To move to the Org Chart Options form, shown in Figure 5-10, from the Organization Chart form, press F8-Options. You can return to the Organization Chart form at any time by pressing F8-Data.

### Displaying Less than the Entire Organization

The first two options on the Org Chart Options form (shown in Figure 5-10) permit you to define the manager that will be displayed at the top level of the organization, as well as the number of levels to display. If you set the "Start chart at" option to Top, the organization chart will start at the top manager. If you set the "Start chart at" option to

## Organization Charts 117

```
┌─────────────────────────────────────────────────────────────────────┐
│                          Org Chart Options                          │
├─────────────────────────────────────────────────────────────────────┤
│                                                                     │
│         Start chart at  │ ►Top    Current manager                   │
│         Levels to show  │ ►All    1   2   3   4   5   6   7         │
│                         │                                           │
│         Show titles     │ ►Yes   No                                 │
│         Show comments   │  Yes  ►No                                 │
│         Abbreviations   │  Yes  ►No                                 │
│         Shadow          │  Yes  ►No                                 │
│                         │                                           │
│         Names           │ ►Light  Italic  Bold  Color: 1  Split: ►Yes  No │
│         Titles          │  Light ►Italic  Bold  Color: 1  Split:  Yes ►No │
│         Comments        │ ►Light  Italic  Bold  Color: 1  Split:  Yes ►No │
│                                                                     │
│                                 Last Level                          │
│                         ┌──────────────────────────────────┐        │
│              Show titles│      Yes  ►No                    │        │
│              Show comments│    Yes  ►No                    │        │
│                         │                                  │        │
│              Arrangement│     ►Vertical    Horizontal      │        │
│                                                                     │
│  F1-Help                                                            │
│  F2-Draw chart            F6-Colors      F8-Data      F10-Continue  │
└─────────────────────────────────────────────────────────────────────┘
```

**Figure 5-10.**   Org Chart Options form

Current manager, the highest manager depicted in the chart will be the manager who is currently displayed in the "Manager" column on the Organization Chart form.

You define the maximum number of levels to display using the "Levels to show" option. If you set it to All, all levels of the chart, starting with the level set at "Start chart at," will be displayed. If you want to restrict the number of levels displayed, set "Levels to show" to the desired number of levels.

When you are setting the "Start chart at" and "Levels to show" options, keep in mind that when you save your chart, Harvard Graphics remembers which individual is the current manager. You can use this feature to save the same organization chart many different times (using different chart names), each with a different individual selected as the current manager. If each of these charts is saved with "Start chart at" set to Current manager, each chart will display a different subsection of the organization.

*Note:* Harvard Graphics counts the top level as one of the levels. If you set "Levels to show" to 1, only one individual, the top manager, will be displayed in the organization chart.

## Customizing the Information Displayed

By default, Harvard Graphics displays the name and title of each of the individuals represented in the organization chart. If you like, you can also display the comment information for each individual or suppress the display of the title. The "Show titles," "Show comments," and "Abbreviations" options on the Org Chart Options form (shown in Figure 5-10) are used to define what information Harvard Graphics will display in your organization chart for all but the last level. (The information displayed at the last level is specified separately on the form at the "Last Level" options, described later in this chapter.)

When "Show titles" is set to Yes, the information you supplied in the "Title" row of the "Manager" column will be displayed for each individual. Similarly, the "Show comments" setting indicates whether your chart will include the information entered in the "Comment" row.

When "Abbreviations" is set to No, Harvard Graphics utilizes the name, title, and comment information entered in the "Manager" column on the Organization Chart form. For example, if "Show titles" is set to Yes, "Show comments" is set to No, and "Abbreviations" is also set to No, Harvard Graphics will display the name and title that you entered in the "Manager" column for each individual in your chart, with the exception of the lowest level. Alternatively, if "Abbreviations" is set to Yes, Harvard Graphics will use the versions you entered into the "Abbrev." column on the Organization Chart form. If you set "Show titles" or "Show comments" to Yes, Harvard Graphics will display the abbreviated version of this information as well.

### Adding a Shadow to Organization Boxes

The name, title, and comments for each individual in the organization are printed in boxes on your organization chart (except for the last level, which may or may not be, depending on the settings described later in "Setting the Last Level Display Characteristics"). You can add a drop shadow effect to these boxes by setting "Shadow" to Yes. Figure 5-11 shows an organization chart with and without the shadow.

## Shadow

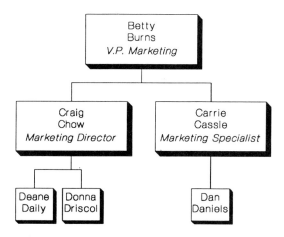

## No Shadow

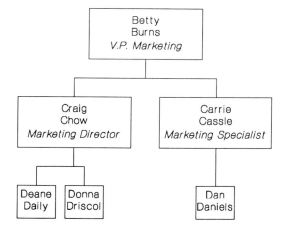

**Figure 5-11.**   "Shadow" set to Yes adds a drop shadow to boxes

### Setting Organization Text Attributes

Harvard Graphics allows you to define the text attributes for each of the three text fields (name, title, and comment) displayed on your organization chart. You set text attributes for these text fields on the three rows in the middle of the Org Chart Options form. The attributes you can define for each text field are type style (Light, Italic, or Bold), "Color," and "Split."

Move to the type style option (Light, Italic, or Bold) at the "Names," "Titles," or "Comments" row. The cursor will be at one of the settings when you move to this line. Press the SPACEBAR if you want to change the current setting to one of the others.

To set a different color for your text, move to "Color" and press the SPACEBAR until the desired color number is displayed. Alternatively, you can press F6-Colors to display the Color Selection overlay shown in Figure 5-12. On the overlay, highlight the desired color name and then press ENTER or F10-Continue to return to the Org Chart Options form.

Use the "Split" option to divide longer text fields onto two lines. When "Split" is set to Yes, Harvard Graphics may optionally divide a

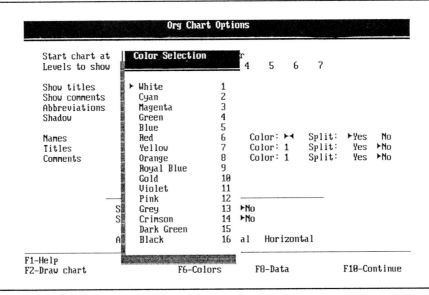

**Figure 5-12.**   Color Selection overlay

text line onto two consecutive lines. Setting "Split" to No tells Harvard Graphics to keep each of the text fields on its own line.

If you have used the ¦ character in the "Name," "Title," or "Comment" fields on the Organization Chart form to force Harvard Graphics to divide a text line at a particular point, you must also set "Split" to Yes at the corresponding "Names," "Titles," or "Comments" row on the Org Chart Options form.

### Setting the Last Level Display Characteristics

The characteristics of the last level of the organization chart are specified separately from the higher levels. Options for the last level are listed at the bottom of the form under "Last Level" (see Figure 5-10). These options give you the option of displaying the titles and comments for individuals in the last level, and allow you to define the orientation of the last level display.

If you want to display the title of each individual in the last level, set the "Show titles" option for the last level to Yes. To display the comments for the last level individuals, set "Show comments" to Yes.

The "Arrangement" option for the last level has several major effects on the appearance of the chart. The default setting is Vertical. When "Arrangement" is set to Vertical, individual entries at the last level are displayed in a vertical list and are not enclosed in boxes. When "Arrangement" is set to Horizontal, last level entries are arranged from left to right and each is enclosed in a box, in the same manner as the higher level entries. If the "Shadow" option is set to Yes, these boxes will be displayed with shadows. Figure 5-13 depicts the difference between vertical and horizontal last levels.

## Clearing Values

You can clear all text entered and options set for your organization chart using the <Clear values> option on the Create New Chart menu. Since <Clear values> removes all values entered for the organization chart, it has essentially the same effect as selecting <Create new chart> from the Main Menu, followed by <Organization> from the

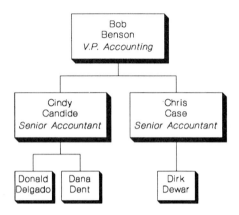

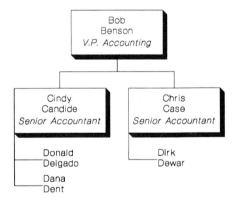

**Figure 5-13.** Possible arrangements for subordinates at the last level

Create New Chart menu. You can use either method to create a new organization chart when your current chart is also an organization chart. To use <Clear values>, press ESC until you return to the Main Menu and select <Create new chart>. Select <Clear values> from the Create New Chart menu. If you have not saved your chart since creating or modifying it, Harvard Graphics will display the message "Chart values are about to be cleared. Press Enter to continue; Esc to Cancel." If you want to save your current chart, press ESC, save your chart, and then repeat the preceding steps.

When you have cleared the values from your chart, Harvard Graphics will remove all the text entered on your chart and return the option settings to the defaults.

# XY Charts: Bar/Line, Area, and High/Low/Close

**S I X**

Creating XY Charts
XY Chart Styles Overview
Specifying the X Data Type
Automatic X Data Entry
Entering XY Chart Data
Using Calculations
Specifying XY Chart Text
Specifying XY Chart Characteristics
Clearing Data from XY Charts
Changing Data Chart Styles

This chapter covers three of the Harvard Graphics chart styles: bar/line, area, and high/low/close charts. These chart styles, collectively referred to as XY charts, represent three of the four styles of data charts that you can create with Harvard Graphics. The fourth data chart style, pie chart, is covered in the next chapter.

An overview of the steps involved in creating XY charts begins this chapter. The rest discusses the details of creating these charts. If you are unfamiliar with creating any of these chart styles, you should read this chapter in its entirety. If you are experienced with XY charts, you may want to read only the sections that interest you.

Throughout the chapter it is assumed that you are familiar with the names that Harvard Graphics uses for the various chart elements and characteristics. These terms, such as grid lines, tick marks, and axes, as well as other more general charting concepts, are described in detail in Part Three of this book. If you find you are unfamiliar with some of the terms, you will benefit by first reading Chapter 17, "Effective Data Charts," and Chapter 18, "Advanced Data Topics."

## Creating XY Charts

An XY chart is any chart where data are represented as symbols, and these symbols are displayed with respect to a horizontal and a vertical axis, labeled X and Y, respectively. Hence the name XY charts. The axes are somewhat like rulers. That is, you use them to determine the values represented by each of the symbols plotted on the chart. In bar charts, for example, you determine the value a bar represents by comparing the height of the bar to the value labels displayed on the Y axis.

To create an XY chart, follow these steps:

1. At the Main Menu, select <Create new chart>.

2. At the Create New Chart menu, select <Bar/Line>, <Area>, or <High/Low/Close>, depending on your needs.

3. Specify the X data type on the X Data Type Menu overlay (as described in "Specifying the X Data Type").

4. Enter your data on the Chart Data form specific to your chart style (as described in "Entering XY Chart Data").

5. Optionally, define any calculations or formulas that should be applied to your data to create additional series on the Calculate overlay (as described in "Using Calculations").

6. Press F8-Options to display the Titles & Options form for your particular XY chart (as described in "Specifying XY Chart Text"). Although this step is also optional, you will want to at least define axis labels. The Titles & Options form also lets you set the attributes of your text, customize its size and placement, specify the symbol type for your chart, define the colors for chart elements, and customize the legend, to name just a few alternatives.

At this point your XY chart is complete. If you want to save your chart without any additional modifications, skip to step 11. You may, however, want to consider some of the following optional steps to improve or enhance your chart:

7. To check the spelling of text in your chart, return to the Main Menu and press F4-Spell check. Additional information about spell checking your charts is provided in Chapter 2, "Harvard Graphics Basics."

8. To change the font used for text on your chart or to select a different chart border or orientation, return to the Main Menu and press F8-Options. Set the "Orientation," "Border," and "Font" options on the displayed Current Chart Options overlay. See Chapter 3, "Setup and Default Settings," for additional detail.

9. You may also want to embellish your XY chart by using Harvard Graphics' drawing and annotating features to add text or drawings, or incorporate any Harvard Graphics symbols in your chart. You can also reduce the overall size of your chart. See Chapter 9, "Drawing and Annotating," for more information.

10. If you want to print, plot, or record your chart on film, return to the Main Menu and select <Produce output>. See Chapter 8, "Producing Output," for more information.

11. Save your chart to disk if you want to use it at a later time. See Chapter 2, "Harvard Graphics Basics," for information on saving charts.

## XY Chart Styles Overview

Each of the XY chart types permits you to create a wide variety of different chart styles. The following sections briefly describe the charts you can create with XY chart selections. If you would like more information about the uses of these various chart styles, see Chapter 17, "Effective Data Charts."

### Bar/Line Chart

The <Bar/Line> selection from the Create New Chart menu allows you to create a variety of bar charts. Figure 6-1 shows a selection of the bar styles you can create. <Bar/Line> also allows you to create several types of line charts and point charts (also called scatterplots, crossplots, or scattergraphs). Examples of line and point charts created with Bar/Line are shown in Figure 6-2. On all of these charts, the height of the bars, lines, or points represents the value of your data.

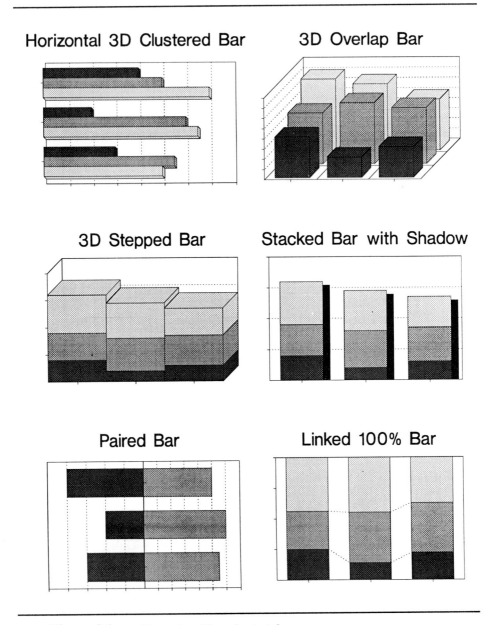

**Figure 6-1.** Examples of bar chart styles

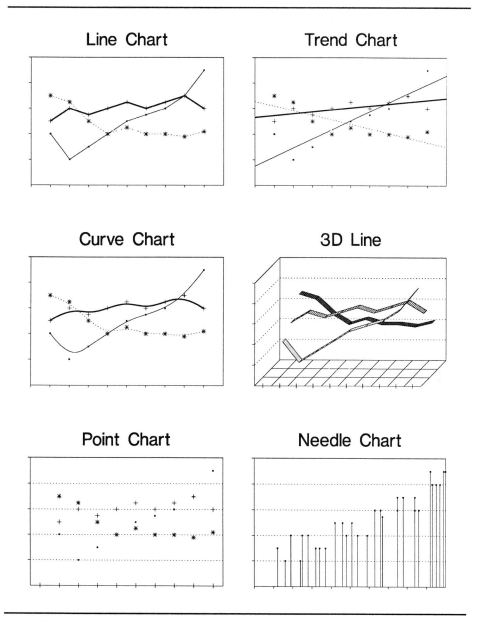

**Figure 6-2.** Examples of line and point chart styles

## Area Chart

An area chart is ideal for displaying your data as areas. The height of an area is determined by the values of your data. Figure 6-3 shows a few of the different types of charts you can create with the <Area> selection.

## High/Low/Close Chart

The <High/Low/Close> selection from the Create New Chart menu allows you to create range bar charts, error bar charts, and band charts. You are probably familiar with the use of range charts to display stock prices. Not only is the highest value that the stock reached displayed, but also the lowest value, and often the closing value. This is where the name *high/low/close* comes from. Several variations of charts created with <High/Low/Close> are shown in Figure 6-4.

## Specifying the X Data Type

Whenever you create an XY chart, Harvard Graphics requires you to first identify what type of X data you have, using the X Data Type Menu overlay, before you can start entering data for the chart. The most important benefit of defining your X data type is that Harvard Graphics uses this information to determine which charting options are valid for your data type. For instance, if your X data are numerical, Harvard Graphics knows that a bar chart is not suitable for displaying these data. Therefore, when you set your "X data type" option to Number and the "Type" option to Bar, Harvard Graphics will produce a needle chart instead of a bar chart.

Another benefit of defining your X data type is that it allows Harvard Graphics to verify that your X data are valid. For instance, if you tell Harvard Graphics the X data are months, and then you enter the month name **Januaru** instead of **January**, Harvard Graphics will spot this error and make you correct it before you can continue. Defining your X data type also permits Harvard Graphics to accurately

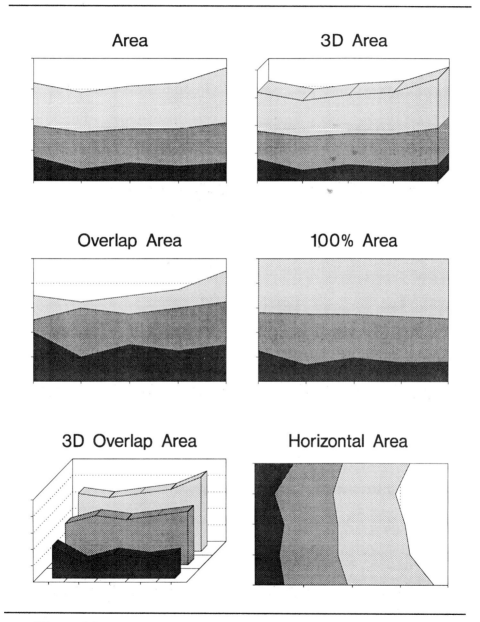

**Figure 6-3.** Examples of area chart styles

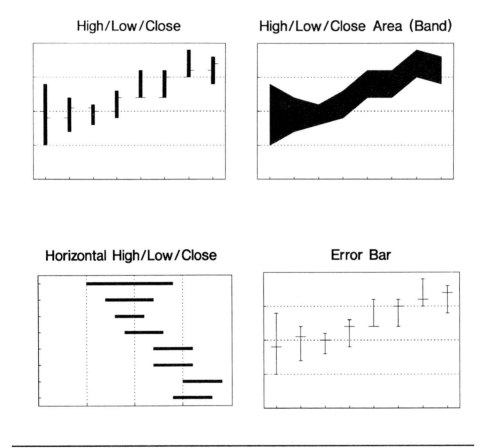

**Figure 6-4.**  Examples of high/low/close chart styles

sort your data by the X data values (for most but not all X data types). Sorting X data is described later in this chapter in the "Using Calculations" section.

For many of the available X data types, you can have Harvard Graphics automatically place your X data in the "X Axis" column of the Chart Data form. However, it can only do this when the X data for a series can be predicted. For instance, if your X data are months,

Harvard Graphics can predict your data (the names of the months), and put them in the "X Axis" column. However, Harvard Graphics cannot predict your X data if your X data are the names of salespeople in your company. You will have to enter these names into the "X Axis" column of the Chart Data form manually.

Harvard Graphics automatically displays the X Data Type Menu overlay (shown in Figure 6-5) after you select one of the XY chart styles from the Create New Chart menu. To identify your X data type on this overlay, press the SPACEBAR until the desired setting is highlighted. Alternatively, press the first letter of the desired setting until it appears at the option "X data type." Each of the X data types has slightly different properties. Table 6-1 displays a list of the X data types, their uses, and samples of valid data for each type.

There are 11 X data types in Harvard Graphics, and these can be roughly divided into four categories: name, calendar, time, and number. If your X data are merely labels for defining groups, set "X data

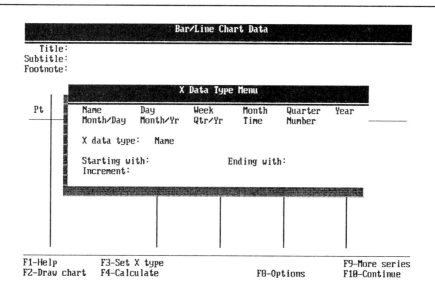

**Figure 6-5.** X Data Type Menu overlay

| X Data Type | Valid Data Entries | Comments |
| --- | --- | --- |
| Name | Alabama, Alaska, ...<br>100, 200, ...<br>Part #1, Part #2, ... | Data can be letters, numbers, and/or special characters. X data must be entered manually. |
| Day | Sunday, Monday, ...<br>Sun, Mon, ... | Automatic X data entry is available. |
| Week | 1, 2, 3, ... | Only numbers (up to 240) can be used. Automatic X data entry is available. |
| Month | January, February, ...<br>Jan, Feb, ...<br>1, 2, ... | Automatic X data entry is available. |
| Quarter | first, second, ...<br>1, 2, ... | Automatic X data entry is available. |
| Year | 1990, 1991, ...<br>90, 91, ... | Automatic X data entry is available. |
| Month/Day | Oct 1, Oct 2, ...<br>10/1, 10/2, ... | Automatic X data entry is available. |
| Month/Yr | Oct 90, Nov 90, ...<br>10/90, 11/90, ... | Automatic X data entry is available. |
| Qtr/Yr | first 90, second 90, ...<br>1/90, 2/90, ... | Automatic X data entry is available. |

**Table 6-1.** X Data Types and Examples of Valid Entries

| X Data Type | Valid Data Entries | Comments |
|---|---|---|
| Time | 1:15 PM, 1:30 PM, ... <br> 12:01 AM, 12:02 AM, ... <br> 13:15, 13:30, ... <br> 0:01, 0:02, ... | Hour:minute format. If you do not specify AM or PM, Harvard Graphics uses the 24-hour format (1:00 - 24:00). Automatic X data entry is available. |
| Number | 10, 20, 30, ... <br> 998.87, ... <br> .000000003, ... <br> 99999999.00, ... | Automatic X data entry is available. Harvard Graphics automatically scales very small and very large numbers (such as the last two entries) for display on the X axis. |

**Table 6-1.**   X Data Types and Examples of Valid Entries (*continued*)

type" to Name. Examples of name data are departments within a company (Marketing, Accounting), political affiliation (Republican, Democrat, Libertarian), sex (Male, Female), and state (Alabama, Alaska, Arizona).

If your X data are calendar based, Harvard Graphics provides you with eight alternative settings: Day, Week, Month, Quarter, Year, Month/Day, Month/Yr, and Qtr/Yr. Set "X data type" to the alternative that best fits your X data. If your X data do not fit one of these categories, you will need to set "X data type" to Name.

When your X data reflect times of day, set "X data type" to Time. And finally, if your X data are numbers, set "X data type" to Number.

Once you have selected the X data type you have two choices. The first is to continue to the Chart Data form and enter your data. If you have set "X data type" to Name, this is your only choice. To continue, press F10-Continue. Harvard Graphics will then display the Chart Data form so you can enter your data. If your "X data type" is any type other than Name, you may be able to take advantage of Harvard Graphics' ability to automatically enter your X data in the Chart Data form.

## Automatic X Data Entry

If your X data are predictable, in other words, if they make up a series such as 1, 2, 3 or January, February, March, then you can instruct Harvard Graphics to enter your data in the "X Axis" column of the Chart Data form. This is done by using the "Starting with," "Ending with," and "Increment" options on the X Data Type Menu overlay. To use this automatic data entry capability, press TAB to move to the "Starting with" option and enter the first value in the series. This value must be valid for the X data type that you specified. For example, you cannot enter .5 when your "X data type" is Month. Next, press TAB to move to the "Ending with" option and enter the last value in the series.

If you now press F10-Continue, Harvard Graphics will assume you want to create a series beginning with the "Starting with" value, and ending with the "Ending with" value. If you do not enter a value at "Increment" Harvard Graphics will default to an increment of 1. This means that the second X value in the series will be one *unit* greater than the first value. A unit is defined as one of whatever the X data type is. For example, if you have defined "X data type" as Day and the "Starting with" value is Monday, the second X value in the series will be Tuesday, since Tuesday is one day more than Monday.

If you want your series to progress in steps other than one unit, you must use the "Increment" option to specify the steps you want. If the X data are defined as one of the calendar types, the "Increment" value must be a whole number. This number will represent the number of units between X data values. For example, if your "Starting with" value is January and your "Increment" is 2, the second X data value in the series will be March, since March is two months later than January.

If your "X data type" is Time, leaving "Increment" blank will cause Harvard Graphics to default to one-hour increments. If you do specify an increment, however, enter the number of *minutes* that should be incremented. For example, if your "Starting with" time is 1:00 and your "Ending with" time is 8:30, set "Increment" to 90 to create the series 1:00, 2:30, 4:00, 5:30, 7:00, 8:30.

When your data are numbers, "Increment" can be any positive, real number. For instance, if you set "Starting with" to 1, "Ending with" to 3, and "Increment" to .5, your series will be: 1, 1.5, 2, 2.5, 3.

After you have defined "Starting with," "Ending with," and "Increment" values, press F10-Continue to continue to the Chart Data form. If the values you entered are valid, Harvard Graphics will enter the requested series in your "X Axis" column on the Chart Data form. If any one of these values is not valid for your defined X data type, Harvard Graphics will display the message, "Invalid X Data type." You must correct the X Data Type Menu overlay options before you can continue.

## Changing the X Data Type

There are several reasons why you may need to change the X data type after you define it. You may decide that the data type you initially chose was not adequate or appropriate for your charting needs. Or you might have used Harvard Graphics' automatic X data entry capabilities, but did not get the X data results that you desired. This could happen if you entered the wrong "Starting with," "Ending with," or "Increment" value.

Fortunately, you can change the X data type at any time. To do so, you must start at the Chart Data form. Press F3-Set X type to display the X Data Type Menu overlay. Harvard Graphics will display the overlay with the current setting displayed at "X data type." The "Starting with," "Ending with," and "Increment" options will be blank (even if you have previously defined them). Press the SPACEBAR until the desired X data type is highlighted and shown at "X data type." If "X data type" is not set to Name, you can now enter values into the "Starting with," "Ending with," or "Increment" options to use Harvard Graphics' automatic data entry feature.

When you have finished redefining your X data, press F10-Continue to continue to the Chart Data form. Harvard Graphics will use the information you entered on the X Data Type Menu overlay to redefine your X data type and/or enter data in the "X Axis" column. If you want to cancel setting your X data type, press ESC rather than F10-Continue. You will return to the Chart Data form and your X data will not have been changed.

### Changing the X Data Type After Entering Series Values

You can change the "X data type" option even after you have entered data into the "Series" columns on the Chart Data form. Changing the X data type will not affect the series data you have already entered. Since your series data will remain unchanged, including its order, you must ensure that the new X data values you enter will appropriately match the series data that appear at the corresponding lines on the Chart Data form. (See the section "Entering Series Data," for a more detailed discussion of the association between X data and series data.)

Consequently, caution should be exercised when making this change. If you follow the next two rules you can change the X data type without having to reenter series data.

- Your new X data should have the same number of values as the previous X data. This holds true whether you use Harvard Graphics' automatic X data entry feature or enter the X data yourself.

- The order of your new X data should be the same as the old order. That is, new X data values should correspond to the appropriate series values.

## Entering XY Chart Data

Harvard Graphics displays the Chart Data form after you have filled out the X Data Type Menu overlay. The Chart Data form for bar/line charts is shown in Figure 6-6. The Area and High/Low/Close Chart Data forms are almost identical to this form except for the name on the title banner. The High/Low/Close Chart Data form, shown in Figure 6-7, has one additional difference: Harvard Graphics automatically names the "Series 1" through "Series 4" columns "High," "Low," "Close," and "Open."

## XY Charts: Bar/Line, Area, and High/Low/Close

```
                    Bar/Line Chart Data
   Title:
Subtitle:
Footnote:

          X Axis      Series 1    Series 2    Series 3    Series 4
   Pt     Name
    1
    2
    3
    4
    5
    6
    7
    8
    9
   10
   11
   12

F1-Help        F3-Set X type                          F9-More series
F2-Draw chart  F4-Calculate            F8-Options     F10-Continue
```

**Figure 6-6.** Bar/Line Chart Data form

```
                   High/Low/Close Chart Data
   Title:
Subtitle:
Footnote:

          X Axis       High        Low        Close       Open
   Pt     Name
    1
    2
    3
    4
    5
    6
    7
    8
    9
   10
   11
   12

F1-Help        F3-Set X type                          F9-More series
F2-Draw chart  F4-Calculate            F8-Options     F10-Continue
```

**Figure 6-7.** High/Low/Close Chart Data form

The top three lines on each of the Chart Data forms can be used to enter a title, a subtitle, and a footnote for your chart. However, it is best to ignore these three lines. You will have greater flexibility if you enter your title, subtitle, and footnote using the Titles & Options form instead. See "Entering a Chart Title, Subtitle, and Footnote" later in this chapter. If you do choose to enter your title, subtitle, and footnote on the Chart Data form, enter the text in the three lines provided.

## Entering X Axis Data

The lower half of the Chart Data form is used to enter the X and series data for your chart. (If you used Harvard Graphics' automatic X data entry feature, the column labeled "X Axis" will contain those data.) Use the keys listed in Table 6-2 to control cursor movement and simplify text entry on the Chart Data form. Use F2-Draw chart frequently to see the layout of the chart you are creating. Then press any key to return to the Chart Data form.

There are six columns for X axis data. From left to right these are labeled "Pt," "X Axis," "Series 1," "Series 2," "Series 3," and "Series 4." The values in the "Pt" column are row numbers. These numbers are used for reference only and cannot be changed. The "X Axis" column is used to enter your X data, and the four series columns are used to enter your series data. (Some people refer to series data as "Y" data.)

Press TAB to move your cursor to the lower part of the Chart Data form. If your X data are not already entered, move to the "X Axis" column. With your cursor on the first line, enter the first value for your X axis. This first X value will appear at the far left of the X axis on your chart for all X data types except Number. (Numeric X data are automatically ordered and need not be entered in any particular order.) After entering your first X data value, press ENTER. Harvard Graphics will move the cursor to the beginning of the second line of the "X Axis" column. Enter the second X data value (the value that will be displayed at the second position on the X axis) and press ENTER. Continue until you have entered all of your X data.

| Key | Function |
| --- | --- |
| BACKSPACE | Moves cursor back one space, deleting any character in the space. |
| CTRL-DEL | Deletes entire contents of line at the cursor. On Chart Data forms, deletes X data value along with all corresponding series values for the line at the cursor. |
| CTRL-DOWN | On Chart Data forms, moves X data value along with all corresponding series values down one position. |
| CTRL-INS | On Chart Data forms, inserts a blank line for an X data value and corresponding series values above the line the cursor is on. |
| CTRL-LEFT | Moves cursor to the previous word in the line. |
| CTRL-RIGHT | Moves cursor to next word in the line. |
| CTRL-UP | On Chart Data forms, moves X data value along with all corresponding series values up one position. |
| DEL | Deletes character at the cursor. |
| DOWN (arrow) | Moves cursor down one line, option, or menu item. |

**Table 6-2.** Cursor Control Keys and Functions for XY Charts

| Key | Function |
|---|---|
| END | Moves cursor to the last option or line on a form. |
| ENTER | Selects highlighted settings for form options and moves cursor to the next option on the form. On Chart Data forms, moves cursor to the next line in the "X Axis" and series columns. |
| ESC | 1. Returns to the previous screen. Press ESC multiple times to "back up" through previous menus and forms to the Main Menu.<br>2. Cancels changes and returns to the previous screen. |
| HOME | Moves cursor to the first option or line on a form. |
| INS | Toggles insert mode on and off; the cursor appears as a block when it is on, and as a small line when it is off. |
| LEFT (arrow) | Moves cursor to the left one character or option setting. |
| PGDN | Displays the next 12 rows of data on the Chart Data form. Displays the next page of the Titles & Options form. |
| PGUP | Displays the previous 12 rows of data on the Chart Data form. Displays the previous page of the Titles & Options form. |

**Table 6-2.** Cursor Control Keys and Functions for XY Charts (*continued*)

| Key | Function |
|---|---|
| RIGHT (arrow) | Moves cursor to the right one character or option setting. |
| SHIFT-TAB | Moves cursor to the previous column or option on a form. |
| TAB | Moves cursor to the next column or option on a form. |
| UP (arrow) | Moves cursor up one line, option, or menu item. |

**Table 6-2.** Cursor Control Keys and Functions for XY Charts (*continued*)

*Note:* For information on using international text characters in your chart, refer to Appendix D, "Harvard Graphics Tables."

### Entering More than 12 Rows of Data

The Chart Data form displays 12 rows for your data by default. You may, however, enter up to 60 rows of data when your X data type is Name, and 240 rows of data when your X data type is any other type (the maximum for an area chart is 100). When you reach the bottom row, which is labeled "12" in the "Pt" column, press either DOWN (to display the next row) or PGDN (to display the next 12 rows). You can continue to display additional rows by pressing DOWN or PGDN, up to the maximum number of rows. After adding additional rows of data, pressing UP or PGUP will move you back to the earlier rows.

### Splitting X Axis Values onto Two Lines

If your X data are of the type Name, you can have Harvard Graphics split long X axis values onto two lines. This is particularly useful when your X axis data consist of people's names. To split X data, type the text splitting character (¦) in the X data entry where you want Harvard Graphics to split the text. When you split X axis data, Harvard Graphics centers the second line of text below the first. Do not follow the ¦ with a space, or the space will appear on the second line, causing it to appear off center.

## Entering Series Data

After you enter your X data, you are ready to enter data in the series columns. The values that you enter in these columns are your measures, which may represent weights, dollars, quantities, percentages, and so on. These values will be used to determine the height of bars, placement of lines, width of areas, or the location of points on your chart.

All series data must be numbers. Indicate negative numbers by placing a minus sign before the number. Fractions are indicated either with a decimal point or with a slash between the numerator and denominator, as in 1/4. You cannot use commas (or periods, in international notation) as separators in whole numbers. For example, **1000** would be a valid entry but **1,000** would not. Table 6-3 contains examples of valid series data entries.

Press TAB to move to the column labeled "Series 1." If you are not at the top line (the line associated with "Pt 1") press UP until you are. Enter the series value that corresponds to the first X data value. Press ENTER to move to the second line and enter the value associated with the second X data value, and so on, until you have entered all the data for "Series 1." If you have a second series, press TAB to move to the "Series 2" column, and then press UP until you are at the first row in the column. Enter your data for "Series 2" just as you did for "Series 1," pressing ENTER to move to the next line in the column. If you have additional series, continue in the same manner and enter data in the "Series 3" and "Series 4" columns.

| To Indicate | Use | Valid Series Data |
|---|---|---|
| Negative number | - | -34 |
| Positive number | Just the number or a + | 873 +873 |
| Fraction | . (decimal point) or / | .75 3/4 |
| Scientific notation | E | 4.5E4 (45000) 6E-5 (.00006) |

**Table 6-3.** Valid Series Data and Indicators

### Entering Data for Series 5 Through 8

Although many charts have only one or two series, it is possible to enter up to eight series for your XY chart. By default, the Chart Data form displays only four columns for series data. You can display an additional four columns by pressing F9-More series. When you do so, the columns labeled "Series 5" through "Series 8" appear in place of "Series 1" through "Series 4." For each X data value, enter the data for each of the remaining series, as needed. Press F9-More series again to return to the display of "Series 1" through "Series 4."

## Changing the Order of X Axis Data

When your X data are any type other than Number, the order of X data in the "X Axis" column determines the left-to-right order that Harvard Graphics uses to display the X data on your chart. When your X data are of the type Number, the tick marks and legend labels on the X axis will be displayed in ascending order, regardless of the corresponding Pt (row) numbers for the X data.

If you wish to change the order of your X axis data, you have two options. The first is to move each row of X data separately. To do this, move your cursor to the row you want to move and press CTRL-UP to move the row up one position and CTRL-DOWN to move the row down one position. When you move a row up or down, Harvard Graphics will move both the X data value and its accompanying series data. This method only moves one row at a time.

The second method is to have Harvard Graphics sort the data in the "X Axis" column. Use this method if your X data are not sorted and you would like them to be displayed in a sorted order. Harvard Graphics cannot sort X data if your data type is Name, however, since it cannot predict the order of the data. If your data are of the type Name, you must move the data manually, as described previously.

To have Harvard Graphics sort the X axis data, follow these steps:

1. Move your cursor to the "X Axis" column.

2. Press F4-Calculate to display the Calculate overlay, shown in Figure 6-8.

3. Press TAB to move to the "Calculation" option.

4. Type **@REDUC** at "Calculation."

5. Press F10-Continue.

The data are then sorted and appear in the "X Axis" column in ascending order (smallest to largest values). For additional information on calculations, see the upcoming section, "Using Calculations."

*Note:* Do not use the @REDUC sorting method if two or more entries in the "X Axis" column have the same values and your data type is other than Number. If you do, Harvard Graphics will combine the duplicate X axis data, summing the values in the corresponding series. When your X data type is Number, however, @REDUC does not combine duplicate X axis data.

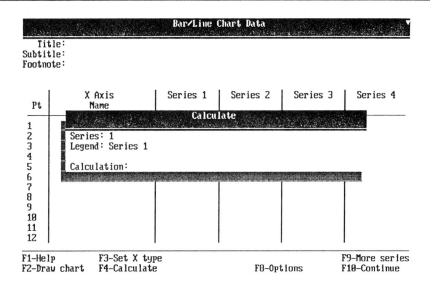

**Figure 6-8.**   Calculate overlay

## Deleting an X Data Value

Harvard Graphics provides you with a simple means of deleting an X data value and all of its corresponding series data. First move to the X axis value you want to delete. Next press CTRL-DEL. Harvard Graphics will delete the X data value, along with data you have entered on the corresponding lines of the series column. If any X data values appear below the deleted value, these values and their corresponding series values will move up one line on the Chart Data form.

## Adding an X Data Value

You can add additional X data values at any time. To do so, move your cursor to the row on the Chart Data form where you want to add the value. Then press CTRL-INS. Harvard Graphics will add a new row at the location of your cursor. The X data value and corresponding series data that were at your cursor will be moved down one row to make room for the inserted row. Enter your new X data value and any desired series data in the new row.

## Using Calculations

After entering your series data, you may want to use one or more calculations. While they are entirely optional, calculations can provide you with a flexible way of modifying or adjusting your data. If you are just learning how to create XY charts, you may want to skip to the section called "Specifying XY Chart Text," and return to this section after you have gained more experience with Harvard Graphics.

In general there are two types of calculations: ones that use *formulas* and ones that use *keywords*. Formulas are mathematical equations that use the arithmetic operators +, −, *, and / to combine series values and/or constants. The results of these calculations are placed in the current series (the series where your cursor is located). Keywords are special Harvard Graphics words that begin with the @ symbol. Keywords tell Harvard Graphics to perform a calculation or operation on one or more series.

To define a calculation, move the cursor to the series column for which you want to perform the calculation. (Note that some calculations, such as @RECALC and @REDUC, are independent of the series where the calculation is performed, and consequently the cursor position does not matter.) Press F4-Calculate to display the Calculate overlay, shown in Figure 6-8. This overlay has two options: "Legend" and "Calculation." The top line of this overlay, which displays "Series:" followed by the name of the current series, is not an option—it merely indicates the name of the current series. The various uses of the Calculate overlay are described in the following three sections.

Once you enter a calculation into the Calculate overlay, press F10-Continue to have the requested calculation performed. To cancel a calculation while the Calculate overlay is displayed, press ESC. If the calculation results in values being calculated for the current series, a diamond appears next to the series name, indicating that a calculation has been performed on this series, as shown in Figure 6-9. However,

# XY Charts: Bar/Line, Area, and High/Low/Close 149

```
                        Bar/Line Chart Data
     Title: 1987 U.S. Population
  Subtitle: By Region
  Footnote: Source:  U.S. Department of Commerce

              X Axis        Millions   ◆Percentage   Series 3    Series 4
      Pt      Name

      1     Northeast        50.3        0.207
      2     Midwest          59.5        0.244
      3     South            83.9        0.345
      4     West             49.7        0.204
      5
      6
      7
      8
      9
     10
     11
     12

  F1-Help          F3-Set X type                              F9-More series
  F2-Draw chart    F4-Calculate                  F8-Options   F10-Continue
```

**Figure 6-9.**   Diamond next to series name signifies a calculated series

when a calculation performs a one-time function, such as clearing a series (@CLR), no diamond appears. When a calculation depends on the data in another series, which most calculations do, Harvard Graphics automatically updates the calculations if you change the data.

*Note:* Calculations are updated when you issue the @RECALC calculation, or you leave and then return to the Chart Data form.

Figures 6-10 and 6-11 display the effects of seven different calculations on a single series of data in the "Series 1" column. The calculations used to produce the displayed data are shown as series legends for reference purposes only. (You can provide any other appropriate series legend.)

## Defining Series Legends Using Calculate

Even if you do not need to use a calculation, you can use the Calculate overlay to give your series names other than "Series 1," "Series 2," and

```
                    Bar/Line Chart Data
    Title: Fictitious Company
    Subtitle: Total Vacation Days, By Month
    Footnote:

         X Axis        Series 1   + @PCT(#1)  + @DUP(#1)  +@SUM(#1,#3
    Pt   Month

     1   January          45        0.092         45          90
     2   February         43        0.088         43          86
     3   March            51        0.104         51         102
     4   April            55        0.112         55         110
     5   May              42        0.086         42          84
     6   June             41        0.084         41          82
     7   July             32        0.065         32          64
     8   August           36        0.074         36          72
     9   September        29        0.059         29          58
    10   October          34        0.07          34          68
    11   November         38        0.078         38          76
    12   December         43        0.088         43          86

    F1-Help         F3-Set X type                         F9-More series
    F2-Draw chart   F4-Calculate              F8-Options  F10-Continue
```

**Figure 6-10.**   @PCT, @DUP, and @SUM calculations were performed on Series 2 through 4, respectively, and were all based on Series 1. (The actual calculations appear as the series legends at the top of each column for reference.)

so forth. To do this, move to the series you want to name and press F4-Calculate to display the Calculate overlay. The cursor will be at the "Legend" option. Press CTRL-DEL to erase the existing series legend and enter a new name for your series.

*Note:* Instead of using the Calculate overlay to rename your series, you can change the names of all the series at once on either Page 1 or Page 4 of the Titles & Options form. For more information, see the section, "Changing the Series Legend," later in this chapter.

If you are using a calculation to create new data in the current series (as described in the following sections), you may enter the name of the new series at the "Legend" option, as described earlier. Alternatively, you can leave the existing series name and change all the names at once on the Titles & Options form.

```
                    Bar/Line Chart Data
  Title: Fictitious Company
Subtitle: Total Vacation Days, By Month
Footnote:

          X Axis        •@RLIN(#1)  • #1 + 20  •@MAVG(#1,1   • #1-#1+3
  Pt      Month                                       ,3)

   1    January         47.346        65         48.5          3
   2    February        46.147        63         47.2          3
   3    March           44.948        71         46.4          3
   4    April           43.748        75         44.2          3
   5    May             42.549        62         41.2          3
   6    June            41.35         61         36            3
   7    July            40.15         52         34.4          3
   8    August          38.951        56         33.8          3
   9    September       37.752        49         36            3
  10    October         36.552        54         36            3
  11    November        35.353        58         38.333        3
  12    December        34.154        63         40.5          3

F1-Help         F3-Set X type                            F9-More series
F2-Draw chart   F4-Calculate            F8-Options       F10-Continue
```

**Figure 6-11.** @RLIN, #1+20, @MAVG, and #1−#1+3 calculations were performed on Series 5 through 8, respectively, and were all based on Series 1. (The actual calculations appear as the series legends at the top of each column for reference.)

## Formula Calculations

Formula calculations permit you to use mathematics to combine values from two or more series and place the results of these calculations in the current series. The arithmetic operators you can use are: +, −, *, and /, which correspond to addition, subtraction, multiplication, and division. You refer to other series in a calculation by preceding the series number with the # sign. For example, to perform a calculation making Series 3 equal to Series 1 plus Series 2, you would place your cursor in "Series 3," press F4-Calculate, and then type #1 + #2 at "Calculation." This specifies that each of the Series 1 values should be added to the corresponding values in Series 2, and placed into the current series, Series 3.

Formula calculations can also use constants. Constants are numbers that do not change (unlike the values in a series, which may be different for each row in the Chart Data form). For example, if you want the values in Series 3 to be twice the value of data in Series 1, you could use this calculation:

2 * #1

This causes each of the values in Series 1 to be multiplied by 2, with the result of this calculation being placed in the current series, Series 3.

Formula calculations are restricted to rather simple formulas. They are always processed in left-to-right order, and you cannot use parentheses to indicate the priority of arithmetic operations. For instance, if you entered #1+3/2 for Series 3, each data entry for Series 3 would be equal to (#1+3)/2 instead of #1+(3/2), as you might expect. Thus, if you have calculations that are complex, and you need to be able to isolate certain operations, you will need to perform the calculation in separate steps. Place the results of each step in a separate series, and then perform an additional calculation in order to combine the different series containing the intermediate steps.

## Keyword Calculations

Keyword calculations use special Harvard Graphics words to perform calculations or operations on your data. Each keyword is preceded by the @ character. See Table 6-4 for a list of all of the keywords and their results.

Keyword calculations can be divided into three categories. The first category consists of calculations that work much like formulas, in that they place values in the current series that are based solely on values in the same row of one or more other series. These calculations are @AVERAGE, @DUP, @MIN, @MAX, and @SUM.

The next category of calculations are those based on values from different rows of the same series. One example of this type of calculation is the @PCT calculation. This calculation computes the percentage of the whole that each value in a series represents. Therefore, it must take into account the sum of all values in the series in order to perform the calculation. For example, if your data values in Series 2 are 1, 1, and 2, the calculation @PCT(#2) would result in the following data being placed in the current series: .25, .25, and .5. (See "Using Arguments in Calculations" for more detail about keyword syntax.) Other calculations that utilize all of the values within a series are @CUM, @DIFF, @MAVG, @REXP, @RLIN, @RLOG, and @RPWR.

## Calculations Based on the Current Row of the Specified Series

| Keyword | Description |
|---|---|
| @AVG(#n, ..., #n) | Average of series values. |
| @MAX(#n, ..., #n) | Maximum value of all series specified. |
| @MIN(#n, ..., #n) | Minimum value of all series specified. |
| @SUM(#n, ..., #n) | Sum across series. |

## Calculations Based on Multiple Rows or All Rows of the Specified Series

| Keyword | Description |
|---|---|
| @CLR | Clears (removes) values in current series*. |
| @COPY(#n) | Copies values from specified series to current series*. |
| @CUM(#n) | Cumulative total of series. |
| @DIFF(#n) | Difference of each value in a series from the value preceding it. |
| @DUP(#n) | Duplicates specified series to current series. Differs from @COPY in that values are maintained (updated). |
| @EXCH(#n) | Exchanges values of specified series with current series*. |
| @MAVG(#n)<br>@MAVG(#n,i,j) | Moving average in the series specified; or from $i$ values prior to, and $j$ values following, the current value in the specified series. |

**Table 6-4.**   Calculation Keywords

| Keyword | Description |
| --- | --- |
| @MOVE(#*n*) | Moves values from the specified series to the current series. Values in the specified series are cleared. |
| @PCT(#*n*) | Percent contribution of each value to the total of values in the specified series. |
| @RECALC | Updates calculations*. |
| @REDUC | Sorts X values, eliminating duplicates. Series values for duplicate X data are summed*. |
| @REXP(#*n*) | Exponential regression curve for the specified series. |
| @RLIN(#*n*) | Linear regression curve for the specified series. |
| @RLOG(#*n*) | Logarithmic regression curve for the specified series. |
| @RPWR(#*n*) | Power regression for the specified series. |

*Note:* #*n* indicates the series number on which the calculation is performed.

* indicates the calculation is performed one time only and is not maintained.

**Table 6-4.** Calculation Keywords (*continued*)

The final class of calculations contains those that perform a one-time function. @RECALC, for example, forces Harvard Graphics to immediately recalculate all the calculations defined for the current chart. The remaining one-time calculations are @CLR, @COPY, @EXCH, @MOVE, and @REDUC. When you perform any of these calculations on a series, a diamond is not displayed next to the "Series" title. The diamonds indicate a calculation is defined for the series, so that the values may change if values in other series are changed.

### Using @REDUC for Data Reduction

The @REDUC calculation was referred to earlier in this chapter as a means of sorting data in the "X Axis" column when the X axis type is not Name. If the X data type is not Number, @REDUC also provides another valuable aid. When two or more X axis values are identical, @REDUC combines them. This data reduction is available even when the X data type is Name (even though @REDUC does not sort Name X data). When X axis values are combined, the series values for duplicate X axis values are added together. The @REDUC calculation is particularly valuable when you are importing data and need to combine duplicate X data values before producing your chart. For more information, see Chapter 12, "Importing and Exporting."

You may use @REDUC from any of the series columns or the "X Axis" column. Press F4-Calculate to display the Calculate overlay. Press TAB to move to the "Calculation" option and enter @REDUC. When you press F10-Continue, Harvard Graphics will perform the data reduction and sorting.

## Using Arguments in Calculations

Most calculations make reference to one or more series. For instance, the @COPY keyword requires you to specify the number of a series that will be copied to the current series. For example, to copy the values in Series 1 to Series 3, move your cursor to the "Series 3" column and press F4-Calculate to display the Calculate overlay. Enter **@COPY(#1)** at "Calculation." The #1 in the @COPY command is called the *argument*. In calculations, an argument is usually a series number. Harvard Graphics uses this argument to carry out your calculation. In the @COPY command, the argument is the name of the series that you want to copy.

Most calculations can use an argument. Some calculations can accommodate one or more arguments. There are five calculations that permit you to specify more than one argument. Four of these are the statistical calculations: @AVERAGE, @MAX, @MIN, and @SUM. For example, if you want Series 5 to contain the average of the values in Series 1 through Series 4, you could apply this calculation to Series 5:

@AVERAGE(#1,#2,#3,#4)

When a calculation has more than one argument they are separated by commas.

The fifth calculation that can accept more than one argument is the only one that can accept arguments other than series numbers. This calculation is @MAVG (moving average) and it can accept three arguments. The first argument defines the series the moving average is calculated on, the second and third arguments indicate how many values before and after, respectively, the moving average should be based on. @MAVG can also be used with a single argument, identifying a series to base the moving average calculation on. In this situation the moving average is calculated based on one point before and one point after the current point.

### Dropping Series Arguments from Keyword Calculations

Any of the keywords that require one or more series as arguments can be used without identifying the arguments. When the keyword calculation requires a single argument, dropping the argument causes Harvard Graphics to assume the argument is the immediately preceding series. For example, if the keyword calculation @PCT were used for Series 2, the effect would be the same as if the calculation @PCT(#1) were used. If the keyword calculation can accept two or more series as arguments, dropping the argument causes Harvard Graphics to assume all of the preceding series as arguments. For instance, using the calculation @SUM in "Series 4" has the same effect as using @SUM(#1,#2,#3).

## Using Calculations that Refer to Calculated Series

When Harvard Graphics recalculates a calculated series for a chart, the recalculation starts at Series 1 and progresses through Series 8. If a calculation uses values in another series, and the values in the other series are the result of a calculation, then the referenced series must be a series earlier than the one referencing it. For example, if Series 2 is the result of the calculation #1 + 100, and Series 3 is the result of the calculation @PCT(#2), then Series 3 will contain the correct values when a recalculation is performed. This is because Series 2 is recalculated before Series 3.

Consider what would happen if the calculations for these series were reversed. When Harvard Graphics recalculates the series, the values in Series 2 will contain the results of calculations performed on Series 3 before the Series 3 recalculation is performed. If any data values in Series 1 were modified, the recalculated Series 2 data might not be correct.

## Specifying XY Chart Text

The Titles & Options forms are used to specify options that affect your chart's appearance. At any time you may switch from the Chart Data form to the Titles & Options form by pressing F8-Options. It is usually a good idea, however, to enter some data in the Chart Data form before you start to customize your chart options. With data entered, you can press F2-Draw chart to see the effects chart options settings are having on your chart.

The first time you display the Titles & Options form, you will you see Page 1 of a four-page form. Page 1 of the Titles & Options form for a bar/line chart is shown in Figure 6-12. You can move between the various pages of this form by pressing PGDN to move to the following page, and PGUP to move to the preceding page. While modifying your chart's titles and options, you can return to the Chart Data form at any time simply by pressing F8-Data. If you press F8-Options again, you will return to the page of the Titles & Options form you were last working on. Also, if you press F2-Draw chart from the Titles & Options form, you will return to the same page on this form once you press any key to remove the chart display from the screen.

The Titles & Options forms for bar/line, area, and high/low/close charts are nearly identical. In fact, there are only six options on all four

```
                Bar/Line Chart  Titles & Options  Page 1 of 4
                        Title:
                        Subtitle:

                        Footnote:

                        X  axis title:
                        Y1 axis title:
                        Y2 axis title:
            Legend                           Type              Display   Y Axis
            Title:                 Bar  Line Trend  Curve  Pt  Yes  No   Y1  Y2

              1 | Series 1                   Bar                Yes      Y1
              2 | Series 2                   Bar                Yes      Y1
              3 | Series 3                   Bar                Yes      Y1
              4 | Series 4                   Bar                Yes      Y1
              5 | Series 5                   Bar                Yes      Y1
              6 | Series 6                   Bar                Yes      Y1
              7 | Series 7                   Bar                Yes      Y1
              8 | Series 8                   Bar                Yes      Y1

        F1-Help                  F5-Attributes    F7-Size/Place
        F2-Draw chart                             F8-Data          F10-Continue
```

**Figure 6-12.**  Page 1 of the Bar/Line Chart Titles & Options form

pages of these forms that are different. Consequently, most of the options discussed in the following pages can be applied to all XY charts. For those few options where differences exist for the different chart types, they will be clearly indicated.

## Entering a Chart Title, Subtitle, and Footnote

The first six lines on the Titles & Options form permit you to enter a one-line title, a two-line subtitle, and a three-line footnote. Each of these lines can contain up to 40 characters. The title and subtitle appear at the top of your chart, and the footnote will appear at the bottom. If you entered a title, subtitle, and/or footnote on the Chart Data form, this text will appear in the first lines of each of these options. You can edit or add to this text on the Titles & Options form.

## Specifying X and Y Axis Titles

The next three options on the Titles & Options form are "X axis title," "Y1 axis title," and "Y2 axis title." (See "Selecting the Series Axis" later in this chapter for descriptions of these axes.) Use these options to provide a brief description for each of your axes. When the measurements for your axes (indicated by your axis labels) are not obvious, it is good practice to supply short, descriptive axis titles. Specify titles only for axes that you are using. If your chart uses only one Y axis, do not enter a Y2 axis title.

### Splitting Axis Titles onto Two Lines

You can force Harvard Graphics to split the text of one or more of your axis titles onto two lines. This feature is useful when your titles are particularly long. To split an axis title, enter the text splitting character (¦) in the axis title where you want Harvard Graphics to split your text. Do not follow the text splitting character with a space or the second line of the axis title will be off center.

## Specifying a Legend Title

By default, Harvard Graphics will not provide your legend with a title. You can specify a legend title by entering the desired title at the "Legend Title" option.

## Changing the Series Legend

When you first create a bar/line or area chart, Harvard Graphics provides each of your series with the default legend names "Series 1," "Series 2," and so on. Similarly, high/low/close charts define the first four series as "High," "Low, "Close," and "Open." Although you could keep your series named in this manner, it is more appropriate to provide your series with names that clearly identify which groups, categories, or measures your series represent.

The series names appear in the first column on the lower half of Page 1 of the Titles & Options form, directly below the "Legend Title" option. Each of the rows in this column corresponds to the eight series from the Chart Data form. To change a series legend, move to the current name for the desired series and press CTRL-DEL to erase it, then type in a new name. You can enter a series legend of up to 20 characters in length.

You can also change your series legends on the Calculate overlay if you wish. (Press F4-Calculate at the Chart Data form to display the Calculate overlay.) See the earlier section, "Defining Series Legends Using Calculate."

## Modifying XY Chart Text Attributes

From Page 1 (or Page 4) of the Titles & Options form, press F5-Attributes to display the Text Attributes overlay, on which you can modify attributes of text entered for "Title," "Subtitle," "Footnote," "X axis title," "Y1 axis title," "Y2 axis title," "Legend Title," and the series legends. The attributes that you define for the "X axis title" option are also used for X axis labels and the data table entries, if they are displayed. (See the section "Using a Data Table" for additional detail). Text attributes defined for the Y axis titles are also used for the Y axis labels and the value labels, if they are displayed. (See the section "Displaying Data Values on an XY Chart" for information about value labels.)

The text attributes you can modify include font weight (bold), style (italics and fill), underlining, and color. (See Appendix D for examples of attribute combinations for each of the six fonts available.) Modifying one or more of these attributes requires two steps. The first involves selecting the text whose attributes you want to modify. The second involves setting the desired text attribute options on the Text Attributes overlay. These steps are detailed in the next two sections.

### Highlighting Text for an Attribute Change

Before you modify text attributes, it is important to place the cursor at the correct location on the Titles & Options form. If you want to modify only a portion of the text that appears on a given line, move the cursor to the left-most character of the text you want to modify. Then press F5-Attributes to highlight the character at your cursor and display the Text Attributes overlay (shown in Figure 6-13) at the bottom of the

# XY Charts: Bar/Line, Area, and High/Low/Close

```
         Bar/Line Chart  Titles & Options  Page 1 of 4
            Title:     1987 U.S. Population
            Subtitle:  By Region

            Footnote:  Source: U.S. Department of Commerce
                       Bureau of the Census

            X  axis title:
            Y1 axis title:
            Y2 axis title:
  Legend                           Type             Display    Y Axis
  Title:                  Bar  Line Trend Curve Pt  Yes  No    Y1  Y2

    1 | Millions                   Bar              Yes        Y1
    2 | Percentage                 Bar              Yes        Y2
    3 | Series 3                   Bar              Yes        Y1
    4 | Series 4                   Bar              Yes        Y1
    5 | Series 5                   Bar              Yes        Y1
    6 | Series 6                   Bar              Yes        Y1
    7 | Series 7                   Bar              Yes        Y1
    8 | Series 8                   Bar              Yes        Y1

 F1-Help                 F5-Attributes     F7-Size/Place
 F2-Draw chart ▶Fill  ▶Bold   Italic   Underline   Color 1   F10-Continue
```

**Figure 6-13.** Text Attributes overlay (with the first line of the subtitle highlighted)

screen. If you want to change the text attributes of one or more entire lines of text, move the cursor to the top line that you want to highlight. Then press SHIFT-F5 to automatically highlight the entire current line and display the Text Attributes overlay at the bottom of the screen.

Use the RIGHT and DOWN arrow keys to extend the highlighting. Press RIGHT to highlight text to the right of the cursor. (In this case, F5-Attributes also acts like RIGHT.) Press DOWN (or SHIFT-F5) to highlight additional lines of text. If you try to highlight the text to the left of the first character you highlighted, no highlighting will occur and the Text Attributes overlay will be removed from the screen.

### Setting Text Attributes for Highlighted Text

Once you have highlighted the desired text, press TAB to move between the various attribute options on the Text Attributes overlay. Press the SPACEBAR to set each attribute option for the highlighted text. (Examples of the attributes for the six different fonts can be found in Appendix D).

The "Fill," "Bold," "Italic," and "Underline" options have two possible settings: On and Off. Whenever one of these attributes is set to On, an arrow appears to the left of the attribute name.

There are two ways to change the "Color" attribute option. The first is to press the SPACEBAR until the desired color number is displayed at "Color." The second way is to press F6-Colors to display the Color Selection overlay, shown in Figure 6-14, and highlight a color in this list. Press ENTER or F10-Continue to return to the Text Attributes overlay.

When you are through setting text attribute options for the highlighted text, press F10-Continue to return to the Titles & Options form.

## Modifying Size and Placement of Chart Text

From Page 1 (or Page 4) of your XY chart's Titles & Options form, you can press F7-Size/Place to modify the size and placement of the titles and labels on your chart. Once you press F7-Size/Place, the Size/Place overlay is displayed over the upper-left corner of the Titles & Options

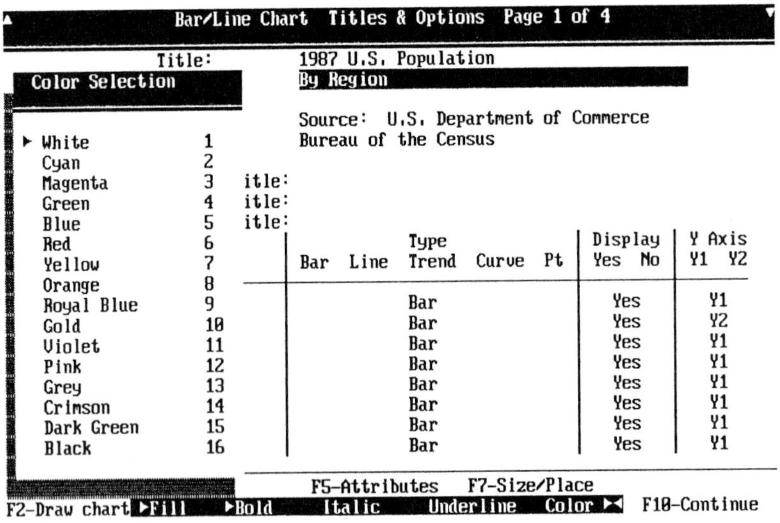

**Figure 6-14.**   Color Selection overlay

form. Set the desired options on this overlay (see Figure 6-15). Press F7-Size/Place or F10-Continue to return to the Titles & Options form.

### Setting the Text Size

Use the "Size" option on the Size/Place overlay to select the size of text to use on your chart. This option is set by entering a number from .1 through 99 in the "Size" column. See Appendix D for examples of different sizes. Each number in this column corresponds to the text on the corresponding line of the Titles & Options form. The Size/Place overlay also displays the options "X labels" and "Y labels" (for Harvard Graphics version 2.1 and later). The text size you set at "X labels" is used to define the size of the labels on the X axis, as well as the size of the legend title and the series legends. The text size that you set at "Y labels" defines the size of the labels on the Y axis, as well as any data values that you display on your chart.

Harvard Graphics provides the default text size values shown in Figure 6-15 for the title, subtitles, footnotes, and axis titles. No sizes are displayed at the "X labels" and "Y labels" options, although the default size of 3 is used for these labels. To use X and Y label sizes other than the default, enter a number in the "Size" column at these options.

*Note:* The size of your titles and labels will influence the size of your chart frame. For example, if you use a large text size for your title, Harvard Graphics will automatically reduce the size of your chart to make room for the title. In addition, if your text size is small, text attributes applied to chart text may not be displayed on your monitor, although they will appear when output.

### Modifying the Placement of Text

The "Place" column on the Size/Place overlay, shown in Figure 6-15, allows you to select the alignment of your title, subtitle, and footnote. Corresponding to each of these text lines are the settings L, C, and R, for left-justified, centered, and right-justified text, respectively. Left-justified text begins at the left margin. Centered text is displayed in the middle. Right-justified text has the right-most character even with the right margin.

```
Size   Place       Bar/Line Chart  Titles & Options   Page 1 of 4
 8     L ►C  R  Title:
 6     L ►C  R  Subtitle:
 6     L ►C  R
 2.5   ►L C  R  Footnote:
 2.5   ►L C  R
 2.5   ►L C  R
 4         ►C     X  axis title:
 3     ►→ ↓        Y1 axis title:
 3     ►→ ↓        Y2 axis title:
                                       Type                Display   Y Axis
            X labels                                       Yes  No   Y1  Y2
            Y labels              Bar  Line Trend Curve Pt

       1  Series 1                          Bar            Yes       Y1
       2  Series 2                          Bar            Yes       Y1
       3  Series 3                          Bar            Yes       Y1
       4  Series 4                          Bar            Yes       Y1
       5  Series 5                          Bar            Yes       Y1
       6  Series 6                          Bar            Yes       Y1
       7  Series 7                          Bar            Yes       Y1
       8  Series 8                          Bar            Yes       Y1

F1-Help                     F5-Attributes     F7-Size/Place
F2-Draw chart                                 F8-Data                F10-Continue
```

**Figure 6-15.**   Size/Place overlay showing default text sizes and placements

*Note:* The placement of the "X axis title" defaults to C and cannot be modified.

The "Place" column also lets you define the orientation of your Y axis titles. On the lines of the "Place" column corresponding to the Y1 and Y2 axis titles are two arrows: one pointing to the right and one pointing down. These arrows correspond to the two orientation alternatives, horizontal and vertical, shown in Figure 6-16. Select the right arrow to display the Y axis titles horizontally and the down arrow to display them vertically.

## Specifying XY Chart Characteristics

The remaining options on the XY Chart Titles & Options form determine the characteristics of your chart. These include the type of symbol

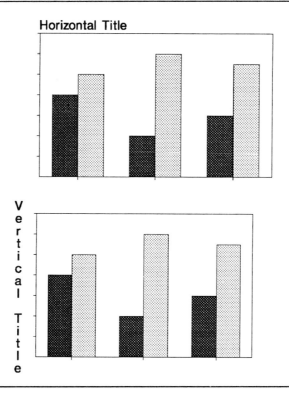

**Figure 6-16.**   Horizontal and vertical Y axis title placements

(bars, lines, markers), symbol enhancements (three-dimensional effects or shadows), placement of the chart legend, chart frame characteristics, and colors of chart elements.

## Selecting Series Symbol Types

The "Type" column on the Titles & Options form allows you to select the type of symbol to display for each of the series in your chart. To make this selection, move the cursor to the row in the "Type" column that corresponds to one of your series. The default setting that appears in this column corresponds to the type of XY chart you are creating. To change a series' type, press SPACEBAR until the desired setting is selected.

Each of the XY data charts offers a different selection of symbols. The following sections detail the "Type" option for bar/line, area, and high/low/close charts.

### Bar/Line Chart Symbols

Page 1 of the Bar/Line Chart Titles & Options form is shown in Figure 6-12. Harvard Graphics provides you with five different symbol types that you can produce on a Bar/Line chart. These are Bar, Line, Trend, Curve, and Pt.

**Bar**   Select Bar if you want to produce one bar for each X data value. If you set "Type" to Bar for more than one series, one bar for each of these series will be displayed at each X data value. The height of each bar will correspond to the series data value. If you have set your "X data type" to Number, selecting Bar will result in a needle chart (points connected to the X axis by a vertical line).

**Line**   When you set "Type" to Line, Harvard Graphics places a point at the coordinates for each X data value and series value, and connects these points with a line. If more than one series are set to Line, the different series are represented by different lines.

**Trend**   Trend is similar to Pt. All of the data values are plotted on the chart. Trend also includes a straight line that approximates the overall trend of the points. This line does not necessarily touch any of the points Harvard Graphics has plotted.

A trend line, also called a regression line or line of best fit, extends beyond the lowest and highest X data value on your chart. This extension, called *extrapolation*, stretches the entire chart frame. Note that this trend line differs from the line produced by Line, which will not extrapolate beyond the entered data.

**Curve**   Curve is nearly identical to Line, except that the line produced by Curve is not necessarily straight. If there is a "bend," or change, in your data, the line produced by Curve will roughly follow this bend. As with Line, Curve will not extrapolate beyond the highest and lowest X data values.

The Trend setting is closely related to the topics of regression and forecasting. For additional details, see "Regression Lines/Trend Lines," in Chapter 17, "Effective Data Charts."

**Pt (Point)**   When you set "Type" to Pt, Harvard Graphics places markers at the coordinates for each X data value and series value, and does not connect them.

## Area Chart Symbols

There are four possible chart type settings for an area chart: Area, Line, Trend, and Bar. The Line, Trend, and Bar settings behave in the same fashion as they do for bar/line charts. For descriptions of these symbol types, refer to the preceding section, "Bar/Line Chart Symbols."

**Area**   An area chart is very similar to a line chart, with the exception that the area below the line is shaded. An area, therefore, is a two-dimensional shape. For any point along the X axis, the height of the area indicates the corresponding series value.

## High/Low/Close Chart Symbols

The High/Low/Close chart style has four unique symbol types (High, Low, Close, and Open) that are automatically defined for Series 1 through Series 4 types. These types are specific to high/low/close charts and cannot be modified. The remaining five symbol types (Bar, Line, Trend, Curve, and Pt) can be selected for Series 5 through Series 8 data. These types are described in the earlier section, "Bar/Line Chart Symbols."

**High, Low, Close, Open**   The series type settings High, Low, Close, and Open, are designed specifically to depict data that vary. The names for these types come from their use in charts depicting stock market fluctuations. The High series is intended for the highest price of the stock, Low for the lowest price, Open for the stock price at the beginning of trading, and Close for the price at the close of trading.

When you use the High series in a High/Low/Close chart, you must also use the Low series, otherwise no symbols will be produced on your chart. The use of the Open and Close series is optional.

You can use a High/Low/Close chart to produce a band chart. In this case the "High/Low style" option is set to Area on Page 2 of the High/Low/Close Chart Titles & Options form, and data are entered for the High and Low series only. Data entered into the Open and Close series will not be displayed when "High/Low style" is set to Area. An example of a band chart is shown in Figure 6-4.

## Displaying Series Symbols

Although you can enter up to eight series of data on the Chart Data forms, it is not necessary to display all of this data on your chart. Set "Display" to Yes to display the series on the current chart (the default), and to No to exclude a series.

*Hint:* You can use this feature to create a number of different charts with the same X data values and option settings. Enter all of the series data and then selectively display the appropriate series for each chart.

## Selecting the Series Axis

Each series in a chart is displayed with respect to the Y axis. On the occasions when more than one type of measurement is depicted in a chart, more than one Y axis is needed. For instance, if your chart includes two series, one representing dollar figures (such as profit), and the other representing count (number of units sold), it is necessary to use two axes on your chart, one for dollars and one for counts. Such an example is shown in Figure 6-17.

Harvard Graphics allows you to define two different Y axes on a single chart: Y1 and Y2. If you have only one series in your chart, use the "Y Axis" column on the Titles & Options form to define which axis (usually Y1) the series will be charted against. If you have more than one series representing different measures, specify which axis each series will be charted against the "Y Axis" column.

## Customizing the Series Symbol Style

The charting options that have the greatest impact on the appearance of your chart are those that influence the symbol style for your series. The

## XY Charts: Bar/Line, Area, and High/Low/Close 169

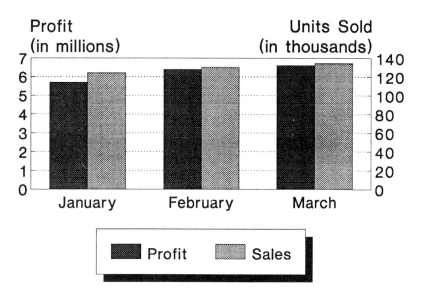

**Figure 6-17.** Dual Y axis chart

most important of these options permit you to fine-tune the type of chart you have selected. For instance, when your series type is set to Bar, you can use the "Bar Style" option to produce a clustered bar chart, a stacked bar chart, or an overlapped bar chart, to name a few alternatives. Other style options allow you to add a three-dimensional effect to your symbols and define the width of your bars or areas.

The symbol style options for each of the three XY charts differ. These options are the first six options located on Page 2 of the Bar/Line and the Area Chart Titles & Options forms, and the first five options on Page 2 of the High/Low/Close Chart Titles & Options form. The following sections on symbol style options are divided by chart type.

Although these symbol styles, in combination, provide you with a large variety of possible settings, be aware that some of these options take precedence over others. For example, in a bar/line chart, when

```
       Bar/Line Chart   Titles & Options   Page 2 of 4

   Bar style          ▶Cluster   Overlap   Stack    100%    Step    Paired
   Bar enhancement     3D        Shadow    Link    ▶None
   Bar fill style     ▶Color     Pattern   Both

   Bar width
   Bar overlap         50
   Bar depth           25

   Horizontal chart    Yes       ▶No
   Value labels        All        Select   ▶None

   Frame style        ▶Full       Half      Quarter  None
   Frame color         1
   Frame background    0

   Legend location     Top       ▶Bottom    Left     Right   None
   Legend justify      ← or ↑   ▶Center    ↓ or →
   Legend placement    In        ▶Out
   Legend frame        Single     Shadow   ▶None

F1-Help
F2-Draw chart                    F6-Colors     F8-Data       F10-Continue
```

**Figure 6-18.**  Page 2 of the Bar/Line Chart Titles & Options form

"Bar Style" is set to Overlap, setting "Bar enhancement" to Shadow will have no effect. In this case, the Overlap setting negates the effect of the Shadow setting.

### Bar/Line Chart Symbol Style Options

There are six options on Page 2 of the Bar/Line Chart Titles & Options form (shown in Figure 6-18) that affect the style of your bar/line symbols. These are "Bar style," "Bar enhancement," "Bar fill style," "Bar width," "Bar overlap," and "Bar depth." These options are discussed in the following sections.

**Bar Style**  You can choose from six styles of bars when your series "Type" option is Bar. These are Cluster, Overlap, Stack, 100%, Step, and Paired. The effects of these settings are shown in Figure 6-19.

XY Charts: Bar/Line, Area, and High/Low/Close    171

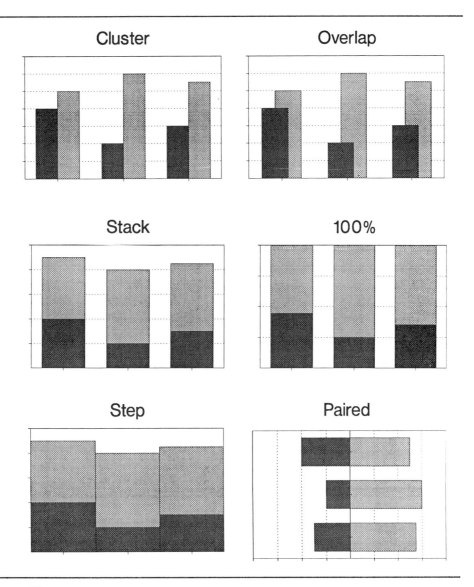

**Figure 6-19.** The six bar styles available on the Bar/Line Chart Titles & Options form

If you have a single series set "Bar style" to Cluster to create a simple bar chart. When you have more than one series, Harvard Graphics produces a true clustered bar chart in which one bar for each series is displayed at each X data value. Both of these bar chart styles are shown in Figure 6-20.

Select Overlap when you have more than one series and you want the bars at each X data value to overlap. The bar for the first series overlaps the bar for the second series, the bar for the second series overlaps the bar for the third series, and so on (see the bar style, "Overlap" in Figure 6-19).

Stack causes the bars for the different series to be stacked on top of one another. The first series appears at the bottom of the stack, the second series is placed above the first series, and so on (see "Stack" in Figure 6-19).

Selecting 100% results in bar charts similar to stacked bar charts—with one important exception. For 100% bar charts, each of the stacks containing the multiple series values are the same height, extending from the X axis to the top of the chart, regardless of the total of the series values for each stack (see "100%" in Figure 6-19). It may help to think of 100% charts as column pie charts, with the series values represented as percentages. The height of each bar segment in a stack is equal to the relative contribution of that segment to the total of the series values for each X data value.

Step bar charts are also similar to stacked bar charts. The difference is that no space appears between the different X axis stacks (see "Step" in Figure 6-19). These bar charts are called *stepped bar charts* because they often look like steps or stairs.

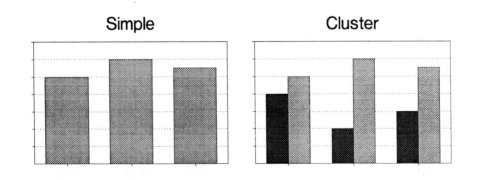

**Figure 6-20.**    Simple and clustered bar charts

## XY Charts: Bar/Line, Area, and High/Low/Close 173

The final "Bar style" setting, Paired, is particularly useful when you want to display the relative patterns of two or more series. A paired bar chart is a horizontal bar chart in which one or more series extend to the left, and one or more series extend to the right of a center line (see Paired" in Figure 6-19). The series that extend to the left are displayed with respect to the Y1 axis, whereas the series that extend to the right are displayed with respect to the Y2 axis.

*Note:* At least one series must be set to each of the Y axes in a paired bar chart.

Bar Enhancement Set to 3D

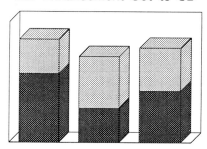

Bar Enhancement Set to Shadow

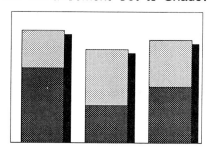

Bar Enhancement Set to Link

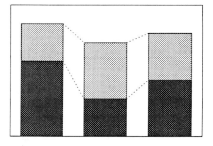

Bar Enhancement Set to None

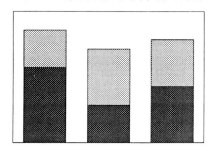

**Figure 6-21.** Examples of bar enhancements

**Bar Enhancement**    Using the "Bar enhancement" option you can add some nice effects to your bar and line charts. See Figure 6-21 for some examples. The most significant of these enhancements is the 3D setting. When you set "Bar enhancement" to 3D, a depth effect is added to your chart symbols. If you have set "Bar style" to Overlap, setting "Bar enhancement" to 3D will cause additional series to be displayed behind the first series in the third dimension. The 3D bar enhancement will also have a three-dimensional effect on Line symbols. However, when the 3D enhancement is used, both Trend and Curve lines are displayed simply as lines.

Setting "Bar enhancement" to Shadow will place a shadow behind bars. As noted previously, setting "Bar style" to Overlap overrides any shadow effects.

The "Bar enhancement" Link setting is used to join corresponding series values in stacked and 100% style bars. The "links" are dashed lines drawn between the bars at each X data value.

Set "Bar enhancement" to None when no bar enhancements are desired.

**Bar Fill Style**    The "Bar fill style" option gives you the choice of using only color, only patterns, or both color and patterns, to fill the bars and 3D lines on your chart. If you are going to print your chart to a black-and-white printer that does not support grey scaling, select either Both or Pattern. If you are producing your chart on a color output device, or plan to display the chart on a color monitor, select Color, Pattern, or Both, to suit your needs. See Chapter 8, "Producing Output," for more detail on the impact of color selections on printing.

**Bar Width**    The "Bar width" setting affects the percentage of the chart frame width your charts' bars or 3D lines use. When the "Bar width" option is blank, Harvard Graphics will default the "Bar width" to 60. If you set "Bar width" to 100, no space will appear between your bars. Alternatively, if you set "Bar width" to a small number, say 10, the bars will be quite narrow, and there will be large spaces between the bars or clusters. Figure 6-22 shows examples of different bar widths.

**Bar Overlap**    The "Bar overlap" option has two uses. First, when you are displaying an overlap bar chart with "Bar enhancement" set to

None, "Bar overlap" controls the amount of overlap of the bars. Set "Bar overlap" to any number between 1 (almost no overlap) and 100 (total overlap).

Second, when "Bar enhancement" is set to 3D, "Bar overlap" influences the amount of rotation of the chart frame. Enter a value between 1 (almost no rotation), and 100 (maximum permissible rotation). The influence of the number entered at "Bar overlap" depends on other option settings as well as the number of X data values you are displaying (the more data values, the more precisely the "Bar overlap" settings affect the rotation). You may have to experiment with this setting to

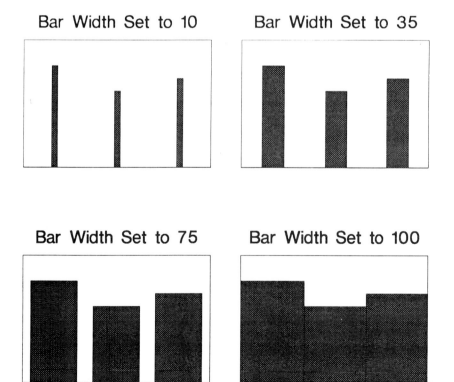

**Figure 6-22.** Examples of bar widths

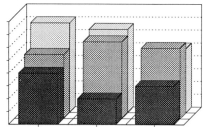
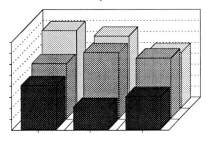
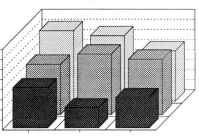

**Figure 6-23.**  Bar overlap settings with a 3D bar enhancement

achieve the desired effect. Figures 6-23 and 6-24 show examples of different "Bar overlap" settings with and without 3D effects.

**Bar Depth**  Use "Bar depth" to control the size of the 3D effect on bars and lines. The default value for "Bar depth" is 25. Decrease this value to reduce the 3D effect. Similarly, increase this value to create a larger effect. Although settings from 1 through 100 typically result in the desired effect, "Bar depth" settings are also influenced by "Bar width" settings. For example, if you use a small bar width, you can

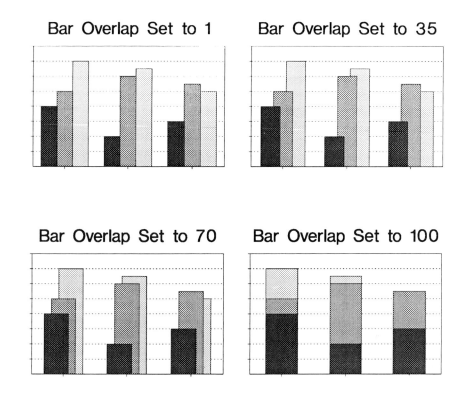

**Figure 6-24.**   Bar overlap settings with no bar enhancements

set "Bar depth" to values much greater than 100. See Figure 6-25 for examples of different "Bar depth" settings with 3D bars.

### Area Chart Symbol Style Options

There are six options on Page 2 of the Area Chart Titles & Options form (shown in Figure 6-26) that influence the style of area chart symbols. These six options ("Chart style," "Chart enhancement," "Chart fill style," "Bar width," "3D overlap," and "3D depth") are described in the following sections.

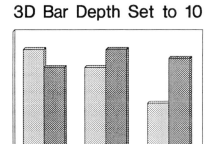
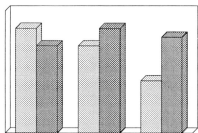
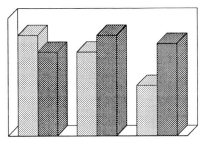
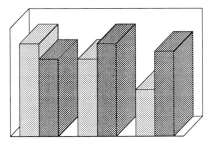

**Figure 6-25.**   Examples of depths for 3D bars

**Chart Style**   The "Chart style" option gives you a choice of three alternative settings: Stacked, Overlap, and 100%. The effects of these settings can be seen in Figure 6-27.

If you set "Chart style" to Stack, the areas will be stacked on top of one another. The area depicting Series 1 values is placed at the bottom. The next area in the stack depicts Series 2 values, and so on. Stacked areas are cumulative; that is, the height at the top of any given area represents the sum of the values of that area and those areas beneath it.

In contrast, Overlap causes all of the areas to start at the same level. The Series 1 area is always displayed in front and the Series 2

```
         ▲          Area Chart  Titles & Options  Page 2 of 4           ▼

            Chart style        │ ▶Stack    Overlap    100%
            Chart enhancement  │  3D       ▶None
            Chart fill style   │ ▶Color    Pattern    Both

            Bar width          │
            3D overlap         │  50
            3D depth           │  25

            Horizontal chart   │  Yes      ▶No
            Value labels       │  All      Select     ▶None

            Frame style        │ ▶Full     Half       Quarter    None
            Frame color        │  1
            Frame background   │  0

            Legend location    │  Top      ▶Bottom    Left       Right     None
            Legend justify     │  ← or ↑   ▶Center    ↓ or →
            Legend placement   │  In       ▶Out
            Legend frame       │  Single   Shadow     ▶None

 F1-Help
 F2-Draw chart                             F6-Colors       F8-Data        F10-Continue
```

**Figure 6-26.**  Page 2 of the Area Chart Titles & Options form

area is displayed behind Series 1, and so on. If no chart enhancements are used, it is possible for one series' area to entirely cover a smaller area placed behind it.

The final "Chart style" setting is 100%. The 100% setting is quite similar to the Stack setting. However, the height of the top area is always 100%. The proportion of each area to the whole represents the percentage contribution of each series at each X data value. If you select 100%, your "Type" will be treated as Area, irrespective of the "Type" selected on Page 1 of the Area Chart Titles & Options form.

**Chart Enhancement**  You can choose from two "Chart enhancement" options. These are 3D and None. To add a three-dimensional effect to your area charts, set "Chart enhancement" to 3D. Otherwise, set "Chart enhancement" to None. The influence of the 3D setting is shown in Figure 6-28.

*Note:*  The 3D setting will not have an effect if "Chart style" is set to Stack when you include bars or lines on your area chart (by setting

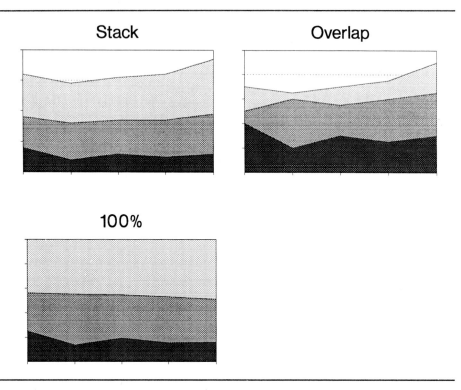

**Figure 6-27.**   The three chart styles available on the Area Chart Titles & Options form

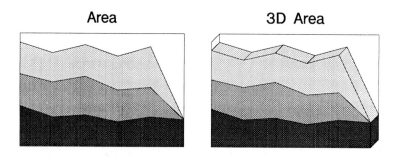

**Figure 6-28.**   Chart enhancements for area charts

"Type" to Line, Trend, or Bar on Page 1 of the Area Chart Titles & Options form).

**Chart Fill Style**   The "Chart fill style" option gives you the choice of using only color, only patterns, or both color and patterns to fill the areas in your chart. If you are going to print your chart to a single-color device that does not support grey scaling, select either Both or Pattern. If you are producing your chart on a color output device, or plan to display the chart on a color monitor, select Color, Pattern, or Both. See Chapter 8, "Producing Output," for more detail on the impact of color selections on printing.

**Bar Width**   Like the "Bar width" option on the Bar/Line Chart Titles & Options form, this "Bar width" option permits you to define the width of bars displayed on an area chart (if any series uses the Bar "Type" option). If "Bar width" is blank, the width of bars will cover 60 percent of the chart frame's width by default. To make your bars wider or thinner, set "Bar width" to the percentage of the chart frame that you want the bars to use.

If you are displaying areas instead of bars, and have set "Chart style" to Overlap and "Chart enhancement" to 3D, "Bar width" influences the width of the area in the third dimension. This option and the "3D depth" option for area charts have related effects on the depth of the third dimension (see the section, "3D Depth"). You may have to experiment with combinations of these settings to achieve the desired effect. Figure 6-29 shows examples of different bar width settings.

**3D Overlap**   The "3D overlap" option only affects area charts when you have set "Chart style" to Overlap and "Chart enhancement" to 3D. In these cases, "3D overlap" allows you to adjust the amount of rotation of your chart in the third dimension. Set "3D overlap" to a number from 1 to 100. If you set "3D overlap" to 1, the 3D areas overlap almost completely. Setting "3D overlap" to 100 results in the maximum possible rotation. Figure 6-30 shows examples of "3D overlap" settings.

*Note:*   Like the "Bar overlap" setting available for bar/line charts, "3D overlap" is influenced by the number of data points. With few data points, the highest "3D overlap" setting that has an effect may be substantially lower than 100.

**3D Depth** Use the "3D depth" option to define the width of areas and bars in the third dimension when the "Chart enhancement" option is set to 3D and "Chart style" is set to either Overlap or 100%. A smaller number reduces, and a larger number increases, the size of bars and areas in the third dimension. "Bar width" and "3D depth" settings interact. If you leave the "Bar width" setting at its default (60), enter a "3D depth" from 1 to 100. If you reduce the "Bar width" you may be able to use a "3D depth" setting over 100. You may have to experiment

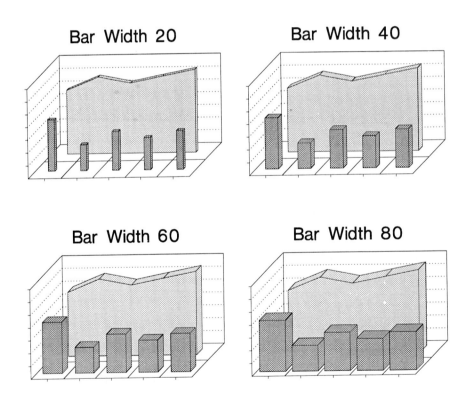

**Figure 6-29.** Examples of bar widths for area charts

## XY Charts: Bar/Line, Area, and High/Low/Close

with combinations of these settings to achieve the effect desired for your chart. Figure 6-30 shows examples of "3D depth" settings.

### High/Low/Close Chart Symbol Style Options

Unlike the other Titles & Options forms, Page 2 of the High/Low/Close Chart Titles & Options form (shown in Figure 6-31) has only five options for modifying your symbol styles. These options ("Bar style," "High/Low style," "Bar fill style," "Bar width," and "Bar overlap") are covered in the following sections.

**Bar Style**   The "Bar style" option allows you to select either Cluster, Overlap, or Stack for any bars you choose to display on your chart.

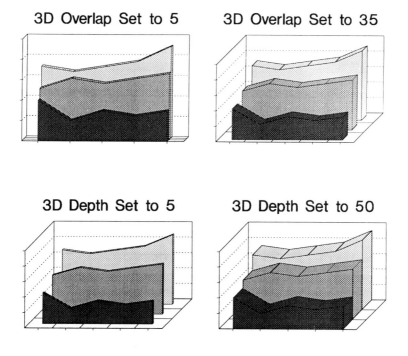

**Figure 6-30.**   Examples of 3D overlap settings for area charts

```
            High/Low/Close Chart  Titles & Options  Page 2 of 4

    Bar style           ▶Cluster    Overlap    Stack
    High/Low style      ▶Bar        Area       Error bar
    Bar fill style      ▶Color      Pattern    Both

    Bar width
    Bar overlap         50

    Horizontal chart    Yes         ▶No
    Value labels        All         Select     ▶None

    Frame style         ▶Full       Half       Quarter   None
    Frame color         1
    Frame background    0

    Legend location     Top         ▶Bottom    Left      Right     None
    Legend justify      ← or ↑      ▶Center    ↓ or →
    Legend placement    In          ▶Out
    Legend frame        Single      Shadow     ▶None

    F1-Help
    F2-Draw chart                   F6-Colors      F8-Data      F10-Continue
```

**Figure 6-31.**   Page 2 of the High/Low/Close Chart Titles & Options form

When "Type" is set to Bar for one or more series (this applies only to Series 5 through Series 8 on high/low/close charts), use the "Bar style" option to define how Harvard Graphics should display the bars. See the earlier section, "Bar Style," for details on the effects of "Bar style" settings.

**High/Low Style**   There are three types of High/Low styles that you can choose from: Bar, Area, and Error bar. Examples of these three different styles are shown in Figure 6-32.

Select Bar to display a standard high/low/close bar. In order to create a band chart, select Area. Harvard Graphics will use the values of your High and Low series to define the upper and lower boundaries of the band on your chart. To create an error bar, select Error bar.

**Bar Fill Style**   See the section "Bar Fill Style," earlier in this chapter for a description of this option.

## XY Charts: Bar/Line, Area, and High/Low/Close 185

**Bar Width**  Use "Bar width" to change the width of bars displayed on your high/low/close chart. When "Bar width" is blank, the width of high/low bars and error bars defaults to 15, while the width of Series 5 through Series 8 bars defaults to 60. To change these settings, enter a number from 1 to 100 to indicate the percentage of the chart space used by the bars. See Figure 6-22 for examples of different bar widths.

**Bar Overlap**  When the "Bar style" option is set to Overlap, use "Bar overlap" to control the amount of overlap for Series 5 through Series 8 bars. The default "Bar overlap" setting is 50. To change this, enter a number from 1 to 100 to indicate the degree of bar overlap. See Figure 6-24 for examples of this effect.

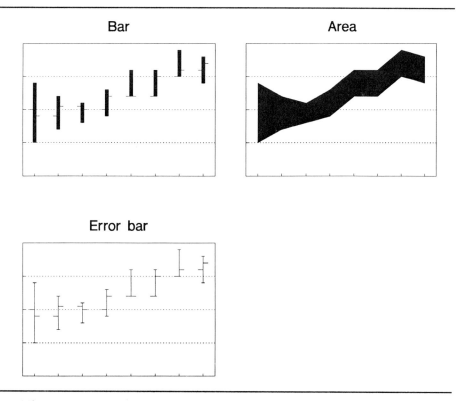

**Figure 6-32.**  The three high/low styles available on the High/Low/Close Chart Titles & Options form

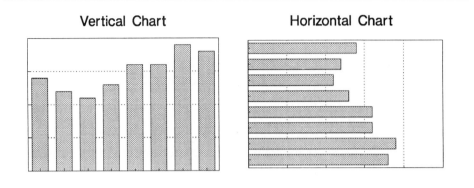

**Figure 6-33.**   Vertical and horizontal chart orientations

## Changing the XY Chart Orientation

When you create an XY chart in Harvard Graphics, the chart is displayed vertically by default (the Y axis is vertical). Figure 6-33 displays vertical and horizontal bar charts. To instruct Harvard Graphics to produce your chart horizontally, set "Horizontal chart" to Yes.

The effects of the "Horizontal chart" settings depend to some extent on your specific XY chart type. For instance, Harvard Graphics can display three-dimensional lines in a vertically oriented bar/line or area chart, but cannot do so with a horizontally oriented chart. On the other hand, paired bar/line charts are horizontal by definition, and the "Horizontal chart" option will not affect the appearance of these charts.

## Displaying Data Values on an XY Chart

Harvard Graphics provides two options for displaying the actual data values on your chart in addition to the bar, line, area, or point symbols. One of these options is to use a data table. This is described in the section "Using a Data Table," later in this chapter.

The second option is to place the data values directly in your chart frame, next to their corresponding symbols. To do this, set "Value labels" to All (on Page 2 of the Titles & Options form). To suppress the display of the data values, leave "Value labels" set to the default, None. Figure 6-34 shows two charts, one chart with and the other without the data values displayed.

# XY Charts: Bar/Line, Area, and High/Low/Close 187

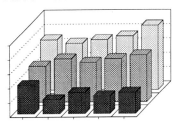

**Figure 6-34.**   Value labels settings

If your chart uses more than one series of data, you may want to display the data values for only selected series. Displaying data values for selected series requires two steps:

1. Set the "Value labels" option to Select.

2. Move to the "Y Label" column at the lower part of Page 4 of the Titles & Options form. Set "Y Label" to Yes for each series whose data values you want to display on the chart. Set "Y Label" to No for all other series.

Harvard Graphics will use the values in the "Y Label" column on Page 4 of the Titles & Options form to determine which series data values to display when "Value labels" on Page 2 is set to Select.

*Note:*   If you set "Value labels" to All, the setting for the "Data Table" option (Page 3 of the Titles & Options form) will be ignored and no data table will be displayed. If you set "Value labels" to Select and also choose to display a data table (see the section, "Using a Data Table"), data values for the selected series will not be displayed in the data table. Any series not selected will appear in the data table.

### Changing the Size of Value Labels

The data values that Harvard Graphics includes in your chart frame are produced using the same text size as the "Y labels" specified on the

Size/Place overlay. See the earlier section, "Setting the Text Size," for information about changing the size of Y labels.

## Customizing the Chart Frame

The "Frame style," "Frame color," and "Frame background" options on Page 2 of the Titles & Options form are used to define the completeness and color of your chart frame (the rectangular region enclosed by the X and Y axes).

The "Frame style" option is used to define the completeness of the chart frame. When you set "Frame style" to Full, a rectangle is drawn entirely around your chart frame. The other "Frame style" settings produce something less than a full frame. The effects of the Half, Quarter, and None "Frame style" settings are dependent on other characteristics of your chart. For instance, if your chart uses a three-dimensional effect, the Half and Quarter settings do not influence the chart frame appearance.

After selecting a "Frame style" setting, press F2-Draw chart to view the effects of your chart frame setting. If the result is not what you desire, try one of the other "Frame style" alternatives. Examples of frame styles for a simple bar chart are shown in Figure 6-35.

The "Frame color" and "Frame background" settings allow you to define the colors for the chart frame and the background within the frame. The color you select for the "Frame color" option will be used to produce the axis lines, tick marks, grid lines, data table frame, and legend frame. Enter a number from 0 to 16 to define the color for your frame color, or press F6-Colors to display the Color Selection overlay and select a color from a list of 16 colors.

*Note:* If you enter 0, no color will be used and the frame elements will be invisible on your chart.

The "Frame background" option allows you to define a background color for your chart's frame and legend. Enter a number from 0 to 16 or press F6-Colors to display the Color Selection overlay and select a color from the list. Similar to the "Frame color" option, a 0 produces no color. Unlike "Frame color," however, using the 0 setting (no color) for the

## XY Charts: Bar/Line, Area, and High/Low/Close 189

frame background is desirable for many chart styles, especially those that will be displayed on a monochrome monitor or printed to an output device that prints in black and white.

## Customizing the Chart Legend

A *legend* is a key that associates a label with each line, marker, pattern, or color that is used to identify the series in the chart. When your chart contains only one series, a legend is often redundant and undesirable.

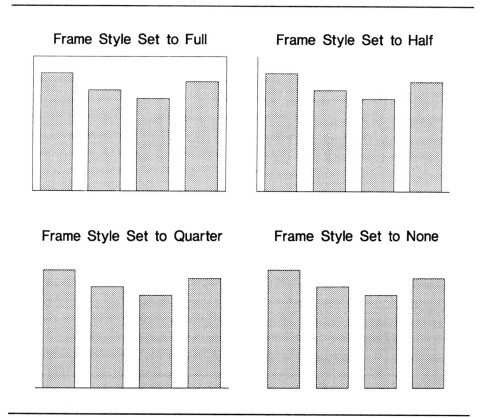

**Figure 6-35.**   Examples of frame styles

To suppress the display of a legend, set "Legend location" to None. When you do want a legend on your chart, Harvard Graphics provides you with four options that let you specify where you want the legend to be placed, and to some extent how you want the legend to look. These options are "Legend location," "Legend justify," "Legend placement," and "Legend frame" on Page 2 of the Titles & Options form. Figure 6-36 displays six combinations of these options. The settings shown in this figure refer to the location, justification, and placement settings for the legend.

The "Legend location" permits you to define the side of the chart where the legend will be placed. When you are using a legend, set "Legend location" to one of the sides of your chart: Top, Bottom, Left, or Right.

The "Legend justify" option permits you to fine-tune the legend's placement. For instance, if "Legend location" is set to Top or to Bottom, "Legend justify" allows you to place the legend to the Left (left arrow), Center, or Right (right arrow) at the top or bottom of the chart. When "Legend location" is set to Left or to Right, the "Legend justify" options are Top (up arrow), Center, or Down (down arrow).

The final adjustment you can make to the legend's placement is to define whether your legend should appear inside or outside of the chart frame. To place the legend within the chart frame, set "Legend placement" to In; otherwise, set it to Out. When you place your legend within the chart frame, Harvard Graphics uses the "Legend location" and "Legend justify" settings to determine where within the frame the legend will be located.

The placement of your legend (if you are using one) usually requires some thoughtful consideration. When a legend appears on your chart, it takes up some of the available space. When your legend is placed outside the chart frame, the size of the frame is reduced to make room for the legend. And although placing your legend within the chart frame will not have a dramatic effect on the frame's size, it is possible that the legend will be placed in front of chart symbols or data values, thereby blocking them from view. It is a good idea to preview your chart using F2-Draw chart to verify that the results of the legend placement are satisfactory.

You can modify your legend's appearance with the "Legend frame" option. When "Legend frame" is set to None, no frame appears around the legend. To use a legend frame, set "Legend frame" to either Single

# XY Charts: Bar/Line, Area, and High/Low/Close    191

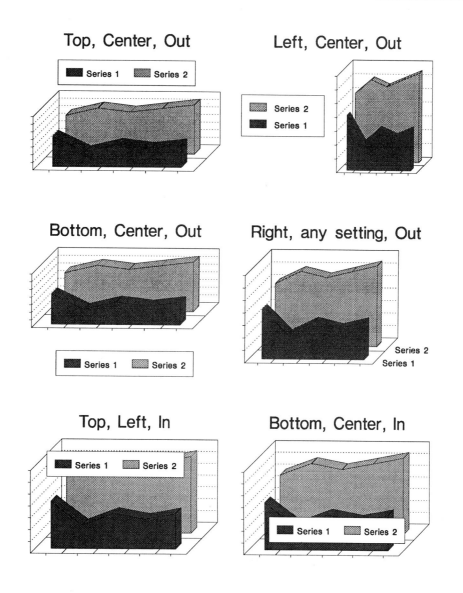

**Figure 6-36.**   The effects of combining legend location, legend justification, and legend placement settings

or Shadow. Single will surround your legend with a single-line frame, while Shadow will frame your legend and produce a drop shadow effect behind the legend. If "Legend frame" is defined as either Single or Shadow, Harvard Graphics will use the values defined at "Frame color" and "Frame background" to color your legend's frame and background. See the previous section, "Customizing the Chart Frame," for more information on setting "Frame color" and "Frame background" options.

## Using a Data Table

Harvard Graphics provides you with two options when you want to display series data values on your chart. One of these options is to display each data value next to the symbol that represents it. This method is described in an earlier section, "Displaying Data Values on an XY Chart." But sometimes it is not desirable to include data values within the chart frame. This is particularly true when a lot of data is plotted on a chart. The second option is to display data values below the chart frame (available since Harvard Graphics version 2.1). You do this by using the "Data Table" option, the first option on Page 3 of the Titles & Options form (shown in Figure 6-37).

In order to display a data table, set "Data Table" to either Normal or Framed. When you set "Data Table" to Normal, Harvard Graphics produces a table of your data below the chart frame. This table has one column for each of the X data values and one row for each of your displayed series. To produce a frame around this data table, select Framed. Several varieties of data tables for the same clustered bar chart are shown in Figure 6-38.

Including a data table in your chart will reduce the size of your chart frame. As the number of series you are displaying on your chart increases, so does the size of the data table. Larger data tables require more of the available space and will result in a corresponding reduction in the size of the chart frame.

*Note:* The setting for the "Data Table" option will be ignored and no data table will be displayed if you set the "Value labels" option on Page 2 of the Titles & Options form to All. If you display a data table when "Value labels" is set to Select, data values for the selected series will not be displayed in the data table, but will still be displayed on the chart

## XY Charts: Bar/Line, Area, and High/Low/Close

next to the corresponding symbol. All other series values will be displayed in the data table. See the earlier section, "Displaying Data Values on an XY Chart" for more information about the "Value labels" option.

### Changing the Size of the Text in a Data Table

Harvard Graphics uses the size of your X labels to define the size of the text in your data table. To change the size of your data table values, see the earlier section "Setting the Text Size."

### Combining a Data Table with a Legend

You can make the legend part of your data table by setting "Legend location" to None, and "Data Table" to either Normal or Framed. An example of a legend within the data table is shown in the lower-left chart in Figure 6-38. If you are using a data table, including the legend in the data table leaves more of the chart space for the chart frame.

```
                Bar/Line Chart  Titles & Options  Page 3 of 4
    Data Table        |  Normal      Framed    ▸None

    X  Axis Labels    | ▸Normal      Vertical    %       None
    Y1 Axis Labels    | ▸Value       $           %       None
    Y2 Axis Labels    | ▸Value       $           %       None

    X  Grid Lines     |  ....        ———        ▸None
    Y1 Grid Lines     | ▸....        ———         None
    Y2 Grid Lines     | ▸....        ———         None

    X Tick Mark Style | ▸In          Out         Both    None
    Y Tick Mark Style | ▸In          Out         Both    None

                      |   X Axis              Y1 Axis              Y2 Axis
    Scale Type        | ▸Linear    Log      ▸Linear    Log      ▸Linear    Log
    Format            |
    Minimum Value     |
    Maximum Value     |
    Increment         |

    F1-Help
    F2-Draw chart                              F8-Data         F10-Continue
```

**Figure 6-37.**   Page 3 of the Bar/Line Chart Titles & Options form

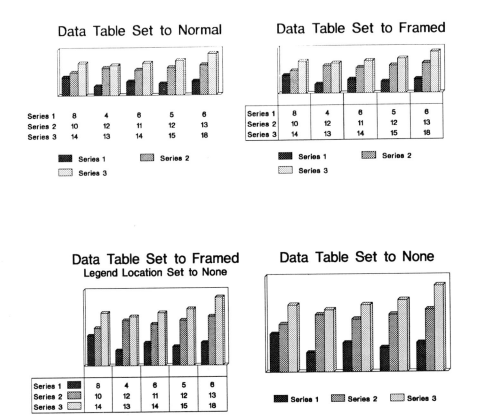

**Figure 6-38.** Examples of data table settings

## Applying Value Labels

When the X and Y labels are displayed on the X and Y axes, these values appear just as you entered them in the "X Axis" and "Series" columns on the Chart Data form. Harvard Graphics provides you with two ways to modify how these labels will appear on your chart. One way is to use the "Format" option for the desired axis. Using "Format" is described later in this chapter in the section "Customizing Axis Label Formats." The other method, which is easier to use but less flexible, involves setting the "X Axis Labels," "Y1 Axis Labels," and "Y2 Axis Labels" options. A selection of different axis label settings is shown in Figure 6-39.

Use the "X Axis Labels" option to define how Harvard Graphics should display the X axis labels. To display the X axis labels with no modifications, set "X Axis Labels" to Normal. To suppress the display of X axis labels altogether, select None. When X axis values are percentages, select the % setting to add a percent sign to each of the X axis labels. Finally, Harvard Graphics will display the X axis labels vertically if you set "X Axis Labels" to Vertical. This setting is particularly useful

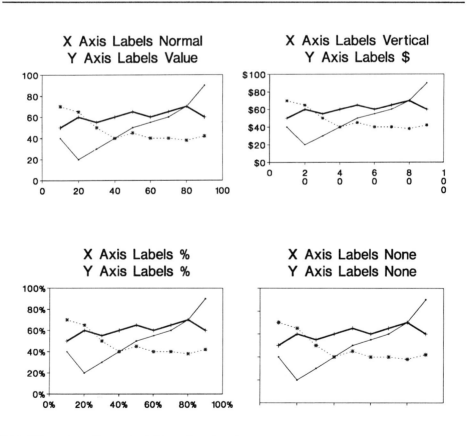

**Figure 6-39.**   Examples of labels for X and Y axes

when your X values are long names and there is not enough room to display them horizontally on the X axis (see also the earlier section, "Splitting X Axis Values onto Two Lines").

You can also have Harvard Graphics display your Y axis labels "as is" by selecting Value, or suppress them by selecting None. When a Y axis consists of dollar values, you can precede each Y axis label with a dollar sign by selecting $. Likewise, if a Y axis displays percentages, select the % setting to add a percent sign to each of the Y axis labels.

## Using Grid Lines

Grid lines are used to help the chart viewer estimate the values of the symbols displayed on a chart. Grid lines extend perpendicularly from the axis. When you first create your chart, Harvard Graphics selects dotted grid lines for the Y axes by default. You can choose solid or dotted grid lines for any of your axes. If desired, select None to suppress the display of grid lines on an axis. The use of grid lines on the X axis is not as common and is usually set to None. Several examples of grid line settings are shown in Figure 6-40.

## Specifying Tick Mark Styles

Harvard Graphics places tick marks along the X and Y axes at the location of each axis label. These marks are set to In by default. You can change the "X Tick Mark Style" and "Y Tick Mark Style" settings to Out, Both, or None. Figure 6-41 displays the effects of each of these settings on the appearance of tick marks.

## Customizing XY Chart Axes

The bottom half of Page 3 of the Titles & Options form contains three columns, one for each of the possible XY chart axes. Each of these columns contains five options: "Scale Type," "Format," "Minimum Value,"

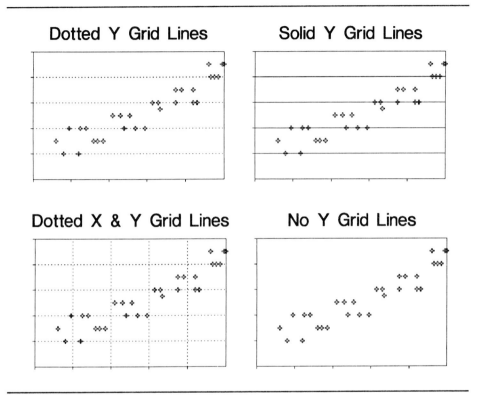

**Figure 6-40.**  Examples of grid lines

"Maximum Value," and "Increment." These options permit you to define the scale and scope of your three XY chart axes. Use of these options is described in the following sections.

### Selecting a Logarithmic Scale

Some specialized business and scientific charts require one or more of the axes to be based on a logarithmic scale. These scales are used to compare very large numbers with very small numbers. To use a logarithmic scale, move to the "Scale Type" option of the appropriate axis and press the SPACEBAR to select Logarithmic.

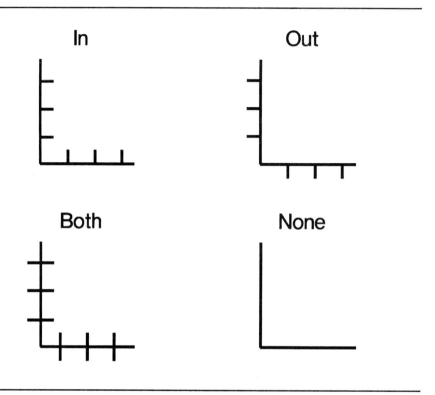

**Figure 6-41.**   Examples of tick mark styles

Figure 6-42 shows two charts that display the same data. The data consist of both very small numbers (less than 1) and very large numbers (greater than 900,000). The chart on the top uses a linear Y axis, whereas the chart on the bottom uses a logarithmic Y axis.

*Note:*   Logarithmic scales are not common in most presentation graphics charts. Unless you are certain you need a logarithmic scale, leave "Scale Type" set to Linear.

### Customizing Axis Label Formats

The "Format" option allows you to define a *format* for each of the axes. A format in this sense, is a command. These formatting commands allow you to add text to your axis labels, define the display characteristics of numeric axis values (such as the number of decimal places to show, the use of scientific notation, and the use of commas), and scale your data. If you are displaying the data on your chart with either the "Value labels" or "Data Table" option, these formatting features will also be applied to your displayed data. Table 6-5 shows the available formatting commands and their effects. These commands are described in the next sections.

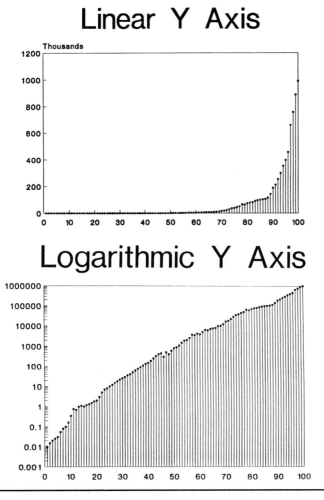

**Figure 6-42.** The same data are shown in each chart

**Adding Text to Axis Labels**   You can add either leading or trailing text to your axis labels. To add leading text, enter the text followed by a space and the ¦ character (a vertical bar) in the "Format" option. For instance, to precede each Y1 axis label with the words *COUNT OF*, enter the format **COUNT OF** ¦. If the number 100 is a Y axis label, this label will appear as "COUNT OF 100." To add trailing text, enter the ¦ character followed by a space and the text. If you set "Format" to ¦ **MILLION**, for example, an axis label of 100 will appear as "100 MILLION."

**Adding Commas to Axis Label Numbers**   When your axis labels are numeric, you can include commas in axis labels greater than 999 by using a comma in the format command. For example, setting "Format" to , will cause Harvard Graphics to display the number 2000 as "2,000."

**Specifying the Number of Decimal Places in Axis Labels**   When your axis labels are numeric, you can also indicate how many decimal places Harvard Graphics should display. To do this, enter a number at "Format" to indicate the number of decimal places to display for each of

| Command Type | Example | Data | Effect |
| --- | --- | --- | --- |
| , (comma) | , | 5000 | 5,000 |
| *num* (decimal places) | 2 | 7.1287 | 7.12 |
| *text* ¦ (preceding) | Part # ¦ | 11 | Part # 11 |
| ¦ *text* (trailing) | ¦ cc | 100 | 100 cc |
| *num* ¦ (division) | 2¦ | 100 | 50 |
| ! (scientific notation) | ! | 1000 | 1.000E+03 |

**Table 6-5.**   Formatting Commands and Their Effects

the axis values. For example, if you set the Y1 "Format" option to 2, Harvard Graphics will display the Y1 axis label 4 as "4.00" and the value 3.3333 as "3.33."

**Displaying Axis Labels in Scientific Notation**  When your axis labels are numeric, you can include the ! character in your "Format" option to specify that Harvard Graphics should display your axis labels in scientific notation.

*Note:*  To use leading or trailing text with scientific notation, use ! in place of the ¦. Also, to modify the number of decimal places displayed in scientific notation, follow the ! with an integer indicating the number of decimal places, for example, !4.

**Using Format to Scale Data**  You can also use the "Format" option to divide all of your data by a number. This division is said to *scale* your data. Scaling retains the relative proportions of your data. To scale data, enter the number that you want to divide the data by, followed by the ¦ character (vertical bar). For instance, if you want to divide all of your Y1 series in half, enter the "Format" option as 2¦. Note that there cannot be a space between the 2 and the ¦, otherwise the 2 would be regarded as preceding text and not as the divisor.

When you scale one of the axes, all data that are displayed against the scaled axis are changed by the divisor. This effect is also carried over to any values you enter into the corresponding "Minimum Value," "Maximum Value," and "Increment" options.

*Note:*  You may use the mathematical properties of division to multiply your axis values. To do this, enter the reciprocal of your multiplier as your divisor. For example, to multiply all of your Y1 axis data by five, divide your data by .2 (1/5 = .2). The "Format" setting to perform this multiplication is .2¦.

**Combining Format Commands**  Any of the preceding formatting commands can be combined to produce an unlimited variety of axis labels. There are several rules that you should observe when combining formatting symbols.

- No spaces can be used between the , (comma), the ¦ character, a decimal place specifier, or a divisor.

- There must be a space between any text (leading or trailing) and any of the format specifiers listed in the first rule.

- The entire "Format" entry is limited to 12 characters.

Consider the following entry in the "Format" option for the Y1 axis:

A 3,¦2 B

This entry would cause the Y1 axis labels to be preceded with the letter A and followed by the letter B, divided by 3, use commas for numbers greater than 999, and display the numbers to two decimal places. Furthermore, if any data are displayed for series charted with respect to the Y1 axis, those data values will also be formatted in this manner.

Table 6-6 contains a list of selected formatting combinations and their effects on specific data values.

### Setting an Axis Range and Increment

The remaining three options on Page 3 of the Titles & Options form are used to define the range of the X and Y axes. The options on these three

| Example | Data | Effect |
| --- | --- | --- |
| 5¦3 | 500 | 100.000 |
| $ ¦,2 | 3000 | $ 3,000.00 |
| Approx. ¦, cc | 1000 | Approx. 1,000 cc |
| 100¦ yrs | 500 | 5 yrs |
| .25¦, | 1000 | 4,000 |
| 10! | 1000 | 1.000E+02 |
| !5 | 12345 | 1.23450E+04 |

**Table 6-6.**   Combined Formatting Commands and Their Effects

rows are "Minimum Value," "Maximum Value," and "Increment." The "Minimum Value" and "Maximum Value" settings define the *range* of an axis, the difference between the lowest and the highest values appearing on an axis. "Increment" allows you define the number of labels to be placed along the axis.

How these options are used for a particular axis depends on whether the data displayed on that axis are numeric or non-numeric. The Y1 and Y2 axes are always used to display numeric data. The X axis, however, displays numeric data if, and only if, the "X Data Type" on the X Data Type Menu overlay is set to Number. All other X data types are considered non-numeric, even when you are using numbers for Time, Day, Week, Month, or Qtr "X data type" option settings. The next two sections discuss how to set the "Minimum Value," "Maximum Value," and "Increment" options for numeric and non-numeric data.

*Note:* Whether your axis data are numeric or non-numeric, "Minimum Value," "Maximum Value," and "Increment" are entirely optional. You may set none, one, or all of these options as long as you conform to the requirements for the option and axis type.

**Setting a Range and Increment for Numeric Data**   The "Minimum Value" option allows you to define the starting value on the axis. If your data are positive, Harvard Graphics defaults to a minimum value of zero. If at least some of the data are negative, Harvard Graphics will default to a negative value slightly lower than the lowest data value on your chart. If you wish to define a minimum value different from the default, enter a value at "Minimum Value." If your "Minimum Value" option setting is higher than the lowest data value for the axis, Harvard Graphics will not use your "Minimum Value" setting.

Similarly, Harvard Graphics will default the "Maximum Value" on an axis to slightly higher than the largest data value to be charted with respect to the axis. To change the default, set "Maximum Value" to any value that is at least as high as the highest data value for that axis.

Set "Increment" to the size of the interval at which you want labels (and tick marks and grid lines, if used) to be displayed on the axis. For instance, if you set "Minimum Value" to 0, "Maximum Value" to 1000, and "Increment" to 250, labels (and tick marks and grid lines) will appear at 0, 250, 500, 750, and 1000.

**Setting a Range and Increment for Non-Numeric Data** When your X data type is not Number, you can use "Minimum Value," "Maximum Value," and "Increment" to define which X data values to include in your chart. For instance, if you have entered 12 months of data, but you want to create a chart that displays only 4 of these months, you can use "Minimum Value" and "Maximum Value" to define which X data values to include in the chart. As you can see in the Area Chart Data form shown in Figure 6-43, each X data value in your chart is numbered. This number appears in the "Pt" column of the Chart Data form. You specify the range of a non-numeric X axis by entering the Pt numbers corresponding to the first and last X data values that you want to include in your chart at the "Minimum Value" and "Maximum Value" options.

For example, if 12 months starting with January and ending with December are entered in rows 1 through 12 of the Chart Data form, you can display the data for only August through November by setting "Minimum Value" to 8 and "Maximum Value" to 11. If you want your

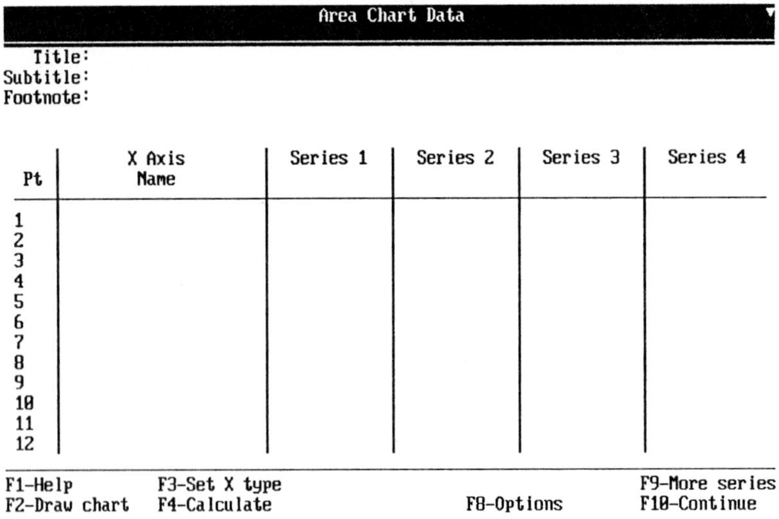

**Figure 6-43.** Area Chart Data form

# XY Charts: Bar/Line, Area, and High/Low/Close

chart to display only January through June, you can leave "Minimum Value" blank and set "Maximum Value" to 6.

Using "Increment" with non-numeric data defines which X values are labeled. If "Increment" is left blank, every X axis value is labeled. If you assign "Increment" a positive integer (1 or greater), Harvard Graphics uses this number to label only those values that fall on the increment (even though all X data are displayed on the chart).

Consider again the example of the 12 months, January through December. If "Increment" is set to 2, only every other data value will be labeled. Tick marks and grid lines, if used, will be displayed at each X data value, however. If "Minimum Value" is set to 1, "Maximum Value" is set to 6, and "Increment" is set to 2, there will be six tick marks on the X axis, one for each month, January through June. However, only the tick marks for January, March, and May will be labeled.

## Page 4 Title, Subtitle, Footnote, Labels, and Legends

Many of the options that appear on Page 4 of the Titles & Options form (shown in Figure 6-44) are repeated from Page 1. You can enter text or

```
                Bar/Line Chart   Titles & Options   Page 4 of 4

            Title:
            Subtitle:

            Footnote:


            X  axis title:
            Y1 axis title:
            Y2 axis title:
  Legend                        Cum        Y Label    Color   Marker/   Line
  Title:                        Yes  No    Yes  No            Pattern   Style

  1  Series 1                   No         No         2       1         1
  2  Series 2                   No         No         3       2         1
  3  Series 3                   No         No         4       3         1
  4  Series 4                   No         No         5       4         1
  5  Series 5                   No         No         6       5         1
  6  Series 6                   No         No         7       6         1
  7  Series 7                   No         No         8       7         1
  8  Series 8                   No         No         9       8         1

  F1-Help                       F5-Attributes    F7-Size/Place
  F2-Draw chart                 F6-Colors        F8-Data          F10-Continue
```

**Figure 6-44.** Page 4 of the Bar/Line Chart Titles & Options form

make changes to the first seven options ("Title" through "Legend Title") and the series legends on either page. For details about setting and modifying these options, see the earlier sections: "Entering a Chart Title, Subtitle, and Footnote," "Specifying X and Y Axis Titles," "Specifying a Legend Title," and "Changing the Series Legend."

## Creating a Cumulative Chart

The "Cum" option permits you to create a *cumulative* chart, one in which the series values that are displayed are accumulated across the X data values (see Figure 6-45).

Consider the values being charted for a single series when "Cum" is set to Yes. The first symbol (bar, line, area, or point), represents the value of the first data value in the series. The second symbol placed in the series represents the sum of the first and second series values. The third point represents the sum of the first three values, and so on.

*Note:* If you use a cumulative series it is critical that you clearly indicate on your chart (in the footnote, for instance) that you are displaying cumulative data.

## Setting Y Labels

When you set the "Value labels" option (on Page 2 of the Titles & Options form) to Select, you must also use the "Y Label" option on Page 4 to indicate which of the series data should be displayed on your chart. Set the "Y Label" option to Yes if you want the corresponding series data values to be displayed in the chart frame, otherwise set "Y Label" to No. If "Value labels" is set to Select, and the "Data table" option (on Page 3 of the Titles & Options form) is set to Normal or Framed, any series for which you set "Y Label" to Yes will be displayed on the chart but not in the data table. See the earlier section, "Displaying Data Values on an XY Chart," for more information.

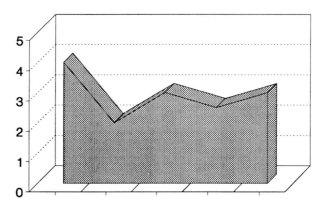

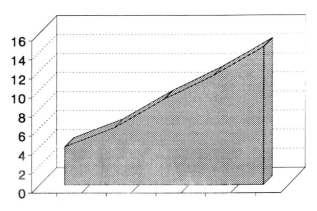

**Figure 6-45.** The same data are shown in each chart; the data in the bottom chart are cumulative

## Defining Chart Symbol Colors

Use the "Color" option on Page 4 of the Titles & Options form to define the colors for your series symbols. These colors only have an impact on your chart if you have set the "Chart fill style" or "Bar fill style" to Color or Both (on Page 2 of the Titles & Options form).

For each series you are displaying on your chart, choose the number that corresponds to the palette color you want Harvard Graphics to

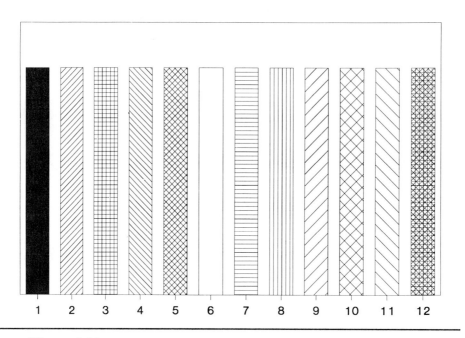

**Figure 6-46.**   The 12 available patterns

use when displaying your chart on a monitor or when recording your chart on film. Rather than typing in the desired palette color number, you can press F6-Colors while your cursor is at the "Color" option. When you do this, Harvard Graphics will display the Color Selection overlay. Select the color you want to use for the corresponding series from this list.

*Note:*   When printing to a color printer or plotter, the names of the colors in your color palette may not correspond to the colors your output device produces. See Chapter 8, "Producing Output," for a more detailed discussion of using color when printing, plotting, or recording.

## Defining Marker and Pattern Styles

When your series symbol is either Bar or Area, and you have set "Chart fill style" or "Bar fill style" to either Pattern or Both, use "Marker/Pattern" to define the pattern for your symbols. For each series, enter a number from 1 to 12 to select one of the 12 available patterns shown in Figure 6-46.

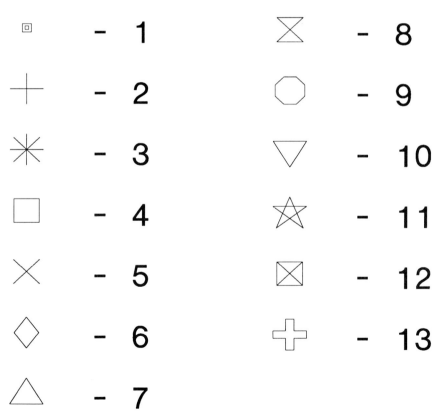

**Figure 6-47.**   The 13 marker styles

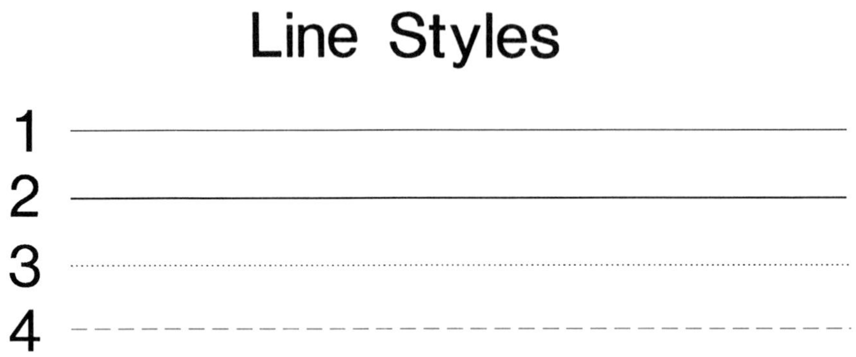

**Figure 6-48.** Line styles for line charts

If your series type is a Line, Trend, Curve, or Point, use the "Marker/Pattern" option to define the type of marker Harvard Graphics will use to mark each data point (although the lines for Trend and Curve symbols may not pass through each data point, a marker *will* be produced at each data point). Harvard Graphics provides you with 13 different marker styles (see Figure 6-47). Set "Marker/Pattern" to the number associated with the desired marker, or to 0 to suppress the display of the marker.

If your chart displays three-dimensional lines, the "Marker/Pattern" option settings will have no effect on the appearance of your lines.

### Defining Line Chart Line Styles

Harvard Graphics can produce four different line styles for use with Line, Trend, and Curve symbol types. Enter a number, 1 to 4, corresponding to one of the line styles shown in Figure 6-48.

If your chart displays three-dimensional lines, the "Line Style" option settings will have no effect on the appearance of your lines.

## Clearing Data from XY Charts

You can clear all the data entered on your Chart Data form (X data and series data) while retaining the settings entered on the Titles & Options form (including the chart title, subtitle, and footnote), the Size/Place overlay, and the Text Attributes overlay. This feature is useful when you need to create a number of XY charts that have the same chart option settings. To clear data values, press ESC until you return to the Main Menu. (If you have not saved your current chart but want to save it, use <Get/Save/Remove> to save your chart before continuing. See Chapter 2, "Harvard Graphics Basics.")

Select <Create new chart> from the Main Menu. Then select <Clear values> from the Create New Chart menu. If you have not saved your chart since creating or modifying it, Harvard Graphics will display the message "Chart values are about to be cleared. Press Enter to continue; Esc to Cancel." Harvard Graphics will then display your Chart Data form. The "X Axis" and series columns will be empty. You can then enter data for your new chart.

## Changing Data Chart Styles

Occasionally you will want to change a data chart (pie chart or one of the XY charts—bar/line, area, or high/low/close) from one style to another while retaining all the data you have entered on the Chart Data form, as well as the comparable settings on the Titles & Options form. Most of these changes work smoothly, especially changing from one type of XY chart to another. See the following section, "Changing XY Chart Styles." Changing from an XY chart to a pie chart is a little more involved. This is described in the next chapter, in the section "Changing an XY Chart to a Pie Chart."

## Changing XY Chart Styles

To change XY chart styles, the original chart must be the current chart. If you have not saved this chart since you created or last modified it, save it before you continue. (See Chapter 2, "Harvard Graphics Basics," for information on saving charts.)

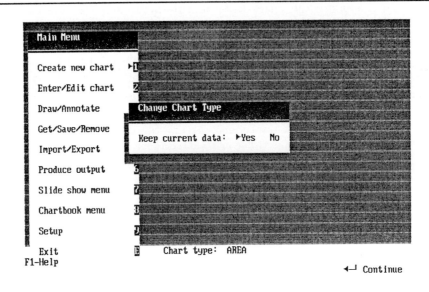

**Figure 6-49.**   Change Chart Type overlay

Return to the Main Menu and select <Create new chart>. Select one of the XY chart styles from the Create New Chart menu. If you select a chart style that is different from the current chart, Harvard Graphics will display the Change Chart Type overlay, shown in Figure 6-49, asking you to indicate whether you want to keep the data entered for the current chart. If you select Yes, Harvard Graphics will use the X data and series data and names already entered for your current chart and copy it to the Chart Data form for the new chart style. Corresponding option settings on the Titles & Options form, the Size/Place overlay, and the Text Attributes overlay will also be transferred to the new chart. If you select No, the Chart Data form for your new chart will be blank.

# Pie Charts

Pie Chart Overview
Creating Pie Charts
Pie Chart Data Form
Pie Chart Titles & Options Form
Page 2 of the Pie Chart Titles & Options Form
Clearing Data from Your Pie Chart
Changing Chart Styles

This chapter describes how to create and customize pie charts in Harvard Graphics. It begins with an overview of the steps involved in creating pie charts, and then moves on to the individual steps used in creating them. Throughout this chapter, it is assumed you are familiar with the names Harvard Graphics uses for the various chart elements and characteristics, such as pie slices and column charts. If you find you are unfamiliar with some of the terms used in this chapter, you will benefit by first reading Chapter 19, "Effective Data Charts," and Chapter 20, "Advanced Data Topics."

## Pie Chart Overview

Pie charts are used to compare the relative sizes of a group of numbers. Each number is represented as a slice of a pie or a section in a column. The size of each slice or section represents its proportion of the sum of all values in the pie or column. Examples of pie charts you can create with Harvard Graphics are shown in Figure 7-1.

Although Harvard Graphics permits you to create both standard, circular pie charts and column pie charts, for ease of discussion, all pies are referred to as if they are circular. Except where noted, all issues regarding circular pie charts also apply to column pie charts.

**214** Harvard Graphics: The Complete Reference

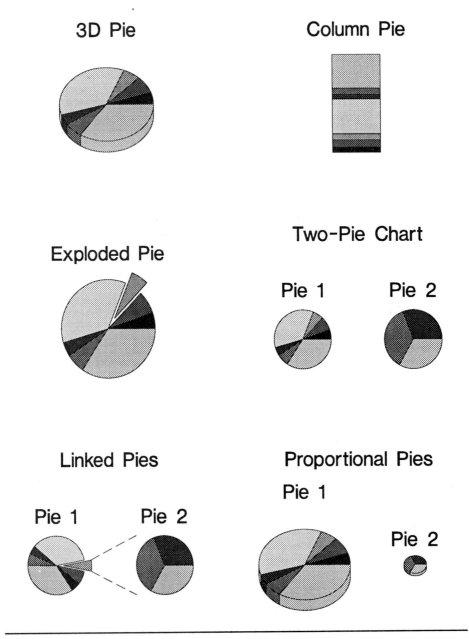

**Figure 7-1.**   Examples of pie chart styles

## Creating Pie Charts

The following list is a summary of the steps involved in creating a pie chart. Use these steps to gain a general understanding of the pie chart creation process. You should refer to the appropriate sections later in this chapter for detailed discussion of these steps.

1. At the Main Menu, select <Create new chart>.

2. At the Create New Chart menu, select <Pie>.

3. Enter your pie labels and data into the "Label" and "Value" columns on Page 1 of the Pie Chart Data form, as described later in the chapter.

4. If you have more than one series of data, for creating more than one pie chart, press F9-More series to display the label and value options for an additional series. Enter the data for your new series as described in the section, "Adding Additional Series." You may enter up to a total of eight series of data by repeating this step. Each series is used to create one pie but only two pies can be displayed at a given time.

5. If you want to produce a pie chart that displays a single pie, make sure the series you want to use for the pie is displayed on Page 1 of the Pie Chart Data form. If it is not, press F9-More series until the desired series is shown on the form.

If you want to display two pies on your chart, you need to select which series will be used for the left pie (Pie 1) and which for the right pie (Pie 2). Make sure the series you want to display as Pie 1 is shown on Page 1 of the Pie Chart Data form. If not, press F9-More series until the desired series is shown on the form.

Press PGDN to display Page 2 of the Pie Chart Data form. If the series you want to display as Pie 2 is not shown on this page of the form, press F9-More series until it is shown. Press PGUP to return to Page 1 of the Pie Chart Data form.

6. If desired, indicate the colors and patterns to be used for each slice of each pie and whether any slices should be exploded (separated) from the pies.

7. Set additional pie options on the Pie Chart Titles & Options form.

At this point your pie chart is finished. You may, however, want to consider some of the following optional steps to improve or enhance your chart. If you do not want to do any of these steps, go to step 12 and save your chart.

8. If you want to check the spelling of text in your pie chart, return to the Main Menu and press F4-Spell check. Additional information about spell checking your charts is provided in Chapter 2, "Harvard Graphics Basics."

9. If you want to change the font used for text in your chart or select a different chart border or orientation, return to the Main Menu and press F8-Options. Set the "Orientation," "Border," and "Font" options on the displayed Current Chart Options overlay. See "Overriding Default Chart Characteristics" in Chapter 3, "Setup and Default Settings," for additional details.

10. If desired, you can enhance your pie chart by using Harvard Graphics' drawing and annotating features. You can reduce the overall size of your chart as well. See Chapter 9, "Drawing and Annotating," for more information.

11. If you want to print, plot, or record your chart on film, return to the Main Menu and select <Produce output>. See Chapter 8, "Producing Output," for more information.

12. Save your pie chart to disk if you want to use it at a later time. See Chapter 2, "Harvard Graphics Basics," for information on saving charts.

## Pie Chart Data Form

The Pie Chart Data form is used to enter the series data Harvard Graphics uses to produce a pie, and to choose the colors and patterns for each pie segment. The Pie Chart Data form also contains options for entering a title, subtitle, and footnote for your chart. Page 1 of this two-page form is shown in Figure 7-2. Page 2 is identical except for the page number in the title banner. It is used to set characteristics for a second pie on your chart.

Although you can enter a title, subtitle, and footnote on the top lines of the Pie Chart Data form, you will have more flexibility if you enter this information on the Pie Chart Titles & Options form. See "Entering a Title, Subtitle, and Footnote," later in this chapter.

On the lower half of the Pie Chart Data form are six columns. The first is labeled "Slice." This column contains the numbers that correspond to each of the 12 possible slices for a pie. These numbers are used for reference only, so you cannot change them.

The next two columns, "Label" and "Value," are used for entering series data for pies. The current series name is displayed under the title of the "Value" column, and indicates the name of the series data in the "Label" and "Value" columns on the Pie Chart Data form. If you are only going to make one pie, you will need only one series, Series 1. You can display additional series by pressing F9-More series. When you do so, the next series' data (Series 2) are displayed in the "Label" and "Value" columns of the Pie Chart Data form.

The final three columns, "Cut Slice," "Color," and "Pattern," are used for customizing the display characteristics of each of the slices of your pie. Unlike the "Value" and "Label" columns, these settings are characteristics corresponding to the page (1 or 2) of the Pie Chart Data

```
                    Pie Chart 1 Data  Page 1 of 2
Title:
Subtitle:
Footnote:

Slice       Label           Value        Cut Slice   Color   Pattern
            Name            Series 1     Yes  No

  1                                           No       2       1
  2                                           No       3       2
  3                                           No       4       3
  4                                           No       5       4
  5                                           No       6       5
  6                                           No       7       6
  7                                           No       8       7
  8                                           No       9       8
  9                                           No      10       9
 10                                           No      11      10
 11                                           No      12      11
 12                                           No      13      12

F1-Help                                              F9-More series
F2-Draw chart              F6-Colors    F8-Options   F10-Continue
```

**Figure 7-2.**   Pie Chart Data form

form, and are not tied to a specific series. (You later choose to display the series data on a given page, thereby applying these characteristics to the pie.)

When you are creating a chart that will display a single pie, you will only need to work with Page 1 of the Pie Chart Data form (shown in Figure 7-2). The settings in the "Cut Slice," "Color," and "Pattern" columns of Page 1 of the Pie Chart Data form define the display characteristics of this pie's slices. The data used for this pie are determined by which series' data you select, that is, which series name is displayed below the "Value" column title. For example, if Page 1 shows "Series 1," the data for this series will be used to create the pie. If Page 1 shows "Series 2," the data for Series 2 will be used.

You can display two pies simultaneously on your chart by using Page 1 to define the left pie, Pie 1, and Page 2 to define the right pie, Pie 2. The data used for Pie 1 and Pie 2 are defined by displaying the appropriate series names on Page 1 and Page 2, respectively. A chart displaying two pies is shown in Figure 7-3. (Although it would not make

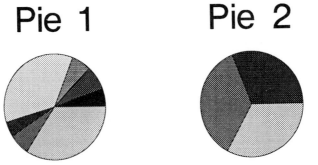

**Figure 7-3.** A chart with two pies

much sense to do so, it is possible to set both Page 1 and Page 2 to the same series. For instance, if both pages of the Pie Chart Data form display "Series 1," Pie 1 and Pie 2 will display the same data. Nearly all of the time, Pie 1 will display one series, Series 1, for example, and Pie 2 will display another, Series 2.)

The options on the Pie Chart Data form are described in the following sections. Use the keys listed in Table 7-1 to control cursor movement and simplify text and data entry on the Pie Chart Data form. Use F2-Draw chart frequently to see the layout of the chart that you are creating. Press any key to remove the chart and return to the form.

## Entering Pie Labels

The pie labels for a particular series are used to name the slices of a pie. The labels in a pie chart are equivalent to the X data in an XY chart. Enter a name for each of the slices in your series in the "Label" column of the Pie Chart Data form. These labels are limited to a maximum of 20 characters each. After typing a label for a pie slice, press ENTER to move the cursor to the next line in the "Label" column.

You may define labels for seven additional series on this form by pressing F9-More series. See the section "Adding Additional Series" later in this chapter for details.

### Splitting Pie Labels onto Two Lines

You may choose to display your pie labels on two lines. To do this, enter the text splitting character ( | ) where you want Harvard Graphics to split the label. When you split a label onto two lines, the text on the second line is centered under the text on the first line. Do not follow the text splitting character with a space, or the second line of the label will appear off center.

## Entering Pie Values

Enter a numeric value in the "Value" column for each of the labels you entered in the "Label" column. These values must be positive numbers. You can use fractions or decimal places, if necessary, but you cannot

| Key | Function |
| --- | --- |
| BACKSPACE | Moves the cursor back one space, deleting any character in the space. |
| CTRL-DEL | Deletes entire contents of line at the cursor, deletes the pie label and corresponding value for the line at the cursor. |
| CTRL-DOWN | Moves the pie label and corresponding value down one position. |
| CTRL-INS | Inserts a blank line for a pie label and value above the line the cursor is on. |
| CTRL-LEFT | Moves the cursor to the previous word in the line. |
| CTRL-RIGHT | Moves the cursor to next word in the line. |
| CTRL-UP | Moves the pie label and corresponding value up one position. |
| DEL | Deletes character at the cursor. |
| DOWN (arrow) | Moves the cursor down one line, option, or menu item. |
| END | Moves the cursor to the last option or line on a form. |
| ENTER | Selects highlighted settings for form options and moves the cursor to the next option on the form, moves cursor to the next line in the "Label" or "Value" column. |
| ESC | 1. Returns to the previous screen. Press ESC multiple times to "back up" through previous menus and forms to the Main Menu. |
| | 2. Cancels changes and returns to the previous screen. |
| HOME | Moves the cursor to the first option or line on a form. |
| INS | Toggles INS on and off; the cursor appears as a block when it is on, and as a small line when it is off. |
| LEFT (arrow) | Moves the cursor left one character or option setting. |
| PGDN | Displays the next page of the form. |
| PGUP | Displays the previous page of the form. |
| RIGHT (arrow) | Moves the cursor right one character or option setting. |
| SHIFT-TAB | Moves the cursor to the previous column or option on a form. |
| TAB | Moves the cursor to the next column or option on a form. |
| UP (arrow) | Moves the cursor up one line, option, or menu item. |

**Table 7-1.** Cursor Control Keys and Functions for Pie Charts

include commas. If your numbers are very large or very small, you can enter your numbers using scientific notation. (See Table 6-3 in Chapter 6 for examples of valid data entries.)

When Harvard Graphics displays your pie, it uses the numbers you enter in the "Value" column to determine the relative sizes of the slices in your pie.

You may define data for seven additional series on the Pie Chart Data form by pressing F9-More series. See the next section for details.

## Adding Additional Series

Although a pie chart can only display two pies at a time, you can enter up to eight different series of data in the Pie Chart Data form. Similar to Harvard Graphics' XY charts, these series are called Series 1 through Series 8.

As you can see in Page 1 of the Pie Chart Data form, shown in Figure 7-2, the name "Series 1" is displayed below the "Value" header of the "Value" column. This means the data displayed in the "Label" and "Value" columns are the data for Series 1. You can switch to one of the other seven series by pressing F9-More series. The first time you do so, the name "Series 2" appears in the "Value" column header. Pressing F9-More series again will display the name "Series 3," and so on, up to "Series 8." When "Series 8" is displayed, pressing F9-More series will display "Series 1."

For any given series, the data displayed in the "Label" and "Value" columns are specific to that series. In contrast, the "Cut Slice," "Color," and "Pattern" settings are specific to the particular page (1 or 2) of the Pie Chart Data form.

To add another series to your Pie Chart Data form, press F9-More series until the name of the series you want to enter is displayed in the header of the "Value" column (for example, you will usually display "Series 2" for a second pie). Next, enter the "Label" and "Value" data for this series. If desired, you can repeat the process until you have entered data for all eight series.

*Hint:* In most instances you will probably not need to use more than one series, or two at most.

## Modifying Pie Series

If you find series data have changed, you can easily edit the appropriate "Label" or "Value" data on the Pie Chart Data form. Other changes, such as adding or deleting a pie slice and changing the order of slices, are described next.

### Adding a New Slice

Move to the form position in the series where you want to add a new slice and press CTRL-INS. Harvard Graphics will insert a new slice at this position. Enter the data in the "Label" and "Value" columns.

### Deleting a Slice

Move your cursor to the slice you want to delete and press CTRL-DEL. Harvard Graphics will delete both the "Label" and "Value" data of the slice.

### Changing the Order of Slices

When Harvard Graphics displays your pie chart, the slices of your pie are arranged in a counterclockwise fashion (starting from three o'clock by default) in the order in which you entered your data in the series. You can change the order of slices if the arrangement displayed when you preview your chart with F2-Draw chart is not satisfactory. The order of slices can be changed in one of two ways. The first is to tell Harvard

Graphics to sort pie slices based on the numbers in the "Value" column, with the largest value placed first, the second largest placed second, and so on. This technique is described in the section "Sorting Pie Slices" later in this chapter.

The second way to modify the order of slices is to change the order of your data in the series. To do this, move the cursor to the entry (in either the "Label" or "Value" column) that corresponds to the slice you want to move. To move the slice up one position in the list, press CTRL-UP. Likewise, press CTRL-DOWN to move the corresponding slice down one position in the list. Both "Label" and "Value" data will be moved.

## Defining a Two-Pie Chart

Harvard Graphics permits you to create a pie chart that displays two pies, one on the left and the other on the right side of the chart. The pie on the left is called Pie 1, and the pie on the right is called Pie 2. Before you can create a two-pie chart, you must enter data for at least two series. You then display the series you want for Pie 1 on Page 1 of the Pie Chart Data form and the series you want for Pie 2 on Page 2.

*Note:* The "Chart style" option for Pie 2 on Page 2 of the Pie Chart Titles & Options form must also be set to the default, Pie, or to Column. Do not change the setting to None. This option is described later in the section, "Pie Chart Titles & Options Form."

## Exploding Slices of a Pie

Sometimes it is desirable to draw attention to one or more specific slices of your pie. A common method for doing this is to separate a pie slice from the pie by a small amount of space. This effect is called *exploding* a slice of the pie. To explode a pie slice, move to the "Cut Slice" column on Page 1 of the Pie Chart Data form and set the desired slice to Yes. You can explode as many slices of a pie as you wish. If your chart will display two pies, you can explode slices for the second pie on Page 2 of the Pie Chart Data form.

*Note:* Harvard Graphics will not explode any pie slices if you have set the "3D effect" option to Yes on Page 1 of the Pie Chart Titles & Options form.

### Selecting the Colors of Pie Slices

You can use color in your pies by setting a color for each pie slice in the "Color" column. To do this, move your cursor to the "Color" column entry corresponding to the desired pie slice. There are two ways to define the color for a given pie slice. One is to enter a number, 0 through 16, for each pie slice in the "Color" column. (Entering 0 makes the corresponding pie slice invisible.) Alternatively, press F6-Colors to display the Color Selection overlay (shown in Figure 7-4) and select a color from the list. Once you highlight a color for the slice, press ENTER to

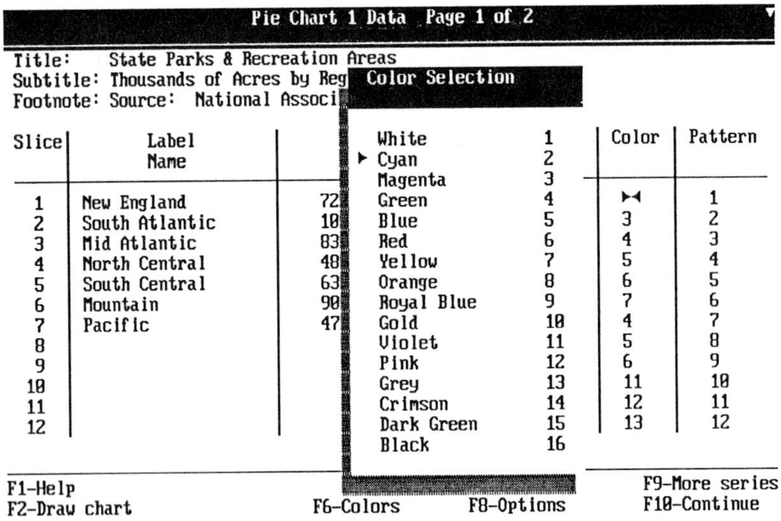

**Figure 7-4.** Color Selection overlay

return to the Pie Chart Data form. (If you are using the Color Selection overlay to select colors, you will have to press F6-Colors for each pie slice.)

To create a chart with one pie, you will only need to define the color settings for Pie 1. To create a two-pie chart, you will also need to define colors for Pie 2 on Page 2 of the Pie Chart Data form.

## Selecting Patterns for Pie Slices

When the "Fill style" option on the Pie Chart Titles & Options form is set to either Pattern or Both, use the "Pattern" column on the Pie Chart Data form to select a pattern for each of your pie slices. To define a pattern for a given pie slice, move your cursor to the corresponding row of the "Pattern" column and enter a number from 1 through 12, corresponding to the 12 patterns shown in Figure 7-5.

Like the "Cut Slice" and "Color" options, you will also need to define these options on Page 2 of the Pie Chart Data form if you are displaying a second pie on your chart.

## Pie Chart Titles & Options Form

From the Pie Chart Data form, press F8-Options to display the Pie Chart Titles & Options form. (You can return to the Pie Chart Data form at any time by pressing F8-Data.) The Pie Chart Titles & Options form is used to define the display characteristics of your pie chart, with the exception of pie slice exploding, colors, and patterns, which are defined on the Pie Chart Data form.

The Pie Chart Titles & Options form is two pages long. From Page 1, press PGDN to move to Page 2. To return to Page 1, press PGUP. Page 1 of the Pie Chart Titles & Options form is shown in Figure 7-6. The options available on the Pie Chart Titles & Options form are described in the following sections.

## Entering a Title, Subtitle, and Footnote

The first six lines on the Pie Chart Titles & Options form permit you to enter a one-line title, a two-line subtitle, and a three-line footnote. Each of these lines can contain a maximum of 40 characters. If you entered a title, subtitle, or footnote on the Pie Chart Data form, this text will

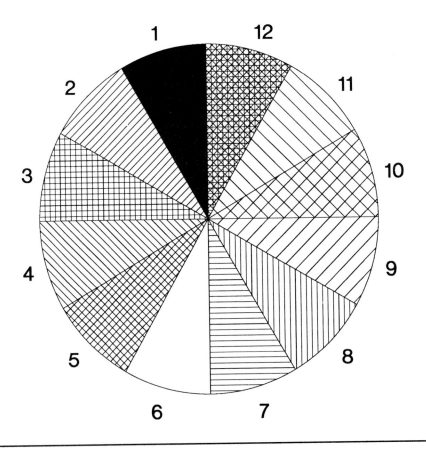

**Figure 7-5.** Patterns available for pie slices

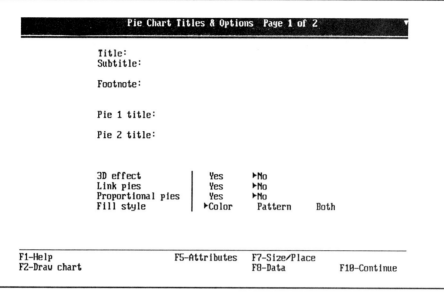

**Figure 7-6.**   Page 1 of the Pie Chart Titles & Options form

appear in the first line of each of these options. You can edit or add to this text on the Pie Chart Titles & Options form. The title and subtitle will appear at the top of the chart and the footnote will appear at the bottom.

*Note:*   For information on using international text characters in your chart, refer to Appendix D "Harvard Graphics Tables."

## Entering Titles for Pie 1 and Pie 2

If your pie chart is designed to display only one pie, the "Pie 1 title" option provides you with two lines for an additional title. This title will be centered directly below the pie. When you are creating a two-pie chart, the "Pie 1 title" and "Pie 2 title" options allow you a two-line title for each pie. The titles will be centered below the corresponding pie. You can change the pie title placement as described later in "Modifying Text Placement."

## Modifying Text Attributes

Press F5-Attributes to display the Text Attributes overlay, which you use to modify attributes of text entered at the options "Title," "Subtitle," "Footnote," "Pie 1 title," and "Pie 2 title." The attributes you define for the "Pie 1 title" option are also used for Pie 1 labels, values, and percentages, if displayed. Likewise, the attributes defined for the "Pie 2 title" option are used for Pie 2 labels, values, and percentages.

The text attributes you can modify include font weight (bold), style (italics and fill), underlining, and color. (See "Fonts and Text Attributes" in Appendix D for examples of attribute combinations.) Modifying one or more of these attributes requires two steps. The first involves selecting the text whose attributes you want to modify. The second involves setting the desired text attribute options on the Text Attributes overlay. These steps are detailed in the next two sections.

### Highlighting Text for an Attribute Change

If you want to modify only a portion of text that appears on a given line, move the cursor to the left-most character of the text you want to modify. Then press F5-Attributes to highlight the character at the cursor and display the Text Attributes overlay (shown in Figure 7-7) at the bottom of the screen. If you want to change the text attributes of one or more entire lines of text, move your cursor to the top line you want to highlight. Then press SHIFT-F5 to automatically highlight the entire current line and display the Text Attributes overlay at the bottom of the screen.

After you have pressed F5-Attributes or SHIFT-F5, use the RIGHT and DOWN arrow keys to extend the highlighting over the desired text. Press RIGHT (or F5-Attributes again) to highlight text to the right of the cursor. Press DOWN (or SHIFT-F5 again) to highlight additional lines of text. If you try to highlight text to the left of the character where you began the highlighting, no highlighting will occur, and the Text Attributes overlay will be removed from the screen.

### Setting Text Attributes for Highlighted Text

Once you have highlighted the desired text, press TAB to move between the various attribute options on the Text Attributes overlay. Press the

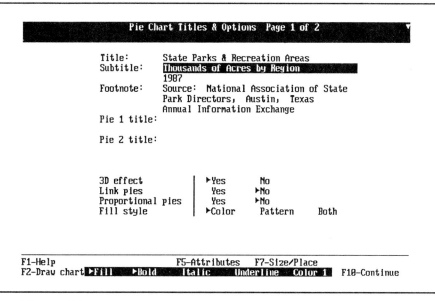

**Figure 7-7.** Text Attributes overlay with text in the first line of the subtitle highlighted

SPACEBAR to set each attribute option for the highlighted text. The "Fill," "Bold," "Italic," and "Underline" options have two possible settings: On and Off. Modify these options by pressing the SPACEBAR to toggle the attribute on or off. Whenever one of these attributes is set to On, an arrow appears to the left of the attribute name.

There are two ways to change the "Color" attribute option. The first is to toggle the SPACEBAR the same way you change settings for the other text attributes. As you press the SPACEBAR, the next sequential color number appears to the right of the "Color" option. The second way is to select a color from a list of colors. With your cursor positioned at the "Color" option, press F6-Colors. Harvard Graphics will display the Color Selection overlay (shown in Figure 7-8) listing the names of all 16 colors in the color palette. Highlight the desired color and then press ENTER or F10-Continue. The Color Selection overlay is removed from the screen and the selected color number appears at the "Color" option on the Text Attributes overlay.

When you are through setting text attribute options for the highlighted text, press F10-Continue to return to the Pie Chart Titles & Options form.

## Modifying the Size and Placement of Text

From Page 1 of the Pie Chart Titles & Options form, press F7-Size/Place to modify the size and placement of the "Title," "Subtitle," "Footnote," "Pie 1 title," and "Pie 2 title" options. Once you press F7-Size/Place, the Size/Place overlay is displayed over the upper-left corner of the Pie Chart Titles & Options form. Set the desired options on this overlay. Press F7-Size/Place or F10-Continue to return to the Pie Chart Titles & Options form.

### Setting Text Sizes

Use the "Size" column on the Size/Place overlay to indicate the size of text to use on your chart. The numbers in this column correspond to the

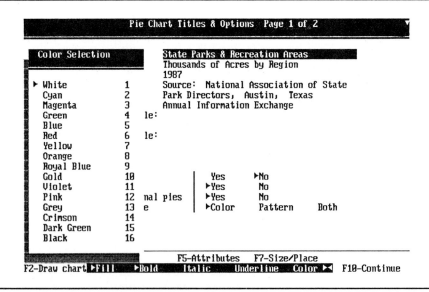

**Figure 7-8.** Color Selection overlay

text on the corresponding line of the Pie Chart Titles & Options form. Harvard Graphics defaults to the text size values shown in the Size/Place overlay in Figure 7-9. To change any of these defaults, move to the appropriate line of the "Size" column and enter a new text size. This number must be between .1 and 99. See Appendix D for examples of different sizes.

*Note:* After changing the size of the text on your pie chart, press F2-Draw chart to verify that the new text size is satisfactory. Large text sizes sometimes cause the text to overlap your chart. On the other hand, if the text size is small, attributes applied to the chart text may not be displayed on your monitor, although they will appear when output.

### Modifying Text Placement

Use the "Place" column on the Size/Place overlay to define the alignment of your title, subtitle, and footnote. Corresponding to each of these text lines are the settings L, C, and R on the Size/Place overlay. These

```
                   Pie Chart Titles & Options  Page 1 of 2
   Size    Place
    8      L ▶C  R  Title:
    6      L ▶C  R  Subtitle:
    6      L ▶C  R
    2.5    ▶L C  R  Footnote:
    2.5    ▶L C  R
    2.5    ▶L C  R
    5      ↑ ▶↓     Pie 1 title:
    5      ↑ ▶↓
    5      ↑ ▶↓     Pie 2 title:
    5      ↑ ▶↓

                  3D effect           Yes    ▶No
                  Link pies           Yes    ▶No
                  Proportional pies   Yes    ▶No
                  Fill style          ▶Color  Pattern   Both


   F1-Help                    F5-Attributes   F7-Size/Place
   F2-Draw chart                              F8-Data         F10-Continue
```

**Figure 7-9.**   Size/Place overlay

settings refer to left-justified, centered, and right-justified text, respectively. Left-justified text is displayed starting at the left margin. Centered text is displayed in the middle. Right-justified text is displayed with the right-most character even with the right margin. Select the appropriate placement for each line of text.

You can also specify the location of your pie titles. On the four lines of the "Place" column corresponding to the "Pie 1 title" and "Pie 2 title" options are two arrows, one pointing up, the other pointing down. Select the up arrow to display the corresponding text above the pie. Select the down arrow to place the text below the pie.

### Adding a Three-Dimensional Effect to Pies

If desired, you can apply a three-dimensional effect to your pie charts. To do this, set the "3D effect" option to Yes. To suppress a three-dimensional effect, set "3D effect" to No. Figure 7-10 shows examples of pies with and without the three-dimensional effect.

*Note:* Harvard Graphics will not explode a three-dimensional pie. If you set the "3D effect" option to Yes, the "Cut Slice" settings on the Pie Chart Data form will be ignored.

### Creating Linked Pies

The "Link pie" option is a special feature that can only be used when your chart displays two pies. It is used to indicate that the right pie is a breakdown of a single slice of the left pie. Harvard Graphics shows this by using dotted lines to connect one of the slices in Pie 1 with the entire Pie 2 area. This link is shown in Figure 7-11.

There are three steps you must follow in order to create linked pies.

1. Define two pies on the Pie Chart Data form. The pie that is defined as Pie 2 must be a breakdown of one of the slices in Pie 1.

2. Set the "Cut Slice" option on Page 1 of the Pie Chart Data form to Yes for the slice of Pie 1 that Pie 2 refers to. Although you can set more than one slice to be exploded, the cut slice that appears first in the chart will be linked to Pie 2. If the slice you want to link

to Pie 2 is not the first cut slice, change the order of the data in the series. (See the section, "Changing the Order of Slices," earlier in this chapter.)

3. Set the "Link pies" option on Page 1 of the Pie Chart Titles & Options form to Yes.

*Note:* Although Harvard Graphics will not explode a slice when the "3D effect" option is set to Yes, you can use "3D effect" in conjunction with "Link pies." The linked slice will not be exploded, however.

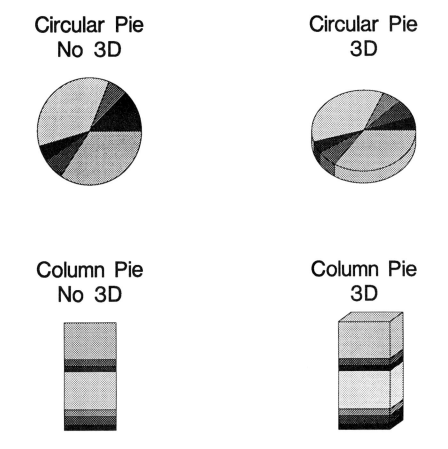

**Figure 7-10.** Effects of 3D settings for pie and column charts

# Linked Pies

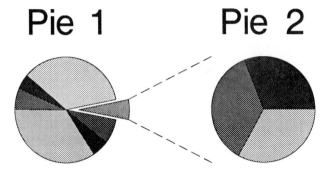

**Figure 7-11.**   Cut slice of Pie 1 linked to Pie 2

## Making Pies Proportional

When your pie chart displays two pies, you can use the "Proportional pies" option to define that the size of your pies should reflect the relative sizes of the pies' series data. When "Proportional pies" is set to No, both pies are identical in size, regardless of the values of each of the pie's data. When "Proportional pies" is set to Yes, Harvard Graphics considers the sum of the series values for each of the pies, and adjusts the size of each pie to reflect this difference. Consider the example displayed in Figure 7-12. Values for Pie 1 are twice as large as values for Pie 2. Setting "Proportional pies" to Yes displays this difference.

*Note:*   When "Proportional pies" is set to No, it is possible to define the size of each pie individually. See "Defining the Pie Size," later in this chapter, for a description of this procedure.

## Selecting a Pie Fill Style

The "Fill style" option gives you the choice of using only color, only patterns, or both color and patterns, to fill pie slices. Set "Fill style" to

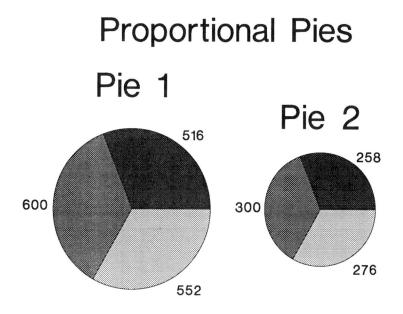

**Figure 7-12.**    Pie 1 is twice as large as Pie 2

Color to display pie slices as solid colors. To display color and patterns, select "Both." To use only patterns to define the slices, set "Fill style" to Pattern. Set the color or pattern for each slice on the Pie Chart Data form, as described previously in the sections "Selecting the Colors of Pie Slices" and "Selecting Patterns for Pie Slices." See Chapter 8, "Producing Output," for more details concerning the impact of color selections on chart output.

## Page 2 of the Pie Chart Titles & Options Form

Page 2 of the Pie Chart Titles & Options form (shown in Figure 7-13) is divided into two columns. The left column is used to set characteristics for Pie 1. The right column is used to set characteristics for Pie 2. The settings available in each column are identical, with one exception: The first option, "Chart style," includes the setting None for Pie 2. This option and the remaining options on Page 2 are described in the following sections.

## Defining Pie Chart Styles

Although pie charts are traditionally shaped like pies, that is, circular, Harvard Graphics allows you to also make column pie charts (Figure 7-10 shows examples of both pie styles). Use "Chart style" to define how Harvard Graphics should display your pies: Pie or Column. In addition, when you want to display only a single pie, set the "Chart style" option for Pie 2 to None.

## Sorting Pie Slices

Use the "Sort slices" option to sort the slices of your pie from largest to smallest. When "Sort slices" is set to No, Harvard Graphics displays the

|  | Pie 1 | | | Pie 2 | | |
|---|---|---|---|---|---|---|
| Chart style | ▶Pie | Column | | ▶Pie | Column | None |
| Sort slices | Yes | ▶No | | Yes | ▶No | |
| Starting angle | 0 | | | 0 | | |
| Pie size | 50 | | | 50 | | |
| Show label | ▶Yes | No | | ▶Yes | No | |
| Label size | 3 | | | 3 | | |
| Show value | ▶Yes | No | | ▶Yes | No | |
| Place value | ▶Below | Adjacent | Inside | ▶Below | Adjacent | Inside |
| Value format | | | | | | |
| Currency | Yes | ▶No | | Yes | ▶No | |
| Show percent | Yes | ▶No | | Yes | ▶No | |
| Place percent | ▶Below | Adjacent | Inside | ▶Below | Adjacent | Inside |
| Percent format | | | | | | |

F1-Help
F2-Draw chart     F8-Data     F10-Continue

**Figure 7-13.**     Page 2 of the Pie Chart Titles & Options form

pie slices using the order in which the series data appear in the Pie Chart Data form. If "Sort slices" is set to Yes, the first slice displayed is the slice with the largest value. The next slice has the second largest value, and so on.

The first slice is displayed starting at the three o'clock position on the pie (as shown in the upper-left pie in Figure 7-14). This position corresponds to a 0 (zero) angle. Each additional slice is added in a counterclockwise direction. If "Chart style" is set to Column, the first slice is the bottom slice, the second slice is stacked on top of the bottom slice, and so on.

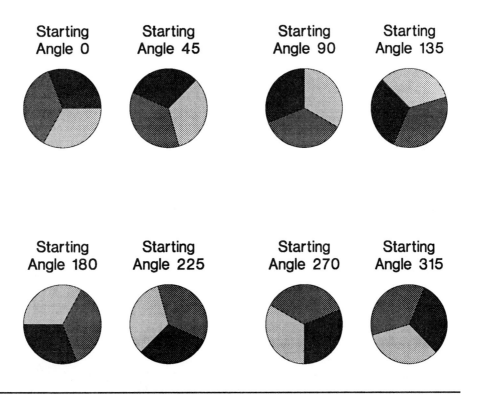

**Figure 7-14.**   Settings for the starting angle of the first (darkest) pie slice

*Note:* When you are displaying linked pies, Harvard Graphics links Pie 1 to Pie 2 on the basis of the first exploded slice displayed on Pie 1. If the "Cut slice" option is set to Yes for more than one slice in Pie 1, setting the "Sort slices" option to Yes for Pie 1 may change the slice Harvard Graphics uses for the link. Use F2-Draw chart to check the order of your pie slices when you use this combination of options.

## Specifying the Starting Angle

The three o'clock position on a pie chart corresponds to an angle of 0, twelve o'clock corresponds to an angle of 90, and nine o'clock corresponds to an angle of 180. To modify the angle at which the first slice in the series will be displayed, set "Starting angle" to a number from 0 to 360. Examples of different starting angles are shown in Figure 7-14.

*Note:* When you are displaying linked pies, Harvard Graphics will override your starting angle for Pie 1 in order to ensure that the cut slice of Pie 1 faces Pie 2.

## Defining the Pie Size

The default pie size is 50. To change this size, set "Pie size" to a number from 1 to 100. This number represents the percentage of the available space the pie will take up when it is displayed or output. The available space for a pie depends on whether one or two pies are displayed, as well as the defined size of the text on your pie chart. Examples of different "Pie size" settings are shown in Figure 7-15.

## Displaying Pie Labels

To display the labels for each pie slice, set "Show label" to Yes. The labels displayed are the names entered in the "Label" column on the Pie Chart Data form. Set "Show label" to No to suppress the display of a

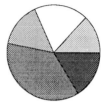
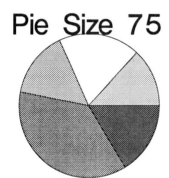
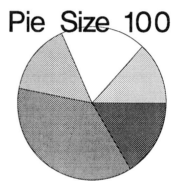

**Figure 7-15.** Examples of pie size settings

label for each pie slice. Pie labels, when displayed, are placed just outside the corresponding pie slice. The effects of "Show label" settings can be seen in Figure 7-16.

### Defining the Pie Label Size

Use the "Label size" option to define the size of the text for pie slice labels, values, and percentages, if displayed. The default value for "Label size" is 3. To change this size, enter a number from .1 to 20.

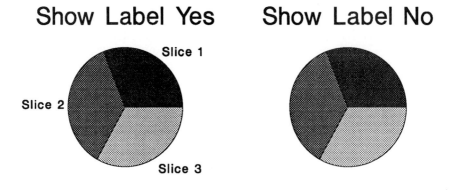

**Figure 7-16.**    Settings for displaying pie labels on the chart

## Displaying Pie Values

You can display the pie values (entered in the "Value" column of the Pie Chart Data form) on your chart. To display these values, set "Show value" to Yes; otherwise, set "Show value" to No.

## Defining the Value Placement

When "Show value" is set to Yes, you can use the "Place value" option to specify where the value is to be displayed. Set "Place value" to Below to center the value below each slice label. Set it to Adjacent to place the value to the right of the label. To place the value within the pie slice, set "Place value" to Inside (the labels will still be displayed outside the pie). Refer to Figure 7-17 for examples of "Show value" and "Place value" settings.

## Formatting Pie Values

The "Value format" option allows you to define a *format* for the pie values displayed on your chart. By entering formatting commands at

"Value format" you can modify how Harvard Graphics will display your pie slice values. This includes adding leading and trailing text to the values, defining the number of decimal places to display, instructing Harvard Graphics to provide commas in values greater than 999, scaling the value data, and displaying the value data in scientific notation. The formats you define for pie values follow the same guidelines outlined for formatting axis values for XY charts. Refer to the section "Customizing Axis Label Formats" and Table 6-6, in Chapter 6, "XY Charts," for a description of the formatting features available in Harvard Graphics.

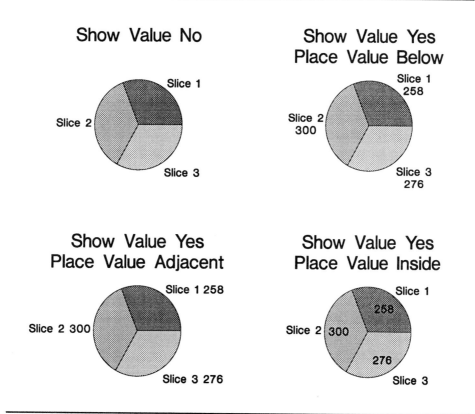

**Figure 7-17.**   Settings for displaying pie values on the chart

## Defining Pie Values as Currency

If your pie values represent dollar amounts, set "Currency" to Yes to display a dollar sign before each pie value, as shown in Figure 7-18. Otherwise, set "Currency" to No.

## Displaying Pie Value Percentages

You can have Harvard Graphics calculate and display the percentage of the pie each slice represents. To do this, set "Show percent" to Yes; otherwise, set "Show percent" to No.

## Defining the Placement of Percentage Values

When you set "Show percent" to Yes, you can define where Harvard Graphics will place the percentage. To define the placement, set "Place percent" to either Below, Adjacent, or Inside. (These are described in the earlier section, "Defining the Value Placement.") See Figure 7-19 for examples of "Show percent" and "Place percent" settings.

*Note:* When "Place value" and "Place percent" are both set to the same placement, the percentage is placed to the right of the value.

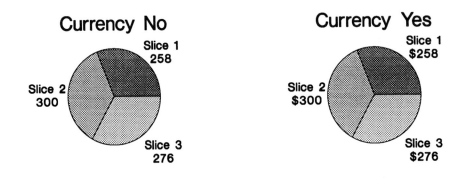

**Figure 7-18.**    Currency settings

Pie Charts 243

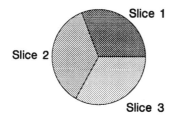
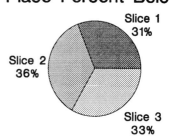
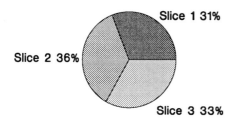
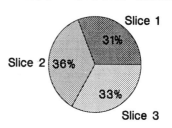

**Figure 7-19.**  Settings for displaying pie percentages on the chart

### Formatting Percentage Values

Similar to the "Value format" option, the "Percent format" option allows you to customize the format of percentages displayed on your chart. Refer to the section "Customizing Axis Label Formats" and Table 6-6, in Chapter 6, "XY Charts," for a description of formatting features available in Harvard Graphics.

## Clearing Data from Your Pie Chart

You can clear all the text and data entered and options set for your pie chart using the <Clear values> option on the Create New Chart menu. Since <Clear values> removes all values entered for the pie chart, it has essentially the same effect as selecting <Create new chart> from the Main Menu followed by <Pie> from the Create New Chart menu. You can use either method to create a new pie chart when your current chart is also a pie chart.

To use <Clear values>, press ESC until you return to the Main Menu, and select <Create new chart>. Select <Clear values> from the Create New Chart menu. If you have not saved your chart since creating or modifying it, Harvard Graphics will display the message "Chart values are about to be cleared. Press Enter to continue; Esc to Cancel." If you want to save your current chart, press ESC, save your chart, and then repeat the preceding steps.

When you have cleared the values from your chart, Harvard Graphics will remove all the text and data entered on your chart and return the option settings to the defaults.

## Changing Chart Styles

To change from a pie chart to a column chart (or the reverse), simply set the "Chart style" option to Column (or Pie) on Page 2 of the Pie Chart Titles & Options form.

Occasionally, you may want to change a pie chart to one of the XY chart styles (bar/line, area, or high/low/close), while retaining all the data you have entered on the Pie Chart Data form. Changing between pie charts and XY charts is described in the following sections.

### Changing a Pie Chart to an XY Chart

To change a pie chart to an XY chart, the pie chart must be the current chart. If you have not saved this chart since you created or last modified it, save it before you continue. (See Chapter 2, "Harvard Graphics Basics," for information on saving charts.)

Return to the Main Menu and select <Create new chart>. Select one of the XY chart styles from the Create New Chart menu. Harvard Graphics will display the Change Chart Type overlay, shown in Figure 7-20, asking you to indicate whether you want to keep the data entered for the current chart. If you select No, the XY Chart Data form for your new chart will be blank.

If you select Yes, Harvard Graphics will use the pie labels specified in the "Label" column on the Pie Chart Data form and place them in the "X Axis" column of the XY Chart Data form. The pie values specified for Series 1 in the "Value" column of the Pie Chart Data form will be placed in the "Series 1" column of the XY Chart Data form. Harvard Graphics also retains the chart title, subtitle, and footnote, and displays them at the appropriate lines of the XY Chart Data form.

If you have more than one series of data for your pie chart, the corresponding pie Series 1 through Series 8 data entered in the "Value" column will be placed in the corresponding "Series 1" through "Series 8" columns. Data from the "Label" column for Pie 1 will *only* be placed in the "X Axis" column on the XY Chart Data form. This means changing

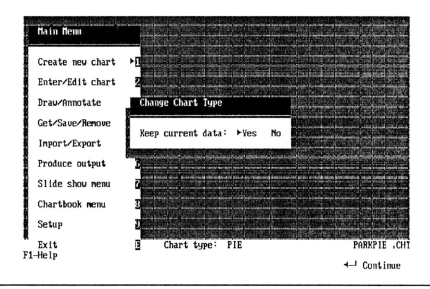

**Figure 7-20.** Change Chart Type overlay

to an XY chart when you have multiple pie series is usually worthwhile only when all the pie series have the same pie labels.

## Changing an XY Chart to a Pie Chart

You can change an XY chart to a pie chart by following the same general steps described in the preceding section. The only difference is that you would start with an XY chart as your current chart, and then select <Pie> from the Create New Chart menu. Since pie charts can only contain a maximum of 12 slices, only the first 12 rows of data will be retained. Data from the series columns on the XY Chart Data form will be placed in the "Value" columns on the Pie Chart Data form for each pie series, Series 1 through Series 8. Data from the "X Axis" column on the XY Chart Data form will be placed in the "Label" column on the Pie Chart Data form for each pie series. This means the pie labels will be the same for all pie series.

# Producing Output

The Produce Output Menu
Preparations for Producing Chart Output
Printing
Plotting
Film Recording
The Effects of Color Settings
Outputting the Charts in a Slide Show
Printing Non-Chart Text

This chapter describes how to produce output. The topics covered include printing and plotting charts, and recording charts on film. In addition to outputting a chart created in Harvard Graphics, several other types of information can be printed. These include the data from your chart, a slide show list, and slide show practice cards.

Once you have set up your printer, plotter, or film recorder (as described in Chapter 3, "Setup and Default Settings"), outputting your chart in Harvard Graphics is as easy as setting options on the appropriate form. If your output device is not yet installed, you will need to refer to your output device manual and the Harvard Graphics manual and install it before you proceed. If your output device is installed but not yet set up, read the appropriate section of Chapter 3.

## The Produce Output Menu

The Produce Output menu (shown in Figure 8-1) allows you to access all Harvard Graphics' outputting facilities. To display the Produce Output

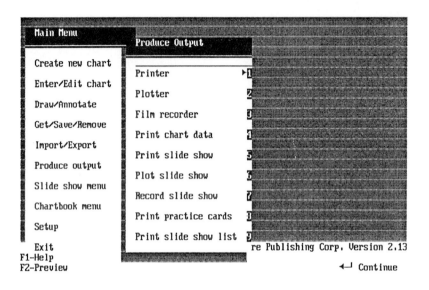

**Figure 8-1.**    Produce Output menu

menu, select <Produce output> from the Main Menu. This menu contains nine options. The first three, <Printer>, <Plotter>, and <Film recorder>, are used to output your current chart. These topics are described in the sections of this chapter entitled "Printing," "Plotting," and "Film Recording." The <Print slide show>, <Plot slide show>, and <Record slide show> options are used to output one or more charts in a slide show. These topics are described in the section "Outputting the Charts in a Slide Show." The <Print chart data>, <Print practice cards>, and <Print slide show list> options do not print charts; instead they allow you to print your chart data, slide show practice cards, and a list of the files in your slide show. These topics are covered in the section "Printing Non-Chart Text" later in this chapter.

## Preparations for Producing Chart Output

The chart you want to output must be the current chart. If it is not the current chart, use <Get/Save/Remove> to retrieve the desired chart. See Chapter 2, "Harvard Graphics Basics," for information about retrieving a previously saved chart.

In order to produce output, your output device must be connected to your computer and must be turned on. In addition, you must have assigned the output device on the appropriate setup form as described in Chapter 3, "Setup and Default Settings." If your output device is not attached to your computer and turned on, or is set up incorrectly, Harvard Graphics will display the message "Output device is not ready. Press Enter to continue; Esc to Cancel." You must resolve the problem before you can produce output.

## Previewing Your Chart Before Outputting

It is always a good idea to first preview your chart before outputting it. Harvard Graphics' previewing feature is only available from the Produce Output menu or one of the produce output forms by pressing F2-Preview. This will display the current chart on your monitor. If you are using a VGA or EGA monitor, the image F2-Preview displays represents Harvard Graphics' best estimate of what your chart will look like when it is output. The image it will display on a CGA monitor is not as accurate.

Harvard Graphics' previewing capabilities on VGA or EGA with F2-Preview are different from the F2-Draw chart view you use while creating a chart. One major difference is the background color used for your chart. Unless you have modified your color palette, the background of your chart using F2-Preview will be white, instead of the black used for F2-Draw chart. Correspondingly, any white text or symbols you have placed on your chart will be displayed in black. This conversion is made because Harvard Graphics translates black to white and white to black for output devices.

If you are previewing your chart on a CGA or monochrome monitor, your chart will appear in black and white only. If you are displaying your chart on an EGA or VGA color monitor, your chart colors will reflect the current color palette settings for your screen (refer to the section "The Color Palette" in Chapter 3, "Setup and Default Settings"), with the exception of the black-white translation. These preview colors may or may not match those used by your color output device. Some output devices use the colors defined in the "Output" columns of the Color Palette Setup form. All other output devices use a set of colors defined by the device.

There are only two background colors Harvard Graphics can display on your monitor in F2-Preview: white and black. If you have changed the background color on your color palette, F2-Preview will not be able to accurately depict the background of your chart and will substitute either white or black for the background. White will be displayed when your palette background is defined as any color other than white. When the background color is set to 1 (white), the background shown using F2-Preview will be black.

The background color defined on your color palette does, however, affect chart output. Refer to the section "The Effects of Color Settings," later in this chapter, for information on using background colors other than black.

If you are satisfied with how your chart looks when you preview it, return to the Produce Output menu and select the appropriate menu option to produce output. If something is wrong with your chart (such as font placement or size), return to the Main Menu and select <Enter/Edit chart> in order to modify the chart.

If your chart includes drawings or annotations, these elements may not be displayed during preview exactly where you originally placed them. This may or may not be a problem. You will probably need to output your chart before you can determine whether the location of drawings or annotations is acceptable. See Chapter 9, "Drawing and Annotating," for details on how Harvard Graphics incorporates drawings and annotations in charts.

## Printing

Select <Printer> from the Produce Output menu to display the Print Chart Options overlay shown in Figure 8-2. This overlay contains six

Producing Output 251

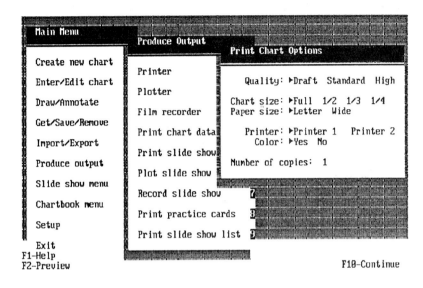

**Figure 8-2.** Print Chart Options overlay

options pertaining to printing your chart: "Quality," "Chart size," "Paper size," "Printer," "Color," and "Number of copies." These options are described in the following sections. Once you set the options on this overlay, press F10-Continue to print your chart.

## Selecting Printing Quality

There are three levels of printer quality: Draft, Standard, and High. One rule of thumb is that the higher the quality you select for your output, the longer it will take Harvard Graphics to print.

On some printers that have internal fonts, these fonts are used when printing quality is set to Draft or Standard. Harvard Graphics fonts are only used in the High quality mode. In addition, text attributes, such as italic or underline, only appear when your chart is printed in High quality.

However, most printers (especially dot matrix printers) will produce text attributes at all levels of output quality. The major difference between output qualities will be the dot density. Harvard Graphics prints more dots when set at the higher output qualities, resulting in a better looking chart.

The "Quality" setting you will use for chart output will depend on a number of factors. Probably the most important of these is your reason for outputting your chart. If your chart is for a report or presentation, you will probably not be satisfied with anything less than High quality. If you are producing your chart to discover or analyze patterns in your data, a chart produced in Draft mode may be adequate.

The type of printer you are using also influences the quality of your chart output. Dot matrix printers in Draft mode rarely produce what is typically considered presentation quality. However, printers that use PostScript will often produce a chart of excellent quality in any mode. Another consideration is that some printers do not support more than one or two output qualities.

If you are printing to a laser printer, the amount of memory your printer has may affect your output. Many earlier models of laser printers that contain only 512K of memory are incapable of producing a full page of graphics at the High setting. You can either reduce your chart size, print at a lower quality setting, or add memory to your printer.

It is worth your time and effort to print a single chart at all three output quality modes (Draft, Standard, and High) on your printer, and use these charts for later reference. This will also allow you to determine how many levels of output quality your printer supports, as well as the approximate amount of time required to print charts at each level of output.

## Selecting Chart Size

There are four chart size settings: Full, 1/2, 1/3, and 1/4. The actual size of your printed chart depends on whether you are using portrait or landscape chart orientation. Figures 8-3 and 8-4 show examples of the four chart sizes as they would be placed on 8 1/2 x 11 inch paper for portrait and landscape orientations, respectively. (Note that for the 1/3 setting, Harvard Graphics actually produces a chart that in overall size is smaller than that produced with the 1/4 setting.)

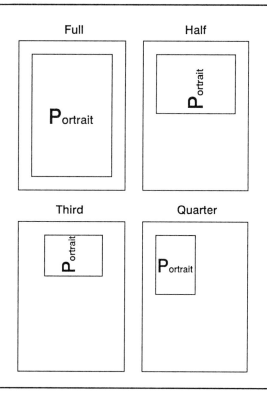

**Figure 8-3.**   Chart sizes used with portrait orientation

## Selecting Paper Size

Harvard Graphics provides two paper sizes. The Letter (8 1/2 x 11 inch) setting is appropriate for most printers. If you have a wide-carriage dot matrix printer (and it is set to print the full width) you can set "Paper size" to Wide to print the chart on 14 x 11 inch paper. The Wide setting will increase your charts' overall size. When "Paper size" is set to Wide, a chart using a landscape orientation is printed vertically (14 x 11 inches) and a chart using a portrait orientation is printed horizontally (11 x 14 inches).

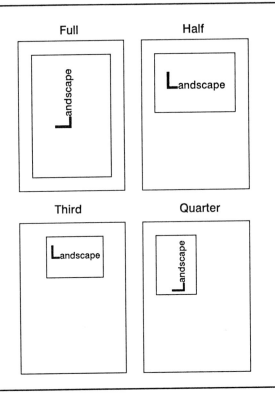

**Figure 8-4.** Chart sizes used with landscape orientation

## Selecting the Printer

Use "Printer" to define which printer, Printer 1 or Printer 2, you wish to use for your chart. The printer you select must have been defined on the Printer 1 or Printer 2 Setup form. (See the section "Setting Default Printers," in Chapter 3, "Setup and Default Settings," for information.)

## Using Color

The "Color" option does not affect printing unless you are using a color printer. When you are printing to a color printer, set "Color" to Yes to print colors and to No to print using only black.

## Printing Multiple Copies

To print more than one copy of the current chart, set "Number of copies" to the number of copies you want to print.

## Plotting

From the Produce Output menu, select <Plotter> to display the Plot Chart Options overlay, shown in Figure 8-5. This overlay contains four options, "Quality," "Transparency," "Pause for pen," and "Number of copies," that are each described in the following sections. Once you set the options on this overlay, press F10-Continue to plot your chart.

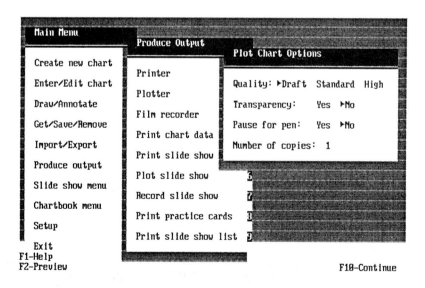

**Figure 8-5.** Plot Chart Options overlay

## Selecting Plotter Quality

There are three levels of plotter quality: Draft, Standard, and High. Similarly to printer output, higher quality output takes longer to plot.

When printing in Draft quality, Harvard Graphics will use your plotter's fonts and patterns instead of solid colors, and will not use text attributes. Standard produces a higher-quality chart, but will also use your plotter's fonts, and will not use text attributes. If you want to use Harvard Graphics' fonts and text attributes, you must plot in High quality.

Some types of charts and some symbols cannot be plotted correctly. For example, Harvard Graphics will not plot a 3D overlap XY chart. These charts will be plotted without the three-dimensional effect. The Harvard Graphics symbols that cannot be plotted are noted in Appendix D.

## Plotting Transparencies

When you are plotting onto transparencies, set "Transparency" to Yes. This will cause Harvard Graphics to move the pens slower, thereby reducing the likelihood of smearing on your chart.

## Pausing for Plotter Pens

If you want Harvard Graphics to stop and wait for you to change pens when you are referencing more colors than your plotter has pen holders, set "Pause for pen" to Yes. When pause for pens is set to No, Harvard Graphics will use all the pens you have holders for, and then start reusing pens in reverse order. For example, if your plotter holds six pens, using color numbers 1 through 6 will cause Harvard Graphics to use the pens in those holders. When color number 7 is requested, Harvard Graphics uses the pen in holder 5, color number 8 uses the pen in holder 4, and so on.

When "Pause for pen" is set to Yes, Harvard Graphics pauses when a pen is requested for which there is no pen holder. In the previous example, if "Pause for pen" is set to Yes and color number 7 is referenced, Harvard Graphics displays the message "Please insert pen for color 7 Yellow. Press Enter to continue; Esc to Cancel." You then place the requested pen in pen holder 2 and press ENTER to continue plotting.

## Plotting Multiple Copies

When you want to plot more than one copy of your chart, enter the number you want at "Number of copies."

## Film Recording

Select <Film recorder> from the Produce Output menu to display the Record Chart Option overlay, shown in Figure 8-6. This overlay contains

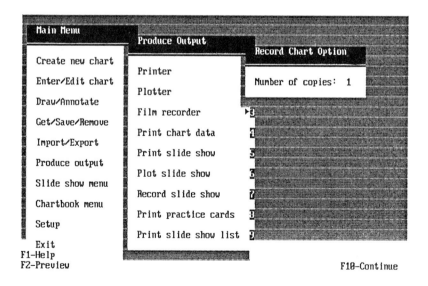

**Figure 8-6.** Record Chart Option overlay

only one option, "Number of copies." Set this option to the number of copies of the chart you want to record, and then press ENTER to begin recording. When you are recording more than one copy of your chart, Harvard Graphics will automatically advance the film between copies.

## Using a Slide Service

You do not need a film recorder in order to create slides of your Harvard Graphics charts. There are many companies that specialize in taking your Harvard Graphics charts and producing them as slides for you. Some of these companies can use a standard Harvard Graphics chart file (.CHT), while others require you to create an output file that can be used by one of the film recorders supported by Harvard Graphics. For more information about these slide services and how to prepare your charts, contact a representative from the service that you are planning to use.

## The Effects of Color Settings

Color settings can influence your chart's appearance whether you output your chart in color or in black and white. For instance, if you change the background setting on your color palette, and the new background color is also a color you are using for other chart elements, these elements will be transparent. This effect will occur whether you are printing to a single-color printer or to a color printer printing either colors or black only.

When you are using a color printer, a pen plotter, or a PostScript capable printer, the effects of your color settings can be even more pronounced. The influence of color on each of these output devices is described in the following sections.

### Color Printing

Not all color output devices can use the 16 colors of the color palette. For example, most color printers can only print eight colors (white, black, and six other colors). In fact only three printers Harvard Graphics supports—CalComp ColorMaster, Hewlett-Packard PaintJet XL, and Tektronix Phaser CP—can produce 16 colors. With the exception of the CalComp ColorMaster, all of the color printers use a color map. This map uses the color number you have assigned to chart elements to determine which color to print. The CalComp ColorMaster uses colors in the palette file called CLRMSTR.PAL, which comes with Harvard Graphics.

Since the colors that appear on your screen may bear little or no resemblance to the colors your printer produces, it is wise to print out your own color reference chart. To do this, print the chart called HG.CHT that comes with Harvard Graphics (make sure the "Color" option on the Print Chart Options overlay is set to Yes). HG.CHT is a two-pie chart that contains one pie slice for each of the 16 color palette settings. Each slice is marked with the color number used to produce the slice. Use this chart to help you select the appropriate colors for your chart elements.

## Color Plotting

The color numbers you define for the elements of your charts and drawings are used to select the pens for your plotter. Any chart element or drawing that is defined as color 1 will be produced using the pen in pen holder 1, elements defined as color 2 will be plotted using pen 2, and so forth. Because Harvard Graphics cannot anticipate the color of the pens you place into your holders, the names that appear in Harvard Graphics' color palette may have no relationship to the colors your plotter will produce.

It is a good idea to use a black pen in holder 1. Although you can fill the remaining holders in any way you choose, it is best to be consistent. For example, always place a blue pen in holder 2, a green pen in holder 3, and so on. After choosing the pen order you intend to use, plot out a reference chart that displays the color of each of these pens. Label these colors with the corresponding pen number so you can use this chart as a color reference.

## Color Film Recording

The colors produced by your film recorder correspond to the color intensity settings defined in the "Output" columns of the Color Palette

Setup form. You should keep in mind that these colors do not necessarily correspond to the colors you see on your monitor. (In fact, they never do match exactly.) In order to aid your color selection when using a film recorder, record the HG.CHT chart that comes with Harvard Graphics (described in the earlier section "Color Printing"). If you use more than one palette with your film recorder, you will want to produce a different HG.CHT chart for each palette.

It is important to keep in mind that there are a number of variables influencing the final output color of the charts you produce with your film recorder. The type of film, as well as the age of your film are among these. If you do not do your own film developing, the company you use to develop the film can also affect the resulting color quality. If you wish to make a number of charts and want to ensure that the colors are consistent, record all of these charts on the same roll or batch of film, and have all your developing done by the same company, preferably one that you have had good service from before.

## Color Settings and Grey Scale Using PostScript

Like color printers that can produce eight different colors, PostScript printers can produce an eight-level grey scale. These eight levels of grey correspond to color palette numbers 1 through 8. Color number 1 produces black, color number 8 produces white, and the remaining numbers produce the intermediate shades of grey. You may want to produce a reference chart, like the one shown in Figure 8-7, that contains these eight levels of grey.

In order to use a grey scale with pie or XY charts, the "Fill style" option on the corresponding Titles & Options form should be set to Color. (See "Bar Fill Style" in Chapter 6, "XY Charts," and "Selecting a Pie Fill Style" in Chapter 7, "Pie Charts.") The "Color" option on the Print Chart Options overlay does not affect these shades, however.

Defining the background color as other than the number 16, the default background color, will have the same effect as on non-PostScript printers. That is, the background of the chart will not be affected or changed. However, if any chart elements are assigned the same color as the background color, these elements will not be visible on the chart.

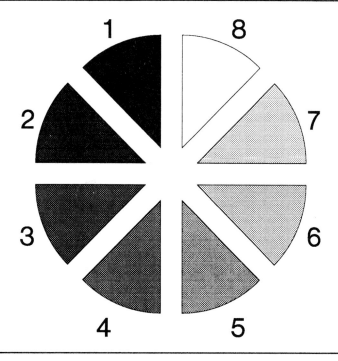

**Figure 8-7.**   A sample grey-scale reference chart

You can trick a PostScript printer into using a background color other than white. To do this, define your printer as Tektronix Phaser CP, which is a color PostScript printer. If you now set your palette background color to a color number other than 16 or 1, the background will appear as a shade of grey as shown in Figure 8-8.

If you do use the color PostScript printer driver for your standard PostScript printer, you must print out the HG.CHT chart for reference. This is especially important because the color PostScript color numbers do not map to the grey scale in a predictable pattern. In other words, although standard PostScript maps to a grey scale using the numbers 1 through 8, a color PostScript does not. Rather, the color PostScript printer driver can use all 16 color numbers, but the eight levels of grey that can be produced are not in an ordered arrangement.

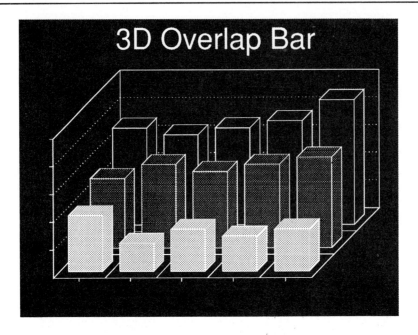

**Figure 8-8.** A sample chart with a shaded background produced with a PostScript printer

## Outputting the Charts in a Slide Show

You can set up Harvard Graphics to print, plot, or record several charts in succession. To do this you must first place the charts that you want to output in a slide show. If you wish to print more than one chart at a time, but are not yet familiar with slide shows, refer to Chapter 13, "Slide Shows," before continuing.

Once your charts are in a slide show, make sure it is the current slide show. Next, select <Print slide show>, <Plot slide show>, or <Record slide show> from the Produce Output menu. If no slide show has been selected, Harvard Graphics will display the message shown in Figure 8-9.

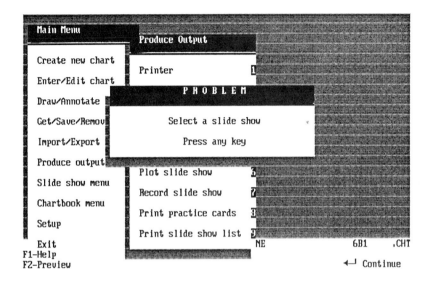

**Figure 8-9.** Message displayed if there is no current slide show

Slide shows can contain four different types of files: Harvard Graphics charts, other Harvard Graphics slide show files, Harvard Graphics templates, and bit-mapped files (files with .PCX or .PIC extensions). Harvard Graphics will not print, plot, or record .PCX or .PIC files. If your slide show includes .PCX or .PIC files, Harvard Graphics will skip over them when producing output.

If you include one or more templates in your slide show, they will influence the charts that come after the template, up until another template is encountered in the slide show. For instance, if the first chart in the slide show is a template that displays your company's logo, and it is the only template in the slide show, all the charts that you print from the slide show will display the logo. The influence of templates in slide shows is discussed in detail in Chapter 13, "Slide Shows."

Including a slide show within a slide show will cause Harvard Graphics to branch to that slide show. When it branches to the included slide show, however, it will not return to the original slide show. For example, if a slide show contains four files, and the third file is another slide show, Harvard Graphics will start producing output from the included slide show when it reaches that point. But the fourth file in the original slide show will not be output.

If you are already familiar with slide shows, you know that slide shows can include special effects called *transitions*. When you display the slide show on a monitor, transitions are used to progress from one file to the next. However, any transitions defined for your slide show will have no effect when you print, plot, or record.

Printing, plotting, or recording a slide show is nearly identical to printing, plotting, or recording a single chart. When you select <Print slide show>, <Plot slide show>, or <Record slide show>, Harvard Graphics displays an overlay. Each overlay is nearly identical to its single-chart counterpart (the Print Chart Options, Plot Chart Options, and Record Chart Option overlays). The difference between these overlays is that the slide show overlays contain three additional options: "From slide," "To slide," and "Collate." Refer to the sections "Printing," "Plotting," and "Film Recording," earlier in the chapter, for descriptions of the duplicated options on these overlays. The three new options are described next.

## Defining the Range of Slides

The "From slide" and "To slide" options allow you to define a range of files to output. These options initially default to the first and last file in the slide show. If you want to print, plot, or record less than an entire slide show, set "From slide" to the slide number you want to start with and set "To slide" to the last slide number you want to output.

## Collating Charts

The "Collate" option is used when you are outputting more than one copy of a slide show. When the "Collate" option is set to Yes, Harvard

Graphics outputs a single copy of all of the files within the defined slide range as one set, and then begins outputting each file again for the second copy, and so on. If you set "Collate" to No, Harvard Graphics outputs the specified number of copies of each file before continuing on to the next file.

## Selecting a Slide Show Chart Size

When you select <Print slide show> from the Produce Output menu, you will see that one of the options on the Print Slide Show Options overlay (shown in Figure 8-10) is "Chart size." When you set "Chart size" to any setting other than Full, Harvard Graphics produces more

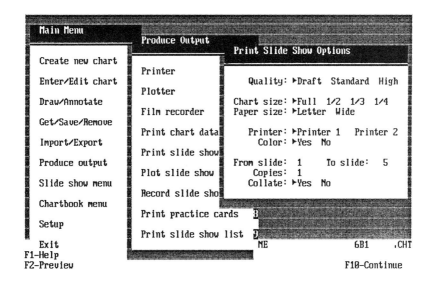

**Figure 8-10.**   Print Slide Show Options overlay

**266** Harvard Graphics: The Complete Reference

than one chart on a page. The number of charts and the order in which they are printed on the page is depicted in Figures 8-11 and 8-12 for each of the "Chart size" settings.

## Printing Non-Chart Text

Besides being able to output your charts, Harvard Graphics permits you to print three types of non-chart text. These are the data for data charts, practice cards for a slide show, and a list of the files in a slide show. These topics are covered in the following sections.

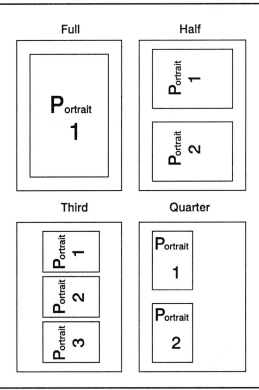

**Figure 8-11.** Portrait-oriented chart output with different size settings

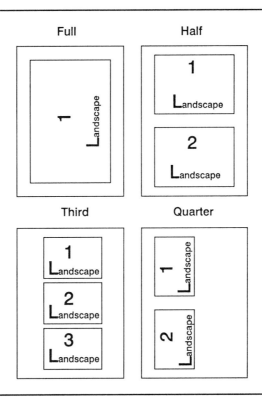

**Figure 8-12.** Landscape-oriented chart output with different size settings

## Printing Chart Data

When your current chart is a data chart (an area, bar/line, high/low/close, or pie chart), you can print the chart data by selecting <Print chart data> from the Produce Output menu. When you do so, Harvard Graphics displays the Chart Data Option overlay, shown in Figure 8-13. Set "Printer" to the desired printer (Printer 1 or Printer 2) on this overlay, and then press ENTER to print the chart data.

## Printing Practice Cards

When you are creating a slide show, you can also create a practice card for each slide to help you prepare for a presentation or to make notes

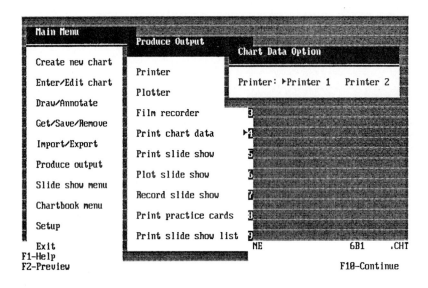

**Figure 8-13.**     Chart Data Option overlay

about your slides (see "Creating Practice Cards" in Chapter 13, "Slide Shows"). The <Print practice cards> selection on the Produce Output menu allows you to print these practice cards.

When you select <Print practice cards> from the Produce Output menu, Harvard Graphics displays the Practice Cards Options overlay, shown in Figure 8-14. This overlay contains four options. The first, "Quality," refers to the printing quality used for the chart associated with each practice card (see the earlier section "Selecting Printing Quality" for information about this option).

When Harvard Graphics prints your practice cards, the chart associated with each practice card is printed below it. (If you set the "Print data" option on a practice card to Yes, Harvard Graphics will also print the data associated with the corresponding chart, if the chart is a data chart.) For more details about practice cards, see "Creating Practice Cards" in Chapter 13, "Slide Shows."

The second option on the Print Cards Options overlay is "Printer." Set "Printer" to the desired printer (Printer 1 or Printer 2) for printing

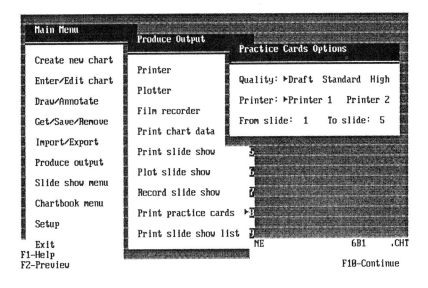

**Figure 8-14.**   Practice Cards Options overlay

your practice cards and any charts. The printer you select must have been defined on the Printer 1 or Printer 2 Setup forms. (See the section, "Setting Default Printers" in Chapter 3, "Setup and Default Settings" for information.)

The remaining two options, "From slide" and "To slide," allow you to define the range of slides for which you want to print the corresponding practice cards. These options default to the first and last files in the slide show. To print practice cards for less than an entire slide show, set "From slide" to the desired starting slide number and "To slide" to the last slide number. Once you have set the desired options, press ENTER to print your practice cards, charts, and any optional data.

## Printing a Slide Show List

When a slide show is current, you can print a list of all of the filenames in the slide show. To do this, select <Print slide show list> from

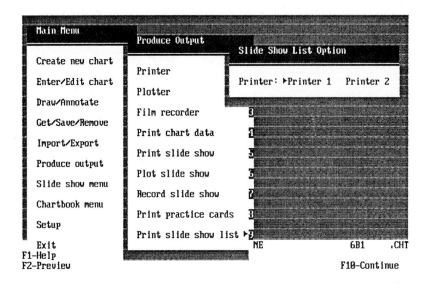

**Figure 8-15.**   Slide Show List Option overlay

the Produce Output menu to display the Slide Show List Option overlay, shown in Figure 8-15. Set the "Printer" option on this overlay to the desired printer (Printer 1 or Printer 2) and then press ENTER.

# Drawing and Annotating

Drawing Overview
Draw Menu Overview
Adding Objects to Your Chart
Modifying Objects
Copying Objects
Deleting Objects
Using a Grid
Using Symbols
Setting Default Options
Advanced Draw/Annotate Topics
Changing the Size and Placement of a Chart

This chapter covers Harvard Graphics' drawing and symbol manipulation features, which you can use to enhance your charts. These enhancements can include annotations (a description added to your chart for information or clarification), your company's logo, a detailed illustration, or a pre-drawn symbol from Harvard Graphics' library of 300 symbols. You can also use Harvard Graphics' drawing features by themselves to create a completely original chart or drawing.

If you have Harvard Graphics' drawing accessory, Draw Partner, you will probably want to use it in conjunction with the drawing and symbol features to create more sophisticated drawings and symbols. Draw Partner is described in Chapter 17, "Introduction to Draw Partner" and Chapter 18, "Drawing and Editing with Draw Partner."

## Drawing Overview

If you have never used Harvard Graphics' drawing and annotating features, there are a number of concepts you should become familiar with before you begin drawing. These include the six types of objects available in Draw/Annotate, the Draw/Annotate screen and its components, the relationship between charts and drawings, cursor movement within the drawing area, adjustment of the default settings for each of the six objects, and using symbols. These topics are discussed in detail in this chapter.

There are six drawing objects you can add to a chart: text, boxes, polylines, lines, circles, and polygons. These objects are referred to as *drawings* when they are added to a chart. Harvard Graphics symbols also consist of drawings. However, a symbol is saved in a separate file from the chart. These files, called symbol files, use the .SYM extension, unlike drawings that are saved as part of a chart, in a .CHT file. A symbol, once it is added to a chart, is nothing more than a collection of one or more drawings.

Harvard Graphics' Draw/Annotate and symbol features are accessed through the <Draw/Annotate> selection of the Main Menu. After selecting <Draw/Annotate>, your screen will resemble Figure 9-1, which shows the Draw/Annotate screen. This screen is divided into

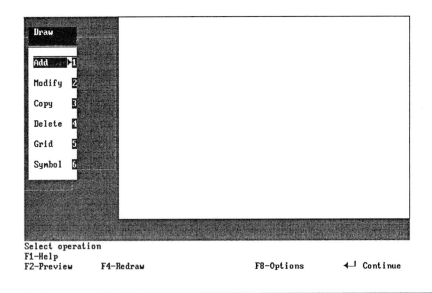

**Figure 9-1.** Draw/Annotate screen

three separate areas: the menu/form area, the drawing area, and the function key banner. As in other areas of Harvard Graphics, the function key banner appears at the bottom of the screen. The menu/form area is on the left side of the Draw/Annotate screen. Any menus or forms related to drawing are displayed in this area. Depending on your computer's monitor and graphics adapter, the precise location of the menus and forms in the menu/form area and the overall look of the Draw/Annotate screen may differ slightly from what you see in the figure. The Draw/Annotate features available, however, are identical.

To the right of the menu/form area is the drawing area—the large rectangle on the right side of the screen. If your current chart has a landscape orientation, the drawing area will be wider than it is tall. If your current chart has a portrait orientation, the drawing area will be taller than it is wide.

*Note:* The Harvard Graphics manual refers to the drawing area of the Draw/Annotate screen as the *chart box*. This area is referred to as the *drawing area* in this book.

## Draw/Annotate and the Current Chart

Drawings and symbols are added to charts. If you want to add drawings or symbols to a chart that already exists, make that chart the current chart, and then select <Draw/Annotate> from the Main Menu. Once you select <Draw/Annotate>, Harvard Graphics displays your current chart in the drawing area. You can then add drawings or symbols. When you save your chart, Harvard Graphics saves these drawings and symbols with the chart in the chart file.

If you want to create a drawing or symbol entirely in <Draw/Annotate>, but do not want the drawing to cover part of your current chart, you must create a blank chart, and then add your drawings or symbols to it. To do this, select <Create new chart> from the Main Menu, followed by <Text> from the Create New Chart menu, and finally <Free form> from the Text Chart Styles menu. Next, press F10-Continue to return to the Main Menu and select <Draw/Annotate>. The drawing area of the Draw/Annotate screen will be blank since you did not add any text to the Free Form Text Chart form. Create your drawings in the drawing area. When you print, plot, record, or display this chart, only the drawings will appear, since there is no chart image present. If you save this chart, Harvard Graphics will save the drawings along with the blank Free Form Text Chart form.

Although you can add drawings to a blank chart of any chart style, the free form text chart is used in the preceding description since it is one that works well for creating a blank chart. Some chart styles do not work as well. Bar/line charts, for instance, display a chart frame even when no text or data has been entered. This frame will appear when you print, plot, record, or display your chart.

## The Drawing Area and Chart Image

When adding drawings to a Harvard Graphics chart, it is important to understand how the chart image and drawings are treated. The chart image and drawings are separate elements of a chart. In Draw/Annotate, when you have a current chart, this chart appears in the drawing area of the Draw/Annotate screen. It is important to note, however, that although the chart appears as if it were on the drawing area, it actually is displayed *behind* the drawing area, as a reference, so you will know where to place your drawings and/or annotations. The drawings you add in Draw/Annotate, on the other hand, are placed directly on the drawing area. This means that any drawings you add will appear in front of, or on top of, the chart image. Figure 9-2, for example, shows that a box and text added in the drawing area appear in front of the chart. You cannot place a drawing behind the chart image.

*Note:* Technically speaking, you cannot place a *drawing* behind a chart. However, if you make your chart a symbol, as described in the section "Saving a Chart as a Symbol," you can make this chart symbol appear in front of other objects. In this situation, however, the chart is not a chart image. Rather, it is a symbol and is placed directly on the drawing area. A drawing *can* be displayed or printed behind a chart, however, when that drawing is placed on a template and included in a slide show. This technique is described in "Including a Template in a Slide Show," in Chapter 13, "Slide Shows."

Because the drawing area is separate from the chart image, if you perform a function that causes the chart elements to move, such as

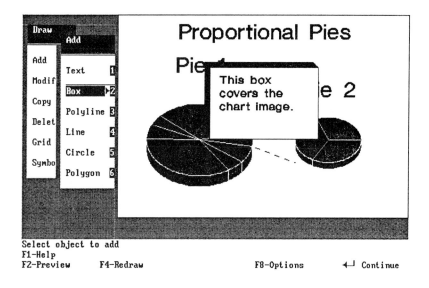

**Figure 9-2.** Chart image is displayed behind the box and enclosed text in the drawing area

adding new data to the chart or modifying chart options that affect the location of objects on the chart, the chart elements will move, but drawings in the drawing area will not move with them. For example, consider the chart on the left in Figure 9-3. An arrow and text were added, using Draw/Annotate to draw attention to one of the series. This chart has a landscape orientation. The right-hand chart in the figure is the same chart converted to portrait orientation. The arrow and text have not moved. Instead, the image of the chart has shifted, and as a result, the arrow no longer points to the desired series. This is just one example of how drawings and chart images are independent in the drawing area.

## Saving Drawings

Although drawings in the drawing area and the chart images Harvard Graphics creates are independent, when you save a chart the drawings you added are saved with it. This is true even if your current chart is

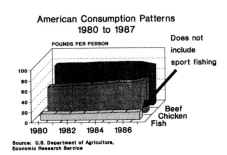 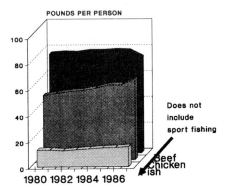

**Figure 9-3.**   Modifying chart orientation affects position but not drawings

blank. To save your current chart after adding drawings, press ESC to return to the Main Menu. Next, select <Get/Save/Remove>, followed by <Save chart> from the Get/Save/Remove menu. Save the chart just as you would save any other chart (see Chapter 2, "Harvard Graphics Basics").

To retrieve your chart once it has been saved to disk, use <Get chart> from the Get/Save/Remove menu. Once you retrieve your chart, Harvard Graphics will display it on the screen, including your drawings. If your chart was blank (no text or data was entered on the chart form), only your drawings will be displayed. Press any key to remove the chart and display the chart form. If you want to add or modify drawings on your chart, return to the Main Menu and select <Draw/Annotate> to display the Draw/Annotate screen.

A second method of saving a drawing created in Harvard Graphics is to save your drawing as a *symbol*. Symbols are drawings that are saved in special files called *symbol files*. Symbols are useful when you want to use the same drawing in a number of different charts (a company logo, for instance). Saving a drawing as a symbol and retrieving symbols for use with charts is discussed in the section "Using Symbols," later in the chapter.

## Draw Menu Overview

When you select <Draw/Annotate> from the Main Menu, the menu/form area contains the Draw menu (see Figure 9-1). The Draw menu contains the six basic drawing functions: Add, Modify, Copy, Delete, Grid, and Symbol. <Add> is used to create objects in the drawing area. <Modify> is used to change objects you have already added in the drawing area. Use <Copy> to duplicate one or more objects and <Delete> to delete one, more than one, or all of the objects in the drawing area. With <Grid> you can create and modify a grid, a tool that assists you with placing objects in the drawing area. Finally, <Symbol> provides you with the tools to create symbols from drawings, retrieve previously saved symbols, and group two or more objects into a single object. Each of these Draw menu options is described in the following sections.

## Adding Objects to Your Chart

All drawings in Harvard Graphics are combinations of one or more of the six basic drawing objects. To add an object to your chart, select <Add> from the Draw menu. The Add menu, shown in Figure 9-4, is displayed, listing the six different objects you can add to your chart.

While you are adding an object, Harvard Graphics permits you to specify options that determine how the object will appear. For instance, you can define the size of the text you add. Likewise, when adding a circle, you can define the color and pattern of the circle's interior. You modify the options for an object on an Options form that lists the

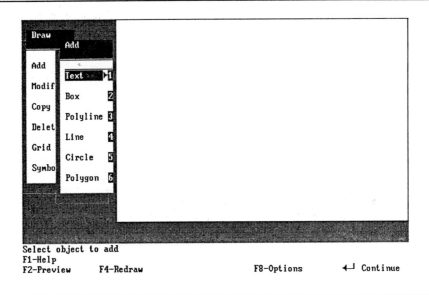

**Figure 9-4.** Add menu

object's default draw settings. To change these settings, press F8-Options, to move your cursor to the Options form. When you set options for an object, you are changing the options for only that addition. You are not changing the default settings. Changing an object's default options is described later in this chapter in "Setting Default Options." Except for the overall size of an object, the effects of an object's option settings will not be apparent until you complete the placement of the object.

Harvard Graphics permits to you add more than one object of the same type without returning to the Add menu. If you do not want to add another drawing of that particular object type, press ESC. Otherwise, continue adding drawings of the selected object type. If you change the option settings for an object while you are adding it, those settings will persist until you either press F8-Options to change them again or you return to the Add menu. When you do return to the Add menu, the options on the Options form revert to their default settings.

If you are not satisfied with the appearance of an object once you add it in the drawing area and/or preview it using F2-Preview, you can modify it (or delete it) as described later, in the section "Modifying Objects."

Each time you add or modify an object, Harvard Graphics updates all the objects in the drawing area. The more objects you add in the drawing area, the longer it takes to update the drawings. However, you can have Harvard Graphics use a quicker mode, so that all the drawing images are not updated with every object addition. (This is particularly useful if you have a slower computer or a number of drawings in the drawing area.) Refer to the later sections "Selecting a Draw/Annotate Display" and "Changing the Redraw Settings" for information.

*Note:* Since the Draw/Annotate screen appears monochrome on a CGA monitor, you cannot view the colors used in objects when the drawing area is displayed, or when you preview your drawings using F2-Preview on this monitor type. To view the colors of your drawings, you must press ESC until you return to the Main Menu, and then use F2-Draw chart. (These colors, however, are your CGA colors, and may not be representative of the colors that will be used if you print, plot, or record your chart and drawings.) Press any key to remove the display, and then select <Draw/Annotate> to return to the Draw/Annotate screen.

## Moving the Cursor in the Drawing Area

When you add an object, select an existing object or group of objects, or move an object or group, you need to move the cursor within the drawing area. You can do this with either a mouse or the cursor keys. Table 9-1 contains a list of the keys you can use to move the cursor in the drawing area.

Three of the keys listed in Table 9-1 permit you to fine-tune this cursor movement: -, +, and *. Press the - key to decrease the distance the cursor travels when you press one of the cursor movement keys. If you press the - key once, subsequent presses of the cursor keys will produce smaller movements than before you pressed the - key. Pressing the - key repeatedly further reduces the size of cursor movements. To increase the distance traveled by the cursor, press the + key. Like the

| Key | Function |
| --- | --- |
| BACKSPACE | Erases last line segment or backs up to reposition first corner of placement box. |
| CTRL-DEL | Deletes entire contents of "Text" line. |
| CTRL-DOWN | Moves cursor to the lower edge of the drawing area. |
| CTRL-END | Moves cursor to the bottom-left corner of the drawing area. |
| CTRL-HOME | Moves cursor to the upper-left corner of the drawing area. |
| CTRL-LEFT | Moves cursor to the left edge of the drawing area. Moves cursor one word to the left in the "Text" line. |
| CTRL-PGDN | Moves cursor to the bottom-right corner of the drawing area. |
| CTRL-PGUP | Moves cursor to the upper-right corner of the drawing area. |
| CTRL-RIGHT | Moves cursor to the right edge of the drawing area. Moves cursor one word to the right in the "Text" line. |
| CTRL-UP | Moves cursor to the upper edge of the drawing area. |
| DEL | Deletes character at the cursor in the "Text" line. |
| DOWN (arrow) | Moves cursor down. |
| END | On the drawing area, moves cursor diagonally, down and to the left. Moves cursor to the last option on a form. |
| ENTER | Places a point in the drawing area. Selects objects in the drawing area. Selects highlighted settings for form options and moves cursor to the next option on the form. |
| ESC | Cancels an operation and returns to the previous screen. For polylines and polygons, completes the placing of the object. |
| HOME | On the drawing area, moves cursor diagonally, up and to the left. Moves cursor to the first option on a form. |

Table 9-1.  Cursor Control Keys and Functions for Drawing

| Key | Function |
| --- | --- |
| INS | Toggles insert mode on and off; the cursor appears as a block when it is on, and as a small line when it is off. |
| LEFT (arrow) | Moves cursor to the left. |
| PGDN | On the drawing area, moves cursor diagonally, down and to the right. |
| PGUP | On the drawing area, moves cursor diagonally, up and to the right. |
| RIGHT (arrow) | Moves cursor to the right. |
| SHIFT | Use in conjunction with mouse or cursor movement keys (DOWN, END, HOME, LEFT, PGDN, PGUP, RIGHT, and UP). Maintains proportions of objects while placing them. Maintains alignment while placing additional lines of text. Maintains vertical or horizontal alignment when moving, sizing, or copying objects, or placing polyline or polygon points. While placing ellipses and boxes, forces them to be perfect circles or squares. |
| SHIFT-TAB | Moves cursor to the previous option on a form. |
| TAB | Moves cursor to the next option on a form. |
| UP (arrow) | Moves cursor down. |
| +, - | Press these keys before using the cursor control keys (arrows, HOME, END, PGUP, and PGDN) in the drawing area to increase or decrease the distance the cursor moves with each keypress. |
| * | Restores default interval for cursor control keys in the drawing area (after they have been changed using + or -). |

**Table 9-1.** Cursor Control Keys and Functions for Drawing *(continued)*

- key, the + key can be pressed repeatedly to further increase the length of the cursor movement. Pressing the * key resets the cursor movement to the original setting.

## Adding Text

To add text in the drawing area, select <Text> from the Add menu. The Text Options form (shown in Figure 9-5) appears in the menu/form area. Enter the text you want to add in the "Text" field, which appears in the top part of the function key banner. The text string you enter can be up to 60 characters in length (the actual number of characters will depend on the text size). You can also enter international text characters, as described in Appendix D. If you want to change the text options, press F8-Options (as described in the next section). You can then return to the "Text" field by pressing F8-Options a second time. When you are ready to place the text you have entered, press F10-Continue or ENTER.

*Note:* You cannot move back to the "Text" field to change your text once you press F10-Continue or ENTER.

After you press F10-Continue or ENTER, Harvard Graphics will display a placement box on the drawing area. This box represents the size of the text you are going to place. Move the box to the location on the drawing area where you want to place the text, and press F10-Continue or ENTER

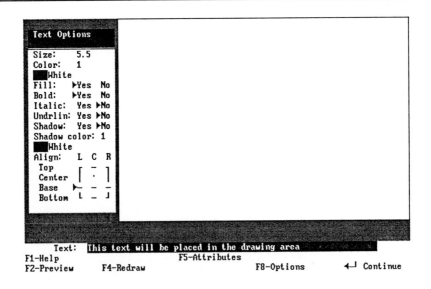

**Figure 9-5.** Text Options form

again. Once the text is added to the drawing area, the "Text" field at the bottom of the screen will once again be empty. You can then enter a new line of text in that field or press ESC to end adding text.

*Hint:* If your text size is too large, Harvard Graphics will not display the placement box. Instead, it will briefly display the message "Text string is too long," and then move the cursor to the Text Options form so that you can change the "Size" option. You cannot edit the text. Change the text size and press F10-Continue or ESC to cancel adding the text.

If you continue adding text, Harvard Graphics will automatically align the text placement box below the line of text that was just added. You can accept this placement or move the placement box to a new location within the drawing area. Press F10-Continue or ENTER to add the text at the selected location. Continue this process until you are done adding text.

When you are adding additional lines of text, pressing the SHIFT key while you move the cursor will help place the text placement box at the same vertical alignment as the previously added text. The farther away the cursor is from the previously placed text, the more helpful the SHIFT key is in aligning the text placement box.

## Setting Text Options

To modify text options, press F8-Options to move the cursor to the Text Options form. The default settings for the options are shown in the form in Figure 9-5. After you set the options on this form, press F8-Options to return to the "Text" field or F10-Continue to place the text placement box in the drawing area.

*Note:* In Harvard Graphics versions 2.13 and earlier, you can only use one text font per chart. To change the font of added text, you must change the default text for the current chart. See "Overriding Default Chart Characteristics" in Chapter 3, "Setup and Default Settings."

## Defining a Text Size

At "Size" enter a number between .1 and 99. Depending on the font, a setting of 5.5 allows about 30 to 35 characters to fit across the drawing area when the current chart is in landscape orientation.

## Selecting a Text Color

At "Color" enter a number from 1 through 16 that corresponds to the desired color for your text. You can also press F6-Choices when the cursor is at "Color" and select a color from the Color Selection overlay, shown in Figure 9-6. The selected color and its name will be displayed

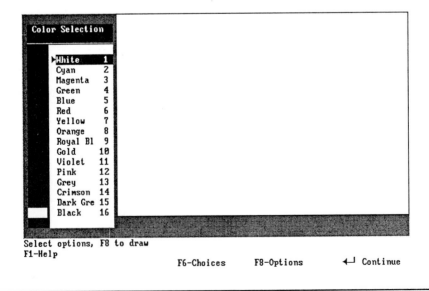

**Figure 9-6.** Color Selection overlay

below the "Color" option on the form. (If you enter a color number manually, the color name will not be updated until you leave the form.)

### Selecting Text Attributes

The following text attributes can be set to either Yes (on) or No (off): "Fill," "Bold," "Italic," "Underline," and "Shadow."

### Selecting a Text Shadow Color

If you set the "Shadow" option to Yes, enter a number from 1 through 16 at "Shadow color" to define the color of the text shadow. Alternatively, with the cursor positioned at "Shadow color," press F6-Choices and select a color from the Color Selection overlay, shown in Figure 9-6. The selected color and its name are displayed below the "Shadow color" option on the form. (If you enter a color number manually, the color name will not be updated until you leave the form.)

### Adjusting Text Alignment

The "Align" option affects the text alignment. The four rows of "Align" correspond to the cursor position in the text placement box. The Top row permits you to align the placement box with the top of such letters as "d" and "l." The Center and Base positions correspond to the top and bottom, respectively, of lowercase letters such as "n" and "w." Bottom aligns to the bottom of such letters as "g" and "p." The three columns of the "Align" option permit you to choose the vertical alignment for the text. Setting align to L, C, or R results in left-justified, centered, and right-justified text, respectively. Choose the align option setting that results in the desired cursor location in the placement box and text alignment.

## Changing Text Attributes

You can define attributes for less than an entire line of text, before adding the text to the drawing area, by using the Text Attributes overlay displayed at the bottom of the screen, as shown in Figure 9-7. The attributes defined on this overlay override the attribute settings on the Text Options form. To define these text attributes, in the "Text" field, first move the cursor to the left-most character of the text whose attributes you want to change. Next, press F5-Attributes to highlight the character at the cursor and display the Text Attributes overlay at the bottom of the Draw/Annotate screen. Use the RIGHT key (or F5-Attributes) to highlight additional characters in the "Text" field. Alternatively, to highlight all the text in the "Text" field, press SHIFT-F5 instead of F5-Attributes. With the desired text highlighted, press TAB to move to the various options on the Text Attributes overlay, and press the SPACEBAR to change the option settings. At the "Color" option, either press the SPACEBAR to select the desired color number, 1 through 16, or press F6-Choices and select a color from the Color Selection overlay, shown in Figure 9-6. Once you have set the desired options, press ENTER

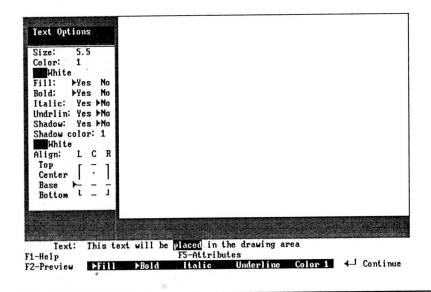

**Figure 9-7.**   Text Attributes overlay

or F10-Continue to remove the Text Attributes overlay and return to the "Text" field to continue with the placement of your text.

### Adding a Bullet

You can place a bullet in the "Text" field by pressing CTRL-B at the desired location in the field. Once you have done so, the Bullet Shape overlay is displayed. Select a bullet shape from this overlay and press ENTER. (See "Adding a Bullet to a Non-Bullet Chart" in Chapter 4, "Text Charts" for more information about chart bullets.)

## Adding a Box

When you select <Box> from the Add menu, Harvard Graphics places the cursor within the drawing area and displays the message "Select first corner" in the function key banner. To place the box, move the cursor to the location where you want to place one of the box corners. It does not matter which corner you place first. With the cursor positioned at the first corner, press ENTER. Harvard Graphics will display the message "Select opposite corner" at the left side of the function key banner. Move the cursor to the opposite corner to define the size of your box. As you move the cursor, Harvard Graphics displays an outline that defines how large your box would be if the location of the cursor were the opposite corner. If the option "Square" on the Box Options form is set to Yes, the box will necessarily be square. When the cursor is at the desired location for the opposite corner of the box, press ENTER.

If you press BACKSPACE after you place the first box corner, but before you place the opposite corner, Harvard Graphics will stop drawing the box, and ask you to place the first corner again. You can then move the cursor to a different location on the drawing area before placing the first corner again by pressing ENTER. Alternatively, you can press ESC before placing the opposite box corner to stop adding a box and return to the Add menu.

Before you place your box (or after you have placed the first corner) you can change the box options by pressing F8-Options, as described in the next section.

## Setting Box Options

Press F8-Options to move to the Box Options form. The default settings for the options are shown in the form in Figure 9-8. After you set the options on this form, press F8-Draw or F10-Continue to return to the drawing area to place your box.

### Selecting a Box Shape

Set "Square" to No to create a rectangular box and to Yes to create a box that is perfectly square. If you set "Square" to No, you can still create a perfectly square box by holding down the SHIFT key while placing the opposite corner of the placement box.

### Selecting a Box Style

Enter a number, 1 through 21, corresponding to one of the box styles shown in the drawing area in Figure 9-8. Alternatively, with the cursor at the "Style" option, you can press F6-Choices to display the Box Styles overlay (shown in Figure 9-9) and select a box style from this list.

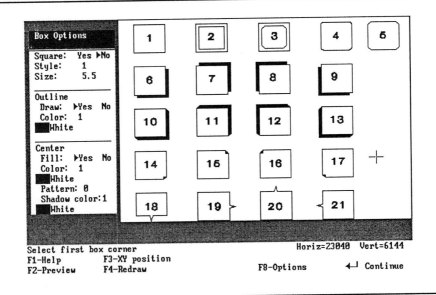

**Figure 9-8.** Box Options form

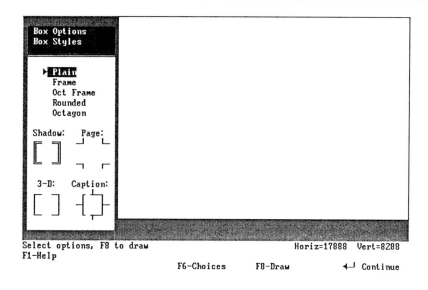

**Figure 9-9.**   Box Styles overlay

### Defining the Size of the Box Style Effect

At "Size" enter a number from .1 to 99. Changing the "Size" number has a different effect on boxes depending on the "Style" selected. These effects are explained in Table 9-2.

| If Your Box Style Is Set To: | The Box Size Setting Affects: |
| --- | --- |
| 2-3 | Width between inner and outer box lines |
| 4 | Roundness of box corners |
| 5 | Size of the diagonally cut corners |
| 6-9 | Width of box shadow |
| 10-13 | Depth of third dimension |
| 14-17 | Width of turned-up page corner |
| 18-21 | Length of caption point |

**Table 9-2.**   Effect of Box Size Setting on Box Style Characteristics

### Selecting a Box Outline and Color

If you want to outline your box, set "Outline Draw" to Yes, and enter a color number, 1 through 16, for the color of the outline at "Outline Color." You can also press F6-Choices when the cursor is positioned at "Outline Color," and select a color from the Color Selection overlay, shown in Figure 9-6. The selected color and its name will be displayed below the "Outline Color" option on the form. (If you enter a color number manually, the color name will not be updated until you leave this form.)

### Selecting a Box Fill, Color, and Pattern

Set "Center Fill" to Yes if you want to fill the center of your box, or to No if you want to display only the box outline (if "Outline Draw" is set to Yes). Enter a color number, 1 through 16, for the color of the box center at "Center Color" or, with the cursor positioned at this option, press F6-Choices and select a color from the Color Selection overlay, shown in Figure 9-6. The selected color and its name will be displayed below the "Center Color" option on the form. (If you enter a color number manually, the color name will not be updated until you leave this form.) Enter a pattern number, 1 through 12, for the pattern of the box center at "Center Pattern." Alternatively, with the cursor positioned at this option, press F6-Choices and select a pattern from the Patterns overlay, shown in Figure 9-10.

*Note:* If both "Outline Draw" and "Center Fill" are set to No, the box will not be visible.

### Selecting a Box Shadow Color

If you select 3D, Shadow, or Page as the box style, set "Shadow color" to a color number, 1 through 16. This color will be used for the third dimension in 3D boxes, the shadow in Shadow boxes, or the turned-up corner in Page boxes. Alternatively, with the cursor positioned at "Shadow color," press F6-Choices and select a color from the Color Selection overlay, shown in Figure 9-6. The selected color and its name

Drawing and Annotating 291

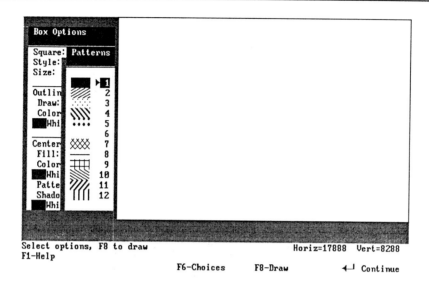

Figure 9-10.     Patterns overlay

will be displayed below the "Shadow color" option on the form. (If you enter a color number manually, the color name will not be updated until you leave this form.)

## Adding a Polyline

A *polyline* is a line that connects two or more points. You place these points by moving the cursor to the desired location on the drawing area and pressing ENTER. Repeat this process until you have placed as many points as you want for your polyline. When you have entered the last point, press ESC. Once you press ESC, Harvard Graphics draws a line from the first point you placed to the second point, then to the third point, and so on until all the points are connected. If the "Close" option has been set to Yes, the last point will be connected to the first point placed. If the polyline option "Shape" is set to Curve, the curved polyline may not actually touch each of the points. Instead, the path of the curved polyline will follow roughly the same pattern as your points.

To place a polyline, select <Polyline> from the Add menu. Harvard Graphics will display the message "Enter to add point, Esc to quit." Place your points as just described. When placing points, you can align the point vertically or horizontally with the preceding point by holding down the SHIFT key. If you make an error while placing a point, press BACKSPACE to erase the last placed point. If you press BACKSPACE more than once, Harvard Graphics will, one at a time, erase the points you placed, in reverse order. When you are done placing your points, press ESC. Harvard Graphics will then draw your polyline.

At any time while you are placing a polyline (or before you begin doing so), you can modify the polyline options by pressing F8-Options. After changing your polyline options, press F8-Draw or F10-Continue to return to drawing the line. If you have already placed one or more points for your polyline, Harvard Graphics will return you to the last point you placed.

Once you have placed a polyline, Harvard Graphics is prepared to place another polyline. If you want to do so, move the cursor to the location of the first point of the new polyline and begin placing points. If you are through placing polylines, press ESC.

## Setting Polyline Options

Press F8-Options to move your cursor to the Polyline Options form, shown in Figure 9-11. After you have set the polyline options on this form, press F8-Draw or F10-Continue to return to the drawing area.

### Selecting a Polyline Color

At "Color" enter a number, 1 through 16, corresponding to the desired color for your line. Alternatively, with the cursor positioned at this option, press F6-Choices and select a color from the Color Selection overlay, shown in Figure 9-6. The selected color and its name will be displayed below the "Color" option on the form. (If you enter a color number manually, the color name will not be updated until you leave this form.)

### Selecting a Polyline Style

At "Style," select one of the four line styles for your polyline: solid, dotted, dashed, or bold. The bold setting is shown on the form as a double line, but the polyline will be bold when it is placed in the drawing area, as shown in the drawing area of Figure 9-11.

### Selecting a Polyline Shape

Set "Shape" to Sharp if you want straight line segments, or to "Curved" to create a curved polyline. When you set "Shape" to Curved, the smoothness of your polyline will be determined by its points. The curve will be smoother if the points are closer together. Examples of both shapes are shown in the drawing area in Figure 9-11. The numbers 1 through 4 indicate the points placed for the polyline.

### Creating a Closed Polyline

Set "Close" to Yes to close the line and form a polygon. This is the only way you can create a rounded polygon in Harvard Graphics. These "rounded polygons," however, cannot be filled, unlike ordinary polygons.

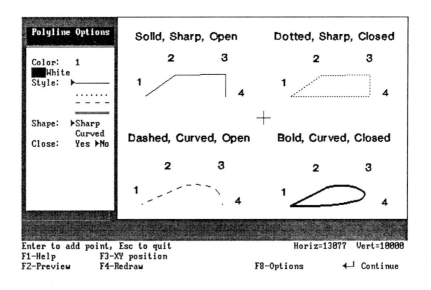

**Figure 9-11.** Polyline Options form

Examples of open and closed polylines are shown in the drawing area in Figure 9-11. The numbers 1 through 4 indicate the points placed for the polyline.

### Making a Curved Polyline Touch a Point

When "Shape" on the Polyline options form is set to Curved, the polyline does not necessarily touch each point you place. To force Harvard Graphics to make the curved polyline touch a specific point, press ENTER three times when you are placing the point you want the polyline to touch.

## Adding a Line or Arrow

To add a line or arrow to your drawing, select <Line> from the Add menu. Harvard Graphics will display the message "Enter to add point, Esc to quit." Press ENTER to add the first point of the line. Next, move the cursor to where you want the line to end, and press ENTER again. Harvard Graphics will draw a straight line between the two points you entered. If you hold down the SHIFT key while moving your cursor to the second point, Harvard Graphics will make the line perfectly horizontal or vertical, depending on the direction of cursor movement. Before adding a line or after you have placed the first point, you can press F8-Options to change the line options, as described in the following section.

## Setting Line Options

Press F8-Options to move the cursor to the Line Options form (shown in Figure 9-12) to modify options for your line. After you set the options on this form, press F8-Draw or F10-Continue to return to the drawing area. (Note that the chart used to create the drawing area in Figure 9-12 has a portrait orientation.)

### Selecting Lines or Arrows

At "Arrows" select either a plain line (the first setting), a left arrow, a right arrow, or a two-way arrow. If you choose the left arrow, the arrowhead will be drawn at the first point you place. Similarly, if you

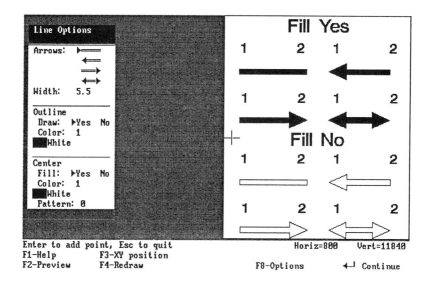

**Figure 9-12.**   Line Options form

select the right arrow, the arrowhead will be drawn at the last (second) point you place. The two-way arrow will result in arrowheads being drawn at both ends of the line.

### Defining the Width of Lines

Enter a number from 1 through 100, for the width of the lines and arrows. This number represents the percentage of chart height that the line width will be.

### Selecting a Line Outline and Color

If you want to add an outline around your line or arrow, set "Outline Draw" to Yes. Enter a color number, 1 through 16, for the color of the outline at "Outline Color." Alternatively, with the cursor positioned at this option, press F6-Choices and select a color from the Color Selection overlay, shown in Figure 9-6. The selected color and its name will be displayed below the "Outline Color" option on the form. (If you enter a color number manually, the color name will not be updated until you leave this form.)

### Selecting a Line Fill, Color, and Pattern

Set "Center Fill" to Yes if you want to fill your line, or to No if you want to display only the line outline (if "Outline Draw" is set to Yes). Enter a color number, 1 through 16, for the line at "Center Color," or with the cursor positioned at this option, press F6-Choices and select a color from the Color Selection overlay, shown in Figure 9-6. The selected color and its name are displayed below the "Center Color" option on the form. (If you enter a color number manually, the color name will not be updated until you leave this form.) Enter a pattern number from 1 through 12 for the pattern used in the line at "Center Pattern" or with the cursor positioned at this option, press F6-Choices and select from the Patterns overlay, shown in Figure 9-10.

*Note:* If both "Outline Draw" and "Center Fill" are set to No, the line placed will not be visible.

## Adding a Circle

To add a circle or ellipse to your drawing, select <Circle> from the Add menu. Once you have done so, Harvard Graphics displays the message "Select circle center." Move your cursor to the location on the drawing area where you want your circle to be centered and press ENTER. Once you define the center, Harvard Graphics displays the message "Select opposite box corner." Move the cursor away from the center of the circle in a diagonal direction. That is, move the cursor both down and away, or up and away, from the circle center. As the cursor moves diagonally from the circle center, Harvard Graphics displays a box that the circle will fill when it is placed. If you set the "Shape" option to Circle, this box will be a perfect square. If the "Shape" option is set to Ellipse, the box may be either rectangular or square. When the placement box is the correct size, press ENTER. Harvard Graphics will then draw the circle or ellipse within the region defined by the box. The box will no longer be visible.

At any time while you are adding a circle, you can change the circle options by pressing F8-Options as described in the following section.

## Setting Circle Options

Press F8-Options to move the cursor to the Circle Options form (shown in Figure 9-13) to modify options for your circle. After you set the options on this form, press F8-Draw or F10-Continue to return to the drawing area.

### Selecting a Circle Shape

Select the desired shape, Circle or Ellipse at "Shape." Examples of both shapes are shown in the drawing area in Figure 9-13. If you select Ellipse, you can still create a perfect circle by holding down the SHIFT key while placing the corner of the placement box.

### Selecting a Circle Outline and Color

If you want to add an outline around your circle or ellipse, set "Outline Draw" to Yes. Enter a color number, 1 through 16, at "Outline Color."

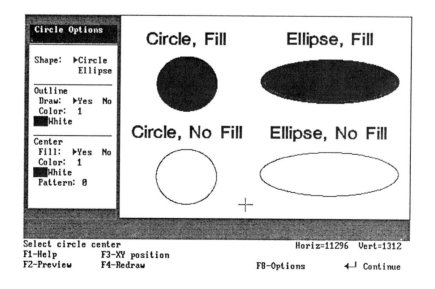

**Figure 9-13.**     Circle Options form

Alternatively, with the cursor positioned at "Outline Color," press F6-Choices and select from the Color Selection overlay, shown in Figure 9-6. The selected color and its name will be displayed below the "Outline Color" option on the form. (If you enter a color number manually, the color name will not be updated until you leave this form.)

### Selecting the Circle Fill, Color, and Pattern

Set "Center Fill" to Yes if you want to fill the center of your circle or ellipse or to No if you want to display only the outline (if "Outline Draw" is set to Yes). Examples of "Fill" settings are shown in the drawing area in Figure 9-13. Enter a color number, 1 through 16, at "Center Color," or with the cursor positioned at this option, press F6-Choices and select a color from the Color Selection overlay, shown in Figure 9-6. The selected color and its name will be displayed below the "Center Color" option on the form. (If you enter a color number manually, the color name will not be updated until you leave this form.) Enter a pattern number, 1 through 12, for the pattern used in the circle or ellipse center at "Center Pattern." Alternatively, with the cursor positioned at this option, press F6-Choices and select from the Patterns overlay, shown in Figure 9-10.

*Note:* If both "Outline Draw" and "Center Fill" are set to No, the circle or ellipse placed will not be visible.

## Adding a Polygon

A *polygon* is a multi-sided object. You define a polygon by entering three or more points. The lines between each of the consecutive points become a side to the polygon. If you enter three points, your polygon will be a triangle, four points will create a quadrangle, and so on. The steps used for adding a polygon are identical to those used for adding a polyline. The only differences between the two are the options on the corresponding Options forms and the shapes of the resulting objects. For example, polygons always close, whereas you choose whether to close polylines. Polygon options are described in the following sections.

## Setting Polygon Options

Press F8-Options to move the cursor to the Polygon Options form (shown in Figure 9-14) to modify options for your polygon. After you set the options on this form, press F8-Draw or F10-Continue to return to the drawing area.

### Selecting a Polygon Outline and Color

If you want to add an outline around your polygon, set "Outline Draw" to Yes. Enter a color number, 1 through 16, for the color of the outline at "Outline Color," or with the cursor positioned at this option, press F6-Choices and select a color from the Color Selection overlay, shown in Figure 9-6. The selected color and its name will be displayed below the "Outline Color" option on the form. (If you enter a color number manually, the color name will not be updated until you leave this form.)

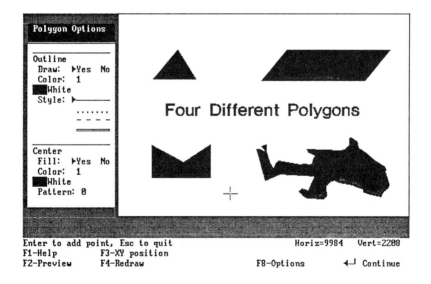

**Figure 9-14.**  Polygon Options form

### Selecting a Polygon Style

At "Style," select one of the four styles for the line: solid, dotted, dashed, or bold.

### Selecting a Polygon Fill, Color, and Pattern

Set "Center Fill" to Yes if you want to fill your polygon, or to No if you want to display only the outline (if "Outline Draw" is set to Yes). Enter a color number, 1 through 16, for the color of the polygon at "Center Color." Alternatively, with the cursor positioned at this option, press F6-Choices and select a color from the Color Selection overlay, shown in Figure 9-6. The selected color and its name will be displayed below the "Center Color" option on the form. (If you enter a color number manually, the color name will not be updated until you leave this form.)

Enter a pattern number from 1 through 12 for the pattern used in the polygon at "Center Pattern." Alternatively, with the cursor positioned at this option, press F6-Choices and select a pattern from the Patterns overlay, shown in Figure 9-10.

*Note:* If both "Outline Draw" and "Center Fill" are set to No, the polygon placed will not be visible.

## Selecting Objects

Once objects are present in the drawing area of the Draw/Annotate screen, you can manipulate and modify them. In order to perform any operations on your objects, however, you need to first select the object or objects to be operated on. This involves two steps. First you indicate what type of operation you want to perform. For example, select <Copy> from the Draw menu to indicate that you want to copy one or more objects. In the second step, you must indicate which object or objects you want to perform the operation on. This is referred to as *selecting* the object.

The next two sections describe how to select single and multiple objects.

## Drawing and Annotating 301

### Selecting a Single Object

Once you select <Copy>, one of the Modify menu selections, or <Delete>, Harvard Graphics displays the message "Select object." To select an object move the cursor in the drawing area until it is positioned on the object you want to select, and then press ENTER. Small markers called *object handles* are then placed at the four corners of an imaginary rectangle that completely encompasses the object you have selected. In addition, a bar appears at the top left of the function key banner with three choices: Choose this, Select next, and Retry. Figure 9-15 displays this bar. If Harvard Graphics has correctly identified your object, select Choose this. The object is now chosen and you can continue with the Draw/Annotate operation.

If you press ENTER and the cursor was not within the imaginary rectangle, Harvard Graphics will not select the object and will display the message "Select opposite box corner." At this point you have two

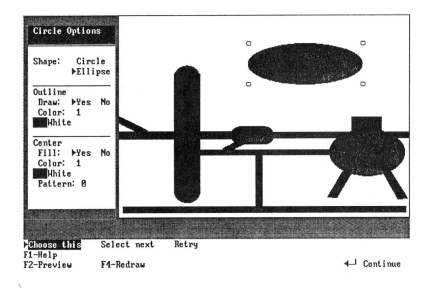

**Figure 9-15.**   Selected object and choices in function key banner

choices. The first, and often the easiest, is to press ESC and start over. Doing so cancels the procedure and returns you to the menu displayed in the menu/form area.

Your second option is to move the cursor to define a box that completely encloses the object you want to select. If you can enclose the object in a box, move the cursor to the opposite corner of this box and press ENTER; otherwise press ESC. If the box you define completely encloses your object, Harvard Graphics will surround it with object handles. Select Choose this and continue with the Draw/Annotate operation. If more than one object is selected, press ESC and start over.

If, while selecting an object, Harvard Graphics identifies an object next to the one you were trying to select, choose Select next or Retry from the bar. If you select Retry, Harvard Graphics will again display the message "Select object." Try again to select your object. If instead you choose Select next, Harvard Graphics will select the next nearest object. If it does not select the correct object this time, you can choose Select next repeatedly until Harvard Graphics selects the correct object. Once it selects the correct object, select Choose this, and continue. If Harvard Graphics cannot find your object, the message "Select opposite box corner" will appear. If this happens, follow one of the procedures described earlier.

### Selecting Multiple Objects

There are two ways to select more than one object. The first is to use the <Group> option from the Symbol menu to combine the different objects into a single object. This is described in a later section entitled "Grouping Objects." The second method is similar to the one used to select a single object. When the "Select object" message appears, identify a box that encloses every object you want to select. (Objects you do not want to select cannot be in this box. If you cannot enclose only the objects you want to select, you cannot use this method to select multiple objects.)

To identify the box, place the cursor at one corner of an imaginary box that will enclose all of the desired objects, and press ENTER. If the cursor was not too close to any one object, Harvard Graphics will display the message "Select opposite box corner."

If Harvard Graphics selects a single object, choose Select next until it stops selecting single objects and displays the message "Select opposite box corner." Move the cursor diagonally until all desired objects are completely enclosed in the box. It is important that every object you want to select is completely within this box. Objects only partially in the box will not be selected.

Once your box is the correct size, press ENTER again. Harvard Graphics will now enclose each of your selected objects in imaginary rectangles with object handles at the corners, as shown in Figure 9-16. If all of your desired objects were selected, select Choose this. Now continue to perform your desired operation.

If no objects were completely enclosed in the box you indicated, Harvard Graphics will again display the message "Select object." If the box you indicated did not contain all the objects you wanted, or contained some objects you did not want, select Retry.

***Hint:*** As you can gather from the previous description, selecting more than one object can be rather difficult. Part of the trick to successfully selecting multiple objects lies in the initial starting point for the selection box. Try to plan which objects will and will not completely lie within your selection box before you use this method of selection.

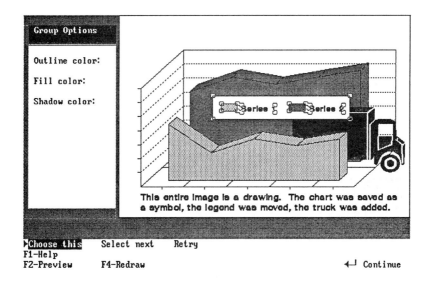

**Figure 9-16.** Group Options form and objects selected for group

## Modifying Objects

After you have placed objects in the drawing area, you can use the <Modify> selection from the Draw menu in order to change them. The Modify menu (shown in Figure 9-17) lists the changes you can perform on an object or objects. These include moving, changing size, changing the options, or changing the relative positions of objects that overlap (front to back). Once you have selected an alternative from the Modify menu, Harvard Graphics will display the message "Select object." If you select more than one object, the modification you selected will be performed on all those objects.

The Modify menu selections are detailed in the following sections. Although these topics discuss modifying a single selected object, you can apply the same modifications to a group of selected objects.

### Moving an Object

<Move> allows you to change the relative location of an object in the drawing area. After selecting <Move> from the Modify menu, select

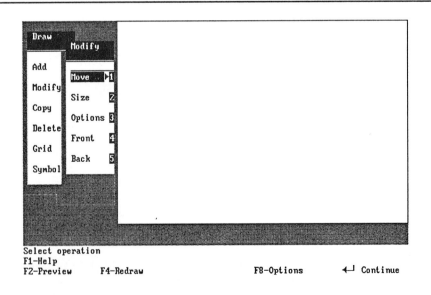

**Figure 9-17.** Modify menu

the object you want to move. Once it is selected, use the cursor to move the box that defines the selected object to the desired location in the drawing area. To maintain the original vertical or horizontal alignment of an object, hold the SHIFT key down while moving the object.

## Changing the Size of an Object

<Size> allows you to change the size of an object in the drawing area. Once you select <Size> from the Modify menu, select the object whose size you want to change. Harvard Graphics will draw a box around the object, placing the cursor at the nearest corner of this box, and will display the message "Select opposite box corner." Use the cursor to move this corner of the box to a new location. When you press ENTER, Harvard Graphics will redraw the object within the box you defined.

*Note:* Harvard Graphics will maintain the width to height proportion of certain types of objects. These include text, boxes that are defined as square, and circles that are defined as circles. Harvard Graphics will modify the size of these objects as long as the newly defined sizes are the same proportions as the objects.

Which corner of the object you move influences the amount of resizing you can do. You can control which corner you use for sizing by keeping in mind that Harvard Graphics lets you size the object using the corner nearest to the cursor when you selected the object.

### Moving and Sizing an Object in One Step

You can both size and move an object at the same time using the <Size> selection from the Modify menu. After selecting the object to size, press BACKSPACE. Harvard Graphics displays the message "Select first box corner." Move the cursor to the position on the drawing area where you want to move the selected object, and press ENTER. Harvard Graphics then displays the message "Select opposite box corner." Move the cursor to the opposite corner of the imaginary box, stretching the box until it is the correct size, and press ENTER. Harvard Graphics will display your object in the new location and size.

*Hint:* To maintain the original proportions of the object, hold down the SHIFT key while moving the cursor to the opposite box corner. Keep the SHIFT key depressed until you press ENTER.

## Modifying Options

You can modify options for an object in the drawing area by selecting <Options> from the Modify menu. Harvard Graphics prompts you with "Select object." Once you select the object, Harvard Graphics displays the Options form for the selected object. Modify the desired options on the Options form and then press F10-Continue to apply the changes and return to the Modify menu. Alternatively, press F8-Draw to further modify the object, as described in the following sections.

### Modifying Text Options

When your selected object is text, Harvard Graphics places the cursor in the "Text" field. You can make any changes to the text, including pressing F5-Attributes to change text attributes for some or all of the text. To change options, press F8-Options or F10-Continue. Once you set options on the displayed Text Options form, press F10-Continue to apply changes to the text and return to the Modify menu. Alternatively, press F8-Draw to both apply changes and select a new location for the text by moving the text placement box to the desired location.

### Modifying Line, Polyline, or Polygon Options

After you select either a line, polyline, or polygon, Harvard Graphics will place the cursor in the corresponding Options form. Change the desired options on this form, and then press F10-Continue to apply the changes and return to the Modify menu.

You can also press F8-Draw to change the shape of the line, polyline, or polygon. If you do so, Harvard Graphics places the cursor at the last point added to the object. To move this point, move the cursor, press BACKSPACE to erase the point (and the points before it as well if you continue to press BACKSPACE); or add additional points (for polylines and polygons only). When you are finished modifying the object, press F10-Continue.

### Modifying Box and Circle Options

After selecting a box or circle, the cursor will be in the Box or Circle Options form. Change the options on this form, and then press F10-Continue to apply your changes and return to the Modify menu. Alternatively, press F8-Draw to apply the changes and modify the location or size of the object. If you press F8-Draw, Harvard Graphics will place the cursor at one of the corners of the box that encompasses the object. To change the size, move the cursor until the box is the desired size. If you want to modify both the size and location of the box or circle, press BACKSPACE and then place the object and size it.

*Note:* If you change the size of a box or circle, you can use SHIFT while placing the opposite box corner to maintain the proportions of the original object.

### Modifying Options of Multiple Objects

When you choose <Options> from the Modify menu, and then select more than one object, the types of modifications you can make depend on the types of objects selected. If all the objects selected are the same type (all text, for example), you can change the options for all of the objects using the Options form specific to that object type. However, if your selected objects are a mixture of object types (a box, a circle, and a polyline, for example) Harvard Graphics will permit you to change only certain characteristics common to all of the objects.

When you select different types of objects, Harvard Graphics displays the Group Options form, shown in Figure 9-16. This form allows you to change the outline color, fill color, and shadow color (as applicable) for all of the objects selected. The outline color affects the outlines of all six types of objects. For text and polylines, the outline color defines the entire color of the object. Fill color modifies the color of any fill used in boxes, lines, circles, and polygons. Shadow color affects the color of any shadows used in text and boxes.

You cannot size or place a group of objects after you modify the options as you can when you modify a single object. To size and place a group of objects, you must use the <Size> and <Move> selections of the Modify menu individually.

## Changing Object Order

Objects that are placed in the drawing area are drawn in the order of their placement. The first item placed is drawn first, the second item placed is drawn second, and so forth. You can see this order of object precedence by pressing F4-Redraw to have Harvard Graphics immediately update the drawing area image. If you overlap objects or place objects on top of existing objects, the front objects will cover some or all of the back objects.

This order, or object precedence, can be changed with the <Front> and <Back> options from the Modify menu. Use <Back> to move the selected object or objects to the back of the drawing area. Likewise, use <Front> to move objects forward, making them the last to be drawn.

For example, imagine you are creating a chart that will be used as an exit sign. After placing the text object, EXIT, onto the drawing area, you decide it would be nice to place a box with a drop shadow entirely around the word. Once you place the box around the text, however, the text will no longer be visible. At this point, select <Back> to move the box object behind the text. Once you press F4-Redraw, EXIT will appear in front of the box, as shown in Figure 9-18.

## Copying Objects

You can copy one or more objects in the drawing area. To do this, select <Copy> from the Draw menu, and then select the object you want to copy. Harvard Graphics will display a box that represents the object you are copying and the message "Position box, press Enter." Move the box to the location in the drawing area where you want to place a copy of the selected object, and then press ENTER to place the copy. To use the

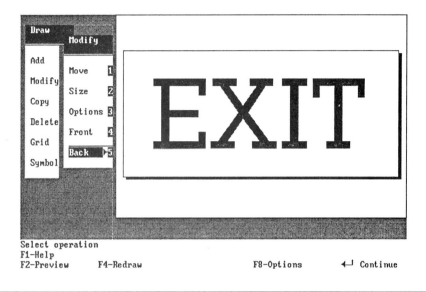

**Figure 9-18.** Final drawing with box moved to the back

same vertical or horizontal alignment as the original object, hold the SHIFT key down while placing the copy.

After the copied object has been placed, Harvard Graphics displays another box representing an additional copy of the object. Harvard Graphics anticipates where you want this second copy based on the difference between the position of the original object and the location where you placed the copy. If you do not want to make another copy of the object, press ESC. Otherwise, place the second copy. You can continue by placing additional copies, as desired. Press ESC when you are finished placing copies of the object.

## Deleting Objects

Select <Delete> from the Draw menu to display the Delete menu shown in Figure 9-19. There are three options on the Delete menu,

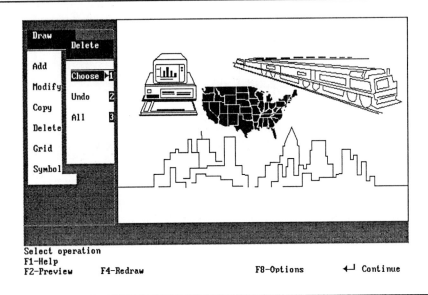

**Figure 9-19.** Delete menu

<Choose>, <Undo>, and <All>, which allow you to delete one or more objects as well as undo (recover) the last deleted object.

## Deleting One or More Objects

If you want to delete one or more objects, but not all the objects in your drawing area, select <Choose>. Then select the object or the group of objects you want to delete.

## Recovering a Deleted Object

Select <Undo> to recover your last deleted object after using <Choose> from the Delete menu. Once you have returned to the Harvard Graphics Main Menu, however, <Undo> is no longer available. If you used <Choose> to delete more than one object, <Undo>

will only recover the front-most object that was deleted. <Undo> cannot recover any objects if you used the <All> selection from the Delete menu.

### Deleting All Objects

Select <All> from the Delete menu to remove all the objects in the drawing area. Harvard Graphics will display the message "Delete all drawings?" and ask you to confirm the deletion. Select Yes to delete all the objects or No to cancel the deletion.

*Note:* Deleting all objects in the drawing area will not affect the chart image, if one is present.

## Using a Grid

A *grid* consists of points that are placed at the intersections of invisible rows and columns in the drawing area, as shown in Figure 9-20. These points are evenly spaced in a grid formation. A grid can help you align and more accurately place objects in the drawing area. Select <Grid> from the Draw menu to display the Grid form (shown in Figure 9-20) to modify the grid options "Size," "Show," and "Snap." The following sections discuss the use of each of these three options.

### Changing Grid Size

The number entered at "Size" affects the distance between points on the grid. You change the grid size by entering a number from 1 through 25. If you select 25, the drawing area will have only four points along the shorter axis. If you select 1, there will be 100 points along the shortest dimension.

*Note:* Not all monitors are able to display all 100 points when "Size" is set to 1.

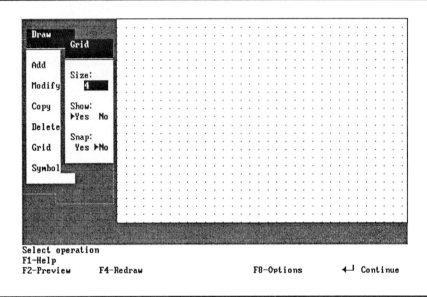

**Figure 9-20.**  Grid form

## Displaying a Grid

You can use a grid (by using the "Snap" feature described next) without actually displaying the points of the grid on your screen. If you want to display the grid, set "Show" to Yes; otherwise, set "Show" to No.

## Using the Snap-to-Grid Feature

When "Snap" is set to Yes, the cursor within the drawing area can only be placed on a point of the grid. The term *snap* is used since the cursor seems to "snap" to each grid point as it moves, as if drawn by a magnet. The snap feature can be helpful when you need to precisely place objects, since the possible cursor locations are limited. To permit free movement of the cursor within the drawing area, set "Snap" to No.

*Hint:* Although "Snap" is helpful for certain drawing tasks, it can make others more cumbersome. It is best to set "Snap" to No until you need the snap-to-grid feature. Return "Snap" to No when it is no longer needed. Setting "Snap" to Yes will not affect objects that have already been placed.

## Using Symbols

*Symbols* are drawings that consist of text, box, polyline, line, circle, and polygon objects. The difference between a symbol and a drawing is that a symbol is stored in a *symbol file*, a special Harvard Graphics file that ends with the extension .SYM. Symbol files can contain anywhere from 1 to 24 symbols each. (Only 20 symbols can be stored in symbol files used with version 2.0.) You can retrieve a symbol from a symbol file and place it in the drawing area. Once it is in the drawing area, it becomes a drawing. You can then add to, modify, copy, or delete this drawing.

The symbols in symbol files can come from a variety of sources. When you loaded Harvard Graphics onto your hard disk, you copied Harvard Graphics' 16 symbol files, which contain a total of 300 symbols. If you do not have a hard disk, these symbol files are on your original Harvard Graphics disk or disks labeled "Symbols." Harvard Graphics' symbol files are listed in Appendix D. You can also use symbols from the Harvard Graphics accessories, Business Symbols and Military Symbols, described in Appendix C. Software Publishing Corporation also markets an accessory called U.S. Mapmaker, also described in Appendix C, that creates maps and turns them into symbols.

Another alternative is to create your own symbols. There are several ways to do this. One is to create a drawing and then save it in a symbol file. Once you have done so you can include it in any of your charts. Another way to create a symbol is to save a chart as a symbol. When a chart is converted to a symbol, you can place it in the drawing area, and then modify it in a wide variety of ways. Converting Harvard Graphics charts to symbols is described later, in the section "Saving a Chart as a Symbol." Symbols can also be made by converting a CGM metafile to a symbol. Converting CGM metafiles is described in Chapter 12, "Importing and Exporting."

When you select <Symbol> from the Draw menu, Harvard Graphics displays the Symbol menu, shown in Figure 9-21. This menu contains

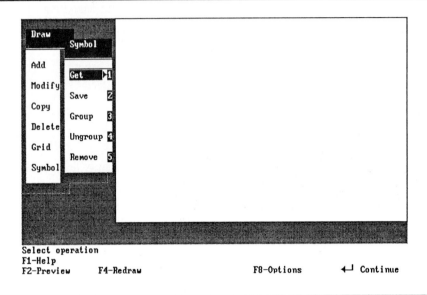

**Figure 9-21.**   Symbol menu

five options for symbols: <Get>, <Save>, <Group>, <Ungroup>, and <Remove>. These options are discussed in the following sections.

## Retrieving a Symbol

You can add any symbol to your chart by retrieving the symbol from the corresponding symbol file. To do this, select <Get> from the Symbol menu to display the Select Symbol File form, shown in Figure 9-22. This form lists all the symbol files in the current directory.

Select the symbol file that contains the desired symbol. Use PGDN and PGUP to display additional files in the current directory. If your symbol file is not in the current directory, change the directory (or drive) by entering the desired path at the "Directory" option, or by pressing F3-Change dir. Refer to the section "Getting Files from Other Directories" in Chapter 2, for information on using F3-Change dir.

Once you select a symbol file, Harvard Graphics displays all the symbols the file contains in the drawing area. (Depending on the speed of your computer and the complexity of the symbols, this may take up to a minute or two.) In Figure 9-23, for example, the Harvard Graphics

Drawing and Annotating 315

```
                    Select Symbol File
Directory: C:\HG
Filename:  ARROWS   .SYM

Filename Ext  |  Date      |  Type   |  Description

ARROWS   .SYM    11-24-87     SYMBOL    Arrow symbols
BUILDING.SYM     12-02-87     SYMBOL    Building symbols
CITIES   .SYM    11-24-87     SYMBOL    City maps
CURRENCY.SYM     11-25-87     SYMBOL    Currency symbols
COUNTRY  .SYM    11-24-87     SYMBOL    Country maps
FLOWCHAR.SYM     12-03-87     SYMBOL    Flowchart symbols
FOODSPRT.SYM     12-02-87     SYMBOL    Food and sports symbols
GREEKLC  .SYM    11-16-87     SYMBOL    Lower case Greek letters
GREEKUC  .SYM    11-16-87     SYMBOL    Upper case Greek letters
HUMAN    .SYM    12-02-87     SYMBOL    People
INDUSTRY.SYM     11-25-87     SYMBOL    Industry symbols
MISC     .SYM    12-02-87     SYMBOL    Miscellaneous
OFFICE   .SYM    12-02-87     SYMBOL    Office symbols
PRESENT  .SYM    12-02-87     SYMBOL    Presentation symbols
STARS    .SYM    11-23-87     SYMBOL    Star symbols

F1-Help        F3-Change dir
                                                       F10-Continue
```

**Figure 9-22.**   Select Symbol File form

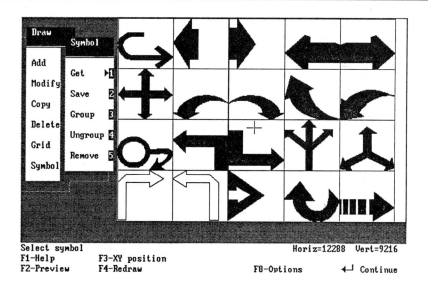

**Figure 9-23.**   Symbols from ARROWS.SYM file displayed in the drawing area

symbol file ARROWS.SYM was selected. All of the symbols in this file are displayed in the drawing area. Select a symbol by moving the cursor to the cell in the symbol file that contains the desired symbol and pressing ENTER. To return to the drawing area without selecting a symbol, press ESC.

Once you select a symbol, Harvard Graphics will remove the symbol file from the screen and display a rectangle in the drawing area that represents the selected symbol. The cursor will be positioned at the upper-right corner of the rectangle, as shown in Figure 9-24. You can move the cursor to adjust the size of your symbol before you place it, if desired. When the symbol is the desired size, press ENTER. To maintain the correct proportions of the symbol, hold down the SHIFT key while setting the symbol's size (keep the SHIFT key depressed until you press ENTER).

You can change both the size and location of your symbol after you retrieve it. Before you press ENTER to define the size of the symbol, press BACKSPACE. Harvard Graphics will display the message "Select first corner." Move the cursor to the corner of the location where you want to

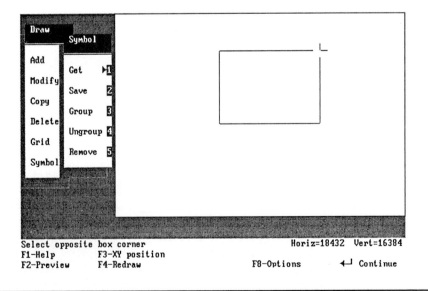

**Figure 9-24.**   Placing a retrieved symbol in the drawing area

place the symbol and press ENTER. Now Harvard Graphics will display the message "Select opposite box corner." Move the cursor to the opposite corner of the rectangle that defines where your symbol should be placed and press ENTER again. You can maintain the proper proportions of your symbol if you press the SHIFT key while placing the opposite box corner and keep it depressed until after you've pressed ENTER.

When the symbol is finally placed in the drawing area it behaves like a single object. If the symbol consists of more than one object (which is nearly always the case), you can ungroup these objects and modify the individual components. This is described in the later section "Ungrouping Objects."

## Saving a Symbol

You can save one or more objects as a symbol. This is useful if you develop a drawing you would like to save for use with more than one chart. To save an object or objects as a symbol, select <Save> from the Symbol menu. Harvard Graphics will display the message "Select object." If you want to save a single object, or you have already grouped the objects you want to save as a symbol, select this object or group.

If you want to save more than one object as a symbol and have not grouped these objects, you will need to select the group of objects. Refer to the earlier section "Selecting Multiple Objects," for a description of this procedure.

Once you have selected the object or objects you want to save as a symbol, Harvard Graphics displays the Select Symbol File form. If you want to save your objects as a symbol, and place the symbol in one of the existing symbol files, select the desired symbol file as described in the preceding section, "Retrieving a Symbol." If you want to create a new symbol file to save the symbol in, enter the name of the new file at the "Filename" option. The name of your symbol file must conform to DOS file naming conventions. Do not enter an extension; Harvard Graphics will add the extension .SYM.

If you select a symbol file from the Select Symbol File form, Harvard Graphics will add the symbol (consisting of the object or group of objects) to this file. If, however, this file already contains 24 symbols (the maximum number permissible), Harvard Graphics will display the message "Symbol file is full." If this happens, press ESC. The Select

Symbol File form will be displayed so you can either select a different symbol file or enter the name of a new one.

If you enter the name of a new symbol file, Harvard Graphics will display the New Symbol File overlay. This overlay contains only one option, "Description." You may then enter an informative description for this symbol file.

Once your symbol is saved to a symbol file, you will return to the Draw/Annotate screen.

## Grouping Objects

Sometimes it is convenient to treat two or more objects as a single entity by grouping them together, creating a *group*. You can then modify, copy, delete, or change options for the entire group.

To group two or more objects, select <Group> from the Symbol menu. Harvard Graphics will display the message "Select objects, Esc when finished." There are several ways to select objects. The first is to move the cursor to one of the objects you want to add to the group and press ENTER. Harvard Graphics will display object handles at the four corners of the imaginary rectangle surrounding the object you have selected, and will ask you to confirm that it has correctly chosen the object you want. If it chose the correct object, select Choose this. If it did not, use Select next. Repeat this process, if necessary, until Harvard Graphics has selected the correct object. Continue to select objects until all the objects you want to group have been selected.

If desired, you can select two or more objects at the same time by defining an imaginary box enclosing all the desired objects. This technique has been described previously in the section "Selecting Multiple Objects."

Once all the objects you want to group are selected press ESC. These objects are now grouped and can be treated as a single object.

You can include up to 100 objects in a single group. If you try to group more than that, Harvard Graphics will display the message "Too many objects for group," as shown in Figure 9-25. If you need to group more than 100 objects, create several subsets of objects, each one containing less than 100 objects, and then group these subsets together.

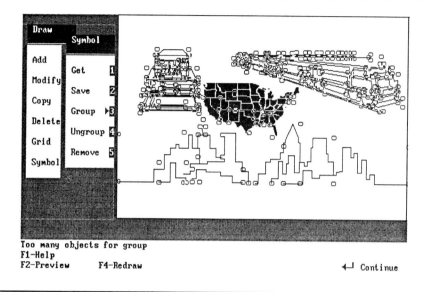

**Figure 9-25.** More than 100 objects cannot be selected for a single group

## Ungrouping Objects

If you want to modify individual objects in a group, you must first ungroup the group of objects. Objects are grouped together in two different situations. The first is when you explicitly group objects together using the <Group> option from the Symbol menu. The second is when objects are saved as a symbol. After you retrieve a symbol and place it in the drawing area, the entire symbol is treated as a single object. If you want to modify individual objects in the symbol group, you must first ungroup the symbol.

To ungroup objects in a group or symbol, select <Ungroup> from the Symbol menu. Harvard Graphics will display the message "Select object." Select the desired group. Harvard Graphics will then display object handles at the four corners of an imaginary rectangle enclosing the group. If the correct group is indicated, select Choose this. Otherwise, use Select next. Once you select Choose this, Harvard Graphics ungroups the objects.

If your group is a group of groups, ungrouping this group will only ungroup the top-level group. For example, if a group consists of two objects, each of which is a group of objects, you can ungroup the group and the result will be two objects, both retaining their status as groups. These groups can then be further ungrouped, if you desire.

## Removing Symbols from Symbol Files

When a symbol is no longer of use to you, you can remove it from its symbol file. To do this, select <Remove> from the Symbol menu. Harvard Graphics will display the Select Symbol File form. Select the symbol file that contains the symbol you want to delete. Once you select a symbol file, Harvard Graphics will display the symbols in the file in the drawing area. Move the cursor to the symbol you want to delete and press ENTER. Harvard Graphics will highlight the selected symbol, and display the message "Delete symbol from file?" Select Yes to delete the highlighted symbol or No to cancel the deletion.

## Setting Default Options

From any menu in Draw/Annotate, press F8-Options to display the Default Options menu, shown in Figure 9-26. This menu allows you to define the default options for each of the six draw objects, as well as define global drawing defaults. You can save time and energy by using the Default Options menu. Select one of the objects listed on the Default Options menu to change the default settings for the corresponding object. These default settings will be used when you add the object from the Add menu.

*Reminder:* When you are adding objects using the Add menu, any changes you make to an object's options on the Options form are in effect only until you return to the Add menu. If you plan to add more than one or two objects with the same option settings, you will want to change the default options rather than changing the option settings when you add an object.

The Options form displayed when you select one of the six object types from the Default Options menu is identical to the Options form displayed when you are adding the object using the Add menu. Although

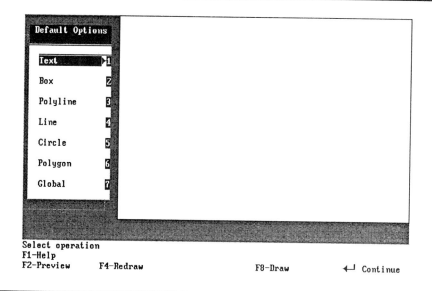

**Figure 9-26.** Default Options menu

you are strongly encouraged to use the Default Options menu to define these options, refer to the earlier sections corresponding to each object type for a detailed description of the Options form ("Setting Text Options," "Setting Box Options," "Setting Polyline Options," "Setting Line Options," "Setting Circle Options," and "Setting Polygon Options").

In addition to changing the default option settings for each type of object, Harvard Graphics permits you to define some global default settings for your drawing session. These are described in the next section.

## Setting Global Options

Global options affect the overall drawing process. You will want to change most of these options only occasionally. You may want to change other options, such as "Target," more frequently, to assist you in particular tasks. To set these options, select <Global> from the Default Options menu to display the Global Options form, shown in Figure 9-27.

### Selecting a Draw/Annotate Display

There are two "Display" modes: Final and Quick. Select Final to immediately display the most accurate image of your chart while you are adding drawings. Select "Quick" to draw charts faster, but with less detail shown in the drawing area.

### Changing the Redraw Settings

At "Redraw," select Yes to redraw the images in the drawing area after modifications are made to any of your objects. The No setting saves time, but does not always show an updated image after modifications are made. When "Redraw" is set to No, you must press F4-Redraw to display the results of your most recent changes to your image. You will probably want to set "Redraw" to No so you can control when the image is

**Figure 9-27.** Global Options form

updated. Once your image becomes even moderately complicated, modifications can take a long time if you have to wait for Harvard Graphics to redraw the image after every change.

### Displaying XY Coordinates

At "Show XY," select Yes to display the horizontal and vertical coordinates of the cursor position in the drawing area. These coordinates will be displayed at the lower-right corner of the Draw/Annotate screen. Select No if you do not want to display the coordinates. Unlike the "Display" and "Redraw" options, the "Show XY" setting does not influence the speed of Draw/Annotate operations.

### Defining the Drawing Area Cursor

You can select a different shape for the cursor in the drawing area at "Target." Select Small if you want small cross hairs for the cursor. Select Large if you want the cross hairs to extend across the entire drawing area. For both Small and Large settings, the intersection of the cross hairs is the active cursor point. Select Arrow if you want the cursor to appear as an arrow rather than cross hairs. The tip of the arrow is the active cursor point. Although the Small setting is preferred by most Harvard Graphics users, the Large setting is particularly well suited to aligning distant objects in the drawing area.

### Changing the Global Alignment

Use "Global align" to define the default alignment position for moving objects as one of the nine positions on the box. For example, if you select the center point, the cursor will be centered in the placement box when you move an object. Alternatively, if you select the lower-left corner alignment position, your target will be positioned in the lower-left corner of the object's rectangular placement box during the movement.

## Advanced Draw/Annotate Topics

The following sections describe some of the advanced features available in Draw/Annotate.

## Editing Symbols

You can modify any symbol, irrespective of whether the symbol came with Harvard Graphics, was created by saving a group of objects as a symbol, was imported from a CGM metafile, or was created when you saved a Harvard Graphics chart as a symbol. Modifying a symbol involves these four steps:

1. Retrieve the symbol using the <Get> selection from the Symbol menu.

2. Ungroup the symbol using the <Ungroup> selection from the Symbol menu.

3. Modify the symbol. You can add new objects to the symbol, modify objects in the symbol, delete objects from the symbol, or copy objects in the symbol.

4. When you are done modifying the symbol, select <Save> from the Symbol menu to save your changes.

*Note:* Saving your symbol modifications will not affect existing versions of the symbol. Even if you add the modified symbol to the same symbol file you retrieved the symbol from originally, both versions of the symbol will exist in the file. If you are editing the symbol exclusively for the purpose of using it on the current chart, and do not wish to save a copy of it for use with another chart, you can skip the fourth step.

## Creating Symbols

When you have created a drawing you would like to use in charts other than the current one, save the drawing as a symbol. Select <Save> from the Symbol menu, and then indicate whether you want to add the drawing to an existing symbol file or create a new symbol file to contain it. Later, when you want to use your saved symbol, select <Get> from the Symbol menu, and then select the symbol file in which you stored the symbol. Harvard Graphics will display all the symbols in the selected file. Once you select the desired symbol, it is placed in the drawing area.

## Saving a Chart as a Symbol

Harvard Graphics allows you to create a symbol from a chart. Once your chart is a symbol, you can make changes to the elements of the chart

Drawing and Annotating 325

(such as the legend components and individual bars, lines, or points) within Draw/Annotate. This is one of the most powerful capabilities that Harvard Graphics provides. It allows you to fine-tune any element of your chart.

To save a chart as a symbol it must be the current chart. If it is not, use the <Get chart> selection from the Get/Save/Remove menu to retrieve it, thereby making it the current chart.

Next, select <Save as symbol> from the Get/Save/Remove menu. Harvard Graphics will display the Save Chart As Symbol overlay, shown in Figure 9-28. This overlay contains three options: "Directory," "Symbol will be saved as," and "For device." The current directory will be displayed at the "Directory" option. If you want to save your symbol to a directory other than the one shown, move to "Directory" and enter the desired drive and directory.

The "Symbol will be saved as" option is used to define the name of the symbol file to which you want to add the symbol (your chart). If you enter the name of an existing symbol file, Harvard Graphics will save your symbol to that file. If you want to create a new symbol file, enter a new symbol filename. The new symbol filename must conform to DOS

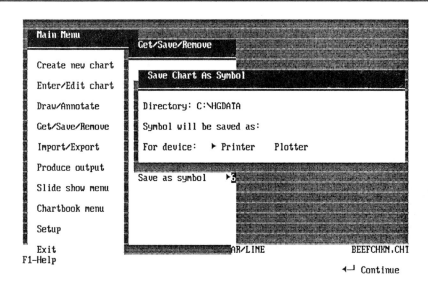

**Figure 9-28.** Save Chart As Symbol overlay

file naming standards. Do not, however, add an extension for this symbol filename as Harvard Graphics automatically adds .SYM.

Finally, you must indicate whether you want to be able to print this symbol using a printer or plotter at "For device." Select Printer if you plan to either print or display the symbol. If you select Plotter, Harvard Graphics will specifically create the symbol file so it can be plotted adequately. This may mean that Harvard Graphics will override one or more of your chart's characteristics. For instance, 3D overlap bar charts will be converted to two-dimensional charts.

When you are finished setting options on the Save Chart As Symbol overlay, press F10-Continue to save your chart as a symbol. If the name you entered at "Symbol will be saved as" is not the name of an existing symbol file on the directory specified at the "Directory" option, Harvard Graphics will display the New Symbol File overlay, shown in Figure 9-29. Enter a description of your new symbol file at the "Description" option, and then press F10-Continue.

*Note:* Once the New Symbol File overlay is displayed, you cannot cancel saving the new symbol file by pressing ESC. If you do press ESC, the symbol file simply will be saved without a description.

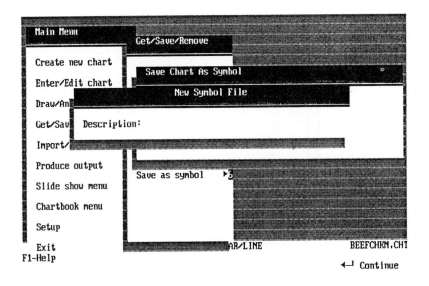

**Figure 9-29.** New Symbol File overlay

The only drawback to saving a chart as a symbol is that it will no longer be associated with data or chart settings. Once you turn the chart into a symbol, it becomes a collection of drawing objects. If you save a chart as a symbol, and then later modify the data or chart options, your chart will reflect the changes, but your symbol will not. You will need to save the chart as a symbol again if you want the symbol to reflect changes made to the chart data or options.

## Using a Chart Saved as a Symbol

There is no limit to what you can do with a chart once it is saved as a symbol. The following is a list of just a few of the many effects you can achieve:

- Display a chart within a second chart (see Figure 9-30)
- Make adjustments to the location of any of the titles or axis labels
- Combine the chart symbol with other drawing objects
- Precisely place the legend anywhere you want on the chart
- Add titles, subtitles, or footnotes longer than 40 characters per line
- Add additional lines of titles, subtitles, or footnotes
- Combine several charts on a single chart (this is how you can create multiple charts containing more than six charts; see also Chapter 10, "Multiple Charts")
- Combine smaller views of an organization chart (saved as symbols) when the organization is too large to display or print as a whole

## Using Draw Partner with Symbols

The Draw Partner accessory to Harvard Graphics can retrieve and save any Harvard Graphics symbol. Draw Partner provides you with a number of powerful drawing tools not available in Draw/Annotate. For this reason, you may want to create more sophisticated drawings entirely in

**Figure 9-30.**   Chart displayed within the frame of another chart

Draw Partner. After creating your drawing in Draw Partner, use Draw Partner's File menu to save the drawing as a symbol. You can then use the <Get> selection from Draw/Annotate's Symbol menu to retrieve the drawing produced in Draw Partner and incorporate it into your Harvard Graphics chart.

You can also use Draw Partner to modify an existing Harvard Graphics symbol in order to make unique modifications to it. Once you have modified the symbol using Draw Partner, you can then bring the symbol into Draw/Annotate and incorporate it in your current chart.

## Changing the Size and Placement of a Chart

Although changing the size and placement of a chart is not actually performed in Draw/Annotate, the Size/Place screen is nearly identical to the Draw/Annotate screen. Likewise, moving the cursor in the Size/Place screen involves the same techniques used in Draw/Annotate. Because of these similarities, you can apply what you know about drawing to changing your chart's overall size.

*Note:* If you have a CGA monitor, the Size/Place screen will appear monochrome.

Chart size is relative. When you create a chart in Harvard Graphics, the chart can be thought of as full size—it will fill a screen or page. The actual size will depend on your output device, the monitor on which you are displaying the chart, and the chart orientation (landscape or portrait). You can make your chart smaller than full size. When you do so, you can choose where it is placed on the screen or page.

To change the size and placement of a chart, you must be at the Main Menu and your chart must be the current chart. While at the Main Menu, press F7-Size/Place. Harvard Graphics will display the Size/Place screen, shown in Figure 9-31. Harvard Graphics will display the message "Select first box corner." Move the cursor within the size/place area to where you want to place a corner of your chart and press ENTER. Harvard Graphics will now display the message "Select opposite box corner." Move the cursor diagonally to the opposite corner of an imaginary box containing the entire chart and press ENTER. (Harvard Graphics will maintain the correct proportions of your chart within this box.) Once you have selected the opposite box corner, Harvard Graphics will redraw the chart in the new location and size. If you are not pleased with the new chart size and placement, you can repeat this process until your chart is sized and placed correctly.

*Reminder:* Table 9-1 contains a list of the keys you can use to move the cursor within the Size/Place screen.

Rather than using the cursor to place the corners of the box, as just described, you can use F3-XY position to move it to a precise position on the size/place area. To do this, press F3-XY position. Enter the horizontal (X) and vertical (Y) coordinates for the box corner at the "Horiz" and

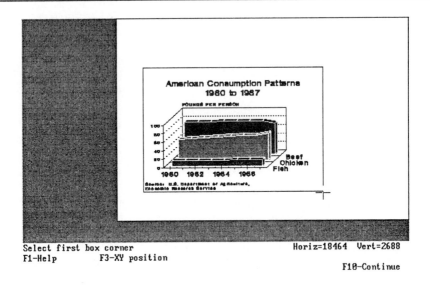

**Figure 9-31.** Size/Place screen with a chart reduced to less than one-half of original size

"Vert" entry fields, located at the top right of the function key banner (as shown in Figure 9-31). When you have entered the desired XY position, press ENTER. Harvard Graphics will move your cursor to the defined position on the size/place area. You can use F3-XY position to move the cursor to the first box corner, the opposite box corner, or both. Remember, however, that once the cursor has been moved using F3-XY position, you still need to press ENTER to select the position.

When you are finished defining your chart's size and placement, press F10-Continue to return to the Main Menu.

*Note:* Drawings and/or symbols placed on your chart will not be moved or sized when you change the size and placement of your chart. If you need to size and place your chart, you should always do so before adding drawings or symbols.

# Multiple Charts

**Multiple Chart Overview**
**Creating Multiple Charts**
**Sizing and Placing a Custom Multiple Chart**
**Changing Multiple Chart Styles**

This chapter describes Harvard Graphics' multiple chart features, which allow you to display the images of two or more charts on one screen or page. Multiple charts are easy to create. They are also particularly useful for creating handouts for presentations, or to display complementary charts simultaneously. This chapter covers how to create multiple charts with two, three, and four charts. It also describes how to create a custom multiple chart with up to six charts. Unlike the other multiple chart styles, custom multiple charts provide you with the flexibility to size and place each of the charts individually.

## Multiple Chart Overview

A multiple chart contains two or more existing Harvard Graphics charts displayed together on the same screen or output together on the same page or slide. A multiple chart can display text, organizational, or data charts (area, bar/line, high/low/close, and pie) in any combination. A multiple chart cannot, however, display another multiple chart.

There are four styles of multiple charts: Two, Three, Four, and Custom. Charts in the Two, Three, and Four multiple chart styles are displayed in a fixed size and position (determined by chart orientation, as discussed later in the section "Edit Multiple Chart Form"). An example of a multiple chart with three charts is shown in Figure 10-1. With a Custom multiple chart you can define the size and placement of up to six charts.

## Chart 1

## Multiple Charts

This multiple chart contains a title chart, a bar chart, and a pie chart.

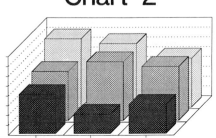

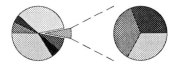

**Figure 10-1.**   A multiple chart with three charts

## Creating Multiple Charts

To be included in a multiple chart, a chart must already exist. (However, you can change the data or options for a chart after it has been included in a multiple chart, and those changes will be reflected in the multiple chart when it is later printed, plotted, recorded, or displayed.) All charts to be included in a multiple chart must be in the same directory. You must save your multiple chart to this directory as well.

The steps for creating a multiple chart are as follows:

1. Select <Create new chart> from the Main Menu.
2. Select <Multiple charts> from the Create New Chart menu.

3. Select the desired multiple chart style from the Multiple Charts Styles menu, shown in Figure 10-2.

4. Select the charts to be included in your multiple chart on the Edit Multiple Chart form, as described in the next section. Press F2-Draw chart once you have created your chart to verify that the charts appear in the desired order in the multiple chart.

5. If you are creating a custom multiple chart, you can optionally press F7-Size/Place and adjust the size and placement of each of the charts in your multiple chart using the Custom Layout screen, as described in the section "Sizing and Placing a Custom Multiple Chart." Press F7-Data to return to the Edit Multiple Chart form.

6. Press F10-Continue to return to the Main Menu.

At this point your multiple chart is complete. However, there are a number of modifications you can make to your multiple chart. If you do not want to make any of these changes, go directly to step 10.

7. You can change the orientation or border for the multiple chart by pressing F8-Options from the Main Menu, as described in the section "Overriding Default Chart Characteristics" in Chapter 3.

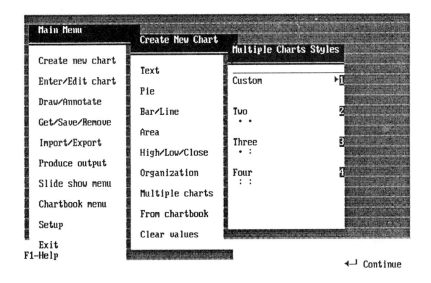

**Figure 10-2.**  Multiple Charts Styles menu

(The "Font" option has no effect on multiple charts, although you can change the font for an individual chart included in a multiple chart.)

8. You can add drawings or annotations to your multiple chart using <Draw/Annotate> from the Main Menu, as described in Chapter 9, "Drawing and Annotating."

9. You can print, plot, or record your multiple chart as described in Chapter 8, "Producing Output." Note that producing output of a multiple chart will generally take longer than producing output of a single chart.

10. If you want to save your chart for future use, save it to disk using the <Save chart> selection from the Get/Save/Remove menu.

*Note:* You must save the multiple chart to the same directory as the directory that contains the charts. If you do not, Harvard Graphics will not be able to print, plot, record, or display your multiple chart.

## Edit Multiple Chart Form

When you select the style of multiple chart you want to create from the Multiple Charts Styles menu, Harvard Graphics displays the Edit Multiple Chart form. The form for the three-chart style is shown in Figure 10-3. The forms for the other multiple chart styles are similar. Differences among them are noted in the following discussion.

The Edit Multiple Chart form is divided into three sections: the file list, multiple chart list, and function key banner. The file list appears at the top of the form and displays the first eight charts in the current directory. When you create a multiple chart, all the charts you add to it must be in the same directory. If you want to create a multiple chart from charts in another directory, you must change directories, as described later in "Changing the Directory." If you want to create a multiple chart that includes charts located in several different directories, you must first copy all the charts to a single directory.

Below the file list is the multiple chart list. This contains lines for the charts that will be included in your multiple chart. The Edit Multiple Chart form for the two-chart style contains two lines, the form for the

```
                    Edit Multiple Chart
  Filename Ext   |   Date   |   Type    |      Description
  HG       .CHT  | 12-01-87 | PIE       | Pie for color palette display
  ANNOUNCE.CHT   | 07-01-87 | FREEFORM  | Sample chart
  INTRO    .CHT  | 07-01-87 | TITLE     | Sample chart
  OPENING  .CHT  | 07-01-87 | TITLE     | Sample chart
  PRODS    .CHT  | 07-01-87 | LIST      | Sample chart
  REGIONS  .CHT  | 07-01-87 | BAR/LINE  | Sample chart
  SALES    .CHT  | 07-01-87 | 2 COLUMN  | Sample chart
  TRISALES .CHT  | 07-01-87 | BAR/LINE  | Sample chart

  - Order -    - Chart -    - Type -              Description
     1      |  HG   .CHT  |           |
     2      |             |           |
     3      |             |           |

      ┌──┬─┐ 2
   1  │  │ │
      └──┴─┘ 3

  F1-Help          F3-Change dir
  F2-Draw chart                                         F10-Continue
```

**Figure 10-3.**   Edit Multiple Chart form

three-chart style contains three lines, and so on. The form for the custom chart style contains six lines, the maximum number permissible for a custom multiple chart. The multiple chart list contains four columns: "Order," "Chart," "Type," and "Description." In the "Order" column are numbers referring to the position of charts in a multiple chart when they are displayed or output.

The actual position of individual charts depends on the orientation of your multiple chart. Figures 10-4 and 10-5 show how Harvard Graphics positions charts for each of the multiple chart styles for landscape and portrait orientations. The positions of the charts in a custom multiple chart are the default positions; but they can be modified, if desired, as described later in "Sizing and Placing a Custom Multiple Chart."

The "Chart," "Type," and "Description" columns contain the filename, type, and description for each of the charts in your multiple chart. When you create a multiple chart, the first chart from the file list will be displayed at the first line in the multiple chart list, with the corresponding chart information shown in the "Chart," "Type," and "Description" columns. You can modify this first chart and add additional charts to your multiple chart, as described later in "Defining Charts in the Multiple Chart List."

A small representation of the chart page is displayed below the multiple chart list at the lower-left corner (as shown in Figure 10-3) for the Two, Three, and Four multiple chart styles. This shows the locations of the charts that will appear in your multiple chart. When you are creating a custom multiple chart, the word "custom" is displayed in place of the page representation, since the number of charts and their locations are not fixed. The function key banner at the bottom of the form shows the active function keys.

### Moving the Cursor on the Edit Multiple Chart Form

While the Edit Multiple Chart form is displayed, the cursor is active in either the file list or the multiple chart list. When you first create a

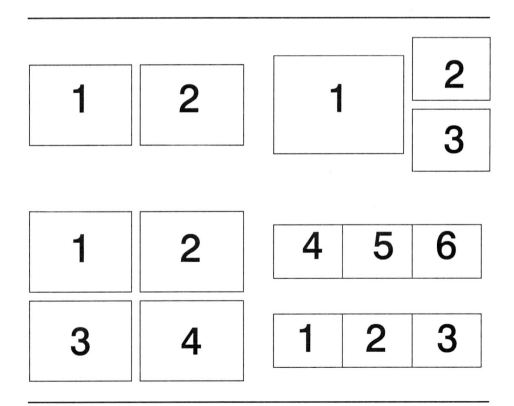

**Figure 10-4.**  Multiple chart positions in landscape orientation

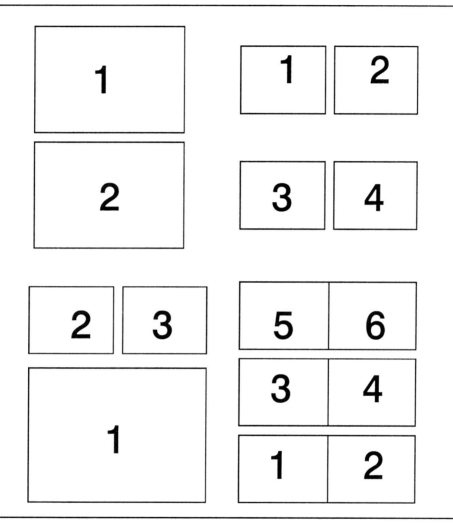

**Figure 10-5.**   Multiple chart positions in portrait orientation

multiple chart, the cursor is active in the file list. To move the cursor from one list to the other press TAB. Pressing the UP and DOWN arrow keys moves the cursor between the chart names in the active list. These and other keys you can use in the Edit Multiple Chart form to create and edit a multiple chart are described in Table 10-1.

### Defining Charts in the Multiple Chart List

There are two methods for adding charts to your multiple chart list: the entry method and the selection method. These methods are described in the next two sections.

Once you have added the names of all of your charts in the multiple chart list, your multiple chart is complete and you can press F10-Continue to return to the Main Menu. (If you are creating a custom multiple chart, you may optionally press F7-Size/Place from the Edit Multiple Chart form to customize the size and placement of your charts, as described later in "Sizing and Placing a Custom Multiple Chart.")

| Key | Function |
| --- | --- |
| BACKSPACE | Moves cursor back one space, deleting any character in the multiple chart list. |
| CTRL-DEL | Deletes entire contents of line at cursor. Use to delete chart name in the multiple chart list. |
| DEL | Deletes character at the cursor in the multiple chart list. |
| DOWN (arrow) | Moves cursor down one position in the file list or multiple chart list. |
| END | Moves cursor to the last line in the multiple chart list. |
| ESC | Cancels an operation and returns to the previous screen. |
| HOME | Moves cursor to the first line in the multiple chart list. |
| INS | Toggles the insert mode on and off; the cursor appears as a block when it is on, and as a small line when it is off. |
| TAB | Activates cursor in either the file list or the multiple chart list. |
| UP (arrow) | Moves cursor up one position in the file list or multiple chart list. |

Table 10-1.    Cursor Control Keys and Functions in the Edit Multiple Chart Form

**Entry Method**   You can enter the names of your charts directly in the multiple chart list. When you first create a multiple chart, the cursor is positioned in row 1 of the multiple chart list. Enter the name of the chart you want to display at location 1 on your multiple chart (see Figures 10-4 and 10-5). Even though the cursor is initially active in the file list, as soon as you begin typing the name of the chart, Harvard Graphics makes the cursor active in the multiple chart list. When you enter the chart name, you do not need to enter the .CHT extension (although you may do so). Press ENTER to move the cursor to row 2 of the multiple chart list, and enter the second chart name in this row. If you selected a Three, Four, or Custom multiple chart style, you may repeat this process to define chart names for any of the remaining rows of the multiple chart list.

If you do not want to display a chart at one of the positions on the multiple chart (that is, you want this position to be blank), leave the corresponding row in the multiple chart list blank. Press DOWN or UP to move past the blank position.

There are two potential drawbacks to using the direct entry method. The first is that Harvard Graphics does not check to see that the chart name you entered is actually a chart on the current directory. You will need to verify this yourself. The second drawback is that when you use the direct entry method, the chart type and descriptions are not listed in the multiple chart list. Depending on your needs, this may not be a problem.

**Selection Method**   To use the selection method, the current directory must contain all your desired charts. If your charts are not in the current directory, press F3-Change dir to change the directory, as described in the section "Changing the Directory."

The cursor must be active in the file list. When you first create a multiple chart this is the case. If it is not, press TAB to activate the cursor in the file list. Use UP and DOWN to highlight the name of the chart you want to place at the first position on the multiple chart, and then press ENTER. Harvard Graphics will enter the name of the selected chart in the multiple chart list. The chart type and chart description will be entered as well. Next, select the chart for the second position in the multiple chart list. Use UP and DOWN to highlight the chart in the file list that you want to appear at the second position on the multiple chart list, and press ENTER again. As before, Harvard Graphics will enter the name, chart type, and description of this chart in the multiple chart list. If you are creating a Three, Four, or Custom multiple chart, continue this process until the names of all your desired charts are displayed in the multiple chart list.

If the chart you want to select is not displayed in the file list (since only eight files can fit in this display at a time), press PGDN or PGUP to display an additional screen of charts from the current directory. Alternatively, press DOWN or UP to scroll one name at a time.

You can leave one or more of the rows of the multiple chart list blank. When you do so, no chart will be displayed at the corresponding position on the multiple chart. To leave a row blank, instead of selecting a chart for a particular position, press TAB to make the multiple chart list active. Then press DOWN to move the cursor to the next position in the multiple chart list where you want to place a chart. Press TAB to reactivate the cursor in the file list. Continue selecting charts for the remaining positions.

### Editing the Multiple Chart List

You can change the charts listed in the multiple chart list at any time. Modifications you may need to make include replacing one chart with another, changing the order of charts, and adding or deleting a chart. You modify the list by changing the entries, one at a time.

To edit the multiple chart list, make sure the desired multiple chart is the current chart, and then display the Edit Multiple Chart form on your screen. (Retrieve it using <Get chart>.) Make the cursor active in the multiple chart list. Then move the cursor to the chart name you want to change. To replace this chart with another chart in the file list, you can use either the entry or the selection method. To use the entry method, press CTRL-DEL (or DEL or BACKSPACE) to delete the name of the chart, and type in the name of the new chart. Use this same technique to modify additional rows as necessary.

To use the selection method, make the cursor active in the multiple chart list and move the cursor to the chart name you want to change. Next, press TAB to make the cursor active in the file list. Move the cursor to the file you want to select and press ENTER. Harvard Graphics will enter your selected chart name into the appropriate row of the multiple chart list.

When you use the selection method to change a chart, what happens next depends on the contents of your multiple chart list. If the row below the chart you have changed is empty, the cursor will remain active in the file list and you can immediately select another chart for this next row, if desired. For example, if you are changing the third chart in a custom multiple chart and row 4 of the multiple chart list is empty, you can immediately select a chart for row 4 after you select a chart for row 3, and then select charts for the fifth and sixth rows, if they, too, are empty.

On the other hand, if the next row is not empty, or you are selecting a chart for the last row in the multiple chart list, the cursor will become active in the multiple chart list as soon as you select a chart from the file list. In this case, you can continue to use the selection method, alternating between positioning the cursor at the desired row in the multiple chart list and pressing TAB to select the new chart from the file list. Continue until you are satisfied with your charts and their order in the multiple chart list.

### Changing the Directory

When you are using the selection method to define your multiple chart list, the directory that contains the charts you want to select must be the current directory. Only files in the current directory can be displayed in the file list. If the desired files are in a different directory, change the current directory by pressing F3-Change dir. Once you do so, Harvard Graphics displays the Select Directory form. Select the desired directory, and then press F3-Select files to return to the Edit Multiple Chart form. See "Getting Files from Other Directories" in Chapter 2, for more information on using the Select Directory form.

## Sizing and Placing a Custom Multiple Chart

You can adjust the size and placement of each of the charts defined in the custom multiple chart. To do this, press F7-Size/Place from the Edit Multiple Chart form to display the Custom Layout screen, shown in Figure 10-6. This screen is very similar to both the Draw/Annotate screen and the Size/Place screen (described in Chapter 9, "Drawing and Annotating").

**342** Harvard Graphics: The Complete Reference

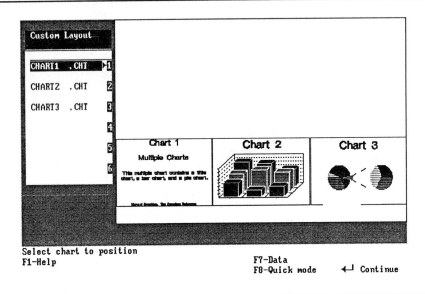

**Figure 10-6.** Custom Layout screen

*Note:* If you have a CGA monitor, the Custom Layout screen will appear in monochrome.

On the left side of the Custom Layout screen is the Custom Layout menu, which lists the charts you defined in the multiple chart list. The custom layout area is the large box on the right side of the screen and initially displays the default layout for your multiple chart. You use this area to define new positions and sizes for your chart. The function key banner is at the bottom of the screen. As you can see in Figure 10-6, Harvard Graphics displays the message "Select chart to position" at the top-left corner of the function key banner when the screen is initially displayed. The keys you can use to position charts in the custom layout area are described in Table 10-2.

| Key | Function |
| --- | --- |
| BACKSPACE | Allows you to reposition first chart corner. |
| CTRL-DOWN | Moves cursor to lower edge. |
| CTRL-END | Moves cursor to bottom-left corner. |
| CTRL-HOME | Moves cursor to upper-left corner. |
| CTRL-LEFT | Moves cursor to left edge. |
| CTRL-PGDN | Moves cursor to bottom-right corner. |
| CTRL-PGUP | Moves cursor to upper-right corner. |
| CTRL-RIGHT | Moves cursor to right edge of custom layout area. |
| CTRL-UP | Moves cursor to upper edge. |
| DOWN (arrow) | Moves cursor down. |
| END | Moves cursor diagonally, down and to the left. |
| ENTER | Places a chart position in the custom layout area. Selects the highlighted chart in the Custom Layout menu. |
| ESC | Cancels an operation and returns to the previous screen. |
| HOME | Moves cursor diagonally, up and to the left. |
| LEFT (arrow) | Moves cursor to the left. |
| PGDN | Moves cursor diagonally, down and to the right. |
| PGUP | Moves cursor diagonally, up and to the right. |
| RIGHT (arrow) | Moves cursor to the right. |
| SHIFT | Use in conjunction with mouse or cursor movement keys (DOWN, END, HOME, LEFT, PGDN, PGUP, RIGHT, and UP). Shows chart proportions when moving or sizing charts in the custom layout area. |
| UP (arrow) | Moves cursor up. |

**Table 10-2.** Cursor Control Keys and Functions for Positioning Charts in the Custom Layout Area

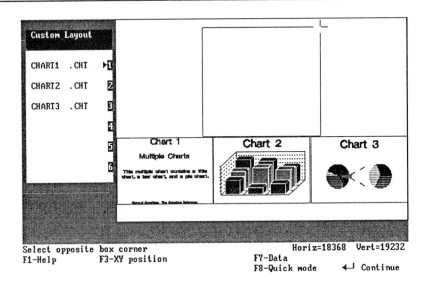

**Figure 10-7.**  Sizing and placing Chart 1 at a different location in the custom layout area

To change size or placement of the charts, follow these steps:

1. Move the cursor on the Custom Layout menu to the name of the chart you want to size and/or place and press ENTER. Harvard Graphics displays the message "Select first box corner" and activates the cursor in the custom layout area.

2. Using the cursor keys or a mouse, move the cursor in the custom layout area to where you want to place the first corner of your chart and press ENTER. Harvard Graphics now displays the message "Select opposite box corner."

3. Move the cursor to the position at which you want to place the opposite corner of your chart, as shown in Figure 10-7. Press ENTER. Harvard Graphics will place your chart where you specified. Regardless of the shape of the placement box, Harvard Graphics will maintain the chart's original proportions, as shown in Figure 10-8. While placing the opposite box corner you can cause the placement box to reflect the chart's proportions by holding down the SHIFT key.

Multiple Charts    345

4. Repeat steps 1 through 4 for any remaining charts you want to position and/or size.

5. When you have finished sizing and placing your charts, press F7-Data to return to the Edit Multiple Chart form.

## Using Quick Mode to Speed Up Custom Chart Layout

Each time you change the position or size of a chart in a custom multiple chart, Harvard Graphics redraws the charts in the custom layout area. Depending on the complexity of your charts and the speed of your computer, this redrawing may take a long time. You can reduce this time by selecting F8-Quick mode. When you press F8-Quick mode, Harvard Graphics draws boxes in place of your charts and labels each box with the name of the represented chart. These boxes can be drawn much faster than the original chart images. Figure 10-9 displays a custom multiple chart in Quick mode.

If you finish sizing and placing your charts and do not want to see the Final mode, press F7-Data to return to the Edit Multiple Chart form. To exit the Quick mode and remain on the custom layout screen, press F8-Final mode.

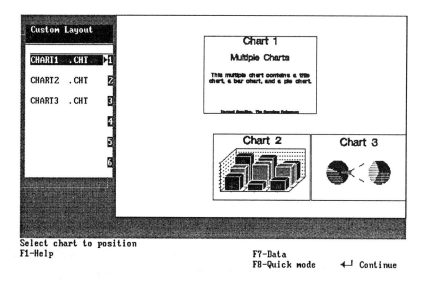

**Figure 10-8.**   The new location for Chart 1

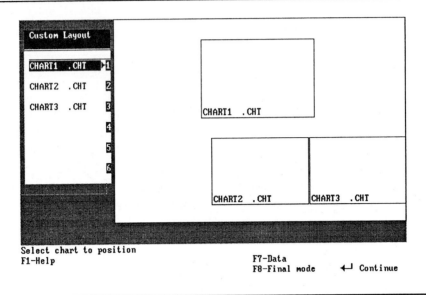

**Figure 10-9.** A custom multiple chart in Quick mode

## Changing Multiple Chart Styles

Once you have created a multiple chart, you can change it to any of the other multiple chart styles, if desired. For instance, you can switch a three-chart multiple chart to a four-chart style. To switch between chart styles, follow these steps:

1. Make the existing multiple chart the current chart. If you just created this chart and have not yet saved it, you must save it before continuing if you want to use this chart at a later time.

2. Return to the Main Menu and select <Create new chart>.

3. At the Create New Chart menu, select <Multiple charts>.

4. At the Multiple Chart Styles menu, select one of the other styles of multiple charts. Harvard Graphics will display the message shown in Figure 10-10. Select Yes to save your existing chart list.

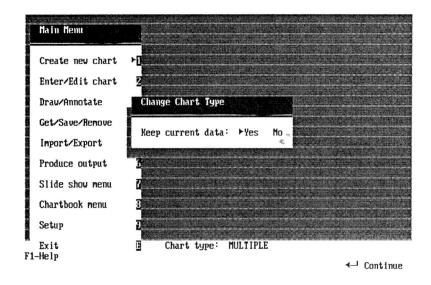

**Figure 10-10.**   Change Chart Type form

If you change from one multiple chart style to a style that can accommodate more charts (for instance, from Four to a Custom style), all the charts will be added to the new multiple chart, and will retain their original positions in the multiple chart list. If you change to a style that supports fewer charts, only those charts defined in the positions available to both styles will be retained.

# Templates and Chartbooks

Template Overview
Saving a Template
Retrieving a Template
Chartbook Overview
Creating a Chart from a Template in a Chartbook

This chapter describes how to create and use a template. A *template* is a saved description of chart settings. When you later use the template to create a chart, much of the work has already been done by the template, and you usually only need to add text and data to complete the chart. In addition to increasing the efficiency of chart production, templates can be used to automate data importation, change Harvard Graphics' default chart settings, and modify characteristics of charts displayed in a slide show.

This chapter also discusses the Harvard Graphics tool called a chartbook. When you make extensive use of templates, a chartbook can be used to organize and group your templates by project or category.

## Template Overview

A template is like a chart, only without any data. It has a chart type and chart settings. You can add drawings or annotations to a template, and you can include a template in a slide show. Templates can be used for any type of chart.

A template is a valuable time-saver if you regularly make charts with specific characteristics (chart option settings, text attributes, text size and placement, drawings) different from Harvard Graphics' default settings for that chart. For example, suppose you create a bar chart every week that uses 3D and overlap settings, displays a legend as part

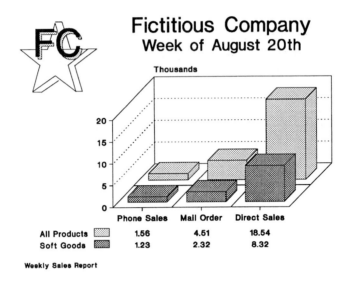

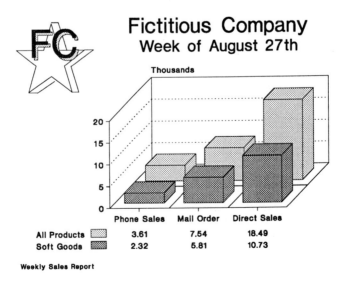

Figure 11-1.    Charts created from the same template

Templates and Chartbooks    351

of a data table, uses the same title and footnote, and presents your company's logo in the upper-left corner of the chart. To create this chart, you would have to apply these settings, enter the title and footnote, and add the logo every time you create your chart. Now suppose you had saved a template the first time you created this chart. The next time you want to create the chart you could simply retrieve your template.

With a template, you only need to add your data. The logo, title and footnote text, and chart settings are already added and set for you. The charts in Figure 11-1, for example, were created with a template; only the data were added.

## Saving a Template

You create a template from the current chart. When you have a chart with settings that you want to save, you can save them as a template as simply as saving the chart itself. The steps for saving a template are as follows:

1. You must have a current chart. Either retrieve an existing chart that has the characteristics you want in your template, or create a new chart. (This chart does not have to contain data.)

2. Ensure all the settings defined for the current chart are settings you want in your template. If they are not, change the settings.

3. If you want to add a drawing or symbol as a part of your template, return to the Main Menu and select <Draw/Annotate>. Add them as described in Chapter 9, "Drawing and Annotating."

4. To specify how the chart as a whole is sized and placed in the template, return to the Main Menu and press F8-Options to display the Size/Place screen. Size and place the chart as described in "Changing the Size and Placement of a Chart" in Chapter 9.

5. When the chart settings and drawings are complete, return to the Main Menu and select <Get/Save/Remove> to display the Get/Save/Remove menu.

6. If you entered data in the chart, and want to save the data as a chart (.CHT) file in addition to saving the template, save the chart before you continue. This is important since your chart data may be deleted when you save a template.

7. From the Get/Save/Remove menu, select <Save template>. Harvard Graphics will display the Save Template overlay.

8. Set the options on the Save Template overlay as described in the next section, and then press F10-Continue to save the template.

## Setting Options on the Save Template Overlay

The Save Template overlay (displayed in Figure 11-2) is used to define the name and characteristics of your template. Once you fill out this overlay, press F10-Continue to save a template based on your current chart settings and characteristics.

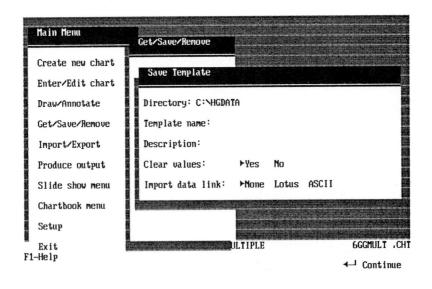

**Figure 11-2.** Save Template overlay

At the "Directory" option, indicate in which directory you want to store the template. If you intend to add this template to a chartbook, the template must be stored in the same directory the chartbook is stored in. The current directory is the default setting. If you want to save your template to a different directory, press SHIFT-TAB to move to "Directory." Press CTRL-DEL to delete the current directory name and enter the name of the desired directory.

At the "Template name" option, define the name of your template. The name you enter must be eight characters or less in length, and conform to MS-DOS file naming conventions. You need not add an extension to this filename since Harvard Graphics will automatically add the extension .TPL when the template is saved, if you have not done so.

There are 12 names you should avoid using when saving a chart as a template. These names are listed in Table 11-1. If you save a template using one of these names, Harvard Graphics will use the settings in the template as the default settings for that particular chart type. The use of this feature to redefine your Harvard Graphics default chart settings is discussed in the section "Changing Default Chart Settings with a Template," later in the chapter.

At the "Description" option, enter information about your template. This description can be particularly helpful, as it will be displayed on the

| Template Name | Chart Type |
| --- | --- |
| AREA | Area chart |
| BARLINE | Bar/Line chart |
| BULLET | Bullet list |
| FREEFORM | Free-form text chart |
| HLC | High/Low/Close chart |
| LIST | Simple list |
| MULTIPLE | Multiple chart |
| ORG | Organization chart |
| PIE | Pie chart |
| TITLE | Title chart |
| 2_COLUMN | Two-column chart |
| 3_COLUMN | Three-column chart |

**Table 11-1.**   Reserved Template Names

Select Template form when you are retrieving an existing template. If you do not enter a description, the title (if there is one) from the chart used to create the template will be used for the description.

The "Clear values" option defaults to Yes, and removes all text and data from your template. Select No to save text and/or data with your template. For instance, if you always use the same X values in a weekly chart you create from a template, you can enter these values (without entering series values) and set "Clear values" to No. When you later retrieve the template, the X data will already be entered in your chart. Likewise, if the title of your chart does not change, you can define the title when you are first creating the chart you will save as a template, and then set the "Clear values" to No when you save it. When you set "Clear values" to No, before you save the template be sure only the text, titles, and data you want to use every time you retrieve the template are the only text and data in your chart.

The final option, "Import data link," is only used when you are saving a data link with your template. This is described later in the section "Saving a Data Link in a Template." Leave "Import data link" set to None to save your template of a chart.

When you have finished setting the appropriate options on the Save Template overlay, press F10-Continue. If "Clear values" is set to Yes, Harvard Graphics will display the message shown in Figure 11-3, informing you that your data are about to be cleared. If you want to save your chart with the text and/or data and have not yet done so, press ESC to return to the Get/Save/Remove menu and save your chart before saving the template. Otherwise, press ENTER to save your template.

## Retrieving a Template

There are two ways to retrieve a template in order to create a chart. The first is to retrieve a template from the Select Template form. This is similar to retrieving a saved chart. To retrieve a template, select <Get/Save/Remove> from the Main Menu, and then select <Get template> from the Get/Save/Remove menu. Harvard Graphics displays the Select Template form, shown in Figure 11-4. Use this form the way you use the Select Chart form (described in "Getting an Existing Chart" in Chapter 2). The only difference between these forms is that the Select Template form displays template files (.TPL) whereas the Select Chart form displays chart files (.CHT).

Templates and Chartbooks   355

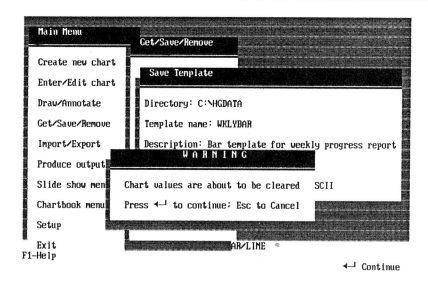

**Figure 11-3.**   Message displayed before data are cleared from a template and the current chart

```
                        Select Template
Directory: C:\HGDATA
Filename:  123AREA .TPL

Filename Ext   Date      Type       Description

MSBAR2   .TPL  08-12-90  BAR/LINE   Michigan Study,  Stack Bars
MSBAR3   .TPL  08-12-90  BAR/LINE   Michigan Study,   Simple bar chart,
WKLYBAR  .TPL  01-08-90  BAR/LINE   Bar template for weekly progress report
MSPIE    .TPL  08-12-90  PIE        Michigan Study,  Linked pie comparison
MSPIE2   .TPL  08-12-90  PIE        Michigan Study,  Single pie, group 1
WKLYPIE  .TPL  01-09-90  PIE        Pie chart for the weekly progress report
WKLYLINE.TPL   03-01-90  BAR/LINE   Trend chart for weekly report
123AREA  .TPL  05-12-90  AREA       Import Hanson Account Totals
123PIE   .TPL  04-30-90  PIE        Import Comparison Figures; Hanson Accnt
Y_T_D1   .TPL  12-28-89  BAR/LINE   Year-to-date trends
AMRPTPIE.TPL   01-09-90  PIE        Annual Report,  Earnings Performance Pie
AMRPTBAR.TPL   01-09-90  BAR/LINE   Annual Report,  Trend w/ bars,
MSPIE3   .TPL  08-12-90  PIE        Michigan Study,  Single pie, group 2
MSLINE   .TPL  08-12-90  BAR/LINE   Michigan Study,  Trends,  Year-to-date
MSLINE1  .TPL  08-12-90  BAR/LINE   Michigan Study,  Regression line

F1-Help        F3-Change dir
                                                              F10-Continue
```

**Figure 11-4.**   Select Template form

Select the desired template from the list. If the template you want is not in the current directory, either enter the desired directory at the "Directory" option, or press F3-Change dir to display the Select Directory form, and select a new directory. For details about changing the directory, see "Getting Files from Other Directories," also in Chapter 2.

The second way to retrieve a template is by selecting the template from a chartbook (you must have previously added the template to the current chartbook, as described later in "Adding Templates to the Chartbook List"). Using this method, you can select <From chartbook> on the Create New Chart menu to display the Select Template form, and then select a template. (See "Creating a Chart from a Template in a Chartbook" later in the chapter.)

## Creating a Chart from a Template

Once you retrieve a template, Harvard Graphics displays a chart form. This form corresponds to the chart type that the template was created from. For instance, if you retrieve a template created from a bar/line chart, the Bar/Line Chart Data form will be displayed. If your template used a data link, Harvard Graphics will import the linked data into your chart form before displaying the form on your monitor. (For information about defining a data link, see the section "Saving a Data Link in a Template," later in the chapter.)

Once the chart form is displayed, you are working with a chart, not a template. If you return to the Main Menu, the "Chart type" shown at the top of the function key banner will show the current type of chart. Of course, this chart has the settings and characteristics defined by the template, rather than the default settings that would have been used if you had created a new chart by selecting the chart type from the Create New Chart menu.

At this point, treat the chart as you would any other chart. Add text and/or data, modify option settings, and add drawings or symbols, if desired. Save your chart by selecting <Save chart> from the Get/Save/Remove menu as described in the section "Saving the Current Chart" in Chapter 2.

## Changing Default Chart Settings with a Template

Table 11-1 lists the 12 reserved template names. When you save a template using one of these names, Harvard Graphics will automatically get and use that template when you select the corresponding chart type from the Create New Chart menu. For example, if you save a template with the name BARLINE, Harvard Graphics will use this template whenever you select <Bar/Line> from the Create New Chart menu.

You can use this feature to customize some or all of Harvard Graphics' chart defaults to suit your needs. You can even define a default drawing or symbol to be added whenever you create a chart of a given type (although this is not recommended).

Use this feature with care, or you may end up spending more time than you save. If you use a template to redefine the default chart settings, only define chart options you want to use for the majority of charts of that type. If you set any of your chart options to settings you need only occasionally, you will find yourself changing these settings nearly every time you use that chart type.

With this caution in mind, the following are suggestions of some characteristics you may find useful to define in one or more default templates:

- Set the default patterns for bars, lines, areas, or pie slices for each series you typically use to the patterns that look best when printed or plotted.

- Set the colors for bars, lines, areas, or pie slices to colors you typically use.

- If you prefer to center your footnote, define this placement.

- If your title charts always display your company's logo, place this symbol on your default title chart template.

### Retaining Harvard Graphics' Default Chart Settings

Once you define a default template using one of the 12 reserved template names, you replace the original default settings defined by

Harvard Graphics. There may be times, however, when you prefer to use the original settings. To retain these settings, save a template that defines Harvard Graphics' original default settings, and give it a different name than one of the reserved template names before you create your new default template. For example, save your template as HGPIE if you are saving the Harvard Graphics template for pie charts. Then create the default template with your desired settings, and give it the reserved template name (PIE, in this example). This new default template will be used whenever you create new charts.

To create a chart with the original Harvard Graphics settings, select the template that contains these settings (such as HGPIE from the previous example) using <Get template> from the Get/Save/Remove menu. Then add the text and data to this chart.

*Hint:* If you use this procedure, consider listing all the templates that describe the Harvard Graphics default settings in a separate chartbook. See the section "Chartbook Overview" for more detail.

## Saving a Data Link in a Template

A data link is created when you import data from a Lotus spreadsheet or an ASCII file. If you import this data into a Harvard Graphics chart regularly, you can save yourself an enormous amount of time by saving a template that "remembers" this data link. When a data link is saved as part of a template, Harvard Graphics will automatically import the data into your chart each time you retrieve the template. This feature is especially useful when you are importing data that change on a regular basis. For example, if you maintain a Lotus spreadsheet of your weekly sales figures, and you want to be able to chart these data, you can save a template that keeps track of where the data are stored. Every time you retrieve the template, Harvard Graphics will import your current data into the chart from the updated Lotus spreadsheet.

To create a template with a data link, import data into a Harvard Graphics chart, and then define any chart options, titles, labels, or text attributes you want to include in future charts. Then save this chart as a template. Note that on the Save Template overlay, the "Import data link" option is set to either Lotus or ASCII, depending on the type of data you just imported. Harvard Graphics automatically sets this option when you import data, as shown in Figure 11-5. Do not change the

Templates and Chartbooks 359

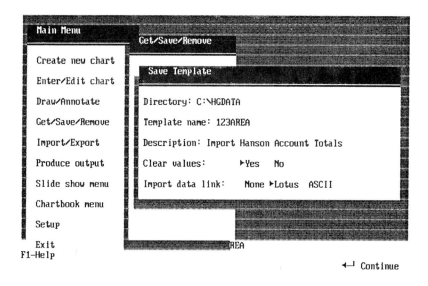

**Figure 11-5.** "Import data link" option reflecting the type of data importation just performed

"Import data link" setting or you will break the data link, and Harvard Graphics will not be able to automatically import the data when you get the template. Press F10-Continue to save the template with the data link.

The next time you need to import the data from this file, simply retrieve your template (using <Get template> from the Get/Save/Remove menu). When you do so, Harvard Graphics will check for a data link, and finding one, will automatically import the data before displaying the chart form on your monitor. Similarly, if you use a template with a data link in a slide show, the data are imported immediately before Harvard Graphics displays the chart in the slide show or prints, plots, or records the chart in the slide show.

In order to successfully use data links saved in templates, you will need to observe these two rules:

- Your data must always be in the same format. For example, Harvard Graphics will remember the cell ranges that contain the data you imported from a Lotus spreadsheet. The new data you want to import must be in this same cell range.

- Harvard Graphics remembers the name and directory of the imported data file. Your data file must always remain in the specified directory and must retain the same filename.

You can find more information about importing data for use with Harvard Graphics charts in "Importing Data" in Chapter 12.

## Using Templates in a Slide Show

Unless it defines a data link, a template in a slide show does not display any data. Rather, the charts that are placed after the template in a slide show simply adopt the settings defined by the template for display on the screen or for producing output. The influence of a template in a slide show continues until another template is encountered in the slide show or the slide show ends. In contrast, templates that define a data link display the imported data and do not influence other charts in the slide show. Including templates in slide shows is covered in detail in Chapter 13, "Slide Shows."

## Chartbook Overview

If you use more than just a few templates, you may want to consider creating a chartbook to keep your templates organized. A chartbook is really nothing more than a list of templates. If you make extensive use of templates, you may benefit from creating and using one or more chartbooks to list related templates. The remaining topics in this chapter will show you how to create, select, and edit a chartbook. If you have only a handful of templates, you will probably not a need a chartbook.

While the advantages of chartbooks are only realized when you manage more than just a few templates, even with a large number you may still not benefit from using chartbooks. Chartbooks are beneficial to the extent that you use many templates, and these templates are specific to two or more functions or projects. For example, if you are responsible for creating charts for a number of different departments, you may want to create a chartbook for each department. Each chartbook would list

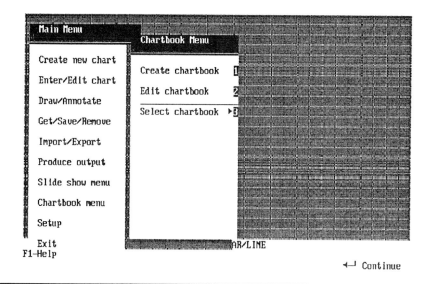

**Figure 11-6.**    Chartbook Menu

only those templates you use for a given department.

Chartbook features are accessed through the Chartbook Menu shown in Figure 11-6. To display it select <Chartbook menu> from the Main Menu. The three options on this menu permit you to create a new chartbook, edit the current chartbook, and select a chartbook in order to make it current. These options are described in the following sections.

## Creating a Chartbook

To create a chartbook, select <Create chartbook> from the Chartbook Menu, which displays the Create Chartbook overlay, shown in Figure 11-7. The current directory is displayed at "Directory." If all the templates you want to list in your chartbook are in another directory, move to "Directory" and enter the name of this directory. Once you create your chartbook, Harvard Graphics will automatically save it to the directory shown on this form.

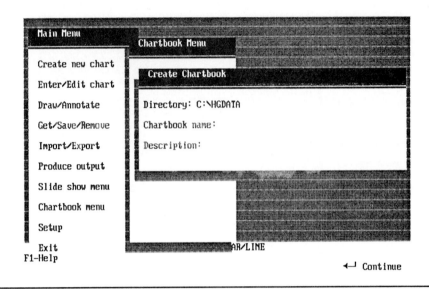

**Figure 11-7.**     Create Chartbook overlay

*Note:* A chartbook can only list templates stored in one directory. If you want a chartbook to list templates located in different directories, you must first copy all the templates to a single directory before you create a chartbook. Then make this directory the current directory.

At "Chartbook name" enter the name of the chartbook you are creating. This name is limited to eight characters and must conform to DOS file naming conventions. Do not add an extension, since Harvard Graphics will automatically add the extension .CBK to this name.

Enter a description for your chartbook at "Description," if desired. This description will be displayed in the Select Chartbook form when you are selecting a chartbook, as described later in "Selecting a Chartbook." Press ENTER or F10-Continue.

Once you press ENTER or F10-Continue, Harvard Graphics displays the Create/Edit Chartbook form, shown in Figure 11-8. The top of this form contains the list that displays all the templates in the current directory. The "Filename Ext," "Date," "Type," and "Description" col-

```
                     Create/Edit Chartbook
    Filename Ext    Date       Type              Description

    TESTFON2.TPL   01-07-90   TITLE
    WKLYBAR .TPL   01-08-90   BAR/LINE   Bar template for weekly progress report
    WKLYPIE .TPL   01-09-90   PIE        Pie chart for the weekly progress report
    WKLYLINE.TPL   03-01-90   BAR/LINE   Trend chart for weekly report
    123AREA .TPL   05-12-90   AREA       Import Hanson Account Totals
    123PIE  .TPL   04-30-90   PIE        Import Comparison Figures; Hanson Accnt

 Chartbook name: ANNUAL   .CBK
 - Order  ——— Template ——— Type ——————— Description ———————
     1       Y_T_D1   .TPL   BAR/LINE   Year-to-date trends
     2       ANRPTPIE.TPL   PIE         Annual Report, Earnings Performance Pie
     3       ANRPTBAR.TPL   BAR/LINE   Annual Report, Trend w/ bars,
     4       WKLYBAR .TPL   BAR/LINE   Bar template for weekly progress report
     5       123AREA .TPL

 Chartbook description: Annual Report Templates

 F1-Help
                                                              F10-Continue
```

**Figure 11-8.**  Create/Edit Chartbook form

umns in this list display the name of the template file, the date it was created, the chart type used to create the template, and a description for each of the templates in the current directory.

"Chartbook name" is displayed at the middle of the form with the name you gave your chartbook on the Create Chartbook overlay. You cannot modify this name.

The lower half of the form contains the chartbook list with its four columns: "Order," "Template," "Type," and "Description." You place the templates you want included in your chartbook in this list (as described in the next section). In the "Order" column are numbers referring to the position in which you place templates in this chartbook. The "Template," "Type," and "Description" columns contain the template filename, the chart type used to create the template, and a description for each of the templates included in the chartbook.

The "Chartbook description" option below the chartbook list contains the description you entered on the Create Chartbook overlay. You can modify this description on the Create/Edit Chartbook form by moving to "Chartbook description." The function key banner at the bottom of the form shows the active function keys.

## Adding Templates to the Chartbook List

When you first create a chartbook, the first template in the template list will be highlighted. This highlighted template name will also appear on the first line in the chartbook list. To change the first template in the chartbook list, move the cursor in the template list until the desired template is highlighted. Add the highlighted template to the chartbook list by pressing ENTER.

Once you press ENTER, Harvard Graphics enters the template name, type, and description in the appropriate columns in the chartbook list, and moves the cursor to the second line in the chartbook list. The cursor is still active in the template list, however. Move the cursor to the next template in the template list you want to include in your chartbook and press ENTER.

If the template you want to select is not displayed in the template list (since only six files can fit in this display at a time), press PGDN or PGUP to display an additional six templates from the current directory. Alternatively, press DOWN or UP to scroll to the next or previous template in the list. Continue to add templates until all the desired templates are listed in the chartbook list. When you are finished, press F10-Continue to return to the Chartbook Menu.

*Note:* You can list the same template in two or more chartbooks.

## Selecting a Chartbook

When you first begin your Harvard Graphics session, the current chartbook is the one defined at the "Chartbook" option of the Default Settings form. (To define this default chartbook, refer to "Default Chartbook" in Chapter 3.) As long as you do not create or select a chartbook different from the default, you can immediately edit the default chartbook using <Edit chartbook> (as described in the next section) or create a chart from a template in this chartbook using <From chartbook>.

If you have not defined a default chartbook, or you want to use a chartbook other than the default, you must select the desired chartbook first in order to make it current. To do this, select <Chartbook menu>

from the Main Menu. Then, choose <Select chartbook> from the Chartbook Menu to display the Select Chartbook form, shown in Figure 11-9. Use this form to select a chartbook just as you use the Select Chart form to select a chart (see "Getting an Existing Chart" in Chapter 2).

If the chartbook you want to select is on another directory, enter the desired directory at "Directory" or press F3-Change dir, and select a directory from the Select Directory form. See "Getting Files from Other Directories" also in Chapter 2, for more information on selecting a different directory.

Once you select a chartbook, press F10-Continue and you will return to the Chartbook Menu.

## Editing a Chartbook

At any time, you can change the templates listed in the current chartbook list. Modifications you can make include adding and deleting templates and changing the order of templates. These modifications are described in the next three sections.

```
                          Select Chartbook

Directory: C:\HGDATA
Filename:  WEEKLY  .CBK

  Filename Ext  |   Date    |   Type    |         Description
  
  WEEKLY   .CBK |  03-05-90 | CHRTBOOK  | Weekly Report Progress Report Templates
  ANNUAL   .CBK |  12-28-89 | CHRTBOOK  | Annual Report Templates
  HANSON   .CBK |  05-21-90 | CHRTBOOK  | Templates for the Hanson Account
  WASHINTN.CBK  |  07-15-90 | CHRTBOOK  | Washington Presentation Templates




  F1-Help       F3-Change dir
                                                              F10-Continue
```

**Figure 11-9.**     Select Chartbook form

To edit a chartbook, select it as described in the preceding section, "Selecting a Chartbook," if the desired chartbook is not the current chartbook. Then select <Edit chartbook> from the Chartbook Menu to display the Create/Edit Chartbook form on your screen. The keys you can use in the Create/Edit Chartbook form are described in Table 11-2. TAB and SHIFT-TAB allow you to activate the cursor in either the template list, the chartbook list, or at the "Chartbook description" option. You can determine if the cursor is active in a list by pressing the UP and DOWN arrow keys. This will move the cursor and highlight the template filenames in the active list. PGUP and PGDN will display additional template

| Key | Function |
| --- | --- |
| CTRL-DEL | Deletes template at cursor in the chartbook list. |
| CTRL-DOWN | Moves template down one position in the chartbook list. |
| CTRL-UP | Moves template up one position in the chartbook list. |
| DOWN (arrow) | Moves cursor down one position in the template list or chartbook list. |
| ENTER | Adds the highlighted template to the chartbook list. |
| ESC | Cancels an operation and returns to the previous screen. |
| PGDN | Displays the next six template files in the template list. |
| PGUP | Displays the previous six files in the template list. |
| SHIFT-TAB | Activates cursor in either the template list, the chartbook list, or the "Chartbook description" option. |
| TAB | Activates cursor in either the template list, the chartbook list, or the "Chartbook description" option. |
| UP (arrow) | Moves cursor up one position in the template list or the chartbook list. |

**Table 11-2.** Cursor Control Keys and Functions in the Create/Edit Chartbook Form

files in the active list. Once you have modified your chartbook list, press F10-Continue to return to the Chartbook Menu.

### Adding Templates to a Chartbook

When the Create/Edit Chartbook form is first displayed after you select <Edit chartbook>, the cursor will be positioned at the last row of the chartbook list. The cursor will be active in the template list, however. Move the cursor to the name in the template list you want to add to the chartbook. When the desired template is highlighted, press ENTER. Continue to add templates to your chartbook as desired. When you are finished, press F10-Continue to return to the Chartbook Menu.

### Deleting Templates from a Chartbook

You can remove a template from a chartbook list without deleting the template file. Press TAB to activate the cursor in the chartbook list (if necessary). Press the UP and DOWN arrow keys to move the cursor to the template you want to remove. When the desired template is highlighted, press CTRL-DEL to delete this template from the chartbook list.

*Note:* If you delete a template file either from DOS or by using the <Remove file> option from the Get/Save/Remove menu, Harvard Graphics will not remove the template from the chartbook list on the Create/Edit Chartbook form. However, when you select <From chartbook>, deleted templates are not listed in the chartbook.

### Changing the Order of Templates in a Chartbook

The order in which templates appear in the chartbook list will also be the order in which the templates are listed in the Template Selection form. You can change the order of templates in the chartbook list, thereby gaining easier access to templates you use most frequently.

To change the order of templates, press TAB to make the cursor active in the chartbook list (if necessary). Highlight the template you want to move in the chartbook list. Press CTRL-UP to move the template up one position or CTRL-DOWN to move it down one position in the chartbook list. When you have finished changing the order of templates, press F10-Continue to return to the Chartbook Menu.

## Creating a Chart from a Template in a Chartbook

To create a chart from a template in the current chartbook, select <Create new chart> from the Main Menu. From the Create New Chart menu, select <From chartbook>. Harvard Graphics will display the Select Template form, shown in Figure 11-4. Move your cursor to the name of the desired template, and press F10-Continue or ENTER. Harvard Graphics will retrieve the template and display the corresponding chart form.

If the desired template is not listed in the current chartbook, first choose <Select chartbook> from the Chartbook Menu to make the appropriate chartbook current. Alternatively, you can select a template without using a chartbook by choosing <Get template> from the Get/Save/Remove menu, as described in the earlier section "Creating a Chart from a Template."

# Importing and Exporting

Importing and Exporting Overview
Importing Data
Preparing a Harvard Graphics Chart for Importation
Saving the Data Link
Importing Lotus Data
Importing ASCII Text Files
Importing Delimited ASCII Files
Importing Graphs into Harvard Graphics
Exporting Charts

This chapter describes how to share data and charts between Harvard Graphics and other software. The Harvard Graphics features described in this chapter allow you to import data from Lotus spreadsheets and two types of ASCII files. You can also import actual charts from Lotus 1-2-3 and PFS:GRAPH. All of these features result in the imported data being placed into a Harvard Graphics chart. This chart can then be modified by changing the chart settings, manipulating the data using calculations, or adding a drawing or annotation. You can display or output this chart, and save it for future use.

Harvard Graphics' exportation features allow you to create a file that can be used by other software. For instance, you can export a chart as an encapsulated PostScript file for use with a desktop publishing program such as Ventura Publisher or a word processing program such as WordPerfect. Three other file formats are also available for exporting charts: HPGL (Hewlett-Packard Graphics Language), CGM metafile, and a special format for creating files for use with Software Publishing Corporation's Professional Write.

## Importing and Exporting Overview

Harvard Graphics' importing and exporting features allow you to share data and charts between Harvard Graphics and other computer soft-

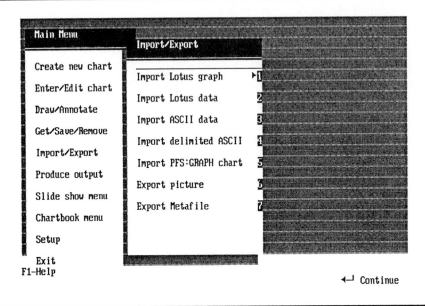

**Figure 12-1.**     Import/Export menu

ware. When you import data, you create a Harvard Graphics chart or a Harvard Graphics symbol. When you export, you create a graphics image that other software packages can use. For instance, you can export an image that many word processing packages can use to include your chart directly in a document. All importing and exporting features (except importing CGM metafiles) are accessed through the Import/Export menu, shown in Figure 12-1.

Exporting and importing are described separately in this chapter. The data importation features are presented first, in the following sections. Data exportation is described in detail later in the chapter.

## Importing Data

The following five types of data can be imported into Harvard Graphics:

- Lotus 1-2-3 spreadsheet data
- Lotus 1-2-3 graphs and data
- ASCII text files
- Delimited ASCII files
- PFS:GRAPH and data

Each of these results in a Harvard Graphics chart that you can then modify. You can change the settings, add a drawing or annotation, modify the data, display or output the chart, and save it for future use.

If you import data from a Lotus 1-2-3 spreadsheet or any ASCII text or delimited ASCII file into a chart, you can save this chart as a template. Templates saved after importing data into a chart contain a *data link*. A data link is a description saved with your template that keeps track of the source of your imported data. You can then use this template to have Harvard Graphics automatically import data from the same file the next time you want to create a chart using data from the same Lotus or ASCII file.

You can also import a CGM metafile in order to create a Harvard Graphics symbol, which can then be included in a chart or displayed by itself in a blank chart. This type of importation is different from importing data since you create a symbol rather than a chart and no actual data (text or numbers) are imported.

Each of these types of importation is presented in the following sections.

## Preparing a Harvard Graphics Chart for Importation

Before you import Lotus 1-2-3 data, an ASCII text file, or a delimited ASCII text file for the first time, you must create a blank chart in which Harvard Graphics will place the imported data. The type of blank chart you create depends on the type of chart you want to use to display the imported data.

To prepare a chart for data importation, select <Create new chart> from the Main Menu. Text charts and pie charts are simple to prepare. If you are going to import text data, select <Text> from the Create New Chart menu, and then select the type of text file you want to import your text into. Alternatively, if the data are labels and numbers, and you want to display these data using a pie chart, select <Pie> from the Create New Chart menu. When the appropriate chart form is displayed, do not add any text or data. Instead, press F10-Continue to return to the Main Menu. You are now prepared to continue with the importation, as described in the following sections.

If the data are appropriate for an XY chart (bar/line, area, or high/low/close) your chart will need a little more preparation. First, select the appropriate XY chart type from the Create New Chart menu. Harvard Graphics next displays the X Data Type Menu overlay. You must select the type of X data you will be importing. The data must conform to the selected X data type. In most cases, setting the X data type to Name will be sufficient. However, if your X data are numbers, or are consistent with one of the Harvard Graphics calendar X data types, set the "X data type" option accordingly.

Do not set the "Starting with," "Ending with," or "Increment" options on the X Data Type Menu overlay since you will be importing these X axis data. When your X data type is defined, press F10-Continue to go on to the chart data form. Do not add any data or text to this form. Instead, press F10-Continue to return to the Main Menu. You are now prepared to continue with the importation, as described in the following sections.

*Note:* You cannot import data into an organization chart.

## Saving the Data Link

After you have successfully imported data from a Lotus spreadsheet or an ASCII file, you can save the link to the data in a template. The data link is automatically recorded when you save a template immediately after importing data into a chart. When you save the data link in a template, Harvard Graphics remembers the file and directory you imported the data from, as well as the data format (spreadsheet cell ranges, for example). When you retrieve the template in the future, Harvard Graphics automatically creates a chart and imports the linked data into it. If you have updated the data file since you last imported the data, the new data will be imported. This feature is especially useful for importing data from a file in which the data change on a regular basis. See "Saving a Data Link in a Template" in Chapter 11, for a complete description of saving the data link using the Save Template overlay.

## Importing Lotus Data

Importing data from a Lotus 1-2-3 spreadsheet to a Harvard Graphics chart is probably the most common data importation performed. Fortunately, it is also the easiest. If you are importing data from the same spreadsheet on a regular basis, you will want to save a template after you have imported your data. This way, you can perform this importation again and again, simply by getting the template.

*Note:* You can only import from Lotus files having the extension .WK1 or .WKS.

Use the following steps to import data from a Lotus 1-2-3 spreadsheet:

1. Create the Harvard Graphics chart as described in an earlier section, "Preparing a Harvard Graphics Chart for Importation."

2. From the Main Menu, select <Import/Export>.

3. From the Import/Export menu, select <Import Lotus data>.

If you specified a Lotus 1-2-3 spreadsheet at the "Import file" option on the Default Settings form, you will see the Import Lotus Data form and you can skip to step 5. (For information on setting a default import file, see "Default Import File" in Chapter 3, "Setup and Default Settings.") Otherwise, continue with step 4.

4. From the Select Worksheet form, shown in Figure 12-2, select a spreadsheet using the same techniques used to select a chart file from the Select Chart form (as described in Chapter 2, "Harvard Graphics Basics"). If your Lotus spreadsheet is not on the directory displayed at the "Directory" option of the Select Worksheet form, change the directory by either entering the desired directory at "Directory" or pressing F3-Change dir and selecting a directory from the Select Directory form (also described in Chapter 2). Select the desired spreadsheet and press F10-Continue. Harvard Graphics then displays the Import Lotus Data form.

5. On the Import Lotus Data form, define the cells and cell addresses for your title, subtitle, footnote, X axis data, and series data, as described shortly in "Using the Import Lotus Data Form." (You may also use named ranges for the X axis data and series data fields).

6. Press F10-Continue to import your data. Harvard Graphics then imports the data and displays the chart data form on your monitor.

The data you imported are displayed on this form.

```
                        Select Worksheet

Directory: C:\HG
Filename:  UNITS    .WKS

    Filename Ext  |  Date     | Type    |   Description

    UNITS    .WKS | 05-07-87  | OTHER
    FUTURE   .WKS | 09-01-90  | OTHER
    HANSON   .WKS | 05-21-90  | OTHER
    WEEKLY   .WKS | 06-12-90  | OTHER
    UPDATE   .WKS | 07-30-90  | OTHER




    F1-Help       F3-Change dir
                                                      F10-Continue
```

**Figure 12-2.**   Select Worksheet form

Once the data have been successfully imported and the chart data form is displayed, your chart can be modified and enhanced like any other Harvard Graphics chart. For example, you may want to add a title, subtitle, or footnote if you did not import this text. You can also modify chart options, add drawings or symbols, produce output of your chart, or include it in a slide show.

7. To save your chart with the imported data, select <Get/Save/Remove> from the Main Menu and <Save chart> from the Get/Save/Remove menu. Save the chart as you would any other Harvard Graphics chart.

8. If you want to save the data link so you can instantly import data in this file later, select <Save template> from the Get/Save/Remove menu, and then save the template as described in "Saving a Data Link in a Template" in Chapter 11.

## Using the Import Lotus Data Form

The Import Lotus Data form, displayed in Figure 12-3, is used to define the title, subtitle, and footnote, as well as the cell ranges for your X data and your series data. The name of the Lotus spreadsheet you will be importing from is displayed at the top of the form. If you want to import data from a different spreadsheet than the one shown, press F3-Select files. Harvard Graphics will return you to the Select Worksheet form so you can select the desired spreadsheet.

There are two ways to define the title, subtitle, footnote, and series legends for your chart. You can type in this text either on the Import Lotus Data form when you are importing your data or on the chart data form after you import the data. Alternatively, you can import this text by specifying the cell address in the spreadsheet where this text information is stored. To enter these cell addresses on the Import Lotus Data form, precede the address with a backslash (\) in the first column of the corresponding "Title," "Subtitle," or "Footnote" option. For example, if cell A1 contains text you want to import as the title of your chart, type in \A1 at the "Title" option.

The middle of the Import Lotus Data form contains two columns. In the first column, "Legend," you can either enter the names of up to

```
                    Import Lotus Data
        Worksheet name: units.wks

                Title:
             Subtitle:
             Footnote:

                     Legend              Data Range

             X   X axis data

             1   Series 1
             2   Series 2
             3   Series 3
             4   Series 4
             5   Series 5
             6   Series 6
             7   Series 7
             8   Series 8

             Append data:  ▶Yes     No

  F1-Help         F3-Select files
                  F4-Clear ranges                         F10-Continue
```

**Figure 12-3.**   Import Lotus Data form

eight series or define the cell location where Harvard Graphics will find the series legends to import. As with the "Title," "Subtitle," and "Footnote" options, you define the cell address by preceding the address with a backslash. See Figure 12-4 for an example of defining cell addresses for the series legend importation.

The second column, "Data Range," is used to enter the cell ranges for your X axis data and series data. Alternatively, if you have created names for the X data and series data ranges in your spreadsheet, you can enter these names on the Import Lotus Data form. If your X axis data and series data are not in one continuous range, you will need to perform the importation more than once, importing the first continuous range and then importing again for the second range, and so on. (See the following section.)

The final option on the Import Lotus Data form, "Append data," is used to add subsequent ranges to data already entered into the chart. If all your Lotus data is in a continuous range and you do not want to keep

```
                    ┌─────────── Import Lotus Data ───────────┐
              Worksheet name: units.wks

                      Title:
                   Subtitle:
                   Footnote:

                             Legend          │   Data Range

                    X   X axis data          │   A4..A6

                    1   \B1                  │   B4..B6
                    2   \C1                  │   C4..C6
                    3   \D1                  │   D4..D6
                    4   Series 4
                    5   Series 5
                    6   Series 6
                    7   Series 7
                    8   Series 8

                    Append data:   Yes   ▶No

   F1-Help          F3-Select files
                    F4-Clear ranges                          F10-Continue
```

**Figure 12-4.**  Defining cell addresses for series legend importation

adding data to your chart each time you import, set this option to No.

### Importing Lotus Data in Non-Continuous Cell Ranges

If your X axis data and series data are not located in a continuous range, importing Lotus data will require several steps, one for each set of ranges. For example, if your Lotus data are in two non-continuous cell ranges in your spreadsheet, you will need to import data twice. The first time you will import the first cell ranges. The second time set "Append data" to Yes, and import the second cell range. These data will then be added to the data imported in the first step. If you have more than two non-continuous cell ranges, continue importing additional data, keeping "Append data" set to Yes for each additional importation.

If at all possible, you should avoid importing data from non-continuous cell ranges since it is not possible to take maximum advantage of a data link in these situations. If possible, modify your spreadsheet so the data you want to use are located in a continuous range.

## Importing ASCII Text Files

The <Import ASCII data> selection on the Import/Export menu is used primarily to import text into a text chart. It can also be used to import numerical data from an ASCII file into a data chart if the data meet certain format requirements. These format requirements, as well as the Harvard Graphics features that permit you to adjust the importation of numerical data, are covered in the section "Importing Tabular ASCII Data."

The steps for importing ASCII data are as follows:

1. Create a Harvard Graphics chart as described in an earlier section, "Preparing a Harvard Graphics Chart for Importation."

2. From the Main Menu, select <Import/Export>.

3. From the Import/Export menu, select <Import ASCII data>.

If you specified a filename at the "Import file" option on the Default Settings form, you will see the Import ASCII Data form and you can skip to step 5. (For information on setting a default import file, see "Default Import File" in Chapter 3). Otherwise continue with step 4.

4. From the Select File form, select the desired ASCII file using the same technique used to select a chart file from the Select Chart form (as described in Chapter 2, "Harvard Graphics Basics"). If the ASCII file is not on the directory shown at the "Directory" option, change the directory either by entering the desired directory at "Directory" or pressing F3-Change dir and selecting a directory from the Select Directory form (also described in Chapter 2). Once you select a file, Harvard Graphics displays the Import ASCII Data form. The selected file is displayed in the ASCII file area.

5. On the Import ASCII Data form, define which lines of data you want to import, as described in the next section. If the data are formatted in columns, you may be able to select which columns of data to import, as described later in "Importing Tabular ASCII Data." Once you have filled out the form, press F10-Continue.

If you are importing the data into a chart data form (bar/line, area, high/low/close, or pie), Harvard Graphics then displays the Import

Titles and Legends overlay. Set the options on this form, and then press F10-Continue. (If you are importing the data to a text chart, the Import Titles and Legends overlay does not apply.)

Harvard Graphics then imports the data and displays the chart form on your monitor. The data you imported are displayed on this form. Once the data have been successfully imported and the chart form is displayed, your chart can be modified and enhanced like any other Harvard Graphics chart. You can modify chart options, add drawings or symbols, produce output of your chart, or include it in a slide show.

6. To save your chart with the imported data, select <Get/Save/Remove> from the Main Menu and <Save chart> from the Get/Save/Remove menu. Save the chart as you would any other Harvard Graphics chart.

7. If you want to save the data link so you can instantly import data from this file at a later time, select <Save template> from the Get/Save/Remove menu. Save the template as described in "Saving a Data Link in a Template" in Chapter 11.

## Using the Import ASCII Data Form

The Import ASCII Data form (shown in Figure 12-5) is divided into three areas: the ASCII file area, the Import ASCII options area, and the function key banner. The contents of the file you are importing are displayed in the ASCII file area, as can be seen in the figure.

While the contents of your ASCII file are displayed in the ASCII file area, use the options on the Import ASCII Data form to define which data in the ASCII file you want to import. When your file is a text file, you only need to set two of the options on this form: "Read from line" and "to line." Harvard Graphics sets these options to the first line and the last line in the ASCII file by default. If you want to import less than the entire ASCII text file, enter the line number corresponding to the first line you want to import at "Read from line" and the last line to import at "to line." For example, to import text from lines 3 through 7 only into your chart, set "Read from line" to 3, and "to line" to 7.

*Note:* There is no way to exclude unwanted lines from importation when they are embedded within the ASCII file. You will need to delete these lines from the chart form once the data have been imported.

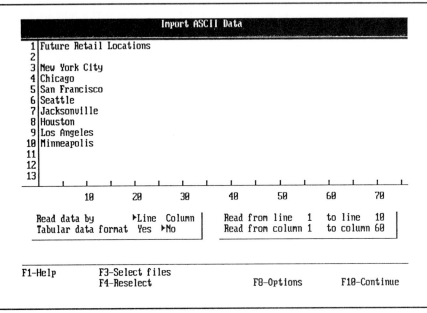

**Figure 12-5.**   Import ASCII Data form

Harvard Graphics automatically sets the "Tabular data format" option to either Yes or No, depending on the format of your data. If your ASCII file meets Harvard Graphics' requirements for importing a tabular data file, this option is automatically set to Yes. You can then set the "Read data by," "Read from column," and "to column" options as described in the next section. If your ASCII file does not meet the requirements of a tabular data file, "Tabular data format" is set to No and the remaining options do not apply. You can change the "Tabular data format" setting, if desired, although changing it to Yes may not result in successful data importation.

Once you have filled out the Import ASCII Data form, press F10-Continue. If you are importing data into a data chart, Harvard Graphics will display the Import Titles and Legends overlay. If you want to import the first three *non-blank* lines in the file (regardless of the "Read from line" and "to line" settings) as the title and a two-line subtitle, set "Import title and subtitle" to Yes. Otherwise, select No. Set "Import first line as series legends" to No if your data are not in a tabular format or to either Yes or No if your data are in a tabular format, as described in the next section.

Press F10-Continue to import your data and display the appropriate chart form.

## Importing Tabular ASCII Data

To import ASCII data into a data chart, the data must be in a tabular format, that is, in columns. Harvard Graphics requires that these columns be separated by at least three spaces. As you can see in the Import ASCII Data form shown in Figure 12-6, the tabular data are displayed in the Import ASCII area of the form. Because there are columns of text or numbers in this ASCII file, Harvard Graphics has automatically set the "Tabular data format" option to Yes.

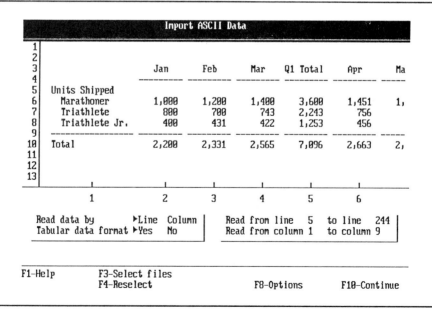

**Figure 12-6.** Importing tabular ASCII data

*Note:* Tabular ASCII data files are generally used only for printing data and are not meant to be imported by another software program. ASCII files that are intended to be imported normally use a special format, such as the delimited ASCII data format. While Harvard Graphics does permit the importation of tabular data files, you may find this importation time consuming and in some cases impossible.

When your data are in a tabular format, the "Read data by" option tells Harvard Graphics how you want the data to be inserted into your data chart (this option has no effect if you are inserting your data into a text chart). If "Read data by" is set to Line, the first values in each line are imported as the X data values for XY charts and the pie labels for pie charts. The remaining values in each line are imported as the series values for both XY charts and pie charts. When "Read data by" is set to Column, the first values in each column are imported as the X data values or pie labels, with the remaining values being imported as the series data.

The "Read from line" and "to line" options are used to define the first and last lines of the data file that will be imported into your chart. When your data are in a tabular format, Harvard Graphics will automatically set "Read from line" to the first line in which a column is detected. The "to line" option is set to the last line in the file by default. Set these options to the first and last lines you want to import. As noted in the preceding section, any lines within this specified line range that you do not want to include in your chart must be deleted from the chart data form after the importation is complete.

The "Read from column" and "to column" options are used to indicate which columns should be included when you import your data (as shown in Figure 12-6). When Harvard Graphics detects that your data are in a tabular format, it numbers each of the columns it detects. These numbers are displayed at the bottom of the ASCII file area. To include only a selected range of columns, set "Read from column" to the number of the first column you want to include in your chart (this should be the X data column when "Read data by" is set to Line, or the first series when "Read data by" is set to Column). Set "to column" to the number of the last column you want to include in your chart. An alternative method of selecting only some of the columns of data is described in the following section.

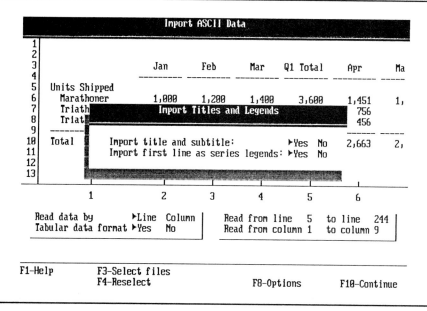

**Figure 12-7.** Import Titles and Legends overlay

Once you have filled out the Import ASCII Data form, press F10-Continue. Harvard Graphics will display the Import Titles and Legends overlay, shown in Figure 12-7. If you want to import the first three *non-blank* lines in the file, the first to be used as a title and the next two as a subtitle, set "Import title and subtitle" to Yes. Otherwise, select No.

If you want Harvard Graphics to import the series legends, set "Import first line as series legends" to Yes. If "Read data by" is set to Line, the first entry in each column of data, starting with the line that "Read from line" is set to, will be used for the series legends. If "Read data by" is set to Column, the first column of data will be used for the series legends (in this case the option on the Import Titles and Legends overlay reads "Import first column as series legends"). Set "Import first line as series legends" to No to suppress the importation of series legends.

Press F10-Continue to import your data and display the appropriate chart data form.

### Customizing Tabular ASCII Data Importation

There are two types of customization you can perform on your data when you are importing tabular ASCII data. You can adjust the size of the columns Harvard Graphics has identified, and you can specifically exclude selected columns from importation. To customize the columns, press F8-Options. Harvard Graphics will enter a special mode, called *customize columns*. While you are in this mode, you will not be able to set any options on the Import ASCII Data form. To exit this mode, press F8-Options again, or press F10-Continue.

In the customize columns mode, you can move the cursor between the various columns in the ASCII file area. Press TAB to move one column to the right and SHIFT-TAB to move one column to the left. Each time you move to a new column, that column is highlighted. While a column is highlighted, you can change its width by using the LEFT and RIGHT arrow keys. As you adjust the width, the size of the highlighted area will change to show you the current width.

There is a trick to customizing the size of a column. With the desired column highlighted, press the LEFT or RIGHT arrow key to indicate which side of the column you want to change. If you press RIGHT first, subsequent presses of both LEFT and RIGHT arrow keys affect the size of the right side of the column. When you are finished adjusting the right side, press ENTER. If you then press the LEFT arrow key, Harvard Graphics interprets this as a sign that you want to adjust the position of the left side of the column. Again, subsequent presses of LEFT and RIGHT arrow keys will adjust this side of the column until you press ENTER. While you are adjusting the size of either side, you cannot use TAB or SHIFT-TAB to move to a new column; you must press ENTER to complete the adjustment before changing columns.

Harvard Graphics also allows you to exclude a column, so that it will not be imported. For example, if you want to import columns 1, 2, 4, and 5, from a file with five columns, you will need to exclude column 3 in order to import the data correctly. To exclude a column, use TAB to highlight the column you want to exclude, and then press CTRL-DEL. The highlight will be removed, indicating that the column will not be imported. As you exclude one or more columns, Harvard Graphics renumbers the remaining columns and displays these numbers at the bottom of the ASCII file area. Columns excluded from importation remain visible on the ASCII file area. They are not, however, labeled with a column number and, consequently, will not be imported.

The following six steps describe how to customize tabular ASCII importation:

1. After you have set the options on the Import ASCII Data form, press F8-Options to enter the customize columns mode. The first column of data will be highlighted.

2. If you want to delete this column from importation, press CTRL-DEL. If you do so, continue to step 5.

3. If you want to adjust the left margin of this column, press LEFT. Now, press LEFT and RIGHT to adjust this left margin, and press ENTER when you are through.

4. If you want to adjust the right margin of this column, press RIGHT. Now, press LEFT and RIGHT to adjust this right margin and press ENTER when you are through.

5. If you want to customize additional columns, press TAB to move to the next column to the right, and then repeat these steps starting with step 2.

6. When you are finished making changes to your column size and selection, press F8-Options or F10-Continue to return to the Import ASCII Data form.

You can undo the column sizing and exclusions by pressing F4-Reselect. When you do so, Harvard Graphics will restore any columns that were excluded and return all columns to their original size. You cannot use F4-Reselect, however, while in the customize columns mode.

## Importing Delimited ASCII Files

Most computer programs that can export data, such as dBASE III+, dBASE IV, and Paradox, can create a delimited ASCII file. Many mainframe computer programs can produce this type of file as well. Thus this file type is one of the best choices for importing data into Harvard Graphics. A delimited ASCII file contains data that are separated, or *delimited*, by specific characters. The most common format is to separate each piece of data with a comma as the delimiter. Each row of data is usually separated with a carriage return and a line feed. Alphanumeric (text) data are identified by quotation marks or other similar identifiers. The following is an example of a delimited ASCII data file:

```
"1980",12.8,49.8,76.4
"1981",9.9,51.3,77.1
"1982",12.3,52.7,76.8
"1983",13.1,53.4,78.25
"1984",13.75,55.2,78.1
"1985",14.4,57.6,78.8
"1986",14.7,100.7,78.4
"1987",15.4,62.7,73.4
```

Harvard Graphics expects that the first value in each record of a delimited ASCII file will contain an X data value that is compatible with the X data type of the XY chart you are importing the data into, or a text value that will be used as a label in a pie chart. The remaining values on each line are the corresponding series values.

Use the following steps to import a delimited ASCII file:

1. Create a Harvard Graphics chart, as described in the section "Preparing a Harvard Graphics Chart for Importation."

2. From the Main Menu, select <Import/Export>.

3. From the Import/Export menu, select <Import delimited ASCII>. Harvard Graphics will display the Select File form.

*Note:* You cannot use the Default Settings form to specify a delimited ASCII file as your default import file. You must use the Select File form.

4. Select the delimited ASCII file that you want to import from the Select File form using the same techniques as used for selecting a chart from the Select Chart form (as described in Chapter 2). If the delimited ASCII file is not on the directory shown at the "Directory" option, change the directory. Either enter the desired directory at "Directory" or press F3-Change dir and select a directory from the Select Directory form (also described in Chapter 2).

Once you select a delimited ASCII file, Harvard Graphics displays the ASCII Delimiters overlay, shown in Figure 12-8.

5. On the ASCII Delimiters overlay, indicate the characters that have been used to delimit the data, as described in the next section. Press F10-Continue when you have defined options on this overlay.

6. Harvard Graphics now asks you to set the "Import first record as series legends" option as described later in "Importing Series Legends from Delimited ASCII Files." When you have set this option, press F10-Continue or ENTER. Harvard Graphics will display the chart data form for the imported chart. Your imported data will appear on this form.

Importing and Exporting 387

Once the data have been successfully imported and the chart data form is displayed, your chart can be modified and enhanced like any other Harvard Graphics chart.

7. Save your chart with the imported data as you would any other Harvard Graphics chart.

8. If you want to save the data link so you can instantly import data from this file at a later time, select <Save template> from the Get/Save/Remove menu. Save the template as described in "Saving a Data Link in a Template" in Chapter 11.

## Defining ASCII Delimiters

After you select <Import delimited ASCII> from the Import/Export menu, Harvard Graphics displays the ASCII Delimiters overlay, shown in Figure 12-8. Use this overlay to indicate the characters that define

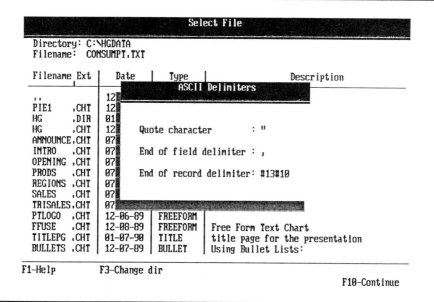

**Figure 12-8.** ASCII Delimiters overlay

the positions of the data you are importing. The "Quote character" option is used to define the character that distinguishes alphanumeric data (text) from numbers. All alphanumeric data in the delimited ASCII file must be enclosed by the defined "Quote character." The "End of field delimiter" option is used to identify the character used to separate individual values on a given line of your data. The most common character used for this purpose is a comma. These files are often called *comma-delimited* ASCII files. The final option, "End of record delimiter," is used to define the character or characters that separate individual records in the delimited ASCII file.

If you need to use ASCII codes for delimiters that cannot be displayed, enter the ASCII code preceded by the # character. For example, Harvard Graphics defaults the end-of-record delimiter to #10#13, the two consecutive ASCII codes for a line feed and a carriage return, respectively. When you have completed the ASCII Delimiters overlay, press F10-Continue or ENTER.

## Importing Series Legends from Delimited ASCII Files

When you press F10-Continue from the ASCII Delimiters overlay, Harvard Graphics displays the option "Import first record as series legends," as shown in Figure 12-9. When you set this option to Yes, Harvard Graphics uses the values in the first row of the delimited ASCII file as the series legends. The first value in this first row is not used, although there must be a value here—two quote characters enclosing nothing is sufficient. The second value is used as the Series 1 legend, the third value is used as the Series 2 legend, and so on. The following is an example of a delimited ASCII file in which "Import first record as series legends" would be set to Yes:

```
"value not used","Fish","Chicken","Beef"
"1980",12.8,49.8,76.4
"1981",9.9,51.3,77.1
"1982",12.3,52.7,76.8
"1983",13.1,53.4,78.25
"1984",13.75,55.2,78.1
"1985",14.4,57.6,78.8
"1986",14.7,100.7,78.4
"1987",15.4,62.7,73.4
```

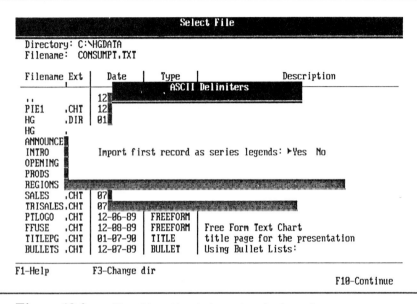

**Figure 12-9.** Use this option to import series legends

## Importing Graphs Into Harvard Graphics

Harvard Graphics allows you to directly import two different types of graphs: Lotus graphs and graphs from PFS:GRAPH. Unlike the data importation described previously, you can import these graph types without first creating a Harvard Graphics chart (unless you want to import only the data from a Lotus graph). When you import either a Lotus graph or a graph from PFS:GRAPH, Harvard Graphics determines the characteristics of this graph and creates a chart that has similar features. The next sections cover importing graphs from Lotus and PFS:GRAPH.

## Importing Lotus Graphs

With Harvard Graphics you can directly import a graph from Lotus 1-2-3 (version 1A or 2) or Lotus Symphony. Harvard Graphics imports all the data associated with a graph; you cannot selectively import data as you can when you import Lotus data. You choose a graph to import by selecting its name. If you did not name your graph, it will have the name MAIN, by default. The graphs cannot be picture files (.PIC) of the graph. (However, you can convert .PIC files into drawings using Draw Partner, as described in Chapter 18, "Drawing and Editing with Draw Partner.") You can import the Lotus graph for the data only, or you can let Harvard Graphics determine the chart type and characteristics and create a chart with these features.

The following steps describe how to import graphs:

1. If you want to import the data only from a Lotus graph, create a chart as described in the earlier section "Preparing a Harvard Graphics Chart for Importation." If you want to also import the graph type and characteristics, do not create a chart first.

2. From the Main Menu, select <Import/Export>.

3. From the Import/Export menu, select <Import Lotus graph>.

If you defined a Lotus spreadsheet as your default import data file on the Default Settings form (as described in "Default Import File" in Chapter 3), Harvard Graphics will display the Import Lotus Graph form. If the graph you want to import is associated with this spreadsheet, continue to step 5. Otherwise, press F3-Select files to display the Select Worksheet form. If you did not define a Lotus spreadsheet as your default import data file, Harvard Graphics will display the Select Worksheet form.

4. Select the spreadsheet that contains your Lotus graph from the Select Worksheet form using the same techniques used to select a chart file from the Select Chart form. If your Lotus spreadsheet is not shown at the "Directory" option of the Select Worksheet form, change the directory. Either enter the desired directory at "Directory" or press F3-Change dir and select a directory from the Select Directory form. Then press F10-Continue. Once you do so Harvard Graphics displays the Import Lotus Graph form.

5. Select the Lotus graph you want to import and set the "Import data only" option to Yes if you want to import the data only or to No to import both the data and the chart. (If you are importing only

the data, you must have first created a chart as described in step 1.) When you have completed this form, press F10-Continue.

If you set "Import data only" to No, the data are imported and the chart data form will be displayed. If you set "Import data only" to Yes, both the data and the chart are imported and Harvard Graphics will first display the chart on your monitor. Press any key to remove the display of the chart and continue to the chart data form.

Once the chart or just the data have been successfully imported and the chart data form is displayed, your chart can be modified and enhanced like any other Harvard Graphics chart.

6. Save your chart with the imported data as you would any Harvard Graphics chart.

7. If you want to save the data link so you can instantly import the chart and data from this file later, select <Save template> from the Get/Save/Remove menu. Save the template as described in "Saving a Data Link in a Template" in Chapter 11.

### Selecting a Lotus Graph from the Import Lotus Graph Form

The Import Lotus Graph form is used to select a graph from a Lotus spreadsheet. The name of the worksheet is displayed at the top of the form at "Worksheet name." The middle of the form contains the graph list area. (If you find your Lotus graph is not in the selected spreadsheet, press F3-Select files to display the Select Worksheet form to select a different spreadsheet.) Highlight the Lotus graph you want to import using the UP and DOWN arrow keys. Once the desired graph is highlighted and its name is shown at the "Graph name" option (just below the graph list area), press ENTER. Harvard Graphics will move the cursor to the "Import data only" option. If you want to import both the data and graph characteristics, set "Import data only" to No. If you want to import only the data, set "Import data only" to Yes. (You must also have prepared a Harvard Graphics chart to import this data into, as described in step 1 of the previous section.)

When you have completed the Import Lotus Graph form, press F10-Continue. Harvard Graphics will now import the graph.

## Importing Graphs from PFS:GRAPH

The following steps describe how to import a graph from PFS:GRAPH:

1. From the Main Menu, select <Import/Export>.

2. From the Import/Export menu, select <Import PFS:GRAPH chart>. Harvard Graphics will display the Select File form.

3. Use the Select File form to select the PFS:GRAPH file you want to import. Select the desired file the same way you retrieve a Harvard Graphics chart. If the PFS:GRAPH file is not shown at the "Directory" option, change the directory. Either enter the desired directory at "Directory" or press F3-Change dir and select a directory from the Select Directory form.

If the file you select is not a PFS:GRAPH file, Harvard Graphics will display the message "File is not of the expected type." Press any key to return to the Select File form.

Once you select a PFS:GRAPH file, Harvard Graphics imports the chart and displays it on your monitor. Press any key to remove the chart displayed and continue to the chart data form. Your chart can now be modified and enhanced like any other Harvard Graphics chart.

4. Save your chart as you would any other Harvard Graphics chart.

Unlike the other types of importation described to this point, you cannot save the importation of a PFS:GRAPH as a template. If you need to later import the same graph again, you must repeat all of the steps just described.

## Importing CGM Metafiles

Harvard Graphics allows you to import a CGM metafile for use as a Harvard Graphics symbol. You can use these symbols the same way you use any drawing or symbol. If you own Draw Partner, use it to import CGM metafiles instead of Harvard Graphics, since Draw Partner makes this importation simple. For details, see the section "Retrieving and Saving Files" in Chapter 17.

If you do not own Draw Partner, how you import a CGM metafile depends on which version of Harvard Graphics you own. If you have Harvard Graphics versions 2.0 or earlier, you cannot import CGM metafiles. If you have Harvard Graphics version 2.10, see the later section "Importing CGM Metafiles Using VDI Device Drivers." If you have Harvard Graphics version 2.12 or 2.13, see the next section.

There may be differences in image appearance between the original CGM metafiles (created with other software) and the symbol files Harvard Graphics creates once it imports the CGM metafiles. This results from the different ways Harvard Graphics and the original program create drawings. Changes that may be apparent once you import the CGM metafile into Harvard Graphics include different element colors, fonts, line thicknesses, and fill patterns. You may also observe changes in the characteristics of some shapes such as circles, boxes, and polygons.

### Using META2HG to Import CGM Metafiles

Harvard Graphics versions 2.12 and 2.13 come with an improved version of the utility called META2HG.EXE. You use META2HG.EXE to convert CGM metafiles to Harvard Graphics symbols. Unfortunately, META2HG.EXE cannot convert large CGM metafiles to Harvard Graphics symbols. If the metafile will result in a symbol that is larger than 32K (32,678 bytes, to be precise), the complete metafile will not be converted.

You must run the utility META2HG.EXE from DOS. To run this utility, exit Harvard Graphics and ensure that META2HG.EXE is on your current directory (your Harvard Graphics directory). For simplicity's sake, copy the metafile to this directory as well. (Although, if you are comfortable with DOS, you can include the path of the metafile as part of its filename when you execute META2HG.EXE to achieve the same effect.) At the DOS prompt, type this command:

**META2HG** *cgmfilename hgsymbolfilename*

That is, type **META2HG**, followed by a blank space, and then type the name of the CGM metafile that you want to convert, followed by another space and the name of the symbol file you want META2HG to create from the metafile. For example, type the following command to convert a CGM metafile called DRAWING.CGM to a Harvard Graphics symbol file called NEWSYM.SYM:

  META2HG DRAWING.CGM NEWSYM.SYM

If the CGM metafile is too large, META2HG will display the message "Warning: not enough room in symbol, some data lost." Unless you are able to simplify the CGM metafile's contents so it is less complex, and therefore takes up less space, you will not be able to convert this entire file.

If your conversion was successful, you will be able to access the newly created symbol using Draw/Annotate in Harvard Graphics. See "Retrieving a Symbol" in Chapter 9.

## Importing CGM Metafiles Using VDI Device Drivers

Importing a CGM metafile with Harvard Graphics version 2.10 requires the use of two of the VDI drivers that accompanied this version of the program. These drivers must be loaded using your CONFIG.SYS file.

You must have installed these VDI drivers in the directory C:\VDI (see the Harvard Graphics manual or "Installing the Virtual Device Interface Drivers" in Appendix B, for information on installing VDI drivers). The following two lines must be added to the end of your CONFIG.SYS file, and must be the last lines in the file:

  DEVICE = C:\VDI\HGSYM.SYS
  DEVICE = C:\VDI\GSSCGI.SYS

You only need to add these commands once. After you add them, you must reboot your system so the commands in the CONFIG.SYS file will be executed.

Finally, you must set the DOS environmental variable called *metafil* once each session before you execute the META2HG.EXE program. From the DOS prompt, enter the command:

  SET METAFIL = HGSYM

You can now use META2HG.EXE to convert a CGM metafile to a Harvard Graphics symbol file. To do this, at the DOS prompt type **META2HG**, followed by the name of the metafile. For example, if your metafile is called DRAWING.CGM, type the following command:

**META2HG DRAWING.CGM**

If your CGM metafile will result in a Harvard Graphics symbol larger than 32K, Harvard Graphics will display the message "Warning: File too large; Symbol file being shortened."

When you convert your first CGM metafile, META2HG will create a file called HG0000.SYM. If you now convert another CGM metafile, META2HG will create a file called HG0001.SYM, then HG0002.SYM, and so on.

*Hint:* You may want to keep a separate version of the CONFIG.SYS file containing the VDI device drivers so that they can be loaded only when you need them. Refer to your Harvard Graphics Manual or the discussion of VDI drivers in Appendix B, "Installation."

## Exporting Charts

You can export Harvard Graphics charts and use them with other software. There are four specific export file formats available in Harvard Graphics: encapsulated PostScript files, HPGL (Hewlett-Packard Graphics Language) files, CGM metafiles, and a special file format that can be imported by Professional Write, a word processing product from Software Publishing Corporation. You should consult the user's manual for the software you want to export your Harvard Graphics chart to for details about which format to use. Many software packages can import more than one of the file formats Harvard Graphics can export.

*Note:* Some software, such as OfficeWriter from Software Publishing Corporation, can import Harvard Graphics symbol files, requiring no special procedure other than saving the chart as a symbol. Refer to your software manuals to help you determine how to import Harvard Graphics charts and symbols.

In all instances, the chart you export is the current chart. If the chart that you want to export is not current, you must first retrieve it. If the chart includes drawings or symbols, these are exported as well. The steps common to exporting the current chart in encapsulated PostScript format, HPGL format, or to Professional Write are described next. Exporting a chart as a CGM metafile is described in the later section, "Exporting a Chart to a CGM Metafile."

1. Make the chart you want to export the current chart.

2. From the Main Menu select <Import/Export>.

3. From the Import/Export menu select <Export picture>. Harvard Graphics will display the Export Picture overlay.

4. Enter the appropriate data on the Export Picture overlay, shown

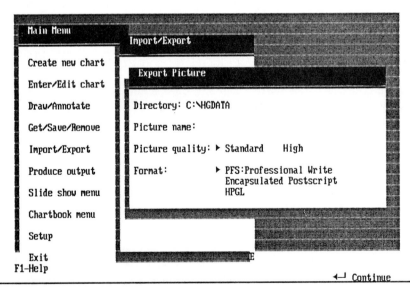

**Figure 12-10.**   Export Picture overlay

in Figure 12-10 (as described in the next section). Then press F10-Continue.

If you set the "Format" variable on the Export Picture overlay to either encapsulated PostScript or HPGL, your chart is exported to the designated directory and filename.

If you set "Format" to PFS:Professional Write, Harvard Graphics will display the Export for PFS:Professional Write overlay. Set the desired options as described later in "Exporting to PFS:Professional Write." Then press F10-Continue to export your chart for use in PFS:Professional Write.

## Using the Export Picture Overlay

Use the Export Picture overlay, shown in Figure 12-10, to specify the characteristics of the file you want to create. At the "Directory" option, specify the path of the directory in which you want Harvard Graphics to write your picture file.

Provide a filename for your picture file at the "Picture name" option. This filename must conform to standard DOS file naming conventions. If you want or need an extension for your filename, you must provide this extension when you enter the name on this overlay.

*Note:* Some software packages will only read files with certain extensions. Consult your software manual for the appropriate file extension.

At the "Picture quality" option, define the output quality of your chart. Although the Standard setting will create a smaller file, the High setting will result in a chart image of higher quality. Setting "Picture quality" to Standard may not produce a suitable image, depending on the software using the chart.

At the "Format" option, indicate the type of file Harvard Graphics should create. These format types are described in the next section.

### Selecting an Export Picture Format

Harvard Graphics provides you with four export picture formats. The PFS:Professional Write format is only applicable if you are creating a chart to be used with PFS:Write, PFS:Professional Write, or Professional Write. The remaining three formats, encapsulated PostScript, HPGL, and CGM metafile, are popular formats usable by most programs that can import charts, such as desktop publishing programs and high-end word processing programs.

*Note:* The CGM metafile format cannot be created using the Export Picture overlay. To export using the CGM metafile format, see the later section, "Exporting a Chart to a CGM Metafile."

Selecting the appropriate format so your chart can be used by other software is not always easy. Each format has both advantages and limitations. To make matters worse, the appropriate format may also depend on the complexity of the Harvard Graphics chart you have created. Although not intended to be exhaustive, the following sections contain information about encapsulated PostScript, HPGL, and CGM metafile formats to help you select the best format for your needs. You may find you will need to experiment a little in order to find the combination that works best with your other software.

**Using the Encapsulated PostScript Export Picture Format**  The first line of the encapsulated PostScript file that Harvard Graphics produces is a header containing non-PostScript information. While some software can read this header and use the information, other software only becomes confused by it. If your software is designed to read encapsulated PostScript, but the files created by Harvard Graphics do not import correctly, you can use a text editor to delete the first line of the file before you attempt to import the file again.

*Note:* Since encapsulated PostScript files support very long line lengths, only text editors capable of editing files with long line lengths can be used.

**Using the HPGL Export Picture Format**  The Hewlett-Packard Graphics Language is a plotter language. Therefore, HPGL files are created with the characteristics of plotted Harvard Graphics charts. Specifically, Harvard Graphics modifies certain characteristics of the chart so a plotter will produce an acceptable image. For instance, since Harvard Graphics cannot plot 3D overlap XY charts, it converts these charts to 2D charts before the export file is created. Also, some symbols cannot be plotted correctly. If these changes are not desirable in your exported charts, you should export your chart using a different format.

**Using the CGM Metafile Export Picture Format**   Considerations for using CGM metafiles are discussed briefly here, although you should refer to the section later in this chapter, "Exporting a Chart to a CGM Metafile," for a complete description of exporting Harvard Graphics charts and symbols using this file format.

CGM metafiles may not maintain all of the characteristics of Harvard Graphics charts. For instance, the chart colors may be changed in the exported file, and lines and text may have a different appearance. Unfortunately, not all CGM metafile conversion programs work equally well. A file created by one software program may be adequately converted by a second, but not by a third. While CGM metafile tends to be a versatile format for exporting a Harvard Graphics chart, you will need to test the adequacy of the resulting images before making this your method of choice.

Another consideration is that CGM metafiles require you to install a VDI device driver (unless you use Draw Partner). You may or may not be able to use these VDI drivers, depending on the amount of memory your computer has, as well as the amount of memory taken up by other memory-resident programs. In addition, you cannot use this format if you are running the Harvard Graphics program from a two-disk system.

**Exporting to PFS:Professional Write**   If you switch "Format" to PFS:Professional Write, Harvard Graphics will display an additional overlay, Export for PFS:Professional Write, shown in Figure 12-11. Set "Printer" to the printer you will use to print the PFS:Professional Write document. This setting assumes that you will print your Professional Write document to a printer you have connected to your computer, and that this printer is defined as one of the two printers you use to print Harvard Graphics charts. Printer 1 and Printer 2 refer to the printers you defined on the Printer 1 and Printer 2 Setup forms (see "Default Printers" in Chapter 3). If you have a color printer, but want to print your output in black and white, set "Color" to No. Otherwise, set "Color" to Yes.

When you include your picture in a Professional Write document, Professional Write will print it in a space measuring 3 1/2 inches tall by 4 1/2 inches wide. When creating your chart for export, keep in mind

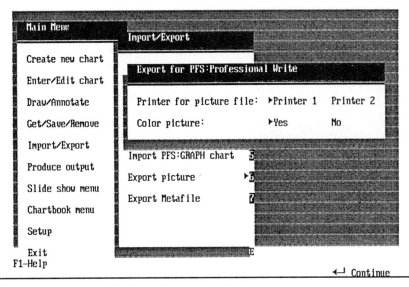

**Figure 12-11.**   Export for PFS:Professional Write overlay

that small text may not be legible when the chart is this size. Also, your Harvard Graphics chart should have a landscape orientation, as this is the orientation that will be used when the chart is printed in Professional Write.

To use the picture you have exported in PFS:Professional Write format, use the *G *file name* command in your Professional Write document. This command must be flush against the left margin of your document. If the file you have exported is not in the same directory as Professional Write, you should include the DOS path of the file in the filename. If the picture file has been exported to the same directory as Professional Write, you do not need to specify the DOS path along with the filename.

For example, if your picture file, called PICTURE.PFS, is located in the same directory as the Professional Write program, include either of these commands to place the chart in your document:

   *GRAPH PICTURE.PFS*

or

   *G PICTURE.PFS*

When you print your document, Professional Write will print the chart file at the location specified by the GRAPH command within the document. Refer to your PFS:Professional Write manual for additional details.

*Note:* You must print your document to the printer defined on the Export for PFS:Professional Write overlay.

## Exporting a Chart to a CGM Metafile

Before you can export to a CGM metafile format, you must have installed the two VDI device drivers for exporting CGM metafiles, as described in the Harvard Graphics manual or in Appendix B. These VDI drivers must be loaded by your CONFIG.SYS file. Assuming that these device drivers are stored in the C:\VDI directory, the last two lines of your CONFIG.SYS file should look like this:

DEVICE = C:\VDI\META.SYS
DEVICE = C:\VDI\GSSCGI.SYS

After you add these two lines to your CONFIG.SYS file, you will need to reboot your computer so these commands will be executed. You are now ready to export a chart as a CGM metafile. The following steps outline this procedure:

1. Exit to DOS if you are already in Harvard Graphics.

2. From the DOS prompt, type

SET METAFIL = META

3. Type **HG** to start Harvard Graphics.

4. Make the chart you want to export as a CGM metafile the current chart (see "Getting an Existing Chart," Chapter 2).

5. Select <Import/Export> from the Main Menu.

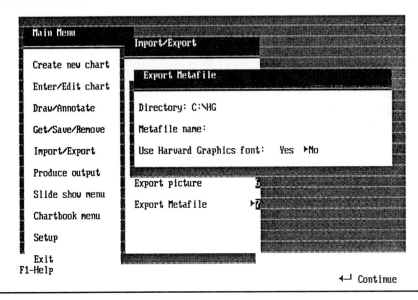

**Figure 12-12.**    Export Metafile overlay

6. Select <Export Metafile> from the Import/Export menu. Harvard Graphics will display the Export metafile overlay.

7. Provide a name for the CGM metafile and press F10-Continue. Harvard Graphics will export your file.

**Using the Export Metafile Overlay**

The Export Metafile overlay is shown in Figure 12-12. This overlay contains three options that permit you to define the characteristics of your CGM metafile. At the "Directory" option, define the path of the directory in which you want to store the metafile. At the "Metafile name" option, define the name, including the extension, of the file that Harvard Graphics will create. Finally, if you want to use Harvard Graphics fonts, set the "Use Harvard Graphics font" option to Yes. If you set "Use Harvard Graphics font" to No, the text in the exported CGM metafile may not accurately depict the font attributes you defined for your chart.

# Slide Shows

Slide Show Overview
Creating a Slide Show
The Create Slide Show Overlay
The Create/Edit Slide Show Form
Selecting a Slide Show
Editing a Slide Show
Including Bit-Mapped Files in a Slide Show
Including a Template in a Slide Show
Including Slide Show Files in a Slide Show
Using Harvard Graphics Screenshows
Adding Screenshow Effects
Special Considerations for Very Large Slide Shows
Using Custom Palettes in a Screenshow
Creating Practice Cards for a Slide Show
Other Slide Show Topics

This chapter describes how to create and customize the Harvard Graphics chart presentation feature called a *slide show*. This feature allows you to produce computerized presentations and interactive information systems. You can also use a slide show to increase your productivity by simultaneously outputting, spell checking, or modifying multiple charts.

## Slide Show Overview

A slide show is a powerful and flexible chart presentation tool in which one chart is displayed after another, the same way slides are shown with a projector. However, Harvard Graphics slide shows provide much more flexibility. The advantages of using a slide show are as follows:

- You can present a series of charts to an audience without having to make each chart current. Special effects called *transitions* can be included to add flair to your presentation.

- Slide shows can be either self-running or user-controlled. Self-running slide shows continue on to the next image after a specified time delay. User-controlled slide shows are not timed; they advance to the next image when you press a key on your keyboard or a mouse button.

- You can extend a user-controlled slide show by defining keys that, when pressed, cause the slide show to continue to a specified image, rather than just the next one. This capability permits you to create interactive presentations.

- Slide shows can be used to output two or more charts with one print, plot, or record command. These slide shows can also include templates with data links that automatically import data just before outputting the chart.

- Slide shows can be used to check the spelling on multiple charts without having to make each chart current. See "Spell Checking Charts in a Slide Show," later in this chapter.

- Slide shows can be used to preview two or more charts without having to make each chart current. If a problem is discovered with one of the charts, you can immediately modify the data or settings for that chart. See "Using a Screenshow to Review Charts," later in this chapter.

- Slide shows can be used to apply the same modification to a group of charts. These modifications can include the overall size and placement of each chart, the addition of a symbol such as your company logo to each chart, or adding the same footnote to each chart. This feature is described later, in the section "Including a Template in a Slide Show."

*Slide show* is a general term used to describe any Harvard Graphics slide show. *Screenshow* is a term used to describe slide shows when they are presented on your monitor or with a screen projection device. While all Screenshows are slide shows, only the slide shows that are used for "live" or on-line presentations are called Screenshows.

## Creating a Slide Show

Four types of files can be included in a slide show:

- Harvard Graphics chart files (.CHT)
- Harvard Graphics template files (.TPL)
- Other slide show files (.SHW)
- Bit-mapped files (.PCX and .PIC)

When a chart is included in a slide show, the chart image can be either displayed or output. Templates have two uses in a slide show. The first is to import and then display or output data linked to a template. The second use is to modify characteristics of charts that follow the template in the slide show. When a slide show file appears in a slide show, Harvard Graphics will immediately *branch*, or switch, to this slide show. Finally, bit-mapped files can be included to display specialized images created using a drawing program, scanned with a digitizing scanner, or captured from your computer screen using screen capture software.

A slide show can display a maximum of 90 charts. While this may seem like a lot, you may occasionally need to include more than 90 charts in a slide show. For instance, this may result if you make extensive use of a technique called build-ups (described later in "Creating and Using Build-Ups"). When your slide show must display more than 90 charts, you can make the last file in the slide show a slide show file in order to continue the slide show.

Creating a slide show involves the following steps:

1. Select <Slide show menu> from the Main Menu.

2. Select <Create slide show> from the Slide Show Menu, shown in Figure 13-1. Harvard Graphics will display the Create Slide Show overlay.

3. Complete the options on the Create Slide Show overlay, as described in the next section. Harvard Graphics will then display the Create/Edit Slide Show form.

4. Select the files to be included in the slide show on the Create/Edit Slide Show form, as described in the section "Entering Files in the Slide Show List."

5. If desired, add special effects to the slide show on the Screenshow Effects form, as described in the section "Adding Screenshow Effects."

At this point, your slide show is complete. Harvard Graphics will have automatically saved this slide show file using the information supplied on the Create Slide Show overlay. You can now display the slide show (as described in "Displaying a Screenshow"), produce output of the charts in the slide show (as described in "Outputting Charts in a Slide Show" in Chapter 8), or spell check the charts in the slide show (as described later in "Spell Checking Charts in a Slide Show").

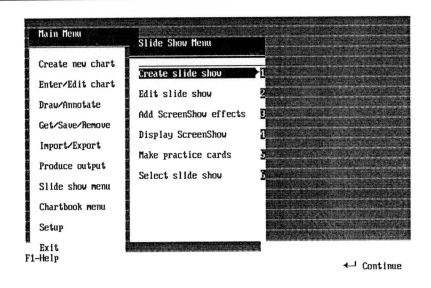

Figure 13-1.   Slide Show Menu

## The Create Slide Show Overlay

The Create Slide Show overlay (shown in Figure 13-2) has three options: "Directory," "Slide show name," and "Description." The "Directory" option defaults to the current directory. If the files you want to include in your slide show are not on the current directory, enter the name of the directory in which they are stored at the "Directory" option.

*Note:* All the files in a slide show must be located in the directory in which your slide show is stored.

Enter the name of your slide show at "Slide show name." This name must conform to standard DOS file naming conventions. If you do not add the .SHW file extension, Harvard Graphics will add it for you. At "Description," enter a description of your slide show. Once you have completed the form, press F10-Continue. Harvard Graphics will then display the Create/Edit Slide Show form described in the next section.

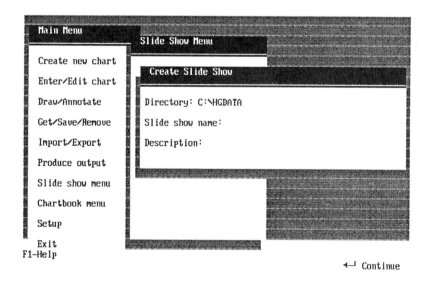

**Figure 13-2.**   Create Slide Show overlay

## The Create/Edit Slide Show Form

The Create/Edit Slide Show form, shown in Figure 13-3, is used to specify the files to be included in the slide show. The top of this form contains a file list in which all the files in the current directory with the extensions .CHT, .TPL, .SHW, .PCX, and .PIC are displayed (up to a maximum of 255 filenames). The "Filename Ext," "Date," "Type," and "Description" columns in the file list contain the name, date of creation, file type, and a description for each of the files displayed.

"Show name," located at the middle of the form, displays the name you gave your slide show on the Create Slide Show overlay. You cannot modify this name.

The lower half of the form contains the slide show list with the four columns "Order," "File," "Type," and "Description." You add files to your slide show by adding the desired filenames to this list (as described in the next section). In the "Order" column are numbers referring to the order of slides in the slide show. You can modify the order of slides as described in the sections "Changing the Order of Files in a Slide Show"

```
                        Create/Edit Slide Show

    Filename Ext     Date      Type        Description

    HG       .CHT   12-01-87   CHART
    ANNOUNCE .CHT   07-01-87   CHART
    INTRO    .CHT   07-01-87   CHART
    OPENING  .CHT   07-01-87   CHART
    PRODS    .CHT   07-01-87   CHART
    REGIONS  .CHT   07-01-87   CHART


    Show name: PRESENT .SHW
    — Order ——————— File ——————— Type ——————————— Description ———
        1         HG       .CHT




    Show description: Slide show for printing charts

    F1-Help                                              F10-Continue
```

**Figure 13-3.**   Create/Edit Slide Show form

and "Changing the File Order from the Screenshow Effects Form." The "File," "Type," and "Description" columns contain the slide filename, the slide type, and a description for each of the slides included in the slide show.

The "Show description" option below the slide show list contains the description you entered on the Create Slide Show overlay. You can modify this description by pressing TAB to move to "Show description" and editing the text. The function key banner at the bottom of the form shows the active function keys.

## Entering Files in the Slide Show List

When you first create a slide show, the first file in the file list will be displayed at the first line in the slide show list on the Create/Edit Slide Show form. To change this file, move the cursor in the file list until the desired file is highlighted. If the file you want to select is not displayed in the file list (since only six files can fit in this display at a time), press PGDN or PGUP to display an additional six files from the current directory. Alternatively, press DOWN or UP to scroll from file to file in the list.

Once the desired file in the file list is highlighted, press ENTER to place this file in the slide show list. Once you do so, Harvard Graphics enters the filename, type, and description in the appropriate columns in the slide show list, and moves the cursor to the second line in the slide show list. The cursor is still active in the file list, however. Move it to the next file in the file list that you want to include in your slide show and press ENTER.

Continue to add files until all the desired files are listed in the slide show list. When you are finished, press F10-Continue to return to the Slide Show Menu. (For additional details concerning the slide show list, see the later section "Editing a Slide Show.")

You can include the same file in any number of slide shows. Likewise, you can include the same file in a slide show list as many times as needed. For example, you may want to create a blank slide (one with no chart or drawings on it) to use for special transitions in a Screenshow.

Once you have added the desired files to your slide show, you may want to print out a list of these files using the <Print slide show list> from the Produce Output menu. For more information, see "Printing a Slide Show List" in Chapter 8.

## Selecting a Slide Show

In order to use a slide show in any way, the slide show must be current. When you first create a slide show, it is the current slide show. However, to access this slide show at a later time, you will need to select the slide show in order to make it current. To do this, choose <Select slide show> from the Slide Show Menu. Harvard Graphics will display the Select Slide Show form, shown in Figure 13-4. Select a slide show either by entering the name of the desired slide show at the "Filename" option, or by highlighting the slide show name, and then pressing F10-Continue or ENTER. If the slide show is not on the directory displayed at the "Directory" option, change directories by entering the name of the desired directory or by pressing F3-Change dir and selecting a directory from the Select Directory form.

```
                         Select Slide Show

Directory: C:\HGDATA
Filename:  ANNUAL   .SHW

Filename Ext  | Date     | Type    | Description

ANNUAL   .SHW | 12-29-89 | SLD SHOW| Print annual report, data linked templat
ORD      .SHW | 07-12-90 | SLD SHOW| Print out product order charts
INTRACTV.SHW  | 08-14-90 | SLD SHOW| Interactive information slide show
ROTATE   .SHW | 08-14-90 | SLD SHOW| Display proposed rotation Screenshow
BUILDUP  .SHW | 04-27-90 | SLD SHOW| Display sales. Use a build-up bar chart
PRODUCTS.SHW  | 08-14-90 | SLD SHOW| Our products slide show
PRESENT  .SHW | 08-03-90 | SLD SHOW| Print charts for the Hanson report
GOALS    .SHW | 08-14-90 | SLD SHOW| Our goals slide show
SERVICES.SHW  | 04-27-90 | SLD SHOW| Our service reputation slide show
FINANCES.SHW  | 08-14-90 | SLD SHOW| Our finances
DEPTPRES.SHW  | 07-02-90 | SLD SHOW| Department presentation


F1-Help     F3-Change dir
                                                      F10-Continue
```

**Figure 13-4.**   Select Slide Show form

## Editing a Slide Show

The Create/Edit Slide Show form (shown in Figure 13-3) is used when you are either creating a new slide show or editing an existing one. Modifications you can make to a slide show include adding, deleting, and changing the order of files in a slide show.

To edit an existing slide show, it must be current. If it is not, select the slide show you want to edit as described in the preceding section. Next, select <Edit slide show> from the Slide Show Menu. The Create/Edit Slide Show form will be displayed and the files in the existing slide show will appear in the slide show list.

The keys you can use in the Create/Edit Slide Show form to edit a slide show are described in Table 13-1. TAB and SHIFT-TAB allow you to activate the cursor in either the file list, the slide show list, or the "Show description" option. You can determine if the cursor is active in a list by pressing the UP and DOWN arrow keys. Pressing UP and DOWN will move the cursor and highlight the filenames in the active list (unless the cursor is active at the "Show description" option). PGUP and PGDN will display additional files in the active list.

| Key | Function |
| --- | --- |
| CTRL-DEL | Deletes file at cursor in the slide show list. |
| CTRL-DOWN | Moves file down one position in the slide show list. |
| CTRL-UP | Moves file up one position in the slide show list. |
| DOWN (arrow) | Moves cursor down one position in the file list or slide show list. |
| ENTER | Adds highlighted file in the file list to slide show list. |
| ESC | Returns to the Slide Show Menu. |
| PGDN | Displays the next six files in the file list. |
| PGUP | Displays the previous six files in the file list. |
| SHIFT-TAB | Activates cursor in either the file list, slide show list, or the "Show description" option. |
| TAB | Activates cursor in either the file list, the slide show list, or at the "Show description" option. |
| UP (arrow) | Moves cursor up one position in the file list or the slide show list. |

**Table 13-1.** Cursor Control Keys and Functions in the Create/Edit Slide Show Form

Adding files to your slide show, deleting files from your slide show, and changing the order of slides in slide shows are described in the following sections. Once you have modified your slide show list, press F10-Continue to return to the Slide Show Menu.

### Adding Files to a Slide Show

When the Create/Edit Slide Show form is first displayed after you select <Edit slide show>, the cursor will be positioned at the last row of the slide show list (if you have just created the slide show, or never added files to the slide show, this will be the first position in the slide show list). The cursor will be active in the file list, however. Move it to the name of the file in the file list you want to add to the slide show. When the desired file is highlighted, press ENTER. Continue adding files to your slide show in this manner. When you are done, press F10-Continue to return to the Slide Show Menu.

### Deleting Files from a Slide Show

You can easily remove a file from a slide show list on the Create/Edit Slide Show form. (Removing a file from the slide show list simply means the file will no longer be part of the slide show; it does not delete the file from your directory.) Press TAB to activate the cursor in the slide show list, if necessary. Press the UP and DOWN keys (and PGUP and PGDN, if necessary) to move the cursor to the file you want to delete from the list. When the desired file is highlighted, press CTRL-DEL to delete the file.

*Note:* If you delete a file either from DOS or with the <Remove file> option from the Get/Save/Remove menu, Harvard Graphics will not remove the file from any of the slide shows in which it appeared. However, when you display or output the slide show, Harvard Graphics will display the message "File not found" when it reaches the deleted file. It will then continue to the next slide in the slide show.

### Changing the Order of Files in a Slide Show

The order in which files appear in the slide show list on the Create/Edit Slide Show form is also the order in which the files will be displayed or output. If your slide show is designed for the purpose of spell checking, outputting, or reviewing a group of charts, the order may not be important to you. However, when your slide show is a Screenshow (for presentation), the order of your files is often very important.

You can change the order of files in a slide show from one of two forms: the Create/Edit Slide Show form and the Screenshow Effects form. The Screenshow Effects form is usually preferred for changing the order of files, since you can use it to preview the slide show, beginning with any file. This allows you to immediately check whether the new order is satisfactory. This process is described later in "Changing the File Order from the Screenshow Effects Form."

To change the order of files using the Create/Edit Slide Show form, press TAB to activate the cursor in the slide show list, if necessary. Highlight the file you want to move. Press CTRL-UP or CTRL-DOWN to move the file up or down one position in the slide show list. When you have finished changing the order of files, press F10-Continue to return to the Slide Show Menu.

*Note:* If you have previously added Screenshow effects to a file (such as a transition or a display time), these effects will still be associated with a given file even after the order has been changed. Screenshow effects are described in the section "Adding Screenshow Effects."

## Including Bit-Mapped Files in a Slide Show

You can use bit-mapped files that are compatible with your graphics adapter in your Screenshow. The bit-mapped files that can be included are .PCX and .PIC file types. A *bit-map* is a pixel-by-pixel record of the colors used to construct an image on your computer monitor. Among the bit-mapped images you may want to include in a Screenshow are images created with a paint or drawing program, images captured from your monitor using a screen capture program, or images scanned with a digitizing scanner.

Using bit-mapped files in a Screenshow can add a sense of realism that can help convey your message. For instance, if your Screenshow is used to describe a special feature of computer software, you can display a screen capture of the actual screen running that software. Similarly, if you are using a slide show as a marketing tool, displaying a bit-mapped image of your product can leave a lasting impression on your audience. You can also overlay a chart or drawing on your bit-mapped image for additional impact. For instance, you can display a chart showing sales figures superimposed on a bit-mapped image of the product. Alternatively, you can overlay an arrow onto your bit-mapped image to draw attention to a specific detail on the screen.

You will need to test whether a given bit-mapped file can be displayed in a Screenshow by including the file in a test slide show. This will determine if Harvard Graphics can present the image on your monitor. In addition to verifying that the .PCX or .PIC file is compatible, you may want to verify whether the color palette used for displaying charts in your slide show and the colors used to create the bit-mapped file are compatible. If these two palettes differ, the transitions between bit-mapped files and your Harvard Graphics charts may result in the temporary loss of one or more colors on your screen.

For example, when a bit-mapped file displays a color that is not available in the Harvard Graphics palette, one or more colors from the Harvard Graphics palette will be modified when the bit-mapped file is displayed. If you are using transitions (see "Adding Screenshow Effects") other than the Replace transition, this loss or distortion of color may be apparent during the transition. The Harvard Graphics palette colors will be restored as soon as the .PCX or .PIC file image is removed from the screen. If palette incompatibility becomes a problem, display a blank chart between your bit-mapped file and the next image.

*Note:* You may want to use more than one palette during a screenshow, and using bit-mapped files is how this is accomplished. See "Using Custom Palettes in a Screenshow" for details.

Although bit-mapped files can be included in slide shows that are output or spell checked, Harvard Graphics cannot print, plot, or record these files, nor will it check the spelling.

## Including a Template in a Slide Show

When certain types of templates are included in a slide show, they affect the display characteristics of the charts in the slide show. In this case the templates themselves are not displayed. Rather, the charts placed after the template adopt the settings defined by the template for display on the screen or for producing output. The influence of this type of template in a slide show continues until another template is encountered in the slide show or the slide show ends.

*Note:* Templates only affect chart files (those with the extension .CHT). If your slide show includes bit-mapped files, the template definition will not affect them. Any charts following the bit-mapped files will again adopt the template definitions.

Templates used in slide shows can be divided into four categories: title chart templates, templates with data links, multiple chart templates, and all others. When you use a template in a slide show that is not one of the first three, slides following the template inherit several of its characteristics. These include

- The text attributes and text size and placement for title, subtitle, and footnote text

- The actual text of the footnote (if you saved the template with "Clear values" set to No on the Save Template overlay)

- The template's Current Chart Options settings (orientation, border, and font)

- Any drawings added to the template (a company logo, for instance)

- Finally, if you have defined the chart size and placement for the template using F7-Size/Place from the Main Menu (as described in "Sizing and Placing a Chart" in Chapter 9), all charts that follow the template will use this size and placement.

*Hint:* Do not use the size/placement feature if any of your charts include drawings, or the drawings may appear displaced. This occurs because changing the size and placement of a chart affects the chart image, but has no influence on added drawings. To avoid this problem, use a multiple chart template instead. See "Including a Multiple Chart Template in a Slide Show," later in the chapter.

Including a template in a slide show to affect chart characteristics can give your charts a consistent appearance. For instance, you can add the date to the footnote of a template before outputting a slide show, thus placing the date on all the charts. In a presentation, you may want to include your company's logo on each chart. If you include this logo as a part of a template, you need to add the logo only once—to the template—rather than adding it to each chart in the slide show.

When a template includes a drawing or symbol, this drawing or symbol is displayed *behind* the charts that follow the template. This is the only way to display a drawing behind a chart without saving the chart as a symbol. There are several valuable uses for displaying a drawing or symbol behind a chart. One is to place a topic-related drawing in the background. For example, if you are making a presentation about a city, you may want to include a template containing a large drawing of a city skyline in the background. All charts displayed after this template will be superimposed on top of the skyline, as shown in Figure 13-5.

Another use is to provide a colored background without having to change your color palette. To do this, create a simple box in Draw/Annotate that uses the desired background color, and make it large enough to cover all, or nearly all, of the drawing area. When this box is displayed as part of the template, all subsequent charts will appear on the background color provided by the box. This allows you to easily use different colored backgrounds for different slide topics by simply inserting templates in the appropriate locations in the slide show. See Chapter 9, "Drawing and Annotating," and Chapter 11, "Templates and Chartbooks," for more information about including drawings in a template and creating templates.

## Including a Title Chart Template in a Slide Show

The title chart template has a special use in a slide show—it cancels the effects of a previous template. Once a title chart template is encountered, all subsequent charts will display their normal settings and characteristics rather than those defined by the preceding template. There is, however, one characteristic a title chart template will apply to subsequent charts. This is the font defined for the title chart template.

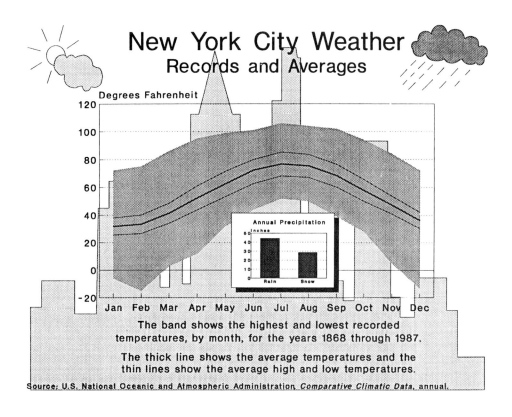

**Figure 13-5.** Skyline template appears behind all following charts in the slide show

## Including a Data-Linked Template in a Slide Show

Use a data-linked template to import chart data immediately before the chart is displayed or output in a slide show. Data-linked templates do not assume the characteristics of other templates in a slide show. In fact, such templates, like title chart templates, cancel the effects of any previous templates.

## Including a Multiple Chart Template in a Slide Show

The last special template you can use in a slide show is a multiple chart template. If a multiple chart template is included in a slide show, each chart that follows the template will be displayed at the position defined for chart 1 in the multiple chart. In addition, any drawings or annotations defined for the multiple chart template will appear as well. However, the position of drawings is *not* restricted to the location defined by chart 1.

The most useful style of multiple charts for templates is the custom multiple chart style. Since Harvard Graphics will display the charts that follow the multiple chart template only in the chart 1 location, you can define the size and placement of that position for the custom chart and save it as a template. Then charts following this template in your slide show will be displayed using the defined size and location.

Although you can also define the chart size and placement in any template (by pressing F7-Size/Place from the Main Menu to display the Size/Place screen), custom multiple chart templates provide an additional advantage that is not available with the other template styles. The size and placement defined for chart 1 on the custom multiple chart template will also affect the size and placement of drawings or symbols.

Figure 13-6 depicts the creation of a custom multiple chart template. This figure shows the placement for chart 1 on the Custom Layout screen. Prior to the placement of chart 1, a city skyline background was added to the custom multiple chart (this background is a Harvard Graphics symbol located in the BUILDING.SYM file). If this multiple chart is now saved as a template, and the template is used as the first slide in a slide show, all charts (and any drawings included in them) will appear in front of the skyline image, as is shown in Figure 13-5.

*Note:* While you are using a multiple chart template in a slide show, you will not be able to display any multiple chart files in the slide show. This is because a multiple chart cannot include a multiple chart. To circumvent this restriction, place a title chart template immediately before your multiple chart. Then include the multiple chart template again immediately following your multiple chart.

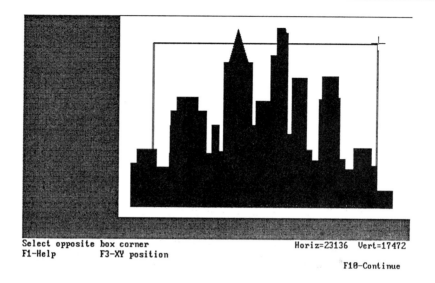

**Figure 13-6.** Placing chart 1 for a custom multiple chart template

## Including Slide Show Files in a Slide Show

When Harvard Graphics encounters a slide show file in a slide show, it immediately switches to that slide show, beginning with the first slide. This feature is useful when you create a slide show that is very long.

When you need to produce a slide show that contains more than 90 files, you can split your show into several slide show files. The last file included in the first slide show should be the next slide show file, so that your show automatically continues and presents all the files in the second slide show. The last file in the second show can refer to yet another slide show, and so on. A slide show file should be the last file in a slide show since Harvard Graphics will not return to the original slide show once it encounters a slide show file. (However, you can tell Harvard Graphics to return to the original slide show by including the original slide show file in the second slide show.)

You can also include multiple slide shows in a single slide show to produce sophisticated, interactive Screenshows. The first slide in an interactive Screenshow usually depicts a menu that displays choices and the corresponding keys the user should press for each choice. Go To keys are used to branch to one of several possible slide shows that displays the requested files. The last file in each slide show names the original slide show, thus returning the viewer to the menu.

## Using Harvard Graphics Screenshows

A *Screenshow* is a real-time presentation of your slide show on a monitor or a screen projection device. Screenshows can be used to review a series of charts, to present a slide show to an audience, and to create automated or fully interactive information systems. Even if you never need to use a slide show for presenting information to others, you may want to experiment with the fun and interesting special effects that can be created using a Screenshow.

When you are creating a chart for the purpose of displaying it on your monitor or a screen projection device, you will want to pay particular attention to details of the chart. These include the colors used, the readability of the text (some font, text attribute, and text size combinations produce better-looking text than others), and the quality of any drawings or symbols used. You can see how the chart will appear in a Screenshow while you are creating or editing the chart by using F2-Draw chart. This view corresponds to how the chart will appear in a Screenshow. The following sections describe how to use Screenshows.

### Hardware Considerations for Screenshows

A good deal of chart production in Harvard Graphics is for the purpose of printing, plotting, or recording one or more charts. In these instances, the quality of the image on your screen is not as important as the quality of the final output. The quality of images displayed in a Screenshow, however, is quite important. For example, although a monochrome or CGA monitor may be fine for chart production in

Harvard Graphics, most users will not be satisfied with the impact of a Screenshow when it is displayed on these types of monitors.

In addition, if you are using a VGA graphics adapter, you may find that many of the Screenshow effects do not work properly (see "Adding Screenshow Effects"). Unfortunately, although individual charts and images may look excellent on your screen, some graphics adapters cannot produce the Screenshow effects. With some VGA graphics adapters, you can circumvent this problem by setting the "Screen" option on the Screen Setup form to EGA color. (See "Setting a Default Screen" in Chapter 3.) If you change your "Screen" option and you still cannot display Screenshow effects, you may want to contact the manufacturer of your graphics adapter to see if there is something you can do to your hardware to display the Screenshow effects.

## Displaying a Screenshow

There are four ways to display a Screenshow. One way is to use the Harvard Graphics Quick Start feature (available in Harvard Graphics version 2.1 and later) to start the Screenshow from DOS. This is described in the section "Quick Start" in Chapter 2. Quick Start is an ideal way to start a Screenshow you are using for a presentation. A second way is to use F2-Preview show from the Screenshow Effects form. This technique is described in "Previewing a Slide Show from the Screenshow Effects Form," later in this chapter.

A third way to display a Screenshow is to use the Harvard Graphics accessory Screenshow Utilities. Screenshow Utilities, which is sold separately from Harvard Graphics, includes a program that permits you to display a Screenshow in the absence of the Harvard Graphics program. See Appendix C, "Harvard Graphics Accessories," for more details.

The fourth way to display a Screenshow is the easiest. Make the Screenshow you want to display the current slide show (if it is not current already). Select <Display Screenshow> at the Slide Show Menu. Harvard Graphics will display your Screenshow starting with the first file. While your Screenshow is being displayed, you can use the keys listed in Table 13-2 to control the presentation. After Harvard Graphics displays the last file, you will return to the Slide Show Menu.

***Note:*** If you have a current chart that you have not saved, you must do so before you display a Screenshow. Displaying a Screenshow displaces the current chart.

| Key | Function |
| --- | --- |
| CTRL-E | Stops the Screenshow and displays the chart form for the chart just displayed. |
| DOWN (arrow) | Displays the next file. |
| END | Displays the last file in the Screenshow. |
| ENTER | Displays the next file. |
| ESC | Stops the Screenshow and returns to the previous screen. |
| HOME | Displays the first file (you can continue the Screenshow from this point). |
| LEFT (arrow) | Displays the previous file. |
| RIGHT (arrow) | Displays the next file. |
| SPACEBAR | Pauses a Screenshow with the current file displayed. Press any key to continue to the next file. |
| UP (arrow) | Displays the previous file. |

| Mouse Button | Function |
| --- | --- |
| Left | Displays previous file. |
| Right | Displays next file. |

**Table 13-2.** Keys and Mouse Buttons Used to Control File Presentation During a Screenshow

## Adding Screenshow Effects

Not only do Screenshows provide you with a flexible means of presenting charts and other images, they also offer two types of special effects: *transitions* and *Go To keys*. Transitions are special effects that provide interesting ways to advance from one file to the next, including Fade, Wipe, and Scroll, to name a few. Go To keys allow you to control the flow of a Screenshow. With a Go To key, you can have Harvard Graphics display any file in a slide show in response to a specific keypress.

To add Screenshow effects, make the desired slide show the current slide show. Next, select <Add Screenshow effects> from the Slide Show Menu. Harvard Graphics will display the Screenshow Effects form, shown in Figure 13-7. This form contains eight columns and as many rows as there are files in the current slide show. The first column contains numbers indicating the order of files in the slide show. The second column, "Filename," lists the names of the files in your slide

```
                    Screenshow Effects

         Filename      | Type     | Draw    | Dir   | Time | Erase  | Dir
         Default       |          | Replace |       |      |        |
    1    SUNRISE .PCX  | BIT MAP  | Fade    | In    |      | Scroll | Down
    2    TITLE   .CHT  | TITLE    | Scroll  | Down  |      |        |
    3    POINTS  .CHT  | BULLET   | Wipe    | Down  |      | Fade   |
    4    BAR1    .CHT  | BAR/LINE | Wipe    | Up    |      |        |
    5    BAR2    .CHT  | BAR/LINE | Wipe    | Up    |      |        |
    6    BAR3    .CHT  | BAR/LINE | Wipe    | Up    |      |        |
    7    BAR4    .CHT  | BAR/LINE | Wipe    | Up    |      | Iris   | In
    8    PRODUCT .PCX  | BIT MAP  | Scroll  | Right |      |        |
    9    MRKTPIE .CHT  | PIE      | Fade    | In    |      | Fade   | Out
   10    BLANK   .CHT  | FREEFORM |         |       | 0:10 |        |
   11    POINTS  .CHT  | BULLET   | Open    |       |      | Close  |
   12    AREA1   .CHT  | AREA     | Fade    | In    |      |        |
   13    AREA2   .CHT  | AREA     | Fade    | In    |      | Scroll | Right
   14    NEWSALES.CHT  | 2 COLUMN | Scroll  | Right |      |        |
   15    SUNSET  .PCX  | BIT MAP  |         |       |      |        |

    F1-Help
    F2-Preview show              F6-Choices    F8-User menu    F10-Continue
```

**Figure 13-7.**  Screenshow Effects form

show. The "Type" column contains the type of each file. If the file is a chart, the type of chart is displayed in this column. Alternatively, if the slide is a template, slide show, or bit-mapped file, this column shows the template type, "SLD SHOW," or "BIT MAP." The remaining five columns are used to define the Screenshow transitions. The use of transitions is described later in the section "Using Transitions to Enhance a Screenshow."

Use the keys listed in Table 13-3 to move the cursor on the Screenshow Effects form.

## Previewing a Slide Show from the Screenshow Effects Form

You can begin previewing your slide show at any point in the slide show list from the Screenshow Effects form. One practical use of this preview capability is to quickly test the effects of transitions and Go To keys while you are developing a Screenshow.

To use this preview feature, move the cursor to the line on the Screenshow Effects form that corresponds with the first file you want to view and press F2-Preview show. Harvard Graphics will begin displaying

| Key | Function |
| --- | --- |
| CTRL-DEL | Deletes current transition, direction, or time entry. |
| CTRL-E | Displays the chart form for the currently displayed chart. |
| CTRL-DOWN | Moves file down one position in the slide show list. |
| CTRL-UP | Moves file up one position in the slide show list. |
| DOWN (arrow) | Moves cursor down one file. |
| END | Moves the cursor to the last column for the last file displayed in the slide show list. |
| ESC | Returns to the Slide Show Menu. |
| HOME | Moves the cursor to the first column for the first file displayed in the slide show list. |
| PGDN | Displays the next screen of files in the slide show. |
| PGUP | Displays the previous screen of files in the slide show. |
| SHIFT-TAB | Moves cursor to the previous column. |
| TAB | Moves cursor to the next column. |
| UP (arrow) | Moves cursor up one file. |

Table 13-3.  Cursor Control Keys and Functions in the Screenshow Effects Form

the slide show from that file on. The influence of templates listed before this file will not be applied. When the Screenshow terminates, either because the last slide is displayed or you have pressed ESC, you will return to the Screenshow Effects form.

## Changing the File Order from the Screenshow Effects Form

While the Screenshow Effects form is displayed you can quickly alter the order of the slides in your slide show. First move the cursor to the file you want to move. Then press CTRL-DOWN to move the file down one position in the list or CTRL-UP to move it up one position. Any Screenshow effects entered for a particular file will be moved with the file. After changing the order of files, you can immediately verify whether the change was satisfactory by using the F2-Preview show feature.

## Using Transitions to Enhance a Screenshow

The five right-most columns on the Screenshow Effects form ("Draw," "Dir," "Time," "Erase," and "Dir") are used to define the transitions

Harvard Graphics will use when displaying your Screenshow. If you print, plot, or record your slide show, these settings will have no influence. However, when you are displaying a Screenshow, these transitions can have a large impact on how your charts and images are perceived. Transitions affect Harvard Graphics chart files (.CHT), bit-mapped files (.PCX and .PIC), and templates with a data link (.TPL). They do not affect slide show files (.SHW) and template files without data links.

The "Draw" column is used to define the transition that will place your file on a computer screen or projection device. To add a transition for a specific file, move the cursor to the "Draw" column for the file, and enter the name of the transition. You can also add a transition by entering just the first letter of the transition, or the first two letters if it shares the same initial letter with another transition. Harvard Graphics will complete the rest of the transition name when the cursor leaves the row or column. Alternatively, with the cursor positioned at the desired row in the "Draw" column, you can press F6-Choices to display the Transitions overlay, which lists all the available transitions, as shown in Figure 13-8. Select a transition from this list by moving the cursor to the desired transition and pressing ENTER. To remove the Transition overlay without selecting a transition, press ESC.

| | Filename | Type | Draw | Transitions | Erase | Dir |
|---|---|---|---|---|---|---|
| | Default | | Replace | ▶Replace | | |
| 1 | SUNRISE .PCX | BIT MAP | Fade | Overlay | Scroll | Down |
| 2 | TITLE .CHT | TITLE | Scroll | Wipe | | |
| 3 | POINTS .CHT | BULLET | Wipe | Scroll | Fade | |
| 4 | BAR1 .CHT | BAR/LINE | Wipe | Fade | | |
| 5 | BAR2 .CHT | BAR/LINE | Wipe | Weave | | |
| 6 | BAR3 .CHT | BAR/LINE | Wipe | Open | | |
| 7 | BAR4 .CHT | BAR/LINE | Wipe | Close | Iris | In |
| 8 | PRODUCT .PCX | BIT MAP | Scroll | Blinds | | |
| 9 | MRKTPIE .CHT | PIE | Fade | Iris | Fade | Out |
| 10 | BLANK .CHT | FREEFORM | | Rain | | |
| 11 | POINTS .CHT | BULLET | Open | | Close | |
| 12 | AREA1 .CHT | AREA | Fade | | | |
| 13 | AREA2 .CHT | AREA | Fade | | Scroll | Right |
| 14 | NEWSALES.CHT | 2 COLUMN | Scroll | Right | | |
| 15 | SUNSET .PCX | BIT MAP | ▶ | | | |

F1-Help

F10-Continue

**Figure 13-8.** Transitions overlay

The "Dir" column immediately to the right of "Draw" allows you to define the direction of the transition specified in the "Draw" column. To add a direction for a transition, move to the "Dir" column for the corresponding file and either enter **Left**, **Right**, **Up**, **Down**, **In**, or **Out**, or enter the first letter of the desired direction. Alternatively, press F6-Choices from the "Dir" column and select a direction from the Directions overlay, shown in Figure 13-9.

Not all transitions have directions, although many do. Table 13-4 displays a list of all of the available transitions, a description of their effects, and their available and default directions. The Scroll transition, for example, slides an image onto the screen. It has four possible directions, Left, Right, Up, and Down, which determine the direction in which the chart will slide onto the screen. If you define a Scroll transition with a Down direction, the chart will slide down the screen from the top until the entire image is visible. Figure 13-10 shows examples of seven transition effects (captured mid-transition) applied to the same chart image. The final chart that would be displayed once each transition is completed is shown in the lower-right corner of the figure.

```
                        Screenshow Effects

         Filename      Type       Draw      Dir        Directions       Dir

       Default                    Replace
                                                       ▶Left
   1   SUNRISE  .PCX   BIT MAP    Fade      In          Right           Down
   2   TITLE    .CHT   TITLE      Scroll    Down        Up
   3   POINTS   .CHT   BULLET     Wipe      Down        Down
   4   BAR1     .CHT   BAR/LINE   Wipe      Up          In
   5   BAR2     .CHT   BAR/LINE   Wipe      Up          Out
   6   BAR3     .CHT   BAR/LINE   Wipe      Up
   7   BAR4     .CHT   BAR/LINE   Wipe      Up                           In
   8   PRODUCT  .PCX   BIT MAP    Scroll    Right
   9   MRKTPIE  .CHT   PIE        Fade      In          Fade            Out
  10   BLANK    .CHT   FREEFORM                 0:10
  11   POINTS   .CHT   BULLET     Open                  Close
  12   AREA1    .CHT   AREA       Fade      In
  13   AREA2    .CHT   AREA       Fade      In          Scroll          Right
  14   NEWSALES .CHT   2 COLUMN   Scroll    Right
  15   SUNSET   .PCX   BIT MAP              ▶

F1-Help                                                         F10-Continue
```

Figure 13-9.    Directions overlay

| Transition | Effect | Directions | Default |
|---|---|---|---|
| Replace | Replaces entire screen. | n/a | |
| Overlay | Presents image over existing image, one element at a time. | n/a | |
| Wipe | Sweeps image on or off the screen. | Left, Right, Up, Down | Right |
| Scroll | Scrolls image on or off the screen. | Left, Right, Up, Down | Up |
| Fade | Image gradually fades on or off the screen. | Down | Full screen |
| Weave | Image weaves on or off from left and right sides of the screen. | n/a | |
| Open | Opens the screen with vertical or horizontal lines from the center. | Left or Right, Up or Down | Up or Down |
| Close | Closes the screen with vertical or horizontal lines to the center. | Left or Right, Up or Down | Up or Down |
| Blinds | Opens or closes the screen in blind-like strips. | Left or Right, Up or Down | Up or Down |
| Iris | Opens or closes the screen from or to the center. | In, Out | Out |
| Rain | Gradually draws or erases the image on the screen. | n/a | |

**Table 13-4.** Screenshow Transitions, Effects, Directions Available, and Default Directions

The "Time" column allows you to specify the maximum amount of time a chart or image will be displayed on the screen before the Screenshow continues on to the next file. You enter a time by specifying the number of minutes and seconds that Harvard Graphics should display the file, using the format MM:SS. For example, to display a given chart for 15 seconds, enter **:15** in the corresponding row in the "Time" column. To display a chart for 1 minute, enter 1:00. If you enter a number

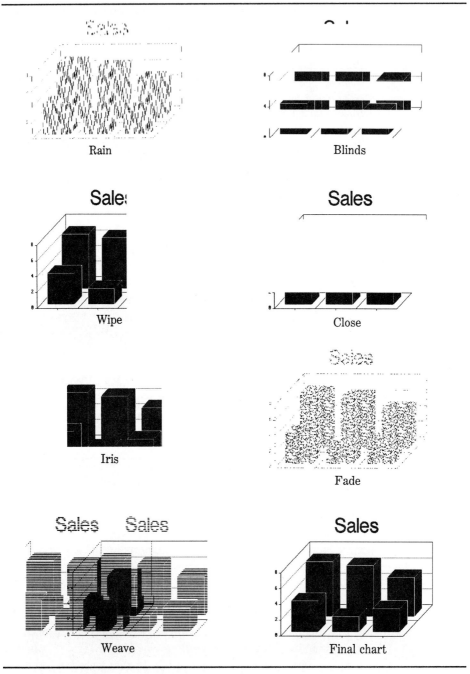

**Figure 13-10.** Examples of transition effects in progress

without adding a colon, Harvard Graphics will assume you are specifying seconds. If the number of seconds entered is greater than 59, Harvard Graphics will convert the number of seconds to the MM:SS format.

If no time value is specified, the chart or image will remain on the screen until one of the user keys listed in Table 13-2 or a Go To key is pressed. (Go To keys are described later in "Using Go To Keys to Create Flexible Screenshows.") It is not uncommon to have a Screenshow in which some charts and images are displayed for a set period of time and other charts and images have no time defined.

*Note:* Some charts and images take longer to display than others. The time you define in the "Time" column is the amount of time Harvard Graphics will display a completed screen before beginning to display the next file. Some files can take up to 15 seconds or more to display, depending on the size of the file being displayed and the speed of your computer. You should take this into account when you are defining display times. Some experimentation may be required to determine the most effective timing.

The last two columns on the Screenshow Effects form, "Erase" and "Dir," allow you to define the transition used to erase a chart or image from the screen and the direction of this transition. Specify these as you would "Draw" and "Dir," by entering a word or letter or pressing F6-Choices to display either the Transitions or Directions overlay. Then select from this overlay.

The word "Default" appears in the row below "Filename," indicating that this row is used to define defaults. Whenever a given file is not assigned a transition, direction, or time, Harvard Graphics will use the values that appear in the default row. Harvard Graphics automatically assigns Replace as the default "Draw" transition and the "Time" default is blank (user-controlled). Although the "Dir" columns do not initially show a default direction, the defaults are determined by transition (see the last column of Table 13-4). You can change any of the default settings by entering the desired transition, direction, or time in the appropriate column of the default row. You can also use F6-Choices to select transitions or directions for the default settings.

*Note:* If you want a Screenshow to run automatically, you can set the default time to the number of minutes and seconds you want each file to be displayed. However, when a default time is defined, any files where a time is not specified will be presented for the default time, and it is not possible to have a single file displayed for an indefinite period of time as you can with a user-controlled display time.

Tasteful use of Screenshow transitions can add a dramatic impact to your presentation. In addition, creative combinations of transitions can be used to display unusual special effects that leave your viewers wondering how you did it. As with many other features in Harvard Graphics, the more you experiment with these transitions, the more effective you will be at using them.

When designing a Screenshow, use F2-Preview show frequently to view the influence of specific transitions. If the combination of transitions is not satisfactory, press ESC to return to the Screenshow Effects form, modify the transitions, and try again. One note of caution is appropriate, however: although variety may be visually stimulating, too many different and seemingly unrelated transitions may spoil an otherwise well-planned Screenshow.

### Using the Overlay Transition

When you use an Overlay transition, Harvard Graphics draws your chart, one element at a time, on the screen. While this may not be desirable in every instance, it can be effective in the right circumstances. To demonstrate this effect, create a number of boxes of exactly the same size and place them behind one another. Alternate the color of the boxes between red and blue. When you view this drawing while you are creating it in Draw/Annotate (using F2-Preview), all you see is the front box. However, remember that Harvard Graphics keeps track of the back-to-front priority of drawings. If you press F4-Redraw while in Draw/Annotate, you will see Harvard Graphics draw the first box, a red box, then the next box, a blue box, then a red box, and a blue box, until only the last box is visible. (Arranging drawn objects this way may require you to use the <Front> and <Back> selections on the Modify menu in Draw/Annotate. See "Changing Object Order" in Chapter 9.

Now imagine that this drawing is used in a Screenshow. If the drawing is placed on a chart that is drawn onto the screen using the Replace transition, only the front box will appear. However, when an

Overlay transition is used, the back box is drawn first, then the box in front of it, and so on. To the viewer, a single box appears to flicker between the colors blue and red. While this example is rather simple, only your imagination can limit what you can do with the Overlay transition and carefully arranged drawings.

Another effective technique with an Overlay transition is to draw an object and then cover it with an object that is the same color as the background, making the first object seem to disappear. If you experiment with this technique, you will find that amazing special effects can be achieved with only a moderate amount of work.

### Using Overlay to Combine Charts and/or Bit-Mapped Images

When a previous chart or image is not removed from the screen with an "Erase" transition, subsequent charts added using the Overlay transition are placed on top of the previous chart or image. Using this technique, it is possible to combine two or more charts, or superimpose a chart on top of a bit-mapped image. Placing two or more charts on the same screen can be an effective way to introduce compatible data, one chart at a time.

This effect works best if the charts do not overlap. You can do this by using the F7-Size/Place function from the Main Menu on each chart you want to overlay, ensuring they are placed in different positions on the screen. Several different templates that define these positions can be used as well.

You can also display a bit-mapped image on the screen and then superimpose a chart on top of it. To do this, place the bit-mapped image onto the screen using any transition you desire. Without erasing it, use Overlay to place a chart on top of the existing image. Figure 13-11, for example, displays a chart that has been overlaid on the Harvard Graphics Main Menu. The Main Menu was captured as a bit-mapped image using the CAPTURE utility provided with Harvard Graphics Screenshow Utilities (see Appendix C, "Harvard Graphics Accessories").

### Creating and Using Build-Ups

A build-up is a technique in which two or more consecutive chart files are used, each chart building on the one displayed previously. Consider

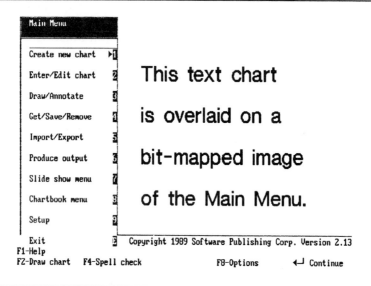

**Figure 13-11.**  Text chart overlaid on a bit-mapped image of Harvard Graphics' Main Menu

the four bullet charts shown in Figure 13-12. Beginning from the top left and moving clockwise, each chart contains the information from the previous chart, plus an additional bullet item. These four charts can be used to make a dramatic Screenshow effect called a *build-up.*

To create a build-up, create the charts first, saving the desired intermediate versions under different names as you develop the final chart. Include these chart files in a slide show, placing the chart with the least amount of information first and the additional charts in succession, with the complete chart placed last. Next, define Screenshow effects to create the build-up. Display each successive chart on the screen using a "Draw" transition that does not disrupt the preceding chart image. Do not use any "Erase" transitions until after the last chart in the build-up has been displayed. One "Draw" transition that works well with build-ups is a Wipe. As long as the first chart in the build-up is not erased from the screen, wiping the next chart onto the screen will make new information appear in addition to the old. Other

**Goals**

**Goals**
- Improve Service

**Goals**
- Improve Service
- Lower Costs
- Increase Sales

**Goals**
- Improve Service
- Lower Costs

**Figure 13-12.** Bullet list used in a build-up, from upper left clockwise to lower left

"Draw" transitions that work well with build-ups include Replace, Overlay, Fade, Iris, Blind, Open, Close, and Rain. The Scroll and Weave transitions do not produce acceptable build-ups.

In order for a build-up to be successful, the following precautions need to be observed:

- Each successive chart in the build-up should add one or more elements.

- Each successive chart should be identical except for the added element. This includes the size and colors of the objects in the chart.

- The transitions used between charts in a build-up should not disrupt the preceding chart image.

The previous example of a build-up (Figure 13-12) used a sequence of text charts. Build-ups can also be created with data charts. Creating data chart build-ups is slightly more involved, because the size of the elements is influenced by the number of series and the amount of data.

Consider the four charts displayed in Figure 13-13. In each chart an additional series was added without changing the size of any of the other elements in the chart. This size was controlled by defining the "Maximum value" and "Minimum value" options on the Y axis (as described in "Setting an Axis Range and Increment" in Chapter 6). In the initial chart zeros were entered for all the Y data. In each successive chart the actual data for an additional series was added to the chart.

*Note:* You must set the "Maximum value" on all charts to a value that is at least slightly larger than the largest series value to be displayed in the final chart.

Build-ups can be used to add the right touch of suspense to your presentation, or simply to focus your audience's attention on one point at a time. However, build-ups can result in the use of many charts in a slide show. If you need to include more than 90 files overall in a slide show, you will need to chain slide shows together. To do this, include a slide show file in a slide show to circumvent the 90-file limit.

## Using Go To Keys to Create Flexible Screenshows

The user keys listed in Table 13-2 can be used to control the flow of a Screenshow. These keys allow you to display the next file (DOWN or RIGHT), the previous file (UP or LEFT), the first file (HOME), or the last file (END) in the slide show. Go To keys, on the other hand, can be used to advance the Screenshow to any file in the slide show.

Go To keys are assigned to a single file. You can assign Go To keys to none, one, or several files in your slide show. When a Go To key is assigned to a file, a diamond appears next to the file number on the Screenshow Effects form. To assign Go To keys to a file, move the cursor to the desired file on the Screenshow Effects form and press

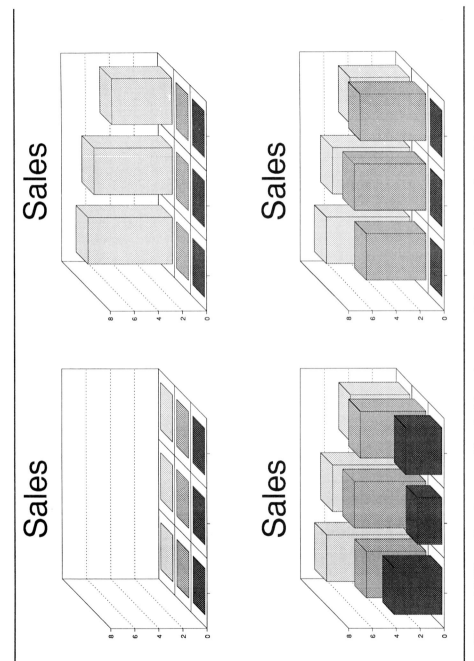

**Figure 13-13.** Bar charts used in a build-up, from upper left corner clockwise to lower left

F8-User menu. Harvard Graphics will display the Go To overlay, shown in Figure 13-14. The arrow pointing to file 2 in this figure indicates that the Go To overlay settings are being applied to file 2.

The Go To overlay contains two columns: "Key" and "Go To." In the "Key" column, enter the single character associated with the key you want to use to control the Screenshow. In the corresponding row of the "Go To" column, enter the number of the file to which you want that key to move the Screenshow. For example, if you want the capability of moving immediately from file 2 to file 4, assign a Go To key to file 2. To do this, move the cursor to the row associated with file 2 and press F8-User menu. Enter a character, **N** for example, in the "Key" column. Then press TAB to move to the "Go To" column and enter 4. Press F10-Continue or ESC to return to the Screenshow Effects form. Whenever you display this Screenshow, you can press **N** when file 2 is displayed to advance immediately to file 4.

| | Filename | Type | Draw | Dir | Time | Key | Go To |
|---|---|---|---|---|---|---|---|
| | Default | | Replace | | | N | 4 |
| | | | | | | P | 8 |
| 1 | SUNRISE .PCX | BIT MAP | Fade | In | | | |
| ▶ 2 | TITLE .CHT | TITLE | Scroll | Down | | | |
| 3 | POINTS .CHT | BULLET | Wipe | Down | | | |
| 4 | BAR1 .CHT | BAR/LINE | Wipe | Up | | | |
| 5 | BAR2 .CHT | BAR/LINE | Wipe | Up | | | |
| 6 | BAR3 .CHT | BAR/LINE | Wipe | Up | | | |
| 7 | BAR4 .CHT | BAR/LINE | Wipe | Up | | | |
| 8 | PRODUCT .PCX | BIT MAP | Scroll | Right | | | |
| 9 | MRKTPIE .CHT | PIE | Fade | In | | | |
| 10 | BLANK .CHT | FREEFORM | | | 0:10 | Close | |
| 11 | POINTS .CHT | BULLET | Open | | | | |
| 12 | AREA1 .CHT | AREA | Fade | In | | | |
| 13 | AREA2 .CHT | AREA | Fade | In | | Scroll | Right |
| 14 | NEWSALES .CHT | 2 COLUMN | Scroll | Right | | | |
| 15 | SUNSET .PCX | BIT MAP | | | | | |

F1-Help                                                F10-Continue

**Figure 13-14.**    Go To overlay

*Note:* Even when Go To keys are defined, you can still use the user keys to control the presentation of files.

### Using Go To Keys to Create Continuous Screenshows

The Go To overlay can be used to create a continuous Screenshow, in which after the last file is displayed the Screenshow starts over again. To achieve this effect, move the cursor to the last file in the Screenshow Effects form (this file should *not* be a slide show itself). Press F8-User menu to display the Go To overlay. Leave the "Key" column blank. Press TAB to move to the "Go To" column and enter the number corresponding to the first file in the slide show (or any other file for that matter). Once the last file is displayed in the Screenshow, Harvard Graphics will advance to the first file (or the file specified) when either the DOWN or RIGHT key is pressed, the right mouse button is pressed, or when the display time expires. If the Screenshow is entirely time controlled, the Screenshow will continue indefinitely until ESC or CTRL-E is pressed.

Although the preceding paragraph describes how to create a Screenshow that continues from the last file in the slide show, you can use this technique to advance to a specified file from any file in the slide show.

### Using Go To Keys to Create Menu-Driven Screenshows

Menu-driven Screenshows are ideal for creating interactive information systems that allow a viewer to select what information is displayed. To create a menu-driven Screenshow, first create a chart that displays a menu of alternatives and the keys users should press to display each alternative. Next, create a slide show that includes the menu chart. This menu chart is often placed as the first file in the slide show on the Create/Edit Slide Show form. On the Screenshow Effects form, assign Go To keys to the menu chart to cause the Screenshow to branch to the appropriate series of files on the basis of each key listed on the menu.

Each series of files specified by a Go To key can contain one or any number of files. The final file in each series, however, should refer back to the file that contains the menu. At the last file in the series, enter the number for the menu chart in the "Go To" column, but do not define a key in the "Key" column.

For example, imagine a slide show that has 41 files. The first file contains a menu that instructs the viewer to press an **A**, **B**, **C**, or **D** to display one of four different series of files. If the viewer presses **A**, the slide show goes to file 2. From file 2, the files continue through file 11, which then automatically returns to file 1. If the viewer presses **B**, the slide show branches to file 12, which continues until file 21, and then returns to file 1. Likewise, **C** will display files 22 through 31, and **D** will display files 32 through 41. Files 31 and 41 return to file 1. With the exception of file 1, all the remaining files are displayed for 10 seconds (as defined in the "Time" column on the Screenshow Effects form). A slide show such as this one is an interactive information system.

The same technique can be used to branch to slide show files. For example, suppose the first file included in a slide show contains a menu instructing the user to press **A**, **B**, **C**, or **D** to display a specific series of files. The Go To overlay used for file 1 in this example is shown in Figure 13-15. Pressing **A** branches to file 2, **B** branches to file 3, **C** branches to file 4, and **D** branches to file 5. All the files referred to are themselves slide show files. In addition, the last file in each of these four

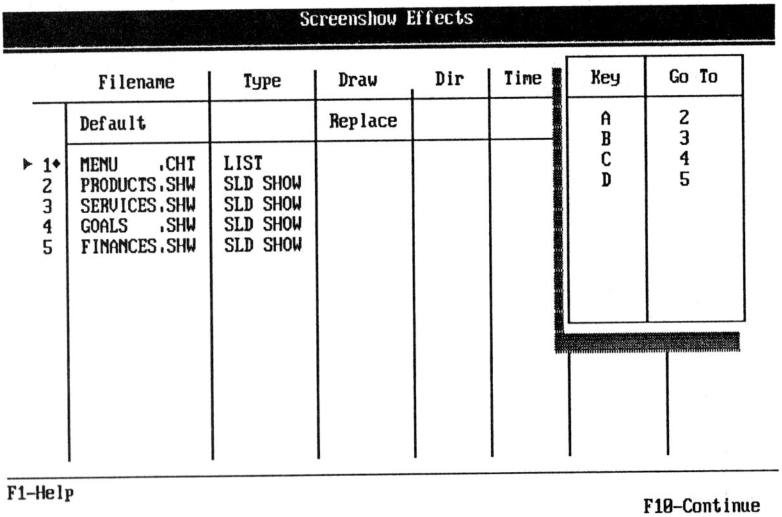

| | Filename | Type | Draw | Dir | Time | Key | Go To |
|---|---|---|---|---|---|---|---|
| | Default | | Replace | | | A B C D | 2 3 4 5 |
| ▶ 1• | MENU    .CHT | LIST | | | | | |
| 2 | PRODUCTS.SHW | SLD SHOW | | | | | |
| 3 | SERVICES.SHW | SLD SHOW | | | | | |
| 4 | GOALS   .SHW | SLD SHOW | | | | | |
| 5 | FINANCES.SHW | SLD SHOW | | | | | |

F1-Help                                                                 F10-Continue

**Figure 13-15.**    Go To overlay settings applied to file 1

slide shows contains the name of the *original* slide show. Once the last file in any of the slide shows is displayed, the show will branch back to the first file of the original slide show and again display the menu. This technique is similar to that previously described, but can be used if the number of files exceeds the 90-file limit for a single slide show.

## Special Considerations for Very Large Slide Shows

When you create a slide show, the list in the file area of the Create/Edit Slide Show form can only display a maximum of 255 files. In this list, chart files are displayed first, followed by slide show files, bit-mapped files, and finally, template files. If you are creating large slide shows that combine three or more slide shows into a single show in which you need to use more than 255 different files overall, you will not be able to create all these slide shows in the same directory. To circumvent this problem, create each of the individual slide shows in its own directory. Once you create each slide show, copy the slide show files into a single directory.

*Note:* Be sure your version of DOS and your computer setup will permit you to maintain more than 255 files in a single directory. Some systems are not set up to do so.

## Using Custom Palettes in a Screenshow

When you display a slide show, Harvard Graphics uses the current palette to display charts. If you display a bit-mapped file that uses a palette different from your current Harvard Graphics palette, the palette will temporarily switch to the palette for the bit-mapped file. If you then overlay a chart onto this bit-mapped file, the chart will use this alternate palette. This is undesirable if you do not want a chart's colors to appear different from the colors you originally defined. However, you can use this palette-switching characteristic in order to use multiple palettes in a single presentation.

To use an alternate color palette, you must first create a bit-mapped file that uses a different palette, as described in the following section. If you want to make this palette "invisible" to your Screenshow viewers, make sure the bit-mapped image is entirely black (or whatever color your Harvard Graphics palette background is).

To use this alternate palette, include the bit-mapped file in your slide show, followed immediately by your chart. Use the Overlay transition to display this chart. Since this chart is overlaid on the bit-mapped file, it will use the palette defined for the bit-mapped file. When you display the next chart, the palette will revert back to the Harvard Graphics palette (unless it too uses an Overlay transition). You can include a number of alternative color palettes in your slide show simply by preceding the desired chart with a bit-mapped file that contains the alternate palette.

## Creating a Bit-Mapped File for an Alternate Palette

The easiest way to produce a bit-mapped file using an alternate palette is to create the palette using the Color Palette Setup form, as described in "The Color Palette" in Chapter 3. Once you create the desired palette, use F2-Draw chart to display a blank chart, thereby producing a blank screen. Capture this blank screen using a screen capture utility such as the one available in the Screenshow Utilities program (see Appendix C, "Harvard Graphics Accessories"). Then save this bit-mapped file to the directory in which your slide show is stored. You can then use this bit-mapped image to change the palette in your slide show, as described in the preceding section.

## Creating Practice Cards for a Slide Show

Practice cards are used to make notes for the files in your slide shows. They can be particularly helpful when your slide show will be used during an oral presentation. If you design practice cards to be used as speaker notes, it is a good idea to print out these practice cards and rehearse your presentation while the Screenshow is being displayed. Practice cards can also be used to maintain information about each of the files in a slide show, or to create handouts that contain descriptive information along with a chart image.

To create practice cards, the desired slide show must be current. (Make the slide show current as described earlier in "Selecting a Slide Show.") Select <Make practice cards> from the Slide Show Menu. Harvard Graphics will display the Practice Cards form, as shown in Figure 13-16. You use this form to create practice cards for each of the files in your slide show. Press PGDN to advance to the next practice card and PGUP to return to the preceding practice card in the slide show. A complete list of the keys used to control movements within the Practice Cards form is shown in Table 13-5. You can also type a file number at the "Slide #" option to move directly to a particular practice card. If you enter a number for a file that does not exist, Harvard Graphics will display the message "Slide or template number is out of range."

The "Slide #," "Name," and "Description" columns at the top of the Practice Cards form display the file number, name of the file, and file description (if the file is a template, chart, or slide show, and you have

```
                         Practice Cards
         Slide #    Name              Description
            6       GOALS5     Current Sales, Anticipated Sales
         Sales have been increasing for the last three years.
         These sales increases are greater than predicted.
         Our sales predictions for next year need to be revised.




         Print data:   Yes  ▶No    │ Display time:


F1-Help
                                                              F10-Continue
```

**Figure 13-16.**    Practice Cards form

| Key | Function |
| --- | --- |
| BACKSPACE | Moves cursor back one space in the text area on the practice card, deleting any character in that space. |
| CTRL-DEL | Deletes current line at cursor in the text area of the practice card. |
| DEL | Deletes character at cursor in the text area of the practice card. |
| DOWN (arrow) | Moves cursor down one line in the text area of the practice card. |
| END | Displays the last practice card in the slide show. |
| ESC | Returns to the Slide Show Menu. |
| HOME | Displays the first practice card in the slide show. |
| INS | Inserts character(s) at cursor in the text area of the practice card. When insert is on, cursor is a block. |
| PGDN | Displays the next practice card in the slide show. |
| PGUP | Displays the previous practice card in the slide show. |
| SHIFT-TAB | Moves cursor between the "Slide #" option, the text area of the practice card, the "Print data" option, and the "Display time" option. |
| TAB | Moves cursor between the "Slide #" option, the text area of the practice card, the "Print data" option, and the "Display time" option. |
| UP (arrow) | Moves cursor up one line in the text area of the practice card. |

**Table 13-5.** Cursor Control Keys and Functions for Creating Practice Cards

defined a description for it). The information in the "Name" and "Description" fields cannot be modified. In the middle of the form is an area for entering notes (text). This area can contain a maximum of 11 lines of text of 60 characters each.

At the bottom of the form are two options: "Print data" and "Display time." The "Print data" option has two settings: Yes and No. If you plan to print the practice cards and also want to print the data associated with the practice card (given that the file is a data chart), set "Print data" to Yes. The data will be printed on a separate page following the practice card. If you set "Print data" to No, the chart data will not be printed when you are printing practice cards. See "Printing Practice Cards" in Chapter 8 for more information. An example of a printed practice card is shown in Figure 13-17.

| SLIDE # | NAME | DESCRIPTION |
|---|---|---|
| 6 | GOALS5 .CHT | Current Sales, Anticipated Sales |

Sales have been increasing for the last three years.

These sales increases are greater than predicted.

Our sales predictions for next year need to be revised.

DISPLAY TIME:

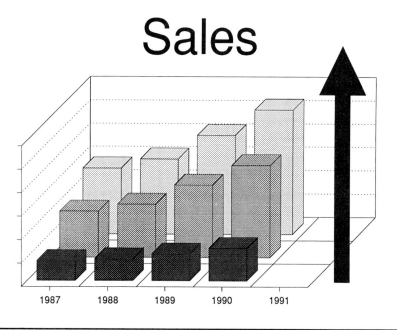

**Figure 13-17.**   A printed practice card

If you assigned a time for the file in the "Time" column on the Screenshow Effects form, the "Display time" option for the corresponding practice card will also display this time. You can modify this time at "Display time." This is useful if you determine a timing change is necessary while you are practicing your presentation. If you change this time, the value in the "Time" column on the Screenshow Effects form will also be modified.

While you are entering notes for each practice card, keep in mind that some files, such as template files and slide show files, are not actually displayed in a Screenshow, and therefore, may not require speaker notes.

## Other Slide Show Topics

Slide shows are flexible and sophisticated, rich in potential, and fun to create. The next sections describe additional uses of slide shows.

## Spell Checking Charts in a Slide Show

You can spell check all the charts in a slide show. To do this, make the desired slide show current. (You can also create a slide show specifically for the purpose of spell checking a group of charts in one step rather than checking them individually.) Once the desired slide show is current, press F4-Spell check while at the Slide Show Menu.

*Reminder:* In order to spell check a slide show you *must* be at the Slide Show Menu. If you press F4-Spell check from the Main Menu, you will only check the current chart.

Harvard Graphics will check the spelling of all of the charts in your slide show, with the exception of bit-mapped files (.PCX or .PIC files), charts in multiple charts, and other slide shows. The text in drawings added to charts will also be checked. Harvard Graphics checks the spelling of each chart in the slide show, one at a time. If it does not recognize a word, it displays the questioned word on the appropriate spelling overlay, as described in "Spell Checking the Current Chart," in

Chapter 2. When you make a correction to a chart while spell checking a slide show, Harvard Graphics will display the Save Chart overlay to allow you to save the modified chart before continuing on to the next chart. To save the chart and continue spell checking, press F10-Continue. Harvard Graphics will continue spell checking the next chart in the slide show. Press ESC at any time to cancel spell checking.

## Creating a Slide Show for Output

Whenever you want to output two or more charts, you can place them in a slide show so you do not have to retrieve and output each chart separately. To do this, first create a slide show that includes each of the charts you want to output, as described earlier in "Creating a Slide Show." Next, return to the Main Menu and select <Produce output>. Select the desired slide show output option: <Print slide show>, <Plot slide show>, or <Record slide show>. Output your slide show as described in "Outputting the Charts in a Slide Show" in Chapter 8.

To create a record of the files you have output, you can select <Print slide show list> and print, as described in "Printing a Slide Show List" in Chapter 8. When you no longer need this slide show, you can delete it using the <Remove file> selection from the Get/Save/Remove menu (see "Deleting Files" in Chapter 2).

## Using a Screenshow to Review Charts

A Screenshow can be used to help you review or edit a group of charts. To do this, simply create a slide show containing the charts you want to review, as described previously in "Creating a Slide Show." Display the Screenshow either by selecting <Display Screenshow> from the Slide Show Menu or by pressing F2-Preview show from the Screenshow Effects form.

If you notice a problem with a chart while viewing the Screenshow, press CTRL-E to immediately display the chart form (for text charts and organization charts) or the chart data form (for data charts). Using this technique, you can save the time involved in retrieving each chart individually. When you are through with the slide show created to review a group of charts, you can delete it using <Remove File> from the Get/Save/Remove menu (see "Deleting Files" in Chapter 2.)

*Note:* If you press CTRL-E to go to a chart form, and then correct or modify the chart, you will return to the Main Menu when you are through changing it. Use <Save chart> from the Get/Save/Remove menu to save any changes. Once you exit a Screenshow by pressing CTRL-E, you do not automatically return to the Screenshow. You will need to display the Screenshow again in order to continue reviewing charts.

# Macros

**Macro Overview**
**Recording a Macro**
**Playing a Macro**
**Customizing a Macro**
**Editing and Writing Macros**

This chapter describes how to create, modify, and use Harvard Graphics macros. Macros can either be a series of recorded keystrokes, which can be played back, or a computer program that you write. Although macros are not for everybody, if you find yourself performing the same task routinely, you can benefit by using one or more macros to automate the task.

## Macro Overview

The term *macro* refers to a record of keystrokes you can *play*, or execute, to automatically perform an entire series of commands, as if you were pressing the keys manually, one at a time. The macro can be recorded while you are pressing keys, or it can be written like a computer program. Most macros are created by recording keypresses while working with Harvard Graphics. Writing a macro, on the other hand, is especially useful when you want to create a fairly long or sophisticated one. However, no matter how your macro was created, you can add features such as displaying customized messages on the screen, permitting user input, and pausing for a specified time before continuing the macro.

When you purchased Harvard Graphics you also received the MACRO software program. (In this chapter, *macro*, lowercase, refers to a record of keystrokes. When the MACRO program is referred to, uppercase letters are used.) MACRO is an independent program, but is designed to be used with Harvard Graphics.

When you installed Harvard Graphics on your computer, you installed a program called MACRO.EXE at the same time (unless you are working with a two-floppy system). This is one of a class of programs called TSRs, which stands for Terminate, Stay Resident (also referred to as memory-resident programs). MACRO is a TSR program because you load it into your computer's memory, and it stays there until you unload it. While MACRO is in memory you can run other software, such as Harvard Graphics.

You can activate MACRO at any time, even while Harvard Graphics is running. When MACRO is activated, you can record macros, play back previously recorded macros, or play programmed macros. When you instruct MACRO to record your keystrokes, it records which keys you press while you operate Harvard Graphics. When you play back the recorded macro, MACRO repeats every keystroke, operating Harvard Graphics as if you were pressing the keys yourself.

Macros are used primarily to automate routines or to simplify tasks you perform repeatedly. For instance, imagine you have created 15 bar charts, each displaying three series of data. When you originally created these charts, you assigned the color numbers 2, 3, and 4 to the three series. After creating these charts, however, you conclude that the colors 5, 9, and 11 would look better on your charts. To change these colors, you can modify each chart, one at a time, or you can simplify these modifications by using a macro.

To use a macro, you first tell the MACRO program that you want to create a macro. You then retrieve the first chart, perform the color modification, and save the chart. MACRO will record your keystrokes while you are working. When you are finished modifying and saving the chart, you tell MACRO the macro is completed.

You can then use this macro to perform the modifications on each of the remaining charts. Simply retrieve each chart and tell MACRO that you want to play the macro you just recorded. When you play the macro, MACRO takes charge and performs all the keystrokes for you, up to and including saving the modified chart. What would have required a dozen or so keypresses has now been compressed into a single command—the command that plays the macro.

This example describes just one of the ways MACRO can help you use Harvard Graphics more efficiently. Here are some other uses for macros:

- You can create a macro that will permit a non-Harvard Graphics user to print out an existing Harvard Graphics chart.

- You can create a macro that will automate the importation of PFS:GRAPH charts.

- You can create a family of macros that move to different directories, which is useful if you keep chart files in separate directories.

- You can create a macro that will print or plot slide shows after hours, when other users are through with the equipment.

While these examples show the potential usefulness of macros, macros also have their limitations. The Harvard Graphics manual recommends you have at least 500K of free memory available to run MACRO with Harvard Graphics. Also, although the manual advises against it, it is possible to run MACRO using a two-disk drive system. However, this may not be worth your while since you will have to copy the MACRO.EXE program onto one of your two Harvard Graphics working copy disks, and then determine whether the memory available with your system is sufficient.

Even if you have a hard disk, you may not have enough memory to run MACRO. Since MACRO is a memory-resident program, it competes for memory with any other memory-resident programs you may be running, such as SideKick, VDI drivers, network interface drivers, and other device drivers—not to mention Harvard Graphics itself. If you find you cannot run Harvard Graphics after MACRO has been loaded, unload MACRO from memory. You will need to find a way to reduce your memory overhead before you can use MACRO with Harvard Graphics.

## Loading MACRO

MACRO is loaded from DOS. To load it, make sure you are in the directory in which both Harvard Graphics and MACRO are stored. At the DOS prompt, type the command

**MACRO**

then press ENTER. You will see the message shown in Figure 14-1 immediately after MACRO is loaded into memory. Once you have loaded MACRO, it is a good idea to avoid loading any other memory-resident programs until you have first unloaded MACRO. This is because you can unload MACRO only when it is the last TSR loaded into memory.

With MACRO loaded into memory, you can invoke it at any time by pressing ALT-0 (zero). When you do so, you will see the MACRO menu, shown in Figure 14-2. The contents of this menu will change once you begin recording a macro. These additional MACRO menu selections are discussed later in this chapter. To remove the MACRO menu without recording or playing a macro, press ESC.

## Unloading MACRO

When you are through using MACRO, you should unload it from memory, since it occupies approximately 60K of RAM (random access memory). If you are still in Harvard Graphics, return to DOS (MACRO cannot be unloaded while Harvard Graphics is running). From DOS, press ALT-0 to display the MACRO menu. From the MACRO menu, select Unload MACRO. If MACRO is not the last TSR loaded into memory, the message "Cannot unload MACRO" will be displayed. If this happens, unload any memory-resident programs loaded after MACRO before attempting to unload MACRO again.

A message will be displayed telling you when MACRO has been successfully unloaded. You will then need to press any key to continue.

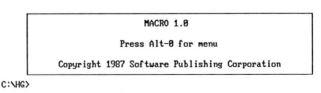

**Figure 14-1.**   Message displayed when MACRO is loaded

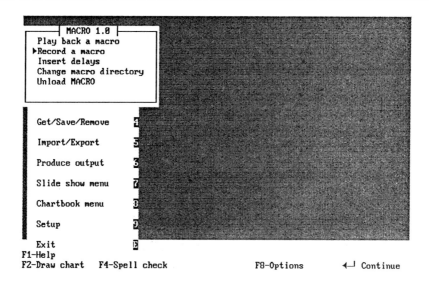

**Figure 14-2.**   MACRO menu

Once it is unloaded, the memory MACRO used will be returned to the general pool for use by other programs. Unloading MACRO will not affect any of the macros you have recorded. These macros are saved in files with the .MAC extension in the current macro directory.

## Recording a Macro

After MACRO is loaded into memory and activated by pressing ALT-0, the menu shown in Figure 14-2 is displayed. From this menu, select <Record a macro>. MACRO will display an overlay like that shown in Figure 14-3. Name your macro on this overlay. The macro name must be eight characters or less in length and cannot contain an extension. MACRO will add the .MAC extension to the name you define. Although you can give your macro any name you desire, if you supply a single-character name, you will be able to play back the macro with a single keystroke (See "Playing a Macro" for additional details.) Press ENTER

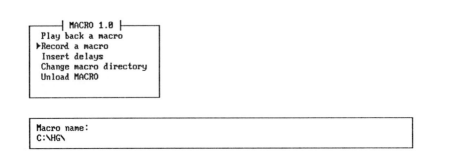

**Figure 14-3.**   Enter the name of the macro you want to record

after you have entered the name to begin recording your macro. If you press ESC instead, you will return to the MACRO menu without recording a macro.

If a macro already exists for the name you entered, MACRO will display the message "File exists, overwrite old." If you want to replace the existing macro, select Yes; otherwise select No. If you select No, enter a new name for the macro.

Once you start recording your macro, each key you press will be recorded, with the exception of a few special keys, listed in Table 14-1. These keys are used to control the MACRO program while you are recording your macro. While recording your macro, perform the tasks you want your macro to record. When you are through with the desired tasks and want to terminate the macro, press ALT-0 again to display the MACRO menu. Next, select <Stop recording macro> to complete the recording of your macro. If you want to cancel the macro while you are recording it, press ALT-F6. A canceled macro is not saved.

For the best performance from a macro, observe the following guidelines:

- A macro does not keep track of which Harvard Graphics screen was displayed nor the exact position of the cursor when you started recording the macro. Therefore, you should always play back a macro beginning at the same position within Harvard Graphics from which you began recording it. If you start at a different position, your macro might make selections from menus or forms that were not present when the macro was recorded, possibly generating undesirable results. Keep this in mind so that you start recording the macro at the same point from which you intend to play it. Also remember the starting point for the macro.

- If you want to make your macro capable of starting from almost any screen in Harvard Graphics, start by pressing ESC three or four times. This should return you to the Main Menu from nearly any screen in Harvard Graphics.

- When recording a macro, select menu items by *typing* rather than *highlighting*. For example, press 4 from the Main Menu to display the Get/Save/Remove menu rather than highlighting the selection and then pressing ENTER. This way the initial position of the cursor on the Main Menu does not matter. The highlighting method will only work when the cursor starts from the same menu option it was at when you recorded the macro.

| Key | Function |
| --- | --- |
| ALT-0 (zero) | Displays the MACRO menu. |
| ALT-END | Stops playback of a macro. |
| ALT-F6 | Cancels the recording of a macro. |
| ALT-F10 | Pauses during the recording of a macro to allow you to type a comment in the macro file. |
| CTRL- (hyphen) | Inserts a variable field into the macro while you are recording the macro. |
| CTRL-ALT | Displays the Pause overlay during the playback of a macro. |
| CTRL-F10 | Pauses during the recording of a macro to allow you to type in a message to be displayed on screen during the playback of a macro. |
| CTRL-RIGHT SHIFT | Cancels a real-time delay or a wait-until delay and continues with the playback of a macro. |
| ESC | Removes the MACRO menu or any overlay in MACRO. |
| F10 | Removes an on-screen message during playback of a macro and continues playback. |

**Table 14-1.** Keys Used to Communicate with MACRO While Recording or Playing a Macro

- Do not use a mouse while recording a macro. MACRO does not recognize mouse movements or button presses.

- You cannot begin recording a macro from Draw/Annotate. In general, it is best to avoid using MACRO with Draw/Annotate altogether, since it may produce unpredictable results.

- If you must use MACRO to size and/or place a chart (this is *not* recommended), use F3-XY position to specify the location of the cursor rather than using the cursor keys. Cursor key movements within the Size/Place screen are unpredictable when recorded by a macro.

## Playing a Macro

There are three ways to play back a macro. First, if you provided your macro with a single-character name, you can instantly play back the macro by holding down the ALT key while pressing the key that defines the macro name. For example, if you named your macro A, you can play your macro instantly by pressing ALT-A. Using a single-character name is an easy way to keep your most useful macros at your fingertips.

*Note:* The macro directory must be set to the directory in which your macro is stored to play a macro using the ALT key. See the next section "Changing the Macro Directory."

Second, you can play back a macro from the MACRO menu. To do this, press ALT-0 to display the MACRO menu and select <Play back a macro>. MACRO will ask you to enter the name of the macro you want to play, as shown in Figure 14-4. Enter the name of the macro, and then press ENTER. If you have already played or recorded a macro since you loaded MACRO, the name of the last macro you played or recorded is already entered for you. If this is not the macro you want to play, press

```
                    Pie Chart 1 Data  Page 1 of 2
       ┌──── MACRO 1.0 ────┐
       │▶Play back a macro │
       │ Record a macro    │
       │ Insert delays     │
       │ Change macro directory │
       │ Unload MACRO      │    Value        Cut Slice  Color  Pattern
       └───────────────────┘  Series A       Yes  No

         1  │ 1               1              Yes         1      1
       ┌─────────────────────────────────┐
       │ Name of macro to play back :    │
       │ C:\HG\                          │
       └─────────────────────────────────┘
         6  │ 6               1              Yes         6      6
         7  │ 7               1              Yes         7      7
         8  │ 8               1              Yes         8      8
         9                                   Yes         9      9
        10                                   Yes        10     10
        11                                   Yes        11     11
        12                                   Yes        12     12

       F1-Help                                      F9-More series
       F2-Draw chart         F6-Colors   F8-Options  F10-Continue
```

**Figure 14-4.**  Enter the name of the macro you want to play

BACKSPACE to erase the current macro name. Then type the name of the macro you want to play and press ENTER.

The third way is to play a macro from another macro. This advanced macro technique is described in the section "Including a Macro Within a Macro."

While your macro is playing, you will see it controlling your computer as if you were pressing the keys yourself. While the macro playback is in progress, you can press ALT-END to cancel it.

## Changing the Macro Directory

The current macro directory is the directory from which you loaded MACRO. Any macros you record will be stored in this directory. If you want to use macros that can be played with a single keystroke, these macros must be stored in the current macro directory. If you use different macros for different charting projects, and these projects are located in different directories, you may want to store the macros for each project in the corresponding project directory. If you do this, you will need to change your macro directory when you change projects in order to play macros with one-character names with a single keypress. (When you play a macro from the MACRO menu, however, you can specify a directory. Or if you are willing to specify the path of the macro, it is not necessary to change the current macro directory.)

To change the macro directory, press ALT-0 to display the MACRO menu. Select <Change macro directory> to display the "New macro directory" option. Enter the name of the new macro directory and press ENTER. Press ESC to return to the MACRO menu without changing the macro directory.

You can also specify a macro directory when you are loading MACRO. Before you load it, use the DOS SET command to assign the environmental variable named MACROS to the desired macro directory. For example, to define the C:\HGDATA directory as your macro directory, type the following command at the DOS prompt *before* you load MACRO:

SET MACROS=C:\HGDATA

## Pausing During Playback

While your macro is playing back, you may want to stop the playback momentarily, perhaps to make changes to the Harvard Graphics environment. For instance, if you notice that you are in the wrong directory after you begin playing back your macro, you can instruct MACRO to pause so you can change directories. Once you have successfully changed directories, you can let the macro continue. Another reason for wanting to pause a macro during playback is to observe what the macro is doing. You can instruct a macro to pause, and then continue playback, one step at a time.

During playback of a macro, press CTRL-ALT to pause the macro and display the Pause overlay, shown in Figure 14-5.

### The Pause Overlay

The Pause overlay displays three options: "Single-step playback," "Pause playback for _ keys," and "Resume macro playback." To use any of these options, either move the cursor to the desired option or

```
                    ┤ Pause ├
        ▶Single-step playback           No
         Pause playback for    keys     No
         Resume macro playback          Yes
```

**Figure 14-5.**   Pause overlay

type the first letter of the option name. Each option can be set to either Yes or No. Press ENTER to toggle the option setting between Yes and No. When you are finished setting these options, press ESC to remove the Pause overlay from the screen.

*Note:* You cannot use the SPACEBAR to set the options as you can in other areas of Harvard Graphics.

Set "Single-step playback" to Yes to play your macro one step at a time. After you remove the Pause overlay from the screen, pressing any key will cause MACRO to execute the next step in the macro. Each additional keypress will cause MACRO to advance to the next step. If you want MACRO to return to executing the macro at normal speed, press CTRL-ALT to display the Pause overlay and reset "Single-step playback" to No. If you want to cancel the macro while executing one step at a time, press ALT-F6.

To pause a macro to allow you to make changes to the Harvard Graphics environment, set "Pause playback for _ keys" to Yes. MACRO will ask you to fill in the blank before "keys." The number you enter here is the number of keystrokes you will be entering manually before you want the macro to take over again (it must be between 1 and 999). If you are not sure how many keys you will need to press, enter a number much higher than you will need. Then press ESC or F10-Continue to remove the Pause overlay and begin typing in Harvard Graphics.

When you are through pressing keys, press CTRL-RIGHT SHIFT (that is, press CTRL and the SHIFT key on the right-hand side of the keyboard simultaneously). MACRO will then resume playing back your macro. If you do not start MACRO by pressing CTRL-RIGHT SHIFT, it will automatically resume playback of the macro once you have pressed the specified number of keys.

You can also use the Pause overlay to cancel the playback of your macro by setting "Resume macro playback" to No and pressing ESC. If you cancel the macro, it will not be saved.

## Customizing a Macro

The macro features described in the preceding sections are sufficient to produce most of the macros you will need. However, MACRO provides a number of features that enable you to create sophisticated, and in some cases, interactive macros. These features include instructing a macro to insert a delay while it is playing, displaying informational messages on the screen during playback, permitting user input during playback, adding comments to the macro while you are recording it, and nesting one macro within another. These topics are discussed in the following sections.

## Adding Delays to a Macro

While you are recording your macro, you can insert a delay so that when the macro is played back, it will wait for a specified amount of time before continuing. While recording your macro, press ALT-0. From the MACRO menu, select <Insert delays>. MACRO will display the Delays overlay, shown in Figure 14-6.

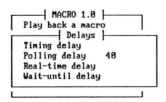

Figure 14-6.    Delays overlay

### The Delays Overlay

The Delays overlay displays four options: "Timing delay," "Polling delay," "Real-time delay," and "Wait-until delay." To set an option, move to the desired option and enter a value, then press ESC to remove the Delays overlay. Once it is no longer displayed, continue recording your macro. The values you define on the Delays overlay are used when the macro is played back.

Use the "Timing delay" option to slow down your macro during playback. Enter a number from 0 to 999. On most computers, a timing delay of 18 creates about a one-second pause between each keystroke executed in your macro. A timing delay is useful for slowing down playback when you are using the macro for a demonstration. Adding a longer timing delay may also be useful when you are trying to *debug* (remove errors from) a complex macro.

"Polling delay" is used to create very brief pauses between keystrokes to make sure your computer does not miss any keystrokes issued by MACRO during playback. Unless you find that MACRO skips keystrokes, leave "Polling delay" set to 40. If keystrokes are being missed, set "Polling delay" to a higher number, for example, 100. Continue to increase "Polling delay," if necessary, until MACRO no longer skips keystrokes while replaying a macro.

The "Real-time delay" allows you to insert a single pause, measured in seconds, in a macro. Enter the number of seconds you want MACRO to pause. You can set the "Real-time delay" option to between 0 and 32,768 seconds (a little more than nine hours). When your macro is playing back, it will pause for the specified time at the point at which you inserted the delay.

Rather than using the "Real-time delay" option, you can set "Wait-until delay" to an actual time, based on your computer's internal clock. Enter the "Wait-until delay" time using the 24-hour time format and then press ENTER. For example, enter **0:00** for midnight, **6:00** for six in the morning, or **18:00** for six in the evening. During playback, your macro will stop at the point at which you placed the delay. It will then wait until the specified time before continuing to execute the macro. This delay can be used for tasks such as printing or plotting a slide show at a late hour when there will be no competition for the printer or plotter. When you play the macro, MACRO will stop when it encounters the delay and wait until the time specified to resume playback and print or plot the charts in your slide show.

*Note:* You will not be able to use your computer for other tasks during this wait.

To cause Harvard Graphics to continue without waiting the full real-time delay or wait-until delay, press CTRL-RIGHT SHIFT (press the SHIFT key on the right side of the keyboard while holding down the CTRL key). MACRO will immediately continue with the macro playback. Alternatively, you can cancel the playback of the macro by pressing ALT-END.

## Displaying On-Screen Messages During Macro Playback

While you are recording a macro, you can create a message that will be displayed on the screen during playback. This is useful if you are creating macros that will be used by other people. To do this, press CTRL-F10 at the point where you want the message to appear while you are recording a macro. MACRO will display a message overlay. Enter a message up to 76 characters long. Press ESC or ENTER when you are finished entering your message. Then continue recording your macro.

During playback, the message will be displayed at the point in the macro where you placed it. MACRO will instruct you to press F10 to continue the macro after you have read the message.

*Note:* Messages of up to 22 lines can be added to the macro by editing. (See "Editing and Writing Macros," later in the chapter.) Recorded messages are limited to one line.

## Permitting User Input During Macro Playback

You may want to permit user input during the playback of a macro. This is a valuable feature if you want the macro to stop and permit the user to retrieve a chart, or select an option, before the macro continues. To permit user input, press CTRL-- (hyphen) to insert a variable field while you are recording your macro. You must then end the variable field while you are recording your macro by pressing ALT-0. Between pressing CTRL-- (hyphen) and ALT-0 in your macro, you should enter keypresses much like those that will be entered into the variable field during macro playback. This ensures Harvard Graphics will be in the same state during macro playback that it is in during macro recording. After pressing ALT-0 to end the variable field, continue recording your macro.

During playback, the macro will stop when it reaches the point at which you entered a variable field and display the message shown at the top left of Figure 14-7. Resume macro playback by pressing ALT-0.

## Adding Comments to a Macro During Recording

While you are recording a macro, you can add one or more comment lines to document the macro. These comments can be invaluable if you later modify the macro with a text editor. Use these comments to remind yourself what the macro is supposed to do at a particular point. To add a comment, press ALT-F10 while you are recording a macro. MACRO will display the overlay shown in Figure 14-8. Enter a comment of up to 76 characters long in this overlay, and then press ENTER to continue recording the macro. If you want to continue the macro without entering a comment, press ESC.

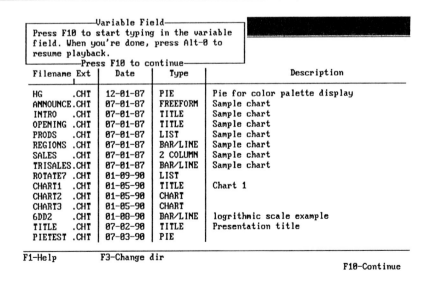

**Figure 14-7.**  Message shown when MACRO pauses for variable field input

```
                    Select Chart
    Directory: C:\HG
    Filename:  HG        .CHT

    Filename Ext  | Date     | Type     | Description
    HG       .CHT | 12-01-87 | PIE      | Pie for color palette display
    ANNOUNCE .CHT | 07-01-87 | FREEFORM | Sample chart
    INTRO    .CHT | 07-01-87 | TITLE    | Sample chart
    OPENING  .CHT | 07-01-87 | TITLE    | Sample chart
    PRODS    .CHT | 07-01-87 | LIST     | Sample chart
    REGIONS  .CHT | 07-01-87 | BAR/LINE | Sample chart
    SALES    .CHT | 07-01-87 | 2 COLUMN | Sample chart
    TRISALES .CHT | 07-01-87 | BAR/LINE | Sample chart
    ROTATE7  .CHT | 01-09-90 | LIST     |
    CHART1   .CHT | 01-05-90 | TITLE    | Chart 1
    CHART2   .CHT | 01-05-90 | CHART    |
    CHART3   .CHT | 01-05-90 | CHART    |
    6DD2     .CHT | 01-08-90 | BAR/LINE | logrithmic scale example

                     Type comment:


                                                       F10-Continue
```

**Figure 14-8.**     Enter comments in this overlay

## Including a Macro Within a Macro

You can include a macro within a macro. Macros called by another macro are called *nested macros*. This allows you to design smaller macros that perform specific functions, and then add them together to create more complex macros. To include a macro within a macro, press ALT-0 while you are recording a new macro and select <Play back a macro>. Then select the macro you want to play. When this macro is done playing, continue to record your new macro. When you play back the new macro, MACRO will load and play the nested macro at the designated place in your macro. Once the nested macro has been played, the macro in which it was nested will resume playing.

## Editing and Writing Macros

Once you have recorded a macro, you may need to modify it. You can do this in one of two ways. First, you can rerecord the macro. This is often the simplest method of fixing a problem macro. To record the macro again, follow the steps described previously in "Recording a Macro." Alternatively, you can edit the commands contained in the macro. Usually this is only done if the macro is complicated or long and is thus difficult to rerecord. The topic of editing the commands in a macro is so closely related to writing macros from scratch that both topics are discussed together in this section.

Macros are simple ASCII text files. You can edit or write a macro using any text editor or word processor that can read and save ASCII files. Harvard Graphics macros consist of keypresses, MACRO *key codes,* and MACRO *commands*. Keypresses represent the alphanumeric keystrokes that are "pressed" when the macro is played back, and are the keyboard characters you press when you record a macro. For instance, imagine that you record a macro starting from the Main Menu. You may press **1** to display the Create New Chart menu, followed by **1** to create a text chart, followed by **2** to create a simple list, and then you enter **WEEKLY REPORT** for the title of the simple list. MACRO would represent these keystrokes as

112WEEKLY REPORT

*Note:* The character recorded when the SPACEBAR was pressed between WEEKLY and REPORT in the above example is a single blank space. When MACRO encounters a blank space in a macro while the cursor is on a Harvard Graphics form or menu, MACRO presses the SPACEBAR.

MACRO key codes are special codes that represent cursor control keys, function keys, ALT and CTRL keys, and nearly every other key on your keyboard that is not an alphanumeric key. Each MACRO key code is enclosed in angle brackets (< and >). For example, the MACRO key code for CTRL-UP is <CTRLUP>.

MACRO commands are special keywords that perform some function in your macro. Most MACRO commands perform functions that can be specified from the MACRO menu while you are recording a macro (such as delays and variable fields). Most MACRO commands begin and end with <CMD>. An example of a MACRO command is

<CMD>W21:00<CMD>

This command includes a wait-until delay, causing MACRO to wait until nine o'clock at night before continuing to the next MACRO command.

The following is an example of a MACRO.

```
<CMD>T0<CMD>
<CMD>P40<CMD>
41<VFLD><VFLD><ENTER><ESC><F10>61
<CMD>R0:0:30:0<CMD>
<F10>
```

The first two lines, <CMD>T0<CMD> and <CMD>P40<CMD> set the timing delay to 0 and the polling delay to 40. The timing- and polling-delay commands must be used to initiate any macro that is recorded or that you write from scratch. (MACRO automatically places these commands in a recorded macro.) The remaining commands select <Get/Save/Remove> from the Main Menu, select <Get> from the Get/Save/Remove menu, and use a variable field to permit the user to get a file. At this point, MACRO will display the message instructing the user to press ALT-F10. The user must select the desired file by pressing ENTER. MACRO then displays a message instructing the user to press ALT-0 to continue the macro. MACRO does these steps automatically, and they need not be specified in your macro program. The macro then returns to the Main Menu, selects <Produce output>, and then selects <Print chart> from the Produce Output menu. The second from the last command inserts a 30-second delay before issuing the last command, an F10-Continue, to print the selected chart.

To edit an existing macro, use a text editor or word processor to add, delete, or change the keypresses, MACRO key codes, or MACRO commands in the macro. To write a macro from scratch, you must first create an ASCII file using a text editor or word processor. Enter the keypresses, the MACRO key codes, and the MACRO commands in this ASCII file.

The available MACRO commands are shown in Table 14-2. Table 14-3 displays the MACRO key codes.

## Inserting a MACRO Command While Recording a Macro

You can include a MACRO command as part of a recorded macro. One way to do this is to record a macro, then edit it. Another way is to issue

| MACRO Command | Function |
| --- | --- |
| <AUTO> | Causes a macro to start playback over again. The macro will play repeatedly until you press ALT-END. |
| <CMD><*text><CMD> | Enter text of up to 22 lines of 76 characters each that you want to appear as an on-screen message to the user. |
| <*comment> | Inserts a comment into the macro file. This comment has no effect on the playback of a macro. |
| <CMD>F[path]filename<CMD> | Plays the macro called *filename*. If the file is not on the current macro directory, optionally specify the directory path, but do not enclose this path in brackets. |
| <CMD>P*num*<CMD> | Enter a number from 1 to 999 to specify the length of the polling delay. |
| <CMD>R*hh:mm:ss:ll*<CMD> | Enter a time in hour:minute:second:millisecond format to specify a real-time delay. |
| <CMD>T*num*<CMD> | Enter a number from 0 to 999 to specify a time delay. |
| <CMD>W*hh:mm*<CMD> | Enter a time in an hour:minute format to specify the time MACRO should wait before continuing playback of a macro. |
| <STOP> | Stops playback of a macro. |
| <VFLD><VFLD> | Waits for variable field input. |

Table 14-2.  MACRO Commands

the MACRO command while you are recording your macro. To do this, press ALT-0 while you are recording your macro. From the MACRO menu, select <Type macro commands>. MACRO will display an overlay in which you can enter MACRO commands (refer to Table 14-2 for a list of commands). You can add as many MACRO commands in this overlay as space permits. When you are done adding the commands, press ENTER and continue recording your macro.

If you want to add more macro commands than space in the overlay permits, press ENTER after you have added some commands. Then press ALT-0 and select <Type macro commands> again. Repeat this procedure until you have added as many MACRO commands as you need.

| MACRO Key Code | Resulting Keypress |
|---|---|
| \<ALT*key*\> | ALT-*key* (ALT-0 or ALT-A, for example) |
| \<ALTF*key*\> | ALT-F*key* (ALT-F1, for example) |
| \<BKS\> | BACKSPACE |
| \<CTRL*key*\> | CTRL-*key* (CTRL-A, for example) |
| \<CTRLDEL\> | CTRL-DEL |
| \<CTRLDN\> | CTRL-DOWN (arrow) |
| \<CTRLEND\> | CTRL-END |
| \<CTRLHOME\> | CTRL-HOME |
| \<CTRLINS\> | CTRL-INS |
| \<CTRLLFT\> | CTRL-LEFT (arrow) |
| \<CTRLPGDN\> | CTRL-PGDN |
| \<CTRLPGUP\> | CTRL-PGUP |
| \<CTRLRGT\> | CTRL-RIGHT (arrow) |
| \<CTRLUP\> | CTRL-UP (arrow) |
| \<DEL\> | DEL |
| \<DN\> | DOWN (arrow) |
| \<END\> | END |
| \<ENTER\> | ENTER |
| \<ESC\> | ESC |
| \<F*key*\> | F*key* (F1 or F10, for example) |
| \<HOME\> | HOME |
| \<INS\> | INS |
| \<LFT\> | LEFT (arrow) |
| \<\<  | < (less than) |
| \<MIN\> | − |
| \<PGDN\> | PGDN |
| \<PGUP\> | PGUP |
| \<PLS\> | + |
| \<RGT\> | RIGHT (arrow) |
| \<SHIFTF*key*\> | SHIFT-F*key* (SHIFT-F10, for example) |
| \<SHIFTTAB\> | SHIFT-TAB |
| \<TAB\> | TAB |
| \<UP\> | UP (arrow) |

**Table 14-3.** MACRO Key Codes

## Creating Macros that Run Continuously

Use the MACRO command <AUTO> to cause a macro to immediately start over again, beginning with the first command in the macro. When <AUTO> is included in a macro it will run continuously. This command should be the last one in your macro. Record your macro, performing all the keystrokes that you want executed as part of the macro. Next, press ALT-0 to display the MACRO menu. Select <Type macro commands>. Enter the macro command <AUTO> and press ENTER. The MACRO menu is again displayed. Select <Stop recording macro> from this menu.

Alternatively, you can record your macro, and then use a text editor to add the <AUTO> statement to the end of the recorded macro.

When you play the macro, the macro will repeat continuously until you press ALT-END.

# Harvard Graphics 2.3

Introduction to Harvard Graphics 2.3
Harvard Graphics 2.3 Features

# Introduction to Harvard Graphics 2.3

**FIFTEEN**

New Features Overview
Starting the On-Line Tutorial
Using Speed Keys
Default Settings
Defining International Formats
Setting Current Chart Options

If you are already a Harvard Graphics user and have upgraded to version 2.3, you will be able to use the new version immediately; the look and feel remain the same. As you use the different menus, however, you will notice changes here and there. While much will be familiar, you will see several additions. These new features have extended the power of Harvard Graphics substantially, while preserving its status as the easiest-to-use graphics program available.

If Harvard Graphics 2.3 is your first introduction to the program, be assured that all the features that have made Harvard Graphics the best selling presentation graphics program for PCs are available in the current version. In addition, the new features respond to the increasingly sophisticated needs of graphics producers at all levels of experience. Some of the additions make creating a great-looking chart as easy as picking the desired style from a gallery of charts. Other features, such as the powerful drawing utility Draw Partner, provide you with a sophisticated set of tools for creating drawings of any level of complexity you could want.

This chapter will introduce you to the new features of Harvard Graphics 2.3, and will describe in detail the Harvard Graphics tutorial, speed keys, new chart default settings and current chart settings, and international formats. For detailed descriptions of the other features introduced in this chapter, see Chapter 16, "Harvard Graphics 2.3 Features," Chapter 17, "Introduction to Draw Partner," and Chapter 18, "Drawing and Editing with Draw Partner."

## New Features Overview

If you are already a Harvard Graphics user, an obvious change you will notice is in the function key banner. Several of the existing function keys have been renamed and some new function keys have been added. The most commonly used function keys, such as F1-Help, F8-Options, and F10-Continue, have remained the same. Others, such as F3-X data type (bar/line, area, and high/low/close) have been changed. These functions are still available; however, they have been relocated to different function keys. For example, the F3-X data type function is now the F5-X data type.

These changes were necessitated by the addition of function keys that permit you to quickly perform certain common functions. For example, from any chart form you can now press F3-Save to save your chart, without having to return to the Main Menu. Similarly, you can press F4-Draw/Annotate to instantly add drawings and annotation to the current chart. While you are working with Harvard Graphics, be sure to examine the function key banner on each screen to see which keys are available. A complete list of function keys for all versions of Harvard Graphics can be found in Chapter 24, "Harvard Graphics Forms and Function Keys."

The following sections contain overviews of new features intended for Harvard Graphics users who have upgraded to version 2.3, or who are thinking of upgrading, or for first-time Harvard Graphics users who are interested in the evolution of the product. If you are new to Harvard Graphics, you may want to skim over these descriptions of the new features in version 2.3 and then refer to Part One of this book for information on using Harvard Graphics.

## On-Line Tutorial

An on-line tutorial is available to familiarize new users with Harvard Graphics features. The tutorial is a separate program that you start from the DOS prompt.

## Integrated Draw Partner

Draw Partner, a drawing accessory that was first shipped with Harvard Graphics in November 1989, is now an integral part of the program. From any of the chart forms, or from the Harvard Graphics Main Menu, you can switch to Draw Partner by pressing CTRL-D. You can also invoke Draw Partner by selecting it from the Applications menu. Specifically, at the Main Menu press F3-Applications to display the Applications menu. Then select <Draw Partner> from this menu. When you are through adding or editing drawings in Draw Partner, you return to Harvard Graphics by selecting <Return to Harvard Graphics> from the Draw Partner Main Menu.

## Improved Draw Partner

Draw Partner has been upgraded from version 1.0 to version 2.3, which includes full compatiblity with Harvard Graphics. Every type of object you can add in Harvard Graphics Draw/Annotate can now be added with Draw Partner. Furthermore, version 2.3 also includes four new drawing objects: arcs, wedges, freehand drawings, and equal-sided polygons.

Other additions to Draw Partner include the ability to change the options for a group of objects, create groups within groups, add shadows and perspective to objects, and bend (or *skew*) objects. With these features added to the already powerful drawing tools included in Draw Partner, an unlimited variety of illustrations and chart enhancements is within reach.

## Chart Gallery

It is sometimes difficult to visualize the right chart style for your data. Since it is easier to identify the type of chart you need if you can see it, Harvard Graphics 2.3 includes a feature called Chart Gallery. When you are in the Chart Gallery, Harvard Graphics displays the chart styles you can choose from. When you see the chart that best matches what you want to create, you simply press F10-Edit + Clear to display the chart form and enter your data.

### Applications

Harvard Graphics 2.3 provides you with a modifiable Applications menu. From this menu, you can easily load other software programs from within Harvard Graphics. For example, if you are creating a chart with a data link to a Lotus 1-2-3 spreadsheet, but you want to update the spreadsheet before you print the chart, select <Lotus 1-2-3> from the Applications menu. When you are finished making modifications to your spreadsheet, exit Lotus 1-2-3 and you will automatically return to Harvard Graphics.

### HyperShow

With Harvard Graphics' new HyperShow capabilities, you can use a mouse to activate a cursor on the screen during a ScreenShow. (The Screenshow feature of the earlier versions appears in 2.3 as Screen-Show.) If you have defined a button on your chart, clicking the mouse while the cursor is on the button can automatically display a file other than the next one in your ScreenShow. HyperShow is an extension of the programmable Go To keys available in earlier versions of Harvard Graphics. Using HyperShow, your interactive presentations can be more intuitive and impressive than ever before.

### Improved International Support

Harvard Graphics' new international formats permit you to easily change the way dates, currency values, and whole number separators are displayed. These settings can be defined as defaults for all your charts, or you can specify them for the current chart.

### Speed Keys

As you use Harvard Graphics, you may find there are certain features you need again and again. Speed keys are included in version 2.3 to simplify access to these common features. With a single control key combination, you can retrieve a previously saved chart, save the changes to your current chart, or invoke Draw Partner, to name a few of the available speed keys.

### New Font

In addition to the six standard fonts that come with Harvard Graphics, a new font has been added. This font, called "Traditional," is a version of the standard Times Roman font.

### Multiple Fonts

Earlier versions of Harvard Graphics do not allow you to use more than one font on a chart. While using only one font per chart is often a good practice, there are some instances in which two or even three fonts can be used tastefully and effectively. Using either Draw/Annotate or Draw Partner, you can add text using any of the seven font styles, regardless of the font specified for your current chart.

### Improved Palettes

Harvard Graphics 2.3 comes with 12 predefined palettes. As with earlier versions, you can also create your own color palette.

Earlier versions of Harvard Graphics display a chart using the current color palette. In the 2.3 version, however, each chart remembers which palette was used to create it. This new feature has several important implications. First, displaying your chart using the appropriate colors is much easier since you do not have to worry about which palette is current. Second, a ScreenShow can be much more colorful since you can easily use a variety of palettes in a single ScreenShow simply by including charts that use different palettes.

### Importing from Excel

In addition to being able to import from Lotus 1-2-3, you can now import charts or data from Excel. As with 1-2-3, this importation can be saved as a data-linked template, thereby automating subsequent importations of the data.

### Viewing Named Ranges for Importing

When you are importing from Excel or Lotus 1-2-3, you can use named ranges to simplify defining the data you want to import. While it was possible to specify named ranges for Lotus spreadsheets in earlier versions of Harvard Graphics, version 2.3 has added a feature that will *display* the named ranges for your selected spreadsheet when you press F6-Select range names.

### Importing CGM Metafiles

Importing CGM metafiles is greatly simplified in version 2.3. To import a CGM metafile you simply select <Import CGM metafile> from the Import/Export menu. The image contained in the imported CGM metafile will be added as a drawing to your current chart.

### ShowCopy

The ShowCopy utility is included to permit you to easily and accurately copy all of the necessary files for a SlideShow to a different directory or drive.

### Animated ScreenShow Examples

A set of ScreenShow sequences employing transition effects that create animation is included with the Harvard Graphics 2.3 package. You can examine these file sequences for ideas on how to use transitions to create animated ScreenShows or even use these file sequences in your own ScreenShow.

### New and Improved Symbols

Harvard Graphics 2.3 comes with over 500 new professionally drawn symbols that you can easily incorporate into your charts. Refer to Appendix D for a list of version 2.3 symbol files or the Harvard Graphics manual to see pictures of all the symbols.

### Support for Additional Output Devices

Support has been added for a number of printers, plotters, and film recorders. Refer to "Printer Setup Form," "Plotter Setup Form," and "Film Recorder Form" in Chapter 24, "Harvard Graphics Forms and Function Keys," to see the output devices supported in Harvard Graphics 2.3. Version 2.3 also supports grey scale printing for all printers. For a complete description of grey scale printing, refer to "Color Settings and Grey Scale Using PostScript" in Chapter 8, "Producing Output."

The remainder of this chapter details the Harvard Graphics tutorial, speed keys, new chart defaults, and international formats. For details concerning any of the other version 2.3 features, see the following chapter. For a complete description of Draw Partner's powerful features, see Chapter 17, "Introduction to Draw Partner," and Chapter 18, "Drawing and Editing with Draw Partner."

## Starting the On-Line Tutorial

To start the tutorial on Harvard Graphics 2.3, you must have installed Harvard Graphics and the tutorial files as described in Appendix B. To start the tutorial, from DOS move to the directory in which the Harvard Graphics program and tutorial files are stored. Then type: **HGTUTOR** and press ENTER. The tutorial is self-paced and prompts you through the various screens.

## Using Speed Keys

Speed keys are control key combinations that permit you to perform specified Harvard Graphics functions without having to return to the Main Menu. From any chart form, hold down the CTRL key while pressing the letter key that corresponds to the desired Harvard Graphics feature. A list of the speed keys and their effects is shown in Table 15-1.

Although all these keys work while you are on a chart form, several work from the Main Menu as well. These include CTRL-D, CTRL-G, CTRL-R, and CTRL-S.

There are three additional control key sequences that you may want to use, although they are not true speed keys. CTRL-B can be used to add a bullet to any text field in Harvard Graphics. This feature is described in Chapter 4, "Text Charts." CTRL-F can be used to activate your cursor in the function key banner so you can select a function key using a mouse or the cursor keys. Finally, CTRL-V can be used to display your current Harvard Graphics version at the top right of the function key banner.

| Speed Key | Result |
|---|---|
| CTRL-D | Go to Draw Partner. |
| CTRL-G | Get a chart. |
| CTRL-L | Get a Lotus spreadsheet. |
| CTRL-P | Print the current chart (display the Print Chart Options overlay). |
| CTRL-R | Go to Draw/Annotate. |
| CTRL-S | Save the current chart (display the Save Chart overlay). |
| CTRL-X | Get an Excel spreadsheet. |

**Table 15-1.**  Speed Keys

## Default Settings

The default settings available in Harvard Graphics 2.3 have changed somewhat from earlier versions. Following is a description of the Default Settings form, shown in Figure 15-1.

Select <Setup> from the Main Menu followed by <Defaults> from the Setup menu to display the Default Settings form. The first six options allow you to simplify file management. The next four—"Default palette," "Orientation," "Border," and "Font"—relate to chart option preferences, and the last option, "Menu colors," allows you to select a color scheme for the Harvard Graphics screen. Once you have set the desired options, press F10-Continue to return to the Setup menu.

As the name suggests, the options you set on the Default Settings form are the default options for your Harvard Graphics sessions. Each of these options except "Menu colors" can be overridden for a specific chart. For instance, even when you have specified a default data directory, you can still get charts from, or save charts to, any directory on your computer. Likewise, if you have set your default font to Executive, you can easily select the Traditional font for a particular chart.

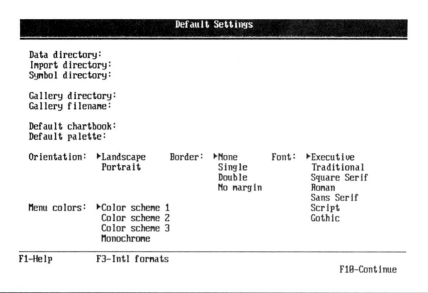

**Figure 15-1.** Default Settings form

*Note:* Changing default option settings that affect chart display characteristics (such as orientation and font) will not influence charts already created. These options are used to define the characteristics of new charts as you create them.

### Setting a Default Data Directory

Most of the time you will want to save the charts you create in one particular directory. If you have not assigned a default data directory, Harvard Graphics will assume you want to store your charts in the current directory. However, if you have created a directory specifically for the purpose of storing Harvard Graphics charts, you will want to define this directory as your default data directory.

On the Default Settings form, enter a drive and directory path at "Data directory" to specify the default directory for storing your charts. For example, type **C:\HGDATA** to tell Harvard Graphics your charts are to be stored in the directory named HGDATA on drive C.

You can always store charts in a different directory by entering that directory name at the "Directory" option on the Save Chart form. When you retrieve a chart from or save a chart to a directory other than the default data directory, Harvard Graphics will use that directory as the default for the remainder of the session. However, the next time you start Harvard Graphics, your default directory will again be the directory specified at the "Data directory" option on the Default Settings form. See Chapter 2, "Harvard Graphics Basics," for more information on getting and saving charts.

### Setting a Default Import Directory

If you generally import data or chart files from a directory other than your default data directory, you can specify this directory at the "Import directory" option. If you do not use Harvard Graphics' importing utilities, leave this option blank.

To enter a default import data directory, move to "Import directory" and enter the directory path. For example, type **C:\LOTUS123** to specify the LOTUS123 directory located on drive C as the directory from which you most often import data. Harvard Graphics will automatically assume this directory when you are importing data and chart files. You can import data from directories other than the default import directory by specifying the appropriate directory path when you are setting up your data importation. For more information about importing data and chart files, see Chapter 12, "Importing and Exporting."

### Setting a Default Symbol Directory

When you first select <Get symbol> or <Save symbol> from the Symbol menu in Draw/Annotate or <Get symbol> or <Save symbol> from the File menu in Draw Partner, the symbol files displayed will be in the default symbol directory specified on the Default Settings form. Set "Symbol directory" to the directory where you store the symbol files you use most often.

### Setting a Default Gallery Directory

The "Gallery directory" option defaults to the Gallery directory, in the path in which you installed the Harvard Graphics program (for example, HG\Gallery). If you have not installed the Chart Gallery, leave this option blank. Most of the time, you will not need to change this option. However, if you create a custom gallery using the Quick-Charts Harvard Graphics accessory, you can set "Gallery directory" to the directory where this gallery is stored.

### Setting a Default Gallery Filename

The "Gallery filename" option defaults to WPICK, which is the name of the chart gallery that comes with version 2.3. If you have not yet installed the Chart Gallery, leave this option blank. As with the "Gallery directory" option, most of the time you will not need to change this option. However, if you create a custom gallery using the Harvard Graphics accessory, Quick-Charts, you can specify the name of that gallery (without an extension) at this option.

*Hint:* A custom gallery is simply a slide show. You can add any charts you regularly want to create to a slide show, and then name this slide show as your chart gallery. When you do so, your slide show will be displayed when you select <From gallery> from the Create New Chart menu. You can then display the slide show using the control keys to control the show. In addition, you can use the keys only available in Chart Gallery: F9-Edit to edit a currently displayed chart, F10-Edit + Clear to remove the existing data from the displayed chart so you can add new data, or ESC to return to the Main Menu.

### Setting a Default Chartbook

If you are one of those Harvard Graphics users who use chartbooks to organize templates, you can specify the chartbook you use most often as the default. (Chartbooks are used to store related templates for easier retrieval.) At "Chartbook," type in the name of this chartbook; do not enter a drive, directory, or extension. If you have defined a default directory, your chartbook must be stored in that directory. Otherwise, your default chartbook must be stored in your current directory. If you do not use a chartbook, leave this option blank.

The next time you create a new chart by selecting <Create chart> from the Chartbook menu, Harvard Graphics automatically gets the chartbook you specified as the default and lists all the templates it contains. You can always get a different chartbook by selecting <Select chartbook> from the Chartbook menu. See Chapter 11, "Templates and Chartbooks," for more information on selecting chartbooks.

## Setting a Default Palette

In Harvard Graphics 2.3, each chart has a color palette associated with it. Set the "Default palette" option to the palette you want to use most often for your charts. Each time you create a new chart, Harvard Graphics will automatically use the default color palette.

*Note:* You can override this default for the current chart by changing the "Palette file" option on the Current Chart Options overlay.

## Setting a Default Chart Orientation

Harvard Graphics uses the default orientation to determine the orientation of the charts you create. *Orientation* is the way Harvard Graphics displays charts on a page. Landscape orientation (the default) produces a chart wider than it is tall, while portrait orientation produces a chart taller than it is wide.

*Note:* To use an orientation other than the default for a specific chart, select that orientation on the Current Chart Options overlay.

## Setting a Default Border

The "Border" option allows you to select the border drawn around charts when they are displayed on the screen or sent to an output device. Harvard Graphics originally defaults to None, which does not draw borders around your charts. To draw single- or double-line borders around your charts, select Single or Double from the "Border" option. If you do not want to use any border and want to have total control over the margins for your chart, set "Border" to No margin.

# Introduction to Harvard Graphics 2.3

This allows you to create a larger chart than is available with the other settings. When you select No margin, you can define your margin by using F7-Size/Place from the Main Menu.

*Note:* To use a border other than the default for a specific chart, select an alternative border on the Current Chart Options form. See "Setting Current Chart Options," later in this chapter.

### Setting a Default Font

You can select one of the seven fonts shown in Figure 15-2 as the default font to be used when you enter text on a chart. Harvard Graphics initially defaults to the Executive font.

Each chart uses only one font for the title, subtitle, footnote, and any other text added to the chart on the chart form. To use a font other than the default for a specific chart, select an alternative font on the Current Chart Options form. You can use additional fonts in conjunction with the current chart font by adding annotations using Draw/Annotate or Draw Partner.

### Setting a Default Menu Colors Scheme

You can change the colors used to display Harvard Graphics menus and forms by selecting one of four different color schemes. If you have a color monitor, Harvard Graphics defaults to Color scheme 1, the color scheme that is used when you first start up Harvard Graphics.

*Hint:* Select Monochrome if you are using a monochrome monitor and a color graphics card. Doing so will improve the appearance of Harvard Graphics' screens by making the text darker and easier to read.

## Defining International Formats

While you are setting your default chart options on the Default Settings form, you can press F3-Intl formats to display the Default International

**Executive**

**Traditional**

**Square serif**

Roman

Sans serif

Script

Gothic

**Figure 15-2.** Fonts available in version 2.3

Settings overlay, shown in Figure 15-3. This overlay is used to specify the default formats used for date, time, and currency values. These defaults will be automatically applied to every chart you create.

If you want to set international formats for only the current chart, press F3-Intl formats while the Current Chart Options form is displayed (when you press F8-Options at the Main Menu, as described later in this

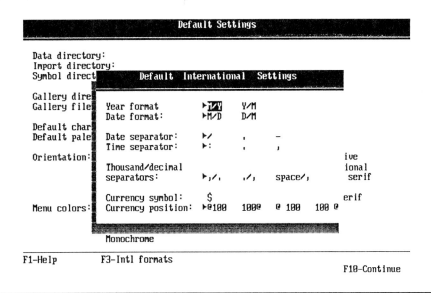

**Figure 15-3.** Default International Settings overlay

chapter), to display the Current International Settings overlay. The options on this overlay are identical to those on the Default International Settings overlay.

The Default International Settings overlay contains seven options. The first three permit you to define the date format. The fourth option is used to define the time format. Use the fifth option to define the default thousand and decimal separators and the final two options to specify the format for currency. When you are through defining the international formats on this overlay, press F10-Continue to return to the Default Settings form. If you displayed the Current International Settings overlay, pressing F10-Continue returns you to the Main Menu.

### Defining Date Formats

Use the "Year format" and "Date format" options to specify how dates should be displayed in Harvard Graphics charts. These settings are used in bar/line, area, and high/low/close charts when your X data type is one of the calendar settings. With the "Year format" option, you can specify that the month be displayed before or after the year. The "Date format" option is used to indicate whether the day will precede or follow the month. Finally, use the "Date separator" option to select which character should be used to separate the day, month, and year values.

The following are examples of possible combinations:

| Year Format | Date Format | Date Separator | Result |
|---|---|---|---|
| M/Y | M/D | / | 12/31/1990 |
| M/Y | D/M | – | 31–12–1990 |
| M/Y | D/M | . | 31.12.1990 |

### Selecting a Time Separator

Use the "Time separator" option to select the character that separates hours, minutes, and seconds. This option is used when your X data type for a bar/line, area, or high/low/close chart is set to Time.

| Time Separator | Result |
|---|---|
| : | 6:30 |
| . | 6.30 |
| , | 6,30 |

### Defining Whole Number Separators

The "Thousand/decimal separators" option is used to define the characters and format of whole number separation. This format is used for all numbers in all chart styles.

| Thousand/Decimal Separator | Result |
|---|---|
| ,/. | 10,000.00 |
| ./, | 10.000,00 |
| space /, | 10 000,00 |

### Defining Currency Format

The final two international format options, "Currency symbol" and "Currency position," are used to specify how Harvard Graphics will denote currency. These formats are used in all chart styles.

To use a currency character other than the dollar sign ($), enter the currency character at the "Currency symbol" option. This option allows you to enter a symbol up to four characters in length. Note that the English pound and Japanese yen symbols are available in the international font styles. See Appendix D for a description of the international fonts.

Using the "Currency position" option, you can specify where the currency symbol will be placed in relation to the currency value. Set this option to one of the four listed positions.

| Currency Symbol | Currency Position | Result |
| --- | --- | --- |
| $ | @100 | $25 |
| £ | 100@ | 25£ |
| S | @ 100 | $ 25 |
| ¥ | 100 @ | 25¥ |

By using the currency options in conjunction with the "Thousand/decimal separator" option, you can completely customize the display of currency values.

## Setting Current Chart Options

Harvard Graphics allows you to override default chart settings for your current chart. The default settings you can modify for your current chart are

- Orientation
- Border
- Font
- Palette file

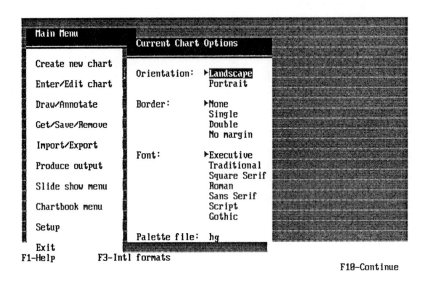

**Figure 15-4.** Current Chart Options overlay

See the earlier section, "Default Settings," for more detailed descriptions of each of these options.

If you want to change one or more of these settings for a chart other than the current chart, you must first retrieve that chart to make it the current chart. The current chart options are changed from the Main Menu rather than the Setup menu. If you are not at the Main Menu, press ESC until you return to the Main Menu. From there, press F8-Options to display the Current Chart Options overlay, shown in Figure 15-4.

The current settings for each option are marked with an arrow. To change the first three options, move to the desired option and press the SPACEBAR until the desired setting is highlighted. To change the "Palette file" option, move to that option and enter the name of the desired palette file. You can enter the number of one of the 12 palettes that comes with the Harvard Graphics package, or the name of a palette you have created. When you are finished setting chart options, press F10-Continue to return to the Main Menu.

# Harvard Graphics 2.3 Features

Chart Gallery Overview
Accessing Other Applications
Changing the Application Options
Including Multiple Fonts in One Chart
ScreenShow Enhancements
Improved Palettes
Improved Importing

This chapter describes the new features added to Harvard Graphics 2.3. Some features, such as the Chart Gallery, are entirely new additions that extend the power and capabilities of Harvard Graphics. Other new features, such as importing from Excel, are similar to previously available features, such as importing from Lotus 1-2-3. When these similar features are described, you will also be referred to the related topics in Part One of this book, where additional details can be found.

## Chart Gallery Overview

The Chart Gallery contains approximately 70 different charts, which can be roughly divided into nine styles. It simplifies the task of choosing the appropriate chart style by displaying these chart styles on your monitor. When you see a chart that looks similar to the one you want to create, a press of a function key will immediately take you to the appropriate chart form. Once on that chart form, you can enter your text and data. The options have already been set to create the style of chart displayed in the gallery.

When you use the Chart Gallery, you are not limited to the chart options and settings that are displayed. You can use the selected chart style from the gallery as a starting point for creating your own customized chart, changing the settings as needed. Additionally, the Chart Gallery permits you to easily choose your chart's colors from one of the 12 standard Harvard Graphics color palettes.

## Using the Chart Gallery

To create a chart using the Chart Gallery, follow these steps:

1. Select <Create new chart> from the Main Menu.

2. Select <From gallery> from the Create New Chart menu. Harvard Graphics displays the Chart Gallery, shown in Figure 16-1, showing the nine general styles of charts. Use the function keys shown in Table 16-1 to move from one level to another in the Chart Gallery.

3. With the mouse, click on the image of the chart style you want to create, or with the keyboard, type the number that corresponds to that chart style. For example, if you want to create an area chart, press 5 or click on the cell labeled 5 in the gallery. Harvard Graphics will display the area chart gallery, shown in Figure 16-2.

4. Once the gallery specific to a chart style is displayed, you can select one of the charts displayed to view in greater detail. For example, if you select chart 2 from the area chart gallery shown in Figure 16-2, the chart shown in Figure 16-3 is displayed.

If the displayed chart is not the style you want, you can press F3-Gallery to return to the previous screen (in this example, the area chart gallery). From this gallery you can select a different chart to examine in greater detail or you can press F3-Gallery once more to return to the Chart Gallery.

If you want to create a chart like the one shown, you can use a special feature of the Chart Gallery to select an alternate color palette for the chart. Press F5-Previous palette or F6-Next palette to show the displayed chart using a different color palette. The use of these keys is described in the next section.

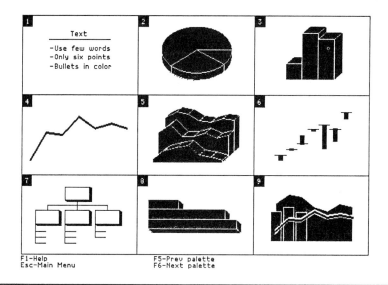

**Figure 16-1.** Harvard Graphics Chart Gallery

| Function Key | Description |
| --- | --- |
| F1-Help | Provides access to on-line help. |
| F3-Gallery | Moves back one screen in the Chart Gallery. |
| F5-Prev palette | Uses the previous numbered palette (1 to 12) to display the Chart Gallery. |
| F6-Next palette | Uses the next numbered palette (1 to 12) to display the Chart Gallery. |
| F9-Edit | When a chart from the Chart Gallery is displayed, moves to the chart form containing the text and data used to create the chart. |
| F10-Edit + Clear | When a chart from the Chart Gallery is displayed, moves to the chart form and clears the text and data from it. |

**Table 16-1.** Function Keys Used in the Chart Gallery

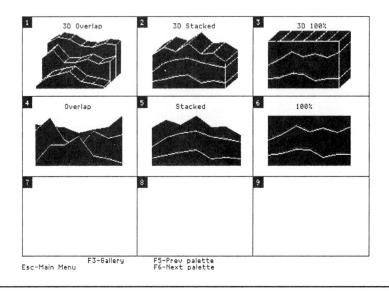

**Figure 16-2.** Area chart gallery

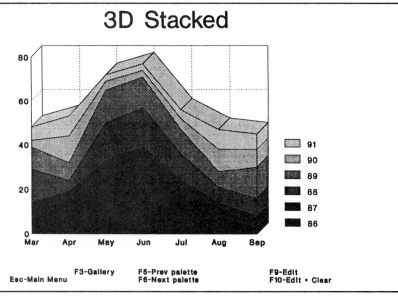

**Figure 16-3.** Area chart number 2

When you are pleased with the color palette selection, you have two ways of creating a chart like the one shown. You can press F9-Edit to display the chart form for the currently displayed chart. This chart form includes the text and data displayed on the chart you are viewing. For example, if you press F9-Edit when the area chart shown in Figure 16-3 is displayed, you will see the Area Chart Data form shown in Figure 16-4. The text and data used to create the number 2 area chart are shown on this form. The Titles & Options form, displayed when you press F8-Options, also includes any option settings necessary to create the chart you selected from the gallery.

Alternatively, you can press F10-Edit + Clear to display the chart form with the text and data cleared from it. This is very similar to F9-Edit except the chart form is cleared. You can then enter your own text and data. All the option settings on the Titles & Options form are retained.

Once you display a chart form by pressing either F9-Edit or F10-Edit + Clear, you can modify the chart just as you would any Harvard

```
                         Area Chart Data

     Title: 3D Stacked
  Subtitle:
  Footnote:

          X Axis          86          87          88          89
     Pt   Name
     ─────────────────────────────────────────────────────────────
     1    Mar             4           10          15          10
     2    Apr             16          3           5           8
     3    May             20          13          17          15
     4    Jun             23          16          18          14
     5    Jul             18          14          12          11
     6    Aug             7           7           7           7
     7    Sep             3           5           8           14
     8
     9
     10
     11
     12
     ─────────────────────────────────────────────────────────────
     F1-Help         F3-Save         F5-Set X type        F9-More series
     F2-Draw chart   F4-Draw/Annot   F6-Calculate  F8-Options  F10-Continue
```

**Figure 16-4.** Area Chart Data form

Graphics chart. You must save the chart in order to keep it permanently (see Chapter 2, "Harvard Graphics Basics").

*Hint:* If you are a new Harvard Graphics user, it may be helpful to select the desired chart using F9-Edit in order to see how text and data are entered in the chart form. You can then press F10-Continue to return to the Main Menu and select <Create new chart> followed by <Clear values>. The sample data will be cleared and you can enter your own data into the chart form.

### Selecting a Color Palette

From any Chart Gallery screen you can press F6-Next palette to display all charts in the gallery using another color palette. If you press F6-Next palette repeatedly, you can cycle forward through the 12 available color palettes. F5-Prev palette cycles backwards through the palettes. When you select a chart from the gallery using F9-Edit or F10-Edit + Clear, the palette that is currently displayed in the gallery will be the palette assigned to the chart you are creating.

## Accessing Other Applications

Harvard Graphics allows you to access other applications while you are in Harvard Graphics. For example, you can suspend Harvard Graphics temporarily while you enter Lotus 1-2-3 to modify a spreadsheet you have linked to a Harvard Graphics chart. When you return from the application, all the characteristics of your Harvard Graphics session are intact. This would not necessarily be the case if you had to exit Harvard Graphics in order to use the other application.

The applications you can start from within Harvard Graphics are displayed on the Applications menu. When you first load Harvard Graphics onto your computer, this menu has only two applications, Draw Partner and AGX Slide Service, as you can see in Figure 16-5. You can add up to seven additional applications to this list.

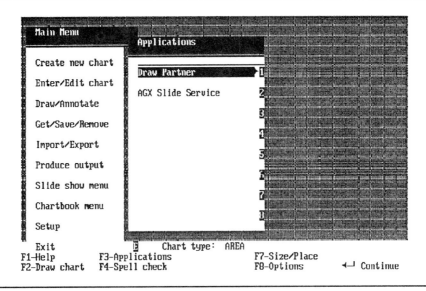

**Figure 16-5.**   Initial Applications menu

## Specifying Applications

You define the applications (software programs and Harvard Graphics accessories) you want to access from within Harvard Graphics on the Applications form, shown in Figure 16-6A. To display this form, select <Setup> from the Main Menu, followed by <Applications> from the Setup menu.

The options on the Applications form are for specifying up to eight applications you want to be able to access from within Harvard Graphics. The applications you define here will be listed on the Applications menu displayed when you press F3-Applications at the Main Menu.

Draw Partner is already displayed at "Menu item 1." You cannot modify this option or the "Maximum size (K)" or "Command" options for the first application. The menu items numbered 2 through 8 can be modified. For instance, although AGX Slide Service appears at Menu item 2, you can change this to any other application that you would like to appear in the second position of the applications menu. To do so,

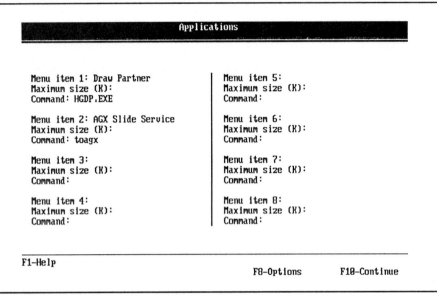

**Figure 16-6A.**   Applications form

move to the "Menu item 2" option, press CTRL-DEL to delete AGX Slide Service, and enter the name of the desired application. This name can be up to 18 characters in length.

If your application does not require much memory, you can use the "Maximum size (K)" option to indicate how much memory it needs. For example, if you have a utility that requires only 256K to run, enter **256** at "Maximum size (K)." The less memory the application requires, the quicker Harvard Graphics will be able to access it. If you do not know how much memory an application requires, or if your application needs all available memory, leave this option blank. When "Maximum size (K)" is blank, Harvard Graphics provides the application with the conventional RAM memory available before you loaded Harvard Graphics, less approximately 13K.

Finally, at the "Command" option, enter the path and name of the application you want Harvard Graphics to execute. For example, if you have entered **Lotus 1-2-3** at "Menu item 2," type **C:\LOTUS123\123** at

"Command" to start the Lotus 1-2-3 program stored in the directory called C:\LOTUS123. If the application is stored on a directory on your DOS path, you only need to enter the name of your application. For example, if your DOS path includes C:\LOTUS123, enter **123** at the "File" option. If your application also requires parameters, these should be specified at the "Command" option following the application name.

If you have additional applications you want to be able to access, enter the appropriate information in the remaining spaces in the Applications form.

*Note:* You cannot add the program MACRO that came with the Harvard Graphics package to the Applications form. You must start MACRO from DOS.

## Changing the Application Options

While you are viewing the Applications form, press F8-Options to display the Application Options overlay shown in Figure 16-6B. This form has two purposes. First, it permits you to define how Harvard Graphics will store a temporary copy of your Harvard Graphics session while the application is running. Second, it permits you to set up Draw Partner for use with Harvard Graphics.

When you load another application, Harvard Graphics creates a temporary file that holds a copy of your Harvard Graphics session. This copy is used to restore your Harvard Graphics session when you return from the application. The first two options on the Application Options overlay are used to instruct Harvard Graphics where to store this information. If your computer is configured with at least 600K of LIM 4.0 compatible expanded memory, the option "Use EMS memory if available" can be set to Yes. This setting results in the fastest access to your applications since it is many times quicker to store the temporary file to RAM than to a disk.

If you do not have EMS, or do not want the temporary file stored in RAM, set "Use EMS memory if available" to No. When "Use EMS if available" is set to No, Harvard Graphics stores the temporary file to disk (there must be at least 600K available on the disk to store this file).

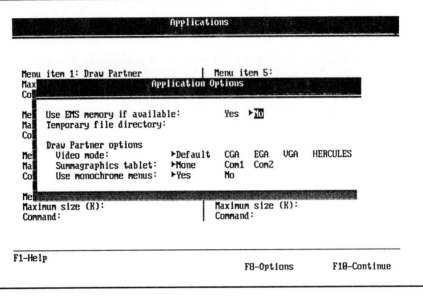

**Figure 16-6B.**   The Application Options overlay

Normally, this file is stored in the current directory. If you want Harvard Graphics to store the file in an alternative directory, enter the path of this directory at "Temporary file dir." For example, if you have created a directory called C:\HG\TEMP for the purpose of storing the temporary file, set "Temporary file dir" to C:\HG\TEMP. If you do not have LIM 4.0 expanded memory, but you have created a RAM disk in extended memory, you can set the "Temporary file dir" to this RAM disk to improve the speed of accessing other applications.

The last three options on the Application Options overlay are used to define the setup characteristics of Draw Partner. Use the "Video mode" option to define the type of graphics card you are using. Most of the time, you can leave this option set to Default. If the video image of Draw Partner looks distorted, set "Video mode" to the type of graphics card that you are using on your computer.

If you are using a Summagraphics tablet, use the "Summagraphics tablet" option to define whether the tablet is using your COM1 or COM2 serial communications port. If you are not using a graphics tablet or if you are using the Kurta/IS One tablet, leave "Summagraphics tablet" set to None (Harvard Graphics and Draw Partner automatically recognize the Kurta/IS One tablet).

The Draw Partner menus can be viewed either in color or monochrome. If you are using a monochrome monitor, set "Use monochrome menus" to Yes.

## Running Applications from Harvard Graphics

To run another application from within Harvard Graphics, return to the Main Menu and press F3-Applications to display the Applications menu. As you can see in Figure 16-7, Draw Partner is the first application listed on this menu. The additional applications you specified on the Applications form will be listed on this menu. Move the cursor to the desired application and press F10-Continue or ENTER to start the application. Perform your tasks in this application. When you are finished, exit the application as you normally would. You will automatically return to the Harvard Graphics Main Menu.

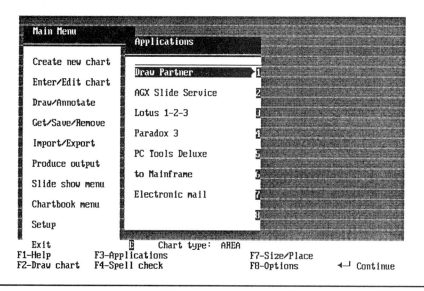

**Figure 16-7.** Applications menu showing added applications

## Including Multiple Fonts in One Chart

Earlier versions of Harvard Graphics do not allow you to use more than one font on a chart. While using only one font per chart is usually good charting practice, there are some instances where two or even three fonts can be used tastefully and effectively. Using either Draw/Annotate or Draw Partner, you can add text using any of the seven font styles, regardless of the style of font specified for your current chart. Using multiple fonts in Draw Partner is described in Chapter 18, "Drawing and Editing with Draw Partner." Using multiple fonts in Draw/Annotate is described next. It may help to refer to the section "Adding Text" in Chapter 9, "Drawing and Annotating."

## Adding Text Using Different Fonts

You can modify the font of any text you are adding in the drawing area just as you modify any of the text options on the Text Options form (described in Chapter 9, "Drawing and Annotating").

To add multiple fonts to a chart, move to Draw/Annotate either by selecting <Draw/Annotate> from the Main Menu or by pressing F4-Draw/Annot from any chart form. Once in Draw/Annotate, select <Add> from the Draw menu, followed by <Text> from the Add menu. Harvard Graphics displays the Text Options form, shown in Figure 16-8, in the menu/form area. The "Text" line for entering text is displayed at the top of the function key banner.

Anytime before you place your text in the drawing area, press F8-Options to activate the cursor in this form. Move to the "Font" option and either enter the number corresponding to the desired font or press F6-Choices to display the Fonts overlay, shown in Figure 16-9, and select a font from this overlay. Press F10-Continue to place the text or F8-Options to return to editing the text. When you place the text, it will be displayed in the font you selected from the Text Options form, regardless of the font for the current chart.

Harvard Graphics 2.3 Features  **501**

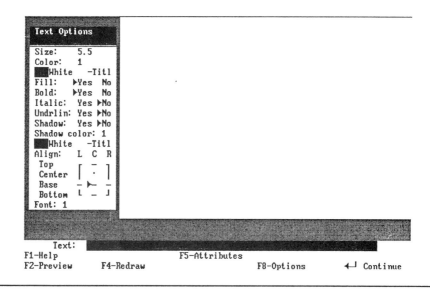

**Figure 16-8.**   Text Options form in Draw/Annotate

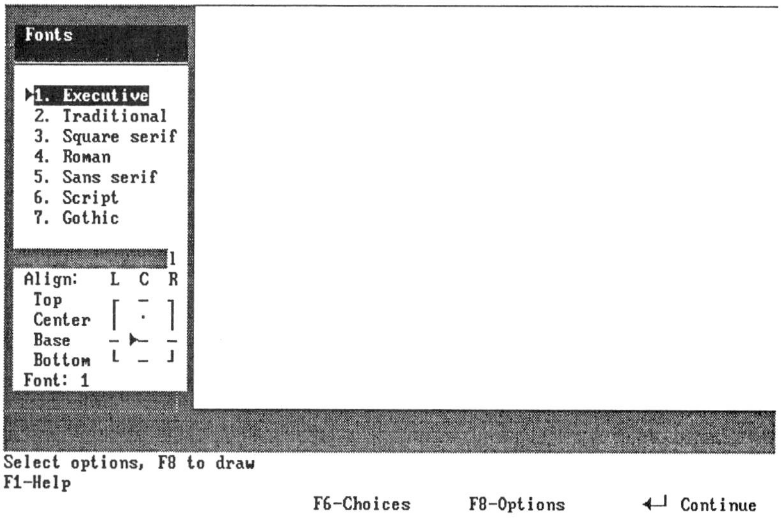

**Figure 16-9.**   Fonts overlay

*Hint:* If you want your title, subtitle, or footnote in a different font, you must use Draw/Annotate or Draw Partner—you cannot add it on the chart form or chart options form. However, in some chart styles— bar/line, for example—when no title has been added the chart frame is larger, leaving you no room to enter a title. In these instances you will need to use F7-Size/Place from the Main Menu to reduce the overall size of the chart. You will then have enough room to place your title, subtitle, or footnote using Draw/Annotate or Draw Partner.

### Modifying the Font of Existing Text

Remember that there are two types of text that can be displayed on your chart: text that is part of the chart, entered from the chart form, and text added in Draw/Annotate or Draw Partner. To modify the text that is part of the chart, press F8-Options from the Main Menu, and then select the desired font from the Current Chart Options overlay (see Chapter 3, "Setup and Default Settings"). All text that is part of the chart must be in the same font.

You can modify the font of any text you added in Draw/Annotate or Draw Partner just as you modify any of the other text options on the Text Options form (described in Chapter 9, "Drawing and Annotating"). To modify the font of text added in Draw/Annotate or Draw Partner, select <Modify> from the Draw menu followed by <Options> from the Modify menu. Harvard Graphics prompts you to select the object for which you want to modify options. Select the text as described in Chapter 9. Once you do so, the Text Options form, shown in Figure 16-8, is displayed. Move to the "Font" option and either enter a number for the font or press F6-Choices and select a font from the Fonts overlay, shown in Figure 16-9. Press F10-Continue to apply the modifications and return to the drawing area.

### Specifying a Default Font

You can select a default font to be used whenever you begin adding text in Draw/Annotate. You can always change the font for a given line of text, as described in the previous two sections. To select a default font, press F8-Options from the Draw menu to display the Default Options menu. Select <Text> to display the Text Options form. Move the cursor to the "Font" option and enter a font number or press F6-Choices and select a font from the Fonts overlay. Press F10-Continue followed by ESC to return to the Draw menu.

## ScreenShow Enhancements

Harvard Graphics 2.3 provides three enhancements to ScreenShow presentations. The first is the inclusion of ten different animated sequences of slides. You can use these sequences, listed in Appendix D, to gain insight into how you can use special ScreenShow effects to create animated sequences of your own, or they can be included, as is in your ScreenShows. The other two additions are described next.

### Using the ScreenShow Pointer

The second enhancement to ScreenShow is the pointer. When you have a mouse connected to your computer, you can activate a small arrow on a file displayed in your ScreenShow. You can use this arrow to point out features of interest, drawing your audience's attention to specific details. This arrow is not present when a file is first displayed. However, if you move the mouse the arrow becomes visible. Subsequent movements of the mouse result in corresponding movements of the arrow on the file.

### Creating a HyperShow

When the arrow is visible on a chart file, you can take advantage of the third enhancement to ScreenShow, called HyperShow. A HyperShow is a ScreenShow that uses a mouse to control the progression of files. This control is gained through the use of *buttons*. In a HyperShow, when you position the arrow on a button and click the left mouse key, the ScreenShow advances to another file. This file does not, however, have to be the next consecutive file in the ScreenShow. It may, in fact, be any file in the ScreenShow.

Before you can use the HyperShow capabilities of ScreenShow, you must do two things. First, you must place one or more buttons on one or more chart files that are part of your ScreenShow. Second, you must instruct ScreenShow which file to progress to when the button is clicked by the mouse. Both of these techniques are described next.

### Placing Buttons

Put simply, a button is like a box object. Buttons can be added in either Draw/Annotate or Draw Partner. When you add a button, you can assign it a button number from 0 to 10, or one of the special button numbers (described in the following section). When a button is assigned number 0, it has no effect on your chart. However, when numbers 1 to 10 are assigned to a button, the button can be used to control a ScreenShow in the same way as Go To keys. You can place a maximum of twenty buttons on a given chart, and two or more buttons may be assigned the same button number.

To place a button in Draw/Annotate, select <Add> from the Draw menu followed by <Button> from the Add menu. Harvard Graphics will move your cursor onto the Button form. Use the Button form to define the button number for the button you are adding. Enter a button number from 1 to 10, or a special button number, and then press F10-Continue to return to the drawing area (see Figure 16-10).

With your cursor in the drawing area, move your cursor to the location where you want to add the button and press ENTER. Next, move your cursor to the opposite corner of a rectangle that will define the size and shape of your button in the drawing area, and press ENTER again.

Once you have placed your button in the drawing area, it will appear as a rectangle defined by dotted lines. These lines are visible only in Draw/Annotate or Draw Partner so you can see the button. When you preview your chart, display your chart as part of a ScreenShow, or output your chart, your buttons will not be visible. In order to make a button visible, you need to place the button on top of a box or other object that will serve as a visual cue to the button's location.

You can overlap one or more buttons on a chart. With these buttons, clicking the overlapped area presses the front-most button. Unless the order of buttons on the chart has been changed using <Modify>, <Front>, or <Back> in either Draw/Annotate or Draw Partner, the

## Harvard Graphics 2.3 Features

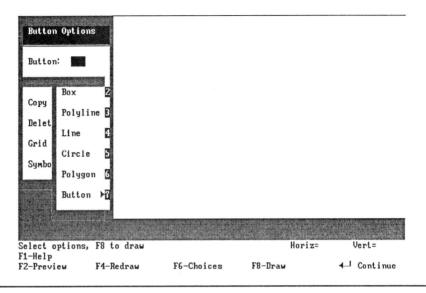

**Figure 16-10.** Button Options overlay

front-most button is the one last placed. This only pertains to overlapping buttons at the position of the tip of the pointer arrow.

### Using Buttons in a HyperShow

To use a button within a ScreenShow, you must instruct Harvard Graphics which file to advance to when you click the button. This is accomplished using the HyperShow menu overlay from the ScreenShow Effects form. With the desired slide show current, select <Add ScreenShow effects> from the Slide Show menu. Move the cursor to the name of the chart file you have added buttons to and press F8-HyperShow. Harvard Graphics will display the HyperShow menu overlay, shown in Figure 16-11.

This overlay has three columns: Button, Key, and Go To. In the "Go To" column, for each button placed on the chart, enter the number

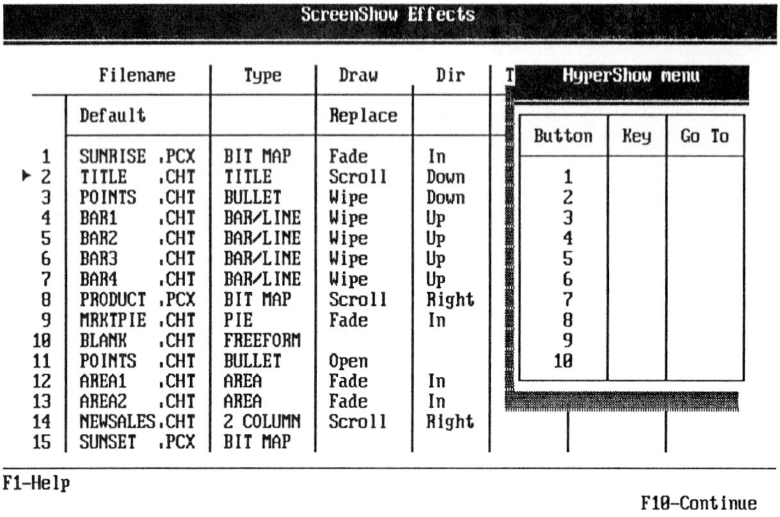

```
                    ScreenShow Effects
   ┌──────────────────────────────────────────┬─────────────────────────┐
   │   Filename     Type       Draw    Dir    │  HyperShow menu         │
   │   Default                 Replace         ├────────┬──────┬────────┤
   │                                           │ Button │ Key  │ Go To  │
   │ 1  SUNRISE .PCX  BIT MAP   Fade    In     │        │      │        │
 ► │ 2  TITLE   .CHT  TITLE     Scroll  Down   │   1    │      │        │
   │ 3  POINTS  .CHT  BULLET    Wipe    Down   │   2    │      │        │
   │ 4  BAR1    .CHT  BAR/LINE  Wipe    Up     │   3    │      │        │
   │ 5  BAR2    .CHT  BAR/LINE  Wipe    Up     │   4    │      │        │
   │ 6  BAR3    .CHT  BAR/LINE  Wipe    Up     │   5    │      │        │
   │ 7  BAR4    .CHT  BAR/LINE  Wipe    Up     │   6    │      │        │
   │ 8  PRODUCT .PCX  BIT MAP   Scroll  Right  │   7    │      │        │
   │ 9  MRKTPIE .CHT  PIE       Fade    In     │   8    │      │        │
   │ 10 BLANK   .CHT  FREEFORM                 │   9    │      │        │
   │ 11 POINTS  .CHT  BULLET    Open           │  10    │      │        │
   │ 12 AREA1   .CHT  AREA      Fade    In     │        │      │        │
   │ 13 AREA2   .CHT  AREA      Fade    In     │        │      │        │
   │ 14 NEWSALES.CHT  2 COLUMN  Scroll  Right  │        │      │        │
   │ 15 SUNSET  .PCX  BIT MAP                  │        │      │        │
   F1-Help                                                  F10-Continue
```

**Figure 16-11.**   HyperShow menu overlay

corresponding to the file you want Harvard Graphics to display when that button is clicked. You must also enter a key in the "Key" column that will cause Harvard Graphics to advance to the indicated file as well. If you fail to provide a key, any press of a key or a button will cause the HyperShow to automatically advance to the file listed in the "Go To" column.

The key you enter in the "Key" column must be an alphanumeric key on the keyboard. Rather than clicking on the button, you can press this key to achieve the same effect. For example, in Figure 16-12, a HyperShow menu overlay is shown for the second file in the Screen-Show. If a button numbered 1 has been placed on this chart, clicking this button with the mouse when the chart is displayed will advance the HyperShow to the eighth file—the file number listed in the "Go To" column corresponding to button 1. Alternatively, pressing **P** on the keyboard will also advance to slide 8 since P is entered into the "Key" column associated with button 1.

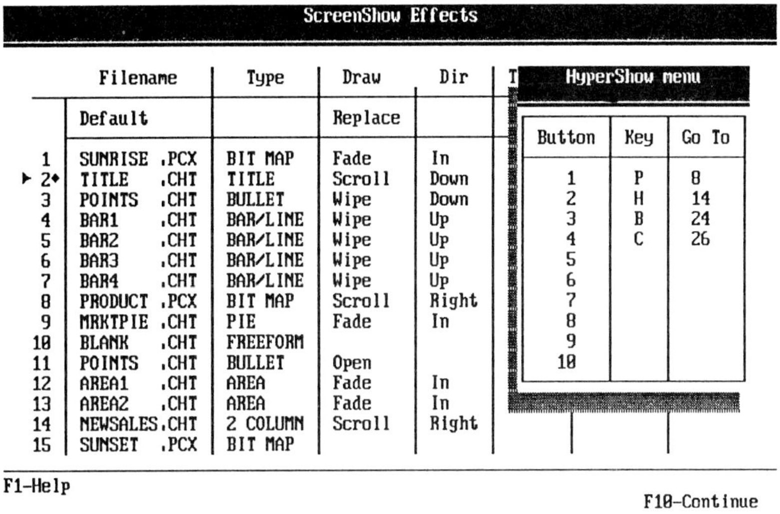

```
                        ScreenShow Effects
         Filename        Type       Draw     Dir    ┌─ HyperShow menu ─┐
       Default                      Replace         │ Button  Key  Go To │
    1  SUNRISE .PCX   BIT MAP    Fade      In       │                    │
  ▶ 2• TITLE   .CHT   TITLE      Scroll    Down     │   1      P     8   │
    3  POINTS  .CHT   BULLET     Wipe      Down     │   2      H    14   │
    4  BAR1    .CHT   BAR/LINE   Wipe      Up       │   3      B    24   │
    5  BAR2    .CHT   BAR/LINE   Wipe      Up       │   4      C    26   │
    6  BAR3    .CHT   BAR/LINE   Wipe      Up       │   5                │
    7  BAR4    .CHT   BAR/LINE   Wipe      Up       │   6                │
    8  PRODUCT .PCX   BIT MAP    Scroll    Right    │   7                │
    9  MRKTPIE .CHT   PIE        Fade      In       │   8                │
   10  BLANK   .CHT   FREEFORM                      │   9                │
   11  POINTS  .CHT   BULLET     Open               │  10                │
   12  AREA1   .CHT   AREA       Fade      In       │                    │
   13  AREA2   .CHT   AREA       Fade      In       │                    │
   14  NEWSALES.CHT   2 COLUMN   Scroll    Right    │                    │
   15  SUNSET  .PCX   BIT MAP                       └────────────────────┘

F1-Help                                                       F10-Continue
```

**Figure 16-12.**  Go To keys assigned to the second file in the ScreenShow

It is not necessary to indicate a file to go to for each of the buttons you have displayed on a chart. If a button has not been assigned a file to go to, Harvard Graphics will treat the click of the mouse as it usually does—to signal that it should display the next file in the slide show.

This HyperShow menu overlay is identical to the Go To overlay described in Chapter 13, "Slide Shows." The only difference is that version 2.3 allows each Go To specification to be associated with a button as well as a key. For more information concerning interactive slide shows using the Go To overlay, see "Using Go To Keys to Create Flexible Screenshows" in Chapter 13.

### Using Special Buttons

Harvard Graphics provides you with seven special button numbers. Buttons using these numbers can be created in either Draw/Annotate or Draw Partner. When you add a button that is assigned a special button number to a chart, that button will be assigned a predefined function.

For instance, if you add a button with the number 217 to a chart, clicking that button during a HyperShow will act as though you pressed the ESC key on your keyboard.

The advantage of special buttons is that they are automatically assigned a function: you do not use the HyperShow menu overlay. By using these special buttons, you can reserve the button numbers 1 through 10 for other purposes. See Table 16-2 for a list of the available special button numbers.

### Using Buttons on Templates

You may add buttons to templates. This is particularly useful when you want to make the appearance of your buttons consistent throughout your entire HyperShow. Buttons that appear on a template will be available on each file that follows the template in the HyperShow (unless another template is encountered). You do not assign an action to a button on a template, however. To assign an action to a button (that is, assign a file to go to, based on the button number), you must use the HyperShow menu for each chart on which the button or buttons are available in order to define how the HyperShow will react to a particular button press.

| Button Number | Purpose |
| --- | --- |
| 211 | Displays the preceding file in the HyperShow |
| 212 | Displays the following file in the HyperShow |
| 213 | Displays the first file in the HyperShow |
| 214 | Displays the last file in the HyperShow |
| 215 | Pauses the HyperShow at the current file |
| 216 | Displays the chart form for the current chart |
| 217 | Terminates the HyperShow |

**Table 16-2.** Special Button Numbers

When you do not assign a file number to a button that appears on a chart as a result of a preceding template, that button will be inactive. The one exception to this is when a template displays buttons that use special button numbers, since special buttons are automatically assigned to an action. See the preceding section for additional information on special buttons.

*Hint:* If you want to permit your entire HyperShow to be advanced forward one file with the press of a button, add a template at the beginning of your HyperShow and place a button with the number 212 on this template. Add the text **NEXT** or **CONTINUE**, or some similar label, to this button. This button will appear on every chart in the HyperShow and will act to advance to the next file in the HyperShow when clicked.

## Using ShowCopy

With the ShowCopy utility, you can copy your ScreenShow to another directory or disk. ShowCopy will assure that all of the necessary files are copied.

### Copying ScreenShows with ShowCopy

SHOWCOPY.EXE is a separate program that is shipped with Harvard Graphics 2.3. Use ShowCopy to copy all the files associated with a ScreenShow from one directory to another. ShowCopy copies all the chart files (.CHT), slide show files (.SHW), template files (.TPL), and bit-mapped files (.PCX and .PIC) listed in the slide show. ShowCopy will also copy each of the palette files from the ScreenShow directory to the destination directory.

Because ShowCopy is a separate program, you must exit Harvard Graphics to use it. You invoke ShowCopy from the DOS prompt by typing the appropriate command. To use ShowCopy to copy a slide show, use the following syntax:

**SHOWCOPY** *sourcename destination*

Here *sourcename* is the name of the slide show and *destination* is the path to which you want ShowCopy to copy the slide show. If the source slide show is on a different directory from the one where SHOWCOPY is stored, you must include the path of the source slide show as part of the SHOWCOPY command. For example, to copy the slide show named PRESENTS.SHW from the C:\HGDATA directory to a floppy disk in drive A, use the following command (noting that the filename extension .SHW is optional but not necessary):

SHOWCOPY C:\HGDATA\PRESENTS A:\

There are two parameters that you can add to the SHOWCOPY command: /S and /U. If you include the /S parameter, ShowCopy will display the name of each of the files it is copying as they are copied. Including the /U parameter causes ShowCopy to update the description column in your slide show as it copies the slide show file. This is useful if you have made changes to descriptions in some of your charts in the slide show since you created it.

You can use one or both of these parameters in a SHOWCOPY command. If you use these parameters, they must be entered after the destination in the SHOWCOPY command, and must follow the destination by at least one space. For example, the previous SHOWCOPY command using these parameters would appear as

SHOWCOPY C:\HGDATA\PRESENTS A:\ /S/U

ShowCopy also has two other uses. First, you can use it to verify that all the necessary files in a slide show are on the same directory as a given slide show file. The syntax for this usage is

SHOWCOPY VERIFY *directory*

This command causes ShowCopy to check each of the slide shows in the specified directory. For each slide show, ShowCopy checks to see if all the necessary files in the directory are present (with the exception of palette files). If any files are not found, ShowCopy displays the message "File not found," and then lists the name of the missing file or files. For example, if you want to verify that all the necessary slide show files for a given slide show are on your floppy disk, you could use the following command:

## Harvard Graphics 2.3 Features

**SHOWCOPY VERIFY A:\**

This version of the SHOWCOPY command is particularly valuable when you have created a slide show sometime ago, and may have since accidentally erased or moved one or more of the files in the show. Using SHOWCOPY VERIFY you can ensure that all the necessary files are present.

The final use of ShowCopy is to create a slide show. From the DOS prompt, enter the command

**SHOWCOPY CREATE** *directory*

ShowCopy will create a slide show called NEWSHOW.SHW. This show will contain all the files in the specified directory.

*Note:* If NEWSHOW.SHW already exists, the SHOWCOPY CREATE command will replace it with a new version. If you want to keep an existing NEWSHOW.SHW file, rename it using the DOS command RENAME.

## Improved Palettes

Using alternative color palettes in Harvard Graphics 2.3 is much easier than in earlier versions. In version 2.3, a color palette is one of the characteristics of a chart. In earlier versions, the color palette was a characteristic of your Harvard Graphics session; if you changed the color palette during your session, all your charts would be displayed using this color palette.

When you create a chart in Harvard Graphics 2.3, the chart is assigned the current color palette. This is usually the palette listed at the "Palette file" option on the Default Settings form. If you did not modify this default, the color palette will be HG23.PAL. Anytime after you create a chart, you can change the color palette for that chart. From the Main Menu, press F8-Options. The last option on the Current Chart Options overlay, shown in Figure 16-13, is "Palette file." Enter an

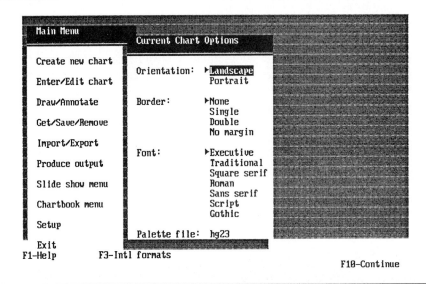

**Figure 16-13.** Current Chart Options overlay

alternative palette name to select a different palette for the current chart. Remember that you must save this chart if you want to keep the current chart settings.

*Note:* One feature common to all of the palettes supplied with Harvard Graphics 2.3 is that they share the same colors numbered 9 through 15. These colors are used for the symbols supplied with Harvard Graphics 2.3. This means that changing your chart palette will not affect the colors used for any symbols that you have added to your chart.

Harvard Graphics 2.3 provides you with several other features to assist you in changing the current palette, editing a palette, and creating a new palette. To access these features, select <Color palette> from the Setup menu, shown in Figure 16-14, to display the Palette menu. The three selections on the Palette menu, shown in Figure 16-15, are described next.

Harvard Graphics 2.3 Features    513

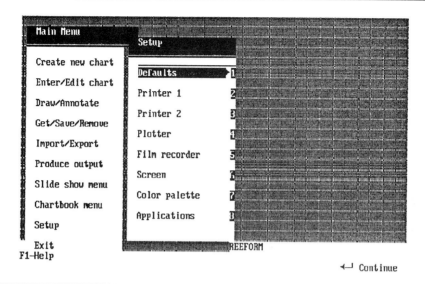

**Figure 16-14.**    Setup menu

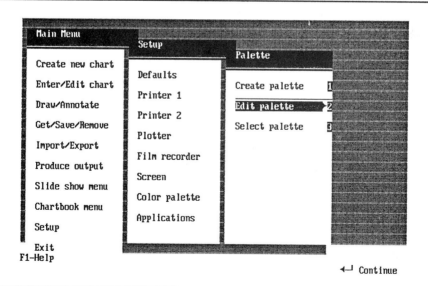

**Figure 16-15.**    Palette menu

## Selecting an Alternate Color Palette

Anytime during your Harvard Graphics session you can change the color palette for your current chart. You can do this by setting the "Palette file" option on the Current Chart Options form. With this method you must know the name of the desired palette. To see the names and descriptions of the available palettes while changing your current chart's palette, use the Select Palette form. From the Palette menu, choose <Select palette>. Harvard Graphics will display the Select Palette form, shown in Figure 16-16. Move the cursor to the name of the palette you want to select and press ENTER. Alternatively, enter the name of the desired palette at the "Filename" option.

If you want to select a palette on a directory other than the current one, move the cursor to the "Directory" option and enter the path. You can also change directories by pressing F3-Change dir. For information on using F3-Change dir, see "Getting Files from Other Directories" in Chapter 2, "Harvard Graphics Basics."

```
                        Select Palette
Directory: C:\HG
Filename:  HG      .PAL

Filename Ext   Date      Type          Description

HG       .PAL  10/20/87  PALETTE
HG23     .PAL  04/13/90  PALETTE
1        .PAL  04/13/90  PALETTE
2        .PAL  04/13/90  PALETTE
3        .PAL  04/13/90  PALETTE
4        .PAL  04/13/90  PALETTE
5        .PAL  04/13/90  PALETTE
6        .PAL  04/13/90  PALETTE
7        .PAL  04/13/90  PALETTE
8        .PAL  04/13/90  PALETTE
9        .PAL  04/13/90  PALETTE
10       .PAL  04/13/90  PALETTE
11       .PAL  04/13/90  PALETTE
PP339    .PAL  10/20/87  PALETTE
PP669    .PAL  10/20/87  PALETTE

F1-Help        F3-Change dir                         F10-Continue
```

**Figure 16-16.** Select Palette form

Once you have selected another palette, Harvard Graphics will assign this palette to your current chart.

### Creating a New Color Palette

From the Palette menu, select <Create palette>. Harvard Graphics will display the Create Palette overlay, shown in Figure 16-17. The directory displayed at the "Directory" option will default to the current directory. If you want to store this palette on a different directory, enter the desired directory at this option. Next, provide a name for your palette. This name can be no longer than eight characters in length and must conform to DOS file naming conventions. It is not necessary to add the .PAL extension to this filename since Harvard Graphics will add it if you do not. Finally, enter a description of the palette you are creating at the "Description" option.

Press F10-Continue to create the new palette and display the Color Palette Setup form, shown in Figure 16-18. This form is described in

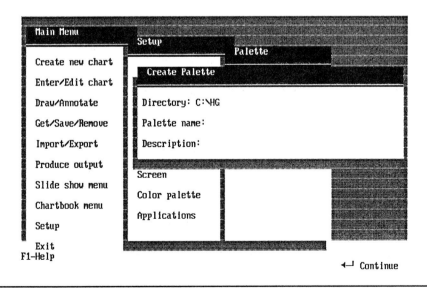

**Figure 16-17.** Create Palette overlay

|  |  | Color Palette Setup | | | | | |
|---|---|---|---|---|---|---|---|
| Palette file: HG | | Screen: EGA | | | Output: Polaroid | | |
| | | Red | Green | Blue | Red | Green | Blue |
| 1 | White | 1000 | 1000 | 1000 | 115 | 35 | 60 |
| 2 | Cyan | 0 | 1000 | 1000 | 0 | 20 | 47 |
| 3 | Magenta | 1000 | 0 | 1000 | 48 | 0 | 47 |
| 4 | Green | 0 | 1000 | 0 | 22 | 20 | 0 |
| 5 | Blue | 0 | 0 | 660 | 0 | 0 | 60 |
| 6 | Red | 1000 | 0 | 330 | 90 | 3 | 6 |
| 7 | Yellow | 1000 | 1000 | 330 | 115 | 35 | 0 |
| 8 | Orange | 1000 | 330 | 0 | 90 | 0 | 0 |
| 9 | Royal Blue | 0 | 0 | 1000 | 0 | 9 | 47 |
| 10 | Gold | 1000 | 660 | 0 | 115 | 24 | 0 |
| 11 | Violet | 660 | 0 | 660 | 20 | 0 | 14 |
| 12 | Pink | 1000 | 0 | 660 | 90 | 0 | 33 |
| 13 | Grey | 660 | 660 | 660 | 25 | 0 | 3 |
| 14 | Crimson | 660 | 0 | 0 | 30 | 1 | 0 |
| 15 | Dark Green | 0 | 330 | 0 | 9 | 0 | 0 |
| 16 | Black | 0 | 0 | 0 | 0 | 0 | 0 |

Background color: 16    Description:

F1-Help
F2-Show palette                                         F10-Continue

**Figure 16-18.**   Color Palette Setup form

Chapter 3, "Setup and Default Settings," and in the next section. When you create a new color palette, the new color palette will inherit the color settings of the palette that was current at the moment you created the new palette.

## Changing an Existing Palette

To change an existing palette, from the Palette menu select <Edit palette>. Harvard Graphics will display the Color Palette Setup form. After you have made your changes to this palette, press F10-Continue to return to the Setup menu.

The Color Palette Setup form is described in detail in Chapter 3, "Setup and Default Settings." The only difference on this form in version 2.3 is the addition of the "Description" option. If you created the palette using the <Create palette> option from the Palette menu, this option displays the description you provided on the Create Palette overlay. You can change this description by moving the cursor to this option and entering a different description.

All the remaining features of the Color Palette Setup form, including the function key selections F3-CGA palette and F6-Shaded Bkgd, are identical to those described in "The Color Palette" in Chapter 3, "Setup and Default Settings." Unlike versions 2.13 and earlier, however, you cannot create a new palette by changing the name shown at the "Palette file" option.

## Printing Using Grey Scale

Prior to Harvard Graphics 2.3, you could only print using grey scale (shades of grey instead of patterns) if you were printing to a PostScript printer. Harvard Graphics 2.3 permits you to print using grey scale from any standard black and white printer.

*Note:* The following technique for printing in grey scale using Harvard Graphics 2.3 is applicable to all printers, including PostScript printers. The technique for printing in grey scale with a PostScript printer using Harvard Graphics 2.13 or earlier is described in Chapter 8, "Producing Output."

Harvard Graphics determines the appropriate level of grey from the red, green, and blue values entered in the output column of the Color Palette Setup form. In general, when the "Color" option on the Print Chart form or the Print Slide Show form is set to Yes, bright colors will produce a darker shade of grey when printed, and dark colors will produce a lighter shade of grey. Since these red, green, and blue values may be different from one palette to the next, the greys that are produced will depend on the palette you are using for a particular chart. The greys produced from the symbols supplied with Harvard Graphics 2.3, however, will be consistent, since the palettes that come with Harvard Graphics 2.3 use the same red, green, and blue values for colors 9 through 15 (the symbol colors).

Unfortunately, not all palettes produce enough variation in the grey scale to be of practical use for some charts. For example, while your clustered bar chart may print fine using the HG23.PAL palette, another palette may result in a virtually identical grey being used for two or more of your series, which is not acceptable in most instances.

There are several approaches that you may want to take in order to effectively use grey scale in Harvard Graphics 2.3. The first is to print the HG.CHT chart, which displays all colors of the color palette, for each of your palettes. You can then select your chart colors based on the greys that a particular palette produces when printed, or select a palette that will produce acceptable greys for the colors that you selected.

A second alternative is to modify the output red, green, and blue values on the Color Palette Setup form in order to adjust the output greys. This approach is difficult since it will require you to experiment with the palette settings in order to create optimal greys. Also, if you need to print your chart from a computer other than the one on which you created the special palette, you will need to copy the palette onto the other computer along with your chart.

Finally, if your computer is connected to a film recorder, you will probably want to define your output colors based on the film recorder output, rather than the grey output of your black and white printer.

If you are unable to produce an acceptable chart using the grey scales, print your chart with the "Color" option on the Print Chart overlay set to No. This setting will cause Harvard Graphics to print your chart using patterns instead of greys.

## Improved Importing

There are four enhancements to the importing and exporting features of Harvard Graphics. These are importation of data from Excel spreadsheets, importation of Excel charts, a function key to display the named ranges in a Lotus 1-2-3 or Excel spreadsheet, and the importation of CGM metafiles. Each of these features is described in the following sections.

### Importing Excel Data

Importing data from an Excel spreadsheet is nearly indistinguishable in procedure from importing data from a Lotus 1-2-3 spreadsheet. There are only two noticeable differences. The first is that the forms used to specify the ranges to import have different names. When you are importing data from an Excel spreadsheet, you select a worksheet from the Select Excel Worksheet, shown in Figure 16-19, and specify the ranges using the Import Excel Data form, shown in Figure 16-20.

The second difference is that you can specify the ranges for importation using a colon. For instance, if your X data are located in cells C1 through C10, you can enter the range either as **C1..C10** or as **C1:C10**. For a complete description, see "Importing Lotus Data" in Chapter 12, "Importing and Exporting." If you use named ranges in your spreadsheet, also see the section later in this chapter, "Selecting Lotus and Excel Named Ranges."

## Importing Excel Charts

If you have created a chart in Excel, you can import it into Harvard Graphics. When Harvard Graphics imports the chart, it will create a chart that closely approximates the features of the Excel chart. As with the importation of Excel data, the importation of Excel charts is nearly

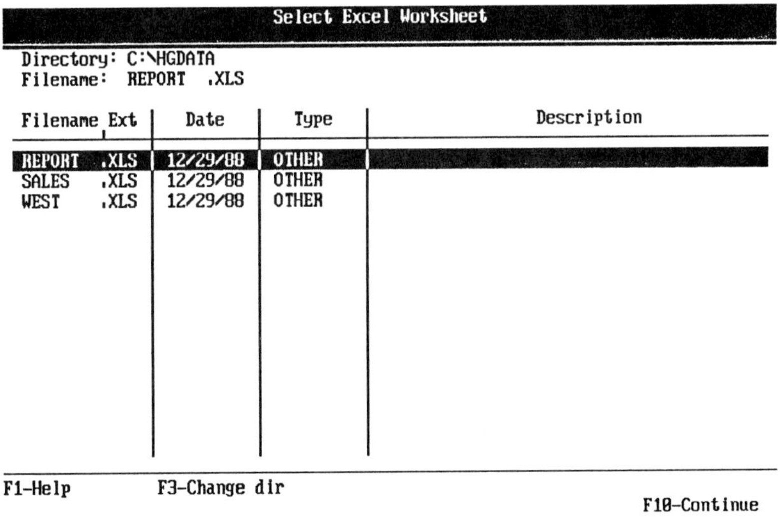

Select Excel Worksheet

Directory: C:\HGDATA
Filename: REPORT .XLS

| Filename Ext | Date | Type | Description |
|---|---|---|---|
| REPORT .XLS | 12/29/88 | OTHER | |
| SALES .XLS | 12/29/88 | OTHER | |
| WEST .XLS | 12/29/88 | OTHER | |

F1-Help F3-Change dir F10-Continue

**Figure 16-19.** Select Excel Worksheet form

```
                    ┌─────────── Import Excel Data ───────────┐
                    Worksheet name: REPORT    .XLS

                         Title:
                      Subtitle:
                      Footnote:

                                 Legend          │  Data Range

                          X  │ X axis data       │
                          1  │ Series 1          │
                          2  │ Series 2          │
                          3  │ Series 3          │
                          4  │ Series 4          │
                          5  │ Series 5          │
                          6  │ Series 6          │
                          7  │ Series 7          │
                          8  │ Series 8          │

                          Append data:  ▶Yes   No

     F1-Help        F3-Select files
                    F4-Clear ranges  F6-Range names                  F10-Continue
```

**Figure 16-20.**   Import Excel Data form

indistinguishable in procedure from the importation of Lotus graphs. For details on importing Excel charts, see "Importing Lotus Graphs" in Chapter 12, and apply the same techniques used to import Lotus graphs.

## Selecting Lotus and Excel Named Ranges

When you are importing from Excel or Lotus 1-2-3, you can use named ranges to simplify defining the data you want to import. This feature is accessed using F6-Range names. When the cursor is in the data range column on the Import Lotus Worksheet form or the Import Excel Worksheet form, press F6-Range names. Harvard Graphics will display the Range Names overlay, shown in Figure 16-21.

If you have not created any range names for the spreadsheet, this form will be empty. If you have created named ranges for the spreadsheet, the first 15 letters of each named range will appear in the form. If more named ranges are available than can be displayed at one time, press PGDN and PGUP to display additional range names. Use the UP and DOWN arrow keys to move the cursor to the appropriate range name and

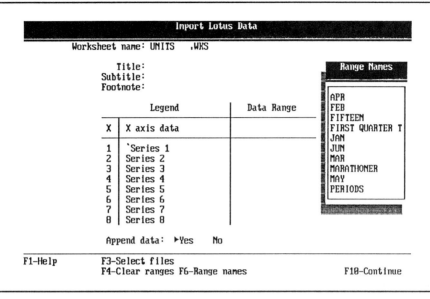

**Figure 16-21.** Range Names overlay

press ENTER. Harvard Graphics will automatically copy the name of the selected range into the appropriate option on the Import Lotus Data form or Import Excel Data form. To return without selecting a range name, press ESC.

## Importing CGM Metafiles

In previous versions of Harvard Graphics, an imported CGM metafile was converted into a symbol in order to be used in Harvard Graphics. This symbol could then be added to the desired chart. In Harvard Graphics 2.3, imported CGM metafiles are added directly to the current chart. Once added, the contents of the metafile are Harvard Graphics drawings. They can be modified using Draw/Annotate or Draw Partner, and can be saved as a symbol, if desired.

To import a CGM metafile, select <Import/Export> from the Harvard Graphics Main Menu. From the Import/Export menu, select <Import CGM metafile>. Harvard Graphics will display the Select CGM Metafile form, shown in Figure 16-22. Move the cursor to the name of the CGM metafile you want to import and press ENTER. Alternatively, you can enter the name of the metafile at the "Filename" option.

```
                 Select CGM Metafile
Directory: C:\HGDATA
Filename:  ..

Filename Ext  | Date     | Type     | Description
..            | 12/03/89 | DIR      | Parent Directory
PIE1     .CHT | 12/03/89 | PIE      | Pie chart number 1.
HG       .DIR | 04/10/90 | OTHER    |
HG       .CHT | 12/01/87 | PIE      | new description
ANNOUNCE .CHT | 07/01/87 | FREEFORM | Sample chart
INTRO    .CHT | 07/01/87 | TITLE    | Sample chart
OPENING  .CHT | 07/01/87 | TITLE    | Sample chart
PRODS    .CHT | 07/01/87 | LIST     | Sample chart
REGIONS  .CHT | 07/01/87 | BAR/LINE | Sample chart
SALES    .CHT | 07/01/87 | 2 COLUMN | Sample chart
TRISALES .CHT | 07/01/87 | BAR/LINE | Sample chart
BUILD4   .CHT | 01/13/90 | BAR/LINE | build-up example
BUILD3   .CHT | 01/13/90 | BAR/LINE | build-up example
BUILD2   .CHT | 01/13/90 | BAR/LINE | build-up example
PTLOGO   .CHT | 12/06/89 | FREEFORM |

F1-Help       F3-Change dir
                                                    F10-Continue
```

**Figure 16-22.**   Select CGM Metafile form

If you want to import a CGM metafile from a directory other than the current one, move the cursor to the "Directory" option and enter the path of this directory. You can also change directories by pressing F3-Change dir. For information on using F3-Change dir, see "Selecting a File from Another Directory" in Chapter 2.

Once you have selected a CGM metafile to import, Harvard Graphics will import the file and display the image on your monitor. Press any key to return to the Main Menu. You can then save your chart including the metafile, or enter Draw/Annotate or Draw Partner to make changes to the image.

If the CGM metafile you are importing is greater than 32K in size, Harvard Graphics will not be able to import the entire file. If this happens, Harvard Graphics will display the message "Metafile is too large: Drawing truncated, Esc continues." If you press ESC, Harvard Graphics will import as much of the metafile as possible; the drawing will not be complete, however. If this happens, try returning to the application in which the CGM metafile was created and simplify the drawing. Then try to import it again. Alternatively, you may want to use the portion of the image Harvard Graphics was able to import and complete it using Draw/Annotate or Draw Partner.

# Draw Partner

**Introduction to Draw Partner**
**Drawing and Editing with Draw Partner**

# Introduction to Draw Partner

Draw Partner Overview
The Draw Partner Screen
Draw Partner Menus
Draw Partner Forms
Using Function Keys
Changing the View with the View Menu
Retrieving and Saving Files
Removing a Symbol from a Symbol File
Using Harvard Graphics Drawings in Draw Partner Version 1.0
Using Draw Partner Drawings in Harvard Graphics

This chapter provides an introduction to Draw Partner, an accessory that extends Harvard Graphics' drawing and annotating features. Draw Partner can be used to create and/or edit Harvard Graphics symbols, import and export CGM metafiles, as well as import Lotus .PIC files. The greatest utility of Draw Partner is its drawing and editing features. With it you can flip and rotate objects, edit individual points in objects, draw freehand, combine two or more polylines into a single polyline, and convert polylines into polygons.

This chapter describes how to use Draw Partner menus, forms, and function keys. Saving drawings and importing and exporting drawings are also discussed. The topics of creating drawings and editing those drawings with Draw Partner are discussed in Chapter 18, "Drawing and Editing with Draw Partner." It is assumed that you have installed Draw Partner along with the Harvard Graphics program as described in Appendix B, "Installation."

There are two versions of Draw Partner. Version 1.0 is a separate accessory for use with Harvard Graphics versions 2.13 or earlier. This version of Draw Partner is started from the DOS prompt. Version 2.3 is an integrated accessory in Harvard Graphics 2.3. You start Draw Partner version 2.3 from within the Harvard Graphics program either by selecting <Draw Partner> from the Applications menu or by pressing CTRL-D. The later section "Starting Draw Partner" covers starting both versions in detail.

## Draw Partner Overview

Draw Partner greatly extends Harvard Graphics' drawing and annotating capabilities. Draw Partner allows you to create drawings for use with Harvard Graphics. With its features you can create much more sophisticated drawings than you can with Harvard Graphics alone. When you create a drawing in Draw Partner, you can save the drawing by itself, as a symbol, or add it to a Harvard Graphics chart. These drawings can also be saved as chart or symbol files, which means they can be printed, plotted, or recorded on film with ease using Harvard Graphics, or included in a Harvard Graphics slide show.

The following is a list of some of the exceptional features offered by Draw Partner:

- You can create boxes, buttons, circles, lines, arrows, wedges, arcs, polylines, polygons, equal-sided polygons, text, and circular text, as well as draw freehand.

- You can use multiple fonts and text attributes in one drawing.

- You can add shadows, flip, rotate, and skew objects, and add perspective to objects to give the appearance of depth.

- You can create a *sweep* of an object—a series of drawings that shows the intermediate stages between two similar objects.

- You can zoom in close on an object, permitting fine adjustments.

- You can edit the points on any non-text object. You can add, delete, align, or reposition a point anywhere on an object .

- You can convert text into polygons, and then make additional modifications using point editing capabilities.

- Polylines can be converted into polygons. Circles, boxes, and polygons can be converted into polylines and two or more polylines can be combined into larger polylines.

- Multiple objects can be automatically aligned with one another.

- You can easily export drawings as CGM metafiles or import CGM metafiles and Lotus .PIC files and turn them into drawings.

These features can be used to create original drawings.

You can also modify and add to any drawings created in Draw/Annotate. Existing Harvard Graphics symbols can be incorporated with drawings, whether they were created previously in Harvard Graphics or Draw Partner, or are a part of the symbol set that came with the Harvard Graphics package. You can save drawings as Harvard Graphics symbols or charts, or in a special Draw Partner format.

## Starting Draw Partner

How you start Draw Partner depends on which verison, 1.0 or 2.3, you have. With version 1.0, you start the program from the DOS prompt. With version 2.3, you start Draw Partner from Harvard Graphics. Both of these methods are described next.

**Starting with Version 1.0**   To start Draw Partner, you must be at the DOS prompt. If you are in Harvard Graphics, exit to DOS before you continue. Start Draw Partner from the directory in which it is stored, unless you have included the Draw Partner program in your DOS path. If you are using a two-disk drive system, Draw Partner should be in drive A and your data disk in drive B.

From the DOS prompt, start Draw Partner by typing **DP** and pressing ENTER. If you are using a digital tablet, you must start Draw Partner using the /T parameter. Type **DP/T** and press ENTER to start Draw Partner with a digital tablet if your tablet is connected to the first serial port (com 1) on your computer. Type **DP/T2** if your tablet is connected to the second serial port (com 2).

**Starting with Version 2.3**   Draw Partner is integrated into Harvard Graphics 2.3. There are two ways to start Draw Partner from Harvard Graphics:

- At the Harvard Graphics Main Menu, press F3-Applications to display the Applications menu, and then select <Draw Partner>.

- Alternatively, from the Main Menu or any chart form, press CTRL-D.

If you have a current drawing created in Draw/Annotate, it will be displayed in the drawing area when you start Draw Partner. You can then modify or add to it just like any Draw Partner drawing. In addition, if you have a current Harvard Graphics chart, it will be displayed behind the Draw Partner drawing area for reference. You can later save both the drawing and chart image in Harvard Graphics as a Harvard Graphics chart (as described later in "Saving a File").

If you want to create an entirely new drawing without an existing Draw/Annotate drawing or chart image being displayed, you can first create a blank chart in Harvard Graphics, and then start Draw Partner. For example, select <Free form> from the Text Chart Styles menu in Harvard Graphics. When the Free Form Chart form is displayed, do not add any text and press CTRL-D to start Draw Partner. The drawing area will then be empty.

## Exiting Draw Partner

You exit Draw Partner from the Draw Partner Main Menu. Press ESC until you return to this menu. With version 1.0, select <Exit> to return to DOS. If you have not saved your current drawing since you created or modified it, Draw Partner will display the Exit menu with the two options: <Resume program> and <Quit program>. Move your cursor to <Resume program> to continue in Draw Partner so you can save your drawing or <Quit program> if you want to exit to DOS without saving it, and press ENTER.

With version 2.3, select <Return to HG>. You will return to Harvard Graphics in the same place you were when you started Draw Partner.

## The Draw Partner Screen

When you first start Draw Partner, you will see the screen shown in Figure 17-1. If you are using a CGA or a monochrome graphics adapter, your screen will be monochrome. Otherwise, Draw Partner will use the colors in the current Harvard Graphics palette. You can change this palette as described later in "Selecting a Color Palette."

On the right side of the Draw Partner screen is the drawing area. This is analogous to the drawing area in Harvard Graphics' Draw/Annotate. On the left side of the screen is the menu/form area, where all Draw Partner menus and forms are displayed. When you first start Draw Partner, this area will contain the Draw Partner Main Menu, as is shown in Figure 17-1. (In version 1.0, the last menu item is <Exit> rather than <Return to HG>.) In the lower part of the screen is the function key banner. Again, this is similar to the function key banner in Harvard Graphics. The area at the top-left corner of the function key banner is used to display Draw Partner messages. When you first load

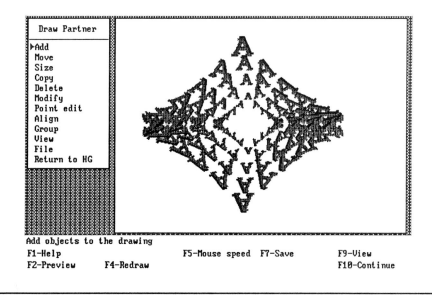

**Figure 17-1.**    Draw Partner screen

Draw Partner, the message "Add objects to the drawing" is displayed in this area. Sometimes these messages instruct you to enter text or a number. Any text or numbers you enter on your keyboard in response to these messages will be displayed on the line immediately below the message.

## Draw Partner Menus

Draw Partner menus are similar, though not identical, to Harvard Graphics menus. When you make a selection from a Draw Partner menu, one of three events may follow. First, selecting a menu option may result in another menu being displayed, similar to the way some Harvard Graphics menus work. Second, selecting a menu option may result in the initiation of a Draw Partner function. For instance, when you select <Move> from the Draw Partner Main Menu, you are asked to select an object to move. This too is similar to how some Harvard Graphics menus work.

A third type of menu selection is used to set Draw Partner parameters. For instance, when you select <View> from the Main Menu, followed by <Auto redraw> from the View menu, Draw Partner displays the Auto redraw menu, shown in Figure 17-2. The Auto redraw menu contains two options: <At all changes> and <When requested>. If you select <At all changes>, you turn the Draw Partner Auto Redraw feature on. If you select <When requested>, you turn the Auto Redraw feature off. (In Harvard Graphics, a form would have been used for this selection rather than a menu.)

When any menu is displayed, you can press HOME to move directly to the first menu option and END to move to the last menu option.

### Selecting Menu Options from the Keyboard

To make a selection from a Draw Partner menu, use the arrow keys to highlight the option you want to select and then press ENTER. You can also press the first character of the option's name to instantly select it. If more than one menu option begins with the same first letter, Draw Partner will highlight the first one, and then cycle through the alterna-

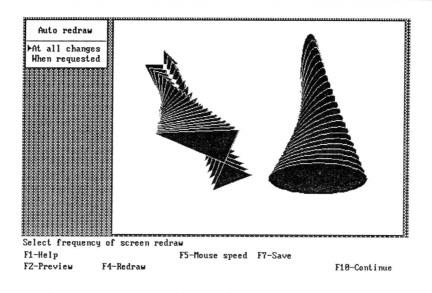

**Figure 17-2.**  Auto redraw menu

tives with additional presses of the same key. When the desired menu option is highlighted, press ENTER.

When a menu other than the Draw Partner Main Menu is displayed, you can press ESC to return to the previous menu.

*Note:*  On EGA and VGA monitors, the menu item appears in reverse video and is marked by an arrow when it is highlighted. On CGA and monochrome monitors, a menu item is only marked by a wedge-shaped arrow when it is highlighted.

### Selecting Menu Options Using a Mouse

Move your mouse up or down to highlight the desired option on the menu. Press ENTER or the left mouse button (which functions as ENTER) to select the highlighted menu option.

When a menu other than the Draw Partner Main Menu is displayed, you can press the right mouse button (which functions as ESC) to return to the previous menu.

## Draw Partner Forms

Draw Partner forms are used to define object settings. All Draw Partner forms contain more than one option. Furthermore, setting options on these forms differs from setting options in Harvard Graphics, as described next.

### Setting Form Options from the Keyboard

Use the arrow keys to move to the options on a form. To change an option setting, move the cursor to that option and press ENTER or F6-Choices to display a list of available option settings. Then move the cursor to the desired setting in the list and press ENTER. Draw Partner will then remove the list and return to the form. When you are through setting the options on a form, press ESC or F8-Draw.

### Setting Form Options Using a Mouse

Use the mouse to move to the options on a form. To change an option setting, move the cursor to that option and press the left mouse button (or F6-Choices) to display a list of the available settings for the option. Move the cursor to the desired setting on the list and press the left mouse button to select that setting. Draw Partner will remove the list and return you to the form. When you are through setting options on a form, press the right mouse button or F8-Draw to remove the form.

### Using Function Keys

As in Harvard Graphics, the function keys available at any given time in Draw Partner are displayed in the function key banner. Function keys listed in the banner can only be selected by pressing the corresponding function key on your keyboard.

In version 2.3, you can also use the mouse to select function keys just as you can in Harvard Graphics. To activate the cursor in the function key banner using a mouse, press the left and right mouse buttons simultaneously. Move the mouse to move the cursor on the screen to the different function keys; then press the left button to select a function key at the cursor. Press ESC to move the cursor from the banner without selecting a function key. Selecting a function key with a mouse is particularly useful while you are using a mouse to draw since it eliminates having to move your hand from the mouse to the keyboard.

While you are at the Draw Partner Main Menu, seven function keys are displayed. These represent most of the function keys available in Draw Partner; they are described in the follwing sections. Other function keys are described throughout this chapter and the following chapter, as appropriate. You can also refer to Chapter 25, "Draw Partner Forms and Function Keys."

## Using On-Line Help

Draw Partner's on-line help system contains two levels: a context-sensitive first level and a help list at the second level. Press F1-Help once to display the context-sensitive help. Press F1-Help again to display the help list.

You can request help about any currently highlighted menu item by pressing F1-Help to display a help screen. Figure 17-3, for example, displays the help screen that is displayed if F1-Help is pressed while the <Add> on the Main Menu is highlighted. If the page reference in the upper-right corner of the help screen indicates there are additional pages of help, you can use PGDN to display the next page and PGUP to display the previous page.

When you are finished, press ESC to return to the previous screen. Alternatively, you can press F1-Help again to display the help list. This list, shown in Figure 17-4, displays the general help topics that describe Draw Partner usage. From the help list, you can move the cursor to highlight one of the topics, and then press ENTER to display help information for that topic. To return to the help list after displaying more help information, press F1-Help again. To return directly to the previous screen, press ESC.

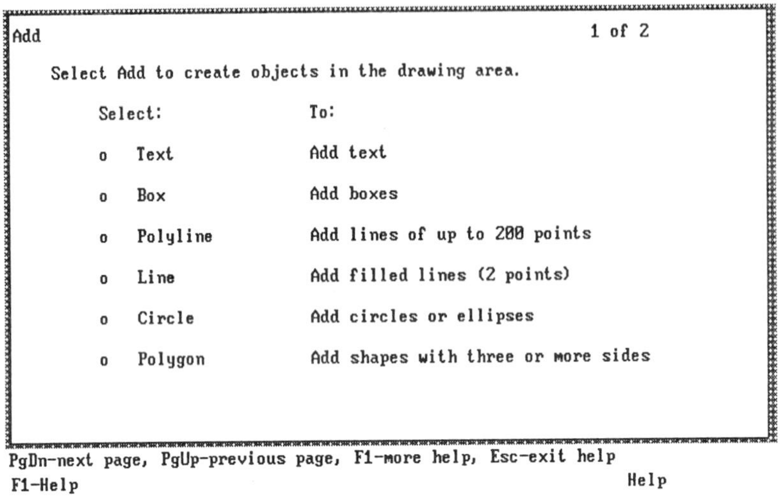

```
Add                                                    1 of 2
    Select Add to create objects in the drawing area.

        Select:          To:

        o  Text          Add text

        o  Box           Add boxes

        o  Polyline      Add lines of up to 200 points

        o  Line          Add filled lines (2 points)

        o  Circle        Add circles or ellipses

        o  Polygon       Add shapes with three or more sides


PgDn-next page, PgUp-previous page, F1-more help, Esc-exit help
F1-Help                                                        Help
```

**Figure 17-3.**  Help screen displayed when you press F1-Help while <Add> on the Main Menu is highlighted

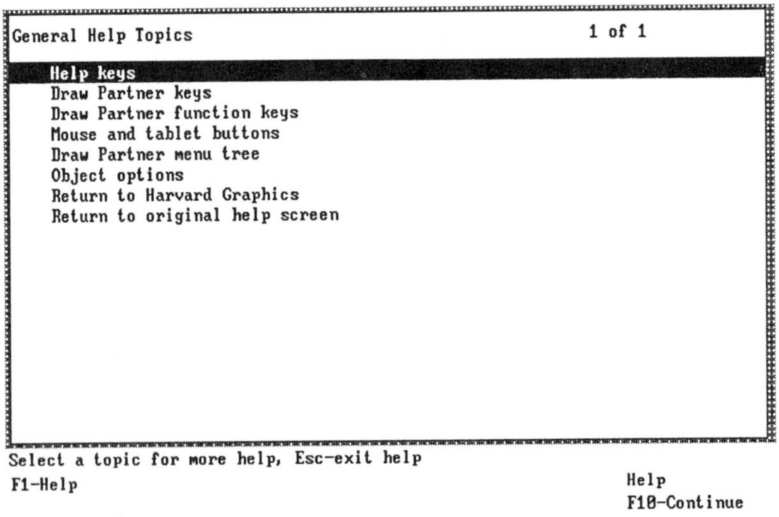

```
General Help Topics                                    1 of 1
    Help keys
    Draw Partner keys
    Draw Partner function keys
    Mouse and tablet buttons
    Draw Partner menu tree
    Object options
    Return to Harvard Graphics
    Return to original help screen




Select a topic for more help, Esc-exit help
F1-Help                                                        Help
                                                               F10-Continue
```

**Figure 17-4.**  Help list

## Previewing a Drawing

While any Draw Partner menu is active, press F2-Preview to view the current drawing. If you have a Harvard graphics chart or symbol in the drawing area, it will also be displayed when you press F2-Preview. When you are finished previewing, press any key to return to the previous screen. If you want to cancel the preview before Draw Partner has completed the drawing, press the SPACEBAR.

## Updating a Drawing Using Redraw

If the Auto Redraw feature is set to When requested, you can press F4-Redraw to update the current image in the drawing area. Auto Redraw is described in the section "Setting the Automatic Redraw."

## Adjusting the Mouse Speed

*Mouse speed* refers to the speed with which the cursor responds to the movements of the mouse. If you want the cursor to be very sensitive to mouse movements, increase the mouse speed using F5-Mouse speed.

When you press F5-Mouse speed, Draw Partner displays the message "Enter new mouse speed (Slow=0, Fast=100, Current=*current*), Esc-no change." Enter a value from 0 to 100 to change the speed of your mouse. Press ESC to return to the previous screen.

## Saving a Drawing

From any menu in Draw Partner, you can save your current drawing in the Draw Partner file format by pressing F7-Save. Once you do so, Draw Partner displays the File screen. Save your drawing as described in the later section "Saving a File."

## Displaying the View Menu

From many of the menus in Draw Partner, you can change your view of the drawing area by pressing F9-View to display the View menu, shown in Figure 17-5. When View is available, the F9-View key will appear in the function key banner. You can also display the View menu by selecting <View> from the Main Menu.

## Changing the View with the View Menu

When you select <View> from the Main Menu, or press F9-View, Draw Partner displays the View menu shown in Figure 17-5. The View menu permits you to *zoom in* on a specific region of the drawing area to see the objects in that region in more detail. You can also move the area viewed while in a zoomed view, add a grid to the drawing area, use the snap-to-grid feature, or use the automatic redrawing feature. These features are described in the following sections.

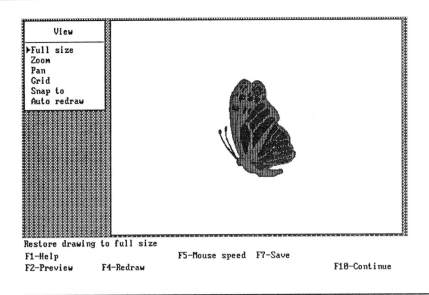

Figure 17-5. View menu

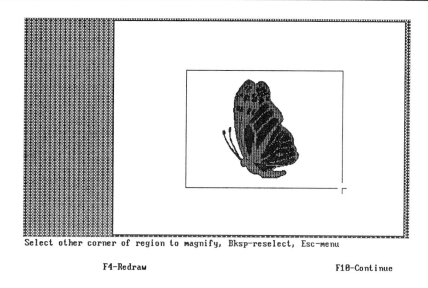

**Figure 17-6.**   Rectangle defining the region of the drawing area to zoom in on

## Using Zoom

While you are working with Draw Partner, you can zoom in on a region of the drawing area. In Zoom mode, Draw Partner does not display the entire drawing area. Instead, only a selected portion of the drawing area is visible and all the objects in the visible area appear larger. Zooming is a valuable tool to assist you in making fine adjustments to objects and to help you place objects more precisely.

To use Zoom, select <Zoom> from the View menu. Draw Partner will display the message "Select first corner of a region to magnify, Esc-menu." Move your cursor to the first corner of a rectangle that encloses the area you want to view and press ENTER. Draw Partner will then display the message "Select other corner of region to magnify, Bksp-reselect, Esc-menu." Move the cursor to the opposite corner of the rectangle and press ENTER. Figure 17-6 shows a region of the drawing area being zoomed in on; Figure 17-7 shows the zoomed view. If you want to change the position of the first corner of the rectangle, press BACKSPACE before you place the second corner. You can cancel the zoom by pressing ESC while you are defining the region to zoom in on.

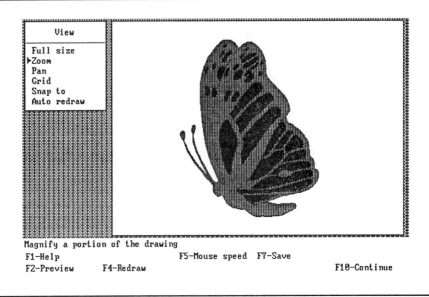

**Figure 17-7.** Resulting zoom view defined in Figure 17-6

Once you no longer require a zoom view, return to the Draw Partner Main Menu and select <View> to display the View menu. Select <Full size> from the View menu to display the entire drawing area again.

## Panning the Zoomed View

You can move a zoomed view by selecting <Pan> from the View menu. (You cannot do this if you have selected <Full size> from the View menu, however.) When panning, the cursor acts as if it has ahold of the corner of the drawing area and can move it to a new location on the drawing. Move the cursor until the zoom window appears to be correctly placed and press ENTER. The region of the drawing area that now lies in the zoom region will be made visible. You may need to experiment with panning to become familiar with how panning works.

The use of <Pan> is shown in Figures 17-8 and 17-9. In Figure 17-8 <Pan> was selected and the zoom window was moved to include the drawing area to the right and above the current zoom window.

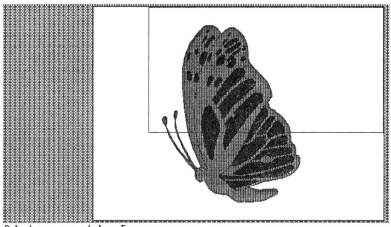

**Figure 17-8.** &lt;Pan&gt; selected and zoom window moved right and above the current zoom window

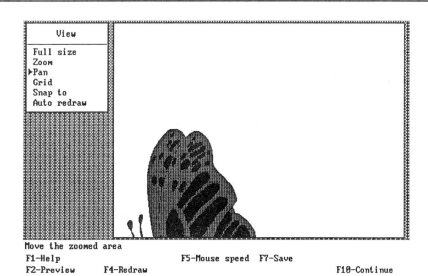

**Figure 17-9.** Resulting zoom view defined in Figure 17-8

Figure 17-9 shows the resulting view. Notice that the lower-left corner of the rectangle in Figure 17-8 is also the lower-left corner of the new zoom area in Figure 17-9.

## Using a Grid

A *grid* is a set of evenly spaced points that are displayed in the drawing area. The grid can help you align and more accurately place objects in the drawing area. When you display a grid in Draw Partner, it will also display vertical and horizontal lines that divide the drawing area into quarters. The grid and these lines, shown in Figure 17-10, are intended as a reference for placing objects; they will not appear in your saved drawing.

If you want to use a grid to aid drawing in Draw Partner, select <Grid> from the View menu. Draw Partner will display the Grid menu shown on the next page.

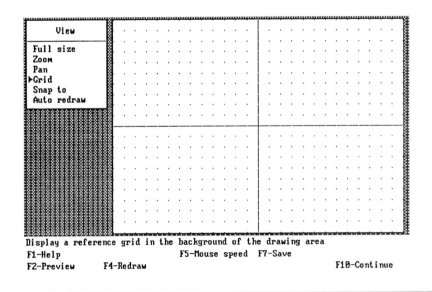

**Figure 17-10.**   Grid with horizontal and vertical lines

Select <Grid on> to display a grid. When you do so, Draw Partner displays the message "Select new grid size (Small=1, Large=25)" on the message line. Enter a value from 1 to 25. Press ESC to return to the Grid menu without adding the grid.

If you are using a grid and want to turn it off, select <No grid> from the Grid menu.

## Using the Snap-to-Grid Feature

When you use the Snap feature with a grid, you can only place the cursor within the drawing area at one of the grid points. The term *snap* is used since the cursor seems to "snap" to each grid point as it moves, as if drawn by a magnet. This feature can be helpful when you need to precisely place and align objects, since the possible cursor locations are limited.

To use the Snap feature, select <Snap to> from the View menu. Draw Partner will display the Snap to menu.

To turn the Snap feature on, select <Snap to grid>. In Draw Partner, you can only use the Snap feature when the grid is turned on. To turn the Snap feature off, select <No snap>.

Although the snap-to-grid capability is helpful for certain drawing tasks, it can make others more cumbersome. It is best to set the Snap to menu to <No snap> until you need the Snap feature. Setting the Snap to menu to <Snap to grid> will not affect objects that have already been placed in the drawing area.

*Note:* The size of your grid determines the size of the objects you can add when you use the snap-to-grid capability. Objects you add when using this feature must be at least as large as an individual grid cell. If you try to add a smaller object, Draw Partner will not recognize it and will not add it. You will need to set this feature to <No snap> or make the grid small enough to accommodate smaller objects (see "Using a Grid").

## Setting the Automatic Redraw

If you want your drawing to be updated after every change you make in the drawing area, you can turn on Draw Partner's Auto Redraw feature. Since redrawing in the drawing area can be time consuming (any chart or symbol present is also redrawn), you will probably want to keep this feature off unless your drawing is fairly simple.

Select <Auto redraw> from the View menu to display the Auto redraw menu, shown in Figure 17-2. To turn the Auto Redraw feature on, select <At all changes> from the Auto redraw menu. To turn this feature off, select <When requested>.

When the Auto Redraw feature is off, you can update your drawing at any time by pressing F4-Redraw. To make Draw Partner stop a redraw, press the SPACEBAR.

## Retrieving and Saving Files

Draw Partner offers you the following file management capabilities:

- Retrieving and saving Harvard Graphics symbols
- Retrieving and saving drawings in a special Draw Partner file format
- Saving drawings as Harvard Graphics charts
- Importing and exporting CGM metafiles
- Importing Lotus .PIC files
- Selecting an alternative Harvard Graphics color palette

When you either retrieve an existing file or save a file, you follow essentially the same procedure regardless of the type of file you are

## Introduction to Draw Partner 543

retrieving or saving. Retrieving a file of any type is described in the next section "Retrieving a File." Likewise, saving files is described in the later section, "Saving a File."

### Retrieving a File

You can retrieve a Draw Partner drawing, a Harvard Graphics symbol, import a Lotus .PIC file or a CGM Metafile, or select an alternate color palette by following these general steps. More specific details on retrieving each of the individual file types are described in "Retrieving Different File Types."

1. From the Draw Partner Main Menu, select <File> to display the File menu.

2. From the File menu, select <Get drawing>, <Get symbol>, <Import>, or <Palette>. If you select <Import>, go to the next step. Otherwise, skip to step 4.

3. From the Import menu, select <Metafile> to import a CGM Metafile or <Lotus> to import a Lotus .PIC file.

4. Select a file from the File screen (similar to the one shown in Figure 17-11). At the top of the File screen is the current directory. All the files in the current directory that match the type of file you want to retrieve are shown below the directory name. For instance, if you select <Get drawing>, Draw Partner drawing files in the current directory will be listed, as shown in Figure 17-11. Similarly, if you select <Metafile> in order to import a CGM metafile, CGM metafiles will be listed in this area. The cursor is represented by a

box that surrounds the selected filename. In Figure 17-11, for example, the cursor is at the file called CIRCULAR. You can select a file to retrieve in one of two ways:

a. Use the cursor keys or mouse to move to the desired filename, and press ENTER to retrieve the selected file. If you want to preview a file before you retrieve it, select the filename and press F2-Preview. This preview feature will not work with symbol or palette files, however.

b. You can immediately retrieve a file by pressing the first letter of the filename. If more than one file begins with the same first letter, pressing this letter will cause Draw Partner to alternate the selection box among the different filenames that share this first letter. When the desired file is selected, press ENTER to retrieve it or F2-Preview to preview it.

Once you select a file, Draw Partner returns to the File menu.

5. Press ESC to return to the Draw Partner Main Menu. When you press ESC, Draw Partner draws the contents of the selected file in

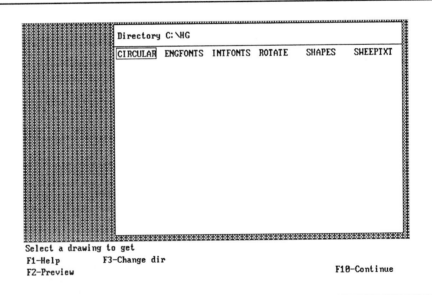

Figure 17-11.    File screen

the drawing area before displaying the Main Menu. While the drawing is being drawn, the message "Press Space bar to stop redraw" is displayed. You can stop the drawing at any point by pressing the SPACEBAR. Doing so will save you time if you have retrieved a complicated drawing. It will not affect the components of the drawing in any way, and they will still be a part of the drawing even though they are not displayed.

If the file you want to select is not in the current directory, you must change directories, as described in the next section. Once the desired directory is selected, you can continue with step 4 to select the desired file.

## Retrieving a File from a Different Directory

While the File screen is displayed, you can change directories in one of two ways. First, you can move your cursor so the box encloses the directory name and then press ENTER. The message "Enter the name of another directory" will be displayed. Type in the directory path and press ENTER. If the path you have entered exists, Draw Partner will move to that directory and display the files in the directory. If you provide the name of a path that does not exist, Draw Partner will display the message "Directory not found, Esc continues." Press ESC to return to the File screen.

*Note:* This is the only way to change to a directory that is located on a different drive.

Alternatively, with your cursor active in the File screen, you can press F3-Change dir. Draw Partner will display the Select Directory screen, which lists all the subdirectories for the current directory. If the current directory is not the root directory on the current drive, the directory name "..\" for the parent directory will also appear in this list. The *parent directory* is the directory within which the current directory is located. If the desired directory is below the current directory, select one of the directory names displayed. If the desired directory is above the current directory, select the parent directory (..) to move up to that directory. Once you select a directory, it becomes the current directory.

**Figure 17-12.**   Symbols in INDUSTRY.SYM displayed in the drawing area

When the desired directory is the current directory, press ESC or F3-Files. Draw Partner will return to the File screen and display the files on the current directory.

### Retrieving Symbol Files

When you select the name of a symbol file from the File screen, Draw Partner will display the contents of the symbol file, as shown in Figure 17-12. Use the cursor to select the desired symbol from this file, and then press ENTER. When you do so, Draw Partner will place it in the drawing area, adding it to any drawings that are already displayed.

When a symbol is added in the drawing area, it is placed in the center using its default size. If you want to change the location or size of the symbol, you must use the Main Menu options <Move> and <Size> as described in Chapter 18, "Drawing and Editing with Draw Partner."

When you retrieve Harvard Graphics symbols into Draw Partner, Draw Partner converts them into a group of Draw Partner drawing objects. Before you can make any changes to components of a symbol, you must ungroup the symbol. See "Ungrouping Objects" in Chapter 18.

*Note:* See the section "Using Harvard Graphics Drawings in Draw Partner Version 1.0" later in this chapter for details on how Draw Partner converts symbols created with Draw/Annotate.

When you retrieve a Draw Partner drawing, or import a CGM metafile or Lotus .PIC file, the current contents of the drawing area are replaced with the contents of the file you imported or retrieved. If you want to save your current drawing, you must do so before you import or retrieve a file.

### Selecting a Color Palette

You can use any Harvard Graphics color palette with Draw Partner. Once you select an alternate color palette, the colors of your drawn objects will reflect those in the new palette. When creating custom symbols, it is a good idea to use the same color palette in Draw Partner that you will use with the chart that you add the symbol to. This way you will see the actual colors that will be applied to your drawings in either application. When you use Draw Partner to add drawings to an existing Harvard Graphics chart, changing the palette in Draw Partner changes the current chart palette.

## Saving a File

You can save a drawing as a Draw Partner drawing (.DP), a Harvard graphics chart (.CHT), a Harvard Graphics symbol (.SYM), or a CGM metafile using the following steps. Additional details about each of these topics are covered individually in following sections.

1. From the Draw Partner Main Menu, select <File> to display the File menu as shown on the next page.

```
         File
▶Get drawing
 Save drawing
 Save as chart
 Get symbol
 Save symbol
 Remove symbol
 Import
 Export metafile
 Palette
```

2. From the File menu, select <Save drawing>, <Save chart>, <Save symbol>, or <Export metafile>. If you select <Export metafile>, Draw Partner will display the Export metafile menu. Otherwise, go directly to step 4.

3. From the Export metafile menu, select whether the metafile should use filled fonts or hardware fonts. Select <Polygon fonts> if you want Draw Partner to draw the fonts. Select <Hardware fonts> if you want to use the fonts of the software or hardware that the CGM metafile is intended for.

4. Select a file from the File screen. The current directory is shown at the top of this screen with all the files of the appropriate type listed below the directory. The selection "New File" is also displayed with the filenames. To replace the contents of one of the existing files with your current drawing, move the cursor to select the existing filename and press ENTER. Before you replace a file, you can preview the file's contents by pressing F2-Preview (this feature is not available for symbol files). F2-Preview permits you to verify that you want to replace the contents of a file. Press any key to remove the previewed drawing and return to the File screen. After previewing a file, you can replace its contents with your current drawing by pressing ENTER, or you can select an alternative file to replace or preview.

If you want to save the current drawing as a new file, select "New File" and press ENTER. Draw Partner displays the message "Enter new filename." Enter a new name for the file and press ENTER. If the filename already exists, Draw Partner will display the message "This file exists—do you want to replace it?" Select <Replace> from the displayed menu to replace the existing file with the current drawing or select <Quit> to cancel saving the drawing. Once you successfully save the drawing or select <Quit> from the displayed menu, Draw Partner will return to the File menu.

If you want to save the file to a directory other than the current directory, you must change directories before continuing with step 4. See the previous section "Retrieving a File from a Different Directory" for details.

*Note:* In version 2.3, if any drawing objects created in Draw Partner are present in the drawing area, they are saved as part of the drawing in the specific file format. A current Harvard Graphics chart image, however, is not saved with the file since it is displayed in the drawing area for reference only. To save a chart with a drawing added in Draw Partner, you must exit Draw Partner and save the chart (with the drawing) in Harvard Graphics, as described later in "Saving a Harvard Graphics Chart with a Draw Partner Drawing."

### Saving a Drawing as a Draw Partner Drawing

You can save drawings using a special Draw Partner file format that uses the extension .DP. When you save a drawing as a Draw Partner drawing, the characteristics of the drawing are maintained. It is a good idea to save a drawing as a Draw Partner drawing until you are certain it can be used satisfactorily in Harvard Graphics. (See "Using Draw Partner Drawings in Harvard Graphics" for a description of changes made in Harvard Graphics to Draw Partner drawings.)

Any time a menu is active in Draw Partner, you can save your drawing as a Draw Partner drawing by pressing F7-Save. Pressing F7-Save is identical to selecting <Save drawing> from the File menu, except that you return to the current menu in Draw Partner rather than returning to the File menu, as occurs when you select <Save drawing>.

### Saving a Drawing as a Harvard Graphics Chart

You can save your drawing as a Harvard Graphics chart. This is useful if you want to print, plot, or record your drawing, or use your drawing in a slide show.

When you save a drawing as a chart, Draw Partner creates a pie chart with no data. Your drawing appears in Harvard Graphics as if you added the drawings to the pie chart using Draw/Annotate. If desired, you can change this pie chart to any of the other data chart styles.

When you save a Draw Partner drawing as a Harvard Graphics chart, Draw Partner also converts its drawing objects into Harvard Graphics drawing objects. These changes are discussed in the section "Using Draw Partner Drawings in Harvard Graphics."

*Note:* In version 2.3, even though drawing objects in the drawing area are saved in a Harvard Graphics chart file, a Harvard Graphics chart displayed in the drawing area will not be saved in this file. This is because the chart is not a part of the drawing and is actually displayed behind the drawing area for reference. You can save a chart with a drawing in Harvard Graphics as described later in "Saving a Harvard Graphics Chart with a Draw Partner Drawing."

### Saving a Drawing as a Harvard Graphics Symbol

When you save a Draw Partner drawing as a Harvard Graphics symbol file, Draw Partner will add the drawing to the existing symbols in the specified symbol file. You can later add this symbol to any number of charts or use the symbol by itself or with other drawings or symbols in either Draw/Annotate or Draw Partner. A Harvard Graphics symbol file can accommodate 24 symbols (20 with Harvard Graphics version 2.0). If you attempt to save a symbol to a symbol file that already contains 24 symbols, Draw Partner will display the message "Cannot append any more symbols to this symbol file, Esc continues." In this case, the symbol will not be saved and you must press ESC to return to the File menu and select another symbol file.

If you select "New File" for your symbol, Draw Partner will ask you for a symbol filename. (You cannot, however, supply your symbol file with a description.)

When you save a Draw Partner drawing as a Harvard Graphics symbol, Draw Partner converts the Draw Partner drawing objects into Harvard Graphics drawing objects. These changes are discussed in the section "Using Draw Partner Drawings in Harvard Graphics."

*Note:* In version 2.3, even though drawing objects in the drawing area are saved in a Harvard Graphics symbol file, a Harvard Graphics chart displayed in the drawing area will not be saved in this file. This is because the chart is not a part of the drawing and is actually displayed behind the drawing area for reference. The next section describes how to save a Harvard Graphics chart with drawings.

### Saving a Harvard Graphics Chart with a Draw Partner Drawing

In version 2.3, a current Harvard Graphics chart is displayed behind the drawing area in Draw Partner for reference. You can save this chart with any drawing objects added in Draw Partner using the following steps.

1. In Harvard Graphics, make the desired chart the current chart.

2. Start Draw Partner (press CTRL-D).

3. Create a Draw Partner drawing.

4. Optionally, save the drawing (without the chart image) in the Draw Partner format (.DP).

5. Exit Draw Partner to return to Harvard Graphics by selecting <Return to HG> from the Draw Partner Main Menu.

6. In Harvard Graphics, select <Get/Save/Remove> from the Main Menu followed by <Save chart> from the Get/Save/Remove menu.

7. Enter the appropriate information on the Save Chart overlay (as described in Chapter 2, "Harvard Graphics Basics") and press ENTER or F10-Continue to save the chart.

The chart will be saved with the drawing. You can later modify the drawing in either Draw/Annotate or Draw Partner by first making the chart current before invoking Draw/Annotate or Draw Partner.

### Saving Complex Drawings

It is possible to create a drawing in Draw Partner that is so complex that it cannot be saved as a Harvard Graphics chart or symbol, even though you can save your drawing successfully as a Draw Partner drawing (.DP) file. Draw Partner will display the message shown in Figure 17-13 when this happens. Draw Partner will save an incomplete chart file (.CHT), which Harvard Graphics cannot read, but will not create an incomplete symbol. If you attempt to use this chart file in Harvard Graphics, you will see the message "File is not the expected file type."

If you encounter the message shown in Figure 17-13, you can try one of two things. First, you can simplify your drawing in Draw Partner and attempt to save it again as a Harvard Graphics chart or symbol. Second, you can save the drawing as a Draw Partner drawing (.DP). Then in Draw Partner, systematically save parts of the drawing as Harvard Graphics *symbols*. This involves deleting some parts of the drawing and saving the drawing as a symbol. Retrieve the drawing (.DP file) again and repeat this process with the other parts of the drawing. You can then attempt to combine these symbols in Harvard Graphics or Draw Partner.

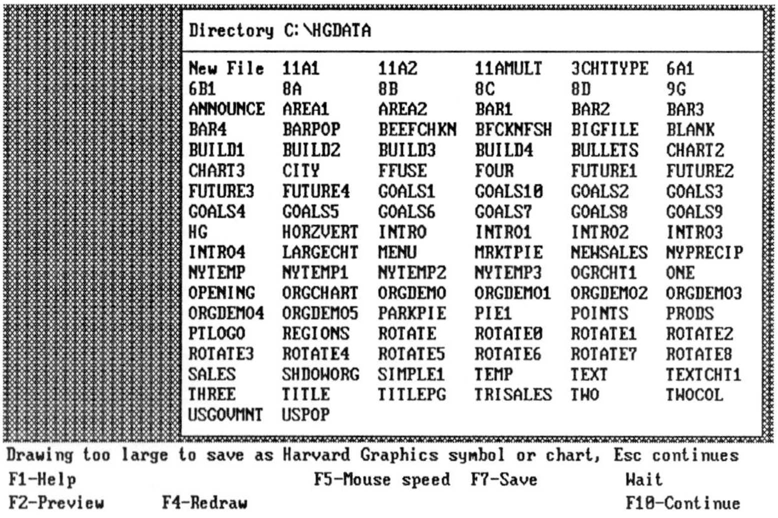

**Figure 17-13.**   Message displayed when drawing is too complex to save as a Harvard Graphics chart or symbol

## Removing a Symbol from a Symbol File

To remove a symbol from a symbol file, select <File> from the Main Menu, and then <Remove symbol> from the File menu. In the File screen, select the symbol file that contains the symbol you want to remove. If the symbol file is not on the current directory, change directories (using the techniques described in the previous section "Retrieving a File from a Different Directory"). Once you select a symbol file, Draw Partner displays the contents of that file. Use the cursor to select the symbol you want to remove and press ENTER.

*Note:* Use care when selecting a symbol to remove. Draw Partner will not ask you to confirm the removal of the selected symbol.

## Using Harvard Graphics Drawings in Draw Partner Version 1.0

Draw Partner verison 1.0 does not support all the features of objects created using Harvard Graphics Draw/Annotate. (These limitations do not apply for Draw Partner version 2.3.) When you bring a symbol created in Harvard Graphics into Draw Partner, the following changes are made to the drawings:

- Harvard Graphics text with the underline attribute is displayed without the underlining.

- Harvard Graphics text is displayed as generic text using one of the four font attributes: Light, Bold, Italic light, or Italic bold.

- The vertical alignment of text added in Harvard Graphics may not be accurately reproduced in Draw Partner.

- Only simple Harvard Graphics boxes (box style 1) are represented as boxes in Draw Partner. All other box styles are converted to polygons.

- Lines and lines with arrowheads are converted to polygons.

- Draw Partner does not recognize groups within groups. When you ungroup a symbol in Draw Partner, all components (including any subgroups) are ungrouped.

## Using Draw Partner Drawings in Harvard Graphics

Some of the objects in Draw Partner, such as circular text, cannot be created using Harvard Graphics. When you select a chart or a symbol created with Draw Partner, the following transformations are performed:

- In version 1.0, any text entered in Draw Partner will adopt the current font setting (Executive, Square serif, Roman, and so on) in Harvard Graphics.

- In version 1.0, Draw Partner drop shadow effects other than lower-right are not supported by Harvard Graphics. Harvard Graphics simulates these effects by converting the text to grouped polygons.

- Rotated text, flipped text, circular text, and text that contains more than 60 characters are converted to polygons if a bold font attribute was used or polylines if a light font attribute was used.

- Text long enough to extend past the edge of the drawing area in Draw Partner is truncated at the edge of the displayed drawing area.

- Objects that are part of a single sweep are grouped.

- Any text created in Draw Partner that was converted to polygons or polylines (either in Draw Partner or when converted for use with Harvard Graphics) cannot be spell checked by Harvard Graphics.

The next chapter describes how to add Draw Partner drawing objects, how to move, size, and modify them, and how to group them.

# Drawing and Editing with Draw Partner

**Drawing and Editing Overview**
**Moving the Cursor in the Drawing Area**
**Overview of Adding Objects**
**Selecting Objects**
**Modifying Objects**
**Editing Polylines and Shapes**

This chapter describes how to draw objects and edit drawings using Draw Partner. It is advisable to read the preceding chapter, "Introduction to Draw Partner," before you read this chapter.

## Drawing and Editing Overview

Draw Partner is a powerful drawing program that permits you to create sophisticated drawings that can be used with Harvard Graphics. It also provides you with editing tools for making changes to drawings and symbols created in either Draw/Annotate or Draw Partner. Together these capabilities of Draw Partner offer you complete control over the final form of the drawings and symbols you create.

In order to familiarize you with the general use of Draw Partner's drawing and editing features, the following section is a quick introduction to each of the drawing and editing-related options (the first nine options) on the Draw Partner Main Menu. Detailed descriptions of the use of these features are provided later in the chapter. The remaining three options, <View>, <File>, and <Return to HG>, are discussed in Chapter 17, "Introduction to Draw Partner."

### Add

<Add> provides you with the tools to add 12 types of objects to a drawing: text, boxes, polylines, lines, circles, polygons, circular text, arcs, wedges, freehand drawings, regular polygons, and buttons.

### Move

<Move> allows to you move an object.

### Size

<Size> allows you to change the size of an object.

### Copy

<Copy> permits you to copy an object.

### Delete

With <Delete> you can delete one, more than one, or all of the objects in the drawing area.

### Modify

Selecting <Modify> displays the Modify menu.

These selections provide you with a number tools for modifying an entire object. These modifications include:

- Rotating an object to a new orientation
- Changing the display options for an object
- Flipping an object either horizontally or vertically
- Moving an object to the front or back of the drawing area
- Editing text
- Creating a sweep of an object
- Adding a shadow to an object
- Skewing an object
- Adding perspective to an object

**Point Edit**

When you select <Point edit>, Draw Partner displays the Point edit menu.

These menu options allow you to make fine adjustments to your drawing objects, as well as change the type of your objects. The following items are a few of the capabilities available with point editing. (Note that the term *shape* is used to refer to boxes, lines, circles, polygons, wedges, and regular polygons. Similarly, the term *polyline* is used to refer to polylines, arcs, and freehand objects.)

- Adding a point to a polyline or shape
- Moving a point in a polyline or shape
- Deleting a point from a polyline or shape

- Breaking a shape into a polyline or a polyline into two smaller polylines
- Joining two polylines together to form a single polyline
- Closing a polyline to form a polygon
- Aligning the points within a polyline or shape
- Converting text (regular or circular), line, or box objects to polylines or polygons

### Align

Using <Align> you can quickly change the position of objects in the drawing area, aligning them with respect to a specified object.

### Group

Use <Group> to display the Group menu.

Using the Group menu options, you can group two or more objects into a single group, or ungroup a previously grouped group.

## Moving the Cursor in the Drawing Area

You will need to move the cursor in the drawing area in order to add an object or change the location or characteristics of one or more objects already added. Once the cursor becomes active in the drawing area (after you make a menu selection), it will move in response to presses of cursor keys, movements of the mouse, or movements of the pen on a digital tablet.

Each time you press a cursor key, the cursor moves a fixed distance on the drawing area. You can decrease the size of this distance by pressing the − (minus) key at any time while the cursor is active in the drawing area. When you press −, the distance the cursor moves with subsequent presses of the cursor control keys is decreased. To return the cursor movement interval to the default distance, press + (plus). (This is different from Harvard Graphics' Draw/Annotate in that there is no way to increase the cursor movement interval to greater than the default.)

Table 18-1 contains a list of all the keys that can be used to control the cursor in the drawing area. You can also use Draw Partner's *zoom* feature described in "Using Zoom" in Chapter 17 to improve the accuracy of cursor placement.

If you use a mouse, its movements will result in corresponding cursor movements in the drawing area. To select an object or add a point, press the left mouse button, which functions as ENTER. The right mouse button functions as ESC.

With a digital tablet, movements of the stylus result in corresponding movements of the cursor in the drawing area. One of the keys on your stylus corresponds to the ENTER key and one to the ESC key. Experiment to determine which keys these are.

## Overview of Adding Objects

From the Draw Partner Main Menu, select <Add> to display the Add menu.

| Key | Function |
| --- | --- |
| BACKSPACE | Undo the last step performed. You cannot undo the previous step once you press ESC to return to the previous menu. (Draw Partner may not be able to undo a step if your drawing is too complex.) |
| DOWN (arrow) | Moves the cursor down. |
| END | Moves the cursor diagonally, down and to the left. |
| ENTER | Selects an object or adds a point at the location of the cursor |
| ESC | Completes the addition of an object. |
| HOME | Moves the cursor diagonally, up and to the left. |
| LEFT (arrow) | Moves the cursor left. |
| PGDN | Moves the cursor diagonally, down and to the right. |
| PGUP | Moves the cursor diagonally, up and to the right. |
| RIGHT (arrow) | Moves the cursor right. |
| UP (arrow) | Moves the cursor up. |
| − | Decreases the interval of cursor movement to allow for finer cursor movements. |
| + | Restores cursor movement interval modified by pressing − to the original movement interval. |

**Table 18-1.**    Keys Used to Control the Cursor in the Drawing Area

The Add menu displays the 12 types of objects you can add to the drawing area. Adding an object of any type follows the same basic steps:

1. Select the type of object you want to add from the Add menu. Unless you have a CGA or monochrome monitor, Draw Partner will display an example of the type of object you are adding in the menu/form area. This example will show the current settings for the object. Figure 18-1, for example, shows a polyline that reflects the current option settings. When you use a CGA or monochrome monitor, the object's options form is displayed, revealing its option settings. An example of an options form for a polyline is shown in Figure 18-2.

2. Follow the instructions displayed on the message line at the top of the function key banner to add the selected object. Before you complete the addition of the object, you can change options by pressing F8-Options. Doing so causes Draw Partner to display the

options form for the object (similar to the one shown in Figure 18-2). With CGA and monochrome monitors, this form is already displayed in the menu/form area; pressing F8-Options causes Draw Partner to make the cursor active in the options form.

3. Change options, if desired, on the options form as described later in this chapter. When you are satisfied with the current option settings, press ESC to return to the drawing area and continue adding objects.

4. For polyline, polygon, and freehand objects, press ESC when you have completed placing the object. For all other objects, press ENTER when you have completed placing the object. (The message line in the function key banner will prompt you to press the appropriate key.)

5. After the object has been placed, Draw Partner will allow you to immediately place another object of the same type. Either continue placing objects by repeating the previous steps, starting with step 2, or press ESC to stop placing objects and return to the Add menu.

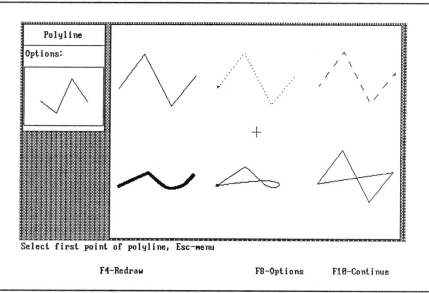

**Figure 18-1.** The polyline reflects the current option settings for polylines added in the drawing area

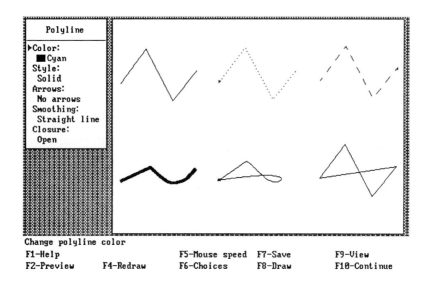

**Figure 18-2.**   Options form for a polyline

There are two important differences between setting options for an object in Draw Partner and setting them in Harvard Graphics. When you change the option settings for an object in Draw Partner, you also change the default settings for that object. (In Harvard Graphics, you would need to set the default options to permanently change the settings as described in Chapter 9, "Drawing and Annotating.") Furthermore, changing the option settings will affect the corresponding options for other objects in Draw Partner. For example, when you select a new pattern for boxes, the pattern used for lines, circles, polygons, wedges, and regular polygons change to this pattern as well. This feature is unique to Draw Partner and is not available in Harvard Graphics' Draw/Annotate.

The objects and options available in Draw Partner differ depending on the Draw Partner version, 1.0 or 2.3. Table 18-2 shows the objects and options available for each of the Draw Partner versions. The following sections describe how to add objects and set object options. If you have Draw Partner version 1.0, refer to Table 18-2 while reading the sections on setting options since more options are available in version 2.3 than in 1.0.

| Object | Version 1.0 options | Version 2.3 options |
|---|---|---|
| Text | Color | Size |
| | Font (attribute) | Color |
| | Height | Weight |
| | Justify | Italic |
| | Drop shadow | Underline |
| | Shadow color | Drop shadow |
| | | Shadow color |
| | | Justify |
| | | Font |
| Box | Outline color | Shape |
| | Fill color | Box style |
| | Pattern | Size |
| | Shape | Outline color |
| | | Outline style |
| | | Fill color |
| | | Pattern |
| | | Shadow color |
| Button | n/a | Button |
| Polyline | Color | Color |
| | Style | Style |
| | Arrows | Arrows |
| | Smoothing | Smoothing |
| | | Closure |
| Line | n/a | Size |
| | | Outline color |
| | | Outline style |
| | | Fill color |
| | | Pattern |
| | | Arrows |
| Circle | Outline color | Shape |
| | Fill color | Outline color |
| | Pattern | Outline style |
| | Shape | Fill color |
| | | Pattern |

**Table 18-2.** Objects and Options Available for Draw Partner Versions 1.0 and 2.3

| Object | Version 1.0 options | Version 2.3 options |
|---|---|---|
| Polygon | Outline color<br>Fill color<br>Pattern | Outline color<br>Outline style<br>Fill color<br>Pattern |
| Circular text | Color<br>Font (attribute)<br>Height<br>Drop shadow<br>Shadow color | Size<br>Color<br>Weight<br>Italic<br>Drop shadow<br>Shadow color<br>Font |
| Arc | n/a | Color<br>Style<br>Arrows<br>Closure |
| Wedge | n/a | Outline color<br>Outline style<br>Fill color<br>Pattern |
| Freehand | n/a | Color<br>Style<br>Arrows<br>Smoothing<br>Closure |
| Regular Polygon | n/a | Outline color<br>Outline style<br>Fill color<br>Pattern<br>Sides |

*Note:* Options are shown in the order in which they are listed on the options form for the object.

**Table 18-2.** Objects and Options Available for Draw Partner Versions 1.0 and 2.3 *(continued)*

## Adding Text

To add text in the drawing area, select <Text> from the Add menu. Draw Partner will display the message "Select location for text, Esc—menu." If you want to change your text options, press F8-Options to display the Text options form before placing the text in the drawing area. When you are finished setting text options (as described in the next section), press ESC to remove the Text options form and return to the drawing area.

Move the cursor to the location where you want to place the text (the text will start at this point) and press ENTER. Draw Partner will display the message "Enter a line of text, F8—character options, Esc—no text entered." Enter a line of text, up to 159 characters in length. As you enter text, the text itself appears below the message line, while the placement box in the drawing area extends to show you the length of the text you are entering. Press ENTER when you are finished to complete the placement. Examples of text added with Draw Partner are shown in Figure 18-3.

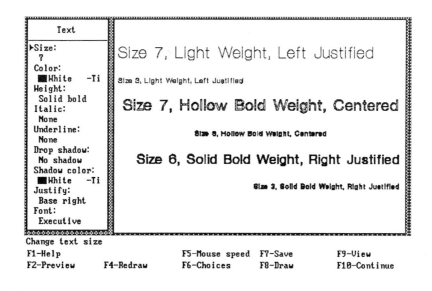

**Figure 18-3.** Text options form

You can press ESC at any time before you finalize the text placement if you want to start over and select a new position for your text. Once you press ENTER and place your text, Draw Partner will prompt you to enter a new line of text. The placement of this line will depend on the justification defined on the Text options form. For instance, if "Justify" is set to Center, the new line will automatically be centered below the preceding line of text. To place the new line of text at a different location, press ESC once and select a new location for your text on the Text options form (as described in the next section). If you are through placing text, press ESC twice to return to the Add menu.

While you are typing your text below the message line, you can modify the options of text within the line you are adding. To do this, move your cursor to the starting position of the text you want to modify and press F8. Draw Partner will ask you to move your cursor to highlight all of the text that you want to modify and then press ENTER again or ESC to cancel. Once you press ENTER, Draw Partner displays an options form with the following options: "Color," "Weight," "Italic," and "Underline." Set the desired options for your highlighted text, and then press ESC. You can now continue to enter the text or press ENTER to add the entered text onto the drawing area.

*Note:* Draw Partner allows you to enter text even when it will extend past the border of the drawing area. The entire text will be saved in the Draw Partner file (.DP file), but will be truncated at the border of the displayed drawing area if you save your drawing as a Harvard Graphics chart or symbol. In addition, text containing more than 60 characters will be converted to either polylines or polygons if you save your drawing as a Harvard Graphics chart or symbol. (Refer to "Using Draw Partner Drawings in Harvard Graphics" in Chapter 17 for more information.)

### Setting Text Options

There are nine options on the Text options form, shown in Figure 18-3. "Size" refers to the relative height of the text and can be any number from 1 to 100. A text size of 1 is equal to one percent of the height of the drawing area, whereas a text size of 100 is equal to 100 percent and completely fills the drawing area. "Color" allows you to select one of 16 colors for your text. "Weight" is used to select a light, hollow bold, or solid bold typeface for your text. Both the "Italic" and "Underline" options permit you to apply these attributes to your text.

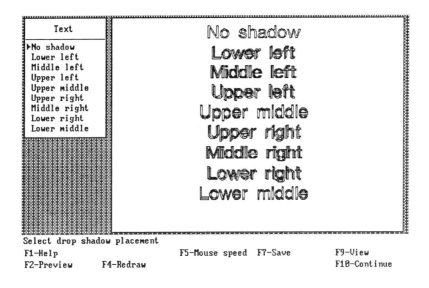

**Figure 18-4.**   List of drop shadows

"Drop shadow" allows you to select one of eight locations for a drop shadow behind the text, as shown in the drawing area in Figure 18-4. Select No shadow if you do not want a shadow behind your text. If you selected a drop shadow location, you can use "Shadow color" to select one of 16 colors for the text shadow.

"Justify" allows you to set the alignment for subsequent lines of text relative to the first line. You have a choice of left-justified, centered, or right-justified. This justification is maintained if you later modify the text using <Edit text> from the Modify menu. And finally, "Font" permits you to select from one of the seven available fonts.

Eight of these options, "Color," "Weight," "Italic," "Underline," "Drop shadow," "Shadow color," "Justify," and "Font," are set by selecting a setting from a list. To change the settings for these options, move the cursor to the option and press ENTER or F6-Choices. Draw Partner will display a list of the available option settings. Figure 18-4, for example, shows the list displayed when you press ENTER or F6-Choices with the cursor positioned at "Drop shadow." Move the cursor to highlight a setting in the list. Then press ENTER to select the desired setting and return to the Text options form. If you do not want to change the option setting after displaying the setting list, press ESC once.

To change the size of the text, move the cursor to "Size" and press ENTER. Draw Partner will display the message "Select new text size (Small=1, Large=100, Current=*current*)." To change the current text size, enter a value from 1 to 100. Press ENTER to return to the Text options form. To return to the Text options form without changing the text size, press ESC once.

*Note:* <Text> and <Circular text> share the same option settings, with the exception of "Underline" and "Justify" which are not circular text options. Any changes made to settings on the Text options form will result in equivalent changes being applied to the Circular text options form. These changes will not affect existing text in the drawing area.

## Adding a Box

From the Add menu, select <Box>. Draw Partner will display the message "Select corner of box, Esc—menu." Move the cursor to the location on the drawing area where you want to place a corner of the box and press ENTER. Draw Partner will then display the message "Select opposite corner of box, Esc—reselect corner." Move the cursor where you want the opposite corner of the box and press ENTER. Before placing the opposite corner, you can press either ESC or BACKSPACE to undo the first corner and place it again.

You can change the box options anytime before you press ESC to complete the placement of your box. To change the options, press F8-Options to display the Box options form. Modify the options on this form as described in the next section. Then press ESC to return to the drawing area and continue placing the box. Examples of boxes added with Draw Partner are shown in Figure 18-5.

Once you have placed your box by pressing ESC, Draw Partner will prompt you to place the first corner of another box. If you do not want to draw another box, press ESC to return to the Add menu.

### Setting Box Options

The Box options form shown in Figure 18-5 contains nine options. "Shape" allows you to create either a square or a rectangular box. At "Box style," select one of the nine styles from the Box Styles list, shown in Figure 18-6. If you set "Box style" to Shadow, 3-D, Page, or Caption,

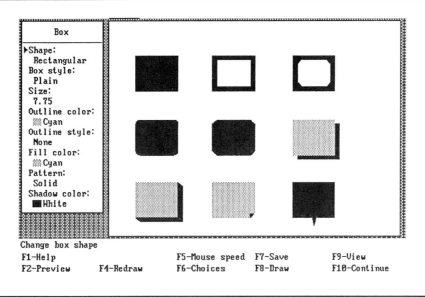

**Figure 18-5.** Box options form

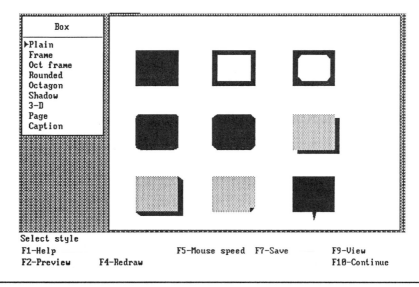

**Figure 18-6.** List of box styles

you will see an additional list (similar to Figure 18-7) from which you select the direction the box style feature will extend. For instance, if you select a 3-D box style, you must choose the direction of the third dimension. Also, when your box style is set to Shadow, 3-D, Page, or Caption, the "Shadow color" option is used to define the color of special box features: "Shadow color" is used to define the shadow on shadow boxes, the third dimension on 3-D boxes, and the up-turned corner on page boxes.

The "Size" option is used to define the size of features for certain box styles. When you select "Size," Draw Partner displays the message "Select new box size (Small=1, Large=100, Current=*current*)." Table 18-3 displays a list of the effects of the "Size" option for each box style.

Use "Outline color" to select either None or one of the 16 colors available for the box outline, and use "Outline style" to choose one of the four line styles to draw the outline. At "Fill color," select one of the 16 colors available for the box center. At "Pattern," select one of the 12 patterns shown in Figure 18-8 for your box.

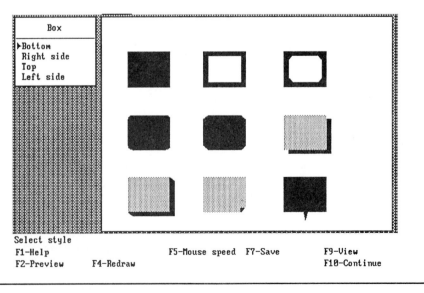

**Figure 18-7.**  Directions list for box style features

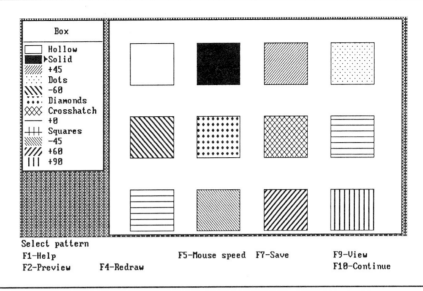

**Figure 18-8.** List of patterns

*Note:* Boxes, lines, circles, polygons, wedges, and regular polygons share the same "Fill color," "Pattern," "Outline color," and "Outline style" option settings. Any changes made to these options on the Box options form will result in equivalent changes being applied to the options forms for line, circle, polygon, wedge, and regular polygon objects.

| Box Style | Size Setting Affects |
| --- | --- |
| Frame, Oct frame | Width between inner and the outer box lines |
| Round | Roundness of box corners |
| Octagonal, Oct frame | Size of the diagonal corners |
| Shadow | Width of box shadow |
| 3-D | Depth of third dimension |
| Page | Width of the turned-up page corner |
| Caption | Length of the caption point |

**Table 18-3.** Effect of Box Size Depends on Box Style

## Adding a Polyline

From the Add menu, select <Polyline>. Draw Partner will display the message "Select first point of polyline, Esc—menu." Move the cursor to the location on the drawing area where you want to place the first point of the polyline and press ENTER. Draw Partner will then display the message "Select point 2 of polyline, Bksp—undo, Esc—done." Move the cursor to the location of the next point in your polyline and press ENTER again. Continue to place each point of the polyline, following the prompts displayed at the message line. You can place up to 200 points for each polyline. After you have placed the last point, press ESC to complete the polyline. Examples of polylines added with Draw Partner are shown in Figure 18-9.

While you are placing the points of your polyline you can cancel the last point placed by pressing BACKSPACE. Doing so moves the cursor to the last point placed and removes it. Position the cursor to place this point again and press ENTER. If you desire, you can press BACKSPACE again, canceling the preceding point. You can continue to press BACKSPACE until you have canceled every point in your polyline, if necessary.

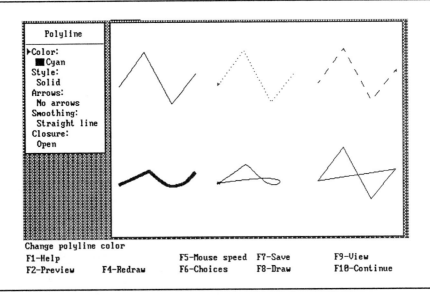

**Figure 18-9.** Polyline options form

You can change the options for the polyline anytime before you press ESC to complete the placement of your polyline. To change the options, press F8-Options. Draw Partner will display the Polyline options form. Modify the desired options on this form as described in the next section. Then press ESC to return to the drawing area and continue placing the polyline.

Once you have placed your polyline, Draw Partner will ask you to place the first point of another polyline. If you do not want to draw another polyline, press ESC to return to the Add menu.

## Setting Polyline Options

The Polyline options form, shown in Figure 18-9, contains five options. Use "Color" to select one of 16 colors for your polyline. "Style" allows you to select either a Solid, Dotted, Dashed, or Thick (bold) line for your polyline. There are four "Arrows" settings: No arrows, Start arrow (the arrowhead appears at the first point placed), End arrow (the arrowhead appears at the last point placed), and Both arrows (arrowheads appear at both ends of the polyline).

There are two "Smoothing" settings: Straight line and Curved line. Straight line displays the line segments exactly as you place them. Curved line smooths out the angles of your polyline to create a curved polyline. If you select Curved line, the line may not touch all the points you place for the polyline. The "Closure" option permits you to define whether the polyline will be a closed or open polyline. When your polyline is closed, Draw Partner connects the last point placed to the first point.

To change the setting of any of these options, move the cursor to the option and press ENTER or F6-Choices. Draw Partner will display a list of the available options settings. Move the cursor to highlight the desired setting in the list. Then press ENTER to select the highlighted setting and return to the Polyline options form. If you want to return to the Polyline options form without changing the original setting, press ESC once.

*Note:* Polylines, arcs, and freehand objects share the same option settings. (The one exception is arcs, which do not have a "Smoothing" option since they are smooth by definition.) Any changes made to these options on the Polyline options form will result in equivalent changes being applied to the Arc and Freehand options forms.

## Adding a Line

From the Add menu, select <Line>. Draw Partner will display the message "Select first point of line, Esc—menu." Move the cursor to the location in the drawing area where you want to place the starting point of the line and press ENTER. Draw Partner then displays the message "Select second point of line, Esc—reselect first point." Move the cursor to the location where you want the line to end and press ENTER. Alternatively, before you press ENTER, you can press ESC to remove the first point of the line and place it at a different location. After you have pressed ENTER you can remove the just-placed line by pressing BACKSPACE, or you can place another line. When you are through placing lines in the drawing area, press ESC to return to the Add menu.

You can change line options anytime before you place the second point of the line. To change these options, press F8-Options. Draw Partner will display the Line options form. Make your changes on this form as described in the next section. Press ESC to return to adding a line once you are through changing your line options. Examples of lines added in Draw Partner are shown in Figure 18-10.

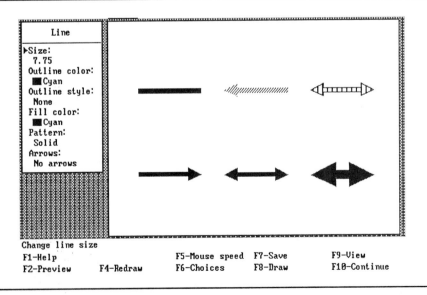

**Figure 18-10.** Line options form

Lines, like boxes, are special objects in Draw Partner. Lines have a "Size" option that determines the thickness of the line. Furthermore, the width of any arrow applied to the line is twice that of the line of itself. Draw Partner automatically maintains these proportions. Draw Partner will not distort a line object. In order to distort a line, you must convert the line to a polygon. See "Converting Text, Lines, or Boxes to Polygons" later in this chapter.

### Setting Line Options

The first option on the Line options form, "Size," permits you to define the width of the line and any arrows that are part of it. With the cursor at the "Size" option, press ENTER. Draw Partner will display the message "Select new line size (Small=1, Large=100, Current=*current*)." Enter the desired size for your line and press ENTER or press ESC to return without changing its size.

The Line options form, shown in Figure 18-10, contains five additional options: "Outline color," "Outline style," "Fill color," "Pattern," and "Arrows." Options two through five are identical to the corresponding options on the Box options form. The "Arrows" option is identical to the "Arrows" option on the Polyline options form. (Refer to the earlier sections "Setting Box Options" and "Setting Polyline Options" for descriptions of these options.) To change the setting for any of these options, move the cursor to the option and press ENTER or F6-Choices. Draw Partner will display a list of the available settings for the option. Move the cursor to highlight the desired setting on the list and press ENTER to select it and return to the line options form.

*Note:* Boxes, lines, circles, polygons, wedges, and regular polygons share the same "Fill color," "Pattern," "Outline color," and "Outline style" option settings. Any changes made to these options on the Line options form will result in equivalent changes being applied to the related forms.

### Adding a Circle

From the Add menu, select <Circle>. Draw Partner will display the message "Select center of circle, Esc—menu." Move the cursor to the location in the drawing area where you want to place the center of your circle and press ENTER. Draw Partner will then display the message "Select size of circle, Esc—reselect center." Move the cursor to define the size (and shape, if the "Shape" option on the Circle options form is set to Ellipse) of the circle and press ENTER. Before setting the circle size, you can press either ESC or BACKSPACE to remove the circle center and place it again.

You can change the circle options anytime before you press ENTER to complete the placement of your circle. To change the options, press F8-Options. Draw Partner will display the Circle options form. Modify the options on this form as described in the next section. Then press ESC to return to the drawing area and continue placing the circle. Examples of circles added with Draw Partner are shown in Figure 18-11.

Once you have placed your circle, Draw Partner will ask you to place the center of another circle. If you do not want to draw another circle, press ESC to return to the Add menu.

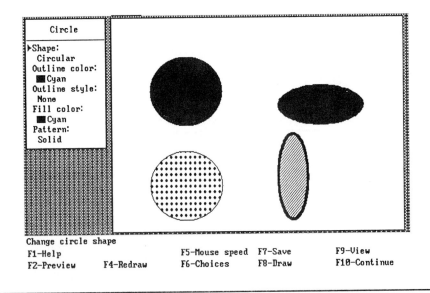

Figure 18-11.   Circle options form

### Setting Circle Options

The Circle options form, shown in Figure 18-11, contains five options: "Shape," "Outline color," "Outline style," "Fill color," and "Pattern." Options two through five are identical to the corresponding options on the Box options form. (Refer to the earlier section "Setting Box Options" for a description of these options.) At "Shape," select either a Circular or an Elliptical shape for your circle.

To change the setting for any of these options, move the cursor to the option and press ENTER or F6-Choices. Draw Partner will display a list of the available settings for the option. Move the cursor to highlight the desired setting on the list and press ENTER to select it and return to the Circle options form. If you want to return to the Circle options form without changing the original setting, press ESC once.

*Note:* Boxes, lines, circles, polygons, wedges, and regular polygons share the same "Fill color," "Pattern," "Outline color," and "Outline style" option settings. Any changes made to these options on the Circle options form will result in equivalent changes being applied to the related forms.

## Adding a Polygon

Placing a polygon involves the same steps as placing a polyline. (Refer to the earlier section "Adding a Polyline.") The only difference is that once you place the last point of a polygon, Draw Partner will automatically connect this point to the first point placed, forming a closed object rather than a polyline. You can place up to 200 points for each polygon. Examples of polygons added with Draw Partner are shown in Figure 18-12.

Anytime before you press ESC to place the polygon, you can change the polygon options by pressing F8-Options to display the options form. Modify the desired options on this form as described in the next section. Then press ESC to return to the drawing area and continue placing the polygon.

### Setting Polygon Options

The Polygon options form, shown in Figure 18-12, contains four options: "Outline color," "Outline style," "Fill color," and "Pattern." These op-

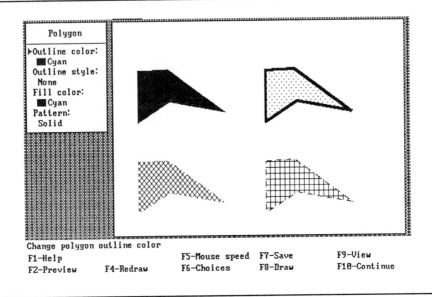

**Figure 18-12.**  Polygon options form

tions are identical to the corresponding options on the Box options form. (Refer to "Setting Box Options" for a description of these options.)

*Note:* Boxes, lines, circles, polygons, wedges, and regular polygons share the same "Fill color," "Pattern," "Outline color," and "Outline style" option settings. Any changes made to these options on the Circle options form will result in equivalent changes being applied to the related forms.

## Adding Circular Text

Circular text is text that follows the arc of a circle, rather than a straight line. Examples of circular text added with Draw Partner are shown in Figure 18-13.

Adding circular text involves three steps. First you define the circle you want the text to follow. You then you indicate whether the text should follow the top or bottom of the circle. And finally you enter the

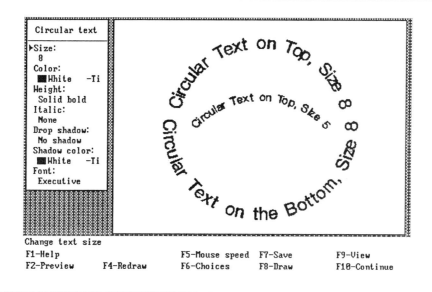

**Figure 18-13.** Circular text options form

text. To add circular text, select <Circular text> from the Add menu. Draw Partner will display the message "Select the center of circle for circular text, Esc—menu." Define the circle whose arc the text should follow by moving the cursor to the position for the center of the circle and pressing ENTER. Now move the cursor away from that point to complete the definition of the circle. When the circle is the desired size press ENTER. Alternatively, press ESC to relocate the center of the circle.

After you have defined a circle, Draw Partner will display the Circular text menu with the two options: <Top> and <Bottom>. Select <Top> to center the text along the top of the circle; the text will read clockwise. Select <Bottom> to center your text along the bottom of the circle. In that case the text will read counter-clockwise. Then press ENTER. Alternatively, press ESC to cancel so you can relocate the center of the circle.

Once you press ENTER, Draw Partner will display the message "Enter a line of text, F8—character options, Esc—no text entered." Enter a line of text, up to 159 characters. As you type, the text you enter will be displayed in the function key banner. Two small lines will be displayed in the drawing area to represent the placement of the text along the arc of the circle. The small lines in the drawing area of Figure 18-14, for example, mark the position of the text shown in the function key banner. When you are finished entering text, press ENTER to place the text along the arc of the circle. Only the text is displayed; the circle you defined will disappear. If you press ESC instead of ENTER, Draw Partner will cancel adding the text and start over, prompting you to define the circle center again.

The size of your text defines the amount of space a line of text will cover along the path of a circle. For example, if your text size is set to 8 and the text covers about half of the circle you defined, changing the text to a size of 5 will result in text that covers less than half of a circle of the same size (see Figure 18-13). If your text is too long to fit around the circle, Draw Partner will reduce the text size so it will fit.

After you have placed your circular text, Draw Partner will be prepared to place another arc of circular text. When you are done adding circular text, press ESC to return to the Add menu.

Any time, while you are typing your text below the message line, you can modify the options of text within the line you are adding. To do

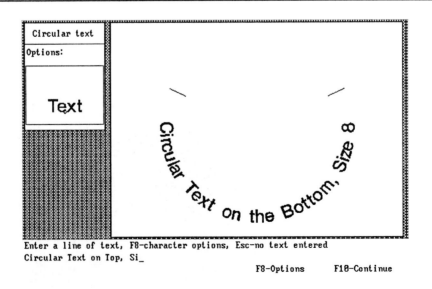

**Figure 18-14.**  Lines in the drawing area marking the text position

this, move your cursor to the starting position of the text you want to modify and press F8. Draw Partner will ask you to move your cursor to highlight all of the text that you want to modify and then press ENTER again or ESC to cancel. Once you press ENTER, Draw Partner displays an options form with the following options: "Color," "Weight," and "Italic." Set the desired options for your highlighted text, and then press ESC. You can now continue to enter the text or press ENTER to add the circular text onto the drawing area.

You can modify options for the circular text anytime before you finish defining the circle. To do this, press F8-Options to display the Circular Text options form. Modify the options as described in the next section. When you are through defining your circular text options, press ESC to return to defining the text circle.

### Setting Circular Text Options

The Circular text options form, shown in Figure 18-13, contains seven options. These options are identical to the corresponding options on the Text options form. See "Setting Text Options," earlier in this chapter, for a description of these options.

*Note:* Text and circular text share the same option settings (except that text has two options, "Justify" and "Underline," not shared with circular text). Any changes made to the Circular text options form will result in equivalent changes being applied to the Text options form.

## Adding an Arc

An *arc* is a segment of a circle. To add an arc, select <Arc> from the Add menu. Draw Partner will display the message "Select center point of Arc, Esc—menu." Move the cursor to the center of a circle on which your arc will be located and press ENTER. Draw Partner will then display the message "Select start point of curve, Esc—reselect center." Move away from the center of the circle to the location where you want your arc to begin. The farther the cursor is from the center of the circle (in other words, the greater the radius), the shallower the curve of the resulting arc.

When the cursor is located where you want to begin placing your arc, press ENTER. Next move the cursor to define the end point of your arc. As the cursor moves, Draw Partner displays an arc with the end point attached to the circle center by a straight line. When the cursor is where you want the arc to end, press ENTER. The straight line will be removed and Draw Partner will draw the arc you have defined.

Anytime while you are placing the arc, you can press ESC to start over and reselect the center of the arc. Once your arc has been placed, you can press BACKSPACE to delete the arc. You can then select the center point for another arc, or you can press ESC to return to the Add menu. Examples of arcs placed in Draw Partner are shown in Figure 18-15.

You can change the options for the arc anytime before you complete its placement. To change the arc options, press F8-Options. Draw Partner will display the options form. Modify the desired options on this form as described in the next section. Then press ESC to return to the drawing area and continue placing the arc.

### Setting Arc Options

The Arc options form (shown in Figure 18-15) contains four options: "Color," "Style," "Arrows," and "Closure." These options are identical to the options found on the polyline options form. For a description of these options, see "Setting Polyline Options."

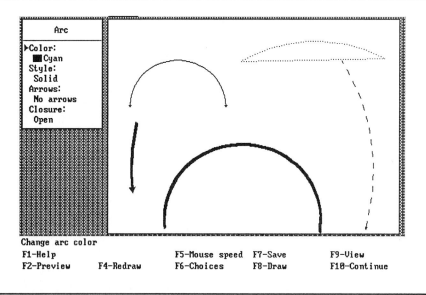

**Figure 18-15.**   Arc options form

*Note:* Polylines, arcs, and freehand objects share the same option settings. (The one exception is that arcs do not have a "Smoothing" option since they are smooth by definition.) Any changes made to these options on the Arc options form will result in equivalent changes being applied to the Polyline and Freehand options forms.

## Adding a Wedge

Adding a wedge in the drawing area is identical to adding an arc. The only difference is that a wedge is a solid object in which the circle center is connected to both the starting and ending points of the arc. Examples of wedges are shown in Figure 18-16. For details on adding a wedge in the drawing area, see the earlier section "Adding an Arc."

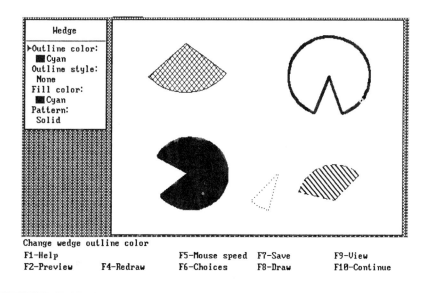

**Figure 18-16.**    Wedge options form

### Setting Wedge Options

The Wedge option form (shown in Figure 18-16) contains four options: "Outline color," "Outline style," "Fill color," and "Pattern." These options are discussed in the section "Setting Box Options."

*Note:* Boxes, lines, circles, polygons, wedges, and regular polygons share the same "Fill color," "Pattern," "Outline color," and "Outline style" option settings. Any changes made to these options on the Wedge options form will result in equivalent changes being applied to the related forms.

## Adding a Freehand Drawing

There are many similarities between adding a freehand drawing and adding a polyline. The major difference is that you do not need to press ENTER to add points while drawing freehand. Draw Partner automatically adds a point each time the cursor, mouse, or stylus changes direction. Freehand drawings can contain up to 200 points.

To add a freehand drawing, select <Freehand> from the Add menu. Draw Partner displays the message "Select first point of freehand, Esc—menu." Move the cursor to the location where you want to begin your drawing and press ENTER. Move the cursor to draw. When you are through drawing, press ENTER or ESC. You can now move the cursor to add another freehand drawing, press BACKSPACE to erase the entire drawing you just placed, or press ESC to return to the Add menu.

Anytime while you are adding a freehand drawing you can press F8-Options to display the Freehand options form. Change the options on this form, and then press ESC to return to adding the freehand drawing. Examples of freehand drawings are shown in Figure 18-17.

*Hint:* If your drawing is so complicated it requires more than 200 points, you can draw segments of the entire drawing in separate freehand drawings.

### Setting Freehand Options

There are five options on the Freehand options form, shown in Figure 18-17. These are the same options that can be found on the Polyline

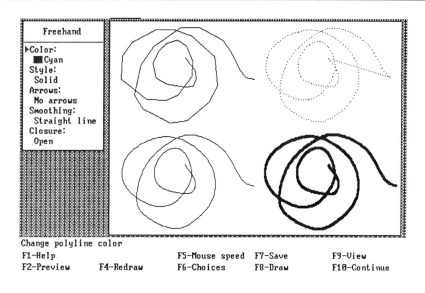

**Figure 18-17.**   Freehand options form

options form. See "Setting Polyline Options" for a description of these options.

*Note:* Polylines, arcs, and freehand objects share the same option settings (except that arcs do not have a "Smoothing" option since they are smooth by definition). Any changes made to these options on the Freehand options form will result in equivalent changes being applied to the Polyline and Arc options forms.

## Adding Regular Polygons

A polygon is an multi-sided solid object in which each side is of equal length. Draw Partner polygons can have from 3 to 200 sides. Adding a polygon is identical to adding a circle. (For details, see "Adding a Circle.") Examples of several regular polygons added in Draw Partner are shown in Figure 18-18.

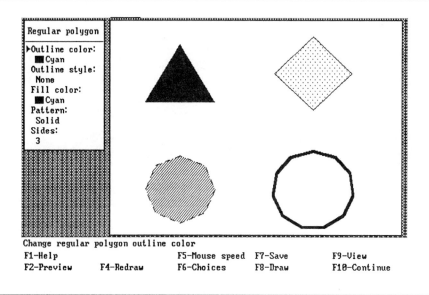

**Figure 18-18.** Regular polygon options form

### Setting Regular Polygon Options

The Regular polygon options form, shown in Figure 18-18, contains five options. The first four options, "Outline color," "Outline style," "Fill color," and "Pattern," are identical to the first four options on the Circle options form. (See "Setting Circle Options" for details.) The fifth option, "Sides," permits you to specify the number of sides for the regular polygon. Move the cursor to the "Sides" option and press ENTER. Draw Partner displays the message "Select number of sides (Small=3, Large=200, Current=*current*)." Enter the number of sides for your regular polygon and press ENTER. A three-sided polygon is a triangle, a four-sided polygon is a diamond (a square rotated 90 degrees), a five-sided polygon is a pentagon, and so on.

*Note:* Boxes, lines, circles, polygons, wedges, and regular polygons share the same "Fill color," "Pattern," "Outline color," and "Outline style" option settings. Any changes made to these options on the Regular polygon options form will result in equivalent changes being applied to the related forms.

## Adding a Button

A button is an invisible rectangle that you can add to your drawing. When a button appears on a chart, you can use the button to control a HyperShow. For information concerning HyperShows, see "Creating a HyperShow" in Chapter 16, "Harvard Graphics 2.3 Features."

To add a button to your drawing, select <Button> from the Add menu. Draw Partner will display the message "Select corner of Button, Esc—menu." Move your cursor to one of the corners where you want to place the button and press ENTER. Next, move your cursor to the opposite corner of a rectangle that defines the size and shape of the button and press ENTER again. Your button will appear on the screen as a hollow rectangle with a dashed outline. The button itself will not be visible on any chart that is previewed, output, or included in a ScreenShow.

Once you have placed the button, Draw Partner will require that you define a number for the button. At the top-left corner of the function key banner, Draw Partner will display the message "Enter Button number (1 .. 10) or special Button number." Type the number for your button, and then press ENTER to complete the placement of the button. You may now place an additional button, or press ESC to return to the Add menu.

*Note:* You are limited to a total of 20 buttons per chart. For additional information about button numbers, including special button numbers, see "Creating a HyperShow" in Chapter 16.

## Selecting Objects

Whenever you need to modify an object or perform an operation on an object in Draw Partner, you need to select that object first. To select an object, move the cursor to the object you want to select and press ENTER. If there is only one object near the cursor, that object will be selected. If the object you select is a group (when two or more objects have been grouped, as described in "Grouping Objects" later in this chapter), the group will be treated as though it were a single object. In either case you can then perform an operation on the selected object.

If two or more objects are near the cursor, Draw Partner will identify the *back-most* object, usually the first object added. (See the later section "Changing Object Order.") Draw Partner identifies the selected object by enclosing it in an imaginary rectangle defined by small markers at the four corners of the rectangle, called *object handles*. Draw Partner also displays a menu (shown in Figure 18-19) with two options: <This object> and <Next object>.

If Draw Partner has identified the correct object, select <This object> from the menu; if it has not, select <Next object>. Repeat this process, as necessary, until Draw Partner selects the correct object. Once you select <This object>, Draw Partner will continue with the operation you requested. You can cancel selecting an object anytime while this menu is displayed by pressing ESC once. You can then either try again to select an object, or press ESC a second time to return to the previous menu.

You cannot select more than one object at a time in Draw Partner, unlike in Harvard Graphics. If you want to treat two or more objects as

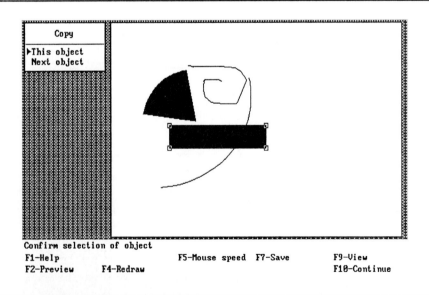

**Figure 18-19.** Object handles marking the object identified by Draw Partner

a group, use the <Group> selection from the Draw Partner Main Menu as described in the later section "Grouping Objects."

## Modifying Objects

The following sections describe how to modify objects. These modifications can be performed on a single object, or on two or more objects that have been explicitly grouped (except for editing text, which can be performed on only one object at a time). Modifications you can perform include:

- Grouping objects
- Ungrouping objects
- Moving an object
- Changing the size of an object
- Copying an object
- Deleting one or more objects
- Rotating an object in any direction
- Flipping an object either horizontally or vertically
- Changing the option settings for an object
- Changing the order of objects
- Editing text and circular text
- Creating object sweep transformations
- Adding a shadow to an object (version 2.3 only)
- Skewing an object (version 2.3 only)
- Adding perspective to an object (version 2.3 only)
- Aligning objects with respect to another object

Draw Partner also permits you to modify individual components of an object using its powerful point editing features. These features are described later in the section "Editing Polylines and Shapes."

## Grouping Objects

Sometimes it is convenient to treat two or more objects as a single entity by grouping them together. When two or more objects have been grouped together, they are referred to as a *group*. When objects are grouped, they can be treated as a single object, which can simplify some operations such as moving or rotating objects.

To group two or more objects, select <Group> from the Draw Partner Main Menu. Draw Partner will display this menu:

The first three options on this menu, <Everything>, <In box>, and <Object>, provide three different ways to group objects. These options are described next. The last option, <Ungroup>, is described in the next section.

If you want to group all the objects in the drawing area, select <Everything>. Draw Partner will display the message "Entire drawing is now grouped, Esc continues." Press ESC to return to the Group menu. Press ESC once more to return to the Draw Partner Main Menu.

If you want to create a group from objects within a section of the drawing area, select <In box>. Draw Partner will display the message "Select first corner of box to include objects, Esc—menu." Move the cursor to one corner of an imaginary box that will contain only the objects you want to group and press ENTER. Now move the cursor to the opposite corner of this box and press ENTER again. Draw Partner groups the objects within this box and displays object handles around the newly formed group, as shown in Figure 18-20.

If Draw Partner selected any objects you did not want to select, or did not select all the objects you wanted in the group, cancel the selection by pressing BACKSPACE and try again. If all the desired objects are selected, press ESC to return to the Group menu. Alternatively, you can draw another box around the next set of objects you want to group. Once you have selected a new set of objects to group or have returned to the Group menu, you can no longer ungroup the last group by pressing BACKSPACE.

### Drawing and Editing with Draw Partner 591

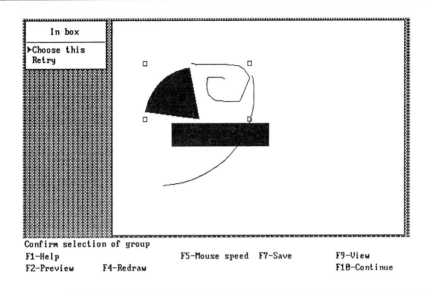

**Figure 18-20.** Object handles indicating which objects will be grouped

The final way to add objects to a group is to add each one individually. To do this, select <Object> from the Group menu. Draw Partner will display the message "Select objects to include in group, Esc—menu." Select the first object to include in the group. Draw Partner will prompt you to add additional objects to the group and press ESC when you are finished. While you are adding objects to the group, you can press BACKSPACE to remove the last added object from the group. If more than one object has been added, you can continue to remove objects from the group by pressing BACKSPACE repeatedly.

Once you have added the desired objects to your group, press ESC. Draw Partner will draw handles around the group to show you the objects you have grouped. You can then begin creating another group by selecting another object or press ESC to return to the Group menu.

In Draw Partner version 2.3, you can group together groups of objects in a way that is similar to Harvard Graphics Draw/Annotate's handling of objects. (This feature is not available with Draw Partner version 1.0.) Specifically, you can create a number of groups, each containing several objects, and then group these groups together. Draw

Partner keeps track of the level of grouping performed. This can be useful if you later need to ungroup objects, as described in the next section.

## Ungrouping Objects

To ungroup the objects in a group, select <Ungroup> from the Group menu. Draw Partner will display the message "Select a group to break apart, Esc—menu." Select the desired group. Draw Partner will then ungroup this group of objects. When it does so, object handles for the individual objects will appear briefly before the prompt to select a group to break apart is again displayed in the function key banner. At this point you can either press BACKSPACE to cancel the ungrouping just performed, or you can select another group to ungroup. When you are done ungrouping groups of objects, press ESC to return to the Group menu.

Similar to Harvard Graphics Draw/Annotate, Draw Partner version 2.3 supports groups within groups. That is, when a group is added to a larger group, it still maintains its identity as a group. When the larger group is ungrouped, all groups contained within the larger group regain their individual status as groups. You can then select any of these groups to ungroup further.

*Note:* Any object that has a shadow is a group. You can separate an object from its shadow by ungrouping.

## Moving an Object

To move an object to a new location in the drawing area, select <Move> from the Draw Partner Main Menu. Draw Partner will display the message "Select an object to move, Esc—menu." Select the object you want to move. Once the object is selected, Draw Partner displays a box that represents the object. Move the cursor to place this box where you want to move the object (as shown in Figure 18-21) and press ENTER. Draw Partner will then move the selected object to the new location. You can continue to move objects or press ESC to return to the Draw Partner Main Menu.

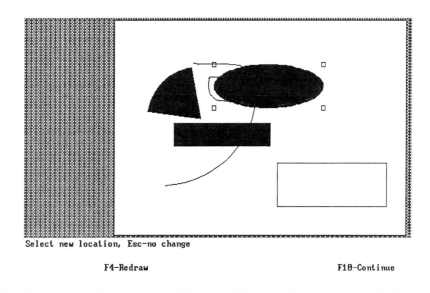

**Figure 18-21.**  Box representing the elliptical object that is being moved

Another method for moving objects involves the use of Draw Partner's Align feature. Using <Align> from the Draw Partner Main Menu, you can move an object into perfect alignment with another object. Align is described in the later section "Aligning Objects."

## Changing the Size of an Object

To change the size of an object, select <Size> from the Draw Partner Main Menu. Draw Partner will display the message "Select an object to size, Esc—menu." Once you select an object, Draw Partner will place the cursor at the upper-right object handle. Move the cursor until the object is the desired size and press ENTER. While you are moving the cursor to define the new size of the object, press SHIFT if you want to maintain the original proportions of the object. Continue to hold down the SHIFT key until you press ENTER to complete the sizing of the object.

When you have finished sizing the object, Draw Partner will prompt you to select another object to size. Select the next object you want to size, if desired. Press ESC when you have finished sizing objects.

## Copying an Object

To copy an object in the drawing area, select <Copy> from the Draw Partner Main Menu. Draw Partner will display the message "Select an object to copy, Esc—menu." Select the object you want to copy. Once the object is selected, Draw Partner displays a box that represents a copy of the object. Use the cursor keys or mouse to move this placement box to the desired location in the drawing area, and then press ENTER. Draw Partner will place a copy of the selected object at the new location defined by the placement box.

Draw Partner assumes you then want to place another copy of the object, and so displays another placement box. It automatically places this second copy of the object the same distance from the first copy as the first copy is from the original object. This feature permits you to quickly place any number of equally spaced copies by simply pressing ENTER repeatedly. In Figure 18-22 this technique was used to copy the circle in the upper-left corner of the drawing area, placing each copy down and to the right.

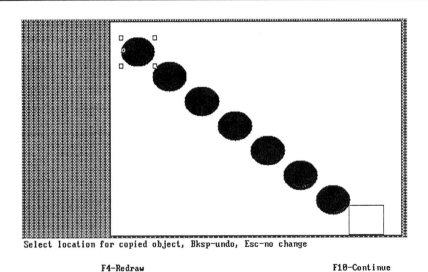

**Figure 18-22.** Circle in upper-left corner copied multiple times by pressing ENTER once the first copy is made

To place the second copy of the object at the position Draw Partner selected, press ENTER. If you want to place the copy somewhere else, move the placement box to the desired location and press ENTER. When you are finished placing copies of the original object, press ESC. Draw Partner will then prompt you to select another object to copy. When you are through copying objects, press ESC once more to return to the Draw Partner Main Menu.

## Deleting Objects

You can delete a single object, a group of objects, or all the objects in the drawing area. To delete objects, select <Delete> from the Draw Partner Main Menu. Draw Partner will display this menu:

To delete individual objects or a group of objects, select <Object> from the Delete menu. Draw Partner will display the message "Select an object to delete, Esc—menu." Select the object or group you want to delete. When you delete an object, Draw Partner will remove it from the drawing area and display the message "Select an object to delete, Bksp—undo, Esc—menu." You can continue to delete objects by selecting the next object to delete.

If you accidentally delete an object you want to keep, press BACKSPACE. When you do so, Draw Partner will restore the *last* object deleted since you selected <Object> from the Delete menu. You can press BACKSPACE again if you have deleted more than one object since you selected <Object> from the Delete menu. Additional presses of BACKSPACE will continue to restore objects in the reverse order in which they were deleted.

*Note:* Once you return to the Delete menu, deleted objects cannot be restored.

When you are through deleting objects, press ESC to return to the Draw Partner Main Menu.

**596** Harvard Graphics: The Complete Reference

To delete all the objects in the drawing area, select <Everything> from the Delete menu. Draw Partner will display a menu with the two options: <Cancel> and <Clear drawing>. Select <Clear drawing> to erase all drawings from the drawing area. Unless you have saved your drawing before selecting <Clear drawing>, you will not be able to recover the deleted drawings. To return to the Delete menu without deleting objects, select <Cancel>.

## Rotating an Object

To rotate an object, select <Modify> from the Draw Partner Main Menu, followed by <Rotate> from the Modify menu. Draw Partner will display the message "Select an object to rotate, Esc—menu." Select the object or group you want to rotate. A rectangle that represents the selected item is displayed. This rectangle contains an arrow that originates from the center of the rectangle and points to the right, as shown in Figure 18-23.

The cursor is positioned at the tip of the arrow. Move the cursor to rotate the selected object. As it moves, the arrow will follow it and the

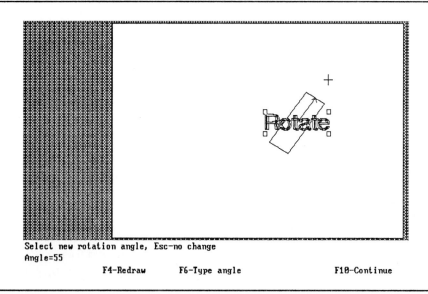

**Figure 18-23.** Rectangle showing the angle of rotation

object will rotate accordingly. If you are using the arrow keys to rotate the object, use the − key to reduce the cursor movement interval and the + key to restore the default cursor movement. As you rotate the object, Draw Partner displays the angle of rotation below a message that reads "Select new rotation angle, Esc−no change." Once you have defined the desired rotation, press ENTER to place the object using this new orientation. You can then select a new object to rotate or press ESC to return to the Modify menu.

Figure 18-24 shows an example of a rotated object, in this case, the text object "Rotate." Seven copies of the original object were made (as described in "Copying an Object"). The copies were then rotated to the desired positions.

*Note:* Draw Partner will not rotate an object if it would result in a part of the object extending beyond the border of the drawing area. If you want to rotate an object that is too close to the drawing area border, move it before attempting to rotate it. You can always move it again after it is rotated.

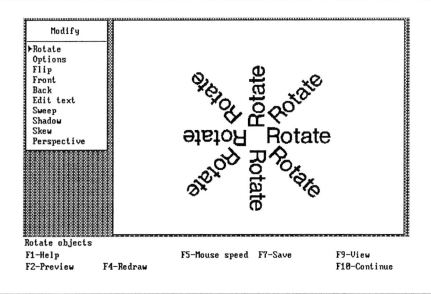

**Figure 18-24.**   Rotated objects

## Flipping an Object

Draw Partner allows you to flip any object either sideways or upside down, as long as the object is not text or a group that contains text. To flip an object, select <Modify> from the Draw Partner Main Menu, followed by <Flip> from the Modify menu. Draw Partner displays the Flip menu with its two options: <Horizontal> and <Vertical>. To flip an object sideways, select <Horizontal>. To flip an object upside down, select <Vertical>. Figure 18-25 shows examples of flipped objects, in this case, text converted to polygons. The original objects are shown along with their flipped copies.

Once you select the direction for the flip, Draw Partner displays the message "Select an object to flip, Esc—menu." Move the cursor to the object you want to flip and press ENTER. You can continue to flip objects in the selected direction. After you flip an object, you can restore it to its original condition either by pressing BACKSPACE or by flipping it back again. When you are through flipping objects or groups, press ESC to return to the Modify menu.

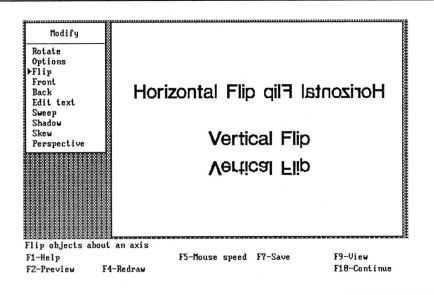

**Figure 18-25.**  Flipped objects

*Note:* Although you cannot flip text, or a group that includes a text object, you can create flipped text like that shown in Figure 18-25 by first converting the text to polygons. See "Converting Text, Lines, or Boxes to Polygons," later in this chapter. Buttons also cannot be flipped.

## Modifying Object Options

To modify the options of an object, select <Modify> from the Draw Partner Main Menu, followed by <Options> from the Modify menu. Draw Partner will display the message "Select an object to change options, Esc—menu." Once you select an object, the options form for that object is displayed. Modify the options and then press ESC to apply the new options to the selected object. If you decide you do not want to change the options of the selected object, press ESC without changing any of the options.

Once you press ESC, Draw Partner displays a message instructing you to select another object to apply these same changes to. The types of objects you can apply these changes to depend on the type of object you originally selected. If you modify the options for a text object (either regular or circular text), you can select another text or circular text object to apply these same changes to. If you modify the options for a shape (a box, line, circle, polygon, wedge, or regular polygon), you can apply these same changes to any other shape object. If you modify the options for a polyline, you can also apply these changes to arcs and freehand objects.

In Draw Partner version 2.3, you can select a group of objects to apply changes to. (Draw Partner version 1.0 will not allow you to modify options for a group.) When you select a group of objects, Draw Partner displays the Group options form, shown in Figure 18-26. This form has six options: "Text color," "Shadow color," "Polyline color," "Outline color," "Fill color," and "Style color."

Use "Text color" to define the color for any text included in the group. The "Shadow color" option is used to change the color of shadows on any shadowed objects in the group (except for shadow-style boxes). If your group includes polylines, arcs, or freehand drawings, change their color using the "Polyline color" option. The "Outline color" option is used to specify a color for the outline of any boxes, lines, circles, polygons, wedges, and regular polygons. Likewise, the "Fill color" option is used to define the fill color for these objects. The final

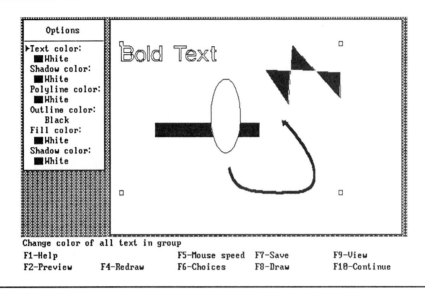

**Figure 18-26.** Group options form

option, "Shadow color," defines the color for the style feature on 3-D, Shadow, and Page style boxes. (See "Setting Box Options" for more details on these features.)

Continue selecting objects to apply the option changes to by moving the cursor to the object and pressing ENTER. When you are through applying these options to objects, press ESC once.

Draw Partner will prompt you to select another object to redefine options for. If you are through modifying options for objects, press ESC once more to return to the Modify menu. Alternatively, select another object, define its options, and apply these new options to other objects, if desired.

## Changing Object Order

Objects in the drawing area are redrawn in the order of their placement. You can see this order by pressing F4-Redraw. F4-Redraw causes Draw Partner to immediately update the drawing area image. The first item placed is drawn first, the second item placed is drawn second, and so forth. When your objects overlap, the front objects will cover some or all of the back objects.

## Drawing and Editing with Draw Partner    601

This order can be changed with the <Front> and <Back> options from the Modify menu. Use <Back> to move the selected object or group to the back of the drawing area. Likewise, use <Front> to move an object or group forward, making it the last to be drawn.

From the Draw Partner Main Menu, select <Modify>. Depending on whether you want to move an object to the front or back, select <Front> or <Back> from the Modify Menu. Draw Partner will display a message instructing you to select an object to move to the front or back of the drawing area. Select an object, or press ESC to cancel and return to the Modify menu. When you select an object, Draw Partner moves it front or back, as requested. After changing the order of an object, you can undo the change, returning the object to its previous position, by pressing BACKSPACE. You can only recover the position of the last selected object as long as you do not select another object or press ESC to return to the Modify menu.

Figure 18-27 shows examples of objects modified by using <Front> and <Back>. The original drawing is shown at the top of the drawing area. The object in the middle of this drawing, a circle, was moved to the back in the drawing on the left and to the front in the drawing on the right.

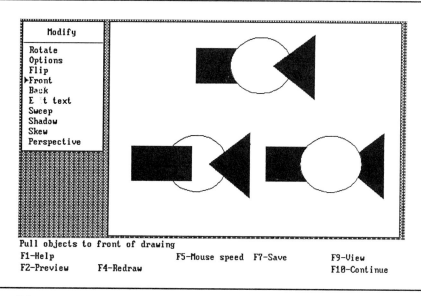

**Figure 18-27.**    Examples of the use of <Front> and <Back>

## Editing Text

To edit regular or circular text, select <Modify> from the Draw Partner Main Menu, followed by <Edit text> from the Modify menu. Draw Partner will display the message "Select text to change, Esc—menu." When you select the text to change, Draw Partner will display the message "Enter new text." Your previously entered text will appear below this message. You can move the cursor within the existing text, and insert text where appropriate—Draw Partner is automatically in an insert mode. Edit the existing text using the following keys:

| | |
|---|---|
| BACKSPACE | Back up, deleting the previous character |
| DEL | Delete the character at the cursor |
| END | Move to the end of the text |
| HOME | Move to the beginning of the text |
| LEFT | Move one character to the left |
| RIGHT | Move one character to the right |

As you add or delete text, a placement box (for text) or line markers (for circular text) appear in the drawing area indicating the size of the text. Press ENTER when you are finished editing the selected text, or press ESC to cancel editing. You can then continue to select more text to edit, or return to the Modify menu by pressing ESC. After you change a line of text, you can cancel your changes by pressing BACKSPACE before you either return to the Modify menu or select a new line of text to edit.

*Note:* If you convert regular or circular text to polygons or polylines, you will not be able to edit the text using <Edit text>.

## Sweeping Objects

Draw Partner provides you with a tool called *sweep*. When you use sweep, Draw Partner will make from 1 to 50 copies of an object. If you want, each of these copies can be slightly different from each of the preceding copies in size, shape, position within the drawing area, and/or rotation. Sweep can be used to create interesting special effects and images. Examples of three sweeps are shown in Figure 18-28.

# Drawing and Editing with Draw Partner 603

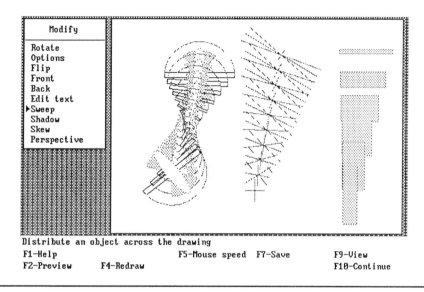

**Figure 18-28.**  Examples of sweeps

To sweep an object, select <Modify> from the Draw Partner Main Menu followed by <Sweep> from the Modify menu. Draw Partner will display the message "Select an object to sweep, Esc—menu." Once you select an object, Draw Partner will create a copy of the object, referred to as the *final object,* and instruct you to move it to the desired location in the drawing area. Place the final object at the desired location and press ENTER. Draw Partner will display this menu:

The first five options on the Sweep menu, <Rotate>, <Move>, <Size>, <Skew>, and <Perspective> allow you to determine the characteristics of the final object. Select <Rotate> to change the orientation of the final object. Select <Move> to change the position of the final object in the drawing area. Use <Size> to change the size of the final object. <Skew> and <Perspective> permit you to distort the final object. (See "Skewing Objects" and "Adding Perspective to Objects" for a description of these distortions.) You can perform any or all of these operations on the final object (with the exception of text, buttons, or groups that contain text or buttons, which you cannot skew or add perspective to in a sweep). If you want to cancel the changes at this point, press BACKSPACE and then redefine an object to sweep.

The orientation, placement, and size of the final object have a dramatic effect on the sweep. If you modify the final object, making it different from the original object, the intermediate copies of the objects created by the sweep will each represent a varying degree of this modification, as is shown in Figure 18-28.

When you are through changing the characteristics of the final object, press ESC or select <Done> from the Sweep menu. Draw Partner will display the message "Enter number of intermediate objects (1..50)." (When you are sweeping a complex object or group, the maximum number of intermediate objects may be less than 50.) To cancel the sweep, press ESC. Otherwise, enter a number from 1 to 50 to indicate the number of intermediate objects you want to add and press ENTER. Draw Partner will create the sweep. If you are satisfied with the sweep results, select another object to sweep or press ESC to return to the Modify menu. You can cancel the last sweep Draw Partner produced before you select another object to sweep or return to the Modify menu by pressing BACKSPACE.

The sweep produced by Draw Partner is a single group. If you want to modify an individual copy of an object within the sweep, you must first ungroup the sweep into its individual objects. (See the earlier section "Ungrouping Objects" for details.)

## Adding Shadows to Objects

With Draw Partner version 2.3 you can add a shadow to any object (except buttons) or group by selecting <Shadow> from the Modify menu. Draw Partner will display the message "Select an object to add shadow to, Esc—menu." Select an object or group in the drawing area. Draw Partner will display the Shadow Color menu. Select the desired color of the shadow from this menu and press ENTER. Alternatively, press ESC to reselect an object to add a shadow to. Once you select a shadow color, Draw Partner displays a rectangle representing the shadow, and permits you to define the location for the shadow relative to the original object or group. Move the shadow to the desired location and press ENTER. Examples of several objects with shadows are shown in Figure 18-29.

After placing the shadow, you can select another object to add a shadow to. If you are unhappy with the shadow you have just placed, press BACKSPACE to erase it. When you are done placing shadows, press ESC to return to the Modify menu.

*Note:* When you place a shadow, the shadow is grouped with the object to which you added it. If you want to move an object independently from its shadow, you must first ungroup them.

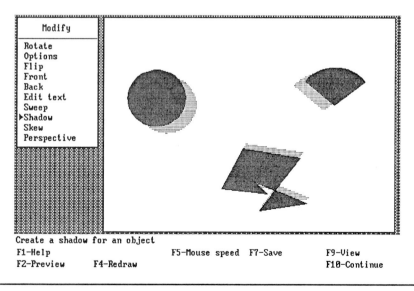

**Figure 18-29.**   Examples of objects with shadows

## Skewing Objects

To *skew* an object is to make it lean to one side or another. With Draw Partner version 2.3 you can skew any object or group by selecting <Skew> from the Modify menu. Draw Partner will then display the message "Select an object to skew, Esc—menu." Once you have selected an object or group, Draw Partner encloses the object in a box and places the cursor at the upper-left corner of the box. Move the cursor right or left to make the box lean in that direction. When the box is tilted to the desired angle, press ENTER. Draw Partner will then redraw the object to fit within the box. Depending on the complexity of the object and the speed of your computer, this redraw may take up to a minute or so.

Once you have skewed an object, you may either select another object to skew, press BACKSPACE to undo the previously applied skew, or press ESC to return to the Modify menu. An example of several objects that have been skewed is shown in Figure 18-30.

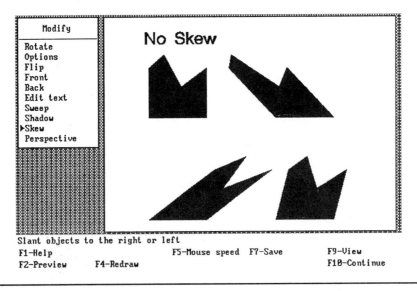

**Figure 18-30.**   Skewed objects

*Note:* You cannot skew text, buttons, or any groups that contain text or buttons. If you want to skew text, you must first convert the text to a group of polygons. Also, if you skew a box or line, the resulting object will lose its identity and become a polygon.

### Adding Perspective to Objects

Adding perspective to an object gives it an appearance of depth. Perspective permits you to make the top of an object appear either closer to or farther from the viewer than the bottom of the object. You can add perspective with Draw Partner version 2.3.

To add perspective to an object, select <Perspective> from the Modify menu. Draw Partner will display the message "Select an object to add perspective to, Esc—menu." Select the object to add perspective to. Draw Partner will enclose the selected object in a box. Move the cursor to the right or left to make the top of the box bigger or smaller than the bottom of the box. Making the top of the box bigger than the bottom will result in the top of the object appearing closer than the bottom. A smaller top will make the top of the object appear farther away. When the top of the box is the desired size, press ENTER. Draw Partner will redraw the object with the specified perspective. Depending on the complexity of the object and the speed of your computer, this redraw may take up to a minute or so.

Once you have added perspective to an object, you may either select another object to add perspective to, press BACKSPACE to undo the previously applied perspective, or press ESC to return to the Modify menu. Examples of objects to which perspective was added are shown in Figure 18-31.

*Note:* You cannot add perspective to text, buttons, or any groups that contain text or buttons. If you want to add perspective to text, you must first convert it to a group of polygons. Likewise, if you add perspective to a box or line, the resulting object will automatically be converted to a polygon.

### Aligning Objects

Draw Partner provides you with a convenient method for aligning objects within the drawing area. You can align a number of objects either

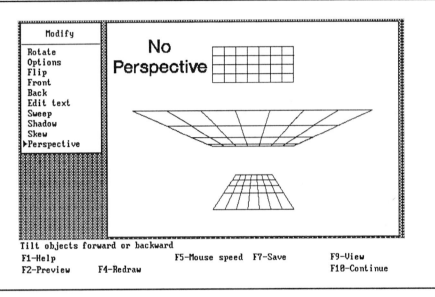

**Figure 18-31.** Examples of objects with perspective applied

horizontally, vertically, or both horizontally and vertically, with respect to another object in the drawing area.

*Note:* Do not confuse this alignment feature with the ability to align points within a single object. See "Aligning Points in a Polyline or Shape" later in this chapter for information on the latter.

To align objects in the drawing area, select <Align> from the Draw Partner Main Menu. Draw Partner will display the message "Select an object to use to line up other objects, Esc—menu." Select an object to be used as a reference object. Once you select this object, Draw Partner displays the Align menu, shown in Figure 18-32. The positions listed on the Align menu determine how objects are aligned with the reference object. Select the desired alignment, or press ESC to cancel and reselect the reference object.

If you select <Center point>, any selected item will be directly centered on the reference object—in other words, aligned both horizontally and vertically with respect to the reference object. If you select <Top>, any selected item will be moved so that its top is aligned

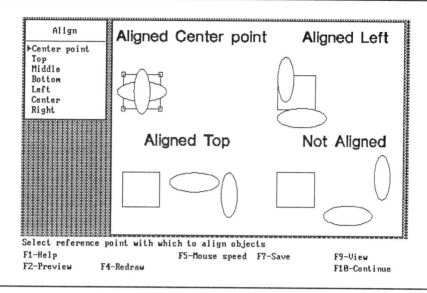

**Figure 18-32.** Align menu and aligned objects

vertically with the top of the reference object. The horizontal position of the object will not change. The <Middle> and <Bottom> options result in alignment of the middle or bottom of the selected object with the middle or bottom of the reference object. The horizontal position of the object will not be affected.

If you select <Left>, the left side of the selected object is aligned with the left side of the reference object. The object is moved horizontally and its vertical position is not affected. Likewise, <Center> and <Right> result in the object being centered or right-aligned with the center or right side of the reference object, respectively. Selecting <Center> and <Right> will not affect the vertical position of the aligned object.

Once you select the desired alignment, Draw Partner prompts you to select an object to align. When you select an object, Draw Partner moves the object into the selected position. If you want to restore the object to its original position, press BACKSPACE. Continue to select objects to align to the reference object. When you are through aligning objects, press ESC. Draw Partner will prompt you to select another reference object, or press ESC to return to the Draw Partner Main Menu.

Figure 18-32 displays some different alignment settings. The square is the reference object and the two ellipses are aligned with respect to the square.

## Editing Polylines and Shapes

All non-text objects consist of two or more points. The location of the points in these objects define their size and shape. When you create a polyline, line, or polygon, you explicitly place these points each time you press ENTER. When you create a box, line, circle, arc, or wedge, the size of the object defines where Draw Partner places the points. With regular polygons, the number of sides determines the number of points and the size determines their placement. Finally, when you draw a freehand object, Draw Partner places a point each time the cursor changes direction.

*Note:* For the remainder of this discussion, all non-text objects are categorized as either polylines or shapes. Polylines, arcs, and freehand drawings are all forms of *polylines*, whereas boxes, lines, circles, polygons, wedges, and regular polygons are referred to as *shapes*.

Draw Partner provides you with four tools for modifying points in objects. These tools allow you to add, delete, and move points, and align points with another point in the same object. It also provides you with tools that permit more fundamental changes to objects. These tools allow you to change a shape into a polyline, to convert a polyline into a polygon, and to add two polylines together to make a new, larger polyline. A final tool provided by Draw Partner permits you to convert text (regular or circular) into a group of polygons. This conversion tool also permits you to convert lines and boxes to polygons.

Taken together, these editing tools allow you to create an infinite number of variations of objects. All of these editing tools are available from the Point edit menu.

## Drawing and Editing with Draw Partner

The Point edit menu is displayed when you select <Point edit> from the Draw Partner Main Menu. Following is a brief list of some of the uses of Draw Partner's point editing features:

• You can connect two short polylines together to form a longer polyline.

• You can break a polyline, forming two smaller polylines. These individual polylines can then be moved to separate areas of the drawing area.

• You can convert a polyline into a polygon in order to fill it with a color or pattern.

• You can add a point to a rectangle to create a pentagon, or you can delete a point to create a triangle.

• You can move several points in a circle to create a more interesting shape.

• You can convert a circle into a polyline, join this polyline to another polyline, and then convert the new polyline back into a polygon to create a unique shape.

• You can convert text to polygons and then make unique modifications to the font by adding points to each character.

These features are covered in the sections that follow.

## Adding Points to a Polyline or Shape

To add one or more points to a polyline or shape, select <Add> from the Point edit menu. Draw Partner will display the message "Select a polyline or shape to add points to, Esc—menu." Once you select the object, Draw Partner will ask you to indicate where you want to add the new point. A small diamond-shaped cursor will be displayed on the outline of the polyline or shape. This diamond is placed between two consecutive points on the object, as shown in Figure 18-33. You can add a point at this location, or you can move the cursor to select a location between any other two consecutive points. As you move the cursor, Draw Partner displays the diamond at different locations around the object. It is always, however, between the two consecutive points closest to the cursor.

When the diamond is located where you want to add a point, press ENTER. Draw Partner will then display lines connecting the point you are adding with the two points on either side. Next move the cursor to the position where you want to place the new point (anywhere in the drawing area) and press ENTER. Once you press ENTER, Draw Partner

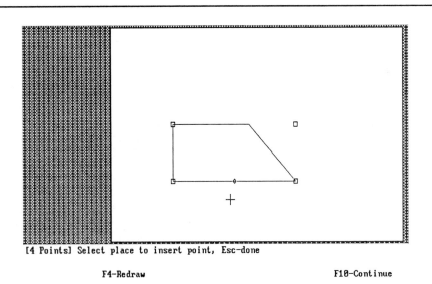

**Figure 18-33.** Small diamond cursor displayed between two consecutive points on the object

adds this point to the object and updates the image of the object in the drawing area. Figure 18-34 displays the object shown in Figure 18-33 with the new point added.

You can continue to add points to this object, as desired. While you are adding points, you can cancel the placement of the last added point by pressing BACKSPACE. Subsequent presses of BACKSPACE will continue to erase any added points in the reverse order in which you added them.

When you are through adding points to your object, press ESC once. Draw Partner will give you three options. You can select another object to add points to, press BACKSPACE to start deleting points added to the previous object, or you can press ESC once more to return to the Point edit menu. If you select another object or return to the Point edit menu, you will not be able to undo points added to the previous object. (You can, however, use the <Delete> selection from the Point edit menu to remove any points from an object, as described in "Deleting Points from a Polyline or Shape.")

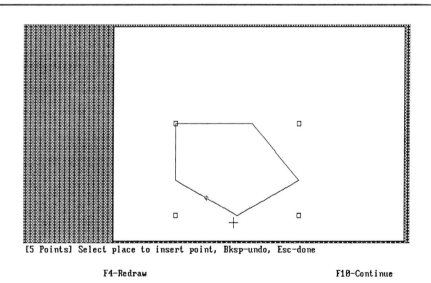

**Figure 18-34.** Object shown in Figure 18-33 with the new point added

## Moving Points in a Polyline or Shape

To move an existing point of a polyline or shape, select <Move> from the Point edit menu. Draw Partner will display the message "Select an object to move points of, Esc—menu." When you select the object, Draw Partner will draw object handles around it and display a diamond (representing the cursor position) at the existing point closest to the cursor. If the object is a straight line or a box, the diamond may be obscured by the nearest object handle. Move the cursor, if necessary, until the diamond identifies the point you want to move and press ENTER. Next, move the cursor to the location where you want to move this point and press ENTER.

To move another point in the object, move the cursor until the diamond identifies the point and press ENTER to select it. Then move this point to the desired location and press ENTER again. When you are through moving points, press ESC. You can restore the previously moved point by pressing BACKSPACE. Additional presses of BACKSPACE will restore the original position of previously moved points, in reverse order.

Once you are finished moving points for a given object, you have three options. You can select another object and move its points, you can press BACKSPACE once to cancel *all* point movements made to the previous object, or you can press ESC to return to the Point edit menu. Once you select another object or return to the Point edit menu, you will not be able to use BACKSPACE to cancel the changes made to the previous object.

## Deleting Points from a Polyline or Shape

You can delete points from any polyline or shape that contains three or more points. To delete an existing point from an object, select <Delete> from the Point edit menu. Draw Partner will display the message "Select an object to delete points from, Esc—menu." Once you select an object, Draw Partner will enclose the object in object handles and place a diamond at the point on the object nearest the cursor. Move the cursor until the diamond is positioned at the point you want to delete. Press ENTER to delete the point. Continue to delete points as desired. If you want to restore the last point you deleted, press BACKSPACE. If you have deleted more than one point from the current object, you can continue to restore points by pressing BACKSPACE repeatedly. When you are finished deleting points, press ESC.

Figure 18-35 shows three drawings that reflect the various stages of deleting a point. The first drawing shows the original object, a rectangle. The second drawing shows the point at the upper-right corner selected for deletion. The third drawing shows the object once the point has been deleted.

When you have finished deleting points by pressing ESC, you have three choices. You can select another object, you can press ESC to return to the Point edit menu, or you can press BACKSPACE to restore points deleted from the previous object. If you press BACKSPACE, the previous object will become selected again and the last deleted point will be restored. You can continue to restore points by pressing BACKSPACE repeatedly. You cannot restore deleted points once you either select another object to delete points from or return to the Point edit menu.

## Breaking a Polyline or Shape

You can turn any shape into a polyline by *breaking* it. This feature can also be used to divide a polyline into two or more smaller polylines. You

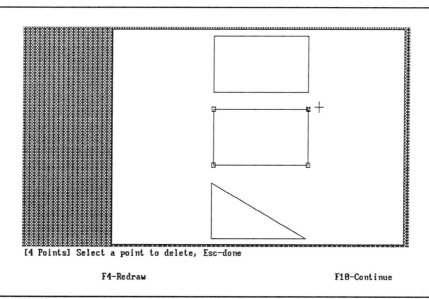

**Figure 18-35.**   Stages of deleting a point

can later move the ends of these lines (using the <Move> point editing feature described in "Moving Points in a Polyline or Shape") to create unique shapes.

To break a polyline or shape, select <Break> from the Point edit menu. Draw Partner will prompt you to select a point on the object at which to break it. Move the cursor until the diamond appears where you want to break the object and press ENTER. At this point, the object is broken at the point you indicated, although it will appear to be joined since the ends still touch. (If you do not want them to touch you can later move them.)

Once you press ENTER to break an object, you have three alternatives. You can select another polyline or shape to break, press ESC to return to the Point edit menu, or press BACKSPACE to restore the last broken object. However, you cannot restore a break in the object once you either select a new object to break or return to the Point edit menu.

When you break a polyline, Draw Partner will add an additional point at the break. This point represents the first point of the new polyline, while the existing point represents the endpoint of the other polyline.

Similarly when you break a shape, Draw Partner will add an additional point at the break. This point represents the first point of the new polyline. The other point represents the endpoint of the polyline. If the shape has a fill color or fill pattern, this fill will be removed since polylines do not have centers.

## Combining Two Polylines

You can create a single polyline out of two polylines as long as the new polyline will not exceed the 200-point maximum. To combine polylines, select <Join> from the Point edit menu. Draw Partner will display the message "Select a polyline to combine, Esc—menu."

Once you select the first polyline you want to join, Draw Partner will display the Join menu with its two options, <Start point> and <End point>. Select one of these options to indicate which point, starting or ending, you will use to combine this polyline with another. If you select <Start point>, a diamond will appear at the starting point of the selected polyline. If you select <End point>, a diamond will appear at the last point of the polyline.

Draw Partner will then display the message "Select next polyline to combine, Bksp—undo, Esc—done." You can press BACKSPACE to start over and select the first polyline to combine again. When you select the second polyline to join to the first polyline, Draw Partner will display the Join menu for the second polyline with two options: <Nearest> and <Farthest>. Select the point on the second polyline to join to the first polyline. By default, <Nearest> is highlighted on this Join menu, and Draw Partner has already drawn a line from the nearest point on the second polyline to the selected point on the first polyline (as shown in the example on the right in Figure 18-36). If you move the cursor to highlight the <Farthest> option on the Join menu, Draw Partner will connect the selected point on the first polyline with the farthest end of the newly selected polyline. Select the connection you want to make and press ENTER. Draw Partner joins these two polylines at the two selected points, as shown in Figure 18-37.

You can then connect another polyline to your newly formed polyline by selecting another polyline to join. If you do so, you will again be

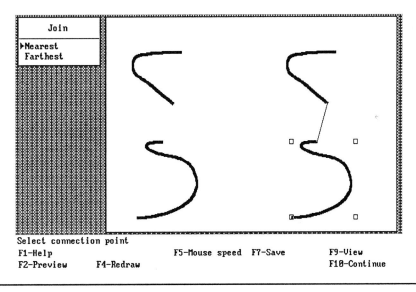

**Figure 18-36.** Original polylines at the left; at right, the nearest point of the second polyline is selected to join endpoint of the first polyline

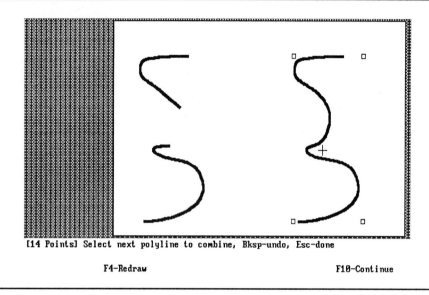

**Figure 18-37.**  Resulting polyline from operation in Figure 18-36

asked to define which point, <Nearest> or <Farthest>, you want to connect to the end of the newly formed polyline. To undo the previous join, press BACKSPACE to reselect a polyline to join to the first polyline. When you are finished joining polylines, press ESC to return to the Point edit menu.

## Converting a Polyline to a Shape

Any polyline can be converted into a polygon by selecting <Close> from the Point Edit menu. Draw Partner will display the message "Select a polyline to convert, Esc—menu." When you select a polyline, Draw Partner will connect the first point in the polyline to the last point and fill in the center of this newly formed polygon with a solid pattern using the same color as defined for the outline color. If you close a curved polyline, the curves between points will be converted to straight lines since polygons do not support curved lines.

You can cancel this conversion by pressing BACKSPACE, or you can select another polyline to convert. When you are finished converting polylines into polygons, press ESC.

## Aligning Points in a Polyline or Shape

You can align points in a polyline or shape with respect to one point in that same polyline or shape. To do this, select <Align> from the Point edit menu. Draw Partner will display the message "Select a polyline or shape to straighten, Esc—menu." When you select a polyline, Draw Partner will display the message "Select a reference point, Esc—cancel." Move the cursor until the diamond indicator is located at the point on the object with which you want to align other points. Then press ENTER.

Draw Partner will then prompt you to indicate whether you want to align objects horizontally or vertically to the reference point. If you want to move other points to the same horizontal plane as the reference point, select <Horizontal>. Select <Vertical> to move other points to the same vertical plane as the reference point. Once you have selected <Horizontal> or <Vertical>, move the cursor to each point you want to align to the reference point and press ENTER. As you do so, Draw Partner will move the point, placing it in the proper alignment. Figure 18-38, for example, shows an original object shape. Figure 18-39 shows

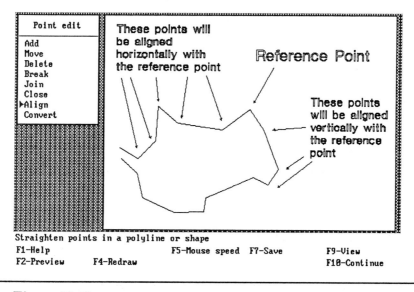

**Figure 18-38.**   Original object

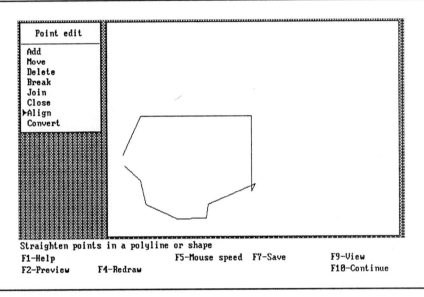

**Figure 18-39.**  Object with points aligned horizontally and vertically to the reference point, as indicated in Figure 18-38

how the object appears once horizontal and vertical alignments to the reference point are performed.

While you are aligning points, you can cancel the alignment of the last-aligned point by pressing BACKSPACE. If you have aligned more than one point, you can restore the object to its original form by pressing BACKSPACE once more. When you are through aligning points, press ESC. You can then select another object within which to align points, press BACKSPACE to restore *all* points in the previous object to their original position, or press ESC once more to return to the Point edit menu.

## Converting Text, Lines, or Boxes to Polygons

Any text (regular or circular) can be converted to a group of polygons. When you convert text to a group, each character is converted to a polygon and these polygons are grouped together. You can then manipulate the group or ungroup it and manipulate the individual polygons.

Once the text is converted, however, you will not be able to edit the text using the <Edit text> selection from the Modify menu. Therefore, before you convert text, make sure it is correct. An example of text converted to polygons is shown in Figure 18-40.

To convert text to a group of polygons, select <Point edit> from the Draw Partner Main Menu followed by <Convert text> from the Point edit menu. Draw Partner will display the message "Select text, line or boxes to convert, Esc—menu." Once you select the text, Draw Partner will convert it to a group of polygons. If the text employed a drop shadow effect, the shadow will be represented by a second set of grouped polygons, located behind the first set.

Once you have converted a text object, you can select more text to convert, press BACKSPACE to restore the previously converted text object, or press ESC to return to the Point edit menu. You will not be able to restore a converted text object once you either select new text to convert or return to the Point edit menu. If you want to make changes to the individual polygons, in converted text, you must first ungroup the polygons, as described in the earlier section "Ungrouping Objects."

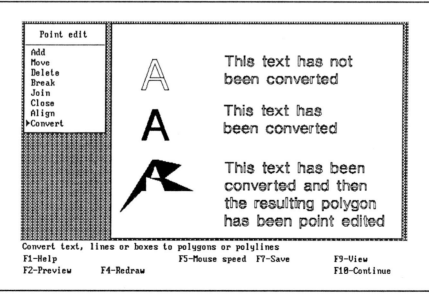

**Figure 18-40.**  Text before and after conversion to polygons

Converting lines or boxes to polygons involves the same steps. When you convert a line object, a single polygon results. When you convert a box that has special features such as a shadow box or a page box, the resulting object is a group of polygons. When either lines or boxes are converted to polygons, these objects lose their original status. For example, once a box is converted, it can be rotated in a sweep, which a box object cannot. Likewise, a line can be sized, skewed, and stretched without maintaining the line-to-arrow proportions required for line objects.

# Part Four: Effective Presentation Graphics

**Effective Data Charts**
**Advanced Data Topics**
**Effective Text and Organization Charts**
**Common Charting Mistakes**
**Using Charts in Presentations and Documents**

# Effective Data Charts

What Is a Chart?
Charts and Data
Data Chart Elements
Types of Data Charts
Guidelines for Creating Data Charts

This chapter introduces you to the principles of data chart design. It defines the elements that make up a chart and describes many of the chart styles you might consider using for reports, presentations, or slide shows, or for the purpose of examining and analyzing data. These topics will familiarize you with concepts you need to select the chart that will best communicate your points and ideas to others.

Text charts and organization charts are treated separately from data charts. See Chapter 21, "Effective Text and Organization Charts," for information concerning these chart styles.

## What Is a Chart?

A chart is a visual representation of data. The data are represented by symbols, such as bars in a bar chart, lines in a line chart, or wedges in a pie chart. By depicting these data as graphical symbols, patterns or trends in the data can be more easily identified.

Data charts are often called *graphs*. All graphs are charts; however, not all charts are graphs. A chart is a graph when the chart depicts data represented as symbols. For instance, a bar chart is a graph just as a pie chart is a graph. Conversely, a table of numbers, although a chart, is not a graph, since it does not use symbols. Instead, the table shows the actual data values. A text chart is another type of chart that is not a graph. Throughout this book, whenever you see a reference to a *data chart*, the word *graph* could just as well have been used.

Charts should be created so viewers can understand and interpret them with a minimum of effort. The ultimate goal of your chart production is to communicate information about the data to chart viewers—including yourself. For example, you may create charts for your own use to assist you in analyzing relationships in data. Charts are a useful tool to help both you and other viewers analyze data and discover trends and relationships within the charted numbers.

## When to Use a Data Chart

Above all, a chart should be used when it will permit you to communicate your data, ideas, or points more clearly. It is not always appropriate to convey this information using a data chart.

Data charts permit chart viewers to analyze relationships among the data as well as discover trends in the data. These two purposes are nearly always the goals of chart use. For instance, when you create a bar chart, your goal may be to find the tallest bar, or the shortest bar, or the difference between the tallest and the shortest bars. In this case, you are interested in the relative height (the relationship) of the bars.

Trends, on the other hand, are the patterns in data represented over time. Trends can also show a relationship to something other than time, but like time, it is always something that is changing at a predictable rate. For example, are the prices of raw materials going up or are they stable? Is the efficiency of a production process improving or declining? Does a chemical reaction generate more or less heat as more of a particular chemical is added? Chart producers usually use line charts, point charts, or area charts to display trend information since these styles make trends readily apparent.

Another useful feature of data charts is that they allow viewers to explore the data. It is not uncommon for data to be rich in content, that is, many conclusions can often be derived from the information presented in a single chart. By placing these data in a data chart, you can permit chart viewers to explore the data, providing much more opportunity for interpretation than a simple verbal description could offer.

Another important advantage of data charts is that they permit you to display a large amount of information within a small space. For example, Harvard Graphics can chart data points for up to 1,920 numbers on a single chart (eight series times 240 X-data values). Even when your *data set* (collection of data) is smaller than this, it may still require a good deal of space to display in a table. Furthermore, if you want to describe the intricate patterns or relationships in your data, it might require many pages in a report or be time-consuming to explain. By displaying the data in a chart, you allow viewers to see the patterns and relationships themselves.

## When to Avoid Using a Data Chart

While it is true that charts can break the monotony of a dull presentation or an otherwise ordinary report or document, a chart should not be included for this reason alone. It should add something else. Charts added gratuitously, where they serve no real purpose, are typically distracting and leave the audience wondering what you are attempting to say.

It is also best to avoid using a chart when another method of presentation would convey your ideas better. For example, when a verbal description of your data would be sufficient, presenting a chart that depicts this information may disrupt the flow of your presentation or report.

If precise numbers are important, you should present your data in the form of a table rather than a data chart. While data charts are ideal for displaying trends and relationships, they are no substitute for actual numbers when very small differences in the data are of critical importance. If both precise numbers and their patterns or trends are important, you will probably want to display both a data chart and a table of the data. Harvard Graphics can present both types of information through the use of a data table in XY charts. And with pie charts, you can display the data values alongside the pie itself.

One way to avoid the inappropriate use of charts is to consider alternative ways your ideas or data can be communicated. Among the most obvious alternatives is a simple verbal description either in writing within a report or document or as part of an oral presentation. Another alternative to a chart, when practical, is to provide a live demonstration. A demonstration of the actual effect you are trying to describe can leave a lasting impact on your audience because it provides them with firsthand evidence and experience with the subject matter.

## Charts and Data

Data charts are used to convey information about measurements that you or someone else has collected. Without these data, you have no chart. The chart itself is a tool for communicating information about the data. The data can come from any number of sources, for example, from a departmental memo or company report. The data might be calculated from a database, or might come from statistics in a journal or document. Or you may collect the information yourself using a survey or other data collection method.

Because the data are so important, the accuracy of your data should be considered before you create a chart. Inaccuracies can occur in a number of ways. Numbers may have been entered inaccurately, for instance. If you want to display the data in a chart that will be scrutinized for information, you must have data that are as free as possible of entry errors. Inaccuracies can also appear as a result of the techniques used to collect the numbers in the first place. The data must have been collected using methodologically sound data collection techniques. Unfortunately, errors in data collection are more common than you might think. If your data are opinions you collected by way of a survey, for example, the wording of the survey questions may have unintentionally biased the results. There is nothing worse than basing conclusions or making policy changes based on "facts" that are shaky or inaccurate.

If you suspect your data are inaccurate or misleading, it is unwise to graph these values. Whether it is your intention or not, a graph seems to have the power of legitimizing data. If you do graph suspect data, a footnote or annotation qualifying that data is an appropriate addition to your chart.

### Understanding Data

Throughout this book, the word *data* is used in the plural form. In recent years, it has become commonplace to see the word *data* used in the singular. This singular usage is fairly common when the discussion concerns computers. However, when data charts are discussed, *data* always refers to many numbers, hence the plural usage here.

One of the most common problems Harvard Graphics users face is deciding how their data fit the Harvard Graphics chart they want to create. Part of the confusion arises because data can often be charted several different ways, any one of which will result in an attractive chart. The style you choose, as well as the data you select to display along the X axis (for XY charts), will determine how your chart is perceived and how effectively the message you want to communicate is conveyed.

The first step toward understanding what type of chart you should use is understanding what type of data you have. At the very least, your data can always be divided into two parts. The first is a definition of what was measured. The second part is the measurement itself, that is, the actual number. In Harvard Graphics terms, the first part of your data is the X axis value (for XY charts) or pie label (for pie charts) that defines what you are measuring. Your actual measurements are the series values. These series values are sometimes referred to as *Y data*, since they are charted with respect to the Y axis in XY charts.

Your series data are *always* numbers. These numbers reflect counts, percentages, averages, amounts, weights, heights, lengths, durations, or some other like measurement. When your data consist of measurements and labels of the things that were measured, you can be assured that the labels are your X data (or pie labels) and the measurements are your series data. If you have two or more measurements for each label, you have two or more series. You can enter each of these measurements into a different series for an XY chart and thus create additional lines in a line chart, additional areas in an area chart, or multiple bars at each X data value in a bar chart. If you are creating pie charts, each extra series can be used to create an additional pie chart.

Which chart styles are most appropriate for your data and how you prepare the data for a particular chart style depend on the characteristics of your X data. For ease of discussion, assume three types of X data: those that are *categories,* those that represent *ordered series,* and those that are themselves *measurements*. These data types, as well as the types of charts appropriate for the different data types, are described next.

## Category Data

When your X data are categories, the X data values are simply names or definitions for the things you measured. For example, if your data set consists of the number of people who work in each of the five departments in your company, your X data would be considered categorical. In this example, the departments are the X data and the numbers of people in each department are the series data. The names of the departments are, thus, categories. With categorical data, X data values do not have a natural order; it may make just as much sense to sort the departments alphabetically as it would by department size or according to the hierarchical structure of the overall organization.

When your X data are categorical, you create data charts in order to compare the series data. For example, you could create a pie chart to compare the proportion of the total staff each department in your company employs. Alternatively, a simple bar chart could be used to chart the actual numbers instead of the percentages reflected in the pie chart.

Some types of charts are not appropriate with categorical X data. For example, it would make no sense to chart the department sizes using a line or area chart. Line charts and area charts are used to represent trends, and departmental names and employee counts do not naturally contain trend information.

## Ordered Data

Another type of X data you have probably encountered consists of an ordered series of values. These X data are often called *continuous X data* because they lie on a continuum. The X data are then divided into equal and meaningful categories. Because the X data are continuous, these categories have a natural order that cannot be altered. For example, if you are interested in the production output of a factory, you might measure the number of units produced every month for a year. In this case, your X data would consist of month names, January to December. Unlike categorical data, the months have a real order to them. Since July 1990 immediately precedes August 1990 it would be displayed this way along the X axis. Other examples of ordered X data include times of day, days of the week, fiscal years, and age groups. These data define the intervals or durations during which the measurements are made.

When your X data belong to an ordered series, it is possible to examine trends in the data. For example, after collecting your factory production data, you can use it to determine whether production output increased, decreased, or remained constant over the course of a year. In this instance, a line chart or area chart would be an appropriate chart style. The fluctuations in the line or area on the chart would permit you to determine the production output level for a particular month, as well as the overall change in production output over a one-year period.

It is also possible to use ordered data in bar charts, although this chart style does not emphasize trends in data as effectively as do line charts or area charts. While it is possible to create a pie chart with these data, it almost never makes any sense to do so. Pie charts reveal relative contributions of individual pie slices to the whole. Trend information is almost entirely lost when a pie chart is used.

### Measurements of Co-Occurrence

In some instances, the distinction between the measurement and what was measured is not appropriate. In these cases, your data consist of two sets of measurements, that is, two sets of numbers. For example, consider a data set consisting of measurements of daily rainfall amounts and daily temperatures in various cities. Both of these are numbers, since they both consist of measurements, rainfall amounts, and temperatures. In this case, you are interested in the relationship between the amount of rainfall and the temperature.

In situations like these, in Harvard Graphics the X data type is Number and you can use either of the measurements as your X data values. Because your X data are measurements themselves, you are restricted in the type of charts you can create with these data. The most common chart used for two sets of measurements is a point chart, which is described later in this chapter.

### Data with Multiple Series

Sometimes your data consist of more than two series values for each X data value. For instance, you may have monthly production output numbers for two or more different factories. When this situation arises, you can use additional series to display the production data for the different factories. These additional series could be displayed as additional lines in a line chart, a cluster of bars for each month in a bar chart, or additional areas in an area chart.

This same situation can occur when the X data are categorical. For example, if you have production output numbers for the day shift, night shift, and swing shift (your X data values), you may want to display these data for two or more different factories. In these instances you can use pie charts, with one pie chart per factory, or bar charts in which the different factories are shown as a cluster of bars for each of the three shifts.

Sometimes, the distinction between what constitutes X data values and the category represented by the additional series is blurred. Figure 19-1 shows an example of how the same data can be charted in two different ways. Depending on the point you want to make, you could display the same data using years or the type of fruit as X data values. In the chart on the top, the X data are years. In this chart you can compare the consumption of different fruits for each of the years. In the chart on the bottom, the type of fruit is depicted along the X axis. In this chart you can compare the consumption of a particular type of fruit over the years.

When your data are such that you are not sure which comparison you want to make, consider whether you want to emphasize the comparison of apples to oranges (top chart in Figure 19-1), or apples to apples (bottom chart). Either of the comparisons may be appropriate for your data. Harvard Graphics does impose restrictions on the number of series per chart, however, which may influence your decision. For example, if there had been more than eight years in the data set, it would not have been possible to show the different years as different series since Harvard Graphics permits only a maximum of eight series per chart. (The only solution to the eight-series limit would be to save the chart as a symbol and then modify it and add additional series in Draw/Annotate.)

Sometimes you have two different types of measurements for each X data value. For example, you can calculate monthly production output for a factory as well as the average cost per unit produced. Likewise, you can calculate the average salary for the employees within each department in a company, and also count the number of employees within each department. In both of these situations, you have two

Effective Data Charts  633

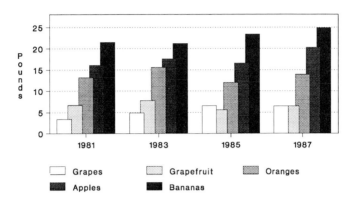

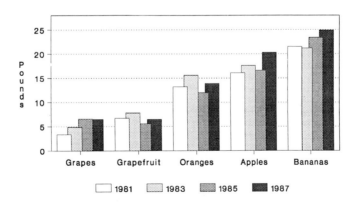

**Figure 19-1.** Example of how the same data can be charted in two different ways

different units of measurement, both relating to the same X data value. Data like these can be displayed either in two separate charts or in one dual-axis XY chart. For example, you may want to use one chart to show average salaries by department and another chart to show the number of employees per department. If you use a dual axis XY chart, however, you can display average salaries with respect to the Y1 axis and number of employees with respect to the Y2 axis.

## Data Chart Elements

The remainder of this chapter defines the graphical elements that make up a data chart, and follows with a discussion of the wide variety of data charts available in Harvard Graphics. These discussions are intended to make you a better chart producer and Harvard Graphics user. As such, the terms defined and the charts described are consistent with those used in Harvard Graphics. Most of this terminology is generic; you can find the terms in any comprehensive book on chart design or graph theory.

If you are not familiar with charting concepts, you may find it useful to refer back and forth between this section, "Data Chart Elements," in which the elements of all types of data charts are described, and the section later in the chapter, "Types of Data Charts," in which the different types of charts are described.

### Titles and Subtitles

A title provides a brief description of the topic, content, or purpose of a chart. It essentially introduces the information the chart contains and can influence how viewers perceive the chart. It is almost always desirable to use a title. Harvard Graphics places the title at the top of a chart. You can choose to center, left-justify, or right-justify the title, although a centered title usually looks the best.

A subtitle is a secondary description that appears directly below the title. A subtitle is used to clarify the information provided in the title. A subtitle may actually be shorter than the title, but does not have to be.

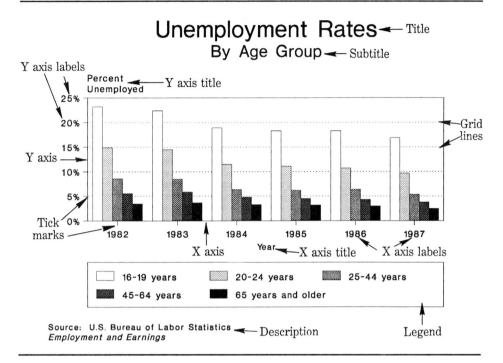

**Figure 19-2.**     Chart elements

For example, you may describe the chart using a title, and use a subtitle to display the date of the chart data. An example of a title and subtitle are shown in Figure 19-2.

The following are a few tips on creating good chart titles:

- A chart title should be brief and succinct.

- A title is usually descriptive in nature only, and does not draw any conclusions or convey an opinion about the data presented in the chart.

- A title should accurately represent the data presented in the chart.

- You may not need a subtitle for your chart. If you can convey the topic, content, or purpose of your chart with the title alone, do not use a subtitle.

- If you want to place a chart title below the chart rather than above it (this may be desirable when you are creating a multiple chart, in which a number of charts are displayed on one screen or page), you can do this in Harvard Graphics by entering this title at the "Footnote" option for the chart. You can then adjust the text size and placement so it looks like a title. In this situation, do not enter text at the "Title" and "Subtitle" options.

## Descriptions

A description contains information in addition to title and subtitle to tell viewers what the chart depicts. Descriptions can be particularly helpful when they further define the quantities or measurements (percentages or counts, for example) and the X data depicted in the chart. Descriptions often indicate the source of the data shown in the chart (as shown in Figure 19-2). If you are using a chart to analyze data for your own needs, you may want to include the date on which the chart was created in a description.

In Harvard Graphics, you enter a description at the "Footnote" option for your XY chart. Harvard Graphics places this footnote below the chart image and left-justifies it by default. You can choose to center or right-justify the footnote.

The following are a few tips on creating good chart descriptions:

- Charts used in reports and presentations usually contain descriptions.

- It is perfectly acceptable to use phrases rather than complete sentences in a description, as long as the essential information is conveyed.

- When possible, descriptions should be no longer than one sentence in length.

- Descriptions can contain information about unique or unusual characteristics of the chart or data. For example, if you performed some kind of data transformation, you should point this out in the description.

## Axes and Axis Titles

The axes on a chart are the vertical and horizontal lines of the chart frame. They show the scale of the data plotted on the chart for all XY chart styles. There are no axes in pie charts.

Every XY chart has at least two axes: X and Y. These axes are shown in Figure 19-2. Usually, the X axis is displayed horizontally, along the bottom of the chart frame, and the Y axis is displayed vertically, along the left side. You can turn the chart on its side, however, to create what is referred to as a *horizontal chart*.

The X axis depicts the scale of continuous X data or the domain for categorical X data. When an X axis scale is numerical, it depicts an ordered series of quantities: counts, times, dates, dollars, or other similar data. If your data are of the type Name (department names or states, for example), then they represent categories and do not represent a numerical scale.

When categories are depicted, the selected categories represent the *domain* of the X axis. The domain refers to the set of selected categories drawn from the set of all possible categories, referred to as the *universe*. The universe of your X axis defines what type of categorical X data your chart contains, while the domain represents selected instances. For example, you may choose to display a selected set of U.S. states on your chart. The states you select define your X axis domain, while the universe consists of all 50 states.

The Y axis depicts the scale for the Y data. This scale is always numerical, without exception, and shows the measurements for the corresponding X data. In most XY charts, you will see the Y axis on the left side of the chart frame. You can place this axis at the right side of your chart in Harvard Graphics, if you feel that it looks better for your chart. XY charts use two Y axes when two or more series contain two different types of measurements; for instance, you can chart both production numbers and production costs in one chart. In this case, the Y axes are typically referred to as the *Y1 axis* and the *Y2 axis* for the axes on the left and right side of the chart, respectively. (If you create a horizontal chart, thereby turning the chart on its side, the Y1 axis will be at the top of the chart and the Y2 axis will be at the bottom.)

The X and Y axis titles are usually one- or two-word descriptions of the corresponding axis, as shown in Figure 19-2. When you provide an X axis title for your chart, Harvard Graphics automatically centers this title below the X axis. You cannot change this placement. The Y axis titles can be placed either horizontally at the very top of the chart frame, next to the Y axis, or vertically along the Y axis.

The following are tips for chart axes and titles:

- The range selected for an axis that depicts numerical data should be slightly larger than the range (lowest to highest values) of the data shown on the chart. Fortunately, Harvard Graphics does a good job of selecting a range for you, although you can define the range yourself if you desire.

- An X axis should have a title if the X data shown at the tick marks on the chart needs further explanation. For example, if your X data are the 12 consecutive months, January through December, you may not want to provide an X axis title (although you might want to further define your X data by displaying the year as an X axis title). If your X data are the numbers 1 through 10, however, an axis title that defines your X data for viewers may be essential.

- Each Y axis should have a title that indicates the unit of measurement—dollars, percentages, units, or temperatures, for example.

- If your data consist of very small or very large numbers, Harvard Graphics will automatically transform the numbers. If it does so, it will also automatically provide a title for the axis that reflects this transformation, such as Thousands or Millions. You may want to change the title Harvard Graphics provides so that it more accurately describes the axis. Examples you may want to use

Dollars (in thousands)
Units Produced (in millions)

## Axis Labels

Axis labels are short descriptors that appear at intervals along each axis (see Figure 19-2). In Harvard Graphics, the X data you enter for your chart are used for the X axis labels, entry for entry, unless your X data are of the type Number. If your X data type is Number, Harvard Graphics will automatically select X data labels for you. The X axis labels are evenly spaced along the X axis and will be centered under the X axis tick marks, if tick marks are used. You can choose to display labels horizontally along the X axis, and add a percent sign (%) if your X data are percentages. You can also display the labels vertically, which is particularly useful if they become crowded when displayed horizontally.

The labels displayed along the Y axis are always numbers. Harvard Graphics selects these labels by default, based on the range it has selected for the Y axis. Harvard Graphics usually does a good job of selecting both a range for your axis and an adequate number of axis labels, although you should always inspect the axis and make adjustments as necessary. You can specify both the range and the number of labels to display (refer to Chapter 6, "XY Charts"). You can also display a dollar sign ($) before each label or a percent sign (%) after each label.

## Data Tables and Data Labels

You may want to display the actual values of your series data on your XY or pie chart. For pie charts, you can display both the values and the percentage each value represents of the whole pie. You can specify the placement of these data to be either adjacent to, below, or within each pie slice.

For XY charts, you can display the values of your series data next to the symbol that represents the data. You can display all of the Y data values (Harvard Graphics refers to these as *Y data labels*) or only selected ones. Harvard Graphics provides a second method of displaying Y data in XY charts. Specifically, you can display a small table of your X data and series data directly beneath the chart image.

The following are a few tips on displaying data on your chart:

- Do not display data either in a data table or next to the symbols unless you feel that it is important that viewers have access to the actual numbers charted.

- In Harvard Graphics, a data table will take up some of the available chart space—how much depends on the amount of data in the table. This may affect the legibility of text elements in your chart.

- Do not display Y data labels on your chart if it makes the chart cluttered or if the labels overlap one another. This can happen when you have many data values in your data set. Try using a data table instead.

- If you display data within the pie slices, the data should be distinguishable against the colors, shades, or patterns used for the slices. If any of the data labels are not legible, place them outside the slice or create a separate text chart that displays the data. If you definitely want data labels within the pie slices, you can try using different colors, shades, or patterns.

## Tick Marks

Tick marks are the small lines on the X and Y axes, as shown in Figure 19-2. These marks serve as a reference for the data values, much as the marks on a ruler help you identify a measurement. Tick marks can be placed inside, outside, or overlapping the chart frame. Or you can suppress the display of tick marks. You will need to experiment to determine which style best suits your chart.

The following are a few tips for using tick marks:

- Y axis tick marks should (almost) always be used.

- X axis tick marks should (almost) always be used in line charts and point charts.

- The use of X axis tick marks in bar charts is optional, depending on your preference.

- If you use grid lines, either do not use tick marks or have them extend out from the chart frame.

## Grid Lines

Grid lines are rules displayed within the chart frame in XY charts (see Figure 19-2). Grid lines originate from the data labels (and tick marks, if used), extending perpendicularly from the axes. These lines serve the same purpose as tick marks. Specifically, they assist chart viewers in determining or estimating data values.

The following are a few tips on using grid lines:

- Y axis grid lines can be used for any XY chart type.

- X axis grid lines are uncommon in XY charts. They are usually not appropriate for bar charts. They can be used with area charts or line charts, but typically are not.

- X axis grid lines in point charts can help viewers identify the X data values.

- Grid lines should not dominate a chart. They should be a part of the background, lighter in shade and thinner than lines, points, bars, or areas on the chart.

- Dotted grid lines are preferable to solid ones.

- Grid lines should be used sparingly. A thick mesh of grid lines can obscure the data presented.

- You do not need grid lines if tick marks are adequate or if determining or estimating the specific data values is not relevant.

## Line Styles and Point Markers

When you are creating a line chart or a point chart, it is important that the different lines or point markers clearly identify the different series depicted on your chart. Harvard Graphics provides four different line styles you can use to distinguish one series from another in a line chart (see "Line Styles" in Appendix D). If you have more than four series, you will need to use some of the line styles twice.

There are 12 markers that can be used to represent points in line charts and point charts (see "Markers" in Appendix D). Since you can only display eight series of data on your chart, these 12 markers are sufficient for most charting needs.

The following are tips on using line styles and point markers:

- Do not be afraid to experiment with different line style or point marker combinations. Some combinations will look better than others, depending on the characteristics of your data.

- When you have more than one series of data, it is preferable to use varied line styles and/or point markers to represent the different series rather than using only one style or marker.

- When you have more than four lines on your line chart, try to assign line styles to series so that the series using the same line style do not appear next to each other on the chart.

- It is often preferable to use different markers in addition to, or instead of, the different lines on your line chart. This is especially important when you have more than four series and, consequently, must duplicate one or more of the same line styles on your chart.

- On a line chart, you may want to use a single line style, usually the style Solid, and then vary the point markers to represent the different series. This can create an effective and attractive chart as long as the lines are not close or overlapping.

- Make certain you select point markers that are distinguishable from one another. You may need to output or display a sample of your chart in order to make this determination.

- If you are depicting a large number of data points on your point chart, use the simpler marker styles.

## Patterns and Shading

Effective use of patterns or shades in a chart can greatly enhance the visual quality of your chart when it is printed or plotted in black and white. Different patterns can be used to uniquely identify the specific symbol (area, bar, or pie slice) that represents each of the series in your chart. Alternatively, you can use shading (different shades of grey) to achieve the same purpose.

Harvard Graphics provides 12 patterns to choose from for your different series. Since you can include a maximum of eight series per chart, there are more than enough patterns to choose from for most charting needs. The shades in Harvard Graphics result when you print a color chart to a black and white printer. (In versions 2.13 and earlier, this is true only for PostScript printers.) The colors you indicate will define the shade of the symbols.

The following are tips on using shades and patterns in charts:

- Shading or patterns should contribute to a chart by assisting chart viewers to identify the different series. You may have to experiment with different shades or patterns to find the combination that looks best in your chart.

- The different shades or patterns used in your chart should be distinctive from one another so chart viewers can easily distinguish the series.

- It is best not to place extremely different shades or patterns directly beside one another.

- When a crosshatching pattern is used, a distracting visual interference effect, called the *moir effect*, can result. This can make the chart difficult to view and can even distort its appearance. This effect is described in Chapter 22, "Common Charting Mistakes."

- In bar or area charts in which the bars or areas are stacked vertically, darker patterns or shades should be used for segments at the bottom and lighter patterns or shades should be used for those segments at the top.

- Above all, shades or patterns should be used because they contribute to the chart—not simply because they are available.

## Colors

The effective use of color can greatly enhance the appearance of your chart when it is displayed on a color monitor, printed or plotted on a device that can produce color, or when you produce a slide of your chart using a film recorder. Color in a chart serves the same purpose as do patterns and shades—it provides chart viewers with a means of identifying the different series shown in a chart. Color can add texture to a chart and greatly enhance its subjective visual quality.

The following are a few tips on using color in charts:

- Keep in mind that more than four percent of the population has some form of color blindness. Thus color coding should not be the only means of distinguishing one series from another. The order in which symbols are arranged on a chart can be reflected by the order in which they appear in a legend to provide this duplicate information. Adding labels next to symbols is another way to help viewers distinguish series.

- The use of more than five to seven colors in a chart can be distracting, making the chart difficult to view and interpret.

- Although color can make a chart more attractive, some color combinations can be distracting. For example, colors that contrast sharply with one another, such as red and green, should not be used side by side.

- Examine colors used to distinguish different groups to see if they are so close in shade or pigment that they may lead to confusion.

- In bar or area charts in which the bars or areas are stacked vertically, use a darker color for segments at the bottom of the chart and a lighter color for those segments at the top.

- If you have any form of color blindness (or are simply not adept at matching and mixing colors), ask others to inspect your chart and give you suggestions on better color combinations before producing your final chart for display or output.

- Make sure the colored elements in your chart (title, chart frame, symbols, axis labels, and so on) are distinguishable from the background.

## Legends

When more than one series is present on a chart, they are distinguished from one another with a coding scheme. In Harvard Graphics, the coding schemes used are the different line styles in line charts, the marker styles in point charts, and the colors, shades, or patterns in the areas, bars, or pie slices of those chart styles. These coding schemes must be adequately labeled so that viewers can match the appropriate symbol characteristic (color or line, for example) with the series it represents.

In Harvard Graphics, a legend can be used in any XY chart to match the symbol characteristics with the corresponding series names (see Figure 19-2). The series names used in a legend are those you specify for the chart (or the default, Series 1, Series 2, and so on, if you do not specify your own names). A legend associates a label with the color, shade, pattern, line style, or point marker used to identify each series. The entire legend can be enclosed in a box or a box with a shadow.

The following are tips on using legends:

- If you choose to display a legend within the frame of your chart, inspect the chart to make sure the legend does not cover any of the symbols.

- It is a good idea to provide a title for your legend, although it is not always necessary if your series names are self explanatory (such as years).

- If you are displaying a data table in your XY chart, you can combine the legend with the table of data for an effective yet compact way of displaying both types of information.

## Fonts and Text Attributes

Fonts are collections of letters that share similar shapes. In Harvard Graphics versions 2.13 and earlier, there are six fonts available for use in your chart: Executive, Square serif, Roman, Sans serif, Script, and Gothic. Harvard Graphics 2.3 added a font, Traditional. Examples of these fonts are shown in "Fonts and Text Attributes" in Appendix D.

When you create a chart in Harvard Graphics, you can only use one font per chart. Although this may seem limiting, it is actually a good charting practice since using more than one font can make a chart look cluttered or gaudy. In version 2.3, you can use more than one font in either Draw/Annotate or Draw Partner. You can vary the appearance of text in a chart by modifying the attributes used for different text elements. There are five text attributes, which you can apply in any combination: Fill, Bold, Italic, Underline, and Color. For example, you may want your title to appear in boldface, your footnote to be italicized and underlined, and the remainder of the text to appear in a plain font (with no attributes defined). However, not all text attributes are available for every font.

The following are a few tips on using fonts and text attributes:

- Fonts with complex letters (Gothic, Roman, and Script fonts) are typically more difficult to read than less elaborate fonts (Executive, Sans serif, and Square serif). This is especially important when you are creating a text chart that contains a good deal of text. Keep in mind that you may need to use a larger text size with Gothic, Roman, and Script fonts to guarantee they are legible than you would with the other font types.

- The topic or content of a chart may render certain fonts inappropriate. For example, if you are charting sales figures for your high-tech company, you will probably not want to use a Gothic or Script font in your chart.

- In general, text using both upper- and lowercase letters is easier to read than text in all capital letters. All capitals can be used, if desired, for very short titles and labels.

- Avoid displaying more than about three different combinations of text attributes on a single chart. You should especially refrain from using a different text attribute for each text element (title, subtitle, labels, and so on).

## Text Sizes

The physical size of text can greatly affect your chart's overall appearance as well as the readability of the text. Using different sizes for different text elements is encouraged to the extent that it enhances the readability and appearance of your chart.

The size used for text elements in Harvard Graphics is a relative size. For example, it is almost impossible to create text that is exactly 1/2 inch tall on your first try. This is because the actual text size differs depending on the font, overall size of the chart (Full, 1/2, 1/3, or 1/4 size), as well as on whether you are printing on letter-size or wide paper, recording to film, or plotting on any number of sized plotters.

The text size number you specify in Harvard Graphics is a percentage of the chart space (which is influenced by some of the factors just mentioned) that is used by the text. A text size of 99, for example, takes up almost the entire chart space. The ultimate point here is that you will have to experiment with different text sizes to find those satisfactory for your chart.

The following table is a general guideline for defining the relative sizes of different text elements on your chart:

| Text Size | Chart Element |
|---|---|
| Large | Title |
| Medium | Subtitle |
| Small to medium | Axis titles |
| Small | Footnote |
| Small | X and Y axis labels and data values |

If a different combination of text sizes than these looks better in your chart, use it. Just be sure that all text is legible, whether you are displaying your chart on a monitor or projection device, producing a slide or overhead transparency of your chart, or outputting a printed or plotted chart.

Here are some additional tips on text sizes:

• A title should be in a large enough text size so that it is clearly readable, but not so large as to overpower the chart itself. The text size of a title is usually the largest used in the chart.

• A subtitle usually looks best when its size is slightly smaller than that of the title.

• Although X and Y axis labels and data labels are usually smaller than other text elements in your chart, they should be large enough to read easily when the chart is output or displayed on a monitor or projection device.

• Be aware that if your text size is small, attributes applied to the text may not appear when your chart is displayed or output, depending on the resolution capability of your display or output device. If this occurs, either do not use the attributes or use a larger text size.

## Types of Data Charts

The following are descriptions of the many types of charts you can produce with Harvard Graphics. These discussions make extensive use of the terms defined in the preceding sections of this chapter. If this is your first exposure to many of these chart styles, you may want to refer back to those definitions whenever necessary.

The discussion of each of these chart styles follows a similar format. The style of chart is described and an example of the chart style is shown. This includes a discussion of the type of data the chart is appropriate for, followed by the advantages and disadvantages of the particular chart style over others.

## Bar Charts

Bar charts depict data in the form of bars or columns. Each bar is associated with one X data value. The height (or length) of each bar represents the corresponding series value. You can determine the series value represented by each bar by comparing the height of the bar to the Y value labels displayed on the Y axis. For example, Figure 19-3 shows the number of people in the U.S. labor force by seven different age groups. The X data are the age groups and the series data are the number of workers. Although this bar chart is oriented vertically, bar charts can also be displayed horizontally.

Bar charts are ideally suited for comparing the measurements for different groups. For example, in Figure 19-3 you can compare the number of workers for each age group almost without effort. This chart permits you to quickly determine the age group that provides the largest number of workers, the age group that provides the least, as well as the differences among the age groups.

A disadvantage of using bar charts is that they are not ideally suited for displaying a large amount of data. Although you may occasionally see bar charts with as many as 50 bars, or even more, these charts are usually difficult to interpret since the resulting bars become quite thin. When you have a large amount of data, you should consider whether you can split the data between several bar charts. Another

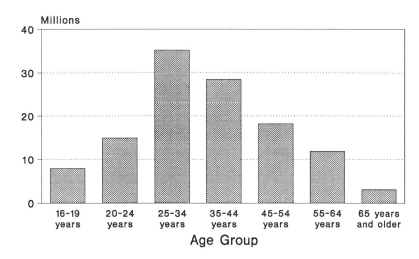

**Figure 19-3.**   Simple bar chart

alternative is to use one of the data reduction techniques described in Chapter 20, "Advanced Data Topics," to reduce the total number of bars.

Bar charts are also not appropriate when your X data type is Number, since the bars cannot show a continuum. Fortunately, Harvard Graphics knows this and will not allow you to create a bar chart when your X data type is Number. It will create a needle chart instead.

There are a number of bar chart styles in addition to a simple bar chart. These include

- Clustered bar charts
- Stacked bar charts

- 100% and column bar charts
- Stepped bar charts
- Paired bar charts
- High/low/close charts
- Error bar charts

These bar chart styles are described individually in the next sections. Creating bar charts in Harvard Graphics is covered in Chapter 6, "XY Charts."

### Clustered Bar Charts

A clustered bar chart is used when each X data value is associated with two or more measurements (series). A cluster of bars (representing the different series values) is displayed at each X data value. For example, in Figure 19-4, there are six years of data represented along the X axis. For each year, employment figures are charted by age group. The data for each age group was entered into a separate series on the XY chart data form. While the employment figure for each age group for each year is represented as an individual bar, Harvard Graphics has clustered the bars on the basis of the X data value, in this case, the year. To assist viewers with distinguishing between the different series, a different color, shade, or pattern is used for each series.

Clustered bar charts are ideal when you want to show the relationship between two different groups of data. In the chart in Figure 19-4, these groups are years and age groups. How you orient these groups can affect how viewers interpret the data. For example, the chart in Figure 19-4 was designed to compare the percentage of unemployed persons by age group for each of the years listed. It would have been just as easy to produce a chart in which the X axis data were the different age groups and the series data were the six years. In that case, the chart would be suited for examining the change in unemployment over the six years for each age group. This alternate chart is displayed in Figure 19-5. Although the data are the same, the conclusions you draw from these data might be influenced by which chart you were shown.

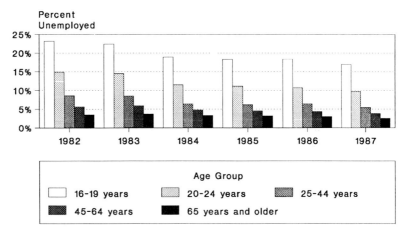

**Figure 19-4.**   Clustered bar chart

In some sense, the advantage and disadvantage of clustered bar charts is the same feature. Since the decision about which data to display along the X axis influences the appropriateness of the chart, care must be taken to design the chart to be consistent with the point you want to make.

### Stacked Bar Charts

Stacked bar charts are similar to clustered bar charts in that they can chart the same kind of data. That is, more than one series is charted for each X data value. The individual bars from each cluster, however, are stacked one on top of another to form one whole bar at each X data

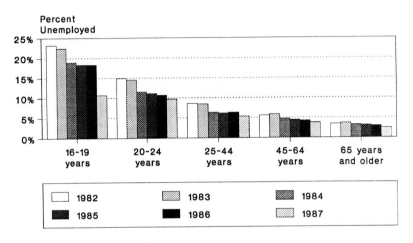

**Figure 19-5.** Alternate presentation of data shown in Figure 19-4

value. Figure 19-6, for example, shows consumption of five different types of fruit. In a clustered bar chart, the types of fruit would be displayed using five side-by-side bars instead.

There are two advantages to stacking the bars in this manner. First, you can still examine the individual segments of a bar. By measuring bottom and top points of each bar segment against the labels shown along the Y axis, you can estimate the values of each bar segment. Second, the sums of the stacked bar segments can provide additional information. For example, the top of each bar in Figure 19-6 represents the sum total of fruit consumption for each of the years shown. Whether you choose to display your data using a clustered bar chart or a stacked bar chart should depend on whether you want to emphasize individual values or the overall total values at each X data value.

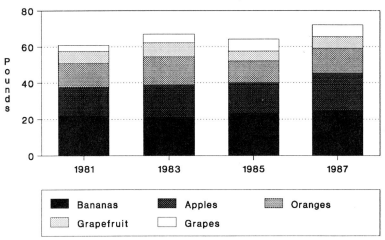

**Figure 19-6.** Stacked bar chart

The disadvantage of stacked bar charts is that it is more difficult to estimate the individual values of the segments within each bar. This is because the segments of the bars, other than the bottom segment, do not share the same starting point. It is necessary to calculate the difference between the bottom and the top of these segments in order to calculate the value they represent.

### 100% and Column Bar Charts

An example of a 100% bar chart is shown in Figure 19-7. Bar charts in which the stack at each X data value is the same size and represents the total are called *100% bar charts*. They are very similar to stacked bar charts, except that the size of each segment within each bar represents

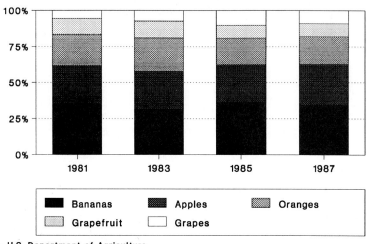

**Figure 19-7.**   100% bar chart

the contribution of that series to the total bar. That is, for each X data value, values for each series are converted to percentages. These charts, then, are essentially columnar forms of pie charts, called *column charts*. Both 100% bar charts and column charts (which, in Harvard Graphics, consist of only one bar) contain the same information (percentages) as would be displayed in pie charts. An example of a column chart is shown in Figure 19-8.

The advantage of a 100% bar chart is that it shows you changes in proportions across different X data values. The disadvantage is that the actual data values are not represented. When only percentages are displayed, potentially important information about the absolute values is not available.

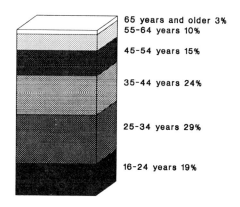

**Figure 19-8.**   Column chart

## Stepped Bar Charts

Stepped bar charts are nearly identical to stacked bar charts. The identifying characteristic of these charts is that the bars appear side by side, extending continuously across the entire chart frame. Stepped bar charts are essentially a hybrid of stacked bar charts and stacked area charts. Stepped bar charts (called this because they often look like steps) are sometimes referred to as *frequency distributions* or *histograms* since they are ideal for displaying distributions. An example of a stepped bar chart is shown in Figure 19-9.

Stepped bar charts are appropriate for data that are ordered yet have discrete steps (for instance, monthly production figures). The bars

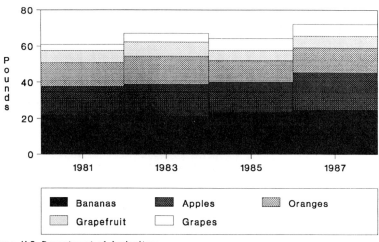

**Figure 19-9.**   Stepped bar chart

in Figure 19-9, for example, represent the per capita consumption of selected fruits over the years. Each year is represented by a successive bar and is a discrete group. By using a stepped bar chart instead of an area chart, the actual consumption of selected fruit for a given year can be more easily estimated. An area chart would be more appropriate for depicting the change in consumption patterns over the years. As with area charts, the X data must represent an ordered set of data for the stepped bar style to be appropriate.

The disadvantage of stepped bar charts is the same as that for stacked bar charts. That is, some computation may be necessary to estimate the values of series that are not displayed at the bottom layer of the chart.

## Paired Bar Charts

Paired bar charts allow you to directly compare two series of data. In Figure 19-10, for example, expenditures for books versus other selected forms of entertainment (TV, radio, and sound equipment) are compared for different regions of the country. Paired bar charts are oriented horizontally (and you cannot change this orientation in Harvard Graphics). The Y axis is displayed along the bottom of the chart frame and the X axis is displayed vertically. The two series of data extend outward from a center line, one in either direction. If more than two series are plotted with respect to either the Y1 or the Y2 axis, these series will be stacked on that side of the bar chart.

Paired bar charts are useful for comparing the relative patterns of two or more series. However, since Harvard Graphics adjusts the size of

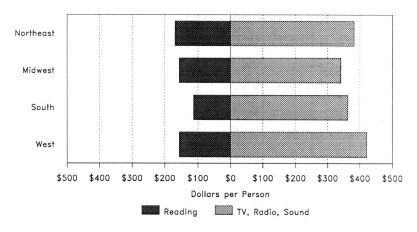

**Figure 19-10.**    Paired bar chart

the Y1 and the Y2 axes individually, you may need to use the formatting features on Page 3 of the Bar Chart Titles & Options form in order to ensure that the two axes display the same range. When the ranges for these axes are not similar, the relative differences between the two sides of the paired bar chart may become distorted.

Paired bar charts are not a common bar style. Most data you can display using a paired bar chart may be better displayed using a clustered bar chart.

### High/Low/Close Charts

High/low/close charts are actually a variety of bar chart, since they too display data in the form of bars. They are most commonly used to display stock market prices, although they can be used to display any data that contain natural ranges. Because high/low/close charts show a range of values, they are also called *range bar charts*. Figure 19-11, for example, shows the average high, the average low, and the average daily temperatures in Houston, Texas, for each month.

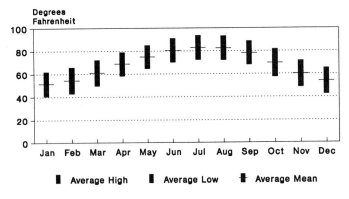

Figure 19-11.    High/low/close chart

At least two values must be used to create each bar in the high/low/close chart. The bottom of the bar represents the lowest value and the top of the bar represents the highest value for each X data value. Additional values can be displayed to further reveal patterns in the data, such as the average temperatures in Figure 19-11. When stock market prices are displayed, the opening and closing prices of the stock are often included along with the high and low prices. Depending on your data, you may want to display averages (means) or medians in addition to the highest and lowest values for each bar.

High/low/close charts are well suited for data that contain natural ranges. The primary disadvantage of using these charts is that viewers must perform some mental computations in order to compare the ranges depicted in each bar. In many applications of high/low/close charts, however, precise estimates of the ranges are not as important as their relative sizes.

### Error Bar Charts

Error bar charts are very similar to high/low/close charts. The bars in these charts, however, are only the width of a single line. In Figure 19-12, for example, the highest and the lowest temperatures ever recorded for Chicago, Illinois, are displayed by month. While the error bars can display the same information as high/low/close bars, the error bar style is often the style of choice in scientific applications.

Error bars get their name from the assumption in some areas of science that the ranges observed when measuring certain effects are due in part to errors in measurement. The tops and bottoms of these bars, therefore, represent the actual effect plus error. The unattainable "true value" of the measurement is assumed to lie within the range depicted by the error bars.

### Line Charts

A line chart is an XY chart in which points are placed at the coordinates of each X value and its corresponding Y (series) value. These points are then joined together to form a line. If there is more than one series of data, more than one line is charted, one for each series.

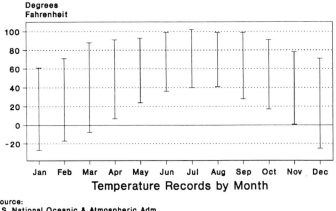

**Figure 19-12.**    Error bar chart

The rise and fall of lines in a line chart allow viewers to observe trends in the data. This is possible only when the X data are an ordered series. Thus line charts often contain time or calendar X data types, permitting viewers to observe changes to the series values over a period of time. The trends displayed in a line chart are often used for extrapolation to time periods not yet measured—making predictions about trends based on the information currently available.

When more than one line is displayed on a chart, you can compare trends for different series of data (see Figure 19-13). The use of multiple series in a line chart is only effective when chart viewers can discriminate between the different lines displayed on the chart. Lines that cross, touch, or overlap can be difficult to differentiate. When you use multiple series in a line chart, ensure they are distinguished through the use of different styles (dotted, dashed, and so on) and/or point marker types.

In Harvard Graphics, you have the option of selecting a number of different classes of lines. Trend lines, for instance, do not connect the

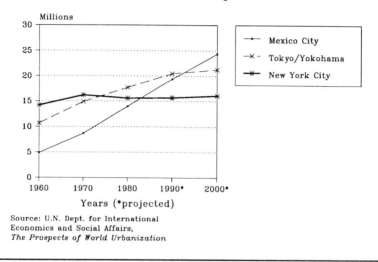

**Figure 19-13.**    Line chart

data points. Instead, they display a straight line that represents the overall increase or decrease in the series values over the length of the X axis. In Harvard Graphics, trend lines are simple linear regression lines (see "Point Charts").

Curved lines are also available. These lines are not straight, but instead display a smoothed representation of the pattern represented by the series values (see Figure 19-14). While these lines can be useful for summarizing the patterns in the data, they should be presented as an addition to the actual data points, not as a substitute for them, since curved lines are a distortion of the data.

If your X data are categorical (and your X data type is set to Name), then a line chart is not appropriate for your data. Because categorical data do not have a natural order, examining the fluctuations of lines for a trend is misleading. Since there is no natural order for categorical data, you could alter the positions of the categories along the X axis, thereby changing any "trends" implied by the lines.

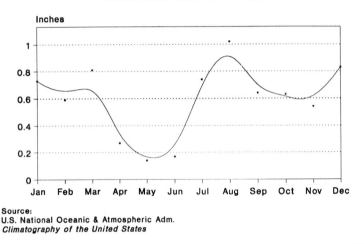

**Figure 19-14.**    Curved line chart

## Band Charts

Band charts are similar to line charts in which two lines representing two different series of data are displayed. In a band chart, however, the area between the two lines is filled with a color, shade, or pattern. This area emphasizes the differences between the two series at each X data value. The top and bottom positions of the band also reflect trends in the two series. It is only appropriate to use a band chart when your X data represent a continuous series or natural progression. Band charts are also similar to what a high/low/close chart would be if the tops of the bars were connected and the bottoms of the bars were connected to form a band. Band charts are sometimes referred to as *net difference band charts*. An example of a band chart is shown in Figure 19-15.

Since a band chart is used to emphasize the difference between two series, it is not appropriate to use a band chart when the two series are based on different measures. For example, if one series contains dollars of profit, and the other series contains number of units produced, producing a band chart of this data would be useless—the band would not

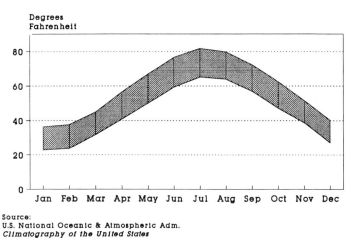

**Figure 19-15.**  Band chart

represent anything meaningful. In contrast, if a band chart displays the difference between income and expenses, the band represents profit, a meaningful measure on its own.

In Harvard Graphics, you create a band chart by selecting <High/Low/Close> from the Create New Chart menu. You then enter the series that represents the top of the band in the "High" series and the bottom series in the "Low" series on the High/Low/Close Chart Data form. You must also set the "High/Low style" option on the Titles & Options form to Area in order to create the band. Harvard Graphics disregards values entered into the "Open" and "Close" series when "High/Low style" is set to Area.

## Point Charts

Point charts are probably the most basic of all XY charts. A point chart is an XY chart in which both the X and Y axes represent data that are continuous measurements. That is, both the X data and the Y (series) data are numeric. In Harvard Graphics, your X data type would be set to Number. Markers are then placed at the coordinates of each X value and its corresponding series value (when you have one series) or series values (when you have two or more series).

Point charts are generally used to display the relationship between the X data values and the series values. Specifically, when you create a point chart you are interested in whether the relationship is positive, negative, or neutral. The relationship is positive when a change in the X data values is accompanied by a similar change in series values. In Figure 19-16, for example, as temperature increases, the average amount of rainfall also increases. This is an example of a positive relationship. A negative relationship, on the other hand, is one in which changes for X data values are accompanied by a change in the opposite direction for the series values. For instance, when the availability of some commodity increases, the price typically decreases.

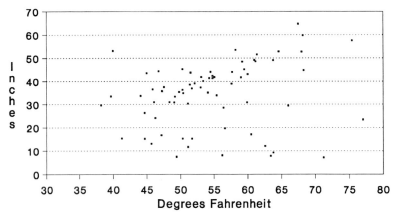

**Figure 19-16.**     Point chart

A neutral relationship means that changes in the X data values bear no similarity to changes in the series values. For example, there should be a neutral relationship between a place's elevation above sea level, in feet, and the number of letters in its name. In a neutral relationship, the point chart would show one big cloud of scattered points with no apparent pattern. Because most relationships that are charted using a point chart are not perfect, in that the relationships are general trends and a great deal of variation in data is typical, the points in point charts are usually scattered about the chart, as they are in Figure 19-16. For this reason, point charts are sometimes referred to as *scatterplots* or *scattergrams*.

Because both the X data and the series data are numeric, the selection of which data to use on the X axis is determined by the point that you want to make with the chart. In Figure 19-16, for example, temperature could have been shown on the Y axis and the amount of precipitation could have been shown on the X axis.

Advantages of point charts include being able to depict a number of different types of numeric data and being able to display a large amount of data in a small space. They can present all the data without adding excess clutter to a chart, which is often a problem when displaying a large amount of data using another chart style. Point charts with hundreds of points are not at all uncommon.

One of the disadvantages of point charts is that, although used for determining the relationship between two or more sets of numbers, most people are not very good at estimating the relationships displayed in a point chart. In order to assist chart viewers, most chart producers add trend lines to their point charts. Trend lines show the best estimate of the relationship between the two sets of numbers (based on least-squares linear regression). A trend line is also referred to as a *regression line* or a line of *best fit*. You can use trend lines even when your data consist of more than one series. For example, if you are displaying the relationships between temperature and rainfall for both U.S. cities and European cities, you can show two trend lines, one for U.S. cities and one for European cities.

Using a trend line makes observing the relationship between X data values and series easy. If the trend line increases in height from left to right, the relationship between the numbers is positive. If the trend line decreases in height from left to right, the relationship is a negative one. If the trend line is approximately flat, neither increasing nor decreasing in height, the relationship is neutral. Figure 19-17 shows a trend line added to the data displayed in Figure 19-16.

When more than one series are displayed on the point chart, you must make sure the different series are distinguishable. Different point markers should be used to differentiate the different series. For example, if selected European cities were also shown in the chart in Figure 19-16, these cities could be shown using a different marker, for example a star. Likewise, when more than one trend line is displayed on a point chart, these lines should be distinctive.

## Needle Charts

Needle charts are simply a variation of point charts. From each point shown on the chart, a vertical line attaches to the X axis, as shown in

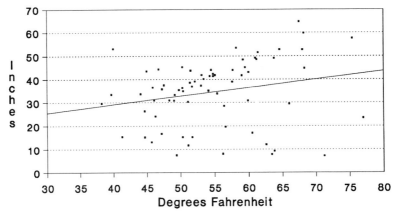

**Figure 19-17.**   Point chart with a trend line

Figure 19-18. These lines can give you a better idea of how the data are distributed along the X axis than a point chart. Because of the lines that drop down from the points to the X axis, it is not appropriate to add trend lines to needle charts—they would only clutter the chart. In all other respects, however, issues that concern point charts can be applied to needle charts.

In Harvard Graphics, needle charts are created under the <Bar/Line> selection from the Create New Chart menu. Your symbol type must be set to Bar and your X data type must be set to Number.

## Area Charts

Area charts are similar to line charts, except that the area below the lines is filled. Area charts emphasize the volume or quantity represented

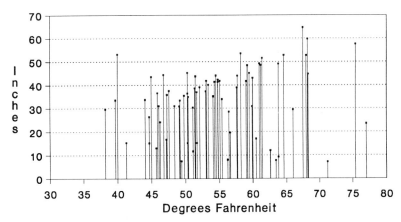

**Figure 19-18.**  Needle chart

because the areas provide a sense of the relative sizes of the series. When an area chart contains only one series, only one area is displayed. The height of the area for each X data value represents the corresponding series value. Because area charts are similar to line charts, area charts are only meaningful when the X axis data represent an ordered series. An example of a simple area chart is displayed in Figure 19-19.

There are three styles of area charts in addition to the simple area chart. The most common style is a stacked area chart. You can also create 100% and overlapped area charts. These styles are described next.

### Stacked Area Charts

Stacked area charts contain two or more areas. Like the segments in a stacked bar chart, the areas in a stacked area chart are added on top of

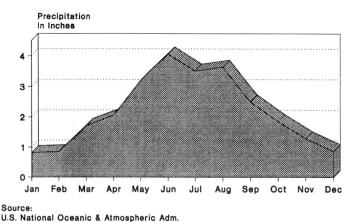

**Figure 19-19.**    Simple area chart

one another. Stacked area charts are useful when the sum of the areas reveals additional information. Consider the area chart shown in Figure 19-20. By reading the top of the area representing the population of Mexico City, you can estimate the combined total population for the three cities shown.

Although stacked area charts provide a great advantage when you are particularly interested in the combined contribution of a number of series to an overall trend, they make it difficult to estimate the individual contributions of each series. Estimation is even more complicated when the lower areas show a large amount of variation or fluctuation.

### 100% Area Charts

Similar to stacked area charts are 100% area charts. However, in these charts the entire chart frame is used to display the areas, with all the

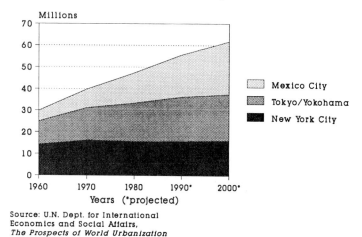

**Figure 19-20.** Stacked area chart

areas together forming a rectangular shape. In addition, the series values are converted to percentages, with each area reflecting the proportion of contribution by that series at each X data value. The 100% area chart style makes it easy to compare the changes in the relative contributions of different series to the total. In this respect, 100% area charts are similar to 100% bar charts. However, 100% area charts are only appropriate when your X data are ordered or continuous data. This is because the areas also convey trends, similar to stacked area charts.

An example of a 100% area chart is shown in Figure 19-21. This chart shows that the relative contribution by Tokyo/Yokohama is predicted to remain constant. Furthermore, the relative contribution to population by New York City is predicted to decline, while that by Mexico City is predicted to increase substantially.

Because 100% area charts depict percentages as opposed to actual numbers, you may need to supplement them with other data or charts that can provide chart viewers with a perspective on the amount of data represented at each X data value.

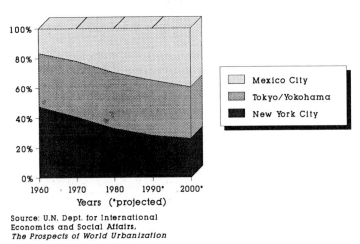

**Figure 19-21.**    100% area chart

### Overlapped Area Charts

Overlapped area charts can be thought of as line charts in which the area between the X axis and each of the different lines is filled in with a different color or pattern. The areas representing the different series will overlap. In overlapped area charts, you should always enter the series with the smallest series values as the first series (Series 1) so that it appears in front of the other areas. The last series entered should be the series with the largest series values, so it does not cover up any other areas displayed in the chart. An example of an overlapped area chart is shown in Figure 19-22.

Overlapped area charts allow you to compare trends by examining the positions of the tops of the areas; they are similar to line charts in this respect. The filled-in areas, however, provide a sense of volume or quantity that is not emphasized in a line chart. You may want to try charting your data using each of these styles to determine the effect you

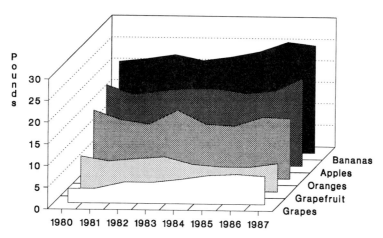

**Figure 19-22.**   Overlapped area chart

## Pie Charts

Pie charts are used to display data as a percentage of a whole, much like the sections or slices of a pie. The area of the pie represents 100 percent. The pie is then divided into from 2 to approximately 12 slices. The size of each slice maintains the relative proportion of a single series value to the sum of all of the values in the series. A pie chart is shown in Figure 19-23.

Because percentages do not provide information about the actual size of the values depicted, it is important that slices of a pie are labeled

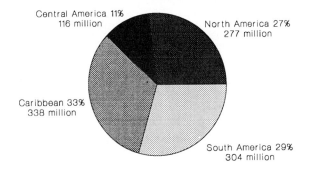

Figure 19-23.    Pie chart

with the X data they represent. In addition, it is often desirable to display the actual percentage each pie slice represents, since most people are not very good at estimating the percentage represented by a slice of a pie. Fortunately, Harvard Graphics allows you to display all this information.

If you want to emphasize one slice in a pie, you can *explode* it from the pie. When you explode a pie slice, you separate it by a small amount of space from the center of the pie, as shown in Figure 19-24. In Harvard Graphics, you can explode more than one slice in a pie, if desired.

You can also create a two-pie chart in Harvard Graphics, which is simply a chart with two pie charts displayed side by side. Two-pie charts provide a convenient way of comparing the relative proportions of two different series. However, keep in mind that pie charts are not appropriate for displaying trend information. Many two-pie charts display data that would have been better displayed using a clustered bar chart.

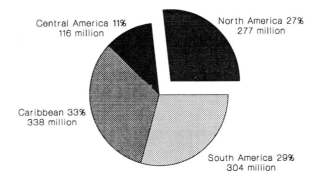

**Figure 19-24.** Pie chart with an exploded pie slice

## Specialty Charts

Sometimes data cannot be adequately represented by one of the types of charts covered in the preceding sections. These situations often call for a more creative use of charts. Several alternative chart styles available in Harvard Graphics are described next.

### Cumulative Charts

Cumulative charts are charts in which series values are cumulated, or summed, across X data values. In Figure 19-25, for example, annual precipitation for Minneapolis-St. Paul, Minnesota, is shown cumulatively. January precipitation is approximately 1 inch. This amount is then added to the amount of precipitation for February and plotted at February. Each additional month contains all the previous precipitation amounts plus that added for the current month. December shows the average precipitation for the entire year. Cumulative charts are appropriate when a total of series values over time is of interest.

One of the dangers of using a cumulative chart is that chart viewers

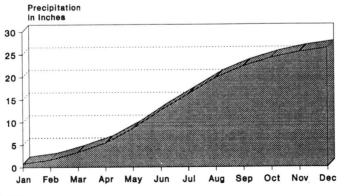

Figure 19-25.   Cumulative chart

may not realize that the displayed data are cumulative. To avoid this misinterpretation, it is essential to adequately identify a cumulative chart.

## Dual-Axis Charts

Dual-axis charts are charts with two Y axes. In these charts two Y axes are required because the data of two or more series that share the same X data values have different units of measurement, for example heights and weights, dollars and units sold, and temperatures and quantities. All series displayed on a dual-axis chart must use the same X data values. An example of a dual-axis chart is shown in Figure 19-26. The Y1 axis on this chart displays the average daily temperature in degrees Fahrenheit, while the Y2 axis depicts the average rainfall in inches for San Francisco, California.

Because dual-axis charts can display two different types of information on a single chart, effective use of these charts can reveal patterns that would not be apparent if the data were displayed in separate charts. It is important, however, to ensure that your axes and symbols

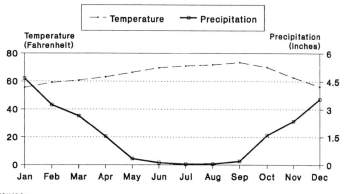

**Figure 19-26.**   Dual-axis chart

are clearly (and correctly) marked. Failure to do so will result in a muddled chart that causes more confusion than enlightenment.

When you first create a dual-axis chart in Harvard Graphics, sometimes it will produce two sets of grid lines, one set for each axis. This is not desirable. If you want to display grid lines on your chart, use the minimum, maximum, and increment settings on Page 3 of the Titles & Options form to adjust the Y1 and Y2 axes so they display the same number of grid lines. When you do this, the grid lines for the two axes will overlap, as they do in Figure 19-26.

## Combination Charts

Combination charts are charts that include two different symbol types (bars, lines, point markers, or areas) on a single chart. They are particularly useful for comparing two related but different types of series information in one chart. The bars in Figure 19-27, for example, show the average amount of precipitation for each month in San Francisco, California. The area shows the same data cumulated so that it is easy to see the pattern of annual precipitation. Note that both the bar and the area symbols use the same X data. This is a necessary characteristic of combination charts. If your different series did not share the same X data values, you would not be able to show them on the same chart.

Although the series shown using the bars and areas in Figure 19-27 are both displayed with respect to the same Y axis, this is not a requirement of a combination chart. You can create a combination chart in which the different symbol types represent data based on different measurements, and are therefore displayed with respect to different axes (Y1 and Y2). For example, you could show monthly precipitation in inches on Y1 and the average number of traffic accidents on Y2. You could then represent the monthly rainfall amounts using bars and the traffic accident counts using a line. Showing both data on the same chart allows you to compare the different types of data. Using different symbols emphasizes that the data are distinct.

You must use caution when creating a combination chart. Since you are essentially combining two charts in one, there is a potential for the chart to become crowded and difficult to interpret.

## Data Maps

Data maps are appropriate when your data are geographical in nature. Data that you may want to display using a data map include census

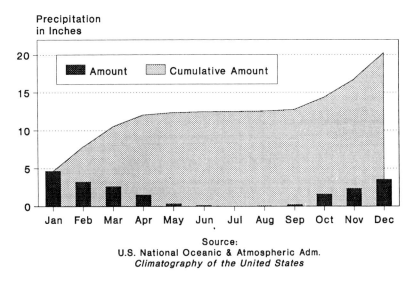

**Figure 19-27.**   Combination chart

data, sales figures, market percentages, growth by geographical region, and so on. Data maps give the data a frame of reference not available with a more standard chart style.

Consider Figure 19-28. This chart was created from a symbol in the Harvard Graphics symbol file called COUNTRY.SYM (included with the Harvard Graphics package). Each of the states was color coded in Draw/Annotate. Note that 48 data values are easily displayed on this one data map, and the patterns of population are readily apparent. A more standard chart style would not be able to display these data anywhere near as effectively. For example, you would need to display all 48 states along the X axis for a bar chart. Similarly, a table of these data would not reveal the population patterns as readily.

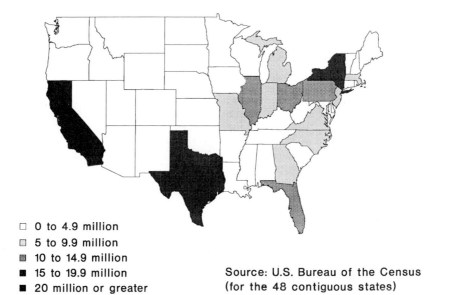

**Figure 19-28.**  Data map

## Guidelines for Creating Data Charts

Table 19-1 provides a general guide to selecting the appropriate chart type for your data. The following sections summarize the processes involved in creating a data chart. These processes are divided into those steps that you perform before you create your chart and those that you perform after creating your chart.

|  | Category Data | | X Data — Ordered Data | | Measurement Data | |
|---|---|---|---|---|---|---|
| Series (Y) Data: | One | Multiple | One | Multiple | One | Multiple |
| **Chart Type** | | | | | | |
| Simple bar | ☆ | | ✓ | | | |
| Clustered bar | | ☆ | | ✓ | | |
| Stacked bar | | ☆ | | ✓ | | |
| 100% bar | | ☆ | | ✓ | | |
| Column bar | ☆ | | ✓ | | | |
| Stepped bar | | | ☆ | ✓ | | |
| Paired bar | | ☆ | | ✓ | | |
| High/Low/Close | | | | ☆ | | |
| Error bar | | ✓ | | ☆ | | |
| Line | | | ☆ | ☆ | | |
| Band | | | ☆ | ☆ | | |
| Point | | | ✓ | ✓ | ☆ | ☆ |
| Needle | | | | | ☆ | |
| Simple area | | | ☆ | | | |
| Stacked area | | | | ☆ | | |
| 100% area | | | | ☆ | | |
| Overlapped area | | | | ☆ | | |
| Pie | ☆ | ☆ | | | | |
| **Specialty** | | | | | | |
| Cumulative | | | ✓ | ✓ | | |
| Dual-Axis | | ✓ | | ✓ | | ✓ |
| Combination | | ✓ | | ✓ | | ✓ |
| Data map | | ✓ | | | | |

Note: ☆ = Best match between data and chart type
 ✓ = Acceptable match between data and chart type

**Table 19-1.** Guidelines for Selecting Appropriate Chart Type

## Before You Create Your Chart

The following are steps you should take to plan your charts:

- **Collect your data**  The data you will use in your chart may originate from any number of sources. They might originate in a company report, be downloaded from the company mainframe computer, be listed as statistics in a newspaper or journal, or you may collect them yourself using a survey or other data collection method.

- **Identify your viewers**  Who will see the chart? Is the chart intended for your own personal use or will it be shown to others?

    Consider also the chart viewers' familiarity with the subject matter. Are you trying to inform the viewers about subjects that may be new to them, or are you providing an update on a subject that the viewers are knowledgeable about? If you are the only intended viewer, titles and other labels can be limited to those that remind you of the source and date of the data.

- **Identify the main goal**  What is the purpose of creating the chart? Do you want to compare data, or discover trends and patterns in the data? What points do you want to make to your viewers by presenting your data in a chart?

- **Identify the type of data**  Do your X data consist of categories, ordered series, or continuous measurements?

    For XY charts, what scale range would best display your series data?

    What form are your series (Y) data in? Should a data reduction, transformation, or adjustment be performed on your data? (Chapter 20, "Advanced Data Topics," covers these topics.)

- **Select the appropriate chart type**  To select the appropriate chart type, you must carefully consider both the goal or purpose of your chart and the type of data you have. Choose the chart type that is easiest to interpret and best illustrates the point or points you are trying to convey. Keep in mind that a particular chart style, although it attractively displays your data, may not be the most appropriate style for your data. You may need to try several different chart types to determine which type is best for your particular data.

- **Select a method for producing your chart** Decide on the output quality and chart size that best suits your charting needs. If your chart must be of the highest possible output quality, you may want to create a slide of your chart using a film recorder or a slide service. For reports or presentations, you may only need to print or plot your chart to paper or transparencies. Another option for presentations is to add your chart to a slide show.

## After You Have Created Your Chart

Once you have created a chart, you should carefully examine it to determine that it is satisfactory. The following are guidelines for evaluating whether or not your chart meets your needs:

- **Does the chart convey your point?** Take a step back and try to analyze exactly what the chart itself suggests, rather than the point you are trying to convey with your chart. Evaluate whether there is any possibility your viewers may be confused by the chart.

- **Does the chart contain the necessary elements?** Examine each of the elements in the chart (title and subtitle, description, axes and axis labels, symbols, fonts, text attributes, text size, tick marks, grid lines, and legend). Are the elements present on your chart correct? Are there any missing elements you should add?

    Evaluate characteristics of the symbols used in the chart (patterns, shades, colors, line styles, point markers, chart enhancements such as shadows and 3D effects, bar widths, and exploded pie slices). Evaluate whether any of the symbol characteristics are distracting or distorting. (See Chapter 22, "Common Charting Mistakes.") Take charge of Harvard Graphics. If the chart settings defined by Harvard Graphics are unsatisfactory for your chart, change them.

# Advanced Data Topics

**Data Reduction**
**Transformations and Adjustments**
**Other Data Topics**

The data you want to chart may not all be in a form that is ready to use. For example, you may be interested in the average monthly output of one your company's factories. This output may be recorded on a daily basis, however. In order to look at the data by month, you will need to calculate monthly totals from the daily figures before creating your chart. While this example is a simple one, it is just one of the many data manipulation topics described in this chapter.

The topics presented in this chapter are divided into three general sections, "Data Reduction," "Transformations and Adjustments," and "Other Data Topics." These discussions are designed more to familiarize you with these types of data issues than to provide you with a comprehensive description of the presented techniques.

It would be ideal if data were always in the form appropriate for the chart you want to create. This is rarely the case, however. What you want to discover in your data will determine the manipulations you need to perform. For example, if you want to compare the productivity of two different factories, you would probably need to calculate mean production figures for each factory. However, with data that represents daily output of each factory, you could determine the overall trends in production for both factories. Which question you wanted to address would determine how you would manipulate the data.

This brings up another very important point. Terms like *manipulating data* or *transforming data* are used to describe the process by which patterns or trends in data can be made available. They in no way imply the data are being contrived or faked. These changes to your data are legitimate ways of defining data, discovering trends or patterns, or adjusting the data, as long as there are valid reasons for doing so.

## Data Reduction

The most common changes to data are those of reducing an overwhelming amount of information to a more manageable size. This reduction might involve calculating averages, which are then charted instead of the individual data points, or using scientific notation in order to display very large or very small numbers more succinctly.

Most of the topics covered under the subject of data reduction involve statistics. Since it is not the purpose of this chapter to describe these topics in great detail, you may want to make reference to a beginning statistics textbook for additional information on averages, sums, minimums, maximums, and ranges. For details on the topic of regression, you will need to consult a more advanced statistical reference source.

### Averages and Totals

Calculating averages and totals are ways to combine multiple data points. Two of the most common examples of arithmetic calculations include a *mean* (also called an *arithmetic average*), and a *total* or *sum*. Both of these calculations can be used to reduce a vast number of data points down to a manageable level, while maintaining much of the informational value of the data.

For example, imagine you want to display a chart that depicts the quantities of some product produced by a factory over the last year. Furthermore, you would like to see if this production has increased or decreased during that period. If your data consist of daily totals, you would need to chart 365 data points (assuming the factory is running seven days a week). Since Harvard Graphics can only display a maximum of 240 points along the X axis, you will not be able to produce this chart.

In addition, daily figures tend to fluctuate. On any given day a particular machine may be down for repair and, consequently, factory output may be near zero. A more accurate picture of the output levels would result if you summed the output by month. After calculating these totals, you have 12 values to chart, and these values will be less affected by events such as short-term equipment failure.

These types of calculations are often performed *before* the data are added in Harvard Graphics. For instance, the data may be stored in a database or spreadsheet on your PC computer or a mainframe computer. In that case, you can extract only the summary information from the database or spreadsheet, rather than the individual data. These summary data can then be imported directly into your chart, or you can enter them by hand.

If you are creating an XY chart, Harvard Graphics provides you with the @REDUC function to calculate totals within Harvard Graphics. As long as your X data type is not Number, the @REDUC function will sum all series values for each X data value. To use this feature you must have more data points (rows in the XY data chart form) than there are unique X data values. For example, in Figure 20-1 there are several sales entered for each month, with the amount of each sale listed separately in the Series 1 column. You may, however, be more interested in the total sales for each month. In that case you can perform a @REDUC on this series to create the series shown in Figure 20-2, in which all January sales amounts are totaled, all February sales amounts are totaled, and so on. Additional details about the @REDUC calculation can be found in Chapter 6, "XY Charts."

## Minimums, Maximums, and Ranges

Calculations such as totals or averages are only one way to discover trends in your data. There are a number of other calculations that can help you and your viewers discover more about the dynamics of your data. Three of these calculations are the *minimum, maximum,* and *range* of your data.

The minimum, maximum, and range can be calculated for groups of data. For example, instead of calculating the total output of a factory for each month, you could calculate the maximum daily output within each month—the value for the day on which output was greatest. If you were to calculate the minimum, you would be calculating the lowest output figure for each month. The range is a value that represents the difference between the minimum and maximum values.

When you are specifically interested in how much your data are

```
                    Bar/Line Chart Data
     Title:
  Subtitle:
  Footnote:

          X Axis         Series 1    Series 2    Series 3    Series 4
     Pt   Month

     1    January        1000.5
     2    January        1250.2
     3    January        1749.1
     4    January        2000.1
     5    January        2000.1
     6    February       1256.74
     7    February       1521
     8    February       1629.54
     9    February       1921.01
     10   February       2212.87
     11   March          2408.12
     12   March          2354.32

  F1-Help         F3-Set X type                          F9-More series
  F2-Draw chart   F4-Calculate              F8-Options   F10-Continue
```

**Figure 20-1.**   Original series values before data reduction is performed

```
                    Bar/Line Chart Data
     Title:
  Subtitle:
  Footnote:

          X Axis         Series 1    Series 2    Series 3    Series 4
     Pt   Month

     1    January        8000
     2    February       8541.16
     3    March          9262.44
     4    April          10233.24
     5    May            10243.87
     6    June           10742.87
     7    July           10543.96
     8    August         10641.43
     9    September      10751.92
     10   October        10954.48
     11   November       11017
     12   December       11349.71

  F1-Help         F3-Set X type                          F9-More series
  F2-Draw chart   F4-Calculate              F8-Options   F10-Continue
```

**Figure 20-2.**   Series values after @REDUC has been performed

Sample Data Set
Minimum, Maximum, and Range

| Series (Y) Data | |
|---|---|
| 34 | Minimum Value |
| 76 | 23 |
| 87 | |
| 34 | Maximum Value |
| 65 | 87 |
| 47 | |
| 23 | Range |
| 84 | 23-87 = 64 |

**Figure 20-3.** Sample data set and minimum, maximum, and range calculations

fluctuating, the range may be the appropriate value for you. Figure 20-3 contains a sample data set and the minimum, maximum, and range calculations.

You may think these calculations do not provide any information you cannot glean from an average or total. However, these values can provide alternative impressions of your data. For instance, consider the example of the daily factory production figures. If one factory produces about the same output every day, and another factory produces variable output depending on the reliability of the machinery on a given day, total and average production figures of the two companies may not be that different. However, the minimums, maximums, and ranges may differ a great deal. By looking at the maximum figures, for example, you would be able to compare both factories based on days when all the machinery was running properly.

## Frequency Counts

The most fundamental type of data reduction technique is to simply count instances of occurrence. When your chart includes counts, the series data consist of tabulations for each X data value. Returning to the factory example, rather than summing the total production for each month, you could simply count the number of days in each month on which the factory exceeded some established quota. The advantage to this type of data reduction is that it can be accomplished quickly and easily, even when you perform the calculation manually.

## Regression and Regression Lines

*Regression* is a name for a family of sophisticated statistical techniques used to estimate trends in data. The result of a regression calculation is a series of points that lie on the same line, called the *regression line.* This line represents a function that best describes the trends in your data. Because the regression calculation results in the estimation of a regression line, it is appropriate to use a regression equation only when your data are appropriate for a line chart, point chart, or area chart.

Harvard Graphics offers four calculations for four different regression estimations: linear, exponential, power, and logarithmic. When you calculate a linear regression line, the calculated points lie on a straight line, (thus the name *linear.*) An example data set and estimated data values (calculated by the @RLIN calculation in Harvard Graphics) are shown in Table 20-1. (These data are shown in the chart in Figure 19-17.) Note that for a given temperature in the Average Temperature column in Table 20-1, the estimated data value in the Estimated Precipitation column lies on the regression line displayed in Figure 19-17.

The remaining three regression equations—exponential, power, and logarithmic—estimate the corresponding functions that best fit your data. These lines, unlike the linear regression line, are usually curved.

Regression lines are convenient ways to view a trend or trends in your data. However, it is important to remember that the regression calculations available in Harvard Graphics estimate the simple regression lines, but do not provide any details concerning confidence intervals or statistical significance tests. Therefore, these types of charts are not a substitute for a conventional regression analysis.

| Average Temperature | Observed Precipitation | Estimated Precipitation |
| --- | --- | --- |
| 67.5 | 64.64 | 39.177 |
| 51.1 | 30.34 | 33.205 |
| 40.0 | 53.15 | 29.164 |
| 49.4 | 37.49 | 32.586 |
| 71.2 | 37.11 | 40.524 |
| 45.9 | 36.53 | 31.312 |
| 61.0 | 49.20 | 36.810 |
| 53.1 | 41.93 | 33.934 |
| 62.6 | 12.08 | 37.393 |
| 56.2 | 8.12 | 35.062 |
| 60.5 | 17.10 | 36.628 |
| 47.3 | 35.74 | 31.822 |
| 63.8 | 9.32 | 37.830 |
| 47.6 | 37.52 | 31.931 |
| 56.6 | 19.71 | 35.208 |
| 54.5 | 44.12 | 34.443 |
| 50.3 | 15.31 | 32.914 |
| 60.0 | 43.16 | 36.446 |
| 46.8 | 44.39 | 31.640 |
| 59.0 | 41.76 | 36.082 |
| 54.8 | 41.38 | 34.553 |
| 41.3 | 15.36 | 29.637 |
| 57.6 | 39.00 | 35.572 |
| 53.4 | 40.14 | 34.043 |
| 68.0 | 52.76 | 39.359 |
| 49.8 | 35.40 | 32.732 |
| 75.4 | 57.55 | 42.053 |
| 51.7 | 36.97 | 33.424 |
| 61.2 | 48.61 | 36.883 |
| 59.9 | 30.89 | 36.410 |
| 77.0 | 23.47 | 42.636 |
| 53.0 | 37.39 | 33.897 |
| 51.1 | 11.71 | 33.205 |

**Table 20-1.** Average Annual Temperatures, Precipitation Amounts, and Estimated Precipitation Amounts Calculated @RLIN. Temperatures and Precipitation Amounts Are for a Selected Sample of U.S. Cities from 1951 to 1980

| Average Temperature | Observed Precipitation | Estimated Precipitation |
|---|---|---|
| 54.3 | 41.42 | 34.370 |
| 49.2 | 33.34 | 32.514 |
| 50.3 | 36.30 | 32.914 |
| 50.4 | 34.89 | 32.950 |
| 50.3 | 45.32 | 32.914 |
| 52.1 | 39.12 | 33.569 |
| 63.8 | 49.12 | 37.830 |
| 49.1 | 30.83 | 32.477 |
| 46.3 | 24.12 | 31.458 |
| 56.4 | 28.61 | 35.135 |
| 61.4 | 51.57 | 36.956 |
| 58.2 | 53.56 | 35.791 |
| 59.2 | 48.49 | 36.155 |
| 68.2 | 59.74 | 39.432 |
| 66.0 | 29.46 | 38.631 |
| 45.0 | 43.52 | 30.984 |
| 63.4 | 7.82 | 37.684 |
| 55.1 | 41.84 | 34.662 |
| 68.3 | 44.76 | 39.468 |
| 51.5 | 43.81 | 33.351 |
| 51.7 | 15.31 | 33.424 |
| 48.4 | 30.97 | 32.222 |
| 44.1 | 33.69 | 30.657 |
| 39.7 | 33.48 | 29.054 |
| 59.5 | 45.22 | 36.264 |
| 38.2 | 29.68 | 28.508 |
| 57.7 | 40.70 | 35.600 |
| 44.7 | 26.36 | 30.875 |
| 51.4 | 36.00 | 33.300 |
| 64.6 | 52.82 | 38.121 |
| 47.2 | 17.10 | 31.700 |

**Table 20-1.** Average Annual Temperatures, Precipitation Amounts, and Estimated Precipitation Amounts Calculated @RLIN. Temperatures and Precipitation Amounts Are for a Selected Sample of U.S. Cities from 1951 to 1980 (*continued*)

## Transformations and Adjustments

The data manipulations described so far are for the purpose of reducing the overall amount of information being presented to the chart viewer. Another common modification you may need to perform is to transform or adjust the data. These changes can be performed in addition to the data reduction techniques already discussed. When you transform data, you change actual data values. This is done in order to compensate for some other feature of the data that would result in an otherwise misleading chart. Although transformations are not uncommon, it is critical that you perform them only when there is a rational and defensible reason for doing so.

The most common reason for making adjustments to data is to be able to compare data that are inherently unequal. In other words, adjustments attempt to make an otherwise unfair comparison fair. The follow descriptions detail some of the more common transformations.

### Weighting or Equalizing Data

Sometimes measurements that appear equal on the surface are not. For example, if you were to compare the cost of manufacturing a particular product in 1960 versus its cost of manufacturing in 1990, it is likely to appear that manufacturing expenses have increased dramatically. However, if you take into account the fact that the dollar was worth a great deal more in 1960 than in 1990, the difference in costs may be unchanged, or even lower. This type of adjustment is called *weighting* or *equalizing*.

Weighting data provides you with a means of comparing objects of different value, or weight, on the same scale. In the manufacturing example, you may want to compare the cost of manufacturing in terms of 1990 dollars (or 1960 dollars). The actual scale selected is your choice. It is important, however, that your chart clearly indicates how the comparison is being made.

### Percentage Adjustments

When you chart data in order to compare two or more groups, you want to make sure you do not confuse group size with the characteristic that is being compared. For example, consider the chart displayed in Figure 20-4. This chart displays fictitious data that represent the total number of missed work days by the employees at a large manufacturing plant by shift. Since the day shift employees logged more missed days, the implication of this chart is that day shift employees are absent more often. The underlying assumption in a chart of this nature is that the number of possible work days is equal between the two shifts. However, if more employees work the day shift than the swing shift, a comparison of the total number of work days missed is unfair. Since there are more day shift employees, there are more possible work days that can be missed.

Imagine there are twice as many day shift employees as there are swing shift employees (100:50). In order to fairly compare the attendance records of these two shifts, it is appropriate to compute the percentage of missed days. This percentage takes into account the total

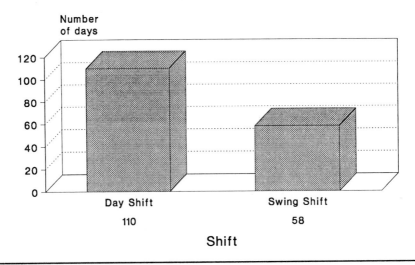

**Figure 20-4.**   Total number of missed work days by employees of different shifts

number of possible days the workers in each shift could work. The percentages of work days missed are displayed in Figure 20-5. As you can see, the percentage adjustment eliminated the unfair comparison and revealed that both day shift and swing shift employees are more or less equally reliable.

## Transformations

Sometimes you must change the scale of your data in order to make it more appropriate for your audience. For example, if you want to chart temperature readings that were recorded in degrees Celsius, but your audience is more familiar with the Fahrenheit scale, it would be necessary to perform a transformation on the data.

Transformations, in the sense used here, are changes in the scale of the data. When data are transformed, there is a one-to-one correspon-

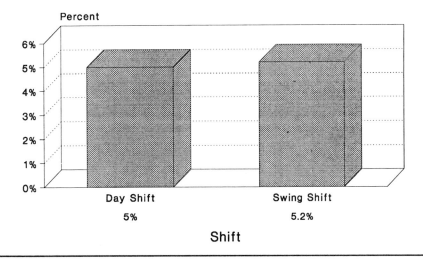

**Figure 20-5.**  Percentage of missed work days by employees of different shifts

dence between the original values and the transformed values. For example, the transformation between degrees Celsius and degrees Fahrenheit is

$$F = C \times (9/5) + 32$$

where F is degrees Fahrenheit and C is degrees Celsius. For any given value of C, there is one, and only one, value of F. With all transformations of this type, the converse is also true. Given any value of F, you could accurately and consistently calculate the value of C. For example:

| Fahrenheit | Celsius |
|---|---|
| 212 | 100 |
| 100 | 23.56 |
| 32 | 0 |
| 14 | -10 |
| 0 | -17.78 |
| -10 | -23.33 |

These transformations are appropriate whenever all your original numbers must be modified, thus maintaining the proportion. For example, if you wanted to compare the prices of a product you are selling in Japan with other similar products, you may want to transform the currency rate from yen to dollars. Although the actual values will be changed, all relative differences will be preserved.

## Logarithmic, Power, and Root Transformations

There are some transformations that are used for data exploration. These transformations change the data in a *nonlinear* fashion, meaning that they do not preserve the proportionality of the original values. Examples of these types of transformations are *logarithmic* transformations, *power* transformations, and *root* transformations.

Because nonlinear transformations change the relative proportions in data, they can be used to exaggerate subtle differences between different series of data, or even between different X data values of the same series. Because of these characteristics, a knowledgeable data analyst can use these transformations to explore and probe the data, searching for patterns that are not otherwise obvious.

By the same reasoning, these transformations should not generally be used with business graphics, unless the audience is familiar with and understands the transformations that have been applied to the data.

## Other Data Topics

The remaining topics in this chapter will describe additional techniques available that you can use to either simplify or enrich the data in your chart.

### Cumulative Data

Cumulating data provides a convenient way to pack additional informational value into your existing data. For example, if your data consist of monthly expenses, but you are primarily interested in your year-to-date expenses, you can create a cumulative chart. When your data are cumulative, each additional data point charted includes the sum of the values for the preceding X data values. For example, the data point charted for March is the sum of the January, February, and March data values. This cumulation occurs within each of the different series in your chart.

Because summation is occurring across X data, it is only appropriate to create a cumulative chart when there is a natural order to your X data values. It is almost never acceptable to create a cumulative chart when your X data are of the type Name.

Adding a series of cumulative data to a chart that contains non-cumulative data is a simple way of including more detail in your chart. Whether you are listing the cumulative data by itself or in addition to other data (using a combination chart), it is critical to always label your chart clearly. If you present cumulative data without the viewers' knowledge, they are likely to come to some very wrong conclusions about the patterns in your data. Refer to Chapter 19, "Effective Data Charts," for an example of a cumulative chart.

## Moving Averages

A *moving average* can be used when your X data are time or calendar values and you want to smooth out incidental variations in your data. The moving average performs this smoothing by converting every value in a series to an average based on adjacent values in the series. The final result is that abnormally high or low values are adjusted by averaging them with their more typical neighboring values.

Figure 20-6, for example, shows original series values in the "Series 1" column and a series consisting of a moving average in the @MAVG column. This moving average was calculated using the Harvard Graphics calculation @MAVG, which calculates the average using the current value and those adjacent to it. Note that the first value in the moving average series column is the average of the first and second data values in the original series column, "Series 1." This is because there is no preceding value in the "Series 1" column. All the remaining moving

| Pt | X Axis Month | Series 1 | @MAVG | Series 3 | Series 4 |
|----|-------------|----------|--------|----------|----------|
| 1  | January     | 45       | 44     |          |          |
| 2  | February    | 43       | 46.333 |          |          |
| 3  | March       | 51       | 49.667 |          |          |
| 4  | April       | 55       | 49.333 |          |          |
| 5  | May         | 42       | 46     |          |          |
| 6  | June        | 41       | 38.333 |          |          |
| 7  | July        | 32       | 36.333 |          |          |
| 8  | August      | 36       | 32.333 |          |          |
| 9  | September   | 29       | 33     |          |          |
| 10 | October     | 34       | 33.667 |          |          |
| 11 | November    | 38       | 38.333 |          |          |
| 12 | December    | 43       | 40.5   |          |          |

**Figure 20-6.** Original series values ("Series 1" column) and moving average values (@MAVG column)

average series values in the @MAVG column, with the exception of the very last value, are based on three values in the "Series 1" column.

With Harvard Graphics, you can calculate your moving average on any range (any number of data values surrounding the current value) by defining the range in your @MAVG calculation. See Chapter 6, "XY Charts," for the syntax of this calculation.

## Scientific Notation

Some numbers, when they are very large or very small, become too lengthy to display conventionally in Harvard Graphics. (Very small numbers are numbers very close to zero and may or may not be negative.) An alternative to displaying these numbers is to use a system called *scientific notation*. Scientific notation is sometimes referred to as *exponential notation*.

Using scientific notation is fairly straightforward. Consider the number 1,000,000,000. This number would be represented in scientific notation as 1.00E+09. There are two parts to a scientific notation. The first is the numerical value, called the *mantissa*, which is always represented with one significant digit. In this case, the number is 1.00. The second part is the *exponent*, in this case, E+09.

Following the letter "E" in scientific notation is typically a two-digit number. This number represents the number of places the decimal point will have to be moved to convert the number back into standard notation. The sign, positive or negative, indicates direction, right or left, of this move. If this sign is positive, the decimal place will be moved to the right, resulting in a number greater than zero. If the sign is negative, the decimal place will be moved to the left, resulting in a number less than zero. For the number 1.00+E09, the decimal point will have to be moved nine positions to the right to represent 1,000,000,000.

The following table shows several numbers and their equivalent scientific notation.

| Conventional Notation | Scientific Notation |
| --- | --- |
| 1,230.00 | 1.23+E03 |
| .00123 | 1.23-E03 |
| -207,650,000 | -2.0765+E08 |
| -.0000000009287 | -9.287-E10 |

One potential disadvantage of using scientific notation is that numbers are typically rounded in order to produce a mantissa of only three digits or so. Most of the time, however, this loss of precision is not a concern because of the magnitude of the numbers to begin with.

# Effective Text and Organization Charts

Types of Text Charts
Considerations for Designing Text Charts
Organization Charts
Considerations for Designing Organization Charts

This chapter describes the different types of text charts and considerations for designing effective text and organization charts.

Text charts are the most common charts used in presentations. They can emphasize points more effectively than a verbal description alone because the combination of seeing the points displayed and hearing a verbal description of them uses both visual and auditory senses. Consequently, your points are much more likely to be remembered and leave an impression on your audience. Text charts also provide variety and can enliven an otherwise ordinary presentation. In reports, these charts can be included to present information in a compact and attractive form as well as to present data in a table.

Organization charts combine both text and symbols (boxes and connecting lines) to graphically display the structure and members of an organization. In most cases, this information would be difficult to convey in a written description. Organization charts are used in presentations and documents as well as for reference.

## Types of Text Charts

You typically use text charts to convey information in a particular format. There are four general categories of text charts.

- Title charts
- List charts

- Column charts
- Free-form charts

Each of these types is described in the following sections. Examples of the layouts of these text chart types are shown in Figure 21-1.

## Title Charts

Title charts, as the name implies, contain the title of a presentation or document. A title chart typically contains a title, the name and affiliation of the author or presenter, and often a date. Harvard Graphics' title charts are set up to display these three pieces of information in an attractive layout. If you want to display a title chart with an alternative format, you can create your chart using the <Free form> selection from the Text Chart Styles menu or using Harvard Graphics' Draw/Annotate. An example of a title chart is shown in Figure 21-2.

## List Charts

List charts contain lists of information. The list is usually fairly short, with no more than about seven lines of information at most. List charts can help viewers structure the information you are presenting. They typically contain an introductory header or title at the top of the chart.

There are two kinds of lists. One is a list in which items are prioritized or have a natural order. Items in these list charts are typically numbered to show their order or priority. The second type of list is one in which the items are given equal weight or importance. In these charts, items are typically preceded by a bullet (a shape such as a dot, square, check mark, or dash) but they can also be listed without being preceded by a bullet.

In Harvard Graphics, you can create a list chart using the <Simple list> selection from the Text Chart Styles menu. If you want to have Harvard Graphics automatically place either a number or a bullet shape before each point in your list, you can use the <Bullet list> selection from the Text Chart Styles menu. An example of a list chart is shown in Figure 21-3.

# Title

Title of Presentation

Name
Affiliation

Date of Presentation

# List

Tips for Presentations

- Have something to say
- Say it
- Stop when you are done

*—Attributed to Tyron Edwards*

# Column

**Population Predictions**
World's Three Most Populous Cities

| Year | New York City | Mexico City | Tokyo/Yokohama |
|------|---------------|-------------|----------------|
| 1960 | 14.2 | 4.9 | 10.7 |
| 1970 | 16.2 | 8.7 | 14.9 |
| 1980 | 15.6 | 14.0 | 17.7 |
| 1990 | 15.7 | 19.4 | 20.5 |
| 2000 | 16.1 | 24.4 | 21.3 |

In Millions

(1990 and 2000 figures are predictions)

# Free-form

*"One rare, strange virtue in speeches, and the secret of their mastery, is, that they are short."*

Fitz-Greene Halleck
Early American Poet

**Figure 21-1.**  Types of text charts

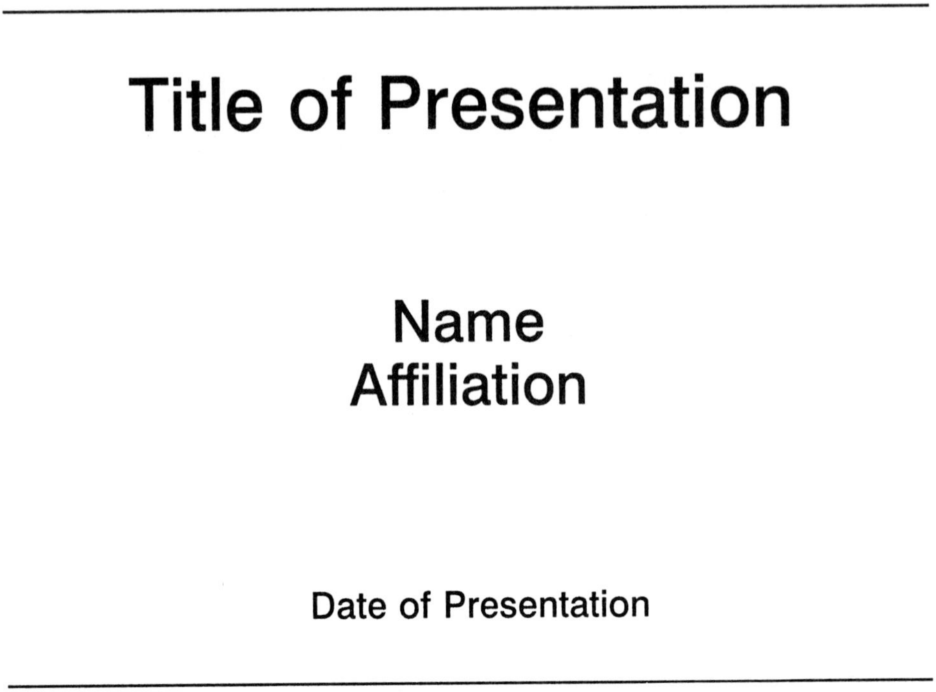

# Title of Presentation

## Name
## Affiliation

### Date of Presentation

**Figure 21-2.**   Title chart

## Column Charts

Column charts contain multiple columns. Column charts are also called *tables*. Typically the columns contain numbers, although text items can be listed side by side in a column format as well. You can use either the <Two columns> or <Three columns> selection from the Text Chart Styles to easily create a column chart with two or three columns. If you want to create a chart with more than three columns, you can use the <Free form> selection from the Text Chart Styles menu or use Harvard Graphics' Draw/Annotate. An example of a column chart is shown in Figure 21-4.

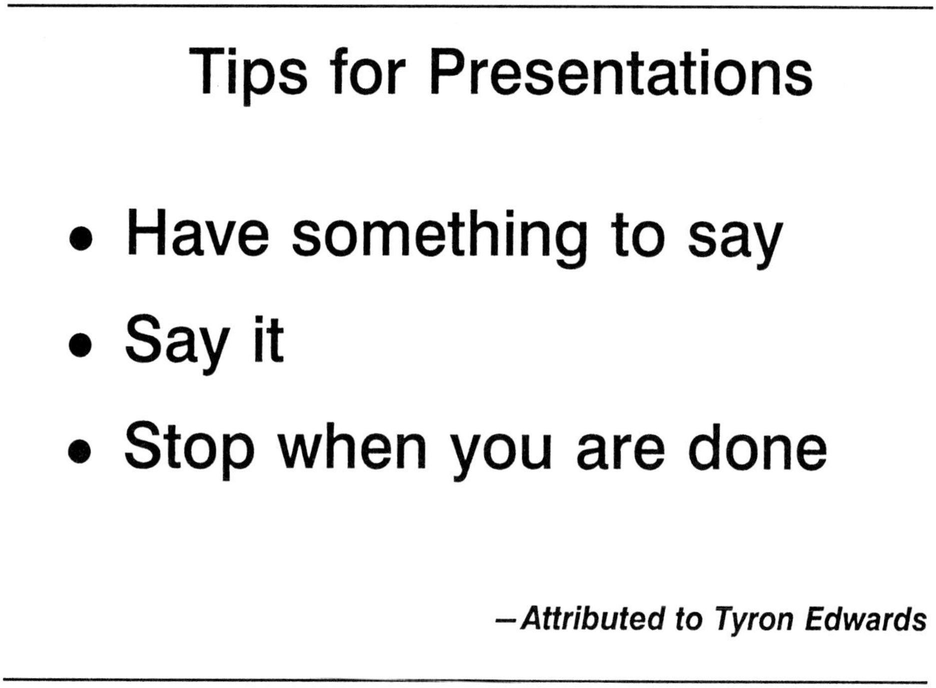

## Tips for Presentations

- Have something to say
- Say it
- Stop when you are done

*—Attributed to Tyron Edwards*

**Figure 21-3.** List chart

## Free-Form Charts

This last type is a catchall category that encompasses any text charts that do not easily fit into one of the preceding categories. Free-form charts may present a single phrase, a sentence, or a paragraph. They may contain information similar to that presented in a list or column chart, but with a layout so different it cannot be categorized as one of these chart styles. For example, you may want to present an outline of your presentation that may not conform to a listing of items conveyed in a list chart.

Although it is fairly easy to lay out a single phrase, sentence, or paragraph on a chart, it can become more difficult to effectively display a more unique, customized layout. This type of layout may take longer to

# Population Predictions
## World's Three Most Populous Cities

| Year | New York City | Mexico City | Tokyo/Yokohama |
|------|---------------|-------------|----------------|
| 1960 | 14.2 | 4.9 | 10.7 |
| 1970 | 16.2 | 8.7 | 14.9 |
| 1980 | 15.6 | 14.0 | 17.7 |
| 1990 | 15.7 | 19.4 | 20.5 |
| 2000 | 16.1 | 24.4 | 21.3 |

In Millions

(1990 and 2000 figures are predictions)

**Figure 21-4.** Column chart

design and to determine whether the layout is effective. In Harvard Graphics, you can create a free-form chart using the <Free form> selection from the Text Chart Styles menu or by using Harvard Graphics' Draw/Annotate features. An example of a free-form chart is shown in Figure 21-5.

## Considerations for Designing Text Charts

The following sections discuss issues to consider in designing effective text charts. The first two topics deal with content. The remaining text chart topics discuss chart components, many of which are shared with data charts, as discussed in Chapter 19 "Effective Data Charts."

*"One rare, strange virtue in speeches,*

*and the secret of their mastery,*

*is, that they are short."*

**Fitz-Green Halleck
Early American Poet**

**Figure 21-5.** Free-form chart

## Simplicity

Keep it simple. Text charts are not meant to be comprehensive. They simply emphasize or summarize the main point or points. Your written or verbal descriptions will complete the picture.

Text charts should be easy to read. If they are, you are more likely to get your point across to your audience. One general recommendation is that your audience should be able to read the entire text chart within at most 30 seconds or so.

Most authorities on text charts recommend you use no more than six lines of text with about six words per line. Although there are no absolutes in business presentation charts, this is the general rule for creating clear and concise text charts. It is up to you, however, to evaluate whether your chart accurately conveys your message. Certainly, tables meant to display numbers or text for reference purposes can contain much more information than a chart created as a bullet list.

## Phrasing

Phrasing is the way in which you convey the information in your chart. This can be summed up as follows:

**Be direct.   Be consistent.   Be clear.**

• Use tense consistently. If one of the points on your chart is in the present tense, the other points should be as well.

• A rule commonly suggested for creating effective text charts is to use an active rather than passive voice. For example, use "Ms. Billings supervises the Marketing Department" rather than "The Marketing Department is supervised by Ms. Billings." However, make sure you are communicating your point as you intend to. There may be times when passive voice is better than active. Using the same example, if you want to stress the marketing department rather than the supervisor, the latter statement is preferable.

• Use consistent phrasing. For example, "Improve sales" and "Increase profits" is consistent whereas "Improving sales" and "Increase profits" is not.

• In list or bullet charts, beginning each item with a verb is often quite effective. For example, "Evaluate current marketing strategies" is more engaging than simply "Current market strategies." The verb involves the reader and provides a direction for the item.

## Fonts and Text Attributes

Fonts are collections of letters and numbers that share similar shapes. There are six fonts available for your chart in Harvard Graphics versions 2.13 and earlier: Executive, Square serif, Roman, Sans serif, Script, and Gothic. Version 2.3 ioncludes an additional font, Traditional. Examples of these fonts (and their available attributes) are shown in "Fonts and Text Attributes" in Appendix D "Harvard Graphics Tables."

In Harvard Graphics, you can use only use one font per chart. Although this may seem limiting, it is actually a good charting practice. You can, if desired, use more than one font in version 2.3 if you create or add to your chart in Draw/Annotate or Draw Partner.

You can vary the appearance of text in a chart by modifying the font attributes used for different text elements. There are five text attributes you can apply in any combination: Fill, Bold, Italic, Underline, and Color. For example, you may want the title or header for your text chart to appear in boldface and the remainder of the text to appear in a plain font (with no attributes defined). You can also use text attributes to highlight or emphasize a particular word or point on your chart. Effective attributes for emphasizing a word or line are bold and italics. Remember, however, that not all text attributes are available for every Harvard Graphics font.

The following are some suggestions for the use of text attributes. (The use of color is described in a following section.)

- Fonts with complex letters (Roman, Script, and Gothic fonts) are typically more difficult to read than are less elaborate fonts (Executive, Sans serif, and Square serif fonts). This is especially important when you are creating a text chart that contains a good deal of text. Keep in mind that you may need to use a larger text size with Roman, Script, and Gothic fonts than with others, in order to guarantee legibility.

- The topic or content of a chart may render certain fonts inappropriate. For example, you will probably not want to use a Gothic or Script font in your text chart if you are describing state-of-the-art services or products.

- In general, text using both upper- and lowercase letters is easier to read than is text in all capital letters. All capitals can be used for very short titles or column labels, if desired.

- If you want to use underlining, it usually looks best to only underline a word or two for emphasis rather than an entire line.

- When varying text attributes in your text chart, avoid displaying more than about three combinations on a single chart. You should especially refrain from using different text attributes for each of the different points or lines in your chart. It is best to display all points using the same attributes.

- Use attributes consistently when two or more similar charts are part of the same presentation or document.

## Text Sizes

The physical size of the text displayed can greatly affect the chart's overall appearance as well as the readability of the text. Using different sizes for different text is appropriate to the extent that it enhances the readability and appearance of your chart. For example, you can use a larger text size to make the primary points in your chart stand out and use a smaller text for additional details.

It is critical that you ensure all chart text is legible, whether you are displaying your chart on a monitor or projection device, using a slide or overhead transparency, or printing or plotting it on paper. Keep in mind that a text chart that is readable in one presentation method may not be readable using another method. It is always a good idea to test whether the text on your chart is legible before you give a presentation or include the chart in a document.

With text charts on paper, it is easy to determine this by simply examining it. If you are presenting the chart in a slide show, test your presentation method first by moving as far from the chart display as you expect the farthest viewer to be. Make sure you can still read the text on the chart. There is nothing worse than presenting an audience with something they cannot read that is supposed to be an integral part of the presentation.

You should also be aware that if your text size is small, attributes applied to the text may not appear when the chart is displayed or output, depending on the resolution capability of your display or output device. If this occurs, you can either not use the attributes or use a larger text size.

You will need to experiment with different text sizes to find what works best for your chart. This is because the size used for text elements in Harvard Graphics is relative. For example, it is almost impossible to create text that is exactly 1/2 inch tall on your first try since the actual text size differs depending on the font; chart size; whether you are printing, recording to film, or plotting; and on the size of the paper or plotter. The text size number you specify in Harvard Graphics is the percentage of chart space—which is influenced by some of the factors just mentioned—used by the text. A text size of 99, for example, takes up almost the entire chart space. The ultimate point is that you will have to experiment with different text sizes to find those satisfactory for your chart.

Here are some other considerations regarding text size:

• The title or header for your text chart is usually the largest text on the chart. However, a title should not be so large as to overpower the chart itself. If you are using a subtitle, it will usually look best when its size is slightly smaller than that of the title.

• Limit yourself to the use of, at most, three or four different text sizes on any one chart.

• You should temper the number of different text sizes you use with the number of different text attributes you use. For example, your text chart might be distracting if you use both three different text sizes and three different text attributes on a single chart. You will need to experiment to find a combination of text sizes and text attributes that looks attractive.

• A sizing technique that is particularly effective in list charts is to display the points in one size, and any supplementary text below each point in a slightly smaller size.

• Use text sizing consistently. For example, use the same text size for all the points on your chart. (Smaller text is acceptable for point details, as mentioned previously.)

• When you have two or more similar charts in a presentation or report, use the same text size for the various chart elements.

## Color

Effective use of color can enhance the appearance of a chart when it is displayed on a color monitor, printed or plotted on a device that can produce color, or when you produce a slide using a film recorder. Color can add texture to a chart and greatly enhance its subjective visual quality. When color is used, it should improve the effectiveness of your chart—not simply display the different colors available.

Other things to consider when using color include

• You may want to distinguish different types of information on your text chart with color. For example, you might want to use a different color for your title. Another use is to present contrasting points, such as pros and cons, in different colors.

- Be consistent in your use of color. All points in a list or bullet chart should be displayed in the same color. Using differing colors for similar topics can be distracting and appear as if you are including colors for the sake of using color.

- It is usually best to use a single color on any given line in your chart. The most common exception to this rule is the use of a different color for bullets in a list chart.

- If two or more similar charts are to be used together in a presentation or document, be consistent with your use of color for the different chart elements. For example, always use the same color for the title.

- In general, text charts should not have more than three different colors per chart. The only exception to this is when you are incorporating a graphic image (such as a Harvard Graphics symbol) either beside the text in your chart or in the background of your text chart. In these situations, the use of from five to seven colors, maximum, may be appropriate for these graphic elements. The use of more colors can be distracting and difficult to view.

- If you use a colored background in your chart, make sure the text is clearly legible against this background.

- If you use a shadow for your text (using Draw/Annotate or Draw Partner), examine the colors selected for text, shadow, and background to ensure the combination of colors is acceptable and the text is legible.

- Keep in mind that more than five percent of the population has some form of color blindness. Color should not be the only feature used to highlight or set off a particular point.

- If *you* have any form of color blindness, or are simply not the best at matching and mixing colors, ask others to inspect your chart for the appropriateness of the colors selected for chart elements.

## Graphic Enhancements

Adding graphics to your text chart can add variety and enhance the message you are trying to convey. Graphic images can be included in text charts either beside the text or as a part of the background.

You may want to add graphical features to set off your text. These include adding shadows, placing text in a box or other shape, or creating circular text. In fact, many Harvard Graphics users create some or all of their text charts entirely within Draw/Annotate or the Draw Partner accessory in order to create simple yet dramatic text chart enhancements. By making extensive use of the text alignment features, shadow effects, and other drawing objects available in Draw/Annotate and Draw Partner, nearly any type of text chart can be produced.

You may also consider adding a drawing to your chart in order to emphasize your point. Graphics you may consider incorporating in your chart include Harvard Graphics symbols, unique symbols you create using either Draw/Annotate or Draw Partner, images originating from another drawing program, or even other Harvard Graphics charts. Any graphic images you include, however, should be closely related to the topic of the chart. You should not include an image simply because it is attractive or interesting. The point of your chart should be to convey a message, not to impress an audience with your artwork. Along these lines, it is important that the text is emphasized over the graphic image.

Whenever you decide to add graphics to your text chart, whether they are enhancements to the text or additional images added to the chart, you must take care to ensure the additions do not reduce the legibility.

## Organization Charts

Organization charts graphically depict the structure of an organization. These charts show the members of an organization and the relationships among them, as shown in Figure 21-6. Although the primary purpose of an organization chart is to represent business organizations, these charts are also useful for displaying other hierarchical relationships. For example, you can graphically depict a family tree, software program menu structure, or the organization of your computer's directories and subdirectories.

In Harvard Graphics, you can easily create organization charts using the <Organization> selection from the Create New Chart menu.

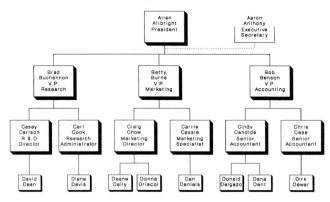

**Figure 21-6.**   Organization chart

Unfortunately, these organization charts are limited, both in the number of levels and the number of individuals who can be displayed at each level. If you are unable to create a correct organization chart using the <Organization> selection from the Create New Chart menu, you might consider drawing an organization chart in Draw/Annotate or Draw Partner.

## Considerations for Designing Organization Charts

All the considerations discussed for text charts in the preceding section, "Considerations for Designing Text Charts," apply to creating effective organization charts as well. The following are additional considerations unique to organization charts:

- It is usually a good idea to include a title for your organization chart.

- Carefully examine the appearance of the text within the boxes of your organization chart. If the text appears crowded or too small, use abbreviated versions of the names, titles, and comments.

- Abbreviations, when used, should be applied consistently. Do not use "Dept." for one comment line and "Department" for another.

- If you use abbreviations, make sure they are ones your viewers will recognize. If you must use abbreviations due to space limitations and think they may be confusing, provide a legend for the abbreviations either in the footnote of your chart or by creating a legend in Draw/Annotate or Draw Partner.

- You do not need to include comments in your organization chart if the title and name text sufficiently describe each member in the organization.

- If you have a number of members at the lowest level in your organization and they cannot all be displayed on one chart, try displaying them using a vertical rather than horizontal orientation.

- Organization charts usually do not include drawings or symbols, with the exception of a company logo. If you include a drawing on your organization chart, make sure it does not interfere with its readability.

- If your organization chart created using <Organization> does not result in a satisfactory chart, bring the chart into Draw/Annotate or Draw Partner and modify it using these tools. Otherwise, create the chart entirely in Draw/Annotate or Draw Partner. Do not let your organization chart suffer because of Harvard Graphics' limitations.

- When several separate organization charts are used together in a presentation or document, ensure the elements are consistent among them.

# Common Charting Mistakes

**Introduction**
**Distortions**
**Illusions**
**Traps**

This chapter introduces you to common mistakes made by chart producers. These mistakes range from poor choice of color or pattern combinations, to chart enhancements that render the chart useless from the viewers' standpoint.

A mistake is something that is unintentional. Sometimes, the distortions or illusions described in this chapter are advantageous. In other words, you can use them to better deliver the information your chart is designed to communicate. For instance, you could use color to draw the viewers' attention to a symbol representing a particular series. However, being able to use these distortions or illusions to your benefit requires that you understand the potential problems these effects can create in your chart. This chapter is designed to give you this understanding.

## Introduction

A great deal of work is involved in getting your point across to the chart viewer. The data must be collected and possibly manipulated. You must then enter the data into Harvard Graphics. You might have to adjust the chart settings. And finally you must create output or add the chart to a slide show. The last thing you want to have happen after all this work is to have your chart fail to adequately communicate your point. Unfortunately, there are many easily overlooked elements of a chart that can either detract from or destroy its effectiveness. In the very worst instances, the resulting chart might be grossly misinterpreted, resulting in unnecessary expense or loss of opportunity.

This chapter details a number of the most common charting mistakes. These can be roughly divided into three categories: distortions, illusions, and traps. A *distortion* results from the text and scale that define your chart. An *illusion* results from features of the charting symbols. *Traps* are common fixations that prevent a chart producer from making more effective charts.

While most of these mistakes occur in data charts, text charts are not entirely immune from these problems. Regardless of your chart type, it is important to always inspect it critically for features that detract from the point you are trying to communicate.

## Distortions

A *distortion*, as the term is used here, is an effect caused by the scale or the accompanying text in a chart. Distortions have an influence on how viewers interpret the chart. Sometimes they pose little more than an inconvenience, requiring chart viewers to work harder to interpret the data. Other times, these distortions can cause the casual viewer to miss the point of the chart entirely.

### Scaling Distortion

All XY charts represent data through the use of symbols (bars, lines, and point markers). The values of these symbols are estimated by comparing their positions against the Y axis. The actual sizes and shapes of the symbols on your chart depend on the *range* of the Y axis—the difference between the smallest and largest axis labels displayed. The range determines the smallest and largest data values that can be represented on your chart. Consider the chart in Figure 22-1. The smallest value that can be displayed against the Y axis is 0 and the largest value is 100. Thus the Y axis range is 100 − 0 = 100.

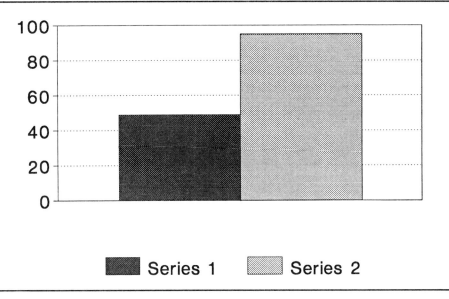

**Figure 22-1.**   Chart with Y axis range of 0–100

When the range of the Y axis is changed, the size of the symbols on the chart change, as do the absolute differences between the sizes of the symbols. If the scale is *increased,* differences between two or more symbols displayed on the chart will decrease in apparent size, while a *reduction* in the scale of the axis will increase the differences in the sizes of the symbols.

The scale distortion is caused when your data values are positive and you reduce the range of your Y axis by not showing the zero point. The result is that the proportionality of your chart symbols is lost. Consider the difference between Figure 22-1 and Figure 22-2, which both chart the same data values. In Figure 22-1, the range has not been distorted. In Figure 22-2, however, the lowest value on the Y axis is much higher than zero, giving the impression that the second bar is many times larger than the first bar, when in fact, the difference is much smaller.

Whether changes in the scale of your axis are valid depends on the purpose of your chart. Specifically, it depends on whether a comparison

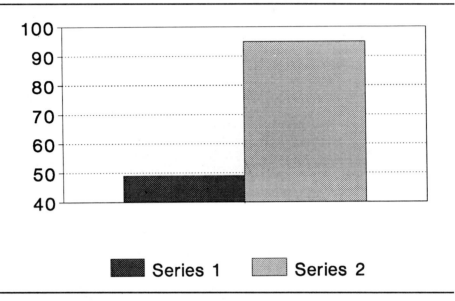

**Figure 22-2.** The Y axis label of 40 gives the impression that the second bar is much larger than the first

between symbols is desirable. When the purpose of the chart is to compare the *relative* size differences between two or more symbols, reducing your scale range can result in a misleading chart. On the other hand, if you are primarily interested in the actual values depicted on a chart, a scale-range distortion can be appropriately applied, and can make the actual values easier to estimate. For example, this is the reason most stock market charts do not include zero. The viewers of these charts are more concerned with the changes in the actual values of stocks rather than the percentage changes.

The following are tips on avoiding this distortion:

- Typically, the Y axis should begin at zero. The exception is when you are also charting negative values (for example, −32, −10, −4). In this case, the lowest Y axis label should be slightly lower than the most negative value you are charting (−35, for example).

- The highest value on the Y axis should be no more than ten percent larger than the largest value being charted. The most common exception to this and the preceding rule is when two or more charts must have the same scale so comparisons can be made across charts. In these instances, the range for all of the charts should be determined by the largest and smallest values of the charts as a whole.

- Avoid limiting the scale of your chart if it is designed to convey information about relative proportions. For example, if you want to show that factory production is ten percent greater this year than the previous year, a zero point should appear on your chart, thereby assuring the proportional differences in the size of your symbols are consistent with the actual percentage change in production.

- If you choose to show less than the full range of the chart, add an annotation or footnote to the chart that warns chart viewers of the nonproportional nature of the symbols when you suspect they might otherwise misinterpret the chart.

## Text Omission Distortion

The text omission distortion occurs when you fail to adequately identify the units being charted. Failure to adequately identify the data, or any transformations, adjustments, or reductions to it, will also result in a text omission distortion. There is never a valid excuse for creating a chart that includes this distortion.

You are probably familiar with the saying that you can prove anything you want by using statistics. This is not entirely accurate. What it should say is that if you omit enough information about your statistics, you can trick people into interpreting them any way you like. In order to communicate effectively with your charts, you must provide viewers with the necessary details for them to accurately interpret the information presented.

A chart should contain all of the following in order to prevent viewers from making assumptions that may be wrong:

- A description of the unit of measurement must be included. For example, your chart should indicate whether a count of units produced or units sold is displayed. If weights are displayed, your chart should specify the unit of weight such as pounds or kilos.

- All transformations or adjustments performed on the data should be clearly indicated.

- Any restrictions or definitions that caused you to include some data in your chart and not other data should be indicated.

- If your data are measured over a period of time, this period must be identified.

- If you use a transformation or adjustment that your viewers may not be familiar with, you need to take extra care to instruct them on the appropriateness of the modification as well as the implications of the change.

Consider the chart shown in Figure 22-3. While it has almost all the elements necessary for a good chart, it is not possible to tell what was

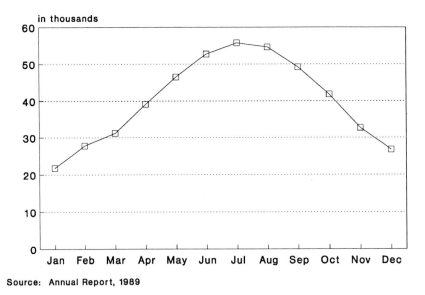

**Figure 22-3.** Chart does not indicate what is being measured

actually measured. Because of this, it would be a mistake for chart viewers to draw conclusions from the data depicted in this chart.

Figure 22-4 shows another example of a text omission distortion that can occur in text charts. In the first statement, viewers may assume that this statement has the same meaning as the statement below it. However, if the statement is taken literally, the unit of measurement must be five years long. In the second statement there is no question about the unit of measurement; it is only one year long. The first statement may imply that the company has regularly sold more ice cream bars than any other company, when in fact the company only managed to do so by having a highly successful year two years ago.

## Misrepresentative Text Distortion

When the text of a data chart describes the effect depicted, and this description is faulty, it tends to mislead viewers into interpreting the data differently than they would otherwise. For example, in Figure 22-5, the text informs viewers that prices of raw materials have remained

---

**In the last five years, we have sold more ice cream bars than any other company in this market.**

**Each year, for the last five years, we have sold more ice cream bars than any other company in this market.**

---

**Figure 22-4.** First statement is not accurately defined

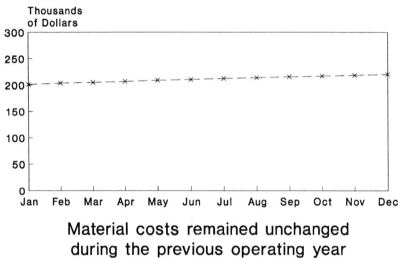

**Figure 22-5.**   Example of a misrepresentative text distortion

unchanged. If you look briefly at this chart, you might come to the same conclusion, in large part because the text leads you to misinterpret the chart. Closer inspection of the chart reveals that a slight, but steady increase in raw material costs has taken place. The overall increase for the period charted is about ten percent, which may be a significant increase.

Misrepresentations can also be present in text charts. It is up to you to carefully and accurately state your points in order to avoid using misleading or confusing words and phrases.

The following are tips on avoiding this distortion:

- Avoid misrepresentative text by including only accurate statements about your data in your chart. If you are unsure about the overall trends in the chart, do not include interpretations in your chart description.

- It is unwise to include descriptions of the size and directions of effects in a data-linked template. Since the data displayed in a chart created from such a template can be updated, it is possible for the effects that are charted to change, which would render the description inaccurate.

## Illusions

An *illusion* is an effect caused by characteristics of the symbols used in data charts. These effects are different from distortions in that all the features of the chart are technically accurate. The illusion arises from incidental features of the otherwise useful symbols. The first two illusions described in the following sections concern charting enhancements that change the apparent size of symbols, making chart elements appear to represent larger or smaller values than they would otherwise. The remaining three illusions can be caused by the colors, shades, and patterns used in your charts.

As a chart producer, you should always be concerned whenever a characteristic other than your data values makes one symbol appear larger or smaller than another.

### Depth Illusion

Chart producers typically love to add a three-dimensional effect to charts. This effect seems to give the chart a sense of concreteness, as well as making it more attractive to viewers. However, three-dimensional effects can dramatically reduce the interpretability of charts if they are not used wisely.

Consider the chart shown in Figure 22-6. Because of the order of the bars and the size of the three-dimensional effect, the bars representing banana consumption obscure the other bars' third dimension, which

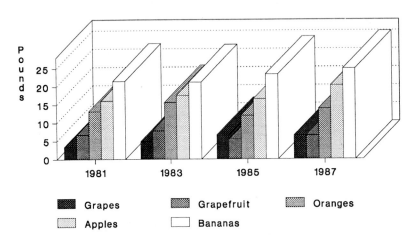

**Figure 22-6.**  Relative order of the bars and three-dimensional effects obscure portions of some bars

suggests that the bars representing bananas are much taller than the others solely because of the three-dimensional effect rather than on actual bar height.

Another concern about three-dimensional distortions is that the chart viewer may not know which part of the chart should be compared to the grid lines in the chart frame. Do you use the front of the bar or the back of the bar? Because a three-dimensional illusion introduces a sense of perspective onto the chart frame (that is, the grid lines in back are higher than the corresponding tick marks on the side), some misinterpretation may result. For instance, the chart viewer may compare the height of the front of the bar to the grid lines in the back of the chart frame. This would result in lower estimates for the series values than would the correct comparison, which is the front of the bars against the tick marks at the front of the Y axis frame or the back of the bars against the back grid lines.

Another serious distortion is displayed in Figure 22-7. This figure includes two charts. Both of these charts depict the same data. The only difference is the inclusion of the three-dimensional effect in the chart on the top. While at first glance the top chart looks fine, closer inspection will reveal that it is nearly impossible to estimate the values represented by the bars in this chart. Although you can compare the consumption of grapes over the years and the consumption of grapefruit over the years, the three-dimensional effect makes it very difficult to compare the consumption of grapes and grapefruit within a given year. By adding this three-dimensional effect, the chart has been rendered almost useless as a tool for estimating and analyzing the data.

To avoid creating an illusion in your chart, consider the following:

- Whenever you add a three-dimensional effect to a chart, it is important you ensure the resulting chart still serves the purpose for which it was created.

- If the three-dimensional effect introduces a distortion that degrades the chart's effectiveness, you should supplement the chart by also displaying a table of the data. While most three-dimensional distortions are not as dramatic as the ones shown in Figures 22-6 and 22-7, care should always be taken before settling on a chart with this enhancement.

- You should use your good judgment. If the distortion to your chart is substantial, make additional adjustments to the chart settings in order to reduce the negative effects of three-dimensional enhancements.

- These same considerations should be taken into account when a shadow effect is added to your chart.

## Size Illusion

The size illusion can occur when drawings other than standard symbols (bars, lines, point markers, or pie slices) are used in your chart. Con-

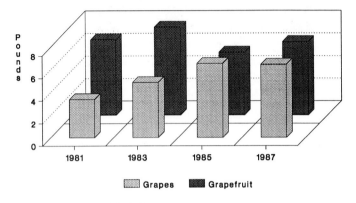

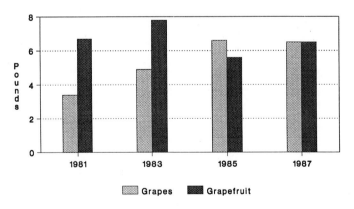

**Figure 22-7.** Same data in charts with and without the three-dimensional effect

sider the charts shown in Figure 22-8. In both charts a Harvard Graphics symbol, in this case a cluster of grapes, has been substituted for the bars in a bar chart. In the chart on the top, however, the use of the symbol created a distortion of the data. This distortion has occurred because, although the data are changing in only one dimension, the symbol has changed size in two dimensions. Although the 1985 data value for grape consumption is actually about twice as large as the 1981 data value for grape consumption, the symbol representing 1985 grape consumption is many times larger in overall volume than the 1981 symbol. The symbols in this chart vary on both height and width dimensions.

In the bottom chart, however, the different data values are shown by stacking the symbols. One dimension of the symbols, their height, varies without adding a change to the width. Another alternative you may want to use is to superimpose more artistic symbols on the standard ones, as was done in Figure 22-9.

The following are considerations for avoiding the size illusion:

- Do not represent a change in data values with changes in two dimensions.

- If you want to use the drawing capabilities of Harvard Graphics to create interesting and novel symbols, you may want to stack the symbols instead of increasing their overall size, as was done in the bottom chart in Figure 22-8. When you stack unique symbols in a bar chart, place partial symbols at the top of the stack rather than at the bottom (as in Figures 22-8 and 22-9). In other words, if a value you want to represent equals 2 1/2 of your symbol's size, place the half symbol at the top of the bar.

## Color Illusion

Not all colors have an equal impact when viewed in your chart; some stand out more than others. In some instances you can use this to your advantage, drawing viewers' attention to a specific bar, line, area, group of markers, or pie slice. However, when most of your chart symbols are of equal importance, it is best to use a selection of colors that do not

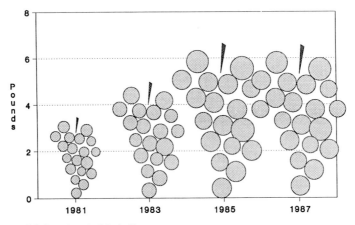

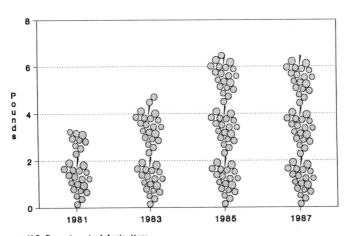

**Figure 22-8.** Symbols in the top chart create a size illusion; symbols in the bottom chart do not

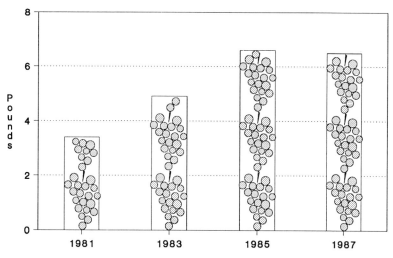

**Figure 22-9.**  Alternative way of incorporating unique symbols in a bar chart

unduly emphasize one of the series, since the result of the color illusion is that dominant colors tend to look larger than less-striking ones.

The following are some general tips for using color:

• Be aware that some colors have meanings of their own within a given industry or area. For example, the color red often has a particular meaning in different industries and areas. Take care so that you do not unintentionally imply something simply by your choice of color.

• Avoid using too many colors in a chart. In general, do not use more than five different colors.

• When you need to use more than five colors, such as when you have more than five series of data in a data chart, display your title, subtitle, and all other text in a single color.

- Do not use colors that are opposites, red and green for example, next to each other. Opposite colors clash and are unpleasant to look at when they appear side by side.

- Use color consistently. For instance, if you have several charts, use the same colors for the same series in each chart. Use the same colors for the text in related chart titles or related text charts.

## Shading Illusion

The shading illusion is similar to the color illusion. When using shades, ensure that the shade for one of your symbols does not dominate the others. An example of a poor selection of different shades is shown in the chart on the top of Figure 22-10; the dark bars dominate the other bars in the chart. A more balanced selection of shading is shown in the chart on the bottom.

The following are tips for avoiding shading problems:

- Do not use strikingly different shades next to one another.

- Ensure that the shades you select are distinguishable.

- Use shades consistently. For example, always select the same shade for a series that will appear in two or more charts.

## Pattern Illusion: The Moiré Effect

Patterns are used when shades or colors cannot be used to distinguish the different chart symbols. Unless you pay some attention to the selection of patterns for your chart symbols, truly appalling charts can result. In particular you should try to avoid, to whatever extent possible, using patterns that consist of sets of parallel lines, especially parallel diagonal lines. Consider the chart shown in Figure 22-11. The patterns

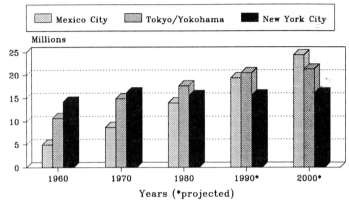

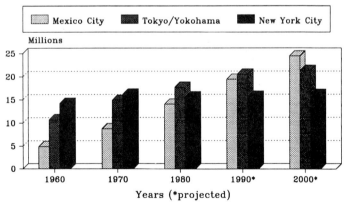

**Figure 22-10.** Top chart shows an example of shading illusion; shades selected in the bottom chart do not

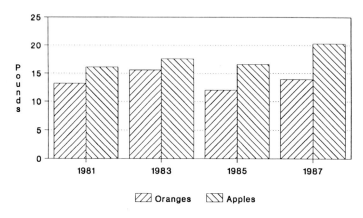

**Figure 22-11.**   Example of the moiré effect

used in the bars of this chart seem to make the bars vibrate or shimmer slightly. This is called the moiré effect.

The following are tips for avoiding illusions with patterns:

- Do not use patterns that create a moiré effect.

- As with colors and shades, use patterns consistently in different charts that will be used in the same presentation or document.

- If you have a single series in an XY chart, either do not use a pattern at all or use a subtle one. A simple outline or a solid color is preferable.

## Traps

This section describes several of the common traps graph producers can get caught in. Unlike distortions and illusions, which are inadvertent characteristics of elements, traps result when you cannot devise alternative ways of creating your chart. There are three basic traps: the artistic trap, the chart-fixation trap, and the equipment/software trap.

## Artistic Trap

The purpose of a chart is always to communicate information about your data or to communicate your points or ideas. This aim is sometimes undermined by the *artistic trap*. When you fall into the artistic trap, the chart itself begins to take on more importance than the data or text it displays. In some cases, the artistic trap results in a chart that is a thing of beauty. Unfortunately, the viewers may be so struck by the sheer magnificence of your chart that the data or points will be entirely overlooked.

More often, however, the artistic trap usually results in a gaudy chart that is distracting to the point of obscuring the data or ideas. This trap can occur in either data or text charts. An example of just such a chart is shown in Figure 22-12. To avoid this trap, keep in mind the following:

- Do not add irrelevant drawings.
- Limit the use of ornate borders.
- Limit the use of colors that do not add to the chart.
- Do not add drawings that obscure important details.
- If you add drawings, limit yourself to one or two.
- Remember, your data and ideas are more important than the chart itself.

## Chart-Fixation Trap

*Chart fixation* means that you become so accustomed to creating a particular style of chart that you fail to consider alternative styles. The result may be to select an inappropriate chart style for your data or ideas. This trap can occur in either data or text charts. The easiest way

**Figure 22-12.** Example of the artistic trap

to avoid it is to always consider the point you want to make, and then consider which type of chart or alternative method will *best* demonstrate this point.

## Equipment/Software Trap

It is easy to get excited about a new piece of high-tech equipment for chart creation, or the newest software on the market for making charts. Both hardware and software, however, are merely tools for creating your charts. The *equipment/software trap* refers to what results when the desire to use a new piece of equipment or software is the driving force behind the creation of a chart, instead of the data or ideas.

Unfortunately, not all equipment or software can create all types of charts or enhancements. Keep the following tips in mind to avoid this trap:

- If the fancy piece of equipment or the new piece of software cannot produce the chart you need, do not use it. Keep in mind that it is better to use the appropriate tool and create the right chart than to create an inadequate one. There will always be an opportunity to work with nice software or hardware in a situation in which your charts will not be adversely affected.

- The creation of a chart should be driven by the need to communicate information. When the tools for creating a chart begin to assume more importance than the data or ideas, there is a danger of using a chart that is less effective than you would otherwise desire.

# Using Charts in Presentations and Documents

**Designing Effective Presentations**
**Using Charts in Documents**
**Using Humor**

This chapter brings together all the topics covered in this part of the book. Uses for the charts you have created in Harvard Graphics, including adding them to a document or using them in a presentation are discussed. The use of charts in presentations takes up the largest portion of this chapter. This is not to imply that charts are not important in documents, only that using charts in presentations is more complicated.

The first section of this chapter focuses on designing presentations. Presentations are a great deal of fun to create, but they also require a fair amount of work and attention to detail. Later sections in this chapter describe how to best use your charts within the body of documents.

## Designing Effective Presentations

Designing presentations requires many of the same considerations you must take into account when designing a single chart. Presentations have many more aspects than a single chart, however. When you design a single chart, you start by identifying the point you want it to make. Given that you have constructed your chart thoughtfully, it will convey this point well. When you create a presentation, you also have a point to make, and this point is usually much broader than the point of a single chart. This broader point is called the *theme* of the presentation. The theme is the glue that holds a presentation together. Without a theme, a presentation lacks focus and impact.

Although the most important step, developing the theme is only the first of five steps involved in creating a quality presentation. These steps are as follows.

1. Develop the theme
2. Define the main points
3. Select the charts you want to include
4. Prepare charts and presentation notes
5. Practice and fine-tune your presentation

The following sections provide a more detailed description of each of these steps. These steps, however, are not intended to be taken as entirely separate. In fact, during the design of most presentations, many of these steps progress simultaneously.

## Develop the Presentation Theme

All well-designed presentations have a theme that defines the global content. This theme is dictated by the data or information you want to present, as well as by the message you want to communicate to your audience. A presentation theme can be general, which is not to say it is not focused. The theme of a presentation is usually direct and suggests a result or conclusion. The following are examples of potential themes of a presentation:

- Our product line needs a new look
- Anticipated market directions
- Sales are increasing

## Define the Main Points

Any theme can generally be divided into from two to five separate but related points. These points are usually defined by the evidence or information you will want to present to your audience. For example, consider the theme "Our product line needs a new look." The points may be as follows:

- Customer demographics are changing
- Our competitor's products look better
- A fresh, new look will attract new customers

These main points form the basis of your overall presentation outline.

### Select the Charts

Each of the main points you have defined can usually be presented visually using charts. These charts can be text charts, data charts, definitions, or illustrations. You select charts based on the type of information that will demonstrate each of the points in your presentation. An example of such a chart layout plan is shown in Table 23-1.

### Prepare Charts and Presentation Notes

This step is often completed simultaneously with the chart layout plan designed in the previous step. As you define the charts that will be presented, you should start to create a set of notes to remind you of the various issues you want to discuss during your presentation. In addition, you may want to anticipate the types of questions your audience may raise at various points in the presentation so that you can quickly respond.

    Before you actually print, plot, or record your charts, make sure that you spell check them. This can also be done in the next step, but it is always best to correct spelling problems before you create output of your charts.

### Practice and Fine-Tune Your Presentation

Finally, you must practice your presentation. This often involves a number of stages. For example, you may give the spoken part of your presentation to an empty room. You would do this to test the flow of

| Chart Style | Purpose |
| --- | --- |
| Title chart | Displays the title of the presentation and your name and affiliation. |
| List chart | Lists the main topics you will cover in the presentation. |
| First buildup chart | Lists first topic, "Customer demographics are changing." |
| Data chart | Chart showing selected demographic data. |
| Data chart | Second chart showing demographic data. |
| Second buildup chart | Adds second topic to previous buildup chart, "Research shows customer tastes have changed." |
| List chart | Lists predictions of what will attract new customers and appeal to old ones. |
| Data chart | Chart depicting data that supports prediction 1. |
| Data chart | Chart depicting data that supports prediction 2. |
| List chart | Lists additional research efforts currently under way. |
| Third buildup chart | Adds third topic to previous buildup chart, "Fresh new look will attract new customers." |
| Illustration | Picture of current product design. |
| Data chart | Chart depicting the change in customer acceptance of current design over time. |
| Illustration | Picture of proposed new look for the product design. |
| Data chart | Chart showing focus group input on new product design. |
| Data chart | Chart showing anticipated sales increases. |
| List chart | Summary list of points. |
| List chart | List of conclusions. |
| Illustration | Picture of new product design superimposed with a statement mentioning its promising future. |

**Table 23-1.** An Example Plan of Charts to Include in a Presentation

your topics and determine if you need to add any additional points or charts. In many instances, there is also a stage in which once all charts are created, you give a practice presentation to others to ensure your timing is acceptable and your charts adequately support your points.

You should expect to make some changes to your presentation at this stage. Most good speakers put a great deal of effort into developing and refining a presentation, making changes to their points and charts and always seeking ways to ensure that they communicate effortlessly and convincingly.

It is during this final stage that you should be your own worst critic. The following are a few tips for including charts in your presentation:

- Examine your charts carefully for aspects of good chart design, as described in the preceding four chapters. Are the charts effective? Are they understandable?

- Each chart you include in your presentation should be displayed long enough for your audience to be able to comfortably read or examine it. Usually this requires, on the average, just under a minute, although the content of the chart should dictate the minimum display time. For example, a text chart that contains one or two short phrases may be displayed for a much shorter period than a table of data or a more complex data chart. If it is reasonable to do so, you may want to leave the chart displayed until you are ready to display the next one.

- While displaying the chart, describe it or state the points it summarizes. There may be situations in which it is appropriate to allow your audience a few moments to examine the chart without your commentary—in other words, pause during your presentation. After a short pause, you should describe or summarize your points or ideas as reflected in the chart.

- Practice coordinating your description of a chart with the display of the chart itself to determine the best timing and presentation method. Do you want to introduce a chart and then display it? Do you want to display the chart first and then describe it? Do you want to display the chart after making your point to summarize your ideas?

- Many times if you are referring to a particular point displayed on your chart, you may want to point to it. Likewise, when referring to symbols (bars, lines, pie slices) in a data chart, pointing to the specific symbol can help ensure the audience is following you.

- Sometime before you give your presentation, verify that all of your notes and charts (whether overhead transparencies, posters, slides, handouts, or charts in a slide show) are all present and in the correct order.

## Putting It Together: Clarity, Consistency, and Context

The three Cs of presentations are clarity, consistency, and context. All good presentations have these three elements. These are not simple to come by, however, and take time and consideration. Failing to include them can result in your entire presentation lacking impact and failing to communicate.

*Clarity* means your points and data are understandable. Whenever possible, use simple, straightforward wording or descriptions rather than complicated ones. Good presenters convey their ideas clearly and with ease. A sure sign of a failed presentation is when the audience leaves thinking, "That presenter sure is intelligent. Most of what was presented was way over my head and I still don't know what the point was."

Achieving clarity in your presentation requires time and planning. The first step is to be knowledgeable about your topic and able to describe it to others. This is more difficult than it sounds. You may want to enlist the services of co-workers or other people unfamiliar with your topic. Describe to them what you want to say. Encourage them to point out where you have not been clear enough. Remember, if your audience cannot understand you, it is because you have not discovered a way to convey the information simply and in an understandable manner—and not because your audience lacks intelligence.

*Consistency* is something that will go far to ensure your presentation is clearly understood. Your charts should be consistent with one another, your terminology should be consistent, and your use of color and emphasis should be consistent. For example, take care not to introduce elements into your presentation that suggest you are making distinctions where none are intended. This can happen innocently when a similar chart element is displayed in one color in one chart and another color in another chart. Consistency does not mean repetitive or bland, however. Instead, it means that your audience will have an easier time understanding your points.

The third C of presentations is *context*. The parts of a presentation are in a context defined by the theme of the presentation and the various points you want to make. Keep the purpose of your presentation in mind to create an integrated, meaningful presentation rather than a collection of separate ideas.

## Incorporating Text Charts

There are three text charts that nearly every presentation includes. The first of these is a title chart, which provides an informative title. Sometimes titles are designed to generate interest in the presentation. While this is an important feature for any presentation, it is even more important when attendance is optional. It is harder to attract an audience to a presentation with a title that sounds dull and boring. On the other hand, your title should not trivialize the presentation topic. A too-glib presentation title can suggest that you do not take the topic or presentation seriously.

The second text chart a presentation nearly always contains is a list of the two to five major points you are going to make. This list works somewhat like a road map. It serves as a guide, indicating to your audience where you plan to take them. This permits your audience to focus on the relevant information you present. This list chart is often displayed several times during a presentation to bring the audience back to the main points and give a sense of continuity.

You might consider displaying this list as a *buildup*. That is, when introducing the first main point, display this chart with only the first point shown. Then when you continue to the second point, redisplay the chart with both the first and second points. This technique can be successfully used to interject novelty as well as continuity into your presentation.

The last of the three charts contains a summary. In some instances, this chart again may be your list of points. While this chart is displayed, you recap your main points and tie together all the loose ends. In other instances, this is a new chart that highlights the major topics or conclusions of your presentation. Again, this chart is presented to summarize. It reminds the audience of your major points and allows them to reflect on the information you presented in light of the entire presentation.

Most presentations will contain many more text charts than the three described here. These additional text charts are often related to the points described in the list chart. For example, one of the items in the list may be discussed with the aid of a table, a paragraph description, or another list that breaks the point down even further.

The following are general rules of good text chart usage in presentations:

- Be consistent in your use of terms and descriptions in the various text charts in your presentation. For example, do not use "Shipping Expenses" on one chart and "Transportation Costs" on another. Doing so may leave your audience wondering whether you are referring to the same or different items.

- Use colors consistently between related text charts. You may want all your titles to be one color, and all your points another. This consistent use of color adds a sense of unity to your presentation and gives it a more professional look.

## Incorporating Data Charts

Data charts are included in order to demonstrate one of the points listed in a list chart. It is not unusual to create a presentation that does not include any data charts. However, if data are available, presenting the data that support your points enables your audience to see the evidence for themselves. This is usually much more convincing than a simple verbal description.

In many presentations, your data charts are crucial to the points you are making. In fact, the points of your presentation may be determined by the patterns and trends in your data. Even so, you typically do not create a presentation with data only. You need to use text charts to introduce the data charts, to explain special measurements or techniques used in data collection, and to summarize the patterns and trends present in the data charts. The data charts are the focus, and the text charts are the guides. The following are tips on incorporating data charts into presentations:

- When you use two or more data charts that contain data your audience should compare, be sure these charts use the same Y axis range. The symbols (bars, lines, areas, markers) can only be directly compared when the different charts have the same range for the Y axes.

- Patterns, shades, and colors should be used consistently when two or more charts display related data. For example, if you have two bar charts, each displaying a bar depicting sales of a specific product, both bars should employ the same pattern, shade, or color.

- When similar data are presented in separate charts, use the same units of measure (such as dollars, percentages, amounts) so viewers can easily compare the charted values.

- If your presentation uses transparencies, slides, or a computerized slide show, consider handing out printed copies of all data charts for reference. This is optional, but is desirable in presentations in which the data are critical.

## Incorporating Illustrations

*Illustrations* are pictures you use in your presentation. They may be used to simplify a difficult description, to display images of interest, or to represent the relationship among a number of different objects. Your illustrations may originate from a number of sources. They can be photographs, captured computer screen images, or drawings created with Harvard Graphics' Draw/Annotate or Draw Partner. The following are guidelines to assist you in using illustrations:

- Make sure any illustrations you use are clean and identifiable. Specifically, do not include pictures of poor quality. If your audience cannot tell what you are showing them, the illustration is not going to leave a good impression.

- If you draw your illustration, avoid falling into the artistic trap described in Chapter 22, "Common Charting Mistakes."

## Special Considerations for Computerized Presentations

Computerized presentations are one of the most important new presentation technologies. It is easy to imagine a time in the near future when many business presentations will use or incorporate electronic capabilities. Some of the advantages of computerized presentations are as follows:

- You can quickly create an attractive presentation.

- You can easily make last-minute modifications to your computerized presentation.

- Special effect transitions and buildups can add interest and a professional quality to your presentation.

- Computerized presentations can be interactive or automated.

- If you can rely on the necessary equipment being available, you can transport your presentation on computer disks.

While this technology can be an important part of your presentations, some cautions are in order. As the old saying goes, if anything can go wrong, it will. By using a computer to present your presentation you are introducing a whole new realm of possible fiascoes. Here is a list of potential problems to consider:

- If you are taking your presentation to another location, you must either bring your own computer or rely on a satisfactory one being available. Even if a computer is available, the graphics adapter may not be satisfactory. Or, an adequate screen projector may not be available. Or, your disks may be damaged en route to the location.

- The computer equipment could fail prior to—or even during—your presentation.

- Computerized presentations are only as flexible as you have planned. For example, if a question arises for which a later chart needs to be displayed, unless you have programmed a Go To key for that chart, you will not be able to easily display it in response to the question.

These problems should not discourage you from using computerized presentations. Rather, they give you some idea of the type of planning you need to do. The following are suggestions for planning a computerized presentation:

- If you are giving a computerized presentation using a computer you are not familiar with, step through the entire presentation in a practice session on the unfamiliar computer prior to the actual presentation.

- If you are transporting your presentation on disks, take along a backup copy, just in case. Do not keep both of these copies in the same place, if possible. Likewise, remember to bring your copy of Harvard Graphics (or the ScreenShow Utilities accessory).

- Have a backup plan. Be able to make your presentation if the computer, disks, power, or whatever is unavailable or fails. Making handouts to go along with the presentation is a good idea. These can be handed out as a supplement even when you are using a computerized presentation.

- If the presentation is self-running, make sure it is also self-explanatory.

- For the best results, start your presentation using Quick Start. (See Chapter 2, "Harvard Graphics Basics.")

## Using Charts In Documents

Documents typically include only data charts, tables, or illustrations. List charts and other text charts are not usually used in documents. Charts serve a number of valuable functions in documents, including adding variety. This should not, however, be the sole reason for including charts in documents. The following are guidelines for using charts in a document:

- Explicit reference should be made to the chart within the body of the document text referring the reader to the chart figure at the appropriate point.

- Your document should include a description of the chart. This description should include suggestions of what the chart viewer should examine.

- Whenever possible, the chart should be included within the body of the document text rather than in an appendix. When the chart is placed within the text of the document, the placement should be as close to the first reference in the text as is reasonable. It is usually not a good idea, however, to place the data chart ahead of the first reference to it.

- You might consider including a table of any data charted in a data chart in the appendix of the document as a supplement if the precise numbers may be of use to document readers. If the actual numbers are *crucial* to the point you are making, however, it is best to include the table of data within the body of the document.

## Using Humor

When used thoughtfully and carefully, humor can be an effective way of getting or keeping your audience's attention. Beginning a presentation with a relevant funny illustration or an entertaining anecdote can go a long way toward making your audience relaxed and responsive. On the other hand, insensitive or inappropriate humor can backfire.

The following are a few thoughts on using humor:

- If you have added a humorous story or illustration to your presentation, you must provide yourself the option of skipping it. This is important if during your presentation you determine that inclusion of the humor would be inappropriate or untimely.

- Do not use humor that is in any way sexist, racist, or otherwise offensive in any manner.

- Be very cautious about using humor in a document. Remember that you cannot be entirely sure who will see a document. Unlike a presentation, once humor is placed in a document, it is not possible to remove it.

# Reference

**Harvard Graphics Forms and Function Keys**
**Draw Partner Forms and Function Keys**

PART FIVE

# Harvard Graphics Forms and Function Keys

## Harvard Graphics Forms

This section consists of a quick reference of all the forms used in Harvard Graphics, listed in alphabetical order. Each reference includes the location in Harvard Graphics where the form can be found, as well as a brief description of the form. Then all the form options and the default setting for each option are described. When a form or option is only available in a particular version of Harvard Graphics, this is noted beside the form or option name.

## Application Options Overlay (Version 2.3)

```
              Application Options

Use EMS memory if available:    Yes  ▶No
Temporary file directory:

Draw Partner options
  Video mode:          ▶Default  CGA   EGA   VGA   HERCULES
  Summagraphics tablet: ▶None    Com1  Com2
  Use monochrome menus: Yes      ▶No
```

**Location**  Select <Setup> from the Main Menu, followed by <Applications> from the Setup menu to display the Applications form. Then press F8-Options to display the Application Options overlay.

**Description**  The first two options on this overlay apply to any application specified on the Applications form. The last three options apply to Draw Partner.

### Use EMS memory if available

**Default:** Yes

Select Yes to save the temporary image of your Harvard Graphics session to expanded memory when you select an application from the Applications menu. Select No if you do not have expanded memory or if you do not want Harvard Graphics to use it.

*Note:*  Harvard Graphics requires that your expanded memory use the LIM 4.0 specification.

### Temporary file directory

**Default:** (Blank)

Enter the name of a directory in which the temporary image of your Harvard Graphics session should be stored when you select an application from the Applications menu. When you quit the other application to return to Harvard Graphics, this temporary file will be deleted from the temporary file directory. At least 600K must be available in the directory you specify at "Temp file dir."

*Hint:*  You can specify a RAM disk at "Temp file dir" to speed processing time.

### Video modes

**Default:** Default

Select the graphics adapter you will be using with Draw Partner. Leave this option set to Default, the setting Harvard Graphics automatically selected when you started the program. If the Draw Partner menus look distorted, you can try one of the other settings.

### Summagraphics tablet

**Default:** None

To use a Summagraphics digitizing tablet with Draw Partner, indicate the port of your computer to which the tablet is connected.

### Use monochrome menus

**Default:** No

Set this option to Yes to have Draw Partner menus displayed in monochrome.

## Applications Form (Version 2.3)

```
                          Applications

       Menu item 1: Draw Partner     Menu item 5:
       Maximum size (K):             Maximum size (K):
       Command: HGDP.EXE             Command:

       Menu item 2:                  Menu item 6:
       Maximum size (K):             Maximum size (K):
       Command:                      Command:

       Menu item 3:                  Menu item 7:
       Maximum size (K):             Maximum size (K):
       Command:                      Command:

       Menu item 4:                  Menu item 8:
       Maximum size (K):             Maximum size (K):
       Command:                      Command:


       F1-Help
                                  F8-Options     F10-Continue
```

**Location**   Select <Setup> from the Main Menu followed by <Applications> from the Setup menu to display the Applications form.

**Description**   Use this form to specify the applications (other programs and Harvard Graphics accessories) you want to be able to access from within Harvard Graphics. The first application on the form is Draw Partner, a Harvard Graphics accessory. You cannot modify this entry. The second entry is AGX Slide Service. You can change this entry, if desired, as well as specify up to six additional applications. Applications specified here will be listed on the Applications menu displayed when you press F3-Applications at the Main Menu.

*Note:* You cannot add the program MACRO that came with the Harvard Graphics package to the Applications form. You must start MACRO from DOS.

### Menu Item (1 through 8)

**Default:** (Draw Partner, AGX Slide Service, ...)

Enter each of the program or accessory names you want to be able to access in Harvard Graphics at the "Program name" options.

### Maximum size (K)

**Default:** (Blank)

If your application requires less than the maximum amount of memory available, enter the number of kilobytes (K) required. Leave this option blank if your application requires all available memory. The maximum amount of memory available is roughly 13K less than was available before you started Harvard Graphics.

### Command

**Default:** (Blank)

For each application specified at a "Program name" option, enter the exact command (including the directory path) that would be required to start the application from the DOS prompt. For example, type **C:\LOTUS123\123** to start the Lotus 1-2-3 program stored in the directory called LOTUS123. The path of the directory is not essential if the directory is included in your DOS path. (See your DOS manual for additional details about your DOS path.)

## Area Chart Data Form

```
                        Area Chart Data
    Title:
 Subtitle:
 Footnote:

              X Axis        Series 1   Series 2   Series 3   Series 4
     Pt        Name

      1
      2
      3
      4
      5
      6
      7
      8
      9
     10
     11
     12

 F1-Help            F3-Save        F5-Set X type                F9-More series
 F2-Draw chart      F4-Draw/Annot  F6-Calculate    F8-Options   F10-Continue
```

**Location**  At the Create New Chart menu, select <Area> to display the Area Chart Data form.

**Description**  The Area Chart Data form is used to enter text and data for an area chart. This form has two areas. At the top are entry spaces for a chart title, subtitle, and footnote. The rest of the form contains columns for the data.

### Title, Subtitle, and Footnote

**Defaults:** (Blank)

Enter a title, subtitle, and/or footnote for your area chart, as desired. If your subtitle or footnote text requires more than one line, enter it on Page 1 of the Area Chart Titles & Options form.

### X Axis

Enter the X axis data in this column. Note that the X data type (Name, Number, Time, or one of the eight calendar-based data types) specified on the X Data Type Menu overlay is displayed at the top of the column under "X Axis." If you used Harvard Graphics' automatic X data entry feature, this column will already contain your X data.

### Series 1 through Series 8

Enter Y axis data in the series columns. The Y axis data must be numeric. If you have more than four series (groups of data), press F9-More series to display additional columns for "Series 5" through "Series 8."

## Area Chart: Size/Place Overlay

**Location** At Page 1 of the Area Chart Titles & Options form, press F7-Size/Place to display the Size/Place overlay.

**Description** Use each row of the Size/Place overlay to define the size and placement of the title, subtitle, footnote, and axis titles entered on the Titles & Options form. Once you set the desired options, press F7-Size/Place or F10-Continue to return to the Titles & Options form.

### Size

**Defaults:** (Vary depending on the line)

```
Size   Place        Area Chart  Titles & Options  Page 1 of 4
 8      L ▸C R  Title:
 6      L ▸C R  Subtitle:
 6      L ▸C R
 2.5    ▸L C  R  Footnote:
 2.5    ▸L C  R
 2.5    ▸L C  R
 4        ▸C      X  axis title:
 3       ▸→ ↓    Y1 axis title:
 3       ▸→ ↓    Y2 axis title:
         X labels                        Type              Display     Y Axis
         Y labels                Area Line Trend Bar       Yes  No     Y1  Y2
     1  Series 1                         Area                Yes        Y1
     2  Series 2                         Area                Yes        Y1
     3  Series 3                         Area                Yes        Y1
     4  Series 4                         Area                Yes        Y1
     5  Series 5                         Area                Yes        Y1
     6  Series 6                         Area                Yes        Y1
     7  Series 7                         Area                Yes        Y1
     8  Series 8                         Area                Yes        Y1

F1-Help                     F5-Attributes    F7-Size/Place
F2-Draw chart                                F8-Data              F10-Continue
```

Enter a number from .1 to 99. This number represents a percentage of the chart height (landscape) or width (portrait).

### Place

**Defaults:** (Vary depending on the line)

Set placement for the title, subtitle, and footnote to either L, C, or R to left-justify, center, or right-justify the text. The X axis title is automatically centered. There are two placement options for the Y1 and Y2 axis titles: vertical and horizontal. Set Y axis title placement to horizontal (the default) to have the titles read left to right at the top of the axes. Set Y axis title placement to vertical to have the titles read vertically along the axes.

## Area Chart Titles & Options Form

**Location**  At the Area Chart Data form, press F8-Options to display the Area Chart Titles & Options form.

**Description**  The Area Chart Titles & Options form contains options that allow you to change the appearance of your area chart. This form is four pages long. Press PGDN and PGUP to move between pages of the form.

## Page 1 of the Area Chart Titles & Options Form

```
                    Area Chart  Titles & Options  Page 1 of 4
                Title:
                Subtitle:

                Footnote:


                X  axis title:
                Y1 axis title:
                Y2 axis title:
   Legend                          Type              Display  | Y Axis
   Title:                    Area Line Trend Bar     Yes  No  | Y1  Y2

   1 | Series 1                    Area                Yes      Y1
   2 | Series 2                    Area                Yes      Y1
   3 | Series 3                    Area                Yes      Y1
   4 | Series 4                    Area                Yes      Y1
   5 | Series 5                    Area                Yes      Y1
   6 | Series 6                    Area                Yes      Y1
   7 | Series 7                    Area                Yes      Y1
   8 | Series 8                    Area                Yes      Y1

F1-Help                  F5-Attributes   F7-Size/Place
F2-Draw chart                            F8-Data           F10-Continue
```

### Title

**Default:** (Blank)

Enter a title for your chart.

### Subtitle

**Default:** (Blank)

Enter a subtitle for the chart; it can be up to two lines long.

### Footnote

**Default:** (Blank)

Enter a footnote for your chart; it can be up to three lines long.

### X axis title, Y1 axis title, Y2 axis title
**Default:** (Blank)

Enter titles for the axes.

### Legend title
**Default:** (Blank)

Enter a name for the chart legend.

### Series
**Default:** Series 1 through Series 8

Enter the series names to be displayed on the chart in this column.

### Type
**Default:** Area

Set "Type" to the type of symbol to be displayed for each series in your chart: Area, Line, Trend, or Bar. Select Area to represent the series as an area. Select Line to place a point at the coordinates for each X data value and series value and connect these points with a line. Trend produces a straight line on the chart that approximates the overall trend of the series data. Select Bar if you want to produce bars for each X data value with the height of each bar corresponding to the series data value.

### Display
**Default:** Yes

For each series, select Yes to display the series on the chart. Select No if you do not want to display the series.

### Y Axis

**Default:** Y1

Select the Y axis each series refers to in this column to create a dual-axis chart. If you are using only one Y axis on your chart, you should leave "Y Axis" set to Y1.

## Page 2 of the Area Chart Titles & Options Form

```
▲                Area Chart  Titles & Options  Page 2 of 4              ▼

      Chart style           ►Stack      Overlap    100%
      Chart enhancement      3D         ►None
      Chart fill style      ►Color      Pattern    Both

      Bar width
      3D overlap             50
      3D depth               25

      Horizontal chart       Yes        ►No
      Value labels           All         Select    ►None

      Frame style           ►Full        Half       Quarter    None
      Frame color            1
      Frame background       0

      Legend location        Top        ►Bottom    Left       Right    None
      Legend justify         ← or ↑    ►Center    ↓ or →
      Legend placement       In         ►Out
      Legend frame           Single      Shadow    ►None
     ─────────────────────────────────────────────────────────────────────
     F1-Help
     F2-Draw chart                      F6-Colors    F8-Data    F10-Continue
```

### Chart style

**Default:** Stack

Select one of the three "Chart style" settings: Stack, Overlap, or 100%. Stack produces an area chart with Series 2 stacked on top of Series 1, Series 3 stacked on top of Series 2, and so on. Overlap produces an area chart with Series 1 placed in front of Series 2, Series 2 placed in front of Series 3, and so on. The 100% setting produces a rectangular area chart in which each series represents a percentage of the whole. If you set "Chart style" to 100%, Harvard Graphics produces an area chart, treating all series as area types regardless of the setting at "Type" on Page 1 of the Area Chart Titles & Options form.

### Chart enhancement

**Default:** None

Set "Chart enhancement" to 3D to add a three-dimensional effect to your chart.

### Chart fill style

**Default:** Color

Set "Chart fill style" to Color to color the sections of the area chart, to Pattern to use a pattern in the area chart sections, or to Both to use both a color and pattern in the area chart sections. The specific colors or patterns used for each series on the chart are specified on Page 4 of the Area Chart Titles & Options form. This setting will also be used for bars if any of the series types are set to Bar.

### Bar width

**Default:** (If you do not specify a width, Harvard Graphics selects a width that corresponds to your other settings.)

The "Bar width" option is applicable only when at least one of the series is set to Bar in the "Type" column on Page 1 of the Titles & Options form. Enter a number from 1 to 100 to indicate the total percentage of chart space used for bars on the chart.

### 3D overlap

**Default:** 50

The 3D overlap setting is applicable when "Chart enhancement" on Page 2 of the Area Chart Titles & Options form is set to 3D. Enter a number from 1 to 100 to influence the angle of perspective of your chart. The effect of this setting is influenced by the number of X data points displayed on your chart.

### 3D depth
**Default:** 25

The 3D depth setting is applicable when "Chart enhancement," on Page 2 of the Area Chart Titles & Options form, is set to 3D. Enter a number from 1 to 100 to indicate the total percentage of the chart space used by bars and bands on the third dimension.

### Horizontal chart
**Default:** No

Select Yes to create a horizontal chart and No to create a vertical chart.

*Note:* Horizontal charts cannot have a three-dimensional effect.

### Value labels
**Default:** None

Set "Value labels" to All to display values for all series in a chart, to None if you do not want values displayed, or to Select to display values for selected series. (Select Series by entering Yes at "Y Label" on Page 4 of the Area Chart Titles & Options form.)

### Frame style
**Default:** Full

Set "Frame style" to either Full, Half, or Quarter to create a full frame, half frame, or quarter frame for your chart, or to None if you do not want a chart frame.

**Frame color**

**Default:** 1

Enter a number from 0 to 16 to indicate the color for the chart frame. Alternatively, you can press F6-Colors to display the Color Selection overlay to select from a list of 16 colors.

**Frame background**

**Default:** 0

Enter a number from 0 to 16 to indicate the color for the chart background. Alternatively, you can press F6-Colors to display the Color Selection overlay to select a color from a list of 16 colors.

**Legend location**

**Default:** Bottom

Set the general location for the placement of the chart legend. Set "Legend location" to None if you do not want a legend displayed on your chart.

**Legend justify**

**Default:** Center

"Legend justify" settings are left or up, center, and down or right. These settings allow you to fine-tune the position of the legend specified at the "Legend location" option.

**Legend placement**

**Default:** Out

Set "Legend placement" to In to place the legend inside the chart frame or Out to place the legend outside the chart frame.

**Legend frame**

**Default:** None

Select Single to draw a line box around the legend or Shadow to add a shadow behind the legend box. Select None if you do not want the legend to be framed.

## Page 3 of the Area Chart Titles & Options Form

```
                Area Chart  Titles & Options  Page 3 of 4

 Data Table       | Normal      Framed    ▶None

 X  Axis Labels   |▶Normal     Vertical   %        None
 Y1 Axis Labels   |▶Value      Currency   %        None
 Y2 Axis Labels   |▶Value      Currency   %        None

 X  Grid Lines    | ....        ——       ▶None
 Y1 Grid Lines    |▶....        ——        None
 Y2 Grid Lines    |▶....        ——        None

 X Tick Mark Style|▶In         Out        Both     None
 Y Tick Mark Style|▶In         Out        Both     None

                        X Axis         Y1 Axis         Y2 Axis
 Scale Type       |▶Linear  Log   ▶Linear  Log    ▶Linear  Log
 Format
 Minimum Value
 Maximum Value
 Increment

 F1-Help
 F2-Draw chart                         F8-Data       F10-Continue
```

**Data Table**

**Default:** None

Set "Data Table" to Normal to display a table of the data at the bottom of the chart, to Framed to also draw a frame around the table of data, or to None if you do not want the chart data displayed in a table. You cannot use a data table if your X data type is Number.

### X Axis Labels

**Default:** Normal

The labels displayed along the X axis of the chart will be the names of the series entered on Page 1 of the Titles & Options form. Set "X Axis Labels" to Normal if you want the labels displayed horizontally or to Vertical if you want the labels to be displayed vertically along the X axis of the chart. The % setting is valid only if "X data type" on the X Data Type Menu overlay is set to Number. If you then set "X Axis Labels" to %, Harvard Graphics adds a percent sign to each number. Select None if you do not want X axis labels on your chart.

### Y1 Axis Labels and Y2 Axis Labels

**Defaults:** Value

The Y1 and Y2 axis labels will be displayed along the Y1 and Y2 axes of the chart. Set these options to Value to display numbers along the Y1 and Y2 axes. Select $, or currency in version 2.3, in order to add a dollar sign at the front of each label. If you select %, Harvard Graphics converts the Y data numbers to percentages and adds a percent sign to each number. Select None if you do not want Y1 and Y2 axis labels on your chart.

### X Grid Lines

**Default:** None

Set "X Grid Lines" to .... or _____ to have dotted or solid grid lines extend from the X axis tick marks. Set it to None if you do not want grid lines.

### Y1 Grid Lines and Y2 Grid Lines

**Default:** ....

Set "Y1 and Y2 Grid Lines" to .... or _____ to have dotted or solid grid lines extend from the Y axis tick marks. Set it to None if you do not want grid lines.

### X Tick Mark Style and Y Tick Mark Style

**Default:** In

Settings for tick mark styles are In, Out, Both, and None. Select In to place tick marks inside the chart axis frame or Out to place tick marks outside the chart axis frame. Select Both to have tick marks that overlap the chart axis frame. Select None if you do not want tick marks.

### Scale Type

**Default:** Linear

Set "Scale Type" to either Linear or Log (logarithmic) in the "X Axis," "Y1 Axis," and "Y2 Axis" columns to specify the scale of data represented along each of the axes.

### Format

**Default:** (Blank)

Enter any formatting instructions in the appropriate columns ("X Axis," "Y1 Axis," and "Y2 Axis") for data represented along each of the axes. Formatting is covered in Chapter 6, "XY Charts."

### Minimum Value

**Default:** (Blank)

Enter values in the appropriate columns ("X Axis," "Y1 Axis," and "Y2 Axis") to specify the minimum data value that should be plotted on the chart for data represented along each of the axes. This value must be lower than the lowest value to be charted on the axis.

**Maximum Value**

**Default:** (Blank)

Enter values in the appropriate columns ("X Axis," "Y1 Axis," and "Y2 Axis") to specify the maximum data value that should be plotted on the chart for data represented along each of the axes. This value must be higher than the highest value to be charted on the axis.

**Increment**

**Default:** (Blank)

Enter values in the appropriate columns ("X Axis," "Y1 Axis," and "Y2 Axis") to specify the increment that should be used for axis tick marks and grid lines between the "Minimum" and "Maximum" data values.

## Page 4 of the Area Chart Titles & Options Form

The first eight options on Page 4 are repeated from Page 1. Any changes you make to these options there will also be reflected on Page 1. See descriptions of the following options under "Page 1 of the Area Chart Titles & Options Form" for more information:

- Title
- Subtitle
- Footnote
- X axis title

```
            Area Chart  Titles & Options  Page 4 of 4
          Title:
          Subtitle:

          Footnote:

              X  axis title:
              Y1 axis title:
              Y2 axis title:
 Legend                     Cum      Y Label   Color   Marker/   Line
 Title:                     Yes No   Yes No            Pattern   Style

 1  Series 1                No       No        2       1         1
 2  Series 2                No       No        3       2         1
 3  Series 3                No       No        4       3         1
 4  Series 4                No       No        5       4         1
 5  Series 5                No       No        6       5         1
 6  Series 6                No       No        7       6         1
 7  Series 7                No       No        8       7         1
 8  Series 8                No       No        9       8         1

 F1-Help                F5-Attributes    F7-Size/Place
 F2-Draw chart          F6-Colors        F8-Data           F10-Continue
```

- Y1 axis title
- Y2 axis title
- Legend Title
- Series

## Cum

**Default:** No

Set "Cum" to Yes if you want the series data to be displayed cumulatively along the X axis.

## Y Label

**Default:** No

"Y Label" is only applicable when you set "Value labels" on Page 2 of the Titles & Options form to Select. Set "Y Label" to Yes to have Y data values displayed on the chart.

## Color

**Default:** 2 through 9 (for Series 1 through Series 8)

Enter a color number, 1 through 16, for each of the series displayed on the chart.

## Marker/Pattern

**Default:** 1 through 8 (for Series 1 through Series 8)

For each series, enter a number, 1 through 12, for the pattern used for areas and bars on your chart. Enter a number, 1 through 13, for the markers used for lines displayed on the chart. Enter a zero to suppress the display of a pattern or marker.

## Line Style

**Default:** 1

Select a "Line Style", from 1 to 4, for the lines on your chart. This option does not have an effect on bars or areas.

# ASCII Delimiters Overlay

```
            ASCII Deliniters

    Quote character         : "
    End of field deliniter  : ,
    End of record deliniter: #13#10
```

**Location** Select <Import delimited ASCII> from the Import/Export menu to display the Select File form and select a delimited ASCII file. Once you select a file, Harvard Graphics displays the ASCII Delimiters overlay.

**Description** Indicate the delimiters used in the data file you are importing. Refer to the software manual that created the file for information on the delimiters used.

### Quote character
Default: "

Define the character used to distinguish alphanumeric text from numbers.

### End of field delimiter
Default: ,

Define the character used to separate individual data values on a line.

### End of record delimiter

Default: #13#10 (These ASCII values represent a carriage return followed by a line feed.)

Define the character or characters that mark the end of each record.

## Bar/Line Chart Data Form

**Location** At the Create New Chart menu, select <Bar/Line> to display the Bar/Line Chart Data form.

```
                    Bar/Line Chart Data
    Title:
 Subtitle:
 Footnote:

            X Axis        Series 1  Series 2  Series 3  Series 4
       Pt   Name
       1
       2
       3
       4
       5
       6
       7
       8
       9
      10
      11
      12

 F1-Help         F3-Save        F5-Set X type              F9-More series
 F2-Draw chart   F4-Draw/Annot  F6-Calculate    F8-Options F10-Continue
```

**Description**  The Bar/Line Chart Data form is used to enter text and data for a bar, line, or point chart. This form has two areas. At the top are entry spaces for a chart title, subtitle, and footnote. The rest of the form contains columns for the data.

### Title, Subtitle, and Footnote

**Default:** (Blank)

Enter a title, subtitle, and/or footnote for your bar or line chart. If your subtitle or footnote text requires more than one line, enter the subtitle or footnote on Page 1 of the Area Chart Titles & Options form.

### X Axis

Enter the X axis data in this column. Note that the X data type (Name, Number, Time, or one of the eight calendar-based data types) specified on the X Data Type Menu overlay is displayed at the top of the column under "X Axis." If you used Harvard Graphics' automatic X data entry feature, this column will already contain your X data.

### Series 1 through Series 8

Enter Y axis data in the series columns. The Y axis data must be numeric. If you have more than four series (groups of data), press F9-More series to display additional columns for "Series 5" through "Series 8."

## Bar/Line Chart: Size/Place Overlay

```
  Size   Place      Bar/Line Chart  Titles & Options  Page 1 of 4
  8      L ►C  R   Title:
  6      L ►C  R   Subtitle:
  6      L ►C  R
  2.5    ►L C  R   Footnote:
  2.5    ►L C  R
  2.5    ►L C  R
  4         ►C     X axis title:
  3        ►  ↓    Y1 axis title:
  3        ►  ↓    Y2 axis title:
         X labels                        Type            Display   Y Axis
         Y labels             Bar  Line  Trend Curve Pt  Yes  No   Y1  Y2
  1  | Series 1                Bar                       Yes       Y1
  2  | Series 2                Bar                       Yes       Y1
  3  | Series 3                Bar                       Yes       Y1
  4  | Series 4                Bar                       Yes       Y1
  5  | Series 5                Bar                       Yes       Y1
  6  | Series 6                Bar                       Yes       Y1
  7  | Series 7                Bar                       Yes       Y1
  8  | Series 8                Bar                       Yes       Y1

  F1-Help                  F5-Attributes    F7-Size/Place
  F2-Draw chart                             F8-Data          F10-Continue
```

**Location**   At Page 1 of the Bar/Line Chart Titles & Options form, press F7-Size/Place to display the Size/Place overlay.

**Description**   Use each row of the Size/Place overlay to define the size and placement of the title, subtitle, footnote, and axis titles entered on the Titles & Options form. Once you set the desired options, press F7-Size/Place or F10-Continue to return to the Titles & Options form.

**Size**

**Defaults:** (Vary depending on the line)

Enter a number from .1 to 99. This number represents a percentage of the chart height (landscape) or width (portrait).

**Place**

**Defaults:** (Vary depending on the line)

Set placement for the title, subtitle, and footnote to either L, C, or R to left-justify, center, or right-justify the text. The X axis title is automatically centered. There are two placement options for the Y1 and Y2 axis titles: vertical (the downward pointing arrow) and horizontal (the arrow pointing to the right). Set Y axis title placement to horizontal (the default) to have the titles read left to right at the top of the axes. Set Y axis title placement to vertical to have the titles read vertically along the axes.

## Bar/Line Chart Titles & Options Form

**Location** At the Bar/Line Chart Data form, press F8-Options to display the Bar/Line Chart Titles & Options form.

**Description** The Bar/Line Chart Titles & Options form contains options that allow you to change the appearance of your bar, line, or point chart. This form is four pages long. Press PGDN and PGUP to move between the pages.

## Page 1 of the Bar/Line Chart Titles & Options Form

```
┌─────────────── Bar/Line Chart  Titles & Options  Page 1 of 4 ───────────────┐
         Title:
         Subtitle:

         Footnote:


         X  axis title:
         Y1 axis title:
         Y2 axis title:
  Legend                              Type              Display  | Y Axis
  Title:                    Bar  Line Trend  Curve  Pt  Yes  No  | Y1  Y2

  1 | Series 1                        Bar                Yes       Y1
  2 | Series 2                        Bar                Yes       Y1
  3 | Series 3                        Bar                Yes       Y1
  4 | Series 4                        Bar                Yes       Y1
  5 | Series 5                        Bar                Yes       Y1
  6 | Series 6                        Bar                Yes       Y1
  7 | Series 7                        Bar                Yes       Y1
  8 | Series 8                        Bar                Yes       Y1

 F1-Help                 F5-Attributes     F7-Size/Place
 F2-Draw chart                             F8-Data          F10-Continue
```

### Title

**Default:** (Blank)

Enter a title for your chart.

### Subtitle

**Default:** (Blank)

Enter a subtitle for the chart; it can be up to two lines long.

### Footnote

**Default:** (Blank)

Enter a footnote for your chart; it can be up to three lines long.

### X axis title, Y1 axis title, and Y2 axis title

**Default:** (Blank)

Enter titles for the axes.

## Legend Title

**Default:** (Blank)

Enter a name for the chart legend.

## Series

**Default:** Series 1 through Series 8

In this column, enter the series names to be displayed on the chart.

## Type

**Default:** Bar

Set "Type" to the type of symbol you want displayed for each series in your chart: Bar, Line, Trend, Curve, or Pt. Select Bar if you want to produce one bar for each X data value, with the height of each bar corresponding to the series data value. If your "X data type" is Number, selecting Bar will result in a needle chart (points connected to the X axis by a vertical line).

Select Line to place a point at the coordinates for each X data value and series value and connect these points with a line. Curve is nearly identical to Line, except the curve that is produced does not necessarily touch the points. Select Pt to place a marker at the coordinates for each X data value and series value. Trend produces the same chart as Pt, with the addition of a straight line on the chart that approximates the overall trend of the data.

## Display

**Default:** Yes

For each series, set Yes to display the series on the chart or No if you do not want to display the series.

### Y Axis

**Default:** Y1

Select the Y axis that each series refers to in this column to create a dual-axis chart. If you are using only one Y axis on your chart, you should leave "Y Axis" set to Y1.

## Page 2 of the Bar/Line Chart Titles & Options Form

```
         Bar/Line Chart  Titles & Options  Page 2 of 4

Bar style            ▶Cluster  Overlap   Stack     100%    Step    Paired
Bar enhancement      3D        Shadow    Link     ▶None
Bar fill style       ▶Color    Pattern   Both

Bar width
Bar overlap          50
Bar depth            25

Horizontal chart     Yes       ▶No
Value labels         All       Select   ▶None

Frame style          ▶Full     Half      Quarter   None
Frame color          1
Frame background     0

Legend location      Top       ▶Bottom   Left      Right    None
Legend justify       ← or →    ▶Center   ↓ or →
Legend placement     In        ▶Out
Legend frame         Single    Shadow   ▶None

F1-Help
F2-Draw chart                   F6-Colors      F8-Data        F10-Continue
```

### Bar style

**Default:** Cluster

You can choose from six styles of bars when your series "Type" option is Bar: Cluster, Overlap, Stack, 100%, Step, and Paired.

If you have a single series, set "Bar style" to Cluster to create a simple bar chart. When you have more than one series, select Cluster to produce a true clustered bar chart, in which one bar for each series is displayed at each X data value. Select Overlap when you have more than one series and want the bars at each X data value to overlap. Stack causes the bars for the different series to be stacked on top of one another, with the first series at the bottom of the stack, the second series stacked on top of it, and so on.

The 100% setting creates bar charts similar to stacked bar charts, except that each bar segment in a stack equals the relative contribution of that segment to the total value for each X data value. Step bar charts are also similar to stacked bar charts, with the difference being that no space appears between the different stacks along the X axis. The final "Bar style" setting, Paired, is a horizontal bar chart in which one or more series extend to the left (represented on the Y1 axis), and one or more series extend to the right (represented on the Y2 axis) of a center line.

### Bar enhancement

**Default:** None

Use "Bar enhancement" to add enhancements to your bar and line charts. Select 3D to add a depth effect to your chart symbols. If you also set "Bar style" to Overlap, setting "Bar enhancement" to 3D will cause additional series to be displayed behind the first series in the third dimension. The 3D bar enhancement will also have a three-dimensional effect on line symbols. However, when 3D is used, both Trend and Curve line styles are displayed simply as lines.

Select Shadow to place a shadow behind bars. Setting "Bar style" to Overlap overrides any shadow effects, however. Select Link to join corresponding series values in stacked and 100% style bars, with dashed lines drawn between the bars at each X data value. Select None when no bar enhancements are desired.

### Bar fill style

**Default:** Color

The "Bar fill style" option gives you the choice of using only color, only patterns, or both color and patterns, to fill the bars and 3D lines on your chart. If you are going to print your chart to a black-and-white printer that does not support grey scaling, select either Both or Pattern. If you are producing your chart on a color output device, or simply plan to display the chart on a color monitor, select Color, Pattern, or Both, to suit your needs.

### Bar width

**Default:** 60 (The default is not displayed on the form.)

The "Bar width" refers to the percentage of the chart frame width that bars or 3D lines use. When the "Bar width" option is blank, Harvard Graphics defaults the bar width to 60. If you set "Bar width" to 100, no space will appear between your bars. Alternatively, if you set "Bar width" to a small number, your bars will be narrow, with large spaces between the bars or clusters of bars.

### Bar overlap

**Default:** 50

The "Bar overlap" option has two uses. First, when you are displaying an overlap bar chart with "Bar enhancement" set to None, "Bar overlap" controls the amount the bars overlap. Set "Bar overlap" to any number from 1 (almost no overlap) to 100 (total overlap).

Second, when "Bar enhancement" is set to 3D, "Bar overlap" influences the amount of rotation of the chart frame. Enter a value between 1 (almost no rotation), and 100 (maximum permissible rotation). The effect of the number entered at "Bar overlap" depends on other option settings as well as the number of X data values you are displaying. (The more data values, the more precisely the "Bar overlap" settings affect the rotation.)

### Bar depth

**Default:** 25

Use "Bar depth" to control the size of the 3D effect on bars and lines. The default value for "Bar depth" is 25. Decrease this value to reduce the chart depth. Similarly, increase this value to create a larger third dimension. Although settings from 1 to 100 typically result in the desired effect, "Bar depth" settings are influenced by "Bar width" settings. For example, if you use a small bar width, you can set "Bar depth" to values much greater than 100.

### Horizontal chart
**Default:** No

Select Yes to create a horizontal chart and No to create a vertical chart.

*Note:* Horizontal charts cannot have a three-dimensional effect.

### Value labels
**Default:** None

Set "Value labels" to All to display values for all series in a chart, to No if you do not want values displayed, or to Select to display values for selected series. (Select series by entering Yes at "Y Label" on Page 4 of the Bar/Line Chart Titles & Options form.)

### Frame style
**Default:** Full

Set "Frame style" to either Full, Half, or Quarter to create a full frame, half frame, or quarter frame for your chart. Select None if you do not want a chart frame.

### Frame color
**Default:** 1

Enter a number from 0 to 16 to indicate the color for the chart frame. Alternatively, you can press F6-Colors to display the Color Selection overlay to select from a list of 16 colors.

### Frame background
**Default:** 0

Enter a number from 0 to 16 to indicate the color for the chart background. Alternatively, you can press F6-Colors to display the Color Selection overlay to select from a list of 16 colors.

### Legend location
**Default:** Bottom

Select the general location for the placement of the chart legend. Select None if you do not want a legend displayed on your chart.

### Legend justify
**Default:** Center

"Legend justify" settings are left or up, center, and down or right. These settings fine-tune the position of the legend specified at the "Legend location" option.

### Legend placement
**Default:** Out

Select In to place the legend inside the chart frame or Out to place the legend outside the chart frame.

### Legend frame
**Default:** None

Select Single to draw a line box around the legend or Shadow to add a shadow behind the legend box. Select None if you do not want the legend to be framed.

## Page 3 of the Bar/Line Chart Titles & Options Form

```
                  Bar/Line Chart  Titles & Options  Page 3 of 4
    Data Table       | Normal      Framed    ▶None

    X  Axis Labels   | ▶Normal     Vertical  %       None
    Y1 Axis Labels   | ▶Value      Currency  %       None
    Y2 Axis Labels   | ▶Value      Currency  %       None

    X  Grid Lines    |  ....       ———       ▶None
    Y1 Grid Lines    | ▶ ....      ———        None
    Y2 Grid Lines    | ▶ ....      ———        None

    X Tick Mark Style| ▶In         Out       Both    None
    Y Tick Mark Style| ▶In         Out       Both    None
                     |      X Axis       |    Y1 Axis      |    Y2 Axis
    Scale Type       | ▶Linear   Log     | ▶Linear   Log   | ▶Linear   Log
    Format           |
    Minimum Value    |
    Maximum Value    |
    Increment        |

F1-Help
F2-Draw chart                               F8-Data         F10-Continue
```

### Data Table

**Default:** None

Set "Data Table" to Normal to display a table of the data at the bottom of the chart, to Framed to also draw a frame around the table of data, or to None if you do not want the chart data displayed in a table on the chart. You cannot use a data table if your X data type is Number.

### X Axis Labels

**Default:** Normal

The labels displayed along the X axis of the chart will be the names of the series entered on Page 1 of the Titles & Options form. Set "X Axis

Labels" to Normal if you want the labels to read horizontally or to Vertical if you want the labels to be displayed vertically along the X axis of the chart. The % setting is valid only if the "X data type" set on the X Data Type Menu overlay is Number. If you then set "X Axis Labels" to %, Harvard Graphics adds a percent sign to each number. Select None if you do not want X axis labels on your chart.

### Y1 Axis Labels and Y2 Axis Labels
**Defaults: Value**

The Y1 and Y2 axis labels will be displayed along the Y1 and Y2 axes of the chart. Select Value to display numbers along the Y1 and Y2 axes. Select $, or Currency in version 2.3, to add a dollar sign at the front of each label. Select None if you do not want Y1 and Y2 axis labels on your chart.

### X Grid Lines
**Default:** None

Set "X Grid Lines" to . . . . or _____ to have dotted or solid grid lines extend from the X axis tick marks or to None if you do not want grid lines.

### Y1 Grid Lines and Y2 Grid Lines
**Default:** . . . .

Set "Y1 and Y2 Grid Lines" to . . . . or _____ to have dotted or solid grid lines extend from the Y axis tick marks or to None if you do not want grid lines.

### X Tick Mark Style and Y Tick Mark Style
**Default:** In

Settings for tick mark styles are In, Out, Both, and None. Select In to place tick marks inside the chart axis frame or Out to place tick marks outside the frame. Select Both to have tick marks that overlap the chart axis frame. Select None if you do not want tick marks.

**Scale Type**

**Default:** Linear

Set "Scale Type" to either Linear or Log (logarithmic) in the "X Axis," "Y1 Axis," and "Y2 Axis" columns to specify the scale of data represented along each of the axes.

**Format**

**Default:** (Blank)

Enter any formatting instructions in the appropriate columns ("X Axis," "Y1 Axis," and "Y2 Axis") for data represented along each of the axes. Formatting is covered in detail in Chapter 6, "XY Charts."

**Minimum Value**

**Default:** (Blank)

Enter values in the appropriate column ("X Axis," "Y1 Axis," and "Y2 Axis") to specify the minimum data value that should be plotted on the chart for data represented along each of the axes. This value must be lower than the lowest value to be charted on the axis.

**Maximum Value**

**Default:** (Blank)

Enter values in the appropriate column ("X Axis," "Y1 Axis," and "Y2 Axis") to specify the maximum data value that should be plotted on the chart for data represented along each of the axes. This value must be higher than the highest value to be charted on the axis.

**Increment**

**Default:** (Blank)

Enter a value in the appropriate column ("X Axis," "Y1 Axis," and "Y2 Axis") to specify the increment that should be used for axis tick marks and grid lines between the "Minimum" and "Maximum" data values.

## Page 4 of the Bar/Line Chart Titles & Options Form

```
                    Bar/Line Chart  Titles & Options  Page 4 of 4
                     Title:
                     Subtitle:

                     Footnote:

                   X axis title:
                   Y1 axis title:
                   Y2 axis title:
   Legend                        Cum      Y Label   Color   Marker/   Line
   Title:                       Yes No    Yes No            Pattern   Style

  1  Series 1                    No        No         2       1        1
  2  Series 2                    No        No         3       2        1
  3  Series 3                    No        No         4       3        1
  4  Series 4                    No        No         5       4        1
  5  Series 5                    No        No         6       5        1
  6  Series 6                    No        No         7       6        1
  7  Series 7                    No        No         8       7        1
  8  Series 8                    No        No         9       8        1

F1-Help                F5-Attributes    F7-Size/Place
F2-Draw chart          F6-Colors        F8-Data              F10-Continue
```

The first eight options on Page 4 are repeated from Page 1. Any changes you make to these options here will also be reflected on Page 1. See descriptions of the following options under "Page 1 of the Bar/Line Chart Titles & Options Form" for more information:

- Title
- Subtitle

- Footnote
- X axis title
- Y1 axis title
- Y2 axis title
- Legend Title
- Series

## Cum
**Default:** No

Set "Cum" to Yes if you want the series data to be displayed cumulatively along the X axis.

## Y Label
**Default:** No

"Y Label" is only applicable when you set "Value labels" on Page 2 of the Titles & Options form to Select. Set "Y Label" to Yes to have Y data values displayed on the chart.

## Color
**Default:** 2 through 9 (for Series 1 through Series 8)

Enter a color number, 1 through 16, for each of the series displayed on the chart.

## Marker/Pattern
**Default:** 1 through 8 (for Series 1 through Series 8)

For each series, enter a number, 1 through 12, for the pattern used for areas and bars on your chart. Enter a number, 1 through 13, for the markers used for lines displayed on the chart. Enter a zero to suppress the display of a pattern or marker.

**Line Style**

**Default:** 1

Select a "Line Style", from 1 to 4, for the lines on your chart. This option does not have an effect on bars or areas.

## Box Options Form

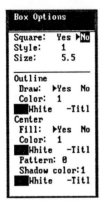

**Location**   The Box Options form appears in Draw/Annotate when you press F8-Options while adding a box in the drawing area, when you select <Options> from the Modify menu and then select an existing box object in the drawing area, or when you select <Box> from the Default Options menu displayed when you press F8-Options at the Draw menu.

**Description** Use the Box Options form to define the characteristics of box objects.

### Square

**Default:** No

Set "Square" to No to create a box with a rectangular shape or to Yes to create a box that is perfectly square.

### Style

**Default:** 1

Enter a number, 1 through 21, corresponding to the desired box style. Alternatively, with the cursor at the "Style" option, you can press F6-Choices to display the Box Styles overlay and select a box style from this list (see "Box Styles Overlay").

### Size

**Default:** 5.5

At "Size" enter a number from .1 to 99. The effect of changing the "Size" number differs depending on the "Style" selected. These effects are described in Chapter 9, "Drawing and Annotating."

### Outline Draw

**Default:** Yes

If you want to outline your box, set "Outline Draw" to Yes.

### Outline Color

**Default:** 1

If you set "Outline Draw" to Yes, enter a color number, 1 through 16, at "Outline Color" for the color of the outline. With the cursor positioned at this option, you can also press F6-Choices and select a color from the Color Selection overlay (see "Color Selection Overlay").

### Center Fill

**Default:** Yes

Set "Center Fill" to Yes if you want to fill the center of your box or to No if you want to display only the box outline (if "Outline Draw" is set to Yes).

### Center Color

**Default:** 1

If you set "Center Fill" to Yes, enter a color number, 1 through 16, at "Center Color" for the color of the box center. Alternatively, with the cursor positioned at this option, press F6-Choices and select a color from the Color Selection overlay (see "Color Selection Overlay").

### Center Pattern

**Default:** 0

Enter a pattern number, 1 through 12, at "Center Pattern" for the pattern of the box center. Alternatively, with the cursor positioned at this option, press F6-Choices and select a pattern from the Patterns overlay (see "Patterns Overlay").

### Shadow color

**Default:** 1

If you select a 3D, Shadow, or Page box style, set "Shadow color" to a color number, 1 through 16. This color will be used for the third dimension in 3D boxes, the shadow in Shadow boxes, and the turned-up corner in Page boxes. Alternatively, with the cursor positioned at "Shadow color," press F6-Choices and select a color from the Color Selection overlay (see "Color Selection Overlay").

## Box Styles Overlay

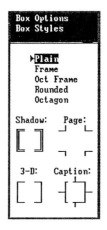

**Location** In Draw/Annotate, position the cursor at the "Style" option on the Box Options form and press F6-Choices to display the Box Styles overlay.

**Description** Highlight the desired style for your box from this list. Press F10-Continue, ENTER, or ESC to select the highlighted box style and return to the Box Options form.

## Bullet List Form

**Location** Select <Create new chart> from the Main Menu followed by <Text> from the Create New Chart menu. Then at the Text Chart Styles menu, select <Bullet list> to display the Bullet List form.

```
                          Bullet List
              Title:
              Subtitle:
              Footnote:
```

```
F1-Help       F3-Save        F5-Attributes   F7-Size/Place
F2-Draw chart F4-Draw/Annot                                   F10-Continue
```

**Description**   The Bullet List form is used to enter text for a bullet list. Bullets are placed automatically at new text lines in the text area in the lower part of the form.

### Title, Subtitle, and Footnote

**Default:** (Blank)

Enter a title, subtitle, and/or footnote for your bullet list.

### Bullet List Text Area

Enter text to be displayed in the lower portion of the bullet list. The first line you add in the text area will be preceded by a bullet. Except for the first line, Harvard Graphics will place a bullet before any line that follows a blank line. If text is placed on a line immediately below an existing line of text, no bullet will appear. You can use this characteristic to create a list of secondary points for each bullet item. You can also change the color of the bullet for emphasis, so that bullets appear in a different color than the text. (For more information on coloring chart bullets, refer to Chapter 4, "Text Charts.")

## Bullet List: Size/Place Overlay

```
 Size    Place              Bullet List
   8     L ▶C  R    Title:
   6     L ▶C  R    Subtitle:
  3.5   ▶L  C  R    Footnote:

  5.5    L ▶C  R

 Bullet Shape
 ▶•  −  ♪  ■  ✟

 Indent: 0




F1-Help          F3-Save         F5-Attributes    F7-Size/Place
F2-Draw chart    F4-Draw/Annot                                   F10-Continue
```

**Location**   At the Bullet List form, press F7-Size/Place to display the Size/Place overlay.

**Description**   Use each row of the Size/Place overlay to define the size and placement of the title, subtitle, footnote, and the text entered in the bullet list text area. Once you set the desired options, press F7-Size/Place or F10-Continue to return to the Titles & Options form.

### Size

**Defaults:** (Vary depending on the line)

Enter a number from 1 to 99.

### Place

**Defaults:** (Vary depending on the line)

Set either L, C, or R to left-justify, center, or right-justify text.

### Bullet Shape

**Default:** • (dot)

Set the desired bullet shape that will be used for all bullets on the chart. The possible settings are a dot, dash, check mark, square, or number (#). Select # to create a sequentially numbered list.

### Indent

**Default:** 0

In order to indent the bullet list, the text in the text area of the Bullet List form must be left-justified. Enter a number, 1 through 100, that corresponds to the percentage of the screen width you want to indent. For instance, 50 will indent text to the center of the screen.

## Bullet Shape Overlay

**Location**   The Bullet Shape overlay can be displayed from any data or text chart form, or from the text line in Draw/Annotate.

**Description** The Bullet Shape overlay is displayed when you press CTRL-B to place a bullet at that location on a chart form. You add a bullet anywhere you can add text. To do this, position the cursor where you want the bullet to appear, and then press CTRL-B. The Bullet Shape overlay will be displayed at the upper-left corner of the screen. Select one of the bullet shapes: dot, dash, check mark, or square. Then press ENTER or F10-Continue. Harvard Graphics will place the selected bullet at the location of the cursor. To cancel adding a bullet once you have displayed the Bullet Shape overlay, press ESC.

## Button Options Form (Version 2.3)

**Location** The Button Options form appears in Draw/Annotate when you press F8-Options while adding a button in the drawing area, or when you select <Options> from the Modify menu and then select an existing button object in the drawing area.

**Description** Use this form to define the button number.

**Button**

Default: 1

Buttons are used in conjunction with slide shows to create an interactive HyperShow, in which the viewer can select a button on the displayed chart to move directly to a specified chart.

To create a button, assign a button number from 1 to 10, or a special button number, to your box. The number you assign must correspond to the number specified in the "Button" column of the HyperShow overlay (see "HyperShow Menu Overlay"). Each chart can contain up to 20 buttons. The duplicate button numbers will perform the same function, that is, move to the same chart specified in the "Go To" column of the HyperShow Menu overlay.

## Calculate Overlay

```
                    Calculate
Series: 1
Legend: Series 1

Calculation:
```

**Location**   The cursor must be positioned in the "Series" column for which you want to perform a calculation on an XY Chart Data form. Press F4-Calculate (versions 2.13 and earlier) or F6-Calculate (version 2.3) to display the Calculate overlay.

**Description**   Define a calculation on this overlay for the series in which the cursor appeared when you pressed F4-Calculate or F6-Calculate. The top line of this overlay displays the name of the current series. To change this name, enter a new name for the series at "Legend." Enter the desired calculation at "Calculation," and press F10-Continue to perform the requested calculation. To cancel performing a calculation while the Calculate overlay is displayed, press ESC. Refer to the section "Using Calculations" in Chapter 6 for more information about calculation commands.

*Note:* Calculations are updated either when you issue the @RECALC calculation or when you leave and then return to the XY Chart Data form.

## CGA Color Palette Overlay

```
          CGA Color Palette
Palette:      ▶Green,Red,Brown
               White,Cyan,Magenta
               White,Cyan,Red
Background
Color:         Black        Dk. Grey
              ▶Blue         Lt. Blue
               Green        Lt. Green
               Cyan         Lt. Cyan
               Red          Lt. Red
               Magenta      Lt. Magenta
               Yellow       Lt. Yellow
               Lt. Grey     White
```

**Location**   In Setup, press F3-CGA palette from the Color Palette Setup form (when the "Screen" option on the Screen Setup form is set to CGA color).

**Description**   Use the CGA Color Palette overlay to define the colors Harvard Graphics will use with a color graphics adapter. Press F10-Continue when you are finished to return to the Color Palette Setup form.

### Palette

Default: Green, Red, Brown

Use the SPACEBAR to highlight the CGA color scheme you want Harvard Graphics to use when displaying your charts.

### Background Color

**Default:** Blue

Use the SPACEBAR to select the color you want Harvard Graphics to use for the background when displaying your chart.

## Change Chart Type Overlay

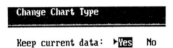

Keep current data: ▶Yes  No

**Location**   The Change Chart Type overlay is displayed whenever you have a current chart and you then select a new chart from the Create New Chart menu that is of a different (but compatible) chart style from that of the current chart.

**Description**   You can change from the current chart to a similar chart style and retain some or all of your data from the previous chart style. From the Create New Chart menu, select a chart style that is compatible with, but different from, your current chart style. When Harvard Graphics displays the Change Chart Type overlay, select Yes to retain some or all of the data or No to create a totally new chart. Additional details concerning which data are retained is located in the appropriate chart chapter: Chapter 4, "Text Charts"; Chapter 6, "XY Charts"; and Chapter 7, "Pie Charts."

### Keep current data

**Default:** Yes

Select Yes if you want to include the text from the old chart in the new chart or No to create an entirely new chart.

## Chart Data Option Overlay

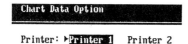

Printer: ▶Printer 1   Printer 2

**Location**   Select <Print chart data> from the Produce Output menu to display the Chart Data Option overlay.

**Description**   This overlay contains only one option. Once you set this option, press F10-Continue to print the data for your current chart.

### Printer

Default: Printer 1

Indicate which printer, Printer 1 or Printer 2, you want to print to. The printer you select must have been defined on the Printer 1 or Printer 2 Setup form. (Refer to "Printer 1 Setup Form.")

## Circle Options Form

**Location**   The Circle Options form appears in Draw/Annotate when you press F8-Options while adding a circle in the drawing area, when you select <Options> from the Modify menu and then select an existing circle object in the drawing area, or when you select <Circle> from the Default Options menu that is displayed when you press F8-Options at the Draw menu.

**Description**   Use the Circle Options form to define the characteristics of circle objects added in Draw/Annotate.

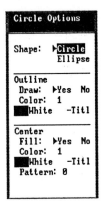

### Shape

**Default:** Circle

Select either a Circle or an Ellipse shape.

### Outline Draw

**Default:** Yes

Select Yes to add an outline around your circle or ellipse.

### Outline Color

**Default:** 1 (white)

If you set "Outline Draw" to Yes, enter a number, 1 through 16, at "Outline Color" for the color of the outline. Alternatively, with the cursor positioned at this option, press F6-Choices and select a color from the Color Selection overlay (see "Color Selection Overlay").

### Center Fill

**Default:** Yes

Select Yes to fill the center of your circle or ellipse or No if you want to display only the outline (if "Outline Draw" is set to Yes).

### Center Color

**Default:** 1 (white)

If you set "Center Fill" to Yes, enter a color number, 1 through 16, at "Center Color" for the color of the circle or ellipse center. Alternatively, with the cursor positioned at this option, press F6-Choices and select a color from the Color Selection overlay (see "Color Selection Overlay").

### Center Pattern

**Default:** 0 (no pattern)

Enter a pattern number, 1 through 12, at "Center Pattern" for the pattern used in the circle or ellipse center. Alternatively, with the cursor positioned at this option, press F6-Choices and select a pattern from the Patterns overlay (see "Patterns Overlay").

## Color Palette Setup Form

**Location** With versions 2.13 or earlier, select <Color palette> at the Setup menu to display the Color Palette Setup form. With version 2.3, select <Color palette> from the Setup menu. Then to edit the current Color palette, select <Edit palette> from the Palette menu to display the Color Palette Setup form. To create a new palette, select <Create palette> and then complete the options on the Create Palette overlay. Once you press ENTER and F10-Continue to remove this overlay, the Color Palette Setup form is displayed.

```
                          Color Palette Setup
Palette file: hg23    Screen: EGA              Output: PCR,QCR
                      Red    Green  Blue       Red    Green  Blue
 1  White   -Title    1000   1000   1000       1000   1000   1000
 2  Cyan dk -Ser 1       0    660    660        660    330    330
 3  Blue    -Ser 2       0    330    660          0    330    825
 4  Blue lt -TextDK    330    660   1000          0    660    660
 5  Cyan LT -Labels    660   1000   1000        660   1000   1000
 6  Yel LT  -Ser 5    1000   1000    660       1000   1000    770
 7  White   -Text     1000   1000   1000       1000   1000   1000
 8  Black   -FrmBkg      0      0      0          0      0      0
 9  White   -Symbol   1000   1000   1000       1000   1000   1000
10  Gray lt -Symbol    660    660    660        660    660    660
11  Black   -Symbol      0      0      0          0      0      0
12  Red     -Symbol    660      0      0        660    110      0
13  Green   -Symbol      0    660      0        110    770    110
14  Blue    -Symbol      0      0   1000          0    165   1000
15  Yellow  -Symbol   1000   1000      0       1000   1000      0
16  Blue DK -Bkgrnd      0      0    330          0      0    330

Background color: 16    Description: Blue bkg, with cyans and blues   = 11.PAL

F1-Help
F2-Show palette                                              F10-Continue
```

## Description

The Color Palette Setup form allows you to display or modify an existing 16-color palette or create a new color palette. Each color palette definition is stored as a separate file with the extension .PAL.

## Palette file

**Default:** In versions 2.13 and earlier, HG (or the default color palette for your output device). In version 2.3, the current (or just named) Palette file.

The name of the current color palette is shown here. In versions 2.13 or earlier, if this is not the palette file you want to examine and/or modify, enter the name of an existing color palette file or enter a new name to create a new color palette. This name is limited to eight characters and must conform to MS-DOS file naming conventions. In version 2.3 you cannot change the Palette file from this form.

## Screen

**Default:** EGA (or the screen previously specified)

Enter the type of screen adapter the palette is intended for at "Screen." You can supply up to 12 characters for this label. This option does not affect your palette settings and is used for reference only.

**Output**

**Default:** (The type of film recorder selected at the Film Recorder Setup form.)

Note the type of film recorder the palette is intended for at "Output." You can supply up to 12 characters. This option does not affect your palette settings and is used for reference only.

**Red, Green, and Blue**

**Defaults:** (Values depend on your color palette.)

Define the intensities of red, green, and blue to produce colors used for the screen display and for recording onto film. For the screen color definitions (the columns under "Screen"), the value 1000 defines full intensity and 0 defines no intensity, or absence of that color.

Although color mixing for an output device follows the same principles (use the columns under "Output"), the numbers you define will depend on the characteristics of the particular output device. Refer to your device manual and the Harvard Graphics manual for color intensity information specific to your output device.

In version 2.3, the output red, green, and blue intensities are used to calculate the shades of grey when you print a chart to a black-and-white printer and the "color" option on the Print Chart Options form is set to Yes.

**Background color**

**Default:** 16 (black)

Define the palette color Harvard Graphics should use in the background of every chart. Enter the number from 1 to 16 corresponding to the palette color you want to use for chart backgrounds.

**Description (version 2.3)**

**Default:** (Blank)

Enter a description for the color palette. This description will be displayed on the Select Color Palette form when you later select a color palette.

## Color Selection Overlay

```
Color Selection

▶White    -Title    1
 Cyan dk  -Ser 1    2
 Blue     -Ser 2    3
 Blue lt  -TextDK   4
 Cyan LT  -Labels   5
 Yel LT   -Ser 5    6
 White    -Text     7
 Black    -FrmBkg   8
 White    -Symbol   9
 Gray lt  -Symbol  10
 Black    -Symbol  11
 Red      -Symbol  12
 Green    -Symbol  13
 Blue     -Symbol  14
 Yellow   -Symbol  15
 Blue DK  -Bkgrnd  16
```

**Location**   The cursor must be at a "Color" option on a form.

**Description**   With the cursor positioned at the "Color" option, press F6-Colors to display the Color Selection overlay. Highlight a color in this list, and then press ENTER or F10-Continue to select the color and return to the previous form.

## Create Chartbook Overlay

**Location**   Select <Create chartbook> from the Chartbook menu to display the Create Chartbook overlay.

Harvard Graphics Forms and Function Keys 803

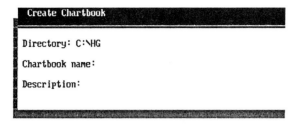

**Description**  Use this form to define a new chartbook.

### Directory

**Default:** (Current directory)

Enter the directory path to store your chartbook. This must be the same directory in which all the templates to be listed in this chartbook are stored.

### Chartbook name

**Default:** (Blank)

Enter a name for the chartbook. It can contain up to eight characters and must conform to DOS file naming conventions. You do not need to include an extension, however, as Harvard Graphics automatically adds the extension .CBK to this name.

### Description

**Default:** (Blank)

Enter a description for your chartbook.

## Create Palette Overlay (Version 2.3)

**Location**  Select <Palette> from the Setup menu followed by <Create palette> from the Palette menu to display the Create Palette overlay.

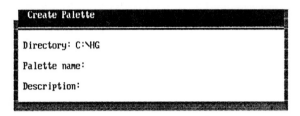

### Description

Use this form to specify the name of a new color palette.

### Directory

**Default:** (Current directory)

Enter the path of the directory in which you want your palette file stored.

### Palette name

**Default:** (Blank)

Enter a name for the palette file. It can contain up to eight characters and must conform to DOS file naming conventions. Do not include an extension, however, as Harvard Graphics automatically adds the extension .PAL to this name.

### Description

**Default:** (Blank)

Enter a description for your palette.

## Create Slide Show Overlay

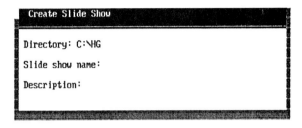

**Location**   Select <Create slide show> from the Slide Show menu to display the Create Slide Show overlay.

**Description**   Use this form to define a new slide show.

### Directory

**Default:** (Current directory)

Enter the path of the directory in which you want your slide show stored. This must be the same directory in which all the files that are to be included in your slide show are stored.

### Slide show name

**Default:** (Blank)

Enter the name of the slide show. It can contain up to eight characters and must conform to DOS file naming conventions. You do not need to include an extension, however, as Harvard Graphics automatically adds the extension .SHW to this name.

### Description

**Default:** (Blank)

Enter a description for your slide show.

## Create/Edit Chartbook Form

```
                    Create/Edit Chartbook
 Filename Ext  |  Date    |  Type      |  Description
 TEST2   .TPL  | 01/06/90 | BAR/LINE   | Units Shipped
 LOTUSGRF.TPL  | 01/07/90 | BAR/LINE   | This is the title
 123AGAIN.TPL  | 01/08/90 | BAR/LINE   |
 WKLYPIE .TPL  | 01/09/90 | PIE        | Pie chart for the weekly progress report
 ANRPTPIE.TPL  | 12/19/89 | PIE        | Annual Report.  Earnings Performance Pie
 ANRPTBAR.TPL  | 12/19/89 | BAR/LINE   | Annual Report.  Trend w/ bars.

 Chartbook name: ANNUAL    .CBK
 - Order ---- Template ----- Type ---------- Description ----------
     1       WKLYPIE .TPL    PIE    Pie chart for the weekly progress report
     2       ANRPTBAR.TPL

 Chartbook description: Annual Report Templates

 F1-Help                                                F10-Continue
```

**Location**   When you are creating a chartbook, this form is displayed once you press ENTER or F10-Continue after completing the Create Chartbook overlay. When you are editing an existing chartbook, this form is displayed once you select <Edit chartbook> from the Chartbook menu.

**Description**   This form is used to select the templates to be listed in a chartbook. Both the chartbook and the templates listed in the chartbook must be stored in the same directory.

### Template File List

The top of this form contains the template list, in which all the templates in the current directory are displayed. The "Filename Ext," "Date," "Type," and "Description" columns in this list display the name of the template file, the date it was created, the chart type used to create the template, and a description of each of the templates in the current directory.

### Chartbook name

The name you gave your chartbook on the Create Chartbook overlay is displayed at "Chartbook name." You cannot modify this name.

### Chartbook File List

The lower half of the form contains the chartbook list with the four columns "Order," "Template," "Type," and "Description." You place the templates to be included in your chartbook in this list. In the "Order" column are numbers reflecting the order in which you place the templates in the chartbook. The "Template," "Type," and "Description" columns contain the template filename, the chart type used to create the template, and a description of each of the templates included in the chartbook. Adding templates to the chartbook list and editing the list are described further in Chapter 11, "Templates and Chartbooks."

### Chartbook description

**Default:** (The description entered on the Create Chartbook overlay.)

Modify or enter a description for your chartbook.

## Create/Edit Slide Show Form

**Location**   When you are creating a slide show, this form is displayed once you press ENTER or F10-Continue after completing the Create Slide Show overlay. When you are editing an existing slide show, this form is displayed once you select <Edit slide show> from the Slide Show menu.

**Description**   The Create/Edit Slide Show form is used to specify the files to be included in the slide show. The slide show file itself and the charts in the slide show must be in the same directory.

```
┌──────────────────────────────────────────────────────────────────────┐
│                       Create/Edit Slide Show                         │
├──────────────┬──────────┬──────────┬──────────────────────────────────┤
│ Filename Ext │  Date    │  Type    │         Description              │
├──────────────┼──────────┼──────────┼──────────────────────────────────┤
│ HG      .CHT │ 04/13/90 │ PIE      │ Color palette display chart      │
│ HGPIE   .CHT │ 12/01/87 │ PIE      │ new description                  │
│ RECEPT  .CHT │ 05/02/90 │ FREEFORM │ Sample Tutorial File             │
│ VTITLE  .CHT │ 03/13/90 │ TITLE    │ Victory Sportshoe - Title Chart  │
│ VEXPENSE.CHT │ 03/13/90 │ PIE      │ Expenses 1990 - original pie     │
│ VPHILOS .CHT │ 04/20/90 │ FREEFORM │ Victory Sportshoe - Company Philosophy │
├──────────────┴──────────┴──────────┴──────────────────────────────────┤
│ Show name: SPCINFO .SHW                                              │
│ - Order ──── File ──────── Type ──────── Description ─────────       │
│    8        HGAINTR4.CHT   FREEFORM    Creating impressive charts is easier and │
│    9        BSYM2   .CHT   FREEFORM    Harvard Graphics Business Symbols │
│   10        MAP4    .CHT   FREEFORM    Harvard Graphics U.S. MapMaker │
│   11        QC      .CHT   FREEFORM    Harvard Graphics Quick Charts │
│   12        MILSYM2 .CHT   FREEFORM    Harvard Graphics Military Symbols │
│   13        HG      .CHT                                             │
│                                                                      │
│ Show description: Registration Info ScreenShow                       │
├──────────────────────────────────────────────────────────────────────┤
│ F1-Help                                                  F10-Continue│
└──────────────────────────────────────────────────────────────────────┘
```

## File List

The top of this form contains a file list, in which files in the current directory with the extensions .CHT, .TPL, .SHW, .PCX, and .PIC are displayed. (A maximum of 255 file names can be listed here.) The "Filename Ext," "Date," "Type," and "Description" columns in the file list contain the name, date of creation, file type, and description for each of the files displayed.

## Show name

The name you gave your slide show on the Create Slide Show overlay is displayed at "Show name." You cannot modify this name.

## Slide Show List

The lower half of this form contains the slide show list with the four columns "Order," "File," "Type," and "Description." You add files to your slide show by adding the desired filenames to this list. In the "Order" column are numbers reflecting the order of your slides in the slide show. The "File," "Type," and "Description" columns contain the slide filename, the slide type, and a description for each of the slides.

### Show description

**Default:** (The description entered on the Create Slide Show overlay.)

Modify (or enter) a description for your slide show.

## Current Chart Options Overlay

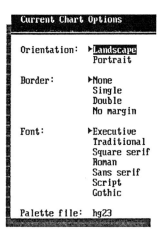

**Location**  At the Main Menu, press F8-Options to display the Current Chart Options overlay.

**Description**  This form is used to set options to override chart default settings for your current chart.

### Orientation

**Default:** Landscape

Set the chart orientation (how you want the charts displayed on the page or screen). Landscape gives the current chart a horizontal orientation and Portrait gives it a vertical orientation.

### Border

**Default:** None

Select a border for your current chart. You can select either a single- or double-line border, or no border in versions 2.13 and earlier. Version 2.3 includes an additional option, No margin. Select No margin to use all the available chart space.

### Font

**Default:** Executive

Select a font for use in your current chart. Versions 2.13 and earlier have six fonts available: Executive, Square Serif, Roman, Sans Serif, Script, and Gothic. Version 2.3 includes these six fonts plus a Traditional font (Times Roman).

*Note:* In version 2.3 you can use more than one font per chart by adding text in Draw/Annotate, although the font selected here is the only one used for text entered on the chart form.

### Palette file (version 2.3)

**Default:** Current palette file

Specify the palette to be used for your current chart. Enter either a number from 1 to 12 corresponding to one of the palettes that came with Harvard Graphics 2.3, HG23 for the standard Harvard Graphics palette, or the name of a palette you have created.

## Current International Settings Overlay (Version 2.3)

**Location**   At the Main Menu, press F8-Options to display the Current Chart Options overlay. Then press F3-Intl formats to display the Current International Settings overlay.

```
        Current International Settings
  Year format       ▶M/Y     Y/M
  Date format:      ▶M/D     D/M

  Date separator:   ▶/        .        -
  Time separator:   ▶:        .        ,

  Thousand/decimal
  separators:       ▶,/.     ./,    space/,

  Currency symbol:      $
  Currency position: ▶@100   100@   @ 100   100 @
```

## Description

This overlay is used to set formats to be used for date, time, and currency values in the current chart. Press F10-Continue when you are finished settings options to return to the Main Menu.

## Year format

**Default: M/Y**

Specify how month and year dates should be displayed in Harvard Graphics charts. You can have the month either precede or follow the year. The setting will be used in bar/line, area, and high/low/close charts when your X data type is one of the calendar settings.

## Date format

**Default: M/D**

Specify how month and day dates should be displayed in Harvard Graphics charts. You can have the day either precede or follow the month. The setting will be used in bar/line, area, and high/low/close charts when your X data type is one of the calendar settings.

### Date separator

**Default: /**

Specify which character should be used to separate the day, month, and year values in Harvard Graphics charts. The choices are a slash, period, or dash. The setting will be used in bar/line, area, and high/low/close charts when your X data type is one of the calendar settings.

### Time separator

**Default: :**

Select the character that will be used to separate hours, minutes, and seconds in Harvard Graphics charts. This option is used when your X data type for a bar/line, area, or high/low/close chart is set to Time.

### Thousand/decimal separators

**Default: ,/.**

Define the characters and format of whole number separation to be used in Harvard Graphics charts. Harvard Graphics will use the selected format to display numbers on data charts (bar line, area, high/low/close, and pie).

| Thousands and Decimal Separators | Result |
| --- | --- |
| ,/. | 10,000.00 |
| ./, | 10.000,00 |
| space/, | 10 000,00 |

### Currency symbol

**Default: $**

You can enter a currency character other than the dollar sign ($), up to four characters in length, at the "Currency symbol" option. The

English pound and Japanese yen symbols are available in the international font styles. See Appendix D for a description of the international fonts.

**Currency position**

**Default:** @100

Specify where the currency symbol should be placed in relation to the currency value. Set this option to one of the four listed positions. The @ sign indicates where the currency symbol will be placed in relation to numeric values.

## Default International Settings Overlay (Version 2.3)

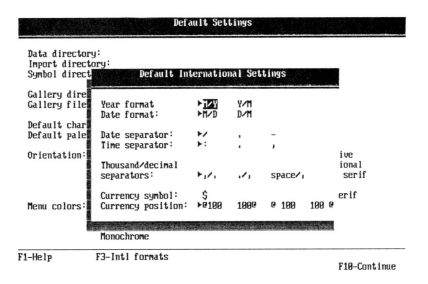

**Location** At the Setup menu, select <Defaults> to display the Default Settings form. Then press F3-Intl formats to display the Default International Settings overlay.

**Description** This overlay is used to set formats to be used for default date, time, and currency values in charts. Press F10-Continue when you are finished setting options to return to the Default Settings form.

### Year format
**Default:** M/Y

Specify how month and year dates should be displayed in Harvard Graphics charts. You can have the month either precede or follow the year. The setting will be used in bar/line, area, and high/low/close charts when your X data type is one of the calendar settings.

### Date format
**Default:** M/D

Specify how month and day dates should be displayed in Harvard Graphics charts. You can have the day either precede or follow the month. The setting will be used in bar/line, area, and high/low/close charts when your X data type is one of the calendar settings.

### Date separator
**Default:** /

Specify which character should be used to separate the day, month, and year values in Harvard Graphics charts. The choices are a slash, period, or dash. The setting will be used in bar/line, area, and high/low/close charts when your X data type is one of the calendar settings.

### Time separator
**Default:** :

Select the character that will be used to separate hours, minutes, and seconds in Harvard Graphics charts. This option is used when your X data type for a bar/line, area, or high/low/close chart is set to Time.

**Thousand/decimal separators**

**Default:** ,/.

Define the characters and format of whole number separation to be used in Harvard Graphics charts. Harvard Graphics will use the selected format to display numbers on data charts (bar/line, area, high/low/close, and pie).

| Thousands and Decimal Separators | Result |
| --- | --- |
| ,/. | 10,000.00 |
| ./, | 10.000,00 |
| space/, | 10 000,00 |

**Currency symbol**

**Default:** $

You can enter a currency character other than the dollar sign ($), up to four characters in length, at the "Currency symbol" option. The English pound and Japanese yen symbols are available in the international font styles. See Appendix D for a description of the international fonts.

**Currency position**

**Default:** @100

Specify where the currency symbol should be placed in relation to the currency value. Set this option to one of the four listed positions. The @ sign indicates where the currency symbol will be placed in relation to numeric values.

## Default Settings Form

```
                      Default Settings
Data directory:
Import directory:
Symbol directory:   C:\HG\symbols

Gallery directory:  C:\HG\gallery
Gallery filename:   vpick

Default chartbook:
Default palette:    hg23

Orientation:   ▶Landscape      Border:  ▶None        Font:  ▶Executive
                Portrait                 Single              Traditional
                                         Double              Square serif
                                         No margin           Roman
                                                             Sans serif
Menu colors:   ▶Color scheme 1                               Script
                Color scheme 2                               Gothic
                Color scheme 3
                Monochrome

F1-Help        F3-Intl formats
                                                         F10-Continue
```

**Location**   At the Setup menu, select <Defaults> to display the Default Settings form.

**Description**   This form allows you to specify default directories and files, chart option preferences, and a default color scheme for the Harvard Graphics screen. Once you set the desired options, press F10-Continue to return to the Setup menu.

### Data directory

**Default:** (Blank)

Enter the directory path where most of your charts are stored. This will be the default directory and will be automatically listed on forms relating to chart file management. For example, type **C:\HGDATA** to tell Harvard Graphics your charts are stored in the directory named HGDATA on drive C.

### Chartbook (versions 2.13 and earlier)

See the "Default chartbook" option that follows.

### Import directory

**Default:** (Blank)

If you import data or chart files from other software applications to Harvard Graphics with any regularity, you can specify an import directory in which these files are stored. Harvard Graphics will automatically assume this directory when you are importing data and chart files. You can find more information about importing data and chart files in Chapter 12, "Importing and Exporting."

### Import File (versions 2.13 and earlier)

**Default:** (Blank)

If you import data or chart files from other software applications to Harvard Graphics, you can specify the one file you import from most often. Enter a filename and include its extension. You can find more information about importing data and chart files in Chapter 12, "Importing and Exporting."

### Symbol directory (version 2.3)

**Default:** Directory called SYMBOLS under the path where you installed Harvard Graphics

Enter the directory in which the symbol files you use most often are stored.

### Gallery directory (version 2.3)

**Default:** Directory called GALLERY under the path where you installed Harvard Graphics

Use this option to define the path of the directory in which your chart gallery is stored. Indicate the name of your chart gallery file at the "Gallery filename" option.

### Gallery filename (version 2.3)

**Default:** WPICK

Use this option to specify your chart gallery file. A chart gallery is nothing more than a slide show file. You can use the provided chart gallery, called WPICK, the chart gallery included in the Harvard Graphics accessory Designer Galleries, or you can create your own slide show to use as a gallery.

### Default chartbook (version 2.3)

**Default:** (Blank)

If you use chartbooks, enter the name of the chartbook you use most often. Do not enter a drive, directory, or extension for the chartbook name. Harvard Graphics assumes your chartbook is in the current directory or the default data directory, if you have defined one. Chartbooks are covered in Chapter 11, "Templates and Chartbooks."

### Default palette (version 2.3)

**Default:** HG23

Enter the name of the palette file you use most often. This palette file will be used whenever you create a new chart. It will be saved with the chart file so that the specified colors are used whenever you display or output the chart.

### Orientation

**Default:** Landscape

Set this option to the orientation you want your chart to be by default. Charts with a landscape orientation are wider than they are tall. Charts with a portrait orientation are taller than they are wide.

### Border

**Default:** None

Define the type of border you want to apply to your charts by default.

### Font

**Default:** Executive

Select a font you want to use for your charts by default. Versions 2.13 and earlier have six fonts available: Executive, Square Serif, Roman, Sans Serif, Script, and Gothic. Version 2.3 includes these six fonts plus a Traditional font (Times Roman). See "Fonts and Text Attributes" in Appendix D for examples of fonts.

### Menu colors

**Default:** Color scheme 1

Select one of the four menu coloring schemes.

*Note:* Select Monochrome if you have a monochrome monitor with a color graphics card. Doing so will improve the appearance of Harvard Graphics' screens by making the text darker and easier to read.

## Delays Overlay

**Location**   At the MACRO menu (press ALT-0 to display the MACRO menu), select <Insert delays> to display the Delays overlay.

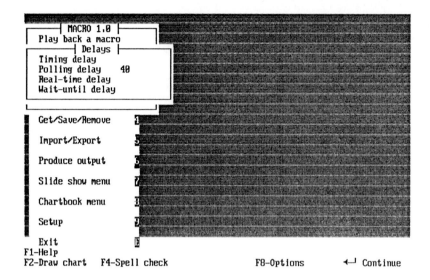

**Description**  Use this overlay to insert a delay in a macro while you are recording a macro. The Delays overlay displays four options: "Timing delay," "Polling delay," "Real-time delay," and "Wait-until delay." To set a delay, move to the desired option and enter a value, then press ESC to remove the Delays overlay. Once the Delays overlay is no longer displayed, continue recording your macro. The values you define on the Delays overlay are used when the macro is played back.

### Timing delay

**Default:** (Blank)

A timing delay slows down your macro during playback. This is useful for displaying a Harvard Graphics demonstration using a macro or when you need to be able to monitor each step the macro executes. Enter a number from 0 to 999. For most computers, a timing delay of 18 creates about a one-second pause after each keystroke executed in your macro.

### Polling delay

**Default:** 40

This delay is used to create very brief pauses between keystrokes to make sure your computer does not miss any keystrokes issued by MACRO during playback. Unless you find that MACRO skips keystrokes during playback, leave "Polling delay" set to the default. If keystrokes are being missed, set "Polling delay" to a higher number (100, for example). Continue to increase "Polling delay" until MACRO no longer skips keystrokes while playing back a macro.

### Real-time delay

**Default:** (Blank)

This delay allows you to insert a single pause, measured in seconds, in a macro. Enter the number of seconds (from 0 to 32,768 seconds) you want MACRO to pause. While your macro is playing back, it will pause at the point at which you inserted the delay.

### Wait-until delay

**Default:** (Blank)

Rather than using the "Real-time delay" option, you can set "Wait-until delay" to an actual time, based on your computer's internal clock. Enter the "Wait-until delay" time using the military time format. For example, enter **0:00** for midnight, **6:00** for six in the morning, or **18:00** for six in the evening. During playback, your macro will stop at the point at which you placed the "Wait-until delay." The macro will then wait until the specified time before continuing to execute the macro.

## Directions Overlay

**Location**  With a current slide show, select <Add ScreenShow effects> from the Slide Show menu to display the ScreenShow Effects

form. Position the cursor in one of the two "Dir" columns on the ScreenShow Effects form and press F6-Choices to display this overlay.

**Description** This overlay is used to select a direction for a display transition assigned to a chart or image in a ScreenShow. To select a direction from this overlay, position the cursor on the ScreenShow Effects form at the line corresponding to the desired file in the "Dir" column. Press F6-Choices and highlight a direction in the Directions overlay. Press ENTER or F10-Continue to select the highlighted direction and return to the ScreenShow Effects form.

## Export for Professional Write Overlay

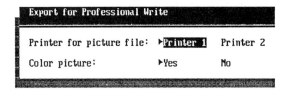

**Location** If you set the "Format" option to Professional Write (version 2.3) or PFS:Professional Write (versions 2.13 and earlier) on the Export Picture overlay, Harvard Graphics displays the Export for Professional Write overlay (version 2.3) or the Export for PFS:Professional Write overlay (versions 2.13 and earlier).

**Description**  Specify the printing characteristics that will be used when printing the chart in a PFS:Professional Write document. Once you set the two options on this overlay, press ENTER or F10-Continue to export your chart.

### Printer for picture file

**Default:** Printer 1

Select which of the printers defined on the Printer 1 and Printer 2 Setup form will be used to print the chart in PFS:Professional Write.

### Color picture

**Default:** No

Select Yes if you plan to print the chart in color in your PFS:Professional Write document.

## Export Metafile Overlay

**Location**  At the Import/Export menu, select <Export CGM metafile> to display the Export Metafile overlay.

**Description**  To export a chart as a metafile, you must have installed the VDI device drivers as described in Appendix B. Once you complete this form, press F10-Continue to export your chart to a metafile.

### Directory

**Default:** (Current directory)

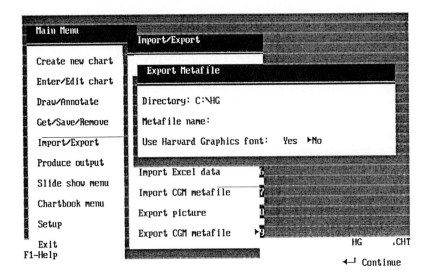

Enter the path of the directory in which Harvard Graphics should store the metafile.

### Metafile name
**Default:** (Blank)

Enter a filename for the exported chart file. Harvard Graphics automatically adds the extension .CGM if you do not provide it.

### Use Harvard Graphics font
**Default:** No

Select Yes to use a Harvard Graphics font or No to use a font in the software you are exporting your chart to.

## Export Picture Overlay

**Location**   At the Import/Export menu, select <Export picture> to display the Export Picture overlay.

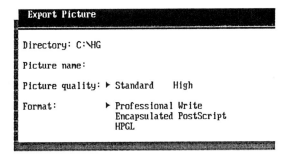

**Description** Enter information about the Harvard Graphics chart you are exporting on this form. When finished, press ENTER or F10-Continue to export your chart.

### Directory

**Default:** (Current directory)

Enter the path of the directory in which Harvard Graphics should store the file you are exporting.

### Picture name

**Default:** (Blank)

Enter a filename, including an extension, for the exported chart file.

### Picture quality

**Default:** Standard

Setting "Picture quality" to High produces a file with greater detail. Standard produces a smaller file with a less detailed image.

### Format

**Default:** Professional Write

Select a file format for your chart: Professional Write, Encapsulated PostScript, or HPGL.

## Film Recorder Setup Form

```
                    Film Recorder Setup

    Polaroid       Palette (CGA)      MATRIX        MVP SCODL (MATRIX fonts)
                   PalettePlus (EGA)                MVP SCODL (HG fonts)
                                                    ChromaScript
    Lasergraphics  RASCOL II/PFR
                   LL compatible      Autographix   Slide Service

    Bell & Howell  CDI IV,1000        General       VideoShow
                                      Parametrics   ColorMetric
    PTI            ImageMaker                       GPC file
                   Montage
                                      VDI           Camera

    Film recorder: Slide Service

    Slide file directory:

    Film type:              ▶Ektachrome   Polachrome   669   339
    Use film recorder's fonts:  ▶Yes      No

    F1-Help                                                F10-Continue
```

**Location**   Select <Film recorder> at the Setup menu to display the Film Recorder Setup form.

**Description**   The Film Recorder Setup form lists the film recorders that Harvard Graphics supports. Select the setting that matches your film recorder. Then press F10-Continue to return to the Setup menu.

### Film recorder

**Default:** In versions 2.13 and earlier, Palette (CGA). In version 2.3, Autographix Slide Service.

To change the current setting, use the cursor keys or press the SPACEBAR to highlight the name of the desired film recorder.

*Note:* If you select a film recorder that requires a VDI device driver (Bell & Howell CDI IV or 1080, Lasergraphics RASCOL II/PFR or compatible, PTI Montage, or Matrix PCR or QCR film recorders), you must install the appropriate VDI device driver before you can produce output with the film recorder. See the Harvard Graphics manual for instructions on installing the VDI device drivers. If you select one of General Parametrics' products (VideoShow, ColorMetric, or GPC file) or select the Autographix Slide Service, you will need to refer to your Harvard Graphics manual for additional information about setting up and using these products with Harvard Graphics.

### Slide file directory

**Default:** (Blank)

Indicate the directory in which you want to store chart files. This is applicable for film recorders that can produce output from files.

### Film type

**Default:** Ektachrome

Indicate the type of film you will use in your film recorder.

### Use film recorder's fonts

**Default:** Yes

To use your film recorder's fonts, if available, set this option to Yes. Harvard Graphics fonts typically provide more font size options, whereas your firm recorder's fonts are typically faster to record and smoother in appearance. (This is called "Use hardware fonts" in versions 2.13 and earlier.)

## Fonts Overlay (Version 2.3)

**Location**   Move the cursor to the "Font" option on the Text Options form in Draw/Annotate and press F6-Choices to display the Fonts overlay.

**Description**   When you are adding or modifying text in the drawing area, you can select a different font for the text. With the cursor positioned at the "Font" option on the Text Options form, press F6-Choices to display the Fonts overlay. Select a font from this list by moving the cursor to the desired font and then pressing F10-Continue or ENTER. The Fonts overlay will then be removed and you will return to the Text Options form.

## Free Form Text Form

**Location**   Select <Create new chart> from the Main Menu followed by <Text> from the Create New Chart menu. Then at the Text Chart Styles menu, select <Free form> to display the Free Form Text form.

```
┌─────────────────────────────────────────────────────┐
│                   Free Form Text                    │
├─────────────────────────────────────────────────────┤
│            Title:                                    │
│         Subtitle:                                    │
│         Footnote:                                    │
├──────┬──────────────────────────────────────────────┤
│      │                                              │
│      │                                              │
│      │                                              │
│      │                                              │
│      │                                              │
│      │                                              │
│      │                                              │
└──────┴──────────────────────────────────────────────┘
F1-Help        F3-Save         F5-Attributes   F7-Size/Place
F2-Draw chart  F4-Draw/Annot                                  F10-Continue
```

**Description**    Enter the text for the chart on this form. Use this form when the format of your text does not easily conform to one of the other text chart styles.

### Title, Subtitle, and Footnote

**Default:** (Blank)

Enter a title, subtitle, and/or footnote for your text chart.

### Free Form Text Area

Enter text in this area. Space the text exactly as you want it to appear in the chart.

## Free Form Text: Size/Place Overlay

**Location**    At the Free Form Text form, press F7-Size/Place to display the Size/Place overlay.

```
Size    Place           Free Form Text
 8     L ►C  R    Title:
 6     L ►C  R    Subtitle:
3.5    ►L  C  R   Footnote:

3.5




F1-Help        F3-Save         F5-Attributes    F7-Size/Place
F2-Draw chart  F4-Draw/Annot                                   F10-Continue
```

## Description

Use each row of the Size/Place overlay to define the size and placement of the title, subtitle, footnote, and text entered on the Free Form Text Chart form. Once you set the desired options, press F7-Size/Place or F10-Continue to return to the Free Form Text Chart form.

## Size

**Defaults:** (Vary depending on the line)

Enter a number from .1 to 99.

## Place

**Defaults:** (Vary depending on the line)

Select L, C, or R to left-justify, center, or right-justify text.

## Global Options Form

**Location**   At the Default Options menu in Draw/Annotate, select <Global> to display the Global Options form.

**Description**   Options on this form allow you to set general characteristics for the drawing area on the Draw/Annotate screen.

### Display

**Default:** Final

Select Final to display the most accurate image of your chart while you are adding objects in the drawing area. Select Quick to draw faster but with less detail.

### Redraw

**Default:** No

Select Yes to update (redraw) the objects in the drawing area after each modification. Select No to control when the objects are updated. If you select No, use F4-Redraw when you want to see modifications made to the objects in the drawing area.

## Show XY

**Default:** Yes

Select Yes to display the horizontal and vertical positions of the cursor. These positions will be displayed while you are adding or modifying objects in the drawing area at the top-right of the function key banner at "Horiz=" and "Vert=."

## Target

**Default:** Small

Select the shape of the cursor that appears in the drawing area: Small (small cross hairs), Large (cross hairs that extend to the edges of the drawing area), or Arrow (an arrow shape).

## Global align

**Default:** (Upper-left corner of the placement box)

Select one of the nine positions of the placement box which the cursor should refer to for moving and placing objects.

# Go To Overlay (Version 2.13)

**Location**   With a current slide show, select <Add Screenshow effects> from the Slide Show menu to display the Screenshow Effects form. Move the cursor to the desired file on the Screenshow Effects form and press F8-User menu. Harvard Graphics will display the Go To overlay.

**Description**   This overlay is used to advance a Screenshow to any file in the slide show. Go To keys are assigned to one file at a time. You

```
                    Screenshow Effects
         Filename      Type    Draw    Dir   Time   Key    Go To
      Default                 Replace
    ▶ 1  20F1  .CHT  FREEFORM
      2  20F2  .CHT  FREEFORM
      3  20F3  .CHT  FREEFORM
```

F1-Help

F10-Continue

can assign Go To keys to none, one, or more than one file in your slide show. Press TAB to move between the "Key" and "Go To" columns. Once you have assigned Go To keys for a file, press ESC or F10-Continue to remove the Go To overlay and return to the Screenshow Effects form.

## Key

Enter the single character associated with the key you want to use to control the Screenshow.

## Go To

Enter the number of the file in the slide show that you want to go to when the corresponding key (defined in the "Key" column) is pressed. This feature allows you to create customized menu-driven Screenshows (see Chapter 13, "Slide Shows").

*Note:* To create a Screenshow that runs continuously, leave the "Key" column blank but enter the file number 1 (or any other file number) in the "Go To" column for the last file in the slide show. Once this last file is displayed in the Screenshow, the file will advance to the first file (or the file specified) when either the DOWN or RIGHT arrow key is pressed, the right mouse button is pressed, or when the display time expires (if one has been defined).

## Group Options Form

**Location** When you select a group of objects to modify in the drawing area of the Draw/Annotate screen, Harvard Graphics displays the Group Options form.

**Description** This form allows you to modify characteristics of selected objects of different types in one step.

### Outline color

**Default:** (Blank)

Enter the number of the color for all text and polylines and for all box, line, circle, and polygon outlines. Alternatively, with the cursor positioned at this option, press F6-Choices and select a color from the Color Selection overlay (see "Color Selection Overlay").

### Fill color

**Default:** (Blank)

Enter the number of the color to be used for the center of box, line, circle, and polygon objects. Alternatively, with the cursor positioned at this option, press F6-Choices and select a color from the Color Selection overlay (see "Color Selection Overlay").

**Shadow color**

**Default:** (Blank)

The number entered at "Shadow color" affects the color of shadows used in text and boxes. You can also press F6-Choices and select a color from the Color Selection overlay (see "Color Selection Overlay").

## High/Low/Close Chart Data Form

```
                     High/Low/Close Chart Data
     Title:
  Subtitle:
  Footnote:

              X Axis
      Pt      Name          High        Low        Close       Open

      1
      2
      3
      4
      5
      6
      7
      8
      9
     10
     11
     12

  F1-Help         F3-Save         F5-Set X type                 F9-More series
  F2-Draw chart   F4-Draw/Annot   F6-Calculate    F8-Options    F10-Continue
```

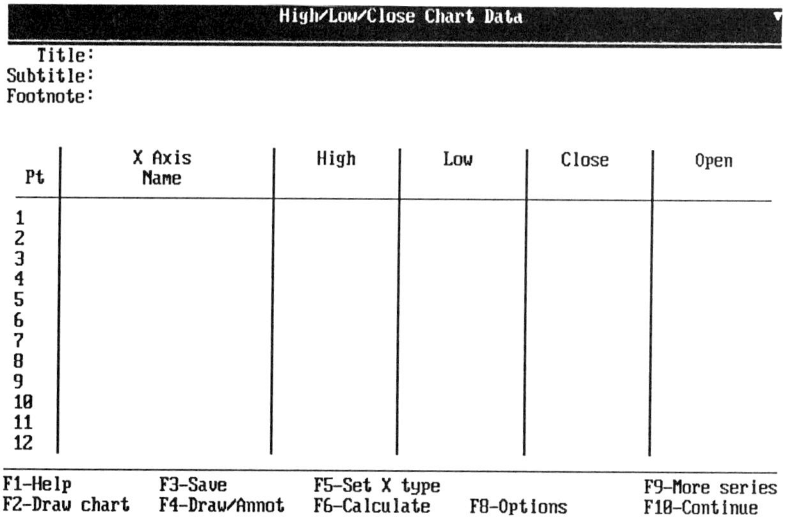

**Location** At the Create New Chart menu, select <High/Low/Close> to display the High/Low/Close Chart Data form.

**Description** The High/Low/Close Chart Data form is used to enter text and data for a high/low/close chart. This form has two areas. At the top are entry spaces for a chart title, subtitle, and footnote. The rest of the form contains columns for the data.

### Title, Subtitle, and Footnote
**Default:** (Blank)

Enter a title, subtitle, and/or footnote for your chart. If your subtitle or footnote text requires more than one line, enter the subtitle or footnote on Page 1 of the High/Low/Close Chart Titles & Options form.

### X Axis

Enter the X axis data in this column. Note that the X data type (Name, Number, Time, or one of the eight calendar-based data types) that was specified on the X Data Type Menu overlay is displayed at the top of the column under "X Axis." If you used Harvard Graphics' automatic X data entry feature, this column will already contain your X data.

### Series 1 through Series 8

The first four series columns, labeled "High," "Low," "Close," and "Open," are designed to create a high/low close chart. You cannot change these names. Enter your Y axis data to be used in a high/low/close chart in these columns. The Y axis data must be numeric. If you have additional data you want on your chart but not in a high/low/close style, press F9-More series to display additional columns for Series 5 through Series 8, and enter the data in these columns.

## High/Low/Close Chart: Size/Place Overlay

**Location** At Page 1 of the High/Low/Close Chart Titles & Options form, press F7-Size/Place to display the Size/Place overlay.

```
Size    Place       gh/Low/Close Chart  Titles & Options  Page 1 of 4
 8      L ►C  R    Title:
 6      L ►C  R    Subtitle:
 6      L ►C  R
 2.5    ►L C  R    Footnote:
 2.5    ►L C  R
 2.5    ►L C  R
 4         ►C      X  axis title:
 3       ►  ↓      Y1 axis title:
 3       ►  ↓      Y2 axis title:
         X labels                              Type              Display    Y Axis
         Y labels           Bar   Line    Trend  Curve   Pt     Yes   No    Y1  Y2

  1   High                                High                   Yes        Y1
  2   Low                                 Low                    Yes        Y1
  3   Close                               Close                  Yes        Y1
  4   Open                                Open                   Yes        Y1
  5   Series 5                            Line                   Yes        Y1
  6   Series 6                            Line                   Yes        Y1
  7   Series 7                            Line                   Yes        Y1
  8   Series 8                            Line                   Yes        Y1

F1-Help                      F5-Attributes       F7-Size/Place
F2-Draw chart                                    F8-Data                F10-Continue
```

**Description**   Use each row of the Size/Place overlay to define the size and placement of the title, subtitle, footnote, and axis titles entered on the Titles & Options form. Once you set the desired options, press F7-Size/Place or F10-Continue to return to the Titles & Options form.

### Size

**Defaults:** (Vary depending on the line)

Enter a number from .1 to 99. This number represents a percentage of the chart height (landscape) or width (portrait).

### Place

**Defaults:** (Vary depending on the line)

Set placement for the title, subtitle, and footnote to either L, C, or R to left-justify, center, or right-justify the text. The X axis title is automatically centered and cannot be changed. There are two placement options for the Y1 and Y2 axis titles: vertical and horizontal. Set Y axis title placement to horizontal (the default) to have the titles read left to right at the top of the axes. Set Y axis title placement to vertical to have the titles read vertically along the axes.

## High/Low/Close Chart Titles & Options Form

**Location**   At the High/Low/Close Chart Data form, press F8-Options to display the High/Low/Close Chart Titles & Options form.

**Description**   The High/Low/Close Chart Titles & Options form contains options that allow you to change the appearance of your high/low/close chart. This form is four pages long. Press PGDN and PGUP to move between the pages.

### Page 1 of the High/Low/Close Chart Titles & Options Form

**Title**

**Default:** (Blank)

  Enter a title for your chart.

**Subtitle**

**Default:** (Blank)

  Enter a subtitle for the chart; it can be up to two lines long.

```
          High/Low/Close Chart  Titles & Options  Page 1 of 4
              Title:
              Subtitle:

              Footnote:

                      X  axis title:
                      Y1 axis title:
                      Y2 axis title:
    Legend                              Type              Display  | Y Axis
    Title:                         Bar Line Trend Curve Pt Yes No  | Y1 Y2

    1 | High                                High             Yes   |  Y1
    2 | Low                                 Low              Yes   |  Y1
    3 | Close                               Close            Yes   |  Y1
    4 | Open                                Open             Yes   |  Y1
    5 | Series 5                            Line             Yes   |  Y1
    6 | Series 6                            Line             Yes   |  Y1
    7 | Series 7                            Line             Yes   |  Y1
    8 | Series 8                            Line             Yes   |  Y1

    F1-Help                  F5-Attributes    F7-Size/Place
    F2-Draw chart                             F8-Data         F10-Continue
```

## Footnote

**Default:** (Blank)

Enter a footnote for your chart; it can be up to three lines long.

## X axis title, Y1 axis title, and Y2 axis title

**Default:** (Blank)

Enter titles for the axes.

## Legend Title

**Default:** (Blank)

Enter a name for the chart legend.

## Series

**Default:** High, Low, Close, Open, Series 5 through Series 8

In this column, enter the series names to be displayed on the chart.

**Type**

**Default:** High, Low, Close, Open (for the first four series)

The first four series symbol types are labeled "High," "Low," "Close," and "Open." These are designed to create a high/low/close chart and cannot be changed. You can set "Type" to the type of symbol to be displayed for each of the remaining series in your chart (Series 5 through Series 8) to one of the following types: Bar, Line, Trend, Curve, or Pt. Each of these symbol types is described at the "Type" option under "Bar/Line Chart Titles & Options Form."

**Display**

**Default:** Yes

For each series, select Yes to display the series on the chart or No if you do not want to display the series.

**Y Axis**

**Default:** Y1

Select the Y axis each series refers to in this column to create a dual-axis chart. If you are using only one Y axis on your chart, you should leave "Y Axis" set to Y1.

## Page 2 of the High/Low/Close Chart Titles & Options Form

**Bar style**

**Default:** Cluster

```
          High/Low/Close Chart  Titles & Options  Page 2 of 4

       Bar style          ▶Cluster   Overlap   Stack
       High/Low style     ▶Bar       Area      Error bar
       Bar fill style     ▶Color     Pattern   Both

       Bar width
       Bar overlap         50

       Horizontal chart    Yes       ▶No
       Value labels        All        Select   ▶None

       Frame style        ▶Full       Half      Quarter   None
       Frame color         1
       Frame background    0

       Legend location     Top       ▶Bottom    Left      Right    None
       Legend justify      ← or ↑   ▶Center    ↓ or →
       Legend placement    In        ▶Out
       Legend frame        Single     Shadow   ▶None

F1-Help
F2-Draw chart                      F6-Colors        F8-Data        F10-Continue
```

When "Type" is set to Bar for one or more series (this applies only to Series 5 through Series 8 on high/low/close charts), use the "Bar style" option to define how Harvard Graphics should display the bars.

### High/Low style

**Default:** Bar

Select one of the three types of styles: Bar, Area, or Error bar. Select Bar to display a standard high/low/close bar. In order to create a band chart, select Area. Harvard Graphics will use the values of your high and low series to define the upper and lower boundaries of the band on your chart. To create error bars, select Error bar.

### Bar fill style

**Default:** Color

Select whether to use color, patterns, or both color and patterns for filling bars on your chart.

## Bar width

**Default:** (Blank)

Use "Bar width" to change the width of bars displayed on your high/low/close chart. When "Bar width" is blank, the width of high/low bars and error bars defaults to 15, while the width of Series 5 through Series 8 bars defaults to 60. To change these settings, enter a number from 1 to 100 to indicate the percentage of the chart space to be used by the bars.

## Bar overlap

**Default:** 50

When the "Bar style" option is set to Overlap, use "Bar overlap" to control the amount of overlap for Series 5 through Series 8 bars. The default bar overlap is 50. To change this setting, enter a number from 1 to 100 to indicate the degree of bar overlap.

## Horizontal chart

**Default:** No

Select Yes to create a horizontal chart and No to create a vertical chart.

## Value labels

**Default:** None

Set "Value labels" to All to display values for all series in a chart, to No if you do not want values displayed, or to Select to display values for selected series. (Select series by choosing Yes at "Y Label" on Page 4 of the Area Chart Titles & Options form.)

## Frame style

**Default:** Full

Set "Frame style" to either Full, Half, or Quarter to create a full frame, half frame, or quarter frame for your chart. Select None if you do not want a chart frame.

**Frame color**

**Default:** 1

Enter a number from 0 to 16 to select the color for the chart frame. Alternatively, press F6-Colors to display the Color Selection overlay to select from a list of 16 colors.

**Frame background**

**Default:** 0

Enter a number from 0 to 16 to select the color for the chart background. Alternatively, press F6-Colors to display the Color Selection overlay to select from a list of 16 colors.

**Legend location**

**Default:** Bottom

Set the general location for the placement of the chart legend. Set "Legend location" to None if you do not want a legend displayed on your chart.

**Legend Justify**

**Default:** Center

"Legend justify" settings are left or up, Center, and down or right. This setting fine-tunes the position of the legend specified at the "Legend location" option.

### Legend placement

**Default:** Out

Set "Legend placement" to In to place the legend inside the chart frame or to Out to place it outside the chart frame.

### Legend frame

**Default:** None

Set "Legend frame" to Single to draw a line box around the legend or to Shadow to add a shadow behind the legend box. Set "Legend frame" to None if you do not want the legend to be framed.

## Page 3 of the High/Low/Close Chart Titles & Options Form

| | High/Low/Close Chart Titles & Options Page 3 of 4 | | | |
|---|---|---|---|---|
| Data Table | Normal | Framed | ▶None | |
| X Axis Labels | ▶Normal | Vertical % | None | |
| Y1 Axis Labels | ▶Value | Currency % | None | |
| Y2 Axis Labels | ▶Value | Currency % | None | |
| X Grid Lines | · · · · | ——— | ▶None | |
| Y1 Grid Lines | ▶· · · · | ——— | None | |
| Y2 Grid Lines | ▶· · · · | ——— | None | |
| X Tick Mark Style | ▶In | Out | Both | None |
| Y Tick Mark Style | ▶In | Out | Both | None |
| | X Axis | Y1 Axis | Y2 Axis |
| Scale Type | ▶Linear  Log | ▶Linear  Log | ▶Linear  Log |
| Format | | | |
| Minimum Value | | | |
| Maximum Value | | | |
| Increment | | | |

F1-Help
F2-Draw chart                                F8-Data       F10-Continue

### Data Table

**Default:** None

Set "Data Table" to Normal to display a table of the data at the bottom of the chart, to Framed to also draw a frame around the table of data, or to None if you do not want the data displayed in a table on the chart. You cannot use a data table if your X data type is Number.

### X Axis Labels

**Default:** Normal

The labels displayed along the X axis of the chart will be the names of the series entered on Page 1 of the Titles & Options form. Set "X Axis Labels" to Normal if you want the labels to read horizontally or to Vertical if you want the labels to read vertically along the X axis of the chart. The % setting is valid only if the "X data type" set on the X Data Type Menu overlay is Number. If you then set "X Axis Labels" to %, Harvard Graphics adds a percent sign to each number. Select None if you do not want X axis labels on your chart.

### Y1 Axis Labels and Y2 Axis Labels

**Defaults:** Value

The Y1 and Y2 axis labels will be displayed along the Y1 and Y2 axes of the chart. Set "Y1 Axis Labels" and "Y2 Axis Labels" each to Value to display numbers along the Y1 and Y2 axes. Set these options to $ to add a dollar sign at the front of each label. If you set "Y1 Axis Labels" or "Y2 Axis Labels" to %, Harvard Graphics adds a percent sign to each number. Select None if you do not want Y1 and Y2 axis labels on your chart.

### X Grid Lines

**Default:** None

Set "X Grid Lines" to .... or _____ to have dotted or solid grid lines extend from the X axis tick marks or to None if you do not want grid lines.

### Y1 Grid Lines and Y2 Grid Lines

**Default:** ....

Set "Y1 Grid Lines" and "Y2 Grid Lines" each to .... or _____ to have dotted or solid grid lines extend from the Y axis tick marks or to None if you do not want grid lines.

### X Tick Mark Style and Y Tick Mark Style

**Default:** In

Settings for tick mark styles are In, Out, Both, and None. Select In to place tick marks inside the chart axis frame or Out to place tick marks outside the chart axis frame. Select Both to have tick marks that overlap the chart axis frame. Select None if you do not want tick marks.

### Scale Type

**Default:** Linear

Set "Scale Type" to either Linear or Log (logarithmic) in the "X Axis," "Y1 Axis," and "Y2 Axis" columns to specify the scale of data represented along each of the axes.

### Format

**Default:** (Blank)

Enter any formatting instructions in the appropriate columns ("X Axis," "Y1 Axis," and "Y2 Axis") for data represented along each of the axes. Formatting is covered in detail in Chapter 6, "XY Charts."

### Minimum Value

**Default:** (Blank)

Enter values in the appropriate columns ("X Axis," "Y1 Axis," and "Y2 Axis") to specify the minimum data value that should be plotted on the chart for data represented along each of the axes. This value must be lower than the lowest value to be charted on the axis.

**Maximum Value**

**Default:** (Blank)

Enter values in the appropriate columns ("X Axis," "Y1 Axis," and "Y2 Axis") to specify the maximum data value that should be plotted on the chart for data represented along each of the axes. This value must be higher than the highest value to be charted on the axis.

**Increment**

**Default:** (Blank)

Enter values in the appropriate columns ("X Axis," "Y1 Axis," and "Y2 Axis") to specify the increment that should be used for axis tick marks and grid lines between the "Minimum" and "Maximum" data values.

## Page 4 of the High/Low/Close Chart Titles & Options Form

The first eight options on Page 4 are repeated from Page 1. Any changes you make to these options here will also be reflected on Page 1. See descriptions of the following options under "Page 1 of the High/Low/Close Chart Titles & Options Form" for more information:

- Title
- Subtitle
- Footnote
- X axis title

- Y1 axis title
- Y2 axis title
- Legend Title
- Series

## Cum

**Default:** No

Set "Cum" to Yes if you want the series data to be displayed cumulatively along the X axis.

## Y Label

**Default:** No

"Y Label" is only applicable when you set "Value labels" on Page 2 of the Titles & Options form to Select. Set "Y Label" to Yes to have Y data values displayed on the chart.

```
┌─────────────────── High/Low/Close Chart  Titles & Options  Page 4 of 4 ──────────────┐
                    Title:
                    Subtitle:

                    Footnote:

               X  axis title:
               Y1 axis title:
               Y2 axis title:
    Legend                          Cum      Y Label    Color    Marker/   Line
    Title:                          Yes No   Yes No              Pattern   Style

    1  High                         No       No         2        1         1
    2  Low                          No       No         3        2         1
    3  Close                        No       No         4        3         1
    4  Open                         No       No         5        4         1
    5  Series 5                     No       No         6        5         1
    6  Series 6                     No       No         7        6         1
    7  Series 7                     No       No         8        7         1
    8  Series 8                     No       No         9        8         1

 F1-Help                  F5-Attributes   F7-Size/Place
 F2-Draw chart            F6-Colors       F8-Data              F10-Continue
```

### Color

**Default:** 2 through 9 (for Series 1 through Series 8)

Enter a color number, 1 through 16, for each of the series displayed on the chart.

### Marker/Pattern

**Default:** 1 through 8 (for Series 1 through Series 8)

For each series, enter a number, 1 through 12, for the pattern used for areas and bars on your chart. Enter a number, 1 through 13, for the markers used for lines displayed on the chart. Enter a zero to suppress the display of a pattern or marker.

### Line Style

**Default:** 1

Select a "Line Style," from 1 to 4, for the lines on your chart. This option does not have an effect on bars or areas.

## HyperShow Menu Overlay (Version 2.3)

| HyperShow menu | | |
|---|---|---|
| Button | Key | Go To |
| 1 | | |
| 2 | | |
| 3 | | |
| 4 | | |
| 5 | | |
| 6 | | |
| 7 | | |
| 8 | | |
| 9 | | |
| 10 | | |

**Location**  With a current slide show, select <Add ScreenShow effects> from the Slide Show menu to display the ScreenShow Effects form. Move the cursor to the desired file on the ScreenShow Effects form and press F8-HyperShow menu to display the HyperShow menu overlay.

**Description**  This overlay is used to advance a ScreenShow to any file in the slide show. Buttons and keys are assigned to one file at a time. You can assign buttons and keys to none, one, or more than one file in your slide show. Press TAB to move among the "Button," "Key," and "Go To" columns. Once you have assigned buttons and keys for a file, press ESC or F10-Continue to remove the HyperShow menu overlay and return to the ScreenShow Effects form.

### Button

These numbers correspond to buttons (boxes created in Draw/Annotate or Draw Partner with numbers 1 to 10). All ten standard button numbers appear on the HyperShow menu overlay, whether or not corresponding buttons have been placed on the chart.

### Key

Enter the single character associated with the key you want to use to control the ScreenShow. If you want to assign a slide number for a particular button, you must assign a corresponding key.

### Go To

Enter the number of the file in the slide show that you want to go to when the corresponding button or the key (defined in the "Key" column) is pressed. This feature allows you to create customized menu-driven ScreenShows (see Chapter 13, "Slide Shows" and Chapter 16, "Harvard Graphics 2.3 Features").

*Note:*  To create a ScreenShow that runs continuously, leave the "Key" column blank but enter the file number 1 (or any other file number) in the "Go To" column for the last file in the slide show. Once this last file is displayed in the ScreenShow, the file will advance to the first file (or file specified) when either the DOWN or RIGHT arrow key is pressed, the right mouse button is pressed, or when the display time expires (if one has been defined).

## Import ASCII Data Form

```
                          Import ASCII Data
 1
 2
 3              Jan      Feb      Mar    Q1 Total   Apr     Ma
 4
 5  Units Shipped
 6    Marathoner      1,000    1,200    1,400    3,600   1,451    1,
 7    Triathlete        800      700      743    2,243     756
 8    Triathlete Jr.    400      431      422    1,253     456
 9
10  Total             2,200    2,331    2,565    7,096   2,663    2,
11
12
13
                   1        2        3        4        5       6

     Read data by       ►Line   Column      Read from line    5  to line    244
     Tabular data format ►Yes   No          Read from column  1  to column    9


  F1-Help         F3-Select files
                  F4-Reselect                        F8-Options      F10-Continue
```

**Location**   This form is displayed when you are importing ASCII data. Select <Import ASCII data> from the Import/Export menu and then select a file to import from the Select File form to display the Import ASCII Data form.

**Description**   The Import ASCII Data form is used to define the data in the ASCII file you want to import. Once you have filled out the Import ASCII Data form, press F10-Continue. Harvard Graphics will display the Import Titles & Legends overlay (see "Import Titles & Legends Overlay").

*Note:* Before you can import ASCII data, you must have first created a blank chart (do not enter text or data in the chart form) in which the imported data will be placed.

### ASCII File Area

This area displays the contents of the file you are importing. Row numbers are displayed at the left of the area and column numbers are displayed at the bottom of the area for reference.

### Read data by

**Default:** Line

Indicate whether the data are arranged by rows (one record per row) or by columns (one record per column). When your data are in a tabular format, the "Read data by" option tells Harvard Graphics how you want the data to be inserted into your data chart. (This option has no effect if you are inserting your data into a text chart.) If "Read data by" is set to Line, the first value in each line is imported as the X data value for XY charts and the pie label for pie charts. The remaining values in each line are imported as the series values for both XY charts and pie charts. When "Read data by" is set to Column, the first value in each column is imported as the X data value or pie label, with the remaining values imported as the series data.

### Read from line _ _ _ to line _ _ _

**Default:** (First and last lines of data in the file)

If you want to import less than the entire ASCII text file, enter the line numbers shown in the ASCII file area of the form that correspond to the first line you want to import ("Read from line") and the last line to import ("to line"). For example, to import text from lines 3 through 7 only into your chart, set "Read from line" to 3, and "to line" to 7.

### Tabular data format

**Default:** (set by Harvard Graphics)

Harvard Graphics automatically sets the "Tabular data format" option to either Yes or No depending on the format of your data. If your ASCII file meets Harvard Graphics' requirements for importing a tabular data file, Harvard Graphics sets this option to Yes. You can then set the "Read data by," "Read from column," and "to column" options. If your ASCII file does not meet the requirements of a tabular data file, "Tabular data format" is set to No and the other options do not apply. You can change the "Tabular data format" setting, if desired, although changing it to Yes may not result in a successful data importation.

**Read from column _ _ _ to column _ _ _**

**Default:** (First and last column of data in the file.)

These options are used to indicate which columns should be included when you import your data. If you want to import less than the entire ASCII text file, enter the column numbers shown in the ASCII file area of the form that correspond to the first column you want to import ("Read from column") and the last column to import ("to column").

The "Read from column" specified should refer to the X data column when "Read data by" is set to Line, or the first series when "Read data by" is set to Column. An alternative method of selecting only some of the columns of data is described in Chapter 12, "Importing and Exporting."

## Import Excel Chart Overlay (Version 2.3)

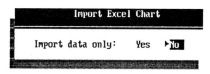

**Location** This overlay is displayed when you are importing an Excel chart to Harvard Graphics. Select <Import Excel chart> from the

Import/Export menu and then select a file to import from the Select Excel Chart form to display the Import Excel Chart overlay.

**Description**  Set the option on this overlay and then press F10-Continue to import the chart and/or data.

### Import data only
**Default:** No

Select Yes to import only the data from the chart without the chart description (graph type). If you set "Import data only" to No, Harvard Graphics automatically creates a chart similar to the Excel chart.

## Import Excel Data Form (Version 2.3)

```
                        Import Excel Data
        Worksheet name: NEWREP    .XLS
                Title:
             Subtitle:
             Footnote:
                        Legend              Data Range
             X    X axis data

             1    Series 1
             2    Series 2
             3    Series 3
             4    Series 4
             5    Series 5
             6    Series 6
             7    Series 7
             8    Series 8

             Append data:  ►Yes    No

F1-Help      F3-Select files
             F4-Clear ranges F6-Range names              F10-Continue
```

**Location**  This form is displayed when you are importing data from an Excel spreadsheet. Select <Import Excel data> from the Import/

Export menu and then select a file to import from the Select Excel Worksheet form to display the Import Excel Data form.

**Description** This form is used to define the title, subtitle, and footnote, as well as the cell ranges for your X data and series data. Once you have filled out the Import Excel Data form, press F10-Continue to import the data into a Harvard Graphics chart form.

*Note:* Before you can import Excel data, you must have first created a blank chart (do not enter text or data in the chart data form) in which the imported data will be placed.

### Worksheet name

The name of the Excel spreadsheet you will be importing from is displayed at the top of the Import Excel Data form. You cannot enter or modify this name. If you want to import data from a spreadsheet other than the one shown, press F3-Select files. Harvard Graphics will return you to the Select Excel Worksheet form so you can select the desired spreadsheet.

### Title, Subtitle, and Footnote

**Default:** (Blank)

There are two ways to define the title, subtitle, and footnote for your chart. First, you can type in this text either on the Import Excel Data form when you are importing your data or on a chart data form after you import the data. Second, you can import this text by specifying the cell address of your spreadsheet where the text information is stored. To enter these cell addresses on the Import Excel Data form, precede the address with a backslash (\) in the first column of the corresponding "Title," "Subtitle," or "Footnote" option. For example, if cell A1 contains text you want to import as the title of your chart, enter \A1 at the "Title" option on the Import Excel Data form.

### Legend

**Default:** Series 1, Series 2 (and so on)

In the "Legend" column, you can either enter the names of the series or define the cell location where Harvard Graphics will find the series legends to import. As with the title, subtitle, and footnote options, you define the cell address by preceding the address with a backslash.

### Data Range

**Default:** (Blank)

Enter the cell ranges or range names for your X axis data and series data in this column. If your X axis data and series data are not in one continuous range, you will need to perform this importation more than once, importing the first continuous range and then importing again for the second range, and so forth. To select from a list of range names, press F6-Range names.

### Append data

**Default:** Yes

This option is used when the data you are importing are not in one continuous range. If all your Excel data are in a continuous range, and you do not want to keep adding additional data to your Harvard Graphics chart each time you import, set this option to No. If your X axis data and series data are not located in a continuous range, set "Append data" to Yes for any additional importations.

*Note:* A data link saved in a template will only be applied to the last data range imported.

## Import Lotus Data Form

**Location** Select <Import Lotus data> from the Import/Export menu. Next, define a spreadsheet to import using the Select Worksheet form. Press F10-Continue to display the Import Lotus Data form.

```
                    Import Lotus Data
         Worksheet name: UNITS    .WKS
              Title:
         Subtitle:
         Footnote:

                      Legend            Data Range

              X | X axis data

              1 | Series 1
              2 | Series 2
              3 | Series 3
              4 | Series 4
              5 | Series 5
              6 | Series 6
              7 | Series 7
              8 | Series 8

              Append data:  ►Yes    No

F1-Help       F3-Select files
              F4-Clear ranges F6-Range names           F10-Continue
```

**Description**   The Import Lotus Data form is used to define the title, subtitle, and footnote, as well as the cell ranges for your X data and series data. Once you have filled out the Import Lotus Data form, press F10-Continue to import the data into a Harvard Graphics chart form.

*Note:*  Before you can import Lotus data, you must have first created a blank chart (do not enter text or data in the chart data form) in which the imported data will be placed.

### Worksheet name

The name of the Lotus spreadsheet you will be importing from is displayed at the top of the Import Lotus Data form. You cannot enter or modify this name. If you want to import data from a spreadsheet other than the one shown, press F3-Select files. Harvard Graphics will return you to the Select Worksheet form so you can select the desired spreadsheet.

### Title, Subtitle, and Footnote

**Default:** (Blank)

There are two ways to define the title, subtitle, and footnote for your chart. First, you can type in this text either on the Import Lotus Data form when you are importing your data or on the chart data form after you import your data. Second, you can import this text by specifying the cell address of your spreadsheet where this text information is stored. To enter cell addresses on the Import Lotus Data form, precede the address with a backslash (\) in the first column of the corresponding "Title," "Subtitle," or "Footnote" option. For example, if cell A1 contains text you want to import as the title of your chart, type in **\A1** at the "Title" option on the Import Lotus Data form.

### Legend

**Default:** Series 1, Series 2 (and so on)

In the "Legend" column, you can either enter the names of the series or define the cell location where Harvard Graphics will find the series legends to import. As with the title, subtitle, and footnote options, you define the cell address by preceding the address with a backslash.

### Data Range

**Default:** (Blank)

Enter the cell ranges or named ranges for your X axis data and series data in this column. If your X axis data and series data are not in one continuous range, you will need to perform this importation more than once, importing the first continuous range and then importing again for the second range, and so forth. To select from a list of range names, press F6-Range names (version 2.3 only).

### Append data

**Default:** Yes

This option is used when the data you are importing are not in one continuous range. If all your Lotus data are in a continuous range, and you do not want to keep adding additional data to your Harvard Graphics chart each time you import, set this option to No. If your X axis data and series data are not located in a continuous range, set "Append data" to Yes for any additional importations.

*Note:* A data link saved in a template will only be applied to the last data range imported.

## Import Lotus Graph Form

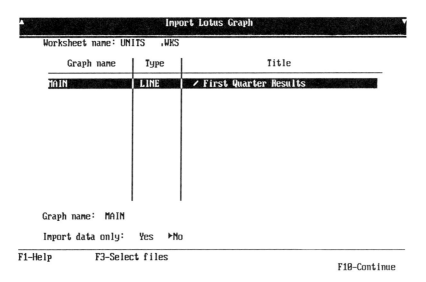

**Location** Select <Import Lotus graph> from the Import/Export menu to display the Select Worksheet form. Select the Lotus spreadsheet that contains the desired Lotus graph from this form to display the Import Lotus Graph form.

**Description** Use this form to select a graph from a Lotus spreadsheet. Once you select a spreadsheet, press F10-Continue to import the graph.

### Worksheet name

Harvard Graphics displays the name of the current worksheet. You cannot change this name. If your graph is not in this worksheet, press F3-Select files to return to the Select Worksheet form and select a different worksheet.

### Graph List

Information about the graphs in the Lotus worksheet is shown in the "Graph name," "Type," and "Title" columns.

### Graph name

**Default:** (First graph in the graph list)

Highlight the Lotus graph you want to import in the graph list using the UP and DOWN arrow keys. Once the desired graph is highlighted and its name is shown at the "Graph name" option, press ENTER to move to the next option.

### Import data only

**Default:** No

Select Yes to import only the data from the graph without the graph description (graph type).

## Import Titles and Legends Overlay

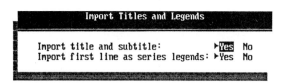

**Location** When you press F10-Continue from the Import ASCII Data form, Harvard Graphics displays the Import Titles & Legends overlay.

**Description** Indicate whether your import ASCII file contains titles and legends you want to import. You can import the first three *non-blank* lines in the file — the first to be used as a title and the next two as a subtitle. (For text charts, only one line will be imported for a subtitle.) When you have set the options on this form, press F10-Continue to import your data and display the appropriate chart form.

### Import title and subtitle

**Default:** Yes

Select Yes to use the first three lines of the imported ASCII file for the chart title and subtitle. Only one line will be imported for the subtitle if your destination chart is a text chart. The value specified at "Read from line" on the Import ASCII Data form will determine the first line.

### Import first line as series legends

**Default:** Yes

Select Yes if the first line (or third line if the "Import title and subtitle" option is also set to Yes) contains the series legends for your chart. If "Read data by" is set to Line, the first line in each column of data will be used for the series legends. (The fourth line in each column will be used for series legends if you also set "Import title and subtitle" to Yes, however.) If "Read data by" is set to Column, the first column of data will be used for the series legends. Set "Import first line as series legends" to No to suppress the importation of series legends.

## Line Options Form

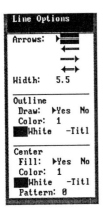

**Location**   The Line Options form appears in Draw/Annotate when you press F8-Options while adding a line in the drawing area, when you select <Options> from the Modify menu and then select an existing line object in the drawing area, or when you select <Line> from the Default Options menu, which is displayed when you press F8-Options at the Draw menu.

**Description**   Use the Line Options form to define the characteristics of line objects.

### Arrows

**Default:** Line

   Select either a plain line (the first setting), a left-arrow line, a right-arrow line, or a dual-arrow line.

### Width

**Default:** 5.5

Enter a number from 1 to 100 to be used for the widths of lines and arrows.

### Outline Draw

**Default:** Yes

Select Yes to outline lines and arrows or No to suppress the outline.

### Outline Color

**Default:** 1

If "Outline Draw" is set to Yes, enter a color number, 1 through 16, for the color of the outline. Alternatively, with the cursor positioned at "Outline Color," press F6-Choices and select a color from the Color Selection overlay (see "Color Selection Overlay").

### Center Fill

**Default:** Yes

Select Yes if you want to fill the center of your lines and arrows or No if you want to display only the line and arrow outlines (if "Outline Draw" is set to Yes).

### Center Color

**Default:** 1

If "Center Fill" is set to Yes, enter a color number, 1 through 16, for the centers of lines and arrows. Alternatively, with the cursor positioned at "Center Color," press F6-Choices and select a color from the Color Selection overlay (see "Color Selection Overlay").

### Center Pattern

**Default:** 0 (no pattern)

If "Center Fill" is set to Yes, enter a pattern number, 1 through 12, for the pattern used in the centers of lines and arrows. Alternatively, with the cursor positioned at "Center Pattern," press F6-Choices and select a pattern from those shown in the Pattern Selection overlay (see "Patterns Overlay").

## New Symbol File Overlay

**Location**  If you enter a new (unique) name on the Save Chart As Symbol overlay when you are saving a chart as a symbol, or on the Select Symbol File form when you are saving a drawing as a symbol, Harvard Graphics displays the New Symbol File overlay.

**Description**  The description entered on the New Symbol File overlay refers to the entire symbol file rather than the individual symbol you are saving in this file.

### Description

**Default:** (Blank)

Enter a description for the new symbol file.

## Organization Chart Form

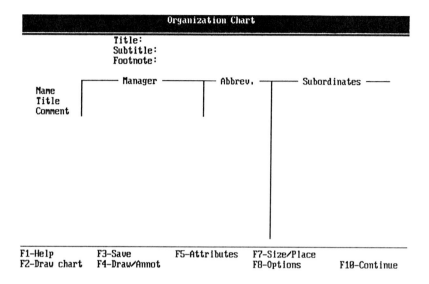

**Location** At the Create New Chart menu, select <Organization> to display the Organization Chart form.

**Description** This form is used to enter the text that will be displayed on the organization chart.

### Title, Subtitle, and Footnote

**Default:** (Blank)

Enter a title, subtitle, and/or footnote for your organization chart. Use F7-Size/Place to adjust the text size and placement for the title, subtitle, and footnote. Use F5-Attributes to define the font attributes for the title, subtitle, and footnote.

### Name

**Default:** (Blank)

Enter a name for the current manager in the "Manager" column. If you plan to use an abbreviated version of the current manager's name, place this abbreviation in the "Abbrev." column.

### Title

**Default:** (Blank)

Enter an optional title for the current manager in the "Manager" column. If you plan to use an abbreviated version of the title, enter this abbreviation in the "Abbrev." column.

### Comment

**Default:** (Blank)

Enter an optional comment for the current manager in the "Manager" column. If you plan to use an abbreviation of the comment, enter this abbreviation in the "Abbrev." column.

### Subordinates

If the current manager is not in the last level of the organization, you can enter subordinates to the current manager in the "Subordinates" column. The names entered in the "Subordinates" column will appear below the current manager in the chart. You may optionally specify one subordinate as a staff person to the top manager in the chart. A staff position is indicated by preceding the staff person's name with an asterisk (*).

## Organization Chart: Size/Place Overlay

**Location**  At the Organization Chart form, press F7-Size/Place to display the Size/Place overlay.

**Description**  Use the Size/Place overlay to define the size and placement of the title, subtitle, and footnote for your organization chart. Once you set the desired options, press F7-Size/Place or F10-Continue to return to the Organization Chart form.

# Harvard Graphics Forms and Function Keys

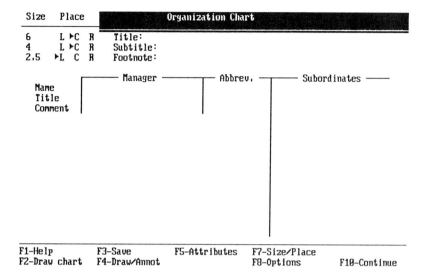

## Size

**Defaults:** (Vary depending on the line)

Enter a number from .1 to 99.

## Place

**Defaults:** (Vary depending on the line)

Set Place to either L, C, or R in order to left-justify, center, or right-justify text.

# Org Chart Options Form

**Location**   From the Organization Chart form, press F8-Options to display the Org Chart Options form.

**Description**   The Org Chart Options form is used to define characteristics of the organization chart.

```
                    Org Chart Options
    Start chart at    │ ▶Top    Current manager
    Levels to show    │ ▶All   1   2   3   4   5   6   7

    Show titles       │ ▶Yes   No
    Show comments     │  Yes  ▶No
    Abbreviations     │  Yes  ▶No
    Shadow            │  Yes  ▶No

    Names             │ ▶Light  Italic  Bold   Color: 1   Split: ▶Yes   No
    Titles            │  Light ▶Italic  Bold   Color: 1   Split:  Yes  ▶No
    Comments          │ ▶Light  Italic  Bold   Color: 1   Split:  Yes  ▶No

                              Last Level
                    Show titles     │ Yes  ▶No
                    Show comments   │ Yes  ▶No

                    Arrangement     │ ▶Vertical   Horizontal

F1-Help
F2-Draw chart                 F6-Colors        F8-Data        F10-Continue
```

### Start chart at

**Default:** Top

Select Top to produce the organization chart starting with the top manager in the organization. Select Current manager to display the organization starting from the current manager, the manager whose name is currently displayed in the "Manager" column of the Organization Chart form. When you select Current manager, only the current manager and the individuals subordinate to the current manager are displayed in the organization.

### Levels to show

**Default:** All

Select the maximum number of organizational levels to display. Select All to display all levels of the organization starting with the top manager. To display less than all levels of the chart, select the number of levels to display. When the "Start chart at" option is set to Current manager, setting "Levels to show" to All will display all levels below the current manager. Setting "Levels to show" to a number will display that number of levels below the current manager.

### Show Titles

**Default:** Yes

Select Yes to display the title information for each individual in the organization. (This option does not affect the individuals at the lowest level.)

### Show comments

**Default:** No

Select Yes to display the comment information for each individual in the organization (this option does not affect the individuals at the lowest level).

### Abbreviations

**Default:** No

Select Yes to use the data entered in the "Abbrev." column instead of the "Manager" column of the Organization Chart form. When the "Abbreviations" option is set to Yes, the title and comment information from the "Abbrev." column will only be displayed if the corresponding "Show title" and "Show comment" options are set to Yes.

### Shadow

**Default:** No

Set "Shadow" to Yes to display a shadow behind the boxes displayed in all but the last level. If "Last level: Arrangement" is set to Horizontal, the "Shadow" setting will apply to the last level as well.

### Text Style, Color, and Split

**Default:**

| Text | Style | Color | Split |
|---|---|---|---|
| Names | Light | 1 | Yes |
| Titles | Italic | 1 | No |
| Comments | Light | 1 | No |

The text style, color, and text split options are defined separately for the name, title, and comment data. Press the SPACEBAR to select a setting for each option. To select a text color you can also press F6-Colors to display the Color Selection overlay and then select a color from this list.

Use "Split" to indicate whether the text may be split onto two lines. If "Split" is set to No, the text will be displayed on one line. If "Split" is set to Yes, Harvard Graphics will split the text onto two lines when necessary, or when the text-splitting character (¦) is placed in the text field. See Chapter 5, "Organization Charts" for more information.

### Last Level: Show titles

**Default:** No

Select Yes to display the titles you provided for the last level entries.

### Last Level: Show comments

**Default:** No

Select Yes to display the comments you provided for the last level entries.

### Last Level: Arrangement

**Default:** Vertical

When "Arrangement" is set to Vertical, the last level entries are shown with a vertical orientation. No box is drawn around the last level entries when the orientation is vertical. To display the last level entries enclosed in boxes, set "Arrangement" to Horizontal. If "Shadow" is set to Yes, the boxes in the last level will be produced with a drop shadow.

## Parallel/Serial Overlay

**Location** Once you select a printer, plotter, or film recorder (certain models only) on the corresponding Printer, Plotter, or Film Recorder Setup form, Harvard Graphics displays the Parallel/Serial overlay.

```
        Parallel              Serial
       ▶LPT1              COM1    COM2
        LPT2       Baud rate: ▶9600  4800  2400  1200  300
        LPT3       Parity:    ▶None  Even  Odd
                   Data bits: ▶8     7
                   Stop bits: ▶1     2
```

**Description**  This overlay is used to define the port on your computer to be used by the printer, plotter, or film recorder you just defined on the corresponding Setup form. If your output device is connected to a parallel port, you only need to define which of the parallel ports it is connected to. If your output device is connected to a serial port, you must also define the baud rate, parity, data bits, and stop bits for the serial communication. Once you have completed this form, press F10-Continue to return to the Setup menu.

## Port

**Default:** LPT1 (the first parallel port)

Select the port to which your output device is connected. LPT1, LPT2, and LPT3 refer to the first, second, and third parallel ports. COM1 and COM2 refer to the first and second serial ports.

## Baud rate

**Default:** 9600

If you selected a serial port, select the baud rate for this serial communication.

## Parity

**Default:** None

If you selected a serial port, select the parity of the serial communication.

## Data bits

**Default:** 8

**872** Harvard Graphics: The Complete Reference

If you selected a serial port, indicate the number of data bits to use in the serial communication.

**Stop bits**

Default: 1

If you selected a serial port, indicate the number of stop bits to use in the serial communication.

## Patterns Overlay

**Location**   On the options forms for objects in Draw/Annotate, position the cursor at a "Pattern" option and press F6-Choices to display the Patterns overlay.

**Description**   Press F6-Choices to display the Patterns overlay listing the 12 patterns that can be used for objects. Highlight a pattern in the list and press F6-Choices or F10-Continue to return to the options form. The pattern number you selected from the Patterns overlay will be displayed at the "Pattern" option on the options form.

## Pause Overlay

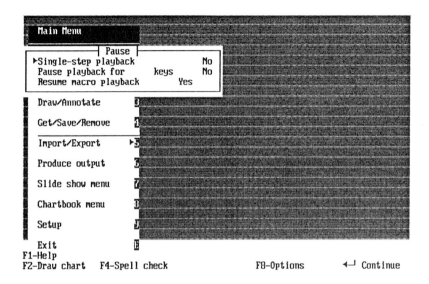

**Location** During the playback of a macro, press CTRL-ALT to pause the macro and display the Pause overlay.

**Description** While your macro is playing back, you can instruct a macro to pause and then continue playback. To use any of the options on the Pause overlay, either move the cursor to the desired option or type the first letter of the option name. Each option can be set to either Yes or No. Press ENTER to toggle an option setting between Yes and No. When you are finished setting the Pause overlay options, press ESC to remove the Pause overlay from the screen.

### Single-step playback
**Default:** No

Press the SPACEBAR to set "Single-step playback" to Yes to play your macro one step at a time with the press of a key. After you remove the Pause overlay from the screen, pressing any key will cause MACRO to execute the next step in the macro. Each additional keypress will cause MACRO to advance one more step. If you want MACRO to return to executing the macro at normal speed, press CTRL-ALT to display the Pause overlay and set "Single-step playback" to No. If you want to cancel the macro while executing one step at a time, press ALT-F6.

**Pause playback for _ _ _ keys**

**Default:** No

To pause a macro in order to allow you to make changes to the Harvard Graphics environment, press the SPACEBAR to set "Pause playback for _ _ _ keys" to Yes. MACRO will ask you to fill in the blank before "keys." Enter the number of keystrokes you will be manually entering in Harvard Graphics before you want the macro to take over again. The number must be from 1 to 999.

If you are not sure how many keys you will need to press, enter a number that is much higher than you will need. Press ESC or F10-Continue to remove the Pause overlay, and begin pressing keys. When you are through pressing keys, press CTRL-RIGHT SHIFT. MACRO will then resume playing back your macro. If you do not start MACRO by pressing CTRL-RIGHT SHIFT, it will automatically resume playback of the macro once you have pressed the specified number of keys.

**Resume macro playback**

**Default:** Yes

To cancel the playback of your macro, press the SPACEBAR to set "Resume playback" to No and then press ESC.

## Pie Chart Data Form

**Location**   Select <Pie> from the Create New Chart menu to display Page 1 of the Pie Chart Data form.

```
                    Pie Chart 1 Data  Page 1 of 2
Title:
Subtitle:
Footnote:

Slice    Label         Value         Cut Slice    Color    Pattern
         Name          Series 1      Yes  No

  1                                       No        2        1
  2                                       No        3        2
  3                                       No        4        3
  4                                       No        5        4
  5                                       No        6        5
  6                                       No        7        6
  7                                       No        8        7
  8                                       No        9        8
  9                                       No       10        9
 10                                       No       11       10
 11                                       No       12       11
 12                                       No       13       12


F1-Help         F3-Save                                F9-More series
F2-Draw chart   F4-Draw/Annot   F6-Colors   F8-Options  F10-Continue
```

**Description**   This form is used to enter data for a pie chart as well as to choose the colors and patterns for each pie segment. This is a two-page form in which Page 1 is used to set characteristics for one pie and Page 2 is used to set characteristics for a second pie on your chart, if a second pie is used. These two pages are identical except for the page number in the title banner. You can display two pies simultaneously on your pie chart by using Page 1 to define the left pie, called *Pie 1*, and Page 2 to define the right pie, called *Pie 2*. The data to be used for Pie 1 and Pie 2 are specified by displaying the appropriate series names on Page 1 and Page 2, respectively. When you are creating a chart that will display a single pie, you will only need to work with Page 1 of the Pie Chart Data form.

### Title, Subtitle, and Footnote

**Default:** (Blank)

Enter a title, a subtitle, and a footnote on the top three lines of this form. If your subtitle and footnote are longer than one line each, enter this text on the Pie Chart Titles & Options form instead.

### Slice

This column contains the numbers that correspond to each of the 12 possible slices for a pie. You cannot change these numbers.

### Label

**Default:** (Blank)

Enter the name of each pie slice in this column.

### Value

**Default:** (Blank)

Enter the value each pie slice represents in this column. These values will determine the relative size of each of the slices in your pie.

### Cut Slice

**Default:** No

Select Yes to cut or explode a pie slice from the pie for emphasis. More than one pie slice can be exploded, if desired.

### Color

**Default:** 2 through 13

Enter a number from 0 through 16 to change the default color number for each pie slice. Entering 0 creates an invisible pie slice. Alternatively, with the cursor positioned at the desired slice in the "Color" column, press F6-Colors to display the Color Selection overlay and select a color from this list.

### Pattern

**Default:** 1 through 12

"Pattern" is used when the "Fill style" option on the Pie Chart Titles & Options form is set to either Pattern or Both. Enter a number from 1 to 12 to change the default pattern number for each pie slice.

## Pie Chart: Size/Place Overlay

```
                  Pie Chart Titles & Options  Page 1 of 2
   Size    Place
    8      L ►C  R Title:
    6      L ►C  R Subtitle:
    6      L ►C  R
    2.5    ►L C  R Footnote:
    2.5    ►L C  R
    2.5    ►L C  R
    5      ↑ ►↓    Pie 1 title:
    5      ↑ ►↓
    5      ↑ ►↓    Pie 2 title:
    5      ↑ ►↓

                    3D effect           Yes    ►No
                    Link pies           Yes    ►No
                    Proportional pies   Yes    ►No
                    Fill style          ►Color  Pattern   Both


   F1-Help                      F5-Attributes   F7-Size/Place
   F2-Draw chart                                F8-Data        F10-Continue
```

**Location** From Page 1 of the Pie Chart Titles & Options form, press F7-Size/Place to display the Size/Place overlay over the upper-left corner of the Pie Chart Titles & Options form.

**Description** Use the Size/Place overlay to define the size and placement of the title, subtitles, footnotes, Pie 1 titles, and Pie 2 titles. Press F7-Size/Place or F10-Continue to return to the Pie Chart Titles & Options form.

### Size

**Defaults:** (Depend on the text)

Use the "Size" column to indicate the size of the text on the corresponding line of the Pie Chart Titles & Options form. To change the default text sizes, move to the appropriate line of the "Size" column and enter a new text size from .1 to 99.

**Place**

**Defaults:** (Depend on the text)

Use the "Place" column to define the alignment of the text on the corresponding line of the Pie Chart Titles & Options form. Set the first six text lines to either L, C, or R for left-justified, centered, or right-justified text, respectively. Set the next four lines (corresponding to the "Pie 1 title" and "Pie 2 title" options) to either the up or down arrow to display this text either above or below the pie.

## Pie Chart Titles & Options Form

**Location**   From the Pie Chart Data form, press F8-Options to display the Pie Chart Titles & Options form.

**Description**   The Pie Charts Titles & Options form is used to define display characteristics of your pie chart (with the exception of pie slice cutting, colors, and patterns, which are defined on the Pie Chart Data form). The Pie Chart Titles & Options form is two pages long. From Page 1, press PGDN to move to Page 2; to return to Page 1, press PGUP. You can return to the Pie Chart Data form at any time by pressing F8-Data.

## Page 1 of the Pie Chart Titles & Options Form

### Title, Subtitle, and Footnote

**Default:** (Blank)

The first six lines on the Pie Chart Titles & Options form permit you to enter a one-line title, a two-line subtitle, and a three-line footnote. Each of these lines can contain a maximum of 40 characters.

### Pie 1 title and Pie 2 title

**Default:** (Blank)

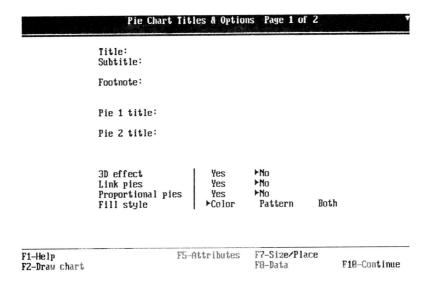

If your pie chart is designed to display only one pie, the "Pie 1 title" option provides you with two lines for an additional title. This title will be centered directly below your pie by default. When you are creating a two-pie chart, the "Pie 1 title" and "Pie 2 title" options allow you provide a two-line title for each pie.

### 3D effect

**Default:** No

To apply a three-dimensional effect to your pie(s), set "3D effect" to Yes. If you set the "3D effect" option to Yes, the "Cut Slice" settings will not result in an exploded pie. To suppress the three-dimensional effect, select No.

### Link pies

**Default:** No

"Link pies" is only applicable when your pie chart displays two pies. Set "Link pies" to Yes to indicate that the right pie (Pie 2) contains a further breakdown of one of the slices in the left pie (Pie 1). You must also set the "Cut Slice" option on Page 1 of the Pie Chart Data form to

Yes for the corresponding slice of the Pie 1 (the slice that Pie 2 refers to). Harvard Graphics will connect this slice in Pie 1 with the entire Pie 2 area using dotted lines.

### Proportional pies
**Default:** No

When your pie chart displays two pies, you can set "Proportional pies" to Yes to indicate that the size of your pies should reflect the relative sizes of the pies' series data. The size of each pie will reflect differences in the sum of the series values for each of the pies. When "Proportional pies" is set to No, both pies are identical in size by default, regardless of the values of each of the pie's series values.

### Fill style
**Default:** Color

Select whether only color, only patterns, or both color and patterns should be used to fill the slices of your pie(s). The specific colors or patterns for each slice are specified on the Pie Chart Data form.

## Page 2 of the Pie Chart Titles & Options Form

Page 2 of the Pie Chart Titles & Options form is divided into two columns. The left column is used to set characteristics for Pie 1 and the right column for Pie 2. The settings available in each column are identical, with one exception: the first option, "Chart style," includes the setting None for Pie 2.

### Chart style
**Default:** Pie

Select Column to create a column pie chart. Set the "Chart style" option for Pie 2 to None if you only want to display one pie when you have entered more than one series data.

```
              Pie Chart Titles & Options   Page 2 of 2

                          Pie 1                    Pie 2

Chart style       ▶Pie    Column         ▶Pie      Column    None
Sort slices        Yes    ▶No             Yes      ▶No
Starting angle     0                      0
Pie size           50                     50

Show label        ▶Yes    No             ▶Yes      No
Label size         3                      3

Show value        ▶Yes    No             ▶Yes      No
Place value       ▶Below  Adjacent Inside ▶Below   Adjacent  Inside
Value format
Currency           Yes    ▶No             Yes      ▶No

Show percent       Yes    ▶No             Yes      ▶No
Place percent     ▶Below  Adjacent Inside ▶Below   Adjacent  Inside
Percent format

F1-Help
F2-Draw chart                    F8-Data            F10-Continue
```

## Sort slices

**Default:** No

Select Yes to sort the slices of your pie from largest to smallest. When you set "Sort slices" to Yes, the first slice displayed (starting at the three o'clock position and moving counterclockwise) on the pie is the slice with the largest value. The next slice has the second largest value, and so on. If "Chart style" is set to Column, the first slice is the bottom slice, the second slice is stacked on top of the bottom slice, and so on.

When "Sort slices" is set to No, Harvard Graphics displays the pie slices using the order of the slices on the Pie Chart Data form.

*Note:* When you are displaying linked pies, Harvard Graphics links Pie 1 to Pie 2 on the basis of the first exploded pie slice displayed on Pie 1. If the "Cut slice" option for more than one slice in Pie 1 is set to Yes, setting the "Sort slices" option to Yes for Pie 1 may change the slice Harvard Graphics uses for the link. Use F2-Draw chart to check the order of your pie slices when you use this combination of options.

## Starting angle

**Default:** 0

The three o'clock position on a pie chart corresponds to an angle of 0 degrees, twelve o'clock is 90 degrees, and nine o'clock is 180 degrees. To modify the angle at which the first slice in the series will be displayed, set "Starting angle" to a number from 0 to 360.

*Note:* When you are displaying linked pies, Harvard Graphics will override your starting angle for Pie 1 in order to ensure that the cut slice of Pie 1 faces Pie 2.

### Pie size

**Default:** 50

To change the default size, enter a number from 1 to 100. This number represents the percentage of the available space the pie will take up when it is displayed or output. The available space for a pie depends on whether one or two pies are displayed, as well as the defined size of the text on your pie chart.

### Show label

**Default:** Yes

To display the labels for each pie slice (positioned just outside the corresponding slice), set "Show label" to Yes. The labels displayed are the names entered in the "Label" column on the Pie Chart Data form. Set "Show label" to No to suppress the display of labels.

### Label size

**Default:** 3

To change the default "Label size," enter a number from .1 to 20. This size will define the size of the text for pie slice labels, values, and percentages, if displayed.

### Show value

**Default:** Yes

To display the values for each pie slice (entered in the "Value" column of the Pie Chart Data form), set "Show value" to Yes. Set "Show label" to No to suppress the display of values.

### Place value

**Default:** Below

When "Show value" is set to Yes, you can use "Place value" to specify where the value is to be displayed. Select Below to place the value below each slice label, Adjacent to place the value to the right of the label, or Inside to place the value within the pie slice.

### Value format

**Default:** (Blank)

The "Value format" option allows you to define a format for the pie values displayed on your chart. The formats you define for the pie values follow the same guidelines outlined for formatting axis values for XY charts. Refer to Chapter 6, "XY Charts" for a description of formatting features available in Harvard Graphics.

### Currency

**Default:** No

If your pie values represent dollar amounts, set "Currency" to Yes to display a dollar sign before each pie value.

### Show percent

**Default:** No

Set "Show percent" to Yes to have Harvard Graphics calculate and display the percentage of the pie that each slice represents.

### Place percent

**Default:** Below

When "Show percent" is set to Yes, you can use "Place percent" to specify where the percentage is to be displayed. Select Below to place the percentage below each slice label, Adjacent to place the percentage to the right of the label, or Inside to place the percentage within the pie slice.

*Note:* When "Place value" and "Place percent" are both set to the same placement, the percentage is placed to the right of the value.

**Percent format**

**Default:** (Blank)

Similarly to the "Value format" option, the "Percent format" option allows you to customize the format of percentages displayed on your chart. Refer to Chapter 6, "XY Charts" for a description of formatting features available in Harvard Graphics.

## Plot Chart Options Overlay

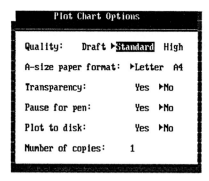

**Location** From the Produce Output menu, select <Plotter> to display the Plot Chart Options overlay.

**Description**  This overlay contains options for plotting your chart. Once you set the options on this overlay, press F10-Continue to plot your chart.

*Note:*  Some chart enhancements and some symbols cannot be plotted correctly. For example, Harvard Graphics will not plot a 3D overlap on an XY chart. These charts will be plotted without the 3D effect. Refer to the Harvard Graphics manual for a complete listing of the symbols that cannot be plotted correctly.

### Quality

**Default:** Draft

Select the desired plotting quality. If you select Draft, Harvard Graphics will use your plotter's fonts, patterns instead of solid colors, and will not use text attributes. Standard produces a higher-quality chart, but will also use your plotter's fonts, and will not use text attributes. If you want to use Harvard Graphics' fonts and apply text attributes, you must plot in High quality. The higher the quality you select, the longer it will take to plot your chart.

### A-size paper format (version 2.3)

**Default:** Letter

29If you are plotting to a size A plotter, select Letter to plot onto 8.5 × 11 inch paper. Select A4 if you are plotting onto 8.25 × 11.7 inch (29.7 × 21 cm) paper.

### Transparency

**Default:** No

Set "Transparency" to Yes if you are plotting a transparency. This will cause Harvard Graphics to move the pens slower, thereby reducing the likelihood of smearing the ink on your chart.

### Pause for pen

**Default:** No

Set "Pause for pen" to Yes if you want Harvard Graphics to stop and wait for you to change pens when you are referencing more pens than your plotter has pen holders. Harvard Graphics will pause when a pen is requested for which there is no pen holder and request that you insert a pen in the specified pen holder. Once you insert the requested pen, press ENTER to continue plotting.

### Plot to disk (version 2.3)

**Default:** No

Select Yes to write the commands that would have been sent to your selected plotter to a disk file. This file will have the name you gave the chart and the extension .PRN. If you have not yet saved the chart and therefore have not yet given it a name, Harvard Graphics will automatically use the default chart style for this name (TITLE.PRN, AREA.PRN, and so on).

### Number of copies

**Default:** 1

When you want to plot more than one copy of your chart, enter the desired number at "Number of copies."

## Plot Slide Show Options Overlay

**Location**  Select <Plot slide show> from the Produce Output menu to display the Plot Slide Show Options overlay.

**Description**  The Plot Slide Show Options overlay is used to define how your slide show will be plotted.

### Quality

**Default:** Draft

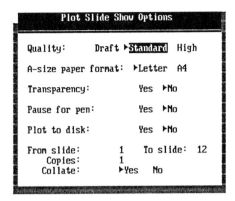

Select the desired plotting quality. If you select Draft, Harvard Graphics will use your plotter's fonts, patterns instead of solid colors, and will not use text attributes. Standard produces a higher-quality chart, but will also use your plotter's fonts, and will not use text attributes. If you want to use Harvard Graphics' fonts and apply text attributes, you must plot in High quality. The higher the quality you select, the longer it will take to plot your charts.

### A-size paper format (version 2.3)

**Default:** Letter

Select Letter if you are plotting onto 8.5 × 11 inch paper. Select A4 if you are plotting onto 8.25 × 11.7 inch (29.7 × 21 cm) paper.

### Transparency

**Default:** No

Set "Transparency" to Yes if you are plotting transparencies. This will cause Harvard Graphics to move the pens slower, thereby reducing the likelihood of smearing ink on your charts.

### Pause for pen

**Default:** No

Set "Pause for pen" to Yes if you want Harvard Graphics to stop and wait for you to change pens when you are referencing more pens than your plotter has pen holders. Harvard Graphics will pause when a pen is requested for which there is no pen holder and request that you insert a pen in the specified pen holder. Once you insert the requested pen, press ENTER to continue plotting.

### Plot to disk (version 2.3)
**Default:** No

Select Yes to write the commands that would have been sent to your selected plotter to a disk file. This file will have the name you gave the chart and the extension .PRN. If you have not yet saved the chart and therefore have not yet given it a name, Harvard Graphics will automatically use the default chart style for this name (TITLE.PRN, AREA.PRN, and so on).

### From slide
**Default:** 1

Enter the number of the first file in the slide show you want to plot.

### To slide
**Default:** (Last file number in the slide show)

Enter the number of the last file in the slide show you want to plot.

### Copies
**Default:** 1

To plot more than one copy of the current chart, enter the number of copies.

## Collate

**Default:** Yes

If you specified that more than one copy of each chart be plotted at "Copies," select Yes if you want the copies to be collated or No if you want Harvard Graphics to plot all copies of a chart before continuing to the next chart.

## Plotter Setup Form

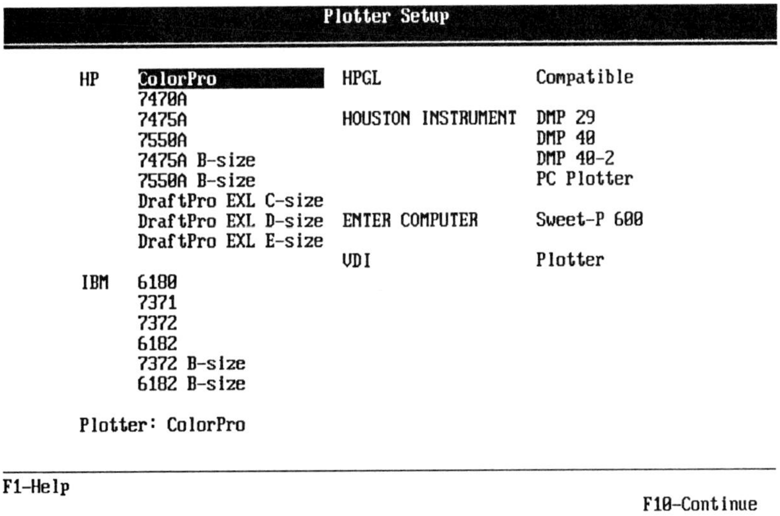

```
                        Plotter Setup

    HP    ColorPro          HPGL              Compatible
          7470A
          7475A             HOUSTON INSTRUMENT DMP 29
          7550A                                DMP 40
          7475A B-size                         DMP 40-2
          7550A B-size                         PC Plotter
          DraftPro EXL C-size
          DraftPro EXL D-size ENTER COMPUTER   Sweet-P 600
          DraftPro EXL E-size
                            VDI                Plotter
    IBM   6180
          7371
          7372
          6182
          7372 B-size
          6182 B-size

    Plotter: ColorPro

F1-Help
                                               F10-Continue
```

**Location**   Select <Plotter> from the Setup menu to display the Plotter Setup form.

**Description**   The Plotter Setup form lists the plotters Harvard Graphics supports. Select the plotter you use most often. Then press F10-Continue to set your default plotter and return to the Setup menu.

## Plotter

**Default:** HP ColorPro

To change the current setting, use the cursor keys or press the SPACEBAR to highlight the desired plotter. You will see the name listed at Plotter change as you scroll through the plotters listed on the form.

*Note:* If your plotter is not listed on the Plotter Setup form and cannot emulate one of the plotters listed, you may be able to use the VDI. Refer to your plotter manual to see if your plotter is supported by the VDI. Also refer to your plotter manual and the Harvard Graphics manual for information on obtaining, installing, and setting up the VDI for your plotter. Then, in Harvard Graphics, select VDI Plotter as the default plotter.

## Polygon Options Form

**Location**  The Polygon Options form appears in Draw/Annotate when you press F8-Options while adding a polygon in the drawing area, when you select <Options> from the Modify menu and then select an existing polygon object in the drawing area, or when you select <Polygon> from the Default Options menu, which is displayed when you press F8-Options at the Draw menu.

**Description**  Use the Polygon Options form to define the characteristics of polygon objects.

### Outline Draw

**Default:** Yes

Select Yes to draw the outline of your polygon or No to suppress the outline.

### Outline Color

**Default:** 1

If "Outline Draw" is set to Yes, enter a color number, 1 through 16, for the color of the outline. Alternatively, with the cursor positioned at "Outline Color," press F6-Choices and select a color from the Color Selection overlay (see "Color Selection Overlay").

### Style

**Default:** (Solid line)

Select one of the four line styles for the line used to draw your polygon: solid, dotted, dashed, or bold. (The bold setting shown on the form appears as a double line but the line will be bold once the polygon is placed in the drawing area.)

### Center Fill

**Default:** Yes

Select Yes if you want to fill the center of your polygon or No if you want to display only the outline (when "Outline Draw" is set to Yes).

### Center Color

**Default:** 1

If "Center Fill" is set to Yes, enter a color number, 1 through 16, for the polygon center. Alternatively, with the cursor positioned at "Outline Color," press F6-Choices and select a color from the Color Selection overlay (see "Color Selection Overlay").

### Center Pattern

**Default:** 0 (no pattern)

If "Center Fill" is set to Yes, enter a pattern number, 1 through 12, for the pattern used in the polygon center. Alternatively, with the cursor positioned at "Center Pattern," press F6-Choices and select a pattern from the Pattern Selection overlay (see "Patterns Overlay").

## Polyline Options Form

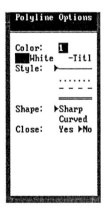

**Location**  The Polyline Options form appears in Draw/Annotate when you press F8-Options while adding a polyline in the drawing area, when you select <Options> from the Modify menu and then select an existing polyline object in the drawing area, or when you select <Polyline> from the Default Options menu, which is displayed when you press F8-Options at the Draw menu.

**Description**   Use the Polyline Options form to define the characteristics of polyline objects.

## Color

**Default:** 1

Enter a number, 1 through 16, corresponding to the desired color for your line. Alternatively, with the cursor positioned at this option, press F6-Choices and select a color from the Color Selection overlay (see "Color Selection Overlay").

## Style

**Default:** (Solid line)

Select one of the four line styles for the line used to draw your polyline: solid, dotted, dashed, or bold. (The bold setting shown on the form appears as a double line but will create a bold line in the drawing area.)

## Shape

**Default:** Sharp

Select Sharp if you want straight line segments or Curved to create a curved polyline. If you select Curved, the smoothness of your polyline will be determined by the points in your polyline. The closer the points of your polyline the smoother the curve.

## Close

**Default:** No

Select Yes to make Harvard Graphics connect the first point in the polyline to the last point, forming a closed object.

*Note:* This is only way you can create a rounded polygon in Harvard Graphics. These "rounded polygons" cannot be filled, unlike ordinary polygons. See, however, "Adding a Wedge" and "Converting a Polyline to a Shape" in Chapter 18, "Drawing and Editing with Draw Partner."

## Practice Cards Form

```
                        Practice Cards
         Slide #    Name              Description
           1        MENU4       For Information on...




         Print data:   Yes  ▶No    | Display time:


F1-Help
                                                    F10-Continue
```

**Location**   The desired slide show must be current. Select <Make practice cards> from the Slide Show Menu to display the Practice Cards form.

**Description**   Practice cards are used to make notes for each of the files in a slide show. They can also be used to maintain information about each of the files in a slide show or to create handouts that contain descriptive information along with a chart image.

Once the Practice Card form is displayed, use PGDN to advance to the next practice card and PGUP to move to the preceding practice card for each file in the slide show.

### Slide #

**Default: 1**

The current file number for the practice card is shown. Instead of using PGDN and PGUP to move between practice cards for a slide show, you can move directly to the desired practice card by entering a file number at the "Slide #" option.

### Name and Description

These options display the name of the file and the file description (if the file is a template, chart, or slide show, and you have defined a description for it). The information in the "Name" and "Description" columns cannot be modified from the practice card.

### Text Area

**Default:** (Blank)

At the middle of the form is an area for entering notes (text). This area can contain up to 11 lines of text with up to 60 characters each.

### Print data

**Default:** No

If you plan to use the <Print practice cards> option from the Produce Output menu, set "Print data" to Yes if you want to also print the data associated with the practice card (given that the file is a data chart). If you set "Print data" to No, the chart data will not be printed when you are printing practice cards. This option does not affect the printing of the charts themselves when you print your practice cards.

### Display time

**Default:** (Time setting from the ScreenShow Effects form)

If you assigned a time for the file in the "Time" column on the ScreenShow Effects form, the "Display time" option for the corresponding practice card will also display this time. You can modify the time here, which is useful if you determine that a timing change is necessary while you are practicing your presentation. If you modify this time, the value in the "Time" column on the ScreenShow Effects form will also be modified.

## Practice Cards Options Overlay

**Location**   At the Produce Output menu, select <Print practice cards> to display the Practice Cards Options overlay.

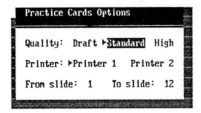

**Description**   Set options for printing practice cards for your slide show. Once you set the options on this overlay, press F10-Continue to print the practice cards.

## Quality

**Default:** Draft

Select one of the three levels of printer quality: Draft, Standard, and High. This option is used to define the output quality of any charts that will be printed along with your practice cards. In general, the higher the quality you select for your output, the longer it will take to print.

## Printer

**Default:** Printer 1

Select which printer, Printer 1 or Printer 2, you want to print to. The printer you select must have been defined on the Printer 1 or Printer 2 Setup form (refer to "Printer 1 Setup Form").

## From slide

**Default:** 1

Enter the file number of the first chart in the slide show for which you want to print a practice card.

## To slide

**Default:** (Last file number in the slide show)

Enter the file number of the last chart in the slide show for which you want to print a practice card.

## Print Chart Options Overlay

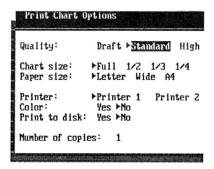

**Location** At the Produce Output menu, select <Printer> to display the Print Chart Options overlay, or press CTRL-P from any chart form (version 2.3 only).

**Description** Set options for printing your current chart on this overlay. Once you set the options on this overlay, press F10-Continue to print your chart.

### Quality

**Default:** Draft

Select one of the three levels of printer quality: Draft, Standard, and High. In general, the higher the quality you select for your output, the longer it will take to print.

The specific printer you print to will affect the appearance of your chart output. For example, some printers do not support more than one or two output qualities. On some printers that have internal fonts, these fonts are used when print quality is set to Draft or Standard. Harvard Graphics fonts are only used in the High quality mode. In addition, text attributes, such as italic or underline, are only displayed when your chart is printed in High quality. Most printers (especially dot matrix printers) will produce text attributes at all levels of output quality, however. The major difference between output qualities will be the dot density. Harvard Graphics prints more dots at the higher output qualities, resulting in a better looking chart.

Some laser printers may not have enough memory to produce a full page of graphics at the High setting. If this occurs, you can either reduce your chart size, print at a lower quality setting, or add memory to your printer.

### Chart size

**Default:** Full

Select one of the four chart sizes: Full, 1/2, 1/3, or 1/4.

### Paper size

**Default:** Letter

The Letter (8.5 × 11 inch) setting is appropriate for most printers. If you have a wide carriage dot matrix printer (and it is set to print wide) you can set "Paper size" to Wide to print the chart on 11 × 14 inch paper. The Wide setting will increase your chart's overall size. When "Paper size" is set to Wide, a chart using a landscape orientation is printed vertically (11 × 14 inch) and a chart using a portrait orientation is printed horizontally (14 × 11 inch).

Version 2.3 includes an additional "Paper size" setting: A4. Select A4 if you are printing onto 8.25 × 11.7 inch (29.7 × 21 cm) paper.

### Printer

**Default:** Printer 1

Select which printer, Printer 1 or Printer 2, you want to use for your chart. The printer you select must have been defined on the Printer 1 or Printer 2 Setup form (refer to "Printer 1 Setup form").

### Color

**Default:** Yes

When printing to a color printer, set "Color" to Yes to print colors or to No to print using only one color, black. When printing to a black-and-white printer, set "Color" to Yes to print using grey scale.

### Print to disk (version 2.3)

**Default:** No

Select Yes to write the commands that would have been sent to your selected printer to a disk file. This file will have the name you gave the chart and the extension .PRN. If you have not yet saved the chart and therefore have not yet given it a name, Harvard Graphics will automatically use the default chart style for this name (TITLE.PRN, AREA.PRN, and so on).

### Number of copies

**Default:** 1

To print more than one copy of the current chart, set "Number of copies" to the number of copies you want to print.

## Print Slide Show Options Overlay

```
Print Slide Show Options

Quality:         Draft ▶Standard  High

Chart size:      ▶Full  1/2  1/3  1/4
Paper size:      ▶Letter  Wide  A4

Printer:         ▶Printer 1   Printer 2
Color:           Yes ▶No
Print to disk:   Yes ▶No

From slide:  1      To slide:  12
Copies:      1
Collate:     ▶Yes  No
```

**Location** Select <Print slide show> from the Produce Output menu to display the Print Slide Show Options overlay.

**Description** Set options for printing charts in the current slide show on this overlay. Once you set the options on this overlay, press F10-Continue to print the charts in the slide show.

## Quality

**Default:** Draft

Select one of the three levels of printer quality: Draft, Standard, and High. In general, the higher the quality you select for your output, the longer it will take to print.

Your printer will affect the appearance of your chart output. For example, some printers do not support more than one or two output qualities. On some printers that have internal fonts, these fonts are used when print quality is set to Draft or Standard. Harvard Graphics fonts are only used in the High quality mode. In addition, text attributes, such as italic or underline, are only displayed when your chart is printed in High quality. Most printers (especially dot matrix printers) will produce text attributes at all levels of output quality, however. The major difference between output qualities will be the dot density. Harvard Graphics prints more dots at the higher output qualities, resulting in a better looking chart.

Some laser printers may not have enough memory to produce a full page of graphics at the High setting. If this occurs, you can either reduce your chart size, print at a lower quality setting, or add memory to your printer.

## Chart size

**Default:** Full

Select one of the four chart sizes: Full, 1/2, 1/3, or 1/4. If you select Full, Harvard Graphics will print one chart on each page. If you select 1/2, Harvard Graphics prints two charts on each page. If you select 1/3, Harvard Graphics will print three charts on each page. If you select 1/4, Harvard Graphics also will print two charts on each page. See Chapter 8, "Producing Output" for more detail, especially on the differences between 1/2 and 1/4 settings.

## Paper size

**Default:** Letter

The Letter (8.5 × 11 inch) setting is appropriate for most printers. If you have a wide carriage dot matrix printer (and it is set to print wide) you can set "Paper size" to Wide to print on 11 × 14 inch paper. The Wide setting will increase your charts' overall size. When "Paper size" is set to Wide, a chart using a landscape orientation is printed vertically (11 × 14 inch) and a chart using a portrait orientation is printed horizontally (14 × 11 inch).

Version 2.3 includes an additional "Paper size" setting: A4. Select A4 if you are printing onto 8.25 × 11.7 inch (29.7 × 21 cm) paper.

## Printer

**Default:** Printer 1

Select which printer, Printer 1 or Printer 2, you want to use for your charts. The printer you select must have been defined on the Printer 1 or Printer 2 Setup form (refer to "Printer 1 Setup form").

## Color

**Default:** Yes

When printing to a color printer, set "Color" to Yes to print colors or to No to print using only one color, black. When printing to a black-and-white printer, set "Color" to Yes to print using grey scale.

## Print to disk (version 2.3)

**Default:** No

Select Yes to write the commands that would have been sent to your selected printer to a disk file. This file will have the name you gave the chart and the extension .PRN. If you have not yet saved the chart and therefore have not yet given it a name, Harvard Graphics will automatically use the default chart style for this name (TITLE.PRN, AREA.PRN, and so on).

## From slide

**Default:** 1

Enter the file number of the first file in the slide show you want to print.

**To slide**

**Default:** (Last file number in the slide show)

Enter the file number of the last file in the slide show you want to print.

**Copies**

**Default:** 1

To print more than one copy of the current chart, enter the number of copies you want to print.

**Collate**

**Default:** Yes

If you specified that more than one copy of each chart be printed at "Copies," select Yes if you want the copies to be collated or No if you want Harvard Graphics to print all copies of a chart before printing the next one.

## Printer 1 Setup Form

**Location**   Select <Printer 1> at the Setup menu to display the Printer 1 Setup form.

**Description**   The Printer 1 Setup form lists the printers Harvard Graphics supports. Select the printer you use most often. Then press F10-Continue to set your default printer and return to the Setup menu.

```
                        Printer 1 Setup
Apple LaserWriter      HP PaintJet,XL (Trans.)  Okidata ML 192,193
AST TurboLaser         HP DeskJet,+             Okidata ML 292,293
Calcomp ColorMaster    HP ThinkJet              Okidata ML 294
Canon LBP8 II,III      IBM Graphics Printer     Okidata LaserLine 6
Epson FX,LX,RX         IBM Proprinter,XL,II     Olivetti PG 108,208 M2
Epson EX,JX            IBM Proprinter X24,XL24  QMS ColorScript 100
Epson MX               IBM Quietwriter II,III   Qume LaserTEN,+
Epson LQ 800,1000      IBM Color Printer        Tektronix 4696
Epson LQ 1500          IBM Color Jetprinter     Tektronix Phaser CP
Epson LQ 2500          IBM Personal PagePrinter Tektronix ColorQuick
Epson GQ 3500          IBM LaserPrinter         Toshiba P1340,P1350,P1351
HP LaserJet            NEC P5,P6,P7             Toshiba P321,P341,P351
HP LaserJet+,II,IID    NEC P5XL,P9XL,CP6,CP7    Toshiba P351C
HP LaserJet IIP,III <2Mb NEC LC-860 (LaserJet)  Toshiba PageLaser 12
HP LaserJet IIP,III    NEC LC-890 (PostScript)  Xerox 4020
HP LaserJet III (HPGL/2) NEC Color PS           Xerox 4045
HP QuietJet,+          Okidata ML 84,92,93
HP PaintJet,XL         Okidata ML 182,183       VDI Printer

Printer: HP LaserJet

F1-Help                                         F10-Continue
```

### Printer

**Default:** In versions 2.13 and earlier, IBM Graphics Printer. In version 2.3, HP LaserJet.

To change the current setting, use the cursor keys or press the SPACEBAR to highlight the name of your printer. You will see the name listed at Printer change as you toggle through the printers listed on the form.

*Note:* If you select a printer (AST TurboLaser, CalComp ColorMaster, or Matrix TT200) that requires the VDI (virtual device interface), you must install the specific VDI for your printer before you can print. See your Harvard Graphics manual for instructions on installing the VDI device drivers.

## Printer 2 Setup Form

**Location** Select <Printer 2> from the Setup menu to display the Printer 2 Setup form.

**Description**    The Printer 2 Setup form allows you to specify a second printer (if you have two connected to your computer). The Printer 1 Setup and Printer 2 Setup forms list the same printers. Refer to "Printer 1 Setup Form."

## Range Names Overlay (Version 2.3)

**Location**    Move the cursor to the data range column on the Import Lotus Worksheet form or the Import Excel Worksheet form and press F6-Select range names to display the Range Names overlay.

**Description**    When you press F6-Select range names from either of the described locations, Harvard Graphics displays the Range Names overlay. Use named ranges to simplify defining the data you want to import.

If you have not created any range names for the spreadsheet, this overlay will be empty. If you have created named ranges for the spreadsheet, Harvard Graphics will display up to 15 characters of each named range in the overlay. If more named ranges are available than can be displayed at one time, press PGDN and PGUP to display additional range names. Use the UP and DOWN arrow keys to move the cursor to the appropriate range name and press ENTER. Harvard Graphics will automatically copy the name of the selected range into the appropriate option on the Import Lotus Data form or Import Excel Data form. To return without selecting a range name, press ESC.

## Record Chart Option Overlay

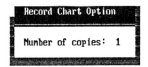

**Location**  At the Produce Output menu, select <Film Recorder> to display the Record Chart Option overlay.

**Description**  This overlay contains only one option, "Number of copies." Set this option and then press ENTER to begin recording. When you are recording more than one copy of your chart, Harvard Graphics will automatically advance your film between copies.

### Number of Copies
Default: 1

Set this option to the number of copies of the chart you want to record.

## Record Slide Show Options Overlay

**Location**  At the Produce Output menu, select <Record slide show> to display the Record Slide Show Options overlay.

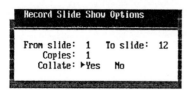

**Description**   Set options for recording charts in your current slide show on this overlay, and then press ENTER to begin recording. Harvard Graphics will automatically advance your film between charts and copies of charts.

### From slide
**Default:** 1

Enter the file number of the first file in the slide show you want to record.

### To slide
**Default:** (Last file number in the slide show)

Enter the file number of the last file in the slide show you want to record.

### Copies
**Default:** 1

Set this option to the number of copies of each chart you want to record.

### Collate
**Default:** Yes

If you specified that more than one copy of each chart be recorded at "Copies," select Yes if you want the copies to be collated or No if you want Harvard Graphics to record all copies of one chart before continuing to the next chart.

## Save Chart As Symbol Overlay

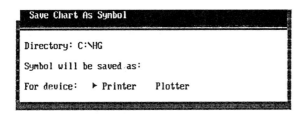

**Location**   At the Get/Save/Remove menu, select <Save as symbol> to display the Save Chart As Symbol overlay.

**Description**   Use this overlay to save your current Harvard Graphics chart in a symbol format (with the .SYM extension). Once you complete the options, press F10-Continue or ENTER.

Refer to Chapter 9, "Drawing and Annotating" for a discussion of the advantages and disadvantages of converting charts to symbols.

### Directory

**Default:** (Current directory)

Enter the drive and directory of the symbol file to which you want to add your symbol.

### Symbol will be saved as

**Default:** (Blank)

Enter the name of the symbol file to which you want to add your symbol. If you enter the name of an existing symbol file, Harvard Graphics will save your symbol to that file. If you want to create a new symbol file, enter a new symbol filename. This filename must conform to DOS file naming standards. Do not, however, add an extension for this symbol filename as Harvard Graphics automatically adds the extension .SYM.

If the name you entered at "Symbol will be saved as" is not the name of an existing symbol file on the directory specified at the "Directory" option, Harvard Graphics will display the New Symbol File overlay in order for you to enter a description of your new symbol file. Refer to "New Symbol File Overlay" for more information.

**For device**

**Default:** Printer

Select Printer if you plan to either print or display the symbol. If you select Plotter, Harvard Graphics will specifically create the symbol file so that it can be plotted adequately. This may mean that Harvard Graphics will override chart characteristics that cannot be plotted. For instance, a three-dimensional overlap bar chart will be converted to a two-dimensional chart.

## Save Chart Overlay

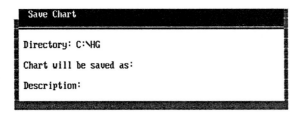

**Location** Select <Save chart> at the Get/Save/Remove menu to display the Save Chart overlay or press F3-Save from any chart form (version 2.3 only).

**Description** This overlay is used to save a copy of the current chart. After you have created or edited a chart, you must save the chart if you want to use it at a later time. Once you complete this overlay, press

F10-Continue or ENTER to save a copy of the current chart. To cancel saving a chart, press ESC.

### Directory

**Default:** (Current directory)

If you have defined a data directory on the Default Settings form, your default data directory will appear at this option. Otherwise, the current directory is listed. If you want to save your chart to a different directory, enter the full directory path. Saving a chart to a directory other than the current directory will make the new directory the current directory.

### Chart will be saved as

**Default:** (Blank)

Enter a name for your chart. This name is limited to eight characters. You do not need to include an extension with this name since Harvard Graphics automatically adds the extension .CHT to this chart name. If this chart has previously been saved, the chart name you used before will appear in this field. If you want to replace the existing copy of your chart with the revised copy, keep the same chart name. If you would like to keep both the old chart and the revised chart, press CTRL-DEL to erase the contents of this field and enter a new name for the chart.

If you enter the name of an existing chart at this option, Harvard Graphics will display a warning. You can either cancel saving the chart or replace the existing chart with the new chart you are saving.

### Description

**Default:** (Title used in your chart)

Enter a description for the chart. If you provided a title for your chart on the chart form, the text from this title will already appear at the "Description" option. You can change this text (this will not change your chart title) or add a description if "Description" is blank. This description is helpful when you later need to retrieve your chart, since the description will be displayed on the Select Chart form along with the chart name.

## Save Template Overlay

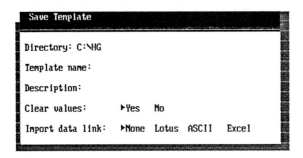

**Location**   At the Get/Save/Remove menu, select <Save template> to display the Save Template overlay.

**Description**   Whenever you have a chart whose settings you would like to save, you can save these settings as a template. The Save Template overlay is used to define the name and characteristics of your template. Once you fill out this overlay, press F10-Continue to save a template based on your current chart settings and characteristics.

If the "Clear values" option is set to Yes, Harvard Graphics will warn you that your data are about to be cleared. If you want to save your chart with the text and/or data and have not yet done so, press ESC to return to the Get/Save/Remove menu and save your chart before saving the template. Otherwise, press ENTER to save your template.

### Directory

**Default:** (Current directory)

Indicate in which directory you want to store the template. If you intend to add this template to a chartbook or slide show, the template must be stored in the same directory as the chartbook or slide show. If you want to save your template to a different directory than the one shown, press CTRL-DEL to delete the current directory name and enter the name of the desired directory.

### Template name

**Default:** (Blank)

Enter a name for your template. The name you enter must be eight characters or less in length, and conform to DOS file naming conventions. You do not need to add an extension to this file name since Harvard Graphics automatically adds the extension .TPL when the template is saved.

*Note:* There are 12 names you should use with care when saving a chart as a template. These are AREA, BARLINE, BULLET, FREEFORM, HLC, LIST, MULTIPLE, ORG, PIE, TITLE, 2_COLUMN, 3_COLUMN. Saving a template with any one of these names will redefine the settings Harvard Graphics will use as the default settings for that particular chart type, as described in Chapter 11, "Templates and Chartbooks."

### Description

**Default:** (Blank)

Enter an informative description for your template. This description is helpful since it will be displayed when you are retrieving an existing template on the Select Template form. If you do not enter a description, the title (if there is one) from the chart used to create the template will be used for the description.

### Clear values

**Default:** Yes

Set "Clear values" to Yes to remove all the text and data from your template. Select No to save text and/or data with your template. When you set "Clear values" to No, be sure that only the text, titles, and data you want to use every time you get the template are the only text and data in your chart before you save the template.

**Import data link**

**Default:** None

If you have just imported data into a chart, the "Import data link" option will be set to the source of the import: Lotus, ASCII, or Excel. (Excel import is available in version 2.3 only.) A template saved with a data link will automatically re-import the data when the template is retrieved. If you do not want to save the data link, or you have not imported data into the current chart, set "Import data link" to No.

# Screen Setup Form

```
                    Screen Setup

              Default screen      VEGA      Deluxe

         IBM  CGA color           HERCULES  Monochrome graphics
              CGA monochrome
              EGA color           TOSHIBA   T3100 monochrome
              EGA monochrome
              VGA                 DGIS      Compatible

                                  VDI       Display


         Screen: Default screen



F1-Help                                           F10-Continue
```

# Harvard Graphics Forms and Function Keys

**Location** Select <Screen> at the Setup menu to display the Screen Setup form.

**Description** The Screen Setup form displays the graphics adapters that Harvard Graphics supports. Press F10-Continue or ENTER to return to the Setup menu.

### Screen

**Default:** Default screen

Typically, you will not need to change the "Screen" option. When you first run Harvard Graphics, the program automatically checks the graphics adapter attached to your computer and sets this graphics adapter type as its default screen. If the Harvard Graphics menus look distorted or fuzzy, however, your screen setting may be incompatible with your computer's graphics adapter.

You may also want to change this setting if you have a second adapter attached to your computer or if ScreenShow special effects do not work on your computer. For VGA adapters, try setting "Screen" to EGA color. For other adapters, try setting "Screen" to CGA color or CGA monochrome. To change this setting, press the SPACEBAR until the appropriate graphics adapter is listed at "Screen."

## ScreenShow Effects Form

**Location** With the desired slide show current, select <Add Screen Show effects> from the Slide Show menu to display the ScreenShow Effects form.

**Description** Use this form to specify display transitions and special effects for your ScreenShow. This form contains eight columns and as many rows as there are files in the current slide show. The first column contains numbers indicating the order of files in the slide show. The second column, "Filename," lists the names of the files in your slide

```
                    ScreenShow Effects

         Filename    | Type     | Draw    | Dir   | Time | Erase  | Dir
         Default     |          | Replace |       |      |        |
    1   MENU4    .CHT  FREEFORM   Fade      In             Wipe     Left
    2♦  REG2     .CHT  LIST       Iris      Out            Wipe     Right
    3♦  GO       .CHT  FREEFORM   Iris      In             Close
    4♦  MENU4    .CHT  FREEFORM   Fade      In             Wipe     Left
    5♦  WHYUP3   .CHT  FREEFORM   Blinds    Right
    6♦  HOWUPGRD .CHT  FREEFORM   Wipe      Down           Close    Right
    7♦  MENU4    .CHT  FREEFORM   Fade      In             Wipe     Left
    8♦  HGAINTR4 .CHT  FREEFORM   Open      Out            Wipe     Up
    9♦  BSYM2    .CHT  FREEFORM   Scroll    Right          Rain
   10♦  MAP4     .CHT  FREEFORM   Scroll    Down           Rain
   11♦  QC       .CHT  FREEFORM   Scroll    Right          Rain
   12♦  MILSYM2  .CHT  FREEFORM   Scroll    Left           Rain

F1-Help
F2-Preview show              F6-Choices     F8-HyperShow    F10-Continue
```

show. The "Type" column contains the type of each file. If the file is a chart, the type of chart is displayed in this column. Alternatively, if the slide is a template, slide show, or bit-mapped file, this column contains the template type, "SLD SHOW," or "BIT MAP," respectively. The remaining five columns ("Draw," "Dir," "Time," "Erase," and "Dir") are used to define the ScreenShow transitions used when you display a ScreenShow.

### Draw

**Default:** Replace

The "Draw" column is used to define the transition that will place each file on your computer screen (or on a projection device). To add a transition for a specific file, move the cursor to the correct row in the "Draw" column for that file, and enter the name of the transition. You can also add a transition by entering the first letter of the transition (or the first two letters of a transition that has the same initial letter as another transition).

Alternatively, with the cursor positioned at the desired row in the "Draw" column, you can press F6-Choices to display the Transitions overlay listing all of the available transitions. Select a transition from this list by moving the cursor to the desired transition and pressing ENTER. To remove the Transition overlay without selecting a transition, press ESC.

## Dir

**Default:** (Depends on the transition selected)

This column allows you to define the direction of the transitions specified in the "Draw" column. If a transition is defined, the default direction for the transition will be used if "Dir" is left blank. To use a transition other than the default, enter a direction or press F6-Choices to display the Directions overlay, and then select a transition from this overlay.

*Note:* Not all transitions have directions, although many do. Refer to Chapter 13, "Slide Shows" for more information.

## Time

**Default:** (Blank)

The "Time" column allows you to specify the maximum amount of time that a chart or image is displayed on the screen before the ScreenShow continues on to the next file. You enter a time by specifying the number of minutes and seconds Harvard Graphics should display the file, using the format MM:SS. For example, to display a given chart for 15 seconds, enter **:15**, or to display a chart for one minute, enter **1:00** in the appropriate row of the "Time" column.

If you enter a number without adding a colon, Harvard Graphics will assume you are specifying seconds. If the number of seconds entered is greater than 59, Harvard Graphics will convert the number to minutes and seconds. If no time value is specified, the chart or image will remain on the screen until one of the user keys, a Go To key, or a button is pressed.)

*Note:* The "Time" column is the amount of time Harvard Graphics will wait before *beginning* to display the next file. Some files, however, can take up to 15 seconds or more to display, depending on the size of the file and the speed of your computer. You may need to experiment to determine the most effective display times.

### Erase

**Default:** (Blank)

Define the transition used to erase a chart or image from the screen. Either enter a transition for the desired file or press F6-Choices to display the Transitions overlay and select a transition from this overlay.

*Hint:* It is not unusual to leave the erase transition blank.

### Dir

**Default:** (Depends on the transition selected)

Define the direction used to erase a chart or image from the screen for the transition defined in the "Erase" column. If an erase transition is defined, leaving "Dir" blank will cause the default direction for the transition to be used. To use a transition other than the default, enter a direction or press F6-Choices to display the Directions overlay and select a transition from this overlay. If the erase transition is blank, you do not need to specify an erase direction.

### Default

The first row below the column headings ("Draw," "Dir," "Time," "Erase," and "Dir") is the "Default" row; it is used to specify default transitions, directions, and timing. Whenever a given file is not assigned a transition, direction, or time, Harvard Graphics will use the values that appear in this row. You can specify any of the default settings by entering the desired transition, direction, or time in the appropriate column of the default row. You can also use F6-Choices to select transitions or directions for the default settings.

*Note:* If you want a ScreenShow to run automatically, you can set the default time to the number of minutes and/or seconds you want each file to be displayed. However, when a default time is defined, all files will be presented for, at most, the default time. Therefore, it is not possible to have a single file displayed indefinitely if you define a default time value.

## Select CGM Metafile Form (Version 2.3)

```
                     Select CGM Metafile
Directory: C:\HG
Filename:  CANADA   .CFG

Filename Ext   | Date     | Type     | Description
CANADA   .CFG  | 10/07/87 | OTHER    |
UK       .CFG  | 10/07/87 | OTHER    |
US       .CFG  | 10/07/87 | OTHER    |
ANNOUNCE .CHT  | 07/01/87 | FREEFORM | Sample chart
INTRO    .CHT  | 07/01/87 | TITLE    | Sample chart
OPENING  .CHT  | 07/01/87 | TITLE    | Sample chart
PRODS    .CHT  | 07/01/87 | LIST     | Sample chart
REGIONS  .CHT  | 07/01/87 | BAR/LINE | Sample chart
SALES    .CHT  | 07/01/87 | 2 COLUMN | Sample chart
TRISALES .CHT  | 07/01/87 | BAR/LINE | Sample chart
SAMPLE   .SHW  | 05/08/90 | SLD SHOW | Sample slide show
PLANSAMP .ASC  | 03/18/87 | OTHER    |
UNITS    .BAK  | 04/12/87 | OTHER    |
UNITS    .WKS  | 03/18/90 | OTHER    |
HG       .PIF  | 07/02/87 | OTHER    |

F1-Help        F3-Change dir                        F10-Continue
```

**Location**  At the Import/Export menu, select <Import CGM metafile> to display the Select CGM Metafile form.

**Description**  This form is used to select an existing CGM metafile. Once the desired file is displayed at the "Filename" option, press F10-Continue to select it.

### Directory

**Default:** (Current directory)

Files in the current directory are listed in the bottom part of the form. To select a CGM metafile from a different directory, enter the name of the desired directory in this field. Alternatively, press F3-Change dir and select a directory from the Select Directory form (see "Select Directory Form").

**Filename**

**Default:** (First file in the list)

Either type in the name of a file (with or without the extension) at "Filename," or use the cursor to highlight the desired filename in the list of files. When a filename is highlighted, its name appears at the "Filename" option.

## Select Chart Form

```
                         Select Chart

Directory: C:\HGDATA
Filename:  GOALS1   .CHT

Filename Ext   Date      Type       Description

GOALS1   .CHT  02/24/90  BULLET
MYTEMP3  .CHT  08/14/90  TITLE      Temperature chart. FOR CITY TPLT
TITLE    .CHT  02/24/90  TITLE      Quarterly Planning Meeting Title
POINTS   .CHT  07/02/90  BULLET     List of points for presentation
BAR1     .CHT  07/02/90  BAR/LINE   first bar of build up.  Sales Figures
BAR2     .CHT  07/02/90  BAR/LINE   Second bar of build up.  Sales Figures
BAR3     .CHT  07/02/90  BAR/LINE   Third bar of build up.  Sales Figures
BAR4     .CHT  07/02/90  BAR/LINE   Final bar of build up.  Sales Figures
MRKTPIE  .CHT  07/02/90  PIE        Market division.
AREA1    .CHT  07/02/90  AREA       Sales Trends
AREA2    .CHT  07/02/90  AREA       Sales Trends.  Area plus symbol
BLANK    .CHT  07/02/90  FREEFORM   blank chart for special effects
NEWSALES .CHT  07/02/90  2 COLUMN   table of current sales figures
GOALS2   .CHT  02/24/90  LIST
GOALS3   .CHT  02/24/90  AREA

F1-Help        F3-Change dir
                                                    F10-Continue
```

**Location**   Select <Get chart> from the Get/Save/Remove menu to display the Select Chart form.

**Description** The Select Chart form is used to retrieve a chart you have previously saved. Once the desired chart is displayed at the "Filename" option, press F10-Continue to retrieve the chart. The chart will then be displayed on the screen. Press any key to remove the chart and display the chart form specific to that type of chart.

### Directory

**Default:** (Current directory)

If the directory displayed does not contain the desired chart file, enter the name of another directory. Alternatively, press F3-Change dir and select a directory from the Select Directory form (see "Select Directory Form").

### Filename

**Default:** (First file in the list)

Enter the name of the chart you want to retrieve. Either type the chart name (with or without the extension) at "Filename," or highlight the name of the file in the file list. When a filename is highlighted, its name appears at the "Filename" option.

## Select Chartbook Form

**Location** At the Chartbook Menu, choose <Select chartbook> to display the Select Chartbook form.

**Description** This form is used to select an existing chartbook in order to make it the current chartbook. Once the desired chartbook file is displayed at the "Filename" option, press F10-Continue to select the file and return to the Chartbook Menu.

### Directory

**Default:** (Current directory)

```
                    Select Chartbook
  Directory: C:\HGDATA
  Filename:  WEEKLY  .CBK

  Filename Ext | Date      | Type     | Description
  WEEKLY  .CBK | 02/21/90  | CHRTBOOK | Weekly Report Templates
  ANNUAL  .CBK | 03/02/90  | CHRTBOOK | Annual Report Templates
  HANSON  .CBK | 05/21/90  | CHRTBOOK | Templates for the Hanson Account
  WASHINTN.CBK | 07/15/90  | CHRTBOOK | Washington Presentation Templates


  F1-Help        F3-Change dir
                                                    F10-Continue
```

If the directory displayed does not contain the desired chartbook file, enter the name of another directory. Alternatively, press F3-Change dir and select a directory from the Select Directory form (see "Select Directory Form").

**Filename**

**Default:** (First file in the list)

Either type in the name of the desired file (with or without the extension) at "Filename," or use the cursor to highlight the name of the file in the list of chartbook files. When a filename is highlighted, its name appears at the "Filename" option.

## Select Directory Form

**Location**  From any form in which you are able to select a file (Edit Multiple Chart form, Select Chart form, Select Chartbook form, Select File form, Select Slide Show form, Select Symbol File form, Select Excel

```
                    Select Directory
Directory: C:\HGDATA
Filename:  ..

Filename Ext | Date      | Type | Description
-------------|-----------|------|------------------
..           | 12/03/89  | DIR  | Parent Directory
HANSON       | 05/29/90  | DIR  | Sub Directory
WSHNGTON     | 08/04/90  | DIR  | Sub Directory
QUEUE        | 09/14/90  | DIR  | Sub Directory
ANNUAL       | 12/23/89  | DIR  | Sub Directory


F1-Help        F3-Select files
                                              F10-Continue
```

Worksheet form, Select Excel Chart form, Select Lotus Worksheet form, Select Worksheet form, or Select Palette form), press F3-Change dir to display the Select Directory form.

**Description**  The Select Directory form is used when you want to select a file from a directory other than the one listed at the "Directory" option on the current form. Once you have selected the desired directory, press F3-Select files or ESC to return to the previous form.

### Directory

**Default:** (Current directory)

You can change directories by moving to "Directory" and entering the path and name of the desired directory.

### Filename

**Default:** (First directory in the list)

Make a subdirectory the current directory by entering the subdirectory name at the "Filename" option and then press ENTER. To make the parent directory the current directory, enter .. at the filename option and then press ENTER.

The names of the subdirectories available for you to enter at "Filename" are shown in the list in the lower part of this form. Instead of entering a name, you can use the cursor to highlight the name of the desired subdirectory in the list. When it is highlighted, the name also appears at the "Filename" option.

## Select Excel Chart Form (Version 2.3)

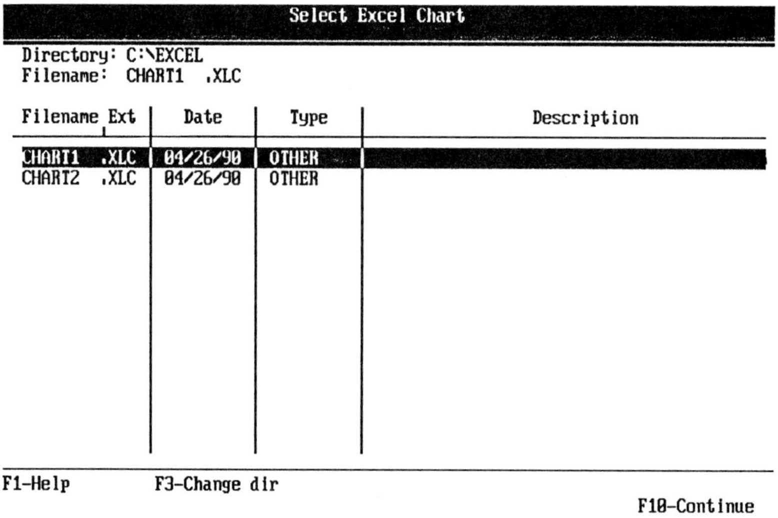

```
                        Select Excel Chart
Directory: C:\EXCEL
Filename:  CHART1   .XLC

   Filename Ext  |   Date    |  Type   |     Description
   CHART1   .XLC | 04/26/90  | OTHER   |
   CHART2   .XLC | 04/26/90  | OTHER   |




F1-Help       F3-Change dir
                                                   F10-Continue
```

**Location**  At the Import/Export menu, select <Import Excel chart> to display the Select Excel Chart form.

**Description**  This form is used to select an existing Excel chart. Once the desired file is displayed at the "Filename" option, press F10-Continue to select the Excel Chart.

### Directory

**Default:** (Current directory)

Files in the current directory are listed in the bottom part of the form. To select a file a from a different directory, enter the name of the desired directory in this field. Alternatively, press F3-Change dir and select a directory from the Select Directory form (see "Select Directory Form").

**Filename**

**Default:** (First file in the list)

Either type in the name of the file (with or without the extension) at "Filename," or use the cursor to highlight the filename in the list of files. When a filename is highlighted, its name appears at the "Filename" option.

## Select Excel Worksheet Form (Version 2.3)

```
                        Select Excel Worksheet
Directory: C:\HGDATA
Filename:  REPORT   .XLS

 Filename Ext  |   Date    |  Type  |         Description
 REPORT   .XLS | 12/29/88  | OTHER  |
 SALES    .XLS | 12/29/88  | OTHER  |
 WEST     .XLS | 12/29/88  | OTHER  |




F1-Help        F3-Change dir
                                                       F10-Continue
```

**Location**  At the Import/Export menu, select <Import Excel data> to display the Select Excel Worksheet form. You can also press F3-Select files from the Import Excel Data form to display the Select Excel Worksheet form, which is useful if you discover you need to select a different file.

**Description** This form is used to select an existing Excel spreadsheet. Once the desired file is displayed at the "Filename" option, press F10-Continue to select the spreadsheet.

### Directory

**Default:** (Current directory)

Files in the current directory are listed in the bottom part of the form. To select a file a from a different directory, enter the name of the desired directory in this field. Alternatively, press F3-Change dir and select a directory from the Select Directory form (see "Select Directory Form").

### Filename

**Default:** (First file in the list)

Either type in the name of the file (with or without the extension) at "Filename," or use the cursor to highlight the filename in the list of files. When a filename is highlighted, its name appears at the "Filename" option.

## Select File Form

**Location** From the Get/Save/Remove menu, select <Remove file> to display the Select File form. From the Import/Export menu, select <Import ASCII data>, <Import delimited ASCII>, or, for versions 2.13 and earlier, <Import PFS:GRAPH> to display the Select File form.

```
                        Select File
Directory: C:\HGDATA
Filename:  MSBAR    .TPL

Filename Ext  |  Date    |   Type    |           Description
MSBAR    .TPL | 08/12/90 | BAR/LINE  | Michigan Study, 3D bars
CHART2   .CHT | 01/05/90 | BAR/LINE  | Chart 2
CHART3   .CHT | 01/05/90 | PIE       | Chart 3
MSBAR2   .TPL | 08/12/90 | BAR/LINE  | Michigan Study, Stack Bars
MSBAR3   .TPL | 08/12/90 | BAR/LINE  | Michigan Study, Simple bar chart.
11A1     .CHT | 01/09/90 | BAR/LINE  | weekly sales performance
WKLYBAR  .TPL | 01/08/90 | BAR/LINE  | Bar template for weekly progress report
WEEKLY   .CBK | 02/21/90 | CHRTBOOK  | Weekly Report Templates
MSPIE    .TPL | 08/12/90 | PIE       | Michigan Study, Linked pie comparison
MSPIE2   .TPL | 08/12/90 | PIE       | Michigan Study, Single pie, group 1
ANNUAL   .CBK | 03/02/90 | CHRTBOOK  | Annual Report Templates
HANSON   .CBK | 05/21/90 | CHRTBOOK  | Templates for the Hanson Account
WASHINTN .CBK | 07/15/90 | CHRTBOOK  | Washington Presentation Templates
WKLYPIE  .TPL | 01/09/90 | PIE       | Pie chart for the weekly progress report
WKLYLINE .TPL | 03/01/90 | BAR/LINE  | Trend chart for weekly report

F1-Help       F3-Change dir
                                                         F10-Continue
```

**Description** This form is used to select an existing file in order to perform your current task. Once the desired file is displayed at the "Filename" option, press F10-Continue to select the file.

### Directory

**Default:** (Current directory)

Files in the current directory are listed in the bottom part of the form. To select a file from a different directory, enter the name of the desired directory at the "Directory" option. Alternatively, press F3-Change dir and select a directory from the Select Directory form (see "Select Directory Form").

### Filename

**Default:** (First file in the list)

Either type in the name of the file (with or without the extension) at "Filename," or use the cursor to highlight the filename in the list of files. When a filename is highlighted, its name appears at the "Filename" option.

## Select Lotus Worksheet Form (Version 2.3)

For versions 2.13 and earlier, see "Select Worksheet Form."

```
                        Select Lotus Worksheet
Directory: C:\HG
Filename:  UNITS    .WKS

Filename Ext    Date       Type         Description

UNITS    .WKS   03/10/90   OTHER
FUTURE   .WKS   09/01/90   OTHER
HANSON   .WKS   05/21/90   OTHER
WEEKLY   .WKS   06/12/90   OTHER
UPDATE   .WKS   07/30/90   OTHER




F1-Help        F3-Change dir                           F10-Continue
```

**Location** At the Import/Export menu, select <Import Lotus data> or <Import Lotus graph> to display the Select Lotus Worksheet form when a default import file is not specified on the Default form. You can also press F3-Select files from the Import Lotus Data form or the Import Lotus Graph form to display the Select Lotus Worksheet form, which is useful if you discover that you need to select a different file.

**Description** This form is used to select an existing Lotus spreadsheet. Once the desired file is displayed at the "Filename" option, press F10-Continue to select the spreadsheet.

### Directory

**Default:** (Current directory)

Files in the current directory are listed in the bottom part of the form. To select a file from a different directory, enter the name of the

## Harvard Graphics Forms and Function Keys 927

desired directory in this field. Alternatively, press F3-Change dir and select a directory from the Select Directory form (see "Select Directory Form").

### Filename

**Default:** (First file in the list)

Either type in the name of the file (with or without the extension) at "Filename," or use the cursor to highlight the filename in the list of files. When a filename is highlighted, its name appears at the "Filename" option.

## Select Palette Form (Version 2.3)

```
                          Select Palette
 Directory: C:\HG
 Filename:  HG23     .PAL

   Filename Ext  |  Date    |  Type    |  Description
   10       .PAL | 04/13/90 | PALETTE  | Lt Gray bkg, with darker colors
   9        .PAL | 04/13/90 | PALETTE  | Lt. Cyan bkg, with darker colors
   8        .PAL | 04/13/90 | PALETTE  | Red bkg, with red green and orange
   7        .PAL | 04/13/90 | PALETTE  | Dk. gray bkg, with warm colors
   6        .PAL | 04/13/90 | PALETTE  | Blue-green bkg, with blue red and cyan
   5        .PAL | 04/13/90 | PALETTE  | Blue bkg, with reds and oranges
   4        .PAL | 04/13/90 | PALETTE  | Blue bkg, with warm colors
   3        .PAL | 04/13/90 | PALETTE  | Blue bkg, with blues and red
   2        .PAL | 04/13/90 | PALETTE  | Blue bkg, with blues
   1        .PAL | 04/13/90 | PALETTE  | Blue bkg, with blue-greens
   HG23     .PAL | 04/13/90 | PALETTE  |
   11       .PAL | 04/13/90 | PALETTE
   PLOT6PEN.PAL  | 04/27/90 | PALETTE
   PLOT8PEN.PAL  | 04/27/90 | PALETTE
   HG23P    .PAL | 05/07/90 | PALETTE

 F1-Help      F3-Change dir
                                                      F10-Continue
```

**Location**   Choose <Select palette> from the Palette menu to display the Select Palette form.

**Description** The Select Palette form is used to select a color palette in order to make it current. You can then edit the selected palette. When you have selected a new palette, press F10-Continue and you will return to the Setup menu.

### Directory

**Default:** (Current directory)

If the directory displayed does not contain the desired palette file, enter the name of another directory. Alternatively, press F3-Change dir and select a directory from the Select Directory form (see "Select Directory Form").

### Filename

**Default:** (First file in the list)

Enter the name of the palette you want to retrieve. Either type the name (with or without the extension) at "Filename," or highlight the name of the palette file in the file list. When a filename is highlighted, its name appears at the "Filename" option.

## Select Slide Show Form

**Location** At the Slide Show Menu, choose <Select slide show> to display the Select Slide Show form.

**Description** This form is used to select an existing slide show file. Once the desired slide show file is displayed at the "Filename" option, press F10-Continue to select the file and return to the Slide Show menu.

### Directory

**Default:** (Current directory)

Files in the current directory (files with a .SHW extension) are listed in the bottom part of the form. To select a file from a different

```
                    Select Slide Show
   Directory: C:\HG
   Filename:  SPCINFO .SHW

       Filename Ext  |   Date    |  Type  |       Description
       SPCINFO .SHW  | 05/17/90  |  SHOW  |




   F1-Help         F3-Change dir
                                                         F10-Continue
```

directory, enter the name of the desired directory in this field. Alternatively, press F3-Change dir and select a directory from the Select Directory form (see "Select Directory Form").

### Filename

**Default:** (First file in the list)

Either type in the name of the file (with or without extension) at "Filename," or use the cursor to highlight the filename in the list of slide show files. When a filename is highlighted, its name appears at the "Filename" option.

## Select Symbol File Form

**Location**  At the Draw menu in Draw/Annotate, select <Symbol> to display the Symbol menu, and then select <Get> from this menu to display the Select Symbol File form.

```
                    Select Symbol File
Directory: C:\HG\SYMBOLS
Filename:  DPSAMPLE.SYM

Filename Ext   Date      Type      Description
DPSAMPLE.SYM   05/03/90  SYMBOL
ARROWS2 .SYM   04/27/90  SYMBOL
BORDERS .SYM   04/27/90  SYMBOL
BUTTONS1.SYM   04/27/90  SYMBOL
BUTTONS2.SYM   04/27/90  SYMBOL
COMPUTR2.SYM   04/27/90  SYMBOL
COMPUTR3.SYM   04/27/90  SYMBOL
FLOWCHT .SYM   04/27/90  SYMBOL
GREEKLC1.SYM   04/27/90  SYMBOL
GREEKLC2.SYM   04/27/90  SYMBOL
GREEKUC1.SYM   04/27/90  SYMBOL
GREEKUC2.SYM   04/27/90  SYMBOL
SIGNS   .SYM   05/02/90  SYMBOL
STARS1  .SYM   04/27/90  SYMBOL
CALENDAR.SYM   05/02/90  SYMBOL

F1-Help        F3-Change dir                          F10-Continue
```

**Description**     This form is used to select an existing symbol file. Once the desired symbol file is displayed at the "Filename" option, press F10-Continue to select the file and display all the symbols in the file in the drawing area of the Draw/Annotate screen.

### Directory

**Default:** (Current Symbol directory [version 2.3] or current directory)

Symbol files in the current directory (files with a .SYM extension) are listed in the bottom part of the form. To select a file from a different directory, enter the name of the desired directory in this field. Alternatively, press F3-Change dir and select a directory from the Select Directory form (see "Select Directory Form").

### Filename

**Default:** (First file in the list)

Either type in the name of the file (with or without the extension) at "Filename," or use the cursor to highlight the filename in the list of symbol files. When a filename is highlighted, its name appears at the "Filename" option. If you enter a filename that does not correspond to one of the symbol files on the current directory, Harvard Graphics will create a new symbol file using that name.

## Select Template Form (<Get template>)

```
                         Select Template
Directory: C:\HGDATA
Filename:  MSBAR2  .TPL

Filename Ext   Date       Type       Description

MSBAR2   .TPL  08/12/90   BAR/LINE   Michigan Study.  Stack Bars
MSBAR3   .TPL  08/12/90   BAR/LINE   Michigan Study.  Simple bar chart.
WKLYBAR  .TPL  01/08/90   BAR/LINE   Bar template for weekly progress report
MSPIE    .TPL  08/12/90   PIE        Michigan Study.  Linked pie comparison
MSPIE2   .TPL  08/12/90   PIE        Michigan Study.  Single pie, group 1
WKLYPIE  .TPL  01/09/90   PIE        Pie chart for the weekly progress report
WKLYLINE .TPL  03/01/90   BAR/LINE   Trend chart for weekly report
123AREA  .TPL  05/12/90   AREA       Import Hanson Account Totals
123PIE   .TPL  04/30/90   PIE        Import Comparison Figures; Hanson Accnt
Y_T_D1   .TPL  12/28/89   BAR/LINE   Year-to-date trends
ANRPTPIE .TPL  01/09/90   PIE        Annual Report.  Earnings Performance Pie
ANRPTBAR .TPL  01/09/90   BAR/LINE   Annual Report.  Trend w/ bars.
MSPIE3   .TPL  08/12/90   PIE        Michigan Study.  Single pie, group 2
MSLINE   .TPL  08/12/90   BAR/LINE   Michigan Study.  Trends.  Year-to-date
MSLINE1  .TPL  08/12/90   BAR/LINE   Michigan Study.  Regression line

F1-Help         F3-Change dir
                                                              F10-Continue
```

**Location**   Select <Get template> from the Get/Save/Remove menu to display the Select Template form.

**Description**   This form is used to select an existing template in order to create a new chart using the settings and characteristics defined in the template. Once the desired template file is displayed at the "Filename" option, press F10-Continue to select the template and display the chart form corresponding to that template.

### Directory
**Default:** (Current directory)

To select a template from a directory other than the current directory, press SHIFT-TAB to move to the "Directory" option and enter the drive and directory path. Alternatively, you can press F3-Change dir and select a directory from the Select Directory form (see "Select Directory Form").

**Filename**

**Default:** (First file in the list)

To select a template, highlight the filename in the list of template files. When a filename is highlighted, its name appears at the "Filename" option.

## Select Template Form (<From chartbook>)

```
                          Select Template
    Chartbook name: WEEKLY    .CBK
    Template name:  MSBAR     .TPL

    Filename Ext  |  Date    |   Type    |        Description
    MSBAR   .TPL  | 08/12/90 | BAR/LINE  | Michigan Study,  3D bars
    MSBAR3  .TPL  | 08/12/90 | BAR/LINE  | Michigan Study,  Simple bar chart,
    MSPIE   .TPL  | 08/12/90 | PIE       | Michigan Study,  Linked pie comparison




    F1-Help                                                  F10-Continue
```

**Location**   If you have a current chartbook that contains the desired template, select <From chartbook> from the Create New Chart menu (versions 2.13 or earlier) or from the Chartbook menu (version 2.3) to display the Select Template form.

**Description**  This form is used to select an existing template from the current chartbook in order to create a new chart using the settings and characteristics defined in the template. Once the desired template file is displayed at the "Template name" option, press F10-Continue to select the template and display the chart form corresponding to that template.

### Chartbook name

The name of the current chartbook is shown at "Chartbook name." You cannot change this name on this form. All the templates (files with a .TPL extension) listed in the chartbook are shown at the bottom of the Select Template form.

### Template name

**Default:** (First file in the list)

To select a template, highlight the filename in the list of template files and press ENTER. When a filename is highlighted, its name appears at the "Template name" option.

## Select Worksheet Form (Versions 2.13 and earlier)

This form contains the same options as the "Select Lotus Worksheet Form," in version 2.3. (See "Select Lotus Worksheet Form.")

## Shaded Background Overlay

**Location**  If your film recorder can support a shaded background, F6-Shaded bkgd will appear in the function key banner of the Color Palette Setup form. From this form, press F6-Shaded bkgd to display the Shaded Background overlay.

```
              ┌─────────Shaded Background─────────┐
              │                                    │
              │ Use shaded background:   Yes  ▶No  │
              │                                    │
              │                 Red  Green  Blue   │
              │ Top color:       0     0     0     │
              │ Bottom color:    0     0     0     │
              │                                    │
              │ Number of levels:   1              │
              └────────────────────────────────────┘
```

**Description**   The Shaded Background form is used to define a top color and a bottom color for a shaded background. You define the number of levels of color to use between the top and bottom colors to achieve the shading effect. Refer to Chapter 3, "Setup and Default Settings" for more information.

### Use shaded background

**Default:** No

To use a shaded background when outputting to your film recorder, press the SPACEBAR to highlight Yes.

### Top color

**Default:** 0 0 0

Define the red/green/blue mix of the color you want to use as the top color of the shaded background.

### Bottom color

**Default:** 0 0 0

Define the red/green/blue mix of the color you want to use as the bottom color of the shaded background.

### Number of levels

**Default:** 1

Define the number of levels of shading you want produced between the top color and the bottom color. A value from 0 to 100 may be entered. If you set "Number of levels" to 50 or higher, the shaded background will appear as a continuous blend between the top and bottom colors.

## Simple List Form

```
                        Simple List
              Title:
              Subtitle:
              Footnote:




F1-Help       F3-Save       F5-Attributes  F7-Size/Place
F2-Draw chart F4-Draw/Annot                              F10-Continue
```

**Location**   Select <Create new chart> from the Main Menu followed by <Text> from the Create New Chart menu. Then at the Text Chart Styles menu, select <Simple list> to display the Simple List form.

**Description**   Enter text for the simple list chart on this form.

### Title, Subtitle, and Footnote
**Default:** (Blank)

Enter a title, subtitle, and/or footnote for your simple list chart.

### Simple List Text Area

Enter a list of words, phrases, sentences, or numbers. You may optionally enter blank lines between the list items.

## Simple List: Size/Place Overlay

```
  Size    Place         Simple List
   8     L ►C  R    Title:
   6     L ►C  R    Subtitle:
   3.5   ►L C  R    Footnote:

   5.5    L ►C  R

   Indent: 0




  F1-Help         F3-Save       F5-Attributes   F7-Size/Place
  F2-Draw chart   F4-Draw/Annot                                  F10-Continue
```

**Location**   At the Simple List form, press F7-Size/Place to display the Size/Place overlay.

**Description**   Use the Size/Place overlay to define the size and placement of the text on the Simple List form. Once you set the desired options, press F7-Size/Place or F10-Continue to return to the Simple List form.

### Size

**Defaults:** (Vary depending on the line)

Enter a number from .1 to 99.

### Place

**Defaults:** (Vary depending on the line)

Set either L, C, or R to left-justify, center, or right-justify text.

### Indent

**Default:** 0

In order to indent the list, the text in the list section of the Simple List form must be left-justified. Enter a number indicating the percentage of the screen width you want to indent. A setting of 50 will indent to the center of the screen.

## Size/Place Overlays

Refer each chart type for a description of the Size/Place overlay for that type: Area, Bar/Line, Bullet List, Free Form, High/Low/Close, Organization, Pie, Simple List, Title, Two Column and Three Column.

## Slide Show List Option Overlay

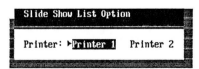

**Location** At the Produce Output menu, select <Print slide show list> to display the Slide Show List Option overlay.

**Description** Set the "Printer" option and then press F10-Continue to print a list of files in the current slide show.

**Printer**

**Default:** Printer 1

Select the printer, Printer 1 or Printer 2, to which you want to print. The printer you select must have been defined on the Printer 1 or Printer 2 Setup form (refer to "Printer 1 Setup form").

## Text Attributes Overlay

```
▶Fill   ▶Bold    Italic    Underline   Color 1
```

**Location** Press F5-Attributes or SHIFT-F5 to display the Text Attributes overlay from the following locations: any text chart form; the Organization Chart form; Page 1 or 4 of the Titles & Options forms for area, bar/line, and high/low/close charts; Page 1 of the Pie Chart Titles & Options form; and the "Text" line on the Draw/Annotate screen that is displayed when you are adding or modifying text.

**Description** You can modify the attributes of most text that appears in your charts and drawings by using the Text Attributes overlay.

In order to modify text attributes, you must first highlight the text to change. To highlight an entire line of text, move the cursor to that line on the form and press SHIFT-F5. To highlight less than an entire line of text, move the cursor to the left-most character of the text you want to highlight and press F5-Attributes. After pressing F5-Attributes or SHIFT-F5 the first time, use the RIGHT and DOWN arrow keys until all the desired text is highlighted. Alternatively, after an initial press of F5-Attributes or SHIFT-F5, additional presses of these keys act like the RIGHT key and DOWN key, respectively.

Once you press F5-Attributes or SHIFT-F5, the Text Attributes overlay is displayed at the bottom of the screen in the function key banner. To change the attributes of the highlighted text, TAB to the desired option on the overlay and press the SPACEBAR to set the attribute option to the desired setting. For the "Fill," "Bold," "Italic," and "Underline" options, the option is set to On when an arrow appears to the left of the option name, and set to Off if no arrow is visible.

With your cursor at the "Color" option, you can press the SPACEBAR until the desired color number is displayed at the "Color" option. Alternatively, you can press F6-Colors to display the Color Selection overlay (see "Color Selection Overlay"). Highlight the desired color in this overlay and then press ENTER or F10-Continue to return to the Text Attributes overlay.

When you are finished setting text attributes for the highlighted text, press F10-Continue to return to the previous form. If you press ESC while the Text Attributes overlay is displayed, your text attribute settings will be cancelled.

See "Fonts and Text Attributes" in Appendix D for examples of different text attribute combinations.

### Fill

**Default:** (On)

Set Fill to Off if you want to display only the outline of the text. Leave Fill set to On if you want your text to appear filled in.

### Bold

**Default:** (Varies between On and Off depending on the text option and chart type.)

Set Bold to On if you want the selected text to appear in a bold font.

### Italic

**Default:** Off

Set Italic to On if you want the selected text to appear in italics.

## Underline

**Default:** (Varies between On and Off depending on the text option and chart type.)

Set Underline to On if you want the selected text to be underlined.

## Color

**Default:** 1

Press the SPACEBAR until the desired color number, 1 through 16, is displayed at the "Color" option. The corresponding color that will be used for the selected text will depend on your current color palette. Alternatively, with the cursor at this option, press F6-Colors and select a color from the Color Selection overlay (see "Color Selection Overlay").

## Text Options Form

**Location** The Text Options form appears in Draw/Annotate when you press F8-Options while adding text in the drawing area, when you select <Options> from the Modify menu and then select existing text in the drawing area, or when you select <Text> from the Default Options menu, which is displayed when you press F8-Options at the Draw menu.

**Description** Use the Text Options form to define the characteristics of text you add in Draw/Annotate.

### Size

**Default:** 5.5

Enter a number from .1 to 99 to be used for the size of text.

### Color

**Default:** 1

Enter a number, 1 through 16, corresponding to the desired color for your text. Alternatively, press F6-Choices when the cursor is positioned at this option and select a color from the Color Selection overlay (see "Color Selection Overlay").

### Fill

**Default:** Yes

Select Yes to fill the center of the text or No to display only the outline of the text.

### Bold

**Default:** Yes

Select Yes to apply boldface to the text.

### Italic

**Default:** No

Select Yes to italicize the text.

### Undrlin

**Default:** No

Select Yes to underline the text.

### Shadow

**Default:** No

Select Yes to add a shadow behind the text.

### Shadow color

**Default:** 1

If you set the "Shadow" option to Yes, enter a number from 1 to 16 at "Shadow color" to define the color of the text shadow. Alternatively, with the cursor positioned at "Shadow color," press F6-Choices and select from the Color Selection overlay (see "Color Selection Overlay").

### Align

**Default:** (Center base)

The "Align" option affects the alignment of your text. The four rows of "Align" correspond to the cursor position on the text placement box. The Top row permits you to align the placement box with the top of letters such as "D" and "l." The Center and Base positions correspond to the top and bottom of lowercase letters such an "n" and "w." Bottom aligns to the bottom of letters such as "g" and "p." The three columns of the "Align" option permit you to choose the type of justification for the text. Setting "Align" to L, C, or R results in left-justified, centered, or right-justified text. Set the "align" option to the setting that results in the desired cursor location on the placement box and text alignment.

### Font (version 2.3)

**Default:** 1 (Executive)

Enter a number from 1 to 7 at "Font" to define the font to be used for the text. Alternatively, with the cursor positioned at "Font," press F6-Choices and select a font from the Fonts overlay (see "Fonts Overlay").

## Three Columns Form

**Location** Select <Create new chart> from the Main Menu followed by <Text> from the Create New Chart menu. Then at the Text Chart Styles menu, select <Three columns> to display the Three Columns form.

**Description** Enter text for a three-column chart on this form.

### Title, Subtitle, and Footnote
**Default:** (Blank)

Enter a title, subtitle, and/or footnote for your three-column chart.

### Column Headers

Enter the text you want to appear at the tops of the columns on the chart.

### Column Text Area

Enter the text to appear within the columns. If the entries in an entire column are numbers only, the text in that column will be right-justified instead of left-justified.

## Three-Column Chart: Size/Place Overlay

```
Size    Place          Three Columns
 8     L ▶C  R   Title:
 6     L ▶C  R   Subtitle:
3.5    ▶L C  R   Footnote:

5.5

5

Column Spacing

S ▶M  L  X


F1-Help       F3-Save        F5-Attributes   F7-Size/Place
F2-Draw chart F4-Draw/Annot                                  F10-Continue
```

**Location**   At the Three Columns form, press F7-Size/Place to display the Size/Place overlay.

**Description**   Define the size and placement of the text that appears on the three-column chart. Once you set the desired options, press F7-Size/Place or F10-Continue to return to the Three Columns form.

### Size

**Defaults:** (Vary depending on the line)

Enter a number from .1 to 99.

### Place

**Defaults:** (Vary depending on the line)

Set either L, C, or R to left-justify, center, or right-justify text.

### Column Spacing

**Default:** M (medium)

Set the spacing that should be used between columns: S (small), M (medium), L (large), or X (extra large). Preview the chart by pressing F2-Draw chart to see the effect of your setting.

## Title Chart Form

```
                        Title Chart
                           Top



                          Middle



                          Bottom



F1-Help        F3-Save        F5-Attributes    F7-Size/Place
F2-Draw chart  F4-Draw/Annot                                    F10-Continue
```

**Location**   Select <Create new chart> from the Main Menu followed by <Text> from the Create New Chart menu. Then, at the Text Chart Styles menu, select <Title chart> to display the Title Chart form.

**Description**   The Title chart form contains three areas for entering text: "Top," "Middle," and "Bottom." A typical title chart may contain the title of a presentation or report, the presenter's or author's name and affiliation, and the date.

## Top

**Default:** (Blank)

Enter up to three lines of text to appear at the top of the chart.

## Middle

**Default:** (Blank)

Enter up to three lines of text to appear at the middle of the chart.

## Bottom

**Default:** (Blank)

Enter up to three lines of text to appear at the bottom of the chart.

# Title Chart: Size/Place Overlay

**Location**  At the Title Chart form, press F7-Size/Place to display the Size/Place overlay.

**Description**  Define the size and placement for each line of text on the Title Chart form. Once you set the desired options, press F7-Size/Place or F10-Continue to return to the Title Chart form.

## Size

**Defaults:** (Vary depending on the line)
Enter a number from .1 to 99.

## Place

**Defaults:** (Vary depending on the line)

Set either L, C, or R to left-justify, center, or right-justify text.

```
                    ┌─────────────────── Title Chart ───────────────────┐
                    
       Size    Place    Top
         8     L ►C  R
         8     L ►C  R
         8     L ►C  R
                       Middle
         6     L ►C  R
         6     L ►C  R
         6     L ►C  R
                       Bottom
         4     L ►C  R
         4     L ►C  R
         4     L ►C  R


       F1-Help           F3-Save         F5-Attributes   F7-Size/Place
       F2-Draw chart     F4-Draw/Annot                                   F10-Continue
```

## Titles & Options Forms

Refer to the name of each chart type for a description of the Titles & Options form for that chart type: Area, Bar/Line, or High/Low/Close.

## Transitions Overlay

**Location** On the ScreenShow Effects form, position the cursor in either the "Draw" column or the "Erase" column and press F6-Choices to display this overlay.

**Description** This overlay is used for selecting a display transition for a chart or image in a ScreenShow. To select a transition from this overlay, position the cursor in the "Draw" or "Erase" column on the ScreenShow Effects form at the line corresponding to the desired file to select a transition for either presentation or removal of the image. Then press F6-Choices and highlight a transition in the Transitions overlay. Press ENTER or F10-Continue to select the highlighted transition and return to the ScreenShow Effects form.

**948** Harvard Graphics: The Complete Reference

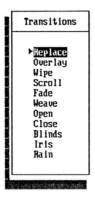

## Two Columns Form

**Location**  Select <Create new chart> from the Main Menu followed by <Text> from the Create New Chart menu. Then at the Text Chart Styles menu, select <Two columns> to display the Two Columns form.

**Description** Enter text for a two-column chart on this form.

### Title, Subtitle, and Footnote
**Default:** (Blank)

Enter a title, subtitle, and/or footnote for your two-column chart.

### Column Headers

Enter the text you want to appear at the tops of the columns on the chart.

### Column Text Area

Enter the text to appear in the columns. If the entries in an entire column are numbers only, the text in that column will be right-justified instead of left-justified.

## Two-Column Chart: Size/Place Overlay

**Location** At the Two Columns form, press F7-Size/Place to display the Size/Place overlay.

**Description** Define the size and placement of the text that appears on the two-column chart. Once you set the desired options, press F7-Size/Place or F10-Continue to return to the Two Columns form.

### Size
**Defaults:** (Vary depending on the line)

Enter a number from .1 to 99.

### Place
**Defaults:** (Vary depending on the line)

Set either L, C, or R to left-justify, center, or right-justify text.

```
Size    Place              Two Columns
 8     L ►C R  Title:
 6     L ►C R  Subtitle:
3.5    ►L C R  Footnote:
─────────────────────────────────────────────
5.5            │                    │
                                    
5                                   
Column Spacing                      
   S ►M  L  X                       
```

```
F1-Help        F3-Save       F5-Attributes   F7-Size/Place
F2-Draw chart  F4-Draw/Annot                              F10-Continue
```

## Column Spacing

**Default:** M (medium)

Set the spacing that should be used between columns: S (small), M (medium), L (large), or X (extra large). Preview the chart by pressing F2-Draw chart to see the effect of your setting.

## X Data Type Menu Overlay

**Location**  Harvard Graphics automatically displays this overlay when you first create a new chart by selecting <Bar/Line>, <Area>, or <High/Low/Close> from the Create New Chart menu. You can also display the X Data Type Menu overlay by pressing F3-Set X type (versions 2.13 and earlier) or F5-Set X type (version 2.3) from the Chart Data form when you want to change your X data type for the chart.

**Description**  This form is used to indicate the type of X data you will be entering for your chart. Harvard Graphics will use the X data type defined on this form to validate the X data entered on the Chart Data form. The X data type you define will also influence, to some degree,

```
              X Data Type Menu
  Name      Day       Week      Month     Quarter   Year
  Month/Day Month/Yr  Qtr/Yr    Time      Number

  X data type:    Name

  Starting with:              Ending with:
  Increment:
```

what type of chart you can create. Once you select your X data type, you have two choices. The first is to continue to the Chart Data form by pressing F10-Continue and enter your data. If you set the "X data type" option to Name, this is your only choice.

If your "X data type" is any type other than Name, you may be able to take advantage of Harvard Graphics' ability to automatically enter your X data into the "X Axis" column of the Chart Data form. You do this by specifying "Starting with," "Ending with," and "Increment" settings on the X Data Type Menu overlay. Harvard Graphics will then automatically enter your X data beginning with the "Starting with" value, ending with the "Ending with" value, and incrementing by the "Increment" value you specify on this overlay.

## X data type

**Default:** Name

Select the type of your X data. There are 11 X data types in Harvard Graphics.

## Starting with

**Default:** (Blank)

If your X data constitute a predictable series, and your X data type is not Name, set "Starting with" to the first X data value in the series.

## Ending with

**Default:** (Blank)

If your X data constitute a predictable series, and your X data type is not Name, set "Ending with" to the last X data value in the series.

**Increment**

**Default:** (Blank)

If you are using the "Starting with" and "Ending with" options, you can use "Increment" to cause your X data series to increment in units other than one. Enter an integer if your X data are any type other than Number. When your X data are of the type Number, you can enter any real number, including fractions.

## Function Keys

This section of the chapter provides you with a quick reference to all of the function keys available in Harvard Graphics. Each reference includes the location within Harvard Graphics where the particular function key is available as well as a brief description of the function key's usage. When a function key is only available within a particular version of Harvard Graphics, this is noted beside the function key name. For more details about each of these function keys, see the index of this book for the pages on which either the function key itself is described or for the Harvard Graphics feature within which the function key is available.

### F1-Help

**Location**  F1-Help is available from any screen in Harvard Graphics.

**Description**  Press F1-Help to display Harvard Graphics' on-line help screen. The help information is context-specific. If there is more information than can fit on one screen, Harvard Graphics will prompt you to press PGDN. Press ESC to exit help and return to the screen from which you pressed F1-Help.

### F2-Draw chart (individual charts)

**Location**  F2-Draw chart is available from the Main Menu, chart forms, options forms, and Draw/Annotate.

**Description**  Press F2-Draw chart to have Harvard Graphics draw the current chart on the screen. If there is no current chart, a blank screen appears. Press any key to return to the previous screen.

## F2-Draw chart (multiple charts)

**Location**  F2-Draw chart for multiple charts is available from the Edit Multiple Chart form.

**Description**  Press F2-Draw chart to display the current multiple chart. Press any key to return to the Edit Multiple Chart form.

## F2-Preview

**Location**  F2-Preview is available from the Produce Output menu.

**Description**  Press F2-Preview before you print, plot, or record your chart to see Harvard Graphics' best approximation of how the chart will look when it is output. The quality of the preview, however, depends on your monitor type. A monitor with a higher resolution will show a more accurate chart image than will a monitor with a lower resolution. In addition, if you are previewing your chart on a CGA or monochrome monitor, your chart will only appear in black and white.

If you are displaying your chart on an EGA or VGA color monitor, your chart colors will reflect the current color palette settings for your screen, with the exception of a reversal of black and white. These preview colors may or may not match those used in your color output device. Once you are done previewing your chart, press any key to return to the previous screen.

Note that F2-Preview will show the black-white translation used for output devices and, thus, differs from the F2-Draw chart display. Only two background colors are used in F2-Preview (black and white). If you have used a background color other than black or white on your chart, the correct background color will be output if your output device can support the colored background.

In addition, F2-Preview may not accurately display the exact location of drawings added to charts. If precise placement of your drawings is critical, you should rely on output rather than F2-Preview to determine if the placement of drawings is acceptable.

## F2-Preview show

**Location**  F2-Preview show is available from the ScreenShow Effects form.

**Description**  Press F2-Preview show to begin displaying your Screen-Show. If the cursor is on a row corresponding to one of the files in your ScreenShow, the display of your ScreenShow will begin with that file. Press ESC anytime during the ScreenShow to return to the ScreenShow Effects form.

## F2-Show palette

**Location**  F2-Show palette is available from the Color Palette Setup form.

**Description**  F2-Show palette displays the current color palette settings on your screen using the current palette file (with extension .PAL). F2-Show palette is particularly useful for checking any modifications you have made to screen color settings on the Color Palette Setup form.

*Note:*  You must save your current chart before you show your palette or any unsaved changes made to your current chart will be lost.

## F3-Applications (version 2.3)

**Location**  At the Main Menu, press F3-Applications to display the Applications menu.

**Description**  Pressing F3-Applications displays the Applications menu, from which you can select another application to run from Harvard Graphics. This is especially useful when you are importing from or exporting to other applications. Once you have finished with the other application, exit it as you normally would. You will automatically return to Harvard Graphics.

## F3-CGA palette

**Location** F3-CGA palette is available from the Color Palette Setup form when the "Screen" option on the Screen Setup form is set to CGA color.

**Description** Press F3-CGA palette to display the CGA Color Palette overlay to define the colors Harvard Graphics will use to display charts using a CGA card and monitor.

## F3-Change dir

**Location** F3-Change dir is available from the following forms: Select Template, Select Chartbook, Select Symbol, Select Slideshow, Edit Multiple Chart, Select CGM Metafile, Select Chart, Select File, Select Worksheet, and Select Palette.

**Description** Press F3-Change dir to display the Select Directory form in order to select a directory other than the current directory.

## F3-Gallery (version 2.3)

**Location** F3-Gallery is available from any screen in the Chart Gallery, with the exception of the initial screen.

**Description** Press F3-Gallery to display the previous screen in the Chart Gallery.

## F3-Intl formats (version 2.3)

**Location** To set international formats for the current chart, press F8-Options at the Main Menu to display the Current Chart Options overlay. Then press F3-Intl formats to display the Current International Settings overlay. To set default international formats, select <Defaults> from the Setup menu to display the Default Settings form. Then press F3-Intl formats to display the Default International Settings overlay.

**Description**   Press F3-Intl formats from either of the locations described to display either the Default International Settings overlay or the Current International Settings overlay. These overlays contain identical options. Use the Default Chart Settings overlay to specify international format settings to be used as defaults and the Current Chart Settings overlay to specify settings for the current chart. Refer to "Default International Settings Overlay" and "Current International Settings Overlay" for more information.

## F3-Save (version 2.3)

**Location**   F3-Save is available from any chart form.

**Description**   Press F3-Save to display the Save Chart overlay when you want to save a copy of the current chart. Once you complete the Save Chart overlay and press F10-Continue to save your chart, the overlay will be removed and you will return to the chart form.

## F3-Select files

**Location**   F3-Select files is available from any Select Directory form.

**Description**   Press F3-Select files to return to the Select File form from the Select Directory form in order to select a file from the current directory.

## F3-Set X type (versions 2.13 and earlier)

For version 2.3, see F5-Set X type.

**Location**   F3-Set X type is available from the Area, Bar/Line, and High/Low/Close Chart Data forms.

**Description**   Press F3-Set X type to display the X Data Type Menu overlay in order to change your X data type or to specify minimum, maximum, and increment values for automatic X data entry on the Area, Bar/Line, and High/Low/Close Chart Data forms.

## F3-XY position

**Location**   F3-XY position is available from the Size/Place screen for sizing and placing charts displayed when you press F7-Size/Place from the Main Menu.

**Description**   Press F3-XY position to directly enter the horizontal and/or vertical coordinates of where you want Harvard Graphics to move the cursor in the Size/Place screen.

## F4-Calculate (versions 2.13 and earlier)

For version 2.3, see F6-Calculate

**Location**   F4-Calculate is available from the Area, Bar, and High/Low/Close Chart Data forms. Position the cursor in the series column in which you want to perform a calculation, and press F4-Calculate to display the Calculate overlay.

**Description**   Enter the calculation at the "Calculation" option. Press F10-Continue or ENTER to perform the calculation and return to the Chart Data form.

You can find more information on performing calculations on data in "Using Calculations" in Chapter 6 "XY Charts."

## F4-Clear ranges

**Location**   F4-Clear ranges is available from the Import Excel Data form (version 2.3) or the Import Lotus Data form.

**Description**   Use F4-Clear ranges to erase all data on the Import Excel Data form (version 2.3) or the Import Lotus Data form. You typically do this when you want to enter new legends, cell addresses, or range names.

## F4-Draw/Annot (version 2.3)

**Location**   F4-Draw/Annot is available from any chart form.

**Description**   Press F4-Draw/Annot to move to Draw/Annotate from the chart form. Once you do so, you will see the Draw menu with the current chart displayed in the drawing area of the Draw/Annotate screen. When you are finished adding drawings or symbols to your current chart, press ESC and you will return to the chart form.

## F4-Redraw

**Location**   F4-Redraw is available from the Draw/Annotate screen.

**Description**   Press F4-Redraw to update the image in the drawing area so it includes all modifications made to it.

## F4-Reselect

**Location**   F4-Reselect is available from the Import ASCII Data form.

**Description**   Use F4-Reselect to reset the column settings when importing tabular ASCII data. When you press F4-Reselect, any changes you have made to the size and/or selection of the columns in a tabular ASCII file using F8-Options will be cancelled.

## F4-Spell check

**Location**   F4-Spell check is available from the Main Menu and the Slide Show menu (when a slide show is current).

**Description**   Press F4-Spell check to use Harvard Graphics' spelling checker to spell check the text in your current chart or the text in all the charts in your current slide show (when you press F4-Spell Check from the Slide Show menu). Harvard Graphics will check your text for incorrect spelling, punctuation, capitalization, and numerical formats, and for repeated words. This spell checking includes text that was added using Draw/Annotate.

If Harvard Graphics does not recognize a word or format, it displays the questioned word or format and waits for you to indicate a course of action. You can select from the alternatives: Word ok, continue, Add to dictionary, and Type correction. Additionally, Harvard Graphics may suggest one or more words that are in the dictionary as possible correct spellings for the unrecognized word. Continue with the spell check by positioning the cursor at one of the three alternatives or one of the suggested words and pressing ENTER. You can terminate spell checking at any time by pressing ESC. Once Harvard Graphics is through spell checking the text in your chart or charts, the message "Spell check complete" is displayed. Press any key to continue.

If you are spell checking the charts in a slide show, and you make corrections to the spelling of the text in a chart, Harvard Graphics will ask if you want to save the chart before continuing on to the next chart. (Harvard Graphics does not check the spelling of files other than chart files.) Press F10-Continue to save the chart with the corrections or ESC if you do not want to save the corrections you made.

## F5-Attributes

**Location**   F5-Attributes is available for text charts from the chart form specific to the style of text chart. For pie and XY charts, it is on the Titles & Options form specific to the style of the data chart. In Draw/Annotate, it is available when you add any text objects or when you modify text options when the Text Options form is displayed.

**Description**   Press F5-Attributes to display the Text Attributes overlay in order to modify text attributes. You can modify attributes of the chart's title, subtitle, and/or footnote text in all styles of Harvard Graphics charts. For text charts, you can also modify attributes for any additional text added to the chart. In pie charts, you can also modify the attributes of pie titles. For XY charts, you can also modify attributes of axes' labels and data values. In Draw/Annotate, press F5-Attributes to change the attributes of text while entering text or modifying the options of text.

Before you define text attributes, you must first move the cursor to the left-most character of the text whose attributes you want to set. Then press F5-Attributes to highlight the character at the cursor and display the Text Attributes overlay (if you press SHIFT-F5 instead, the entire line at the cursor is highlighted). Use the RIGHT arrow key to highlight additional text to the right of the originally highlighted character. Use the DOWN arrow key to highlight additional lines of text.

When you have highlighted the text you want to modify the attributes of, press TAB to move to the desired option on the Text Attributes overlay. Press the SPACEBAR to toggle the option either On or Off for the "Fill," "Bold," and "Underline" options. At the "Color" option, either press the SPACEBAR until the desired color number is displayed, or press F6-Colors and select a color from the Color Selection overlay. Once you set the desired attribute options, press F10-Continue to return to the previous form.

## F5-Prev palette (version 2.3)

**Location**   F5-Prev palette is available from the Chart Gallery.

**Description**   Press F5-Prev palette to display the charts in the Chart Gallery using the preceding palette in the list of 12 consecutive palettes that came with Harvard Graphics. F5-Prev palette is the counterpart of F6-Next palette. See Chapter 16, "Harvard Graphics 2.3 Features" for more information on displaying palettes in the Chart Gallery.

## F5-Set X type (version 2.3)

For versions 2.13 and earlier, see F3-Set X type.

**Location**   F5-Set X type is available from the Area, Bar/Line, and High/Low/Close Chart Data forms.

**Description**   Press F5-Set X type to display the X Data Type Menu overlay in order to change your X data type or to specify minimum, maximum, and increment values for automatic X data entry on the Area, Bar/Line, and High/Low/Close Chart Data forms.

## F6-Calculate (version 2.3)

For versions 2.13 and earlier, see F4-Calculate.

**Location**  In the Area, Bar/Line, and High/Low/Close Chart Data forms, position the cursor in the series column on which you want to perform a calculation and press F6-Calculate to display the Calculate overlay.

**Description**  Enter a calculation at the "Calculation" option. Then press F10-Continue or ENTER to perform the calculation and return to the Chart Data form.

You can find more information on performing calculations on data in "Using Calculations" in Chapter 6.

## F6-Choices (Draw/Annotate)

**Location**  F6-Choices is available on options forms for objects in Draw/Annotate.

**Description**  At all "Color" options, press F6-Choices to display the Color Selection overlay. At all "Pattern" options, press F6-Choices to display a list of patterns. At the "Style" option on the Box Options form, press F6-Choices to display a list of the available box styles. Make your selection from the displayed list by moving the cursor to the desired setting and pressing ENTER. Once you press ENTER, you will return to the previous options form. To return to the options form without selecting a new setting, press ESC.

## F6-Choices (slide show)

**Location**  F6-Choices is available for slide shows from the Screen-Show Effects form.

**Description**  With the cursor in the "Draw" or "Erase" column of the ScreenShow Effects form, press F6-Choices to display the list of possible draw or erase transitions. With the cursor in either of the "Dir" columns, press F6-Choices to display a list of possible transition directions. When a list is displayed, move the cursor to the desired transition or direction and press ENTER to select it. To return to the ScreenShow Effects form without selecting a transition or direction, press ESC.

## F6-Colors

**Location** The cursor must be positioned at a "Color" option on a form. "Color" options that use F6-Colors appear on the Text Attributes form and on Titles & Options forms for data charts.

**Description** Press F6-Colors to display the Color Selection overlay in order to select from a list of 16 colors. Once you highlight the desired color, press F10-Continue or ENTER to select it and return to the previous form. To return without selecting a color, press ESC.

## F6-Next palette (version 2.3)

**Location** F6-Next palette is available from the Chart Gallery.

**Description** Press F6-Next palette to display the charts in the Chart Gallery using the next palette in the list of 12 consecutive palettes that came with Harvard Graphics. F6-Next palette is the counterpart of F5-Prev palette. See Chapter 16, "Harvard Graphics 2.3 Features" for more information on displaying palettes in the Chart Gallery.

## F6-Range names (version 2.3)

**Location** Move the cursor to the "Data Range" column on the Import Lotus Data form or the Import Excel Data form and press F6-Range names.

**Description**   When you press F6-Range names from either of the described locations, Harvard Graphics displays the Range Names overlay. Use named ranges to simplify defining the data you want to import.

If you have not created any range names for the spreadsheet, this overlay will be empty. If you have created range names for the spreadsheet, up to 15 letters of each named range will appear in the overlay. If more named ranges are available than can be displayed at one time, press PGDN and PGUP to display additional range names. Use the UP and DOWN arrow keys to move the cursor to the appropriate range name and press ENTER. Harvard Graphics will automatically copy the name of the selected range into the appropriate option on the Import Lotus Data form or Import Excel Data form. To return without selecting a range name, press ESC.

## F6-Shaded bkgd

**Location**   F6-Shaded bkgd is available from the Color Palette Setup form when the "Film recorder" option on the Film Recorder Setup form is set to a recorder that supports a shaded background.

**Description**   If the film recorder you defined on the Film Recorder Setup form can support a shaded background, F6-Shaded bkgd will appear in the function key banner. Press F6-Shaded bkgd to display the Shaded Background overlay and define the background to be used when you are recording a chart. Enter the color intensities for the top and bottom colors and the number of levels of shading you would like. When at least 50 levels of shading are specified, the background will appear as a continuous transition between the colors defined at the "Top" and "Bottom" options.

## F7-Data

**Location**   F7-Data is available from the Custom Layout Screen (See "F7-Size/Place (Multiple Charts)").

**Description** Press F7-Data to return to the Edit Multiple Chart form. F7-Data is the counterpart to F7-Size/Place for multiple charts. Press F7-Size/Place to display the Custom Layout Screen and F7-Data to return to the Edit Multiple Chart form.

## F7-Size/Place (Individual charts)

**Location** F7-Size/Place is available from the chart forms corresponding to the specific style of text chart, at the Organization Chart form, and at the Titles & Options forms for area, bar/line, high/low/close, or pie charts.

**Description** Press F7-Size/Place to display the Size/Place overlay for the specific type of chart. Define text sizes and placement on your chart in this overlay. For information about the Size/Place overlays, refer to the chart type in this chapter (for example, "Area Chart: Size/Place Overlay").

## F7-Size/Place (Main Menu)

**Location** F7-Size/Place is available from the Main Menu.

**Description** Press F7-Size/Place to display the Size/Place screen. The Size/Place screen permits you to adjust the size and placement of your entire chart on a page.

## F7-Size/Place (multiple charts)

**Location** F7-Size/Place is available from the Edit Multiple Chart form when your multiple chart style is Custom or at the Main Menu when your current chart is a custom multiple chart.

**Description**   Press F7-Size/Place to display the Custom Layout screen to modify the size and location of each chart in a custom multiple chart.

## F8-Data

**Location**   F8-Data is available from the Titles & Options forms for area, bar/line, high/low/close, and pie charts, and at the Org Chart Options form.

**Description**   Press F8-Data to return to the corresponding chart form from the Titles & Options form. F8-Data is the counterpart of F8-Options. You press F8-Options to display the Titles & Options form and F8-Data to return to the chart form.

## F8-Draw

**Location**   F8-Draw is available from Draw/Annotate from the options form for any of the drawing objects (except text) when you are adding an object to the drawing area or modifying the options for an existing object.

**Description**   Once you have made changes on the option form for an object, press F8-Draw to move to the drawing area so you can place the object you are adding or modifying in the drawing area.

## F8-Final mode

**Location**   F8-Final mode is available from the Custom Layout screen for sizing and placing the charts on a custom multiple chart.

**Description** When you are modifying the size and/or placement of charts in a custom multiple chart, press F8-Final mode to show the images of the charts sized and placed on the Custom Layout screen. F8-Final mode is the counterpart to the quick mode view described in "F8-Quick mode."

## F8-HyperShow menu (version 2.3)

For versions 2.13 and earlier, see F8-User Menu.

**Location** F8-HyperShow menu is available from the ScreenShow Effects form.

**Description** Press F8-HyperShow menu to display the HyperShow menu overlay. The HyperShow menu overlay permits you to define go to keys for a ScreenShow, create a HyperShow using on-screen buttons, as well as designate that a ScreenShow repeat continuously.

## F8-Options (Import ASCII Data form)

**Location** F8-Options is available from the Import ASCII Data form.

**Description** Press F8-Options to enter a special mode that permits you to adjust the size of columns being imported in a tabular ASCII data file. While in this mode you can also exclude one or more columns from being imported. To exit this mode, press ESC or F8-Options.

## F8-Options (Main Menu)

**Location** F8-Options is available from the Main Menu.

**Description** Press F8-Options to display the Current Chart Options overlay to modify "Orientation," "Border," "Font," and "Palette file" (version 2.3) settings for your current chart. Once you set options on this form, press F10-Continue to return to the Main Menu. The "Orientation," "Border," and "Font" settings selected on the Current Chart Options overlay will override the default settings used for your current chart only.

## F8-Options (Organization and Data Chart forms)

**Location** F8-Options is available from the Organization Chart form and Chart Data forms for area, bar/line, high/low/close, and pie charts.

**Description** Press F8-Options to display the Titles & Options form specific to your chart type, and set the chart options on this form. For information about the Titles & Options form specific to each chart type, refer to the specific type of chart in this chapter (for example, "Area Chart Titles & Options form"). F8-Options is the counterpart of F8-Data. You press F8-Options to display the Titles & Options form and F8-Data to return to the chart form.

## F8-Quick mode

**Location** F8-Quick mode is available from the Custom Layout screen for sizing and placing the charts on a custom multiple chart.

**Description** When you are modifying the size and/or placement of charts in a custom multiple chart, press F8-Quick mode to have Harvard Graphics display a box for each of the charts on the Custom Layout screen. F8-Quick mode is used to speed the process of sizing and placing the charts in a custom multiple chart since the boxes are drawn much faster than are final charts. F8-Quick mode has no effect on the output of your custom multiple chart. F8-Quick mode is the counterpart to the final mode view discussed previously in "F8-Final mode."

## F8-User menu (versions 2.13 and earlier)

For version 2.3, see "F8-HyperShow menu."

**Location**   F8-User menu is available from the Screenshow Effects form.

**Description**   Press F8-User menu to display the Go To overlay. The Go To overlay permits you to define go to keys for a Screenshow, as well as designate that a Screenshow repeat continuously.

## F9-Edit (version 2.3)

**Location**   F9-Edit is available from the Chart Gallery.

**Description**   In the Chart Gallery, select a chart style from the initial Chart Gallery to display a gallery of charts specific to that style. Then select one of the charts to display it individually in greater detail. At this screen, you can press F9-Edit to move to the chart form for the displayed chart. When you do so, you will see the chart form with the text and data used to create that chart. You can then treat this chart like any Harvard Graphics chart, modifying and saving it, if desired. See also "F10-Edit + Clear."

## F9-More series

**Location**   F9-More series is available from the Area, Bar/Line, High/Low/Close, and Pie Chart Data forms.

**Description**   For area, bar/line, and high/low/close charts, press F9-More series to display additional data columns ("Series 5" through "Series 8") on the Chart Data form. You can enter additional series data in these columns as needed. To return to the original display showing "Series 1" through "Series 4," press F9-More series again.

From the Pie Chart Data form, press F9-More series to advance the series to be displayed to the next series. For example, if Page 1 of the Pie Chart Data form is displaying "Series 1," press F9-More series twice if you want to display "Series 3" as a pie.

## F10-Continue

**Location**  F10-Continue is available from most Harvard Graphics screens.

**Description**  Press F10-Continue to go on to the next Harvard Graphics menu or form.

## F10-Edit + Clear (version 2.3)

**Location**  F10-Edit + Clear is available from the Chart Gallery.

**Description**  In the Chart Gallery, select a chart style from the initial Chart Gallery to display a gallery of charts specific to that style. Then select one the charts to display it individually in greater detail. At this screen, you can press F10-Edit + Clear to move to the chart form for the displayed chart. When you do so, the text and data used to create that chart will be cleared from the chart form although all chart settings will be retained. You can then treat this chart like any Harvard Graphics chart, modifying and saving it, if desired. See also "F9-Edit."

# Draw Partner Forms and Function Keys

This section of the chapter provides you with a quick reference to the forms used in Draw Partner. The forms are listed in alphabetical order. Each reference includes the location within Draw Partner where the particular form is available, as well as a brief description of the form. Then each of the options on the form is described.

## Arc Options Form (Version 2.3)

**Location**   You can move the cursor to the Arc options form by pressing F8-Options while you are adding an arc to the drawing area. If you select <Options> from the Modify menu, the cursor is automatically placed in the Arc options form when you select an arc. When you are through changing the options of your arc, press ESC to return to the previous screen.

**Description** Use the Arc options form to define the characteristics of arc objects in the drawing area. To change a given option, move the cursor to the option and press ENTER. Draw Partner will display a list of possible settings. Move the cursor to the desired setting, and then press ENTER to make the change and return to the Arc options form. To return to the Arc options form without changing the option setting, press ESC.

### Color

Use "Color" to define the color of your arc.

### Style

Use the "Style" option to select one of the four available arc line styles: Solid, Dotted, Dashed, or Thick.

### Arrows

Use the "Arrows" option to select from four different arrow styles: No arrows, Start arrow, End arrow, and Both arrows.

### Closure

When "Closure" is set to Closed, the first and last points of an arc are connected by a straight line.

## Box Options Form

**Location**  You can move the cursor to the Box options form by pressing F8-Options while you are adding a box to the drawing area. If you select <Options> from the Modify menu, the cursor is automatically placed in the Box options form when you select a box. When you are through changing the options of your box, press ESC to return to the previous screen.

**Description**  Use the Box options form to define the characteristics of box objects in the drawing area. To change a given option, move the cursor to the option and press ENTER. To return to the Box options form without changing an option setting, press ESC. For options other than "Size," when you press ENTER Draw Partner will display a list of possible settings. Move the cursor to the desired setting and press ENTER to return to the box options form. For the "Size" option, press ENTER, and then type the size value, from 1 to 100. Press ENTER to apply the new size and return to the Box options form.

*Note:*  Boxes are special objects in Harvard Graphics and Draw Partner. There are two reasons for this. The "Size" option defines the size of the box features in 3D, Shadow, Page, and Caption style boxes. When you change the size of a box, Draw Partner maintains the relative size of the special features.

### Shape

Use "Shape" to define whether your box should be square or rectangular. If you set "Shape" to Square, the sides of your box will be equal in length.

### Box style (version 2.3)

The "Box style" options permit you to select from nine different categories of box style. If you set the style to either 3D, Shadow, Page, or Caption, you will be further asked to identify the direction of the special effect. The combination of these directions and the nine box styles permit you to produce all 21 different box styles supported by Harvard Graphics.

### Size (version 2.3)

Enter a size value, from 1 to 100, to control the size of the following characteristics of boxes: For Frame and Oct frame box styles, "Size" controls the width of the frame. With Rounded boxes, "Size" dictates the roundness of the box corners. If your box is Octagonal, "Size" influences the size of the diagonally cut corners. "Size" also controls the size of the shadow of shadow boxes, the depth of the third-dimension effect in 3D boxes, the size of the folded corner of Page boxes, and the length of the caption point in Caption boxes.

### Outline color

Define the color of the outline of your box with the "Outline color" option.

### Outline style (version 2.3)

Set "Outline style" to the type of box outline you desire: None, Solid, Dotted, Dashed, or Thick.

### Fill color

Use "Fill color" to define the color of your box fill.

### Pattern

The "Pattern" option defines the pattern used for the box fill.

### Shadow color (version 2.3)

The "Shadow color" option is used to define the color of the folded corner of page style boxes, the shadow color of shadow style boxes, and the third dimension in 3D style boxes.

## Button Options Form (Version 2.3)

**Location**   When you want to change the number of an existing button, select <Options> from the Modify menu, and then select a button in the drawing area. Once you do so, Draw Partner displays the Button options form.

**Description**   Use the Button options form to change the number of the selected button for the button that you are adding or modifying. Buttons are used for the Harvard Graphics HyperShow feature. See Chapter 16, "Harvard Graphics 2.3 Features," for information on HyperShows.

### Button number

Enter a number from 1 to 10 (or a special button number) to define a button number for your button. If you set "Button number" to 0, the button will not be active and cannot be used in a HyperShow.

## Circle Options Form

**Location** You can move the cursor to the Circle options form by pressing F8-Options while you are adding a circle to the drawing area. If you select <Options> from the Modify menu, the cursor is automatically placed in the Circle options form when you select a circle. When you are through changing the options of your circle, press ESC to return to the previous screen.

**Description** Use the Circle options form to define the characteristics of circle objects in the drawing area. To change a given option, move the cursor to that option and press ENTER. Draw Partner will display a list of possible settings. Move the cursor to the desired setting and press ENTER to return to the Circle options form. To return to the Circle options form without changing the option settings, press ESC.

### Shape

When "Shape" is set to Circular, the resulting object will be a true circle. Set "Shape" to Elliptical to create an ellipse.

### Outline color

Define the color of the outline of your circle with the "Outline color" option.

### Outline style (version 2.3)

Set "Outline style" to the type of circle outline you desire: None, Solid, Dotted, Dashed, or Thick.

### Fill color

Use "Fill color" to define the color of your circle's center.

### Pattern

The "Pattern" option defines the pattern used for the circle's center.

## Circular Text Options Form

**Location**  You can move the cursor to the Circular text options form by pressing F8-Options while you are adding circular text to the drawing area. If you select <Options> from the Modify menu, the cursor is automatically placed in the Circular text options form when you select a circular text object. When you are through changing the options of your circular text, press ESC to return to the previous screen.

**Description**  Use the Circular text options form to define the characteristics of circular text objects in the drawing area. To change a given option, move the cursor to that option and press ENTER. To return to the Circular text options form without changing an option setting, press ESC. For options other than "Size," when you press ENTER Draw Partner will display a list of possible settings. Move the cursor to the desired setting and press ENTER to return to the Circular text options form. For the "Height" option, press ENTER, and then type the height value, from 1 to 100. Press ENTER to apply the height and return to the Circular text options form.

### Size

Use "Size" to set the size of your text. The value you enter for the "Size" option is a percentage of the chart height.

### Color

Use "Color" to choose the color for your circular text.

### Weight (version 2.3)

Select from three text weight settings: Light, Hollow bold, and Solid bold. Some fonts, such as Script, do not support all three settings. See Appendix D, "Harvard Graphics Tables," for more information.

### Italic (version 2.3)

If you want to produce text in an italic font, set "Italic" to Italic. Otherwise, set "Italic" to None.

### Drop shadow

If you want to add a drop shadow effect to your circular text, select one of the eight drop shadow settings. If you do not want a drop shadow applied to your text, set "Drop shadow" to No shadow.

### Shadow color

When you select a drop shadow effect other than No shadow, use the "Shadow color" option to define the color of the drop shadow.

### Font

In version 2.3 choose one of the seven available fonts for your circular text. In version 1.0, use "Font" to select the font style: Light, Bold, Italic light, or Italic bold.

## Freehand Options Form (Version 2.3)

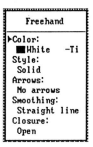

**Location**  You can move the cursor to the Freehand options form by pressing F8-Options while you are adding a freehand object to the drawing area. If you select <Options> from the Modify menu, the cursor is automatically placed in the Freehand options form when you select a freehand object. When you are through changing the options of your freehand object, press ESC to return to the previous screen.

**Description**  Use the Freehand options form to define the characteristics of freehand objects in the drawing area. To change a given option, move the cursor to that option and press ENTER. Draw Partner will display a list of possible settings. Move the cursor to the desired setting and press ENTER to make the change and return to the Freehand options form. To return to the Freehand options form without changing the option setting, press ESC.

### Color

Use "Color" to define the color of your freehand drawing.

### Style

Use the "Style" option to select one of the four available line styles: Solid, Dotted, Dashed, or Thick.

### Arrows

Use the "Arrows" option to select from four different arrow styles: No arrows, Start arrow, End arrow, and Both arrows.

### Smoothing

If you want Draw Partner to smooth out your freehand drawing, set "Smoothing" to Curved line. When "Smoothing" is set to Straight line, the points of your freehand drawing are connected with straight lines.

### Closure

When "Closure" is set to Closed, the first and last points of your freehand drawing are connected by a straight line.

## Line Options Form (Version 2.3)

**Location**  You can move the cursor to the Line options form by pressing F8-Options while you are adding a line to the drawing area. If you select <Options> from the Modify menu, the cursor is automatically placed in the Line options form when you select a line. When you are through changing the options of your line, press ESC to return to the previous screen.

**Description**   Use the Line options form to define the characteristics of line objects in the drawing area. To change a given option, move the cursor to that option and press ENTER. To return to the Line options form without changing an option setting, press ESC. For options other than "Size," when you press ENTER Draw Partner will display a list of possible settings. Move the cursor to the desired setting and press ENTER to return to the Line options form. For the "Size" option, press ENTER, and then type the size value, from 1 to 100. Press ENTER to apply the new size and return to the Line options form.

*Note:*   Lines are special objects in Harvard Graphics and Draw Partner. This is because the "Size" option defines the proportion of the arrowhead size (if applied) to the line width. Draw Partner maintains these proportions when you size a line. If you want to modify a line without maintaining these proportions, you must first transform the line into a polygon using the <Convert> selection from the Point Edit menu.

### Size

Enter a size value, from 1 to 100, to specify the width of the line.

### Outline color

Define the color of the outline of your line with the "Outline color" option.

### Outline style

Set "Outline style" to the type of box outline you desire: None, Solid, Dotted, Dashed, or Thick.

### Fill color

Use "Fill color" to define the color of your line fill.

### Pattern

The "Pattern" option defines the pattern used for the line fill.

### Arrows

Use the "Arrows" option to select from four different arrow styles: No arrows, Start arrow, End arrow, and Both arrows. When you include an arrow on your line, the arrowhead will be twice the width of the line, as defined by the "Size" option.

## Options Form (Version 2.3)

**Location**   When you select <Options> from the Modify menu, and then select an object or group of objects, Draw Partner automatically displays the Options form.

**Description**   This form is sensitive to the object or group that you select. In other words, if you select a single object, or group of same objects, the appropriate object's form is displayed. If you select a group of different objects, the Options form is displayed.

To change a given option, move the cursor to that option and press ENTER. Draw Partner will display a list of possible settings. Move the cursor to the desired setting and press ENTER to make the change and return to the Options form. To return to the Options form without changing an option setting, press ESC.

For a description of the options contained on the Options form, refer to the form description in this chapter for the object or objects in the group (for example, "Line Options Form").

## Polygon Options Form

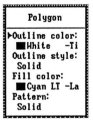

**Location**   You can move the cursor to the Polygon options form by pressing F8-Options while you are adding a polygon to the drawing area. If you select <Options> from the Modify menu, the cursor is automatically placed in the Polygon options form when you select a polygon. When you are through changing the options of your polygon, press ESC to return to the previous screen.

**Description**   Use the Polygon options form to define the characteristics of polygon objects in the drawing area. To change a given option, move the cursor to the option and press ENTER. Draw Partner will display a list of possible settings. Move the cursor to the desired setting and press ENTER to make the change and return to the Polygon options form. To return to the Polygon options form without changing the option setting, press ESC.

### Outline color

Define the color of the outline of your polygon with the "Outline color" option.

### Outline style (version 2.3)

Set "Outline style" to the type of polygon outline you desire: None, Solid, Dotted, Dashed, or Thick.

### Fill color

Use "Fill color" to define the color of your polygon fill.

### Pattern

The "Pattern" option defines the pattern used for the polygon fill.

## Polyline Options Form

**Location**   You can move the cursor to the Polyline options form by pressing F8-Options while you are adding a polyline to the drawing area. If you select <Options> from the Modify menu, the cursor is automatically placed in the Polyline options form when you select a polyline. When you are through changing the options of your polyline, press ESC to return to the previous screen.

**Description**   Use the Polyline options form to define the characteristics of polyline objects in the drawing area. To change a given option, move the cursor to the option and press ENTER. Draw Partner will display a list of possible settings. Move the cursor to the desired setting and press ENTER to make the change and return to the Polyline options form. To return to the Polyline options form without changing the option setting, press ESC.

### Color

Use "Color" to define the color of your polyline.

### Style

Use the "Style" option to select one of the four available line styles: Solid, Dotted, Dashed, or Thick.

### Arrows

Use the "Arrows" option to select from four different arrow styles: No arrows, Start arrow, End arrow, and Both arrows.

### Smoothing

If you want Draw Partner to smooth out your polyline, set "Smoothing" to Curved line. When "Smoothing" is set to Straight line, the points of your polyline are connected by straight lines.

### Closure (version 2.3)

When "Closure" is set to Closed, the first and last points of the polyline are connected by a line. If "Smoothing" is also set to Straight line, this line will be straight. Otherwise it will be curved.

## Regular Polygon Options Form (Version 2.3)

**Location**   You can move the cursor to the Regular polygon options form by pressing F8-Options while you are adding a regular polygon to the drawing area. If you select <Options> from the Modify menu, the cursor is automatically placed in the Regular polygon options form when you select a regular polygon. When you are through changing the options of your regular polygon, press ESC to return to the previous screen.

**Description**   Use the Regular polygon options form to define the characteristics of regular polygon objects in the drawing area. To change a given option, move the cursor to the option and press ENTER. To return to the Regular polygon options form without changing an option setting, press ESC. For options other than "Sides," when you press ENTER, Draw Partner will display a list of possible settings. Move the cursor to the desired setting and press ENTER to return to the regular polygon options form. For the "Sides" option, press ENTER, and then type the number of sides of the regular polygon, from 3 to 200. Press ENTER to apply the new value and return to the Regular polygon options form.

### Outline color

Define the color of the outline of your regular polygon with the "Outline color" option.

### Outline style

Set "Outline style" to the type of regular polygon outline you desire: None, Solid, Dotted, Dashed, or Thick.

### Fill color

Use "Fill color" to define the color of the fill used for the regular polygon.

### Pattern

The "Pattern" option defines the pattern used for the fill.

### Sides

Use the "Sides" option to define the number of sides for the regular polygon, from 3 to 200. Each side in the resulting polygon will be the same length.

## Text Options Form

**Location**  You can move the cursor to the Text options form by pressing F8-Options while you are adding Text to the drawing area. If you select <Options> from the Modify menu, the cursor is automatically placed in the Text options form when you select a text object. When you are through changing the options of your text, press ESC to return to the previous screen.

**Description**  Use the Text options form to define the characteristics of text objects in the drawing area. To change a given option, move the cursor to that option and press ENTER. To return to the Text options form without changing an option setting, press ESC. For options other than "Size," when you press ENTER Draw Partner will display a list of possible settings. Move the cursor to the desired setting and press ENTER to return to the Text options form. For the "Size" option, press ENTER, and then type the size value, from .1 to 99. Press ENTER to apply the height and return to the Text options form.

### Height

Use "Size" to set the size of your font. The value that you enter for the "Size" option is a percentage of the chart height in landscape or chart width in portrait orientation.

### Color

Use "Color" to choose the color for your text.

### Weight (version 2.3)

Select from three text weight settings: Light, Hollow bold, and Solid bold. Note that some fonts, such as Script, do not support all three weight styles.

### Italic (version 2.3)

If you want to produce text in an italic font, set "Italic" to Italic. Otherwise, set "Italic" to None.

### Underline (version 2.3)

If you want to produce underlined text, set "Underline" to Underline. Otherwise, set "Underline" to None.

### Drop shadow

If you want to add a drop shadow effect to your text, select one of the eight drop shadow settings. If you do not want a drop shadow applied to your text, set "Drop shadow" to No shadow.

### Shadow color

When you select a drop shadow effect other than No shadow, use the "Shadow color" option to define the color of the drop shadow.

### Justify

There are two components to the justification of text in the drawing area. The first is the vertical location on the text placement box where the cursor will be placed as you move your text into position. There are four possible positions: Upper, Center, Base, and Lower. Upper will place the cursor at the top of characters such as "t," and "h." Center will place the cursor at the top of characters such as "w" and "n." Selecting Base will position the cursor at the bottom of "n" and "o" characters, while Lower will use the bottom of characters such as "g" and "p."

The second component is the horizontal justification. The three possible positions are Left, Center, and Right. The horizontal justification has two effects. First, it determines the horizontal placement of the cursor on the text placement box while you are moving your text into position. Second, it determines where subsequent lines of text will be placed by default.

**Font**

In version 2.3 choose one of the seven available fonts for your text. In version 1.0, use "Font" to select the font style: Light, Bold, Italic light, or Italic bold.

## Wedge Options Form (Version 2.3)

**Location**  You can move the cursor to the Wedge options form by pressing F8-Options while you are adding a wedge to the drawing area. If you select <Options> from the Modify menu, the cursor is automatically placed in the Wedge options form when you select a wedge. When you are through changing the options of your wedge, press ESC to return to the previous screen.

**Description**     Use the Wedge options form to define the characteristics of Wedge objects in the drawing area. To change a given option, move that cursor to that option and press ENTER. Draw Partner will display a list of possible settings. Move the cursor to the desired setting and press ENTER to make the change and return to the Wedge options form. To return to the Wedge options form without changing the option setting, press ESC.

### Outline color

Define the color of the outline of your wedge with the "Outline color" option.

### Outline style

Set "Outline style" to the type of wedge outline you desire: None, Solid, Dotted, Dashed, or Thick.

### Fill color

Use "Fill color" to define the color of your wedge fill.

### Pattern

The "Pattern" option defines the pattern used for the wedge fill.

## Function Keys

This section of the chapter provides you with a quick reference to all of the function keys available in Draw Partner. Each reference includes the location within Draw Partner where the particular function key is available, as well as a brief description of the key's usage.

## F1-Help

**Location**   F1-Help is available from any screen in Draw Partner.

**Description**   Press F1-Help to display on-line help. Draw Partner's help system contains two levels: a context-sensitive first level and a help list at the second level. Press F1-Help once to display context-sensitive help about the current menu or any currently highlighted menu item. Press PGDN to display the next page of help and PGUP to display the previous page of help. When you are done, press ESC to return to the Draw Partner screen. Alternatively, you can press F1-Help again to display the help list. This list displays general help topics. At the help list, move the cursor to highlight one of the help topics and then press ENTER to display information about the selected topic. To return to the help list after displaying more help information, press F1-Help again. To return directly to the Draw Partner screen, press ESC.

## F2-Preview

**Location**   F2-Preview is available while any Draw Partner menu is active.

**Description**   Press F2-Preview to view the current drawing. When you are finished previewing your drawing, press any key to return to the Draw Partner screen. If you want to cancel the preview before Draw Partner has completed the drawing, press the SPACEBAR.

## F3-Change dir

**Location**   F3-Change dir is available from the File screen

**Description**   Press F3-Change dir to display the Select Directory screen in order to select a directory other than the current directory.

## F4-Redraw

**Location**   F4-Redraw is available from any Draw Partner screen if the Automatic Redraw feature is set to "When requested."

**Description**   Press F4-Redraw to update the current image of your drawing. See "Setting the Automatic Redraw" in Chapter 17.

## F5-Mouse speed

**Location**   F5-Mouse speed is available from the Draw Partner Main Menu.

**Description**   Mouse speed refers to the speed with which the cursor responds to the movements of the mouse. If you want the cursor to be very sensitive to mouse movements, increase the mouse speed using F5-Mouse speed. When you press F5-Mouse speed, Draw Partner displays the message "Enter new mouse speed (Slow=0, Fast=100, Current=*current*), Esc—no change" at the message line of the function key banner. Enter a value from 0 to 100 to change the speed of your mouse. Press ESC to return to the Draw Partner screen.

## F6-Choices

**Location**   F6-Choices is available with the cursor positioned at an option on any of the options forms for objects.

**Description**   Press F6-Choices (or ENTER) to display a list of available settings for the option the cursor is positioned at. Move the cursor to highlight a setting on the displayed list. Then press ENTER to select that setting and return to the options form. If you do not want to change the option setting after displaying the list of settings, press ESC once.

## F7-Save

**Location**    F7-Save is available from any menu in Draw Partner when you have a current drawing.

**Description**    Press F7-Save to display the File screen showing the Draw Partner files in the current directory. To replace one of the existing Draw Partner files with your current drawing, move the cursor to select the existing filename and press ENTER. If you want to save the current drawing as a new file, select "New File" and press ENTER. Draw Partner displays the message "Enter new filename." Enter a new name for the file and press ENTER. If the filename already exists, Draw Partner will display the message "This file exists—do you want to replace it?" Select <Replace> from the displayed menu to replace the existing file with the current drawing, or select <Quit> to cancel saving the drawing. Once you successfully save the drawing or select <Quit>, Draw Partner will return to the previous screen.

If you want to save the file to a directory other than the current directory, you must change directories first. See "F3-Change dir" for details.

*Note:*    Pressing F7-Save is equivalent to selecting <Save drawing> from the File menu. Both display the File screen. However, once you press ENTER to save your drawing, you will return to the previous screen if you originally pressed F7-Save, or to the File menu if you originally selected <Save drawing>.

## F8-Options

**Location**    F8-Options is available when you are adding an object in the drawing area.

**Description**    Press F8-Options to display the options form specific to the type of object you are adding.

## F8-Draw

**Location**   F8-Draw is available while an options form is displayed.

**Description**   Press F8-Draw to move the cursor from the options form to the drawing area so you can continue adding or modifying your drawing.

## F9-View

**Location**   F9-View is available from any menu in Draw Partner.

**Description**   Press F9-View to display the View menu. (You can also display the View menu by selecting <View> from the Main Menu.) Use this menu to set characteristics of your view of the drawing area, including zooming in on a specific area to get a more detailed view of the objects there, add a grid to the drawing area, set the snap-to-grid feature, or set the automatic redraw feature. See Chapter 17, "Introduction to Draw Partner," for a description of View menu options.

## F10-Continue

**Location**   F10-Continue is available from any Draw Partner screen.

**Description**   Press F10-Continue to continue to the next Draw Partner screen, menu, or form.

# Appendixes

Additional Support for Harvard Graphics
Installation
Harvard Graphics Accessories
Harvard Graphics Tables
Harvard Graphics Menus

# Additional Support for Harvard Graphics

Software Publishing Corporation
Slide Services

## Software Publishing Corporation

Your Harvard Graphics package includes a registration card labeled "Preferred Customer Registration Card." Make sure to mail this card (if you have not done so already) so you will automatically be notified about upgrades to Harvard Graphics, as well as receive information on accessory products.

You can find information on upgrading Harvard Graphics and purchasing accessories from software dealers that carry Harvard Graphics. Alternatively, you can write to

Software Publishing Corporation
1901 Landings Drive
P.O. Box 7210
Mountain View, California 94039-7210

## Slide Services

There are a number of companies, both local and international, that specialize in turning Harvard Graphics charts into slides, transparencies, or other output forms. Some of these companies are able to use the standard Harvard Graphics chart file format (.CHT) or a file format used by one of the many film recorders supported by Harvard Graphics.

For information about slide services and how to prepare your charts for slide or other output, contact a representative from the service that you plan to use.

Probably one of the easiest slide services to use is the Autographix Slide Service, since Harvard Graphics directly supports this service. Your Harvard Graphics package includes a utility called ToAGX that allows you to prepare and deliver an order for slides to an Autographix Service Center in your area, either by modem or in person. For more information on the Autographix Slide Service, refer to the accompanying literature in your Harvard Graphics package or call the Autographix Hotline, 800-548-8558.

# Installation

What Comes with Harvard Graphics?
Equipment Needed
Equipment Options
Making Backup and Working Copies
Installing Version 2.3
Installing Version 2.13 or Earlier on a Hard Disk
Preparing to Run Version 2.3 or Earlier from Two 3 1/2-Inch
    Disk Drives
Installing Draw Partner Version 1.0
Installing the Virtual Device Interface (VDI)
Harvard Graphics and Memory-Resident Programs

This appendix is designed to get you started with Harvard Graphics. It describes the product, the computer equipment you will need to use it, installing Harvard Graphics and Draw Partner onto your computer's hard disk, and installing VDI device drivers.

Installation procedures differ depending on the version of Harvard Graphics you purchased. If you have version 2.13 or earlier, install Harvard Graphics as described in the section "Installing Version 2.13 or Earlier on a Hard Disk." The version 2.13 package included the Draw Partner version 1.0 accessory, which is installed separately. If you have Draw Partner version 1.0, refer also to the section "Installing Draw Partner Version 1.0" for installation instructions.

If you purchased Harvard Graphics 2.3, install it using the INSTALL program, as described later in the section "Installing Version 2.3." Since Draw Partner version 2.3 is integrated with Harvard Graphics 2.3, you do not need to install it separately.

If you plan to run Harvard Graphics on a two-disk drive system, refer to the section "Preparing to Run Version 2.13 or Earlier from Two 3 1/2-Inch Disk Drives."

## What Comes with Harvard Graphics?

The Harvard Graphics package includes a reference manual, registration forms, and a set of Harvard Graphics disks, either in the 3 1/2-inch 720K disk format or the 5 1/4-inch 360K disk format, depending on the package you bought.

## Equipment Needed

You will need the following equipment to run Harvard Graphics:

- An IBM or fully compatible PC, XT, AT, or PS/2.

- DOS version 2.0 or later.

- At least 512K (kilobytes) of RAM (random access memory). If you plan to run Harvard Graphics on a network, use a VDI device, import or export CGM metafiles, or use Harvard Graphics' MACRO program, you will need at least 640K of RAM.

- With Harvard Graphics 2.3, a hard disk is required. With version 2.13 or earlier, a hard disk is strongly recommended, although it is also possible to run Harvard Graphics from two 3 1/2-inch disk drives. A hard disk is required with these versions, however, if you plan to import or export CGM metafiles or use Harvard Graphics' MACRO program or a device that requires a VDI device driver.

- An 80-column monochrome or color monitor.

- A graphics adapter. (Compatible graphics adapters are listed on the back cover of the Harvard Graphics package. Most adapters are compatible.)

## Equipment Options

There are many additions you can make to your basic computer system that will improve or enhance Harvard Graphics' performance or ease of use. These additions are described in the following pages. Keep in mind that some of these equipment options may require you to specifically configure Harvard Graphics to take advantage of the equipment. These configurations are created using Harvard Graphics' Setup feature. See Chapter 3, "Setup and Default Settings" for instructions on setting up Harvard Graphics for your particular equipment configuration.

### Mouse

Harvard Graphics fully supports a mouse. This permits you to use a mouse, in place of the keyboard cursor keys, to move the cursor in Harvard Graphics. If you plan to do a fair amount of drawing with Harvard Graphics (or with Draw Partner), a mouse will improve your productivity considerably. Harvard Graphics automatically senses the presence of a mouse so no configuration is necessary.

### Digital Tablet

A digital tablet can be particularly helpful if you need the freehand drawing capabilities of Draw Partner version 2.3. However, little if any advantage is gained from using a tablet with other features in Harvard Graphics.

### Hard Disk Options

A hard disk is required for Harvard 2.3. For versions 2.13 and earlier, a hard disk system is preferable to a two-disk drive system and will greatly increase your efficiency. Not only will Harvard Graphics operate faster on a hard disk system, it is also less likely that you will be affected by limitations in disk space. No special configuration is necessary to use a hard disk.

## LIM 4.0 Expanded Memory (Version 2.3)

Running other applications from within Harvard Graphics 2.3 is faster when you have at least 600K of expanded memory.

## Monitors

Harvard Graphics charts are most attractive when viewed using either an EGA or VGA color monitor. However, if your sole use of Harvard Graphics is to print, plot, or record charts on film, a CGA or monochrome monitor will suffice.

## Output Devices

Most Harvard Graphics users create charts for the purpose of distributing them to others. To do so you will need an output device such as a printer, plotter, or film recorder. Harvard Graphics supports a wide variety of output devices. In order to use a specific output device, you will need to configure Harvard Graphics for your particular brand and model, as described in Chapter 3, "Setup and Default Settings." Some output devices, such as certain models of printers and film recorders, require additional installation procedures. Refer to your Harvard Graphics manual for installation instructions.

## Making Backup and Working Copies

It is a good idea to make at least one complete set of backups of your original Harvard Graphics disks. You can then keep your original disks in a safe place and use the backup as your working copy of Harvard Graphics. If anything happens to these working copies, you will still have your original Harvard Graphics disks.

Before making the backup copies, you should write protect your original disks so that they are *read-only,* meaning that their contents can be copied but cannot be accidentally erased or written over. (Instructions on how to write protect disks are supplied with diskettes when you buy them.)

When you are making backup copies of Harvard Graphics, be aware that some disks contain subdirectories. You must either explicitly back up any subdirectories or use the DISKCOPY command (DOS version 2.0 or later) or the XCOPY command with the /S argument (DOS version 3.2 or later), to ensure any subdirectories are backed up as well. For information about these DOS commands refer to your DOS manual.

## Installing Version 2.3

If you have an earlier version of Harvard Graphics on your hard disk already, you should remove the old Harvard Graphics program files before you install version 2.3. If you have existing Harvard Graphics chart files (.CHT), template files (.TPL), chartbook files (.CBK), slide show files (.SHW), or symbol files (.SYM) that you want to keep, you should not delete these files, since you will be able to use them in Harvard Graphics 2.3.

Harvard Graphics 2.3 comes with an installation utility that makes installation easier than ever before. Start by placing the disk labeled "Disk 1" into drive A of your computer. Next, go to drive A by typing **A:**. Finally, begin the installation by typing **INSTALL**.

Once you begin the installation process, Harvard Graphics displays a series of screens that act as your guide. One of the first screens you see will instruct you to indicate on which drive you want to install Harvard Graphics. If your hard disk has more than one drive, you will be asked to move your cursor onto the name of the drive where you want to install Harvard Graphics. The next prompt will ask you to indicate the name of the subdirectory where you want to install Harvard Graphics. The subdirectory name **\HG\** will be displayed as a default subdirectory. If you are satisfied with this subdirectory, press ENTER. Otherwise, indicate the name of an alternative subdirectory. If the indicated subdirectory does not exist, the installation utility will create it.

Next you will see the Install Harvard Graphics Main Menu. Use this menu to choose the files you want to install. If you are installing Harvard Graphics for the first time, you will want to choose the first selection, "All files except VDI devices." If you have previously installed Harvard Graphics 2.3, and want to install only a subset of files (such as the tutorial), choose the appropriate menu selection.

Next, the installation will display a list of countries. Use this list to define which country configuration Harvard Graphics should use as defaults when displaying numbers, dates, and times.

Once you have indicated the desired country, the program begins the installation process. This process may take a long time, particularly if you are installing all files. As the installation proceeds, the program will prompt you to insert specific Harvard Graphics disks into drive A of your computer. Make sure that you read the messages thoroughly and insert the appropriate disk. Each disk is clearly labeled, so you should have no difficulty figuring out which disk is being requested.

When the installation is complete, the installation program will display a message to inform you that Harvard Graphics has been installed. Before you run Harvard Graphics, refer to the later section in this appendix, "Adding the Harvard Graphics Directory to Your DOS Path."

## Installing Version 2.13 or Earlier on a Hard Disk

Installing Harvard Graphics version 2.13 or earlier on a hard disk is very straightforward. Harvard Graphics comes with an installation program called INSTALL that copies all the files from your Harvard Graphics disks to a drive and directory on your hard disk. Installation will take five minutes, more or less, depending on the speed of your computer and hard disk.

Since all the INSTALL program does is copy all the files from the Harvard Graphics diskettes to your hard disk, it is also possible to install Harvard Graphics onto your hard disk by using the DOS command COPY (DOS version 1.0 or later) or XCOPY (DOS version 3.2 or later). However, since INSTALL prompts you for each of the Harvard Graphics diskettes, you are more likely to have a successful installation if you use INSTALL.

## Preliminary Steps

Before you install Harvard Graphics, your computer must be turned on and DOS (version 2.0 or later) must be installed on your hard disk. The DOS prompt (most likely C:\>) should be displayed. You will need one complete set of disks, either the originals that came with the Harvard Graphics package or your working copies.

If you have an earlier version of Harvard Graphics on your hard disk already, first remove the old Harvard Graphics program files. You can keep any existing Harvard Graphics chart files (.CHT), template files (.TPL), chartbook files (.CBK), slide show files (.SHW), or symbol files (.SYM), since they can be used with your newer version of Harvard Graphics.

At least 2 megabytes of disk space must be available on your hard disk to install Harvard Graphics. If you do not have this much space, do not run the INSTALL program. You will need to remove some existing files from your hard disk in order to free up enough space before continuing with the installation.

You should store the Harvard Graphics program files in a single directory on your hard disk. You can create this directory yourself or have the INSTALL program do it for you. To create this directory yourself, type **MD HG** at the DOS prompt and press ENTER. This creates a directory called HG, in which you can store the Harvard Graphics programs. If you already have a directory called HG, or you wish to choose another name for the Harvard Graphics directory, substitute the "HG" in these commands with any other valid directory name.

It is also a good idea to create a directory that you will use to store the chart files you create in Harvard Graphics. To do so, type **MD HGDATA** at the DOS prompt and press ENTER. This creates a directory called HGDATA that you can use to store your chart files. As with the HG directory, you can supply any other valid directory name in place of HGDATA.

## Installation Instructions

Use the following steps to install Harvard Graphics on your hard disk.

1. Insert the disk labeled Utilities in drive A. Then type **A:** and press ENTER to move to drive A.

2. Type **INSTALL** and press ENTER. The INSTALL program will begin. You will see the on-screen instruction "Type the drive letter and directory of the DESTINATION disk, then press Enter."

3. Type **C:\HG** and press ENTER. This tells INSTALL to copy the Harvard Graphics program into the directory named HG on the C drive. If you want INSTALL to copy the Harvard Graphics program to a different drive and/or directory, enter the appropriate path information.

4. If the directory HG exists, INSTALL proceeds to the next step. If the directory does not exist, meaning that you did not previously create it using the DOS MD command (or using another make directory utility), INSTALL will ask you whether it should create this directory for you. Type **Y** if you want to create the directory or **N** if you want to terminate the installation. Then press ENTER.

5. INSTALL then copies all the files from the Utilities disk to the HG directory. Once it is finished copying the Utilities disk, you are prompted to insert the next disk, Disk 1 Program. Insert this disk and press ENTER. You will be prompted to insert each of the remaining disks until all the necessary files are copied to your hard disk.

If you want to install Draw Partner at this time, refer to the section "Installing Draw Partner Version 1.0."

### Adding the Harvard Graphics Directory to Your DOS Path

In order to run Harvard Graphics, you need to indicate the directory that contains it. You can do this in one of two ways. First, you can use the DOS PATH command every time you start Harvard Graphics. For example, type

**PATH = C:\HG**

to indicate that the directory HG is on the C drive. Then to start Harvard Graphics, type

**HG**

at the DOS prompt. The drawback to this method is that each time you issue the PATH command, your previously defined path is forgotten. This can cause problems if you try to run other software after Harvard Graphics.

The second and most desirable way is to add the Harvard Graphics directory to the PATH command in an AUTOEXEC.BAT file. (If you do not currently use an AUTOEXEC.BAT file, consult your DOS manual for instructions.) If you do so, you will not have to specify the path for your Harvard Graphics directory every time you want to run the program. For example, in this statement, the directory HG located on drive C is added to the path:

**PATH = C:\DOS;C:\HG**

If you want to run the Harvard Graphics program immediately after making this change to the AUTOEXEC.BAT file, you must reset your computer so that the AUTOEXEC.BAT file can be executed with the new path definition. (See your DOS manual for more information about the PATH command and AUTOEXEC.BAT.) Once the DOS prompt is displayed, type

**HG**

to start Harvard Graphics.

You may want to move to the chart directory before starting Harvard Graphics so that the chart directory will be the current directory. Then any chart files you save will be automatically stored in this directory. To move to the chart directory HGDATA, for example, type **CD HGDATA** and then press ENTER. Then, type **HG** to start Harvard Graphics.

## Preparing to Run Version 2.13 or Earlier from Two 3 1/2-Inch Disk Drives

If you do not have a hard disk attached to your computer, you can start Harvard Graphics version 2.13 or earlier from two 3 1/2-inch disks. With Harvard Graphics 2.3, however, a hard disk is required.

To run Harvard Graphics from two 3 1/2-inch disk drives, you first need to prepare a disk that will store Harvard Graphics font and palette files and the chart files that you create. To do this, follow these steps:

1. Insert the Symbols disk in drive A and a blank formatted disk in drive B.

2. At the DOS prompt, type **COPY A:*.FNT B:** and then press ENTER. This copies the font files to the disk in drive B.

3. Type **COPY A:*.PAL B:** and then press ENTER. This copies the palette files to the disk in drive B.

4. Remove the Symbols disk from drive A (leaving the other disk in drive B) and insert the Program disk.

5. Type **PATH = A:\;B:\** and press ENTER. This puts both A and B drives on your path.

6. Type **B:** to make drive B your default drive so that any files you create are automatically stored on the disk in drive B.

7. To start Harvard Graphics, type **HG** and press ENTER.

In the future, all you will have to do to start Harvard Graphics is to insert the Program disk into drive A and the disk you prepared to store your files into drive B, and then repeat steps 5 through 7.

## Installing Draw Partner Version 1.0

You should store the Draw Partner program files in a single directory on your hard disk. To create a directory called DRAW, for example, type **MD DRAW** at the DOS prompt and press ENTER. If you already have a directory called DRAW, or you wish to choose another name for the Harvard Graphics directory, substitute the "DRAW" in these commands with any other valid directory name.

To install Draw Partner version 1.0, copy the program files to your hard disk as follows:

1. Insert the disk labeled Disk 1 in drive A.

2. Type **CD DRAW** and press ENTER.

3. To copy all the files from Disk 1, type **COPY A:*.*** and press ENTER.

If you used a 3 1/2-inch disk, you are finished installing Draw Partner after completing step 3.

4. For 5 1/4-inch disks, remove the first disk and insert the disk labeled Disk 2 in drive A.

5. Type **COPY A:*.*** and press ENTER to copy all the files from this disk to your hard disk.

## Installing the Virtual Device Interface (VDI)

VDI stands for *virtual device interface*. A VDI is a program that comes with Harvard Graphics that permits you to perform specific tasks Harvard Graphics does not directly support. For instance, Harvard Graphics does not come with a device driver to operate the CalComp ColorMaster printer. (A *driver* is a program that can "talk" to a *device*—a device being a printer, plotter, film recorder, monitor, or other piece of hardware. In other words, a driver lets Harvard Graphics control, or "drive," a specific device.) You can, however, use the specific VDI for the ColorMaster to allow Harvard Graphics to print to this machine. In the same fashion, if you want to export Harvard Graphics charts using the CGM metafile format, you will need to use the VDI for exporting metafiles.

Using a VDI requires some additional preparation on your part. This extra effort, however, is very much worth your while if you need to be able to use a device requiring a VDI or if you need to export metafiles. The point here is that if you do not need to use a VDI, do not go to the effort of installing the VDI programs.

One of the difficulties of VDIs is that these programs are *memory-resident*. This means they occupy precious RAM memory; some VDIs require as much as 100K of your computer's RAM. For this reason you will probably want to load the necessary VDIs only when you are using Harvard Graphics and need the capabilities offered by the VDI. The rest of the time, when the VDI is not needed, you should not have the VDI program loaded into memory. Output devices that require VDIs include:

**Printers**

- AST TurboLaser
- CalComp ColorMaster
- Matrix TT200

**Film Recorders**

- Bell & Howell CDI IV
- Bell & Howell 1080
- Lasergraphics PFR and LFR
- Matrix PCR or Matrix QCR
- PTI Montage

For details on installing the VDI drivers, refer to your Harvard Graphics manual.

## Harvard Graphics and Memory-Resident Programs

You may have problems running some memory-resident programs concurrently with Harvard Graphics. If this happens, you may need to remove the memory-resident program from your system.

# Harvard Graphics Accessories

Harvard Graphics accessories extend the power and utility of Harvard Graphics. They are sold separately from Harvard Graphics by Software Publishing Corporation. There are seven accessories available.

- Business Symbols
- Designer Galleries
- Draw Partner
- Military Symbols
- Quick-Charts
- ScreenShow Utilities
- U.S. MapMaker

Each of these utilities is briefly described next. The remainder of this appendix contains more detailed descriptions of all of these accessories with the exception of Draw Partner. Draw Partner is described in detail in Chapters 17 and 18.

**Business Symbols**  This accessory includes over 300 symbols designed for use in business presentation charts.

**Designer Galleries**  This accessory contains a wide variety of charts and templates you can use to simplify the creation of charts in Harvard Graphics.

**Draw Partner**  Draw Partner is a powerful drawing tool that extends the drawing capabilities of Harvard Graphics's Draw/Annotate. It is sold separately for use with Harvard Graphics versions 2.12 and earlier. Draw Partner is included with Harvard Graphics version 2.13 and integrated in version 2.3.

**Military Symbols**   Like Business Symbols, Military Symbols consists of 200 clip-art symbols for use with Harvard Graphics charts.

**Quick-Charts**   Like Designer Galleries, Quick-Charts contains many ready-to-use charts. Select the chart style that you want, then add your own data.

**ScreenShow Utilities**   ScreenShow Utilities provides three programs that you can use to improve ScreenShow presentations: ShowCopy, ScreenShow Projector, and CAPTURE.

**U.S. MapMaker**   This is a powerful accessory that permits you to create maps of the United States and then save these maps for use in Harvard Graphics charts.

## Using Business Symbols

The Business Symbols accessory consists of 19 Harvard Graphics symbols files (.SYM). Contained in these files are approximately 300 symbols you can add to your Harvard Graphics charts. Furthermore, like the standard Harvard Graphics symbols, you can add to or modify these symbols using Draw/Annotate or Draw Partner. Table C-1 lists the symbol files contained in the Business Symbols accessory.

The Business Symbol package contains one 3 1/2 inch disk and two 5 1/4 inch disks. To install Business Symbols, copy the contents of either the 3 1/2 inch disk or the two 5 1/4 inch disks onto your computer using the DOS COPY command. For example, move to the directory where you want to store the symbols, place a Business Symbols disk in drive A, and then type **COPY A:*.***. If you are using the 5 1/4 inch disks, repeat this sequence for the second disk once the files from the first disk have been copied. For best results, place these symbols in a separate directory. (For more information on the DOS COPY command, refer to your

| Symbol File | Description |
|---|---|
| 3DOBJECT.SYM | Three-dimensional objects |
| BUILD2.SYM | Buildings |
| CHEMICAL.SYM | Chemical and scientific symbols |
| COMMUNIC.SYM | Communications symbols |
| COMPUTER.SYM | Computer symbols |
| ELEMENT.SYM | Atomic elements |
| HUMAN2.SYM | People |
| HUMAN3.SYM | More people |
| MATH.SYM | Mathematical symbols |
| MATH2.SYM | More mathematical symbols |
| MISC2.SYM | Miscellaneous symbols |
| MISC3.SYM | More miscellaneous symbols |
| OFFICE2.SYM | Office symbols |
| OFFICE3.SYM | More office symbols |
| PACKAGE.SYM | Packaging symbols |
| TRAFFIC1.SYM | Traffic signs |
| TRAFFIC2.SYM | More traffic signs |
| TRAFFIC3.SYM | More traffic signs |
| WEATHER.SYM | Weather symbols |

**Table C-1.**   Symbol Files in the Business Symbols Accessory

DOS manual.) Once you have copied all the Business Symbols files to your hard disk, you can access the symbols just as you do any Harvard Graphics symbol. See "Using Symbols" in Chapter 9, "Drawing and Annotating," for more information.

## Designer Galleries

Designer Galleries consists of charts, templates, chartbooks, and ScreenShows that help you simplify chart production. The main ScreenShow in Designer Galleries displays a menu of chart styles. You select the desired chart style from this menu to see examples of those charts. When the chart you want to use is displayed, pressing CTRL-E moves you to that chart's chart form. The options are already set for you. All you do is enter your data.

In addition, for each of the charts displayed in the Designer Galleries ScreenShow, Designer Galleries also supplies you with a template. If you desire, you can use these templates to create the corresponding charts. Furthermore, Designer Galleries contains five chartbooks that organize the Designer Galleries templates based on chart style.

Designer Galleries also contains 12 special palette files called the Designer Palettes. These palettes can be used to add special color to your charts or presentations.

## Installing Designer Galleries

Follow these steps to install Designer Galleries:

1. Create a directory where you will store Designer Galleries. For example, you may want to create a directory called C:\DESIGNER.

2. Insert the first 5 1/4 inch Designer Galleries disk or the 3 1/2 inch disk into drive A, and make drive A current by typing **A:** at the DOS prompt.

3. Type **INSTALL** followed by the name of the directory you created in step 1.

For example, to install Designer Galleries in C:\DESIGNER, type the following command at the DOS prompt:

**INSTALL C:\DESIGNER**

The installation program will take over and install the Designer Galleries files. If you are installing Designer Galleries from 5 1/4 inch disks, the installation program will prompt to you insert the second disk once the files from the first one have been successfully copied to your hard disk.

## Using Designer Galleries

There are three ways to use Designer Galleries with Harvard Graphics. First, you can select the desired chart from a ScreenShow; this is the easiest way to choose a chart from the Designer Galleries. Second, if you know the name of the Designer Galleries chart you want to create, select either the template (no data) or the chart itself using <Get template> or <Get chart> from the Get/Save/Remove menu. Finally, you can select the desired template from one of the five Designer Galleries chartbooks.

To use the Designer Galleries ScreenShow, choose <Select slide show> from the Slide Show menu and select the slide show called GALLERY. The first menu in Designer Galleries displays the different styles of charts you can create. Select from the Designer Gallery menus until the desired chart is displayed. Use the following keys to control the Designer Galleries ScreenShow while it is in process:

| Key | Description |
| --- | --- |
| 1-9 | Select an option from a displayed menu. |
| N | Select the next chart or palette file. |
| P | Select the previous chart or palette file. |
| G | Return to the previous menu. |
| CTRL-E | Edit the currently displayed chart. |
| ESC | Exit the ScreenShow. |

If you are using Designer Galleries with Harvard Graphics versions 2.13 or earlier, you can use selection <8> from the Designer Galleries menu to display Designer Palettes. Once you enter Designer Palettes, you can press N or P to display a given sample chart in any one of 12 different palettes. With Harvard Graphics versions 2.13 or earlier, if you want to use one of these palettes you can use the <Palette> selection from the Setup menu to change the current palette to one of the designer palettes. For Harvard Graphics 2.3, you can set a chart to the desired palette using the "Palette" option on either the Current Chart Options form or the Default Settings form.

With Harvard Graphics 2.3, you can make Designer Galleries your default chart gallery. This way you can display the Designer Galleries charts instead of the default chart gallery. From the Setup menu, select <Defaults> to display the Default settings form. Set the "Gallery directory" option to the directory where Designer Galleries is stored, and set "Gallery filename" to PICK. Then, when you select <From gallery> from the Create New Chart menu, the Designer Galleries charts will be displayed.

*Note:* Do not use GALLERY as the "Gallery filename" option in Harvard Graphics 2.3—it will not work.

With Designer Galleries as the default chart gallery, the normal function key banner for the default chart gallery will not be displayed. However, all the normal chart gallery keys will be active. For instance, use F5-Prev palette and F6-Next palette to switch palettes. You do not need to use Designer Galleries selection <8> to see palette changes. Furthermore, F9-Edit and F10-Edit + clear are also functional.

## Military Symbols

The Military Symbols accessory consists of 15 Harvard Graphics symbol files. Contained in these files are approximately 200 symbols you can add to your Harvard Graphics charts. Furthermore, like all Harvard Graphics symbols, you can add to or modify these symbols using Draw/Annotate or Draw Partner. Table C-2 lists the symbol files contained in the Military Symbols accessory.

The Military Symbols package contains one 3 1/2 inch disk and two 5 1/4 inch disks. To install Military Symbols, copy the contents of either the 3 1/2 inch disk or the two 5 1/4 inch disks onto your hard disk using the DOS COPY command. For example, move to the directory where you want to store the symbols, place a Military Symbols disk in drive A, and then type **COPY A:*.***. If you are using the 5 1/4 inch disks, repeat this sequence for the second disk once the files from the first one have been copied. For best results, place these symbols in a separate directory. (For more information on the DOS COPY command, refer to your DOS manual.)

Once you have copied all the Military Symbols files to your hard disk, you can access these symbols just as you do any Harvard Graphics symbols. See "Using Symbols" in Chapter 9 for more information.

## Quick-Charts

Like Designer Galleries, Quick-Charts contains many ready-to-go charts. Select the predefined chart you want, then add your own data.

| Symbol File | Description |
|---|---|
| BOMBREC.SYM | Bombers and reconnaissance aircraft |
| ELECTRON.SYM | Electronic equipment |
| FIGHTER.SYM | Fighter aircraft |
| FVEHICLE.SYM | Fighting vehicles |
| ICONS.SYM | Military icons |
| SHIP.SYM | Ships and submarines |
| SOLDIER.SYM | Soldiers and helicopters |
| TACTICAL.SYM | Tactical unit symbols |
| TRANSAIR.SYM | Transport aircraft |
| USAF.SYM | Air Force insignia |
| USARMY.SYM | Army insignia |
| USMC.SYM | Marine Corps insignia |
| USNAVY.SYM | Navy insignia |
| VEHICLE.SYM | Land vehicles |
| WEAPON.SYM | Military weapons |

**Table C-2.** Symbol Files in the Military Symbols Accessory

Quick-Charts consists of charts, templates, chartbooks, and ScreenShows to help you simplify chart production. When you display the QCHARTS ScreenShow, a menu of chart styles is displayed. You select from this menu to see examples of a given chart style. When the chart you want to use is displayed, pressing CTRL-E moves you to the chart form for that chart. The options are already set for you. All you do is enter your data.

In addition, for each of the charts displayed in the Quick-Charts ScreenShow, Quick-Charts also supplies you with a template. If you desire, you can use these templates to create the corresponding charts. Furthermore, Quick-Charts contains six chartbooks that organize the templates based on chart type.

## Installing Quick-Charts

Follow these steps to install Quick-Charts:

1. Create a directory where you will store Quick-Charts. For example, you may want to create a directory called C:\QCHARTS.

2. Insert the first 5 1/4 inch Quick-Charts disk or the 3 1/2 inch disk in drive A, and make drive A current by typing **A:** at the DOS prompt.

3. Type **INSTALL** followed by the name of the directory you created in step 1.

For example, to install Quick-Charts on C:\QCHARTS, type the following command at the DOS prompt:

**INSTALL C:\QCHARTS**

The installation program will install the Quick-Charts files. If you are installing Quick-Charts from 5 1/4 inch disks, the installation program will prompt you to insert the second disk once the files on the first one have been successfully copied to your hard disk.

## Using Quick-Charts

There are three ways to use Quick-Charts with Harvard Graphics. First, you can select the desired chart from a ScreenShow. This is often the easiest way to choose a chart from Quick-Charts. Second, if you know the name of the Quick-Charts file you want to create, select either the template (no data) or the chart itself by selecting either <Get template> or <Get chart> from the Get/Save/Remove menu. Lastly, you can select the desired template from one of the six Quick-Charts chartbooks.

To use the Quick-Charts ScreenShow, use the <Select slide show> selection from the Slide Show menu and select the slide show called QCHARTS. Next, select <Display ScreenShow>. Select from the Quick-Charts menus until the desired chart is displayed. Use the following keys during the Quick-Charts ScreenShow to control the display:

| Key | Description |
| --- | --- |
| 1-9 | Select an option from a displayed menu. |
| N | Select the next chart. |
| P | Select the previous chart. |
| G | Return to the previous menu. |

| | |
|---|---|
| CTRL-E | Edit the currently displayed chart. |
| ESC | Exit the ScreenShow. |

With Harvard Graphics 2.3, you can define the QCHARTS slide show as your chart gallery. If you do so, you can display the Quick-Charts charts instead of the default chart gallery. From the Setup form, set the "Gallery directory" option to the directory where Quick-Charts is stored, and set "Gallery filename" to QCHARTS. Then, when you select <From gallery> from the Create New Chart menu, the Quick-Charts ScreenShow will be displayed. Although the function key banner you normally see when using the default chart gallery will not be displayed, all the normal chart gallery keys will be active. For example, you can use F5-Prev palette and F6-Next palette to switch palettes and F9-Edit and F10-Edit + clear to display the chart form for the desired chart.

## ScreenShow Utilities

ScreenShow Utilities is a set of three programs you can use to expand the power of the Harvard Graphics ScreenShow feature. This package includes a screen-capture utility, a utility to copy a slide show from one directory to another (ShowCopy), and a ScreenShow Projector, a utility that allows you to display charts and ScreenShows without Harvard Graphics. ShowCopy is described in full in Chapter 16, "Harvard Graphics 2.3 Features," since it is included with version 2.3. The ScreenShow Projector and the Capture Utility are described next.

### Using the ScreenShow Projector

The ScreenShow projector is a program, called SHOW.EXE, that permits you to display a ScreenShow or Harvard Graphics chart. It is not necessary for a copy of Harvard Graphics to be present in order to use SHOW.EXE. Not only does this make it much easier to transport your ScreenShow (since you do not have to bring a copy of Harvard Graphics), it also permits you to display a chart on a computer that does not already have a copy of Harvard Graphics. And when you use ShowCopy in conjunction with ScreenShow Projector, you can easily make copies of ScreenShows and display them on different computers.

To display a ScreenShow using ScreenShow Projector, enter the following command at the DOS prompt:

**SHOW** *showname*

Here *showname* is the name of your slide show (you do not need to add the extension to your slide show name). For example, to display the slide show called PRESENTS.SHW, enter the following command:

**SHOW PRESENTS**

You can use the optional parameter /E after the SHOW command to cause Harvard Graphics to suppress any error messages that may appear.

To use ScreenShow Projector to display a single chart, enter the name of a chart, including its extension, in place of the slide show name. For example, to display the chart SALES.CHT, enter **SHOW SALES.CHT** at the DOS prompt.

To use ScreenShow Projector, you must have both the SHOW.EXE and the SHOW.OVL files available on your disk. You must copy both of these files to the directory where the ScreenShow is stored. This can be either a floppy disk or hard disk. This way you can transport all the files you need on a single disk. Note, however, that the SHOW.EXE and SHOW.OVL files occupy approximately 280K of disk space.

*Note:* If you have any bit-mapped files in your ScreenShow, you can only display these files on a computer with a graphics adapter compatible with the computer used to generate the files. For example, you cannot display a bit-mapped file created with an EGA adapter on a computer using a CGA monitor and card.

## The CAPTURE Utility

CAPTURE is a program that permits you to capture an image from the computer screen and save it using the .PCX file format. These .PCX files can then be included in ScreenShows for special effects.

*Note:* CAPTURE can only be used with an EGA-compatible monitor. In addition, screen images created using CAPTURE can only be displayed on another computer if it has a graphics adapter and monitor compatible with the system used to perform the capture.

## Using CAPTURE

Installing CAPTURE on your computer is quite simple. Use the DOS COPY command to copy the CAPTURE.EXE file from the ScreenShow Utilities disk into the directory of your choice. For instance, to copy CAPTURE from drive A to the C:\HG directory, place the ScreenShow Utilities disk containing the CAPTURE.EXE file in drive A and type:

**COPY A:\CAPTURE.EXE C:\HG**

Then press ENTER.

To load CAPTURE into memory, move to the directory to which you copied CAPTURE and type **CAPTURE**. CAPTURE is a TSR (terminate, stay resident) program. Once CAPTURE has been loaded, activate it using the PRTSC key on your keyboard. This key is normally used to print the text on your screen to a printer. However, when CAPTURE is loaded, pressing PRTSC causes it to display this menu:

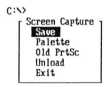

To save the image on screen, select <Save> from the CAPTURE menu. CAPTURE will display the Save Screen overlay:

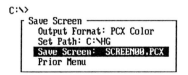

This screen is used to specify the characteristics of the .PCX file. To change the output format of the .PCX file, move the cursor to "Output

Format," and then use the LEFT and RIGHT arrow keys to change the setting. There are three possible output formats: PCX color, PCX BW rev (reverse black and white), and PCX BW norm (normal black and white). The next selection, "Set Path," is used to define the path where the .PCX file will be stored. This path should be the same path where the rest of your ScreenShow files are stored. If it is not, move to the "Set Path" selection and enter the correct path.

The "Save Screen" selection is used to write the screen capture to disk. Move the cursor to "Save Screen" and press ENTER to create a .PCX file. The .PCX file created by CAPTURE is automatically named. The first screen capture is named SCREEN00.PCX, the second is SCREEN01.PCX, and so forth. You cannot change these names from within the CAPTURE program. If you want to rename the captured screen image later, use the DOS RENAME command from the DOS prompt. For instance, to rename the SCREEN00.PCX file to MYFILE.PCX, at the DOS prompt type

   **RENAME SCREEN00.PCX MYFILE.PCX**

Then press ENTER.

The final selection from the Save Screen overlay is "Prior Menu." Highlight "Prior Menu" and then press ENTER to return to the Capture menu.

If you want, you can change the colors of the EGA color palette before you save the .PCX file. To do this, select <Palette> from the Screen Capture menu. CAPTURE displays the Palette menu, shown in Figure C-1. To change a screen color, move the cursor to the row of the Palette menu corresponding to the color you want to change. Use the LEFT and RIGHT arrow keys to change the color number for the EGA display. You can change as many colors as you want using the Palette menu. When you are done, select <Exit>. To return the screen colors back to normal, select <Reset>. Note any colors that you modify using CAPTURE will remained modified after you exit CAPTURE.

Because CAPTURE intercepts a PRTSC keypress, you must use the <Old PrtSc> selection on the Screen Capture menu to print your screen. This selection acts exactly as if you pressed PRTSC without CAPTURE loaded.

To unload CAPTURE from memory, select <Unload>. Note that CAPTURE must be the last program or TSR loaded into memory

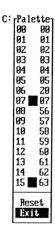

**Figure C-1.**   Palette menu

before you will be able to unload it. For example, if you are using CAPTURE to capture Harvard Graphics screens, you must exit Harvard Graphics before you unload CAPTURE.

To return to your previous screen when you are through using CAPTURE, select <Exit> from the Screen Capture menu.

## U.S. MapMaker Overview

The U.S. MapMaker utility is a powerful accessory that permits you to create maps of the United States and then save these maps as symbols for use in Harvard Graphics charts. U.S. MapMaker can automatically draw the shapes and identify the relative locations of all 50 states, as well as mark the location of over 32,000 cities and towns.

## Installing U.S. MapMaker

Follow these steps to install U.S. MapMaker:

1. Create a directory where you will store U.S. MapMaker. For example, you may want to create a directory called C:\MAP. Make this directory the current directory.

2. Insert the first 5 1/4 inch U.S. MapMaker disk or the 3 1/2 inch disk in drive A.

3. Type **A:\INSTALL**.

4. The installation program will copy all the necessary files into the current directory. At the end of the installation process, you will be asked to indicate whether you have a color or a black-and-white monitor. Indicate your monitor type to complete the installation.

To start U.S. MapMaker after you have installed it, type **USMAP** at the DOS prompt and press ENTER. When you start U.S. MapMaker, you should start from the directory where it is stored.

*Note:* In order to run U.S. MapMaker, you must be able to open at least 15 files simultaneously. This capability is specified in your CONFIG.SYS file using the statement **FILES=15**. If your computer is not configured properly, U.S. MapMaker will display an error message, informing you how to change your CONFIG.SYS file so that the program can run.

## Using U.S. MapMaker

Once you start U.S. MapMaker, you will see the screen shown in Figure C-2. Like the Harvard Graphics Main Menu, this screen contains a menu as well as a function key banner. The following is an overview of how to use U.S. MapMaker.

1. After starting U.S. MapMaker, use the <Add/Edit states> selection or the <Add a group> selection to add states to your map. Indicate the inside and border colors for the added states.

2. If you want to depict city locations on your map, select <Add/Edit cities> or <Add group> to add the desired city locations. For each city you add, indicate the type of symbol to mark the location of the city, the color of the symbol, the text to be placed at the city, and the color of the text.

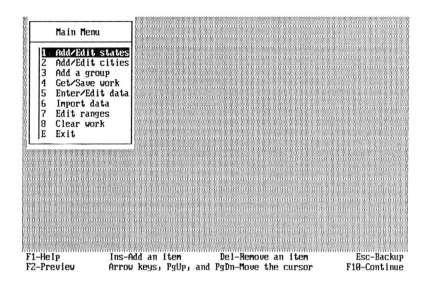

**Figure C-2.**   U.S. MapMaker Main Menu

At this point you can save your map as either a Harvard Graphics symbol (.SYM) or chart (.CHT) file. To do so, continue to step 5.

3. If you want to color code the states in your map on the basis of data ranges, select <Enter/Edit data>. Assign a numeric value to each state.

4. To color code the states by the values added in step 3, select <Edit ranges>. Indicate the maximum value for each range, and identify the inside color, border color, and legend label.

*Note:*   For this color coding to be applied, each state's color must be set to the setting Color code. This is described in more detail in the following sections.

5. Use <Get/Save work> to save your map. You can save your map as a Harvard Graphics symbol (.SYM), chart (.CHT), or in a

special format that can be read by U.S. MapMaker (.MAP). If you save the map using the .MAP format, you can read the map back into U.S. MapMaker at a later time and make changes to the map.

In addition to being able to use U.S. MapMaker as just described, you can import data directly into U.S. MapMaker, edit the ranges, and produce a color-coded map. This is described later in "Importing Data into U.S. MapMaker."

## Adding Cities and States

There are three selections from the U.S. MapMaker Main Menu that permit you to add states and cities to maps. These are <Add/Edit states>, <Add/Edit cities>, and <Add a group>.

To add a state, select <Add/Edit states>. Select from the state list, shown in Figure C-3. When you select a state, U.S. MapMaker will ask you to indicate the inside color and the border color for the state on the form shown in Figure C-4. With the cursor on the "Inside color" or

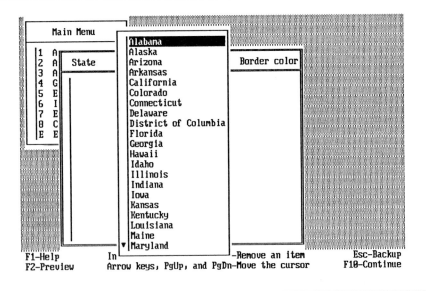

**Figure C-3.** Selecting a state to add to a map

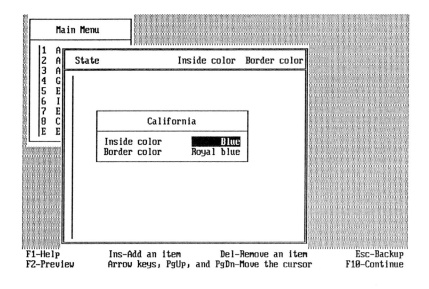

**Figure C-4.** Indicate the colors for the selected state

"Border color" option, press ENTER. U.S. MapMaker will display the color list shown in Figure C-5. Select one of the colors listed. If you select Not drawn, no color will be used. If you select Color code, U.S. MapMaker will use the color coding scheme that you choose when you specify data ranges (as described in "Color Coding Data Ranges").

After selecting the first states, you can use the following keys to continue adding and editing states:

| Key | Description |
| --- | --- |
| ENTER | Change the setting for a state. |
| INS | Add a new state. |
| DEL | Delete a state. |
| UP | Move up one state or option. |
| DOWN | Move down one state or option. |
| PGUP | Move up one screen of states. |
| PGDN | Move down one screen of states. |

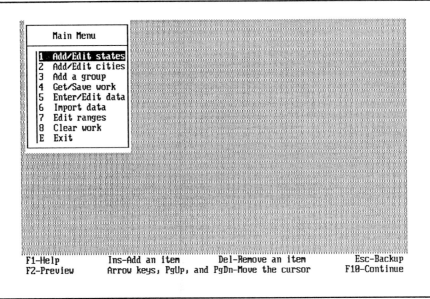

**Figure C-5.** Selecting a color

When you are finished adding states, press ESC to return to the Main Menu.

Adding cities is done in the same fashion. Select <Add/Edit cities> from the Main Menu. At the prompt, enter the city name, or the first two characters of the city name. Press ENTER to display a list of all of the cities that share the entered name or initial characters, as shown in Figure C-6. If the desired city is listed, move the cursor to that city name and press ENTER to add it to the map. If the desired city did not appear in the list, press ESC and try again.

If you add a city that is not located in a state already added, U.S. MapMaker will automatically add the state for you. Thus you do not need to add states before adding cities. However, when U.S. MapMaker adds states, you will need to select <Add/Edit states> to indicate the desired colors for the states.

Once you have added a city, U.S. MapMaker will display the form shown in Figure C-7. Use this form to indicate the label for the city; this label defaults to the city's name. To change the default, move to the

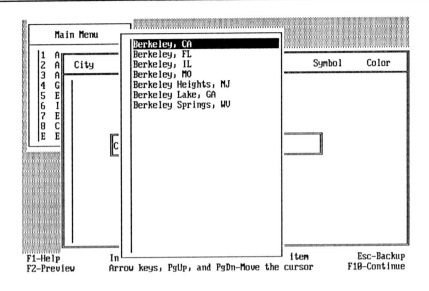

**Figure C-6.**  Indicate the city to add

"Text" option and press ENTER. Edit the label, and then press ENTER again. Use the second option on this form to indicate the color of the label text.

The third and fourth options on this form are used to specify the shape and color of the symbol that marks the location of the city. To change these settings, move the cursor to the desired option and press ENTER. Select a setting from the displayed list and press ENTER to return to the form.

U.S. MapMaker also permits you to add groups of states and/or groups of cities to your map. Select <Add a group> from the Main Menu. U.S. MapMaker will display the list of groups shown in Figure C-8. Select the desired group and fill out the form for the group selected. This group will be added to your list of states and/or cities.

### Editing State and City Lists

Select <Add/Enter states> or <Add/Enter cities>. To add a state or city to the list, move to that state or city name and press INS. To delete a

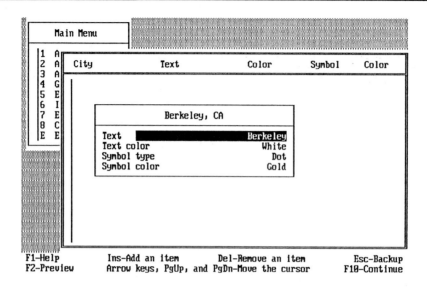

**Figure C-7.**   Indicate the label, colors, and symbols for a city

state or city, press DEL. To change the settings for a city, move to the name and press ENTER. Make changes to the displayed form and press ESC to return to the list.

### Entering Data for States

You can add data in order to color code your states. One way to do this is to import the data; this is covered in the next section. You can also enter or edit data without importing by selecting <Enter/Edit data>. When you do so, U.S. MapMaker displays a list of each of the states in your map followed by a 0 (zero). Change this number to the desired value for each state. See the later section "Color Coding Data Ranges" to complete the color coding of each state.

### Importing Data Into U.S. MapMaker

You can import a list of states and the accompanying data value for each state. This permits you to quickly create color-coded maps. In order to

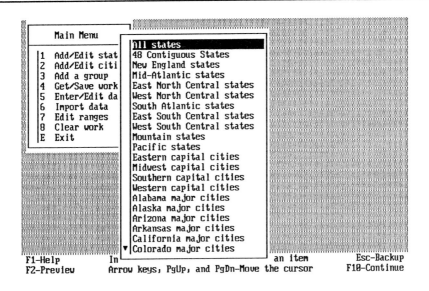

**Figure C-8.**   Groups you can add to a map

import data, your data must be contained in an ASCII text file and must be in the following form: a two-letter state name followed by the numeric value for the state. The state name and state value must be separated by at least one space or a tab character. Only one state may appear on each line.

Once your data are in the correct form, select <Import data>. U.S. MapMaker will display the form shown in Figure C-9. Enter the name of the file that contains your data and press ENTER. U.S. MapMaker will automatically create a state list and data. When you import data, the color for each state will be set to the Color code setting. This prepares your data for color coding. (See the next section.)

After importing the data, you can edit it, if necessary. Figure C-10 displays the Enter/Edit data form after the INCOME.DAT file was imported. INCOME.DAT is a test import file that is part of the U.S. MapMaker package.

*Note:*   Importing data will erase your current map. If you want to save your current map, you must do so before importing data.

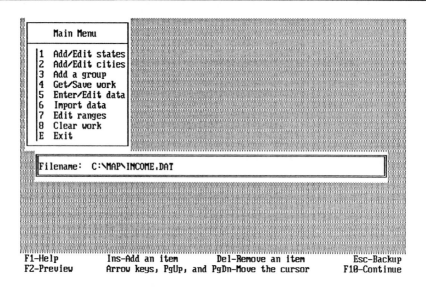

**Figure C-9.**  Specify the filename to import

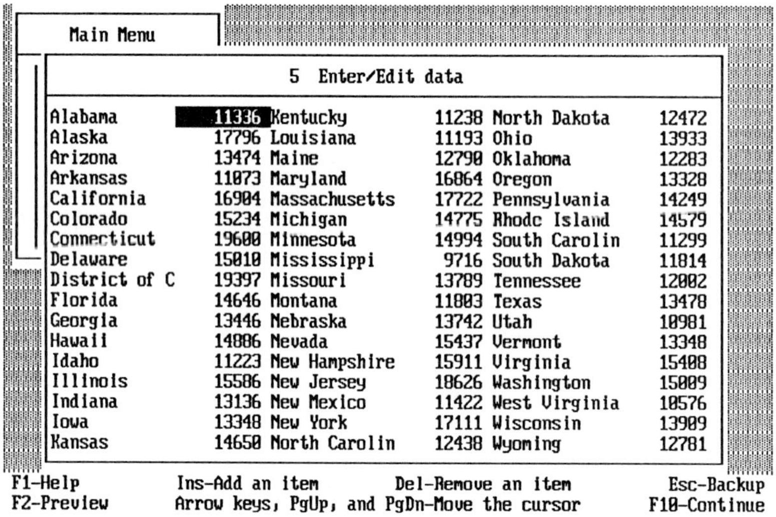

**Figure C-10.**  Enter or edit state data on this form

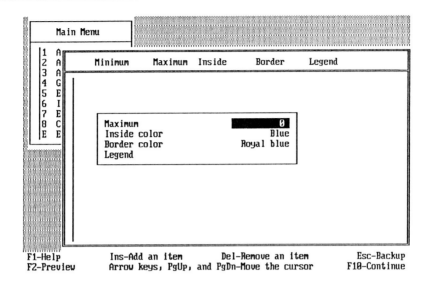

**Figure C-11.**  Specify data ranges for a color-coded map

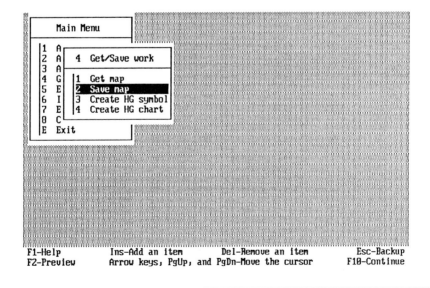

**Figure C-12.**  Get/Save work menu

### Color Coding Data Ranges

Select <Edit ranges>. U.S. MapMaker will display the form shown in Figure C-11. For each range, indicate the maximum value, colors, and legend label. Press ENTER to add the range. U.S. MapMaker will automatically assign a minimum value for each range based on the maximum values for other ranges in your data range list. Press INS to add additional ranges. To delete an existing data range, move the cursor to the data range and press DEL. To edit an existing data range, move the cursor to the desired data range and press ENTER. Press ESC to return to the Main Menu.

### Saving Your Maps

From the Main Menu, select <Get/Save work> to display the Get/Save work menu, shown in Figure C-12. Use <Save map> to save your map using a special U.S. MapMaker file format (.MAP). This is necessary if you want to modify your map sometime in the future. Later, you can use <Get map> to retrieve any maps you have saved using the .MAP format.

The <Create HG symbol> and <Create HG chart> selections permit you to save your map for use with Harvard Graphics charts. When you select <Create HG symbol>, indicate the name of a symbol file to create. Do not enter the name of an existing file or U.S. MapMaker will replace the existing file with your map. Maps saved as symbols can be added to one or more Harvard Graphics charts using Draw/Annotate or Draw Partner. If you simply want to print the map, save it as a Harvard Graphics chart. Then from Harvard Graphics, get the chart using <Get/Save/Remove> and print it using <Produce output>.

# Harvard Graphics Tables

**Fonts and Text Attributes**

## Executive

Fill
No Fill
**Bold Fill**
Bold No Fill
*Italic Fill*
*Italic No Fill*
***Italic Bold Fill***
*Italic Bold No Fill*
<u>Underline Fill</u>
<u>Underline No Fill</u>
<u>**Underline Bold Fill**</u>
<u>Underline Bold No Fill</u>
<u>*Underline Fill Italic*</u>
<u>*Underline No Fill Italic*</u>
<u>***Underline Bold Fill Italic***</u>
<u>*Underline Bold No Fill Italic*</u>

# Traditional

Fill
No Fill
**Bold Fill**
Bold No Fill
*Italic Fill*
*Italic No Fill*
***Italic Bold Fill***
***Italic Bold No Fill***
<u>Underline Fill</u>
<u>Underline No Fill</u>
<u>**Underline Bold Fill**</u>
<u>**Underline Bold No Fill**</u>
<u>*Underline Fill Italic*</u>
<u>*Underline No Fill Italic*</u>
<u>***Underline Bold Fill Italic***</u>
<u>***Underline Bold No Fill Italic***</u>

# Square Serif

Fill
No Fill
**Bold Fill**
Bold No Fill
*Italic Fill*
*Italic No Fill*
***Italic Bold Fill***
*Italic Bold No Fill*
<u>Underline Fill</u>
<u>Underline No Fill</u>
<u>**Underline Bold Fill**</u>
<u>Underline Bold No Fill</u>
<u>*Underline Fill Italic*</u>
<u>*Underline No Fill Italic*</u>
<u>***Underline Bold Fill Italic***</u>
<u>*Underline Bold No Fill Italic*</u>

# Roman

Fill
No Fill
**Bold Fill**
**Bold No Fill**
*Italic Fill*
*Italic No Fill*
***Italic Bold Fill***
***Italic Bold No Fill***
<u>Underline Fill</u>
<u>Underline No Fill</u>
<u>**Underline Bold Fill**</u>
<u>**Underline Bold No Fill**</u>
<u>*Underline Fill Italic*</u>
<u>*Underline No Fill Italic*</u>
<u>***Underline Bold Fill Italic***</u>
<u>***Underline Bold No Fill Italic***</u>

# Sans Serif

Fill
No Fill
**Bold Fill**
**Bold No Fill**
*Italic Fill*
*Italic No Fill*
***Italic Bold Fill***
***Italic Bold No Fill***
<u>Underline Fill</u>
<u>Underline No Fill</u>
<u>**Underline Bold Fill**</u>
<u>**Underline Bold No Fill**</u>
<u>*Underline Fill Italic*</u>
<u>*Underline No Fill Italic*</u>
<u>***Underline Bold Fill Italic***</u>
<u>***Underline Bold No Fill Italic***</u>

# Script

Fill
No Fill
Bold Fill
Bold No Fill
Italic Fill
Italic No Fill
Italic Bold Fill
Italic Bold No Fill
<u>Underline Fill</u>
<u>Underline No Fill</u>
<u>Underline Bold Fill</u>
<u>Underline Bold No Fill</u>
<u>Underline Fill Italic</u>
<u>Underline No Fill Italic</u>
<u>Underline Bold Fill Italic</u>
<u>Underline Bold No Fill Italic</u>

# Gothic

Fill
No Fill
Bold Fill
Bold No Fill
Italic Fill
Italic No Fill
Italic Bold Fill
Italic Bold No Fill
<u>Underline Fill</u>
<u>Underline No Fill</u>
<u>Underline Bold Fill</u>
<u>Underline Bold No Fill</u>
<u>Underline Fill Italic</u>
<u>Underline No Fill Italic</u>
<u>Underline Bold Fill Italic</u>
<u>Underline Bold No Fill Italic</u>

## Text Sizes

5

10

25

50

## International Characters

To add these characters to your chart, hold down the ALT key while typing the three-digit code, then release.

| | | | | | | | |
|---|---|---|---|---|---|---|---|
| ä | 132 | ç | 135 | ñ | 164 | Ü | 154 |
| Ä | 142 | Ç | 128 | Ñ | 165 | ú | 163 |
| á | 160 | ë | 137 | ö | 148 | ù | 151 |
| à | 133 | é | 130 | Ö | 153 | û | 150 |
| â | 131 | É | 144 | ó | 162 | ÿ | 152 |
| å | 134 | è | 138 | ò | 149 | £ | 156 |
| Å | 143 | ï | 139 | ô | 147 | ¡ | 173 |
| æ | 145 | í | 161 | º | 167 | ¿ | 168 |
| Æ | 146 | ì | 141 | ß | 225 | « | 174 |
| ª | 166 | î | 140 | ü | 129 | » | 175 |

## Line Styles

1 ─────────────
2 ─────────────
3 ·············
4 - - - - - - -

## Markers

- ⊡ - 1
- ✚ - 2
- ✳ - 3
- ☐ - 4
- ✕ - 5
- ◇ - 6
- △ - 7
- ⧖ - 8
- ⬡ - 9
- ▽ - 10
- ☆ - 11
- ⊠ - 12
- ✛ - 13

## Screen Patterns

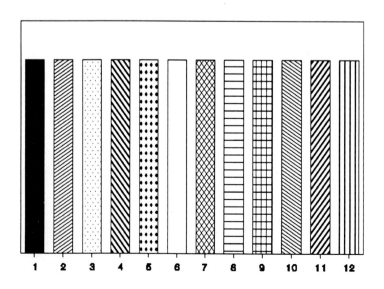

## Printer Patterns (HP LaserJet)

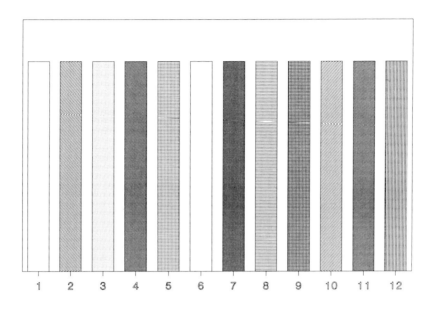

## Printer Patterns (PostScript)

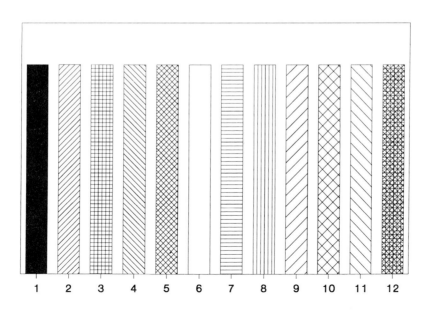

## Grey Scale (Version 2.13 and Earlier)

In version 2.3, grey scale output is determined by the Chart Palette. See Chapter 16 for details.

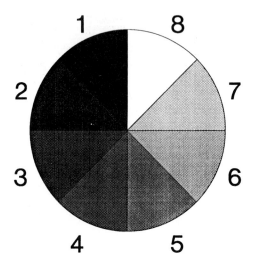

## Symbols

### Symbol Files for Version 2.0

Harvard Graphics version 2.0 comes with 92 predrawn symbols in the following symbol files. For pictures of these symbols, see Appendix G in your Harvard Graphics manual. You can also retrieve a symbol file when you are in either Draw/Annotate or Draw Partner and examine the symbols in the file on your screen.

| Symbol File | Description |
| --- | --- |
| MAP.SYM | Maps |
| FLOWCHAR.SYM | Flowchart symbols |
| BLDGTRAN.SYM | Buildings and transportation vehicles |
| INDUSTRY.SYM | Industrial symbols |
| GENERAL.SYM | Miscellaneous symbols |

### Symbol Files for Versions 2.1 Through 2.13

Harvard Graphics versions 2.1 through 2.13 come with 284 symbols. The names of the files containing these symbols are listed in Table D-1. For pictures of these symbols, see Appendix G in your Harvard Graphics manual. You can also retrieve a symbol file when you are in either Draw/Annotate or Draw Partner and examine the symbols in the file on your screen.

| Symbol File | Description |
| --- | --- |
| ARROWS.SYM | Arrows |
| BUILDING.SYM | Buildings |
| CITIES.SYM | Maps of U.S. and European cities |
| COUNTRY.SYM | Maps of countries |
| CURRENCY.SYM | Currency symbols |
| FLOWCHAR.SYM | Flowchart symbols |
| FOODSPRT.SYM | Foods and sports |
| GREEKLC.SYM | Greek alphabet, lowercase letters |
| GREEKUP.SYM | Greek alphabet, uppercase letters |
| HUMAN.SYM | People |
| INDUSTRY.SYM | Industry symbols |
| MISC.SYM | Miscellaneous symbols |
| OFFICE.SYM | Office symbols |
| PRESENT.SYM | Borders, symbols for presentations |
| STARS.SYM | Stars |
| TRANSPT.SYM | Transportation vehicles |

**Table D-1.** Symbol Files for Version 2.13

| Symbol File | Description |
|---|---|
| ANIMALS.SYM | Animals |
| ANIPLANT.SYM | Animals and plants |
| ARROWS2.SYM | Arrows |
| BORDERS.SYM | Borders |
| BUILD3.SYM | Buildings |
| BUTTONS1.SYM | Buttons |
| BUTTONS2.SYM | Buttons and switches |
| CALENDAR.SYM | Calendar symbols |
| COMNOBJ1.SYM | Common objects |
| COMNOBJ2.SYM | Common objects |
| COMPUTR2.SYM | Computer related objects |
| COMPUTR3.SYM | Computer related objects |
| DPSAMPLE.SYM | Draw Partner bicycle wheel example |
| FLAGS1.SYM | Flags of coutries, A-E |
| FLAGS2.SYM | Flags of coutries, F-Ma |
| FLAGS3.SYM | Flags of coutries, Me-Si |
| FLAGS4.SYM | Flags of coutries, Sp-Z and miscellaneous |
| FLOWCHT.SYM | Flow chart symbols |
| GREEKLC1.SYM | Greek alphabet, lowercase letters |
| GREEKLC2.SYM | Greek alphabet, lowercase letters |
| GREEKUC1.SYM | Greek alphabet, uppercase letters |
| GREEKUC2.SYM | Greek alphabet, uppercase letters |
| HUMANS4.SYM | People |
| HUMANS5.SYM | People |
| INDSTRY1.SYM | Industry symbols |
| INDSTRY2.SYM | Industry symbols |
| MAPS1.SYM | Maps of countries and world |
| MAPS2.SYM | Maps of countries |
| MONEY.SYM | Money and currency symbols |
| OFFICE4.SYM | Office objects |
| PRESENT2.SYM | Presentation symbols |
| PRESENT3.SYM | Presentation symbols |
| SIGNS.SYM | Traffic and information signs |
| TRANSPT1.SYM | Transportation vehicles |
| TRANSPT2.SYM | Transportation vehicles |

**Table D-2.**   Symbol Files for Version 2.3

## Symbol Files for Version 2.3

Harvard Graphics 2.3 comes with over 500 symbols. The names of these symbol files are listed in Table D-2. For pictures of these symbols, see your Harvard Graphics manual. You can also retrieve a symbol file when you are in either Draw/Annotate or Draw Partner and examine the symbols in the file on your screen.

# Animated Sequences (Version 2.3)

| Name of Sequence | What It Displays |
| --- | --- |
| Fireworks | Fireworks over city skyline |
| Hourglass | Sand sifting through hourglass |
| Ratmaze | Rat racing through a maze |
| Shooting ducks | Shooting ducks at a shooting gallery |
| William Tell | Arrows shot at a man with an apple |
| Fish eating fish | Smaller fish being eaten by bigger fish |
| Dartboard | Darts hitting a dart board |
| Fish story | Man describing a fish, which grows |
| Birdman | Man with wings tries to fly, falls |
| Cash register | Cash register rings up sales |

To display the animated sequences, select the slide show called ANIMATOR.SHW and display it. This slide show should be located in the SAMPLES directory, located under the directory where you installed Harvard Graphics.

To use the animated sequences in your own slide show, add the three to seven files from the desired part of ANIMATOR.SHW to your own slide show. To do this, you must copy the files to the directory where your slide show is stored. Remember that once you add these files to your own slide show, you must use the same Draw, Time, Erase, and Dir settings that are defined for these files in the ANIMATOR.SHW show.

To see a list of all of the files and their Draw, Time, Erase, and Dir settings, select ANIMATOR.SHW and then select <ScreenShow effects> from the Slide Show menu.

# Menus

## Harvard Graphics Version 2.1 - 2.13 Menus

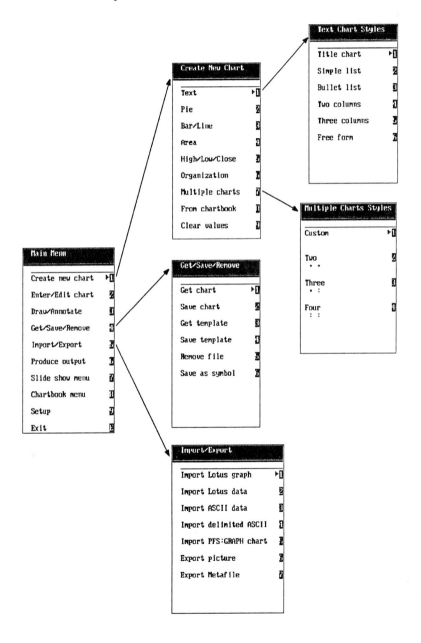

**1052** Harvard Graphics: The Complete Reference

## Harvard Graphics Version 2.1 - 2.13 Menus (continued)

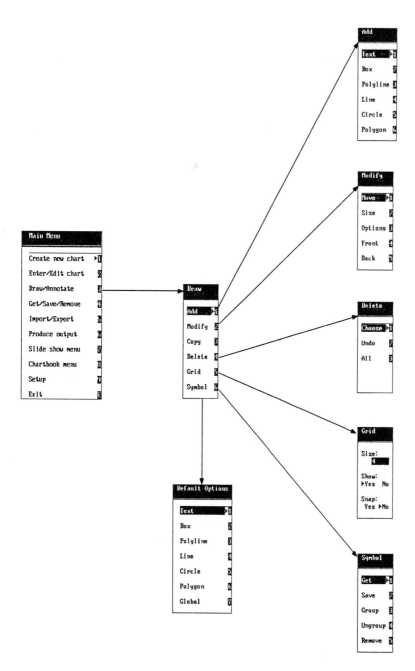

Menus 1053

# Harvard Graphics Version 2.1 - 2.13 Menus (continued)

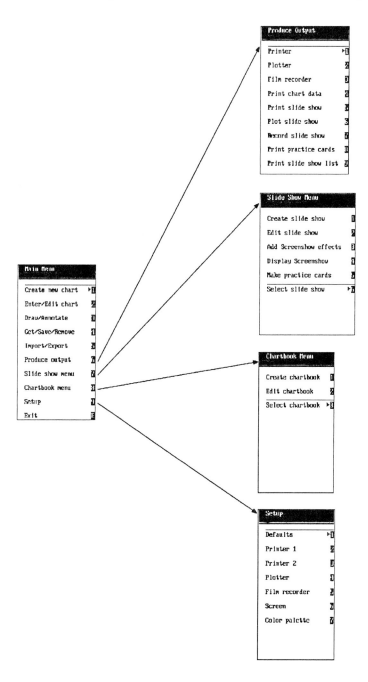

## Harvard Graphics 2.3 Menus

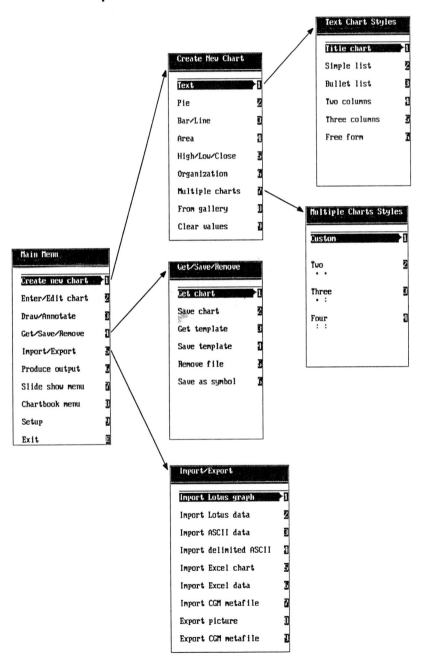

# Harvard Graphics 2.3 Menus (continued)

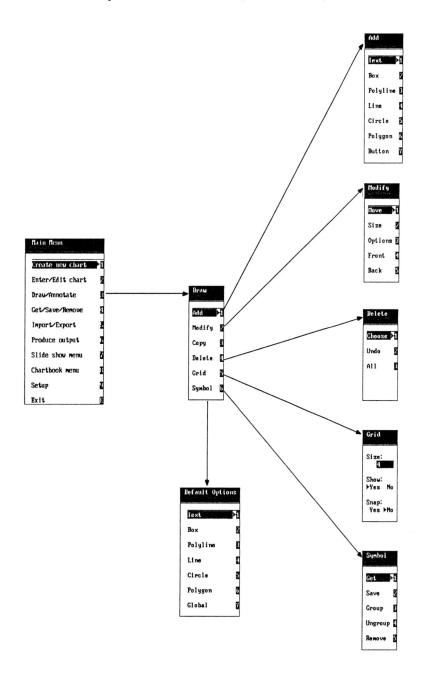

## Harvard Graphics 2.3 Menus (continued)

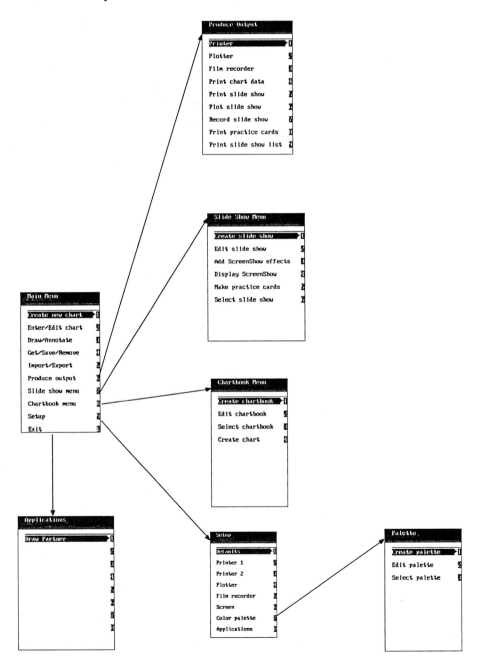

## Draw Partner Version 1.0 Menus

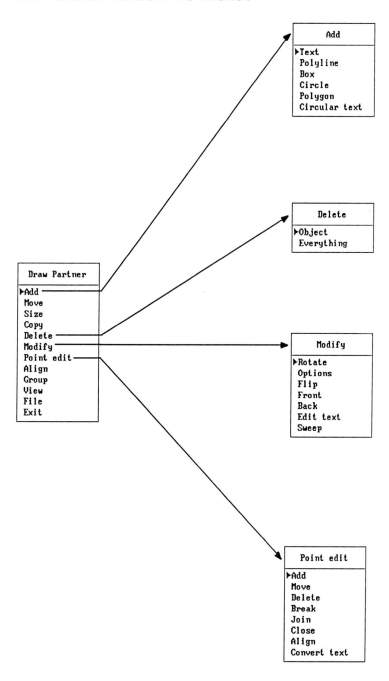

# Draw Partner Version 1.0 Menus (continued)

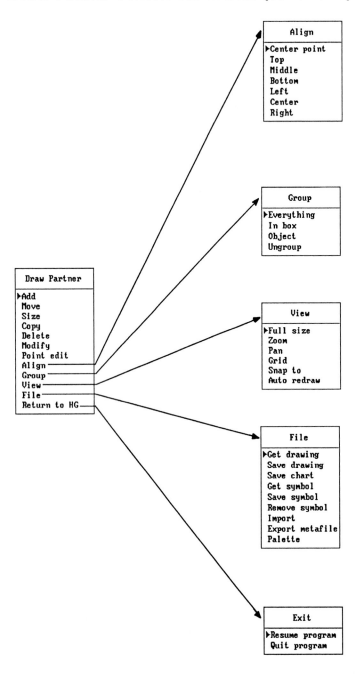

## Draw Partner Version 2.3 Menus

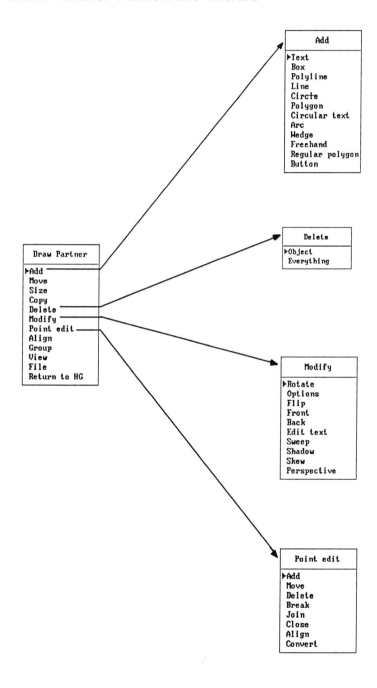

## Draw Partner Version 2.3 Menus (continued)

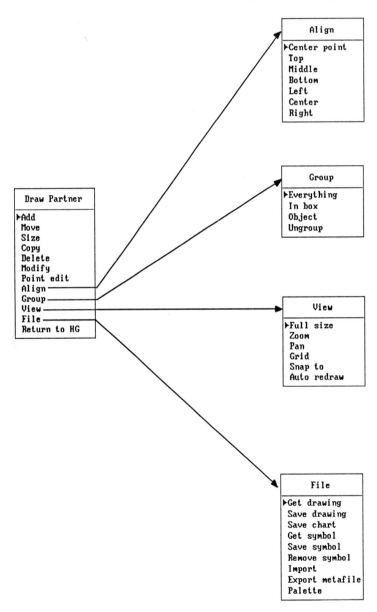

# INDEX

@AVG, 153, 156
@CLR, 153, 154
@COPY, 153, 154, 155
@CUM, 153
@DIFF, 153
@DUP, 153
@EXCH, 153, 154
@MAVG, 153, 696-697
@MAX, 153
@MIN, 153
@MOVE, 154
@PCT, 152, 153
@RECALC, 148, 154
@REDUC, 148, 154, 155, 685-686
@REXP, 154
@RLIN, 154, 688-690
@RLOG, 154
@RPWR, 154
@SUM, 153, 156

## A

Abbreviations in organization charts, 109
Accessories for Harvard Graphics
    Business Symbols, 1011-1013
    Designer Galleries, 1011, 1013-1016
    Draw Partner. *See* Draw Partner
    Military Symbols, 1011-1012, 1016
    Quick-Charts, 1011-1012, 1016-1019
    ScreenShow Utilities, 1011-1012, 1019-1023
    U.S. MapMaker, 1011-1012, 1023-1034
Add menu in Draw/Annotate, 277-279
Aligning
    objects in Draw Partner, 607-610
    points in objects in Draw Partner, 619-620
Animated sequences, 476, 503, 1049
Annotating. *See also* Draw/Annotate and Draw Partner
    defined, 11, 271
Applications
    accessing others from Harvard Graphics, 494, 499
    menu, 494-495, 499, 954-955
    options setup, 497-499, 751-753
    setup, 495-497, 753-755
Arcs
    adding in Draw Partner, 581-582
    options in Draw Partner, 582-583, 971-972
Area Chart Data form, 138-140, 755-756

Area Chart Titles & Options form, 157-158, 177-183, 757-769
Area charts. *See also* XY charts
    defined, 130-131, 167, 667-668. *See also* XY chart
    100%, 131, 171-180, 669, 670
    overlapped, 131, 178-180, 671-672
    Size/Place overlay, 756-757
    stacked, 131, 178, 180, 668-669
    style options, 177-183
    3D (three-dimensional), 179-180
Arithmetic operators, 151-152. *See also* Calculations
Arrows, drawing. *See* Lines
ASCII data
    customizing tabular import, 384-385
    importing, 378-385, 851-853
    importing delimited ASCII, 385-389, 769-770
ASCII Delimiters overlay, 387-388, 769-770
Attributes, text. *See* Text attributes
Auto redraw in Draw Partner, 535, 542, 992
Autographix Slide Service, 495-496, 998
Average, mean, 684-685. *See also* @AVG

## B

Back, moving drawing objects to
    in Draw Partner, 600-601
    in Draw/Annotate, 308
Backing up Harvard Graphics disks, 1002-1003
Band charts. *See also* High/low/close charts
    creating, 184, 663
    defined, 130, 132, 185, 662-663
Bar charts. *See also* XY charts
    clustered, 128, 171-172, 650-651
    defined, 127-128, 166, 648-650
    100% or column, 128, 171, 653-655
    paired, 128, 171, 173, 657-658
    stacked, 128, 171, 651-653
    stepped, 128, 171-172, 655-656
    3D (three-dimensional), 128, 173-174
Bar/Line charts. *See also* XY charts
    Size/Place overlay, 772-773
    style options, 170-172
Bar/Line Chart Data form, 138-140, 770-772
Bar/Line Chart Titles & Options form, 157-158, 773-786
Bold. *See* Text attributes
Border, 52-53, 70-71, 482-483, 819

Boxes
    adding in Draw Partner, 568
    adding in Draw/Annotate, 287
    options in Draw Partner, 568-571, 972-974
    options in Draw/Annotate, 288-291, 786-789
    styles, 789
Breaking objects
    in Draw Partner, 615-616
Buildups in ScreenShows. *See* ScreenShows
Bullet List form, 76, 79, 81, 789-791
Bullet lists, 79, 700
    Size/Place overlay, 791-792
Bullet Shape overlay, 792-793
Bullets
    adding, 90-91, 93, 792-793. *See also* Bullet lists
    adding in Draw/Annotate, 287
    changing, 91-92
    coloring, 92-93
Business Symbols accessory, 1011-1013
Buttons
    options form in Draw Partner, 975
    options form in Draw/Annotate, 793-794
    placing on charts in Draw Partner, 504-505
    placing on charts in Draw/Annotate, 587
    placing on templates, 508-509
    special button numbers, 507-508

## C

Calculate overlay, 794-795, 957-958, 961-962
Calculations
    formulas (XY charts), 148, 151-152
    keywords, 148, 152-155
    order of recalculation, 156-157
    series legends, 149-150
    using, 148-149, 957-958, 961-962
    using arguments in, 155-156
CAPTURE utility, 1020-1023
CGA Color Palette overlay, 795-796
CGM metafiles
    exporting to, 399, 401-402
    importing, 371, 392-395, 521-522, 542-545, 917-918
    saving a drawing as, in Draw Partner, 547-549
Change chart type, 796
    multiple charts, 346-347
    pie chart to XY chart, 244-246

Change chart type (*continued*)
    text charts, 95-96
    XY chart to pie chart, 246
    XY charts, 211-212
Chart box, 273. *See also* Draw/Annotate screen, drawing area
Chart forms (chart data forms)
    area, 138-140, 755-756
    bar/line, 138-140, 770-772
    bullet list, 76, 79, 81, 789-791
    free form, 76, 82, 84, 828-829
    high/low/close, 138-140, 835-836
    organization, 102, 104, 105, 865-866
    pie, 216-221, 874-876
    simple list, 76, 79-80, 935-936
    three columns, 76, 79, 83, 943-944
    title, 945-946
    two columns, 76, 79, 82, 948-949
Chart Gallery
    color palettes, 490-494
    creating chart from, 493-494
    default directory/filename, 817-818
    definition, 489-490
    function keys in, 491, 955, 961, 963, 969, 970
    using, 490-494
Chartbook
    Create/Edit Chartbook form, 362-363, 806-807
    adding templates to, 364
    create, 361-363, 802-803
    creating a chart from a template in a, 368
    default, 817, 818
    defined, 12, 349, 360-361
    modifying, 365-368, 806-807
    selecting, 364-365, 919-920
Charting mistakes
    distortions, 716-723
    illusions, 723-732
    traps, 732-735
Charts. *See also* Organization charts, Pie charts, Text charts, and XY charts
    change chart type. *See* Change chart type
    creating, 33-34
    creating from a template in a chartbook, 368, 932-933
    current chart options, 70-71
    defined, 625-626
    deleting, 39-41
    elements of, 634-647
    film recording, 257-258, 905
    getting, 36-38, 918-919

## Index

Charts (*continued*)
  guidelines for creating data charts, 678-682
  orientation, 51-52
  printing, 250-255, 897-899
  saving, 34-36, 909-910, 956
  saving a drawing as, from Draw Partner, 547-550
  saving as template, 352-354, 910-912
  saving as symbol, 324-327, 907-908
  saving drawings with charts, 272, 551
  selecting, 37
  sizing, 329-330, 957
  spell checking, 41-45
Circles
  adding in Draw Partner, 575-576
  adding in Draw/Annotate, 296-297
  options in Draw Partner, 577, 975-977
  options in Draw/Annotate, 297-298, 797-799
Circular text
  adding in Draw Partner, 578-581
  options in Draw Partner, 581, 977-978
Clear values
  XY charts, 210-211
  organization charts, 121-123
  pie charts, 244
  text charts, 93-94
Closing polylines in Draw Partner, 618
Color
  palettes. *See* Palettes
  text. *See* Text attributes
  use of, considerations, 709-710
Color Palette Setup form, 63-66, 516-517, 799-802. *See also* Palettes
Color Selection overlay, 802, 963
Column charts (table). *See* Two-column charts, Three-column charts
Combination charts, 676
Combining polylines in Draw Partner, 616-618
Computerized presentations. *See* ScreenShows
Converting text, boxes, and lines in Draw Partner, 620-622
Copying drawing objects
  in Draw Partner, 594-595
  in Draw/Annotate, 308-309
Create Chartbook overlay, 361-362, 802-803
Create New Chart menu, 33-34
Create Palette overlay, 515, 803-804
Create Slide Show overlay, 407, 805

Create/Edit Chartbook form, 362-364, 806-807
  adding templates to, 364
  cursor control, 366
  modifying chartbook, 365-368
Create/Edit Multiple Chart form, 334-336
  cursor control on, 336-338
Create/Edit Slide Show form, 408-409, 411-412, 807-809
  cursor control, 411
Creating a new chart, 33-34
Cumulative charts, 205-207, 674-675. *See also* XY charts
Current chart, 31-33
Current chart options, 70-71, 809-810, 967-968
  international settings, 484-487, 810-813
  version 2.3 options, 487-488
Cursor control, 24-26
  editing keys, 27
  movement keys, 25
Custom Layout screen for multiple charts
  cursor control, 343
  placing multiple charts, 341-345, 965-966
  quick mode/final mode, 345-346, 966-968

**D**

Data, 628-634, 683
  average (mean), 684. *See also* @AVG
  frequency counts, 687-688. *See also* @REDUC
  minimum and maximum, 685-687. *See also* @MIN, @MAX
  moving averages, 696-697. *See also* @MAVG
  percentage adjustments, 691-693. *See also* @PCT
  range, 685-687
  regression and regression lines, 688-690. *See also* @REXP, @RLIN, @RLOG, @RPWR
  scientific notation, 200-203, 697-698
  total, sum, 684. *See also* @SUM
  transformations and adjustments, 691-698
  weighting/equalizing, 691
Data charts. *See also* XY charts and Pie charts
  defined, 9, 625-626
  using in documents, considerations, 747-748
  using in presentations, 744-745
Data link, save with template, 358-360, 372-373
Data maps, 676-678. *See also* U.S. MapMaker

Defaults
    change chart settings with a template, 353, 357-358
    default settings, 49-54, 816-819
    default settings version 2.3, 478-483
    international settings, 483-487, 813-815
Delays in macros, 458-460, 819-821. *See also* Macros
Deleting files, 39-41
Deleting drawing objects
    in Draw Partner, 595-596
    in Draw/Annotate, 309-311
Deleting points in drawing objects in Draw Partner, 614-615
Delimited ASCII importing
    defined, 385-387
    defining delimiters, 387-388
    importing series legends, 388-389
Designer Galleries accessory, 1011, 1013-1016
Desktop presentations. *See* ScreenShows
Digital tablet
    using, 25-26, 1001
    using in Draw Partner, 498-499, 559, 753
Dir (direction) of transition in ScreenShows, 426, 429, 821-822, 915-916
Directories, changing, 38-39
Distortions. *See* Charting mistakes
Documents
    using charts in, considerations, 747-748
    using humor in, considerations, 748
Draw menu in Draw/Annotate, 277
Draw Partner
    adding objects, 559-564
    adding points, 611-613
    aligning objects, 607-610
    aligning points in objects, 619-620
    arc options, 582-583, 971-972
    arcs, adding, 581-582
    auto redraw, 535, 542, 992
    back, moving objects to, 600-601
    box options, 568-571, 972-974
    boxes, adding, 568
    breaking objects, 615-616
    button options, 975
    buttons, adding, 587
    changing directories, 545-546
    circle options, 577, 975-977
    circles, adding, 575-576
    circular text options, 582-583, 977-978
    circular text, adding, 581-582
    closing polylines, 618
    combining polylines, 616-618

Draw Partner (*continued*)
    conversions to Harvard Graphics drawing objects, 553-554
    converting text, boxes, and lines, 620-622
    copying objects, 594-595
    cursor control, 530-531, 532, 559-560
    defined (version 1.0), 13-14, 525-527
    defined (version 2.3), 525-527
    deleting objects, 595-596
    deleting points in objects, 614-615
    digital tablet, 498-499, 559, 753
    editing text, 602
    exiting, 528
    flipping objects, 598-599
    freehand drawings, adding, 584
    freehand options, 584-585, 979-980
    front, moving object to, 600-601
    getting drawings (.DP file extension), 542-544
    getting symbols, 542, 546-547
    grid, displaying, 540-541
    grouping objects, 558, 590-592
    installing version 1.0, 1008-1009
    line options, 575, 980-982
    lines, adding, 574-575
    modifying objects, 556-557, 589-622
    modifying objects defined, 589
    modifying options, 599-600, 982
    modifying symbols, 327-328
    mouse speed, 535, 992
    mouse, using, 531-533, 559
    moving a drawing object, 592-593
    moving points in objects, 614
    1.0 vs. 2.3 objects comparison, 563-564
    panning a zoomed view, 538-540
    perspective, adding to objects, 607-608
    point editing, 557-558, 610-622
    polygon options, 577-578, 982-983
    polygons, adding, 577
    polyline options, 573, 984-985
    polylines, adding, 572-573
    previewing drawing, 535
    regular polygon options, 586, 985-986
    regular polygons, adding, 585
    removing symbols from symbol files, 553
    rotating objects, 596-597
    saving complex drawings, 551-552
    saving drawing (.DP file extension), 535, 547-549, 993
    saving drawing as a CGM metafile, 547-549
    saving drawing as a chart, 547-550

Draw Partner (*continued*)
  saving drawing as a symbol, 547-549, 550-551
  saving drawing with a Harvard Graphics chart, 551
  selecting objects, 587-589
  selecting palettes, 542-545, 547
  setup options, 497-499, 753
  shadows, adding to objects, 604-605
  sizing objects, 593
  skewing objects, 606-607
  snap-to-grid, 541-542
  starting with a blank drawing area, 528
  starting with version 1.0, 527
  starting with version 2.3, 528
  sweeping objects, 602-604
  symbols, 542-551, 553
  text options, 566-568, 987-989
  text, adding, 565-566
  ungrouping, 592
  view options, 535-536, 994
  wedge options, 584, 989-990
  wedges, adding, 583
  zooming, 537-540
Draw Partner object conversions, 554
Draw Partner 1.0 installation, 1008-1009
Draw Partner Main Menu, 529, 555-558
Draw Partner screen, 529-530
  CGA or monochrome, 497-499, 529
  drawing area, 529
Draw Partner symbols. *See* Symbols
Draw transition in ScreenShows, 425, 914-915, 947-948
Draw/Annotate
  back, moving objects to, 308
  box options, 288-291, 786-789
  box styles, 289
  boxes, adding, 287
  circle options, 297-298, 797-799
  circles, adding, 296-297
  copying objects, 308-309
  creating symbols, 317-318, 324
  cursor control, 279-281
  default options, 320-323
  deleting objects, 309-311
  drawing behind a chart, 274
  drawing defined, 271-272
  drawing on current chart, 273-275
  front, moving objects to, 308
  getting symbols, 314-317, 929-931
  global options, 321-323, 831-832
  grid, 311-313

Draw/Annotate (*continued*)
  group options, 834-835
  grouping objects, 318-319
  line options, 294-296, 862-864
  lines, adding, 294
  modifying objects, 304-308
  modifying symbols, 324-327
  moving objects, 304-305
  patterns, 872
  polygon options, 299-300, 890-892
  polygons, adding, 298
  polyline options, 292-294, 892-893
  polylines, adding, 291-292
  redraw, 958-959
  saving drawings, 275-277
  saving symbols, 317-318, 324
  saving chart as symbol, 324-327
  selecting objects, 300-303
  sizing drawing objects, 305-306
  starting with a blank drawing area, 273-274
  text options, 283, 285, 940-942
  text, adding, 282, 283
  ungrouping, 319-320
Draw/Annotate screen, 272-273
  CGA, 279
  Draw menu, 277
  drawing area, 273
Draw/Annotate symbols. *See* Symbols
Dual-axis charts, 168, 675-676

# E

Entry options, defined, 20
EPS (encapsulated PostScript) file format, exporting to, 398, 825-826
Erase transition in ScreenShows, 429, 916, 947-848
Excel
  importing charts, 519-520, 853-854, 922-923
  importing data, 518-519, 854-856, 923-924
Expanded/extended memory, 498, 1002
Exploded pies, 223-224. *See also* Pie charts
Export Metafile overlay, 402. *See also* CGM metafiles
Export Picture overlay, 396-399, 824-826
Exporting
  CGM metafiles, 399, 401-402, 823-824
  CGM metafiles, saving drawing as in Draw Partner, 547-549
  HPGL (Hewlett-Packard Graphics Language), 398-399, 825-826

Exporting *(continued)*
    Professional Write (PFS:Professional Write), 397-398, 399-401, 822-823, 825-826
    defined, 369-370, 395-397
    EPS (encapsulated PostScript), 398, 825-826

## F

F1-Help, 23, 952
F1-Help, Draw Partner, 533, 990
F2-Draw chart, 33, 952-953
F2-Preview, 249-250, 953-954
F2-Preview, Draw Partner, 535, 990
F2-Preview show, 421, 954
F2-Show palette, 64, 954
F3-Applications, 499, 954-955
F3-CGA palette, 795, 955
F3-Change dir, 38, 955
F3-Change dir, Draw Partner, 990
F3-Gallery, 490-491, 955
F3-Intl formats, 483, 955-956
F3-Save, 956
F3-Select files, 956
F3-Set X type, 957
F3-XY position, 329-330, 957
F4-Calculate, 794, 957-958
F4-Clear ranges, 958
F4-Draw/Annot, 958
F4-Redraw, 958-959
F4-Redraw, Draw Partner, 535, 992
F4-Reselect, 959
F4-Spell check, 42, 444, 959-960
F5-Attributes, 85-86, 960-961
F5-Mouse speed, Draw Partner, 535, 992
F5-Prev palette, 490-491, 494, 961
F5-Set X type, 961
F6-Calculate, 957-962
F6-Choices, Draw Partner, 992
F6-Choices, Draw/Annotate, 962
F6-Choices, slide shows, 962-963
F6-Colors, 963
F6-Next palette, 490-491, 494, 963
F6-Range names, 520, 963-964
F6-Shaded Bkgd, 69, 933, 964
F7-Data, 964-965
F7-Save, Draw Partner, 535, 993
F7-Size/Place, charts, 965
F7-Size/Place, Main Menu, 329, 965
F7-Size/Place, multiple charts, 965-966
F8-Data, 966
F8-Draw, 966

F8-Draw, Draw Partner, 994
F8-Final mode, 345, 966-967
F8-HyperShow menu, 850, 967
F8-Options, Draw Partner, 993
F8-Options, Import ASCII Data form, 967
F8-Options, Main Menu, 967-968
F8-Options, organization and data charts, 157, 968
F8-Quick mode, 345-346, 968
F8-User menu, 436, 969
F9-Edit, 491, 493, 969
F9-More series, 969-970
F9-View, Draw Partner, 535-536, 994
F10-Continue, 970
F10-Continue, Draw Partner, 994
F10-Edit + Clear, 491-493, 970
Fill. *See* Text attributes
Film recording
    charts, 257-258, 905
    colors, 259-260
    hardware fonts, 61
    recorder connection, 870-872
    saving slides to disk, 60-61
    setup, 59-61, 826-827
    slide shows, 262-266, 445, 905-906
Flipping objects in Draw Partner, 598-599
Fonts, 53-54, 70-71, 483, 484, 819, 828, 1035-1041
    multiple fonts in charts, 475, 500
    use of, considerations, 645-646, 706-707
Formats, data
    XY charts, 198-205
    currency, 487
    date, 485-486
    pie charts, 240-241, 243, 883-884
    thousand/decimal separators, 486
    time, 486
Forms
    options, 20-22
    options defined, 19, 20
    overlays, defined, 19
    using forms, 19-20
Free-form charts, 82, 701, 703, 705
    Size/Place overlay, 829-830
Free Form Text form, 76, 82, 84, 828-829
Freehand drawing
    adding in Draw Partner, 584
    options in Draw Partner, 584-585, 979-980
Frequency counts, 687-688
Front, moving drawing objects to
    in Draw Partner, 600-601
    in Draw/Annotate, 308

Function keys, 952-970
    function key banner, 22
    in Draw Partner, 990-994

## G

Getting
    charts, 36-38, 918-919
    CGM metafiles, 521-522, 917-918
    chartbooks, 364-365, 919-920
    directories, a different, 38, 920-922
    Excel charts, 519-520, 922-923
    Excel worksheets, 519, 923-924
    files, 924-925
    Lotus worksheets, 374, 390, 926-927, 933
    palettes, 514, 927-928
    slide shows, 410, 928-929
    symbol files, 314-315, 929-931
    templates, 354-356, 368, 931-933
Global options form in Draw/Annotate, 831-832
Go To keys. See HyperShows and ScreenShows
Go To overlay, 436-439, 832-834, 969. See also HyperShow menu overlay
Graphics adapter (video card), 61-62, 1002
Graphs. See also Charts
    defined, 625
Grey scale printing, 260-262, 517-518, 1046
Grid
    in Draw Partner, 540-541
    in Draw/Annotate, 311-313
Group options
    in Draw Partner, 982
    in Draw/Annotate, 834-835
Grouping objects
    in Draw Partner, 590-592
    in Draw/Annotate, 318-319
    ungrouping in Draw Partner, 592
    ungrouping in Draw/Annotate, 319-320

## H

Harvard Graphics
    accessories. See Accessories for Harvard Graphics
    default settings, 49-54
    defined, 1
    exiting, 28
    features, 7-13
    Main Menu, 16-18, 29-31
    quick start, 28
    starting, 26-28
Harvard Graphics 2.3
    introduced, 471-477
    tutorial, 477

Help, 23, 952
    in Draw Partner, 533, 990
High/Low/Close Chart Data form, 138-140, 835-836
High/Low/Close Chart Titles & Options form, 157-158, 183-185, 838-849
High/low/close charts. See also Band chart and XY charts, area.
    defined, 130, 132, 184-185, 658-659
    error bars, 130, 132, 184, 659
    Size/Place overlay, 836-838
    style options, 183-185
Horizontal charts, XY charts, 186
HPGL (Hewlett-Packard Graphics Language)
    file format, exporting to, 398-399, 825-826
HyperShows. See also ScreenShows
    buttons, 503-509, 587
    creating, 503-509, 849-851, 967
    defined, 503
    HyperShow menu overlay, 505-507, 849-851, 967

## I

Illusions. See Charting mistakes
Import ASCII Data form, 379-385, 851-853
Import Excel Chart overlay, 853-854
Import Excel Data form, 519-520, 854-856
Import Lotus Data form, 375-377, 856-859
Import Lotus Graph form, 391, 859-860
Import Titles and Legends overlay, 380-381, 383, 860-861
Importing
    ASCII data, 378-385, 851-853
    CGM metafiles, 371, 392-395, 521-522, 542-544, 917-918
    data link, defined, 371
    data-linked template, using, 358-360, 371, 372-373
    default directory/file, setting, 817
    defined, 369-371
    delimited ASCII data, 385-389
    Excel charts, 519-520, 922-923
    Excel data, 518-519, 923-924
    Lotus data, 373-377, 856-859, 926-927
    Lotus graphs, 389-391, 859-860, 926-927
    Lotus .PIC files, 542-544
    PFS:GRAPH charts, 389, 392
    preparing a chart for, 371-372
    range names, 519, 520-521, 904-905, 963-964

Installation, 999-1010
    Draw Partner 1.0, 1008
    equipment options, 1001-1002
    equipment required, 1000
    version 2.13 or earlier, floppy disks, 1008
    version 2.13 or earlier, hard disk, 1004-1007
    version 2.3, 1003-1004
    virtual device interface (VDI), 1009-1010
International settings
    current, 484-487, 810-813, 955-956
    default, 483-487, 813-815, 956
International text characters, 1043
Italic. *See* Text attributes

## K

Keys. *See* HyperShows and ScreenShows

## L

Line charts. *See also* XY charts
    curved, 129, 166, 661-662
    defined, 127, 129, 166, 659-661
    trend, 129, 166, 660-661, 665-666
Lines
    adding in Draw Partner, 574-575
    adding in Draw/Annotate, 294
    options in Draw Partner, 575, 980-982
    options in Draw/Annotate, 294-296, 862-864
    styles of, 1043
List options, defined, 21-22
Logarithmic scale, 154, 197-198, 694-695
Lotus 1-2-3
    importing .PIC files, 542-545
    importing data from, 373-377, 856-859, 926-927
    importing graphs, 389-391, 859-860, 926-927

## M

Macros
    MACRO commands, 463-465, 467
    MACRO key codes, 463-466
    MACRO program, 447-449
    adding comments to, 461-462
    changing macro directory, 455-456
    continuous running macros, 467
    control keys, 453
    defined, 13, 447-449
    delays, 458-460, 819-821

Macros (*continued*)
    displaying messages during, 460
    editing and writing, 462-464
    loading MACRO, 449-450
    nesting (macros within macros), 462
    pausing during playback, 456-458, 873-874
    playing, 454-455
    recording, 451-454
    unloading MACRO, 450-451
    user input during, 460-461
Main Menu, 16-18, 29-31
Manager in organization charts, 107
Manipulating data. *See* Calculations and Data
Markers, 1044
Menus
    Draw Partner version 1.0 menu tree, 1057-1058
    Draw Partner version 2.3 menu tree, 1059-1060
    Harvard Graphics version 2.1 through 2.13 menu tree, 1051-1053
    Harvard Graphics 2.3 menu tree, 1054-1056
    color scheme, 53-54, 819
    using, 16-18
META2HG.EXE, 392-393. *See also* CGM metafiles
Microsoft Excel. *See* Excel
Military Symbols accessory, 1011-1012, 1016
Minimum and maximum, 153, 685-687
Mistakes. See Charting mistakes
Modifying charts. *See* Organization charts, Pie charts, Text charts, XY charts, modifying
Modifying drawing object options
    in Draw Partner, 599-600
    in Draw/Annotate, 306-308
Modifying drawing objects
    in Draw Partner, 589-622
    in Draw/Annotate, 304-308
Moiré effect, 730, 732
Mouse
    button functions, 26
    in Draw Partner, 531-533, 535, 559, 992
    using, 24-25, 1001
Moving averages, 153, 696-697
Moving drawing objects
    in Draw Partner, 592-593
    in Draw/Annotate, 304-305
Multiple charts
    adding charts to, 338-340
    creating, 332-336
    defined, 331

Multiple charts (*continued*)
    modifying, 340-341
    placing custom multiple charts, 341-345, 965-966
    quick mode/final mode, 345-346, 966-967, 968
    sizing custom multiple charts, 341-345

## N

Named ranges. *See* Importing, range names
Navigating. *See* Cursor control
Needle charts. *See* Point charts, needle
New Symbol File overlay, 864

## O

Object handles. *See* Draw/Annotate or Draw Partner, selecting objects
1-2-3. *See* Lotus 1-2-3
Org Chart Options form, 116, 867-870
Organization Chart form, 102, 104, 107-111, 865-866
Organization charts
    abbreviations, specifying, 109
    adding organization levels, 111
    creating, 100-102
    cursor control, 103
    defined, 9, 97-99, 711-712
    design considerations, 712-713
    manager, specifying, 107
    modifying organization levels, 115-116
    options, 116-121, 867-870
    Size/Place overlay, 106-107, 866-867
    staff position, 109-111
    subordinates, specifying, 109
Orientation, 51-52, 70-71, 482, 818-819
Outputting. *See* Film recording, Plotting, and Printing
Overlay. *See* Forms

## P

Palettes
    CGA color settings, 65-67, 955
    background color, 68-69
    color palette setup, 63-70, 799-802
    color settings, 67-68
    creating, 515-516, 803-804
    current chart, for, 488, 810
    default, 482, 818
    displaying current, 954
    editing, 63-64, 516-517

Palettes (*continued*)
    grey scale setup, 518
    selecting, 514-515, 927-928
    selecting in Draw Partner, 542-545, 547
    shaded background in slides, 69-70, 933-935, 964
    symbol colors, 512
    version 2.3 default, 511
    version 2.3 features, 511-512
Panning, a zoomed view in Draw Partner, 538-540
Parallel/Serial overlay, 56-57, 870-872
Patterns, 1044-1045
    Patterns overlay, 872
    use of, considerations, 642-643, 730, 732
Pause in macros, 456-458, 873-874. *See also* Macros
.PCX file format. *See* Slide shows
Percentage adjustments to data, 152, 153, 691-693. *See also* Data
Perspective, adding to objects in Draw Partner, 607-608
PFS:GRAPH charts, importing, 389, 392
PFS:Professional Write. *See* Professional Write
.PIC file format. *See* Slide shows
Pie Chart Data form, 216-219, 874-876
Pie Chart Titles & Options form, 225, 235-235, 878-884
Pie charts
    Size/Place overlay, 230-232
    adding and selecting series, 221-222, 223, 969-970
    changing data order, 222-223
    colors and patterns, 224-225, 234-235
    column pie charts, 233, 236, 880
    creating, 215-216
    cursor control, 220
    cut slices (explode), 223-224, 673
    defined, 213, 672-673
    formatting values, 240-241, 243, 883-884
    design considerations, 678-682
    labels and values, 219, 221
    labels and values, displaying, 238-243, 882-884
    linked, 232-234, 879-880
    modifying data, 222
    modifying options, 232-243, 878-884
    proportional, 234, 235, 880
    3D (three-dimensional), 214, 232-233, 879
    titles, 227
    two pies, 218-219, 223, 673

Pie charts (*continued*)
    types of, 214
    using in documents, considerations, 747-748
    using in presentations, 744-745
Placing a chart, 329-330, 957, 965. *See also* Size/Place screen
Plotting
    charts, 255-257, 884-886
    charts to disk files, 886
    colors, 259
    plotter connection, 56-58, 870-872
    setup, 58-59, 889-890
    slide shows, 262-266, 445, 886-889
    slide shows to disk files, 888
Point charts. *See also* XY charts
    defined, 127, 129, 167, 663-666
    needle, 129, 166, 666-667
    trend, 129, 166-167, 660-661, 665-666
Point editing in Draw Partner, 557-558, 610-622
    adding points, 611-613
    aligning points, 619-620
    breaking objects, 615-616
    closing polylines, 618
    combining polylines, 616-618
    converting text, boxes, and lines, 620-622
    deleting points, 614-615
    moving points, 614
Polygons
    adding in Draw Partner, 577
    adding in Draw/Annotate, 298
    options in Draw Partner, 577-578, 982-983
    options in Draw/Annotate, 299-300, 890-892
Polylines
    adding in Draw Partner, 572-573
    adding in Draw/Annotate, 291-292
    options in Draw Partner, 573, 984-985
    options in Draw/Annotate, 292-294, 892-893
PostScript
    exporting in EPS (encapsulated PostScript) file format, 398
PostScript printing. *See* Printing
Practice cards
    creating, 440-444, 894, 895
    cursor control, 442
    printing, 267-269, 442, 895-897
Presentations
    computerized, considerations for, 745-747
    design considerations, 737-743

Presentations (*continued*)
    using data charts in, 744-745
    using humor in, considerations, 748
    using illustrations in, 745
    using text charts in, 743-744
Previewing a chart, 249-250
Printing
    charts, 250-255, 897-899
    charts to disk files, 899
    chart data, 267, 797
    color, 254, 258-259
    grey scale, 260-262, 517-518, 1046
    PostScript, 260-262, 517
    practice cards, 267-269, 442, 895-897
    printer connection, 56-57, 870-872
    setup, 55-57, 902-904
    size of output, 252, 253, 254
    slide show list, 269-270, 445, 937-938
    slide shows, 262-266, 445, 899-902
    slide shows to disk files, 901
Produce Output menu, 247-248. *See also* Film recording, Plotting, and Printing
Professional Write, exporting to, 397-398, 399-401, 825-826

## Q

Quick start, 28
Quick-Charts accessory, 1011-1012, 1016-1019

## R

Range, defined, 685-687
Range names, importing, 519-521, 914-915, 963-964
Redraw in Draw/Annotate, 958-959
Regression and Regression lines, 688-690. *See also* @REXP, @RLIN, @RLOG, and @RPWR
Regular polygons
    adding in Draw Partner, 585
    options in Draw Partner, 586, 985-986
Removing files, 39-41
Reports. *See* Documents
Rotating drawing objects in Draw Partner, 596-597
Running applications from Harvard Graphics. *See* Applications

## S

Saving
    chart as symbol, 324-327, 907-908
    charts, 34-36, 908-909, 956

Saving (*continued*)
Draw Partner drawing as CGM metafile, 547-549
Draw Partner drawing as chart, 547-550
Draw Partner drawing as symbol, 547-549, 550-551
Draw Partner drawings, complex, 551-552
drawings with charts, 272, 551
templates, 352-354, 910-912
Scaling data, 201. *See also* Format
Scientific notation, 200-202, 697-698. *See also* Format
Screen Setup form, 61-62, 912-913
ScreenShow Effects form, 422-434, 913-917
changing file order from, 424
cursor control, 424
ScreenShow Utilities accessory, 1011-1012, 1019-1023
ScreenShows. *See also* HyperShows
buildups, 431-435
color palettes in (versions 2.13 and earlier), 439-440
default transitions, 429
defined, 404, 420. *See also* Slide shows
Dir (directions) of transition, 426, 429, 821-822, 915, 916
displaying, 421-422
Draw transition, 425, 914-915, 947-948
Erase transition, 429, 916, 947-948
Go To keys, 422, 434-439, 969
hardware considerations, 420-421
overlay transition, 430-431
pointer, 503
previewing, 423-424, 954
ShowCopy, 509-511
special effects, 422-423, 424-434
time of transition, 427, 915-916
transitions, 422, 424-434, 947-948
use of, considerations, 745-747
Select CGM Metafile form, 521-522, 917-918
Select Chart form, 36-38, 918-919
Select Chartbook form, 364-365, 919-920
Select Directory form, 38, 920-922
Select Excel Chart overlay, 922-923
Select Excel Worksheet form, 519, 923-924
Select File form, 924-925
Select Lotus Worksheet form, 374, 390, 926-927
Select Palette form, 514, 927-928
Select Slide Show form, 410, 928-929
Select Symbol File form, 314-315, 929-931
Select Template form, 354-356, 368, 931-933

Select Worksheet form, 926-927, 933
Series data (Y data), 144-145, 629, 631-632
Setup menu, 48
Shaded background. *See* Palettes, shaded background in slides
Shadows, adding to objects in Draw Partner, 604-605
Shapes, defined, 610
ShowCopy, 509-511
.SHW file format. *See* Slide shows
Simple List form, 79, 80, 935-936
Simple lists, 79, 700-701, 703
Size/Place overlay, 936-937
Size/Place overlays
area charts, 162-164, 756
bar/line charts, 162-164, 772-773
bullet lists, 791-792
free form charts, 829-830
high/low/close charts, 162-164, 836-838
organization charts, 106-107, 866, 867
pie charts, 230-232, 877-878
text charts, 88-92
three-column charts, 88, 90, 944-945
title charts, 946-947
two-column charts, 88, 90, 949-950
Size/Place screen, 329-330, 957, 965
Sizing a chart, 329-330, 957
Sizing drawing objects
in Draw Partner, 593
in Draw/Annotate, 305-306
Skewing objects in Draw Partner, 606-607
Slide services, 258, 997-998
Slide shows. *See also* ScreenShows
creating, 405-409, 805
creating large slide shows, 439
defined, 403-404
file limits of, 405, 434
file types in, 405
film recording, 262-266, 445, 905-906
for reviewing charts, 445-446
including bit-mapped (.PCX, .PIC) files in, 413-414
modifying slide show list, 411-413, 807-809
plotting, 262-266, 445, 886-889
practice cards, 440-444, 894-895
practice cards, printing, 267-269, 442, 895-897
print slide show list, 269-270, 445, 937-938
printing, 262-266, 445, 899-902
selecting, 410, 927-929
slide show files in, 419-420

Slide shows (*continued*)
    spell check charts in, 444-445
    templates in, 360, 414-418
Snap (to grid)
    in Draw Partner, 541-542
    in Draw/Annotate, 312-313
Software Publishing Corporation, 5, 997
Speed keys, 477-478
Spell checking
    charts, 41-45, 959-960
    slide shows, 444-445, 959-960
Splitting text
    X axis values (XY charts), 144
    axis titles, 159
    organization chart, 107-108
    pie labels, 219
Staff position in organization charts, 109-111
Subordinates in organization charts, 109
Sweeping objects in Draw Partner, 602-604
.SYM, symbol file extension, 272, 313
Symbol colors (version 2.3), 512
Symbols
    Business Symbols accessory, 1011-1013
    creating, 324
    default directory, 817
    defined, 272, 276-277, 313
    getting in Draw Partner, 542-545, 546-547
    getting in Draw/Annotate, 314-317, 929-931
    grey scale, 517
    grouping, 318
    Military Symbols accessory, 1011-1012, 1016
    modifying in Draw/Annotate, 324-327
    modifying in Draw/Partner, 327-328
    New Symbol File overlay, 864
    removing, 320
    removing using Draw Partner, 553
    saving, 276-277, 317-318
    saving a chart as, 324-327, 907-908
    saving a drawing as, in Draw Partner, 547-549, 550-551
    ungrouping, 319-320
    version 2.0 symbol files, 1046-1047
    version 2.1 to 2.13 symbol files, 1047
    version 2.3 symbol files, 1048-1049

**T**

Templates
    creating a chart from, 356
    data linked, 358-360, 372-373
    default chart settings, 357-358

Templates (*continued*)
    defined, 349-351
    getting, 354-356, 931-933
    in slide shows, 414-418
    placing buttons on, 508-509
    reserved template names, 353, 357-358
    saving, 351-354, 910-912
Text
    adding in Draw Partner, 565-566
    adding in Draw/Annotate, 282-283
    charts. *See* Text charts
    editing in Draw Partner, 602
    multiple fonts on one chart, 500-503
    options in Draw Partner, 566-568, 987-989
    options in Draw/Annotate, 283-287, 940-942
Text attributes, 645-646, 938-940, 960-961, 1035-1041
    Draw Partner, in, 566-568, 602, 987-989
    Draw/Annotate, in, 285-287, 940-942
    organization charts, 104-105, 120-121
    pie charts, 228-230
    text charts, 84-87
    XY charts, 160-162
Text charts. *See also* names of charts and lists
    artistic enhancements, considerations, 710-711
    changing chart styles, 95-96
    chart forms, 76-84
    creating, 73-75
    cursor control, 77
    defined, 9
    design considerations, 704-711
    types of, 74, 699-705
    using in documents, considerations, 747-748
    using in presentations, considerations, 743-744
Text placement. *See also* Size/Place overlays
    organization charts, 106-107
    pie charts, 231-232
    text charts, 88, 89-90
    XY charts, 163-164
Text size. *See also* Size/Place overlays
    examples of, 1044
    organization charts, 106-107
    pie charts, 230-231
    text charts, 88-89
    XY charts, 162-163, 164
    use of, considerations, 646-647, 708-709
Three Columns form, 943-944

Three-column charts, 79, 82, 83, 702
    Size/Place overlay, 944-945
3D (three-dimensional)
    area charts, 131, 179-180
    bar charts, 128, 173-174
    line charts, 129
    pie charts, 214, 232-233, 880
    use of, 723-726
Time of transition in ScreenShows, 427, 915-916
Title Chart form, 77-78, 945-946
Title charts
    defined, 76, 700-702
    Size/Place overlay, 88-90, 946-947
Titles & Options
    XY charts, 157-158
    area charts, 157-158, 757-769
    bar/line charts, 157-158, 773-786
    high/low/close charts, 157-158, 838-839
    pie charts, 225, 235-236, 878-884
    XY charts, 157-158
Toggle options, defined, 22
Total (sum) 684
.TPL, template file extension, 353
Transformations, 691-698. *See also* Calculations and Data
    logarithmic, power, and root, 197-198, 694-695
Transitions, 422, 424-434, 947-948. *See also* ScreenShows
Traps. *See* Charting mistakes
Two Columns form, 76, 79, 82, 948-949
Two-column charts, 79, 82, 83, 702
    Size/Place overlay, 88, 90, 949-950
Two-pie charts, 218-219, 221-223, 673

## U

U.S. MapMaker accessory, 1011-1012, 1023-1034
Underline. *See* Text attributes
Ungrouping drawing objects
    in Draw Partner, 592
    in Draw/Annotate, 319-320

## V

Virtual device interface (VDI), 1009-1010

## W

Wedges
    adding in Draw Partner, 583
    options in Draw Partner, 584, 989-990

Weighting/equalizing data, 691. *See also* Data
.WK1 and .WKS (Lotus files), 373

## X

X data
    automatic entry, 136-137
    types, 630-631
    valid entries, 134-135
X data type
    changing, 138, 950-952, 957, 961
    selecting, 130, 132-137, 950-952
X Data Type Menu overlay, 950-952
XY charts
    axis titles, 158-159, 637-639
    changing data order, 145-146
    chart frame, 188-189
    creating, 126-127
    cumulative, 206-207, 674-675
    cursor control, 141-143
    customizing axes, 194-205
    customizing symbols, 168-185
    data table, 192-194, 206, 639-640
    defined, 125
    displaying data values, 186-188, 192-194, 206
    displaying series symbols, 168
    entering X axis data, 138-144
    entering series data, 138-140, 144-145, 969-970
    guidelines for creating, 678-682
    grid lines, 196, 197, 640-641
    horizontal, 186
    legend, 189-192, 644-645
    line styles, 210, 641-642, 1043
    modifying, 147-148
    selecting series axis, 168, 675-676
    selecting series symbol type, 165-168, 176
    symbol colors, markers and patterns, 207-210, 641-644, 727-732, 1044
    tick marks, 196, 198, 640
    types of, 127-130, 648-672, 674, 676
    using in documents, considerations, 747-748
    using in presentations, considerations, 744-7

## Y

Y data (series data), 144-145, 629, 631-632, 969-970

## Z

Zooming, a view in Draw Partner, 537-540

The manuscript for this book was prepared and submitted
to Osborne/McGraw-Hill in electronic form. The
acquisitions editor for this project was Elizabeth Fisher,
the associate editor was Ilene Shapera, the
technical reviewer was John Levy, and
the project editor was Judith Brown.

Text design by Stefany Otis, Patricia J. Beckwith and
Roger Dunshee, using Century Expanded for text body
and Eras Demi for display.

Cover art by Bay Graphics Design, Inc. Color separation
and cover supplier, Phoenix Color Corporation. Screens
produced with InSet, from Inset Systems, Inc. Book
printed and bound by R.R. Donnelley & Sons Company,
Crawfordsville, Indiana.

# ▷ Expand Your Skill Even More

with help from our expert authors. Now that you've gained greater skills with **Harvard Graphics: The Complete Reference**, let us suggest the following related titles that will help you use your computer to full advantage.

### Harvard® Graphics 2.3 Made Easy
*by Mary Campbell*

(Includes One 5 1/4" Disk) Create memorable presentations with Harvard® Graphics 2.3 for the IBM® PC and Mary Campbell's outstanding book. This book takes you step-by-step through the creation of charts, animation, presentation-quality slide shows with text, and tells you about new integrated features and accessory products that help you expand Harvard Graphics. A handy supplementary disk offering template samples, exercises and macros is included.
$24.95p ISBN: 0-07-881692-0, 568 pp., 7 3/8 X 9 1/4 Covers Releases 2.12 & 2.3

### 1-2-3®: The Pocket Reference, Second Edition
*by Mary Campbell*

Next time you're wondering how to format a 1-2-3® calculation, set up a print option, or copy a column, reach for this *Pocket Reference*. All the most frequently used Lotus 1-2-3 commands and functions for releases 2.01, 2.2, 3.0 and 3.1 are listed alphabetically and are briefly described. Allways®, which gives 1-2-3 release 2.2 presentation graphics capabilities, and WYSIWYG® (Impress®), which gives release 3.0 presentation graphics capabilities, are also covered. It's a 1-2-3 memory jogger you won't want to be without.
$7.95p ISBN: 0-07-881702-1, 225 pp., 4 1/4 X 7

### 1-2-3® Release 2.2: The Complete Reference
*by Mary Campbell*

This indispensable reference covers Lotus Release 2.2, as well as existing Releases 2.0 and 2.01. You'll find every Release 2.2 feature, command, and function thoroughly described for beginners and pros alike. Lotus expert Campbell has organized the book so you can quickly find information on entering data, macros, graphics, printing, and more.
$27.95p ISBN: 0-07-881588-6, 1100 pp., 7 3/8 x 9 1/4 Covers Releases 2.0, 2.1 & 2.2

▶ _____**Osborne McGraw-Hill** ■ Available at local book and computer stores.

### 1-2-3® Release 2.2 Made Easy
*by Mary Campbell*

Whether you're a first-time 1-2-3® user or experienced in 1-2-3 but new to Release 2.2, Campbell takes you step-by-step from the basics of spreadsheet organization to more complex Release 2.2 functions, including file-linking and macro recorders. With the skills you'll learn here, you'll be handling Release 2.2, as well as Releases 2.0 and 2.01, like a pro in no time.
$19.95p ISBN: 0-07-881554-1, 600 pp., 7 3/8 x 9 1/4 Covers Releases 2.0, 2.01, & 2.2

### Excel® 2.1 Made Easy: IBM® PC Version
*by Martin S. Matthews*

Even if you've never worked with Excel, spreadsheets, or Windows before, you can easily follow Matthews' detailed instructions. Part One of this book introduces Windows and the Excel environment. Part Two discusses the basic steps that everyone needs to know to use Excel. Part Three describes the use of Dynamic Data Exchange to share data with other Windows applications. You'll also find out about linking worksheets, the macro language and other advanced features. Part Four includes a handy command reference. Covers All Versions Through 2.1.
$19.95p ISBN: 0-07-881677-7, 600 pp., 7 3/8 X 9 1/4

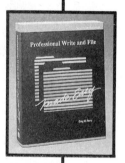

### Professional® Write and File Made Easy
*by Greg M. Perry*

This step-by-step tutorial will have everyone editing documents and creating databases in no time. Perry covers both the word processor and database software packages in detail before showing how to combine the two for more advanced applications. Appendixes display menu maps, speed keys, and DOS subdirectories, make Software Publishing Company's Professional® Write and File easier to use than ever.
$19.95p ISBN: 0-07-881592-4, 450 pp., 7 3/8 x 9 1/4 Covers Version 1.0

### DOS Made Easy
*by Herbert Schildt*

Previous computer experience is not necessary to understand this concise, well-organized introduction that's filled with short applications and exercises. Begin with an overview of a computer system's components and a step-by-step account of how to run DOS for the first time. Edit text files, use the DOS directory structure, and create batch files.
$19.95p ISBN: 0-07-881295-X, 385 pp., 7 3/8 x 9 1/4 Covers MS-DOS/PC-DOS Version 3.3

▶ _____ Osborne **McGraw-Hill** ■ **Available at local book and computer stores.**